William Dunbar

The Complete Works

Middle English Texts

General Editor

Russell A. Peck
University of Rochester

Associate Editor

Alan Lupack
University of Rochester

Assistant Editor

Dana M. Symons
University of Rochester

Advisory Board

Rita Copeland
University of Pennsylvania

Thomas G. Hahn
University of Rochester

Lisa Kiser
Ohio State University

R. A. Shoaf
University of Florida

Bonnie Wheeler
Southern Methodist University

The Middle English Texts Series is designed for classroom use. Its goal is to make available to teachers and students texts that occupy an important place in the literary and cultural canon but have not been readily available in student editions. The series does not include those authors, such as Chaucer, Langland, or Malory, whose English works are normally in print in good student editions. The focus is, instead, upon Middle English literature adjacent to those authors that teachers need in compiling the syllabuses they wish to teach. The editions maintain the linguistic integrity of the original work but within the parameters of modern reading conventions. The texts are printed in the modern alphabet and follow the practices of modern capitalization, word formation, and punctuation. Manuscript abbreviations are silently expanded, and *u/v* and *j/i* spellings are regularized according to modern orthography. Yogh is transcribed as *g*, *gh*, *y*, or *s*, according to the letter in modern English spelling to which it corresponds. Distinction between the second person pronoun and the definite article is made by spelling the one *thee* and the other *the*, and final *-e* that receives full syllabic value is accented (e.g., *charité*). Hard words, difficult phrases, and unusual idioms are glossed on the page, either in the right margin or at the foot of the page. Explanatory and textual notes appear at the end of the text, along with a glossary. The editions include short introductions on the history of the work, its merits and points of topical interest, and also contain briefly annotated bibliographies.

William Dunbar

The Complete Works

Edited by
John Conlee

Published for TEAMS
(The Consortium for the Teaching of the Middle Ages)
in Association with the University of Rochester

by

MEDIEVAL INSTITUTE PUBLICATIONS
College of Arts & Sciences
Western Michigan University
Kalamazoo, Michigan
2004

Library of Congress Cataloging-in-Publication Data

Dunbar, William, 1460?-1520?
 [Works. 2004]
 William Dunbar : the complete works / edited by John Conlee.
     p. cm. -- (Middle English texts)
 "Published for TEAMS (The Consortium for the Teaching of the Middle Ages) in
Association with the University of Rochester."
 Includes bibliographical references and index.
 ISBN 1-58044-086-X (paperbound : alk. paper)
 1. Scotland--Poetry. I. Conlee, John W. II. Consortium for the Teaching of the
Middle Ages. III. Title. IV. Middle English texts (Kalamazoo, Mich.)
 PR2265.A5C66 2004
 821'.2--dc22

                                                        2004014606

ISBN 1-58044-086-X

Printed in the United States of America

Cover design by Linda K. Judy

Contents

Poems Public and Private

Acknowledgments

I wish to thank Professor Russell A. Peck for inviting me to undertake this project, and also for his encouragement and assistance during my work on it. Throughout the process he made a great many helpful suggestions for revision and notes. Many other members of the Middle English Texts Series staff helped bring this edition to completion: Dana M. Symons gave the volume its initial formatting and final proofreading; Michael Livingston checked the poems against the manuscripts, expanded the textual notes, proofread the volume, made numerous suggestions for revision and for explanatory notes, wrote the Glossary, entered corrections, and gave the volume its final formatting; Emily Rebekah Huber reviewed the volume and added suggestions for revision, writing numerous explanatory notes based on recent scholarship.

I am greatly indebted to the many scholars and editors who, down through the years, have studied the poems of William Dunbar and his Middle Scots contemporaries, scholars and editors who have contributed a vast amount to our knowledge and understanding of these late medieval writers. In particular, I wish to acknowledge my debt to Priscilla Bawcutt, whose two-volume edition for the Association for Scottish Literary Studies will undoubtedly remain the authoritative work on Dunbar for many years to come. I would like to thank Patricia Hollahan and her staff at Medieval Institute Publications for seeing this volume through to the press. Finally, I wish to thank the National Endowment for the Humanities for its generous support of the Middle English Texts Series.

The Works of William Dunbar

Introduction

The Scottish poet William Dunbar lived during the final decades of the fifteenth century and the initial decades of the sixteenth. Although his early years and final years are shrouded in uncertainty, throughout much of his adult life he was closely associated with the royal court of James IV of Scotland (r. 1488–1513), a court that provided the social backdrop as well as the specific impetus for many of Dunbar's poems. Dunbar belongs to a significant group of late-medieval Scottish poets who are generally known as the Middle Scots Poets or the Scottish Makars, a group that includes the author of *The Kingis Quair* (possibly James I of Scotland), Richard Holland, Robert Henryson, Gavin Douglas, and Sir David Lindsay. Henryson and Dunbar are usually considered the two major writers from among the Middle Scots Poets and are often viewed as being two of the most important figures in fifteenth-century British literature. Dunbar, moreover, may lay claim to being the finest lyric poet writing in English in the century and a half between the death of Chaucer in 1400 and the appearance of *Tottel's Miscellany* in 1557.

Dunbar's poems offer vivid depictions of late-medieval Scottish society and serve up a striking pageant of colorful figures at James IV's court. Some of these figures are portrayed favorably but more often they are targets of the poet's satire, satire that tends to be scornful and derisive rather than bemused and good-natured. Several of Dunbar's poems also offer hints and suggestions about the poet himself, suggestions that have sometimes been used as a basis for speculations about Dunbar's life. But the truth is that we possess very little information about William Dunbar that can be verified by external documentation. What information we do possess comes primarily from three sources: the *Acta* of the University of St. Andrews, *The Register of the Privy Seal*, and, most importantly, *The Treasurer's Accounts* (*Accounts of the Lord High Treasurer of Scotland*), which contain the records of expenditures for the royal household during James IV's reign.

The date and place of the poet's birth are not known, but there is little doubt that William Dunbar was a Lowland Scot whose origins were in the Lothian area of southeastern Scotland. Perhaps the poet actually grew up in or near the town of Dunbar, which is located on the North Sea midway between Berwick-upon-Tweed and Edinburgh. It is very likely that William Dunbar the poet is the same William Dunbar who attended St. Andrews University, "determining" (receiving his bachelor's degree) in 1477, and becoming "licentiate" (receiving his master's degree) in 1479. If this is so, and if Dunbar was about twenty years old when he received his first degree from St. Andrews, then he was probably born in the late 1450s. For the first decades of Dunbar's adulthood, 1480 to 1500, no documentary evidence has come to light. Several of his poems suggest that at some period during his life he engaged in extensive foreign travels, and it is possible that those travels would have occurred during this time. The historical records do indicate that during 1500–01 Dunbar was in England, for the *Treasurer's Accounts* show that a payment was made to him in 1501, "efter he com furth of Ingland" (2.95). It is quite possible that Dunbar was among the group of Scots who were making arrangements for the marriage of James IV to Princess Margaret, the daughter of the English monarch Henry VII. It is also possible that Poem 29, for which the Maitland Folio colophon reads "Quod Dumbar at Oxinfurde" (i.e, Oxford), was written about this time.

For the years 1501 to 1513, when the poet was serving in the court of James IV, many entries in the *Treasurer's Accounts* refer to Dunbar. Most of these entries record payments made to him such as his *pensioun* (his annual pay), his livery (a clothing allowance he periodically received), and other minor gifts and remuneration. During this period Dunbar was clearly a "servitour" at the court of James IV, although we can not be certain about the specific capacities in which he served. Very likely he was employed within the royal secretariat as a scribe, secretary, or envoy (quite possibly some combination of these things), and perhaps he also served during this time as a court chaplain. It is even possible that for some portion of this time Dunbar may have served as either the king's or the queen's personal priest. Dunbar's petition poems (Poems 37–53), which were almost certainly written between 1501 and 1510, offer some of the best internal evidence for Dunbar's activities during this period. These poems reflect very clearly the poet's intense desire to be granted a benefice, an endowed church office that provided its holder with a secure, and sometimes substantial, annual income. They also suggest that Dunbar had long aspired to attaining a position of prominence within the church, but it appears that this last aspiration was never fulfilled. The records do show, however, that Dunbar's pension was doubled in 1507 to £20 a year, and that in August of 1510 it was raised yet again, this time to the very substantial sum of £80 a year.

The final mention of Dunbar in the historical records occurs in May of 1513. In the following September the reign of James IV came to a tragic end at the Battle of Flodden, where the Scottish king and 9,000 of his fellow Scots, including many earls, bishops, and abbots, perished at the hands of the English army. It is possible that Dunbar was one of those who died at Flodden Field on that early fall day in 1513, but most scholars incline to the view that he survived on into the reign of James V. There is no documentary evidence to prove that this was so because the *Treasurer's Accounts* for the period from August of 1513 until June of 1515 no longer exist. It is possible that Poem 34, which was written to provide comfort for a grieving widow, is Dunbar's expression of sympathy for Queen Margaret following James IV's death; if so, it would indicate that Dunbar was alive after the Battle of Flodden. But Poem 34 is one of the poems of disputed authorship (Priscilla Bawcutt excludes it from her recent edition), and, furthermore, the poem does not identify the widow who is being addressed, and there were many widows of Scottish noblemen following the Battle of Flodden (if indeed her widowhood is meant to be tied to that event). We can be certain, however, that Dunbar died sometime prior to 1530, when Sir David Lindsey wrote his *Testament of Papyngo*, for, in the opening verses of that poem, Lindsey laments the deaths of the great Scottish poets, including Dunbar.

Dunbar's Poetry

Scholars and editors agree that William Dunbar is the author of slightly more than eighty poems. Although Dunbar's possible authorship of a small number of poems continues to be a matter of debate, on the whole there is a good deal of consensus about which poems comprise the Dunbar canon. The principal difficulty for modern editors in establishing the poet's canon stems from the fact that the Bannatyne Manuscript and the Maitland Folio, two of the most important early witnesses of Dunbar's poetry, sometimes disagree in their attribution of poems. In several instances one of these sources will credit a particular poem to Dunbar when the other source considers that same poem to be anonymous or even attributes it to some other poet. In fact, there are a few poems that Dunbar's editors believe to be his that are not actually attributed to him in any of the early witnesses. But at this point Dunbar's canon has been established with a good deal of certitude, and we can be confident that the eighty-three or eighty-four poems usually attributed to him are very likely his.

Dunbar's poems are remarkable both for their diversity and variability and for their multiplicity of voices, styles, and tones. They treat a wide range of subjects and themes and reflect the characteristics of many different literary genres, forms, and modes. They range from the sacred to the profane, including devotional poems of the greatest seriousness and rarified beauty, and comic and parodic poems of extreme salaciousness and scatological coarseness. Many of them are highly traditional and conventional, while others are highly innovative and experimental. Some are backward looking and thoroughly medieval, and some seem completely imbued with the spirit of the English Renaissance. Dunbar's poems praise and sometimes imitate his great English predecessors — Chaucer, Gower, and Lydgate — and it is accurate to say that his poetry represents the culmination of medieval poetic practice. At the same time, it is also appropriate to point out that some of his poems seem to anticipate the poetry of such sixteenth- and seventeenth-century poets as Wyatt and Donne, Herbert and Milton, and, in Scottish literary tradition, the poetry of Robert Burns.

The great variety of poems within Dunbar's canon includes religious hymns of exaltation, moral poems on a wide range of serious themes, general satires against the times, and satires with much more specific targets, often a single individual. Dunbar's canon also includes allegorical poems and dream visions, poems that celebrate or critique or repudiate courtly love, laudatory poems and panegyrics, poems of vituperation and invective, and precatory poems (poems of request, or petition poems) addressed to the king or queen. There are also wildly exuberant comic poems and various kinds of literary burlesques and parodies, and there are a few longer poems that are more narrative than lyrical. Clearly, pinning labels to Dunbar's poems is not always easy; many of them reflect simultaneously the distinctive characteristics of several poetic sub-categories, and the classification of some of his poems remains a matter of scholarly dispute.

But perhaps above all else Dunbar is a satirist. A large number of his poems are undoubtedly satiric in intent and fall clearly within this mode. Others that are not so obviously subversive in their intentions contain satiric elements and asides. It is the poet's impulse towards satire that is perhaps the single most common feature of his literary art, and for Dunbar that mode is usually tinged with the darker emotional hues — often suggesting the poet's own sense of anger, frustration, disappointment, and disillusionment. Thus the satire in Dunbar's poems more often tends to be derisive and scornful rather than light-hearted and gently mocking, and several of his poems appear to have been written with the explicit intention to expose and humiliate. They are much more akin to the darker and more cynical tone found in a work such as Swift's *Gulliver's Travels* than they are to the subtler varieties of satire seen in Chaucer's *Canterbury Tales*. Dunbar, in contrast to Chaucer, rarely works by indirection. He does occasionally employ irony, but he is usually overt and direct in his comic subversions. Dunbar rarely leaves any doubt in his satiric poems about the thoughts and emotions in his mind and heart.

Dunbar's poems reflect several distinctive voices and styles. One of the voices often sounded in his moral poems, for example, is that of a stern preacher who is admonishing his hearers to attend to their spiritual and moral needs. Many of Dunbar's petition poems, on the other hand, seem to reflect a very personal voice, a voice that gives every appearance of being the poet's own voice. Stylistically, Dunbar's poems are marked by the use of several highly contrastive forms of diction. The most distinctive feature in several of his poems is what scholars call aureation or aureate diction, a very formal and artificial diction that uses many words of Latin derivation, some of which appear to be original coinages. A term that Dunbar himself might use for such language is *annamalit* ("enameled"), which aptly describes the brilliant, glossy surface so characteristic of these poems. Dunbar's aureate diction is found in several of his formal, ceremonial poems (e.g., "The Thistle and the Rose" — Poem 30), in some of his courtly love poetry (e.g., *The Golden Targe* — Poem 65), and perhaps most pronouncedly in his poem in praise of the Virgin, "A Ballad of Our Lady" (Poem 4). Contrasting with Dunbar's aureate diction is his use of the language of colloquial insult; indeed there can be little doubt but that Dunbar has mastered the fine art of name-calling. Several of his poems, both from among his petition poems and from among his satiric poems, reflect his genius in this regard. "To the King" (Schir, ye have mony servitouris — Poem 46) is one of the best examples, as is *The Flyting of Dunbar and Kennedy* (Poem 83). An especially intriguing example of it occurs in "In a Secret Place"(Poem 72), in which the catalogue of extremely colloquial names the speakers apply to each other are meant to be terms of endearment rather than degrading insults.

Another important characteristic of Dunbar's versatility may be seen in the poet's metrical virtuosity. A few of his poems are written in rhyming couplets (Poems 5, 45, 46, and 81) and one, *The Tretis of the Tua Mariit Wemen and the Wedo* (Poem 84), is written in the Middle English alliterative long line.[1] The vast majority of his poems, however, are written in short stanzas with complex rhyme schemes. In most of these poems the stanzas contain anywhere from four to eight verses, with most of them having refrains. One of Dunbar's favorite forms is the five-line stanza rhyming *aabba*, a form he uses sixteen times. Nearly as common is his use of quatrains rhyming *aabB*, with the final line being a refrain, a form he uses eleven times. In the case of these two much-favored stanzaic forms, there does not appear to be any common denominator — regarding such things as theme or tone or subject matter — that would logically group them together. But that *does* seem to be the case with some of the other verse forms that Dunbar employs. For example, all the poems written in the seven-line stanza with the *aabbcbc* rhyme scheme are pieces of comic or satiric verse (Poems 56, 60, 69, 72, and 74). Similarly, all of the poems written in the seven-line stanza form known as rhyme royal (iambic pentameter poems with an *ababbcc* rhyme scheme) are serious and/or courtly poems, in accordance with established practice in the later Middle Ages. Another form Dunbar uses for serious and/or celebratory poems is the *ballade*, an eight-line stanza rhyming *ababbcbC* in which the final line is a refrain; he employs this verse form in sixteen poems. The only exception to this general rule is *The Flyting of Dunbar and Kennedy* (Poem 83), where he uses the *ballade* form (though without the refrain) for comic purposes. A final stanzaic form that Dunbar sometimes employs is the tail-rhyme stanza. Although he only uses it a few times (Poems 54, 55, 67, and 77), when he does, it is always for comic or satiric purposes.

The Arrangement of the Poems

Most previous editors of Dunbar's poetry have tended to arrange the poems according to their subject matters or their formal characteristics or some combination of the two. Although such arrangements are inevitably subjective and somewhat arbitrary, there are few attractive or feasible alternatives. Priscilla Bawcutt, Dunbar's most recent editor, has chosen to present the poems alphabetically according to the first word of the first line. This neutral arrangement has a distinctive advantage in that it "permits poems to be read without over-explicit labeling of their subject or 'kind'" (Bw 1.21). Certainly, such an ordering of the poems has much to be

---

[1] For a discussion of Dunbar's use of alliterative conventions in his poetry, see A. A. MacDonald, "Alliterative Poetry and Its Context: The Case of William Dunbar."

said for it, but in practical terms it also has some very significant drawbacks; Bawcutt herself recognizes this when in a handful of instances she is forced to deviate from her own plan. Indeed, perhaps the advantages to such a "neutral" ordering of the poems are offset by the inconvenience to the reader who wishes to view Dunbar's poems in relationship to each other. For that simple reason it seems better to do what other editors have done and attempt to arrange the poems into logical groupings. A second reason to do this is that many of Dunbar's poems are obviously companion pieces to each other, and there are even several short sequences of poems that are directly interconnected. It makes little sense not to place such poems adjacent to one another. Furthermore, it makes a good deal of sense to print all of Dunbar's petition poems together as a group, and to print all of his courtly love poems as a group. To do this is not to deny that there will always be differences of opinion in regard to which of his poems actually are his petition poems or actually do pertain to courtly love.

The plan adopted here is to begin with Dunbar's serious poems and to end with his comic ones. Within this scheme Dunbar's poetry has been divided into four large categories. The first of them includes Dunbar's religious and moral poems, which comprise about a third of his canon. The second sub-grouping includes the poems that directly relate to the poet's life as a figure in the court of James IV. This group is followed by the small number of poems that Dunbar wrote in the medieval tradition of *fin'amor* — his poems pertaining to courtly love. The final group is a sprawling and rather heterogeneous set of poems that are comic, satiric, and parodic, and in the case of some of them, scatological and obscene.

Poems Devotional and Moral

About a third of the poems in the Dunbar canon provide serious treatment of religious or moral topics. Poems 1–3 — which have many of the characteristics we associate with church hymns — celebrate biblical events of great importance to medieval Christians: the Nativity, the Crucifixion, and the Resurrection. "A Ballad of Our Lady" (Poem 4), similarly, reflects the medieval theme of the Adoration of the Virgin Mary. "In Praise of Women" (Poem 5) is less specifically religious in nature and appears to celebrate women in general and mothers particularly, yet it is also clearly intended to venerate the Holy Mother of God. Indeed, it is possible that the poem as we have it is the opening section of what was once a much longer poem celebrating the Virgin.

Among Dunbar's devotional poetry is a small group of penitential poems, Poems 6–9, works closely associated with the liturgical season of Lent. These poems are especially concerned with the spiritual preparation Christians should make prior to going to confession during Holy Week. The speaker in "The Manner of Going to Confession" (Poem 6) admonishes his audience to search their consciences and reflect upon their sins in order to achieve the spiritual condition known as contrition, while the speaker in "The Table of Confession" (Poem 7)

6

provides a comprehensive guide to the sins and reminds its audience of the fundamental tenets of medieval Christian doctrine. "All Earthly Joy Returns to Pain" (Poem 8) and "Of Man's Mortality" (Poem 9) focus on Ash Wednesday, the day that initiates the Lenten season; this pair of poems also introduces us to the poet's concern with human mortality and earthly mutability, but their main focus continues to be on penitence, contrition, and confession. In "An Orison" (Poem 10), a brief and simple devotional poem, the speaker acknowledges his sensual desires but also expresses his heartfelt wish to atone for his sins. "Of the World's Vanity" (Poem 11), one of Dunbar's most conventional expressions of the theme of earthly mutability, is not explicitly about confession, but that concern is perhaps implied. In this poem, as in several others, the speaking voice is that of a preacher who is admonishing his listeners to heed his words.

A few of Dunbar's moral poems are concerned with "the four last things" — Death, Judgment, Heaven, and Hell. "Of Life" (Poem 12) suggests that we can experience a short-lived torment and an everlasting bliss, or a short-lived joy and an everlasting sorrow. "Of the Changes of Life" (Poem 13) focuses on the alternation of joy and woe in this life but offers no suggestions about how to achieve a more lasting joy when this life ends. Two of Dunbar's most acclaimed moralities are "The Lament for the Makars" (Poem 14) and "A Meditation in Winter" (Poem 15). "The Lament for the Makars" is a poignant meditation on the inevitability of death in the *memento mori* tradition. The speaker tells us that Death comes for everyone, regardless of social class or professional accomplishments, and no exception is made for poets. Despite the poem's somber tone, however, there is a slight upswing at the end when we are reminded that life in this world should be viewed as preparation for the life to come. In "A Meditation in Winter" the speaker's melancholy stems from the oppressive winter weather with its long nights and dark, cheerless days; in this case the speaker is able to dispel his dreary thoughts by contemplating the joyful return of spring.

Boethian elements appear in many of Dunbar's moral poems but are especially prominent in Poems 16–22, works that share some similarities with the Chaucerian lyrics "Truth," "Fortune," and "Lak of Stedfastnesse." "None May Assure in this World" (Poem 16), one of Dunbar's more intriguing moral poems, reflects the characteristics of several poetic types including the Boethian lyric (it specifically recalls Chaucer's "Lak of Stedfastnesse"), while Poems 17–19 are more narrowly concerned with achieving consolation in this world in the face of life's adversities. These poems counsel their hearers to be content with their lot, despite the apparent unfairness of life. "Best to Be Blithe" (Poem 17) is imbued with a strong sense of the speaker's personal pain, while "Without Gladness No Treasure Avails" (Poem 19), the most cheerful of these poems, encourages the listener to be merry and to enjoy what life has to offer. "His Own Enemy" (Poem 20) is one of Dunbar's more problematic moral poems, for while it seems to be advising its audience to enjoy what they are fortunate enough to possess, there is a sardonic quality to the poem that sets it apart from the others.

"Spend Thine Own Goods" (Poem 21) and "Of Covetise" (Poem 22), while reflecting many conventional elements of the poem of moral advice, also begin to reflect the elements of courtly satire that seem to lie at the heart of the final sub-group of Dunbar's moral poems. The advice these poems offer is more secular and practical and concerns how to survive in the complex and often hostile environment existing at court. Several of Dunbar's moral poems focus on the importance of money and worldly goods and thus may be closely related to Dunbar's petition poems. "Of Deeming" (Poem 23) offers advice about how to cope with malicious gossip (ignore it and live as virtuously as you can); "How Should I Conduct Myself" (Poem 24) offers practical advice about how to conduct oneself; and "Rule of Oneself" (Poem 25), one of the most sententious in the Dunbar canon, suggests more broad-based counsel on how to cope with the uncertainties of life at court. Poems 26–28 are a series of interconnected poems that consider the "discretion" one should possess in regard to asking, giving, and taking. The three poems in this sequence share a common poetic form and employ similar refrains, yet each of them has a distinctive flavor. "Dunbar at Oxford" (Poem 29) is the final poem in this section. Here the moral advice is directed specifically at scholars, who are urged to pursue their intellectual achievements while maintaining a strong moral grounding.

Poems Public and Private

The poems in this section reflect Dunbar's life and his professional responsibilities at court during the reign of James IV of Scotland. Some grow out of the poet's important public responsibilities at court, and a great many more of them stem from his more personal inter-actions with members of the court, including the king and the queen. The first group of poems, Poems 30–36, are occasional poems written to commemorate important public events. In some cases, as in "The Thistle and the Rose" (Poem 30), which concerns the royal marriage of James to Margaret Tudor in 1503, these were events of national consequence. These celebratory poems suggest that Dunbar was often called upon to provide poems for special occasions. That appears to be the case in the group of the poems addressed to Queen Margaret (Poems 31–34) and in the two poems written in praise of Bernard Stewart (Poems 35 and 36). These great display pieces of public celebration contrast sharply with Dunbar's many other poems that concern the court of James IV, poems that are probably intended for a much more selective audience and whose purpose is primarily comedic and/or satiric rather than celebratory (Poems 50–60).

Far less easy to fathom, however, is the extensive group of poems comprising Dunbar's petitions. There are more than a dozen of these poems, many of which are addressed to "Schir" — undoubtedly King James IV himself — and most of them are direct or indirect appeals for the king's financial and professional support. It is also likely that the king was not their exclusive audience and that they were circulated among a small circle of the poet's friends, though just how private or public they actually were is impossible to determine. Some readers of Dunbar have found these poems unseemly and embarrassing, both because there are so many of them and because they often seem self-serving and sometimes self-pitying. These poems are intriguing because of the various suggestions they make about the poet's relationship to the king. Also within this group are a few poems of considerable artistic merit. Dunbar scholars generally agree that "To the King" (Schir, ye have mony servitouris — Poem 46) is one of the poet's most subtle and artful poems; and every reader of Dunbar has been intrigued by the brief, somewhat enigmatic, and apparently highly personal poem often called "The Headache" (Poem 43). One of the poems in this group that especially appeals to the editor of this volume is "To the King" (That I suld be ane Yowllis yald — Poem 49), which develops and sustains a clever metaphorical comparison involving men and horses.

Poems 51–60 focus on a variety of people who were associated with the royal court. Some the poet admires, some he humorously satirizes or mocks, and some he scorns and viciously maligns. Poems 51–53 stand in close relationship to Dunbar's petition poems and once again testify to the poet's difficulties in securing the financial support he feels he deserves, and also to his worries about managing money once he has some. "To the Lord Treasurer" (Poem 52) and "To the Lords of Chalker" (Poem 53) are addressed to important financial officers of the court, the Lord Treasurer and the Lords of Chalker. The first of this pair of poems expresses the poet's delight at the treasurer's speedy return to Edinburgh, which means that he will be able to receive his pension without further delay. The second comically reveals to the Lords of Chalker, who were the auditors of the exchequer, that he is unable to account for the sudden and mysterious disappearance of the funds he had received. "The Antichrist" (Poem 51) and "A Ballad of the Friar of Tungland" (Poem 54) heap scorn and ridicule upon John Damian, a colorful and flamboyant figure at James' court whom Dunbar considered a fraud and a charlatan, but who nonetheless received substantial support from the king, to Dunbar's considerable chagrin. Poems 56–58 concern figures belonging to Queen Margaret's personal entourage, and these poems may suggest that Dunbar was himself attached to the queen's service. And three of Dunbar's poems about figures at court — Poems 55, 59, and 60 — are apparently denunciations of actual people against whom Dunbar felt particularly aggrieved.

Poems in the Courtly Tradition

The eight poems in this small group are all concerned with *fin'amor* (or "courtly love"), a pervasive and influential literary phenomenon that flourished from the twelfth century into the sixteenth. *Fin'amor* was an elaborate code of behavior and discourse that established guidelines for the conduct of amorous relationships between the sexes. It is a complex and controversial literary phenomenon and one that appears in many guises and permutations throughout the Middle Ages. In brief, it posited the sovereignty and superiority of the lady, whose male wooer was expected to perform long service and endure great suffering before his suit could be entertained or his amorous desires reciprocated. Some medieval writers seem to take the doctrines of *fin'amor* very seriously and others, particularly in the later Middle Ages, are more inclined to satirize them. One group of Dunbar's poems appears to celebrate *fin'amor* (Poems 61–64), while another clearly repudiates it (Poems 66–68). Posed between these two starkly contrasting attitudes is Dunbar's *The Golden Targe* (Poem 65), which critics have variously interpreted, although it seems quite likely that the poem is more negative in its attitude toward courtly love than positive. Dunbar wrote relatively few poems in the courtly love tradition, but two of them — "Sweet Rose of Virtue" (Poem 61) and *The Golden Targe* — are often ranked among his most impressive works.

Poems Comic, Satiric, and Parodic

The sixteen poems in this group, although extremely heterogeneous, are all essentially comic. And, while they surely reflect a wide range of purposes and intentions, one of the central intentions in each of them is to provide amusement. Indeed, several of them were almost certainly written for public performances at court (Poems 71, 77, 83, and possibly 84). Several of them focus on various kinds of sexual comedy (Poems 69, 70, 72, 73, and 84), several humorously satirize members of the non-noble classes within Scottish society (Poems 74, 75, 76, 77, 78, 79, and 82), and several are essentially literary parodies (Poems 71, 72, 80, and 81). By far the most celebrated poem within this group is *The Tretis of the Tua Mariit Wemen and the Wedo* (Poem 84), which Dunbar critics and scholars, without exception, consider one of his most important works. There is far less consensus on the literary merits of the poem which here precedes the *Tretis*, Poem 83, a poem containing Dunbar's war of words with his fellow poet Walter Kennedy — *The Flyting of Dunbar and Kennedy*. There can be little doubt, though, that these two final poems represent the most extreme and outrageous examples of excremental humor and sexual obscenity to be found within the Dunbar canon.

The Early Texts and Manuscripts

The texts of Dunbar's poems are preserved in a small number of sixteenth- and seventeenth-century witnesses. Five of these early sources — a pair of printed texts, the Aberdeen Sasine Register, the Asloan Manuscript, and the Arundel Manuscript — all date from the poet's own lifetime or shortly thereafter. These sources, however, contain only a small number of Dunbar's poems. Far more are preserved in the three great Renaissance anthologies commonly known as the Bannatyne Manuscript, the Maitland Folio, and the Reidpeth Manuscript. An additional source is the late sixteenth-century Osborn Manuscript, which contains the text of just one poem.

1. *The Early Printed Texts*
 A) *Chepman and Myllar* (Edinburgh, National Library of Scotland).
The texts of three of Dunbar's poems (Poems 35, 65, and 83) are contained in a series of small booklets that were printed in 1508 by Walter Chepman and Andrew Myllar, Scotland's first printers.
 B) "*The Rouen Print*" (Edinburgh, National Library of Scotland).
This early print also contains three of Dunbar's poems (Poems 14, 80, and 84); it is undated and typographically distinct from the Chepman and Myllar prints. Kinsley called it "the Rouen print," but some scholars believe that it was printed in Edinburgh rather than on the continent, possibly by Myllar before he and Chepman began their collaboration.

2. *The Aberdeen Sasine Register* (Aberdeen, City Charter Room, The Town House).
Also called "The Aberdeen Minute Book," this multi-volume work, which was begun in 1484, is primarily a record of property transactions for the royal burgh of Aberdeen. In the margins and on some originally blank pages other writings are recorded, including several vernacular poems. Three of them (Poems 19, 33, and 82) are attributed to Dunbar; they are found in Volumes II and III (for the years 1502–07 and 1507–13, respectively).

3. *The Asloan Manuscript* (Edinburgh, National Library of Scotland MS 16500).
This large miscellany, which contains works in both prose and verse, was probably compiled between 1515 and 1525. It bears the name of its primary scribe, John Asloan (or Sloane), a public notary in Edinburgh from the 1490s to the early 1530s. It contains the partial texts of three Dunbar poems (Poems 2, 54, and 77). It is especially important for preserving the only extant text of Poem 4, one of the finest examples of Dunbar's use of the aureate style, and his only poem written exclusively in praise of the Virgin Mary.

4. *The Arundel Manuscript* (London, British Library MS Arundel 285).
This manuscript, which probably dates to about the middle of the sixteenth century, is a fairly homogeneous collection of devotional pieces — poems, verse meditations, and prayers. It contains the texts of three of Dunbar's religious poems (Poems 2, 6, and 7).

5. *The Bannatyne Manuscript* (Edinburgh, National Library of Scotland Advocates' MS 1.1.6).
The compiler of this important manuscript collection of early Scottish poetry was George Bannatyne (1545–1608), an Edinburgh merchant. Bannatyne states that he assembled his anthology in 1568, during a "tyme of pest." This extensive collection is in two parts. The main

section contains 375 leaves, and the shorter section, which is either a partial draft or a partial duplicate copy, contains fifty-eight. The contents of the manuscript are quite varied, including both Scottish materials and English materials, and materials derived from both manuscript sources and early printed sources. Its overall design is indicated by Bannatyne's decision to arrange his materials in five major sections (each of which has several sub-sections), sections to which he gave the titles "ballatis of moralite," "ballettis mirry," "ballatis of theoligie," "ballattis of luve," and "fabillis." Each of Bannatyne's sections includes poems attributed to Dunbar, and in all, the Bannatyne MS preserves the texts of about forty of Dunbar's poems, nearly half the poet's canon.

6. *The Maitland Folio* (Cambridge, Pepys Library, Magdalene College MS 2553).
This great miscellany of 366 pages was compiled between 1570 and 1586. It contains poems by many poets, including a large number written by Sir Richard Maitland (1496–1586) and many others that were written in honor of Maitland. Interspersed throughout the folio are fifty-two poems that are specifically attributed to Dunbar, and ten more poems that Bannatyne had attributed to Dunbar. Thus the Maitland Folio preserves the texts of more than sixty Dunbar poems — nearly three-quarters of the entire canon. At one time this manuscript had contained even more of Dunbar's poems, as the Reidpeth MS indicates.

7. *The Reidpeth Manuscript* (Cambridge, Cambridge University Library MS Ll.v.10).
This manuscript, which is named for its copyist John Reidpeth, is a partial transcript of the Maitland Folio. It is a folio volume of sixty-nine leaves, and as the copyist indicates, was begun in December of 1622. It contains fifty poems that scholars attribute to Dunbar. The special importance of the Reipeth MS, however, is that it is the only one of the earliest witnesses to preserve the texts for eight of Dunbar's poems. These poems were copied from a gathering of the Maitland Folio that is now lost. They are Poems 33, 36, 37, 42, 43, 52, 53, and 75.

8. *The Osborn Manuscript* (New Haven, CT, Beinecke Rare Book and Manuscript Library, Yale University, Music MS 13).
Also called the "Osborn Commonplace Book" and the "Braye Lute Book," this late sixteenth-century miscellany of fifty-seven leaves has been of particular interest for the music it preserves for the lute. In addition, this small quarto volume contains various written items, including recipes and about a dozen poems. One of these is a version of Dunbar's "In a Secret Place" (Poem 72).

Introduction

The Presentation of the Texts

Modern conventions for punctuation and capitalization have been followed in presenting the texts of Dunbar's poems. The early witnesses contain many abbreviations that have been silently expanded. The refrains in the texts of many of the poems, which are often abbreviated after the initial stanza, are printed in full. In a small number of instances, the spelling conventions of the original texts have been altered for the convenience of the modern reader with the assumption that the revised spelling reflects the original pronunciation of the word more accurately than the orthographic convention of the day:

1) *u/v*: *obseruance* is here printed as *observance*; *vpoun* is printed as *upoun*.
2) *w/u/v*: *hewinlie* is here printed as *hevinlie*; *ws lewit* is printed as *us levit*.
3) *i/j*: *iugis* is here printed as *jugis*; *Iudas* is printed as *Judas*
4) The only archaic letter that regularly appears in the early witnesses is yogh; it is here printed as *y* or *g* in most instances, though in a few instances as *z*, as in *Lazarus*.
5) In several of the poems there are personified figures such as "Trewth" or "Honour." They have been treated as proper names and thus capitalized.
6) The second person familiar pronoun is here printed as *thee* /þe/ in order to distinguish it from the article *the*, which was pronounced /þə/.
7) Titles: Medieval lyrics rarely possess titles, and the titles by which we may know them are more often than not the creations of modern editors. The same is true for the poems of William Dunbar. Many of Dunbar's poems, however, are widely known by their various popular titles — e.g., "The Lament for the Makars," *The Golden Targe*, and "The Thistle and the Rose" — titles which for the most part were given to the poems by Dunbar's eighteenth- and nineteenth-century editors. Because these titles have been in common usage for some time, there is value in preserving them. The "titles" of Dunbar's poems given here attempt to follow such current practice, but also provided in brackets for some poems is a secondary set of titles that might include other familiar titles or briefly descriptive titles (such as refrains) that may make it easier for users of this volume to identify particular poems. An index of first lines is provided in the back of the volume for additional ease of cross-referencing.

Select Bibliography

Modern Editions

The Poems of William Dunbar. Ed. Priscilla Bawcutt. 2 vols. Association for Scottish Literary Studies 27 and 28. Glasgow: Association for Scottish Literary Studies, 1998.

The Poems of William Dunbar. Ed. James Kinsley. Oxford: Clarendon Press, 1979.

The Poems of William Dunbar, Now First Collected. With Notes, and a Memoir of His Life. Ed. David Laing. Edinburgh: Laing and Forbes, 1834; *Supplement*, 1865.

The Poems of William Dunbar. Ed. W. Mackay Mackenzie. London: Faber and Faber, 1932. Rev. 1960, with corrections by Bruce Dickins.

The Poems of William Dunbar. Ed. J. S. Schipper. 5 parts. Vienna: K. Akademie der Wissenschaften, 1891–94.

The Poems of William Dunbar. Ed. John Small, Walter Gregor, and Æ. J. G. Mackay. 3 vols. Scottish Text Society 2, 4, 16, 21, 29. Edinburgh and London: W. Blackwood, 1883–93.

Primary Texts and Reference Works

Aberdeen Council Register. Extracts from the Council Register of the Burgh of Aberdeen. Ed. John Stuart. Spalding Club 12. Aberdeen: William Bennett, 1844–48.

Accounts of the Lord High Treasurer of Scotland. Ed. Thomas Dickson, James Balfour Paul, C. T. McInnes, and Athel L. Murray. 13 vols. Edinburgh: H. M. General Register House, 1877–.

Ancient Scottish Poems, Never Before in Print, but Now Published from the Ms. Collections of Sir Richard Maitland, of Lethington, Knight, Lord Privy Seal of Scotland, and a Senator of the College of Justice; Comprising Pieces Written from about 1420 till 1586, with Large Notes, and a Glossary; Prefixed Are: An Essay on the Origin of Scottish Poetry; A List of All the Scottish Poets, with Brief Remarks; and an Appendix is Added, Containing, among Other Articles, an Account of the Contents of the Maitland and Bannatyne Mss. Ed. John Pinkerton. 2 vols. London: C. Dilley, 1786.

Asloan, John. *The Asloan Manuscript: A Miscellany in Prose and Verse.* Ed. W. A. Craigie. 2 vols. Scottish Text Society n.s. 14, 16. Edinburgh: W. Blackwood and Sons, 1923–25.

The Bannatyne Manuscript. National Library of Scotland, Advocates' MS. 1.1.6. Intro. Denton Fox and William A. Ringler. London: Scolar Press, in association with the National Library of Scotland, 1980.

Introduction

Bannatyne, George. *The Bannatyne Manuscript Written in Tyme of Pest, 1568*. Ed. and intro. W. Tod Ritchie. 4 vols. Scottish Text Society n.s. 22–23, 26; third ser. 5. Edinburgh: W. Blackwood and Sons, 1928–34.

Barbour, John. *Barbour's Bruce: A Fredome Is a Noble Thing!* Ed. Matthew P. McDiarmid and James A. C. Stevenson. 3 vols. Scottish Text Society fourth ser. 12–13, 15. Edinburgh: Scottish Text Society, 1980–85.

The Bible of the Poor [Biblia Pauperum]: A Facsimile and Edition of the British Library Blockbook C.9.d.2. Trans. and com. Albert C. Labriola and John W. Smeltz. Pittsburgh, PA: Duquesne University Press, 1990.

Bower, Walter. *Scotichronicon in Latin and English*. Ed. D. E. R. Watt et al. 9 vols. Aberdeen: Aberdeen University Press, 1987–98.

Brown, Carleton, and Rossell Hope Robbins. *The Index of Middle English Verse*. New York: Columbia University Press, 1943.

The Buke of the Howlat. Ed. Richard Holland. In *Longer Scottish Poems*, ed. Bawcutt and Riddy, 1987. Pp. 43–84.

Chaucer, Geoffrey. *The Riverside Chaucer*. Gen. ed. Larry D. Benson. Third ed. Boston: Houghton Mifflin Co., 1987.

The Chepman and Myllar Prints: Nine Tracts from the First Scottish Press, Edinburgh, 1508, Followed by the Two Other Tracts in the Same Volume in the National Library of Scotland: A Facsimile. Intro. William Beattie. Edinburgh: Edinburgh Bibliographical Society, 1950.

Colkelbie Sow and the Talis of the Fyve Bestes. Ed. Gregory C. Kratzmann. Garland Medieval Texts 6. New York: Garland, 1983.

Devotional Pieces in Verse and Prose from Ms. Arundel 285 and Ms. Harleaian 6919. Ed. J. A. W. Bennett. Scottish Text Society third ser. 23. Edinburgh: W. Blackwood and Sons, 1955.

Douglas, Gavin. *Aeneid. Translated into Scottish Verse by Gavin Douglas*. Ed. David F. C. Coldwell. 4 vols. Scottish Text Society third ser. 25, 27–28, 30. Edinburgh: W. Blackwood and Sons, 1957–64.

Douglas, Gavin. *The Palis of Honoure*. Ed. David Parkinson. Kalamazoo, MI: Medieval Institute Publications, 1992.

The Ever Green, Being a Collection of Scots Poems Wrote by the Ingenious before 1600. Ed. Allan Ramsay. 2 vols. Edinburgh: Thomas Ruddiman, 1724.

The Floure and the Leafe, The Assembly of Ladies, The Isle of Ladies. Ed. Derek Pearsall. Kalamazoo, MI: Medieval Institute Publications, 1990.

Geoffrey of Monmouth. *History of the Kings of Britain*. Trans. and intro. Lewis Thorpe. London: The Folio Society, 1969.

Greene, Richard Leighton. *The Early English Carols*. Rev. ed. Oxford: Clarendon Press, 1977.

Hary's "Wallace" (vita nobilissimi defensoris Scotie Wilelmi Wallace militis). Ed. Matthew P. McDiarmid. 2 vols. Scottish Text Society fourth ser. 4–5. Haddington, UK: Scottish Text Society, 1968–69.

Henryson, Robert. *The Poems of Robert Henryson*. Ed. Denton Fox. Oxford: Clarendon Press, 1981.

Higden, Ranulf. *Polychronicon Ranulphi Higden monachi Cestrensis, together with the English Translations of John Trevisa and of an Unknown Writer of the Fifteenth Century*. Ed. Churchill Babington and J. Rawson Lumby. Rolls Series 41. 9 vols. London: Longman and Co., 1865–86.

Lindsay, Sir David. *The Works of Sir David Lindsay of the Mount, 1490–1555*. Ed. Douglas Hamer. 4 vols. Scottish Text Society third ser. 1–2, 6, 8. Edinburgh: W. Blackwood and Sons, 1931–36.

Longer Scottish Poems. Volume 1: *1375–1650*. Ed. Priscilla Bawcutt and Felicity Riddy. Edinburgh: Scottish Academic Press, 1987.

Lydgate, John. *The Minor Poems of John Lydgate: Part I*. Ed. Henry Noble MacCracken. EETS e.s. 107. London: Oxford University Press, 1911; rpt. 1962.

The Maitland Folio Manuscript, Containing Poems by Sir Richard Maitland, Dunbar, Douglas, Henryson, and Others. Ed. W. A. Craigie. 2 vols. Scottish Text Society n.s. 7, 20. Edinburgh: W. Blackwood and Sons, 1919–27.

Malory, Thomas. *Malory: Works*. Ed. Eugène Vinaver. New York: Oxford University Press, 1971.

Medieval English Lyrics: A Critical Anthology. Ed. R. T. Davies. London: Faber and Faber, 1963.

Middle English Debate Poetry: A Critical Anthology. Ed. John W. Conlee. East Lansing: Colleagues Press, 1991.

Middle English Dictionary. Ed. Hans Kurath, Sherman M. Kuhn, John Reidy, and Robert E. Lewis. Ann Arbor: University of Michigan Press, 1952–.

Middle English Lyrics: Authoritative Texts, Critical and Historical Backgrounds, Perspectives on Six Poems. Ed. Maxwell S. Luria and Richard L. Hoffman. New York: W. W. Norton, 1974.

The Owl and the Nightingale. Ed. Eric Gerald Stanley. London: Nelson, 1960.

Religious Lyrics of the XIVth Century. Ed. Carleton Brown. Oxford: Clarendon Press, 1924.

Religious Lyrics of the XVth Century. Ed. Carleton Brown. Oxford: Clarendon Press, 1939.

Robbins, Rossell Hope, and John L. Cutler. *Supplement to the Index of Middle English Verse*. Lexington, KY: University of Kentucky Press, 1965.

Rotuli scaccarii regum Scotorum: The Exchequer Rolls of Scotland, A.D. 1264–1600. Ed. John Stuart, George Burnett, Æ. J. G. Mackay, and G. P. McNeill. 23 vols. Edinburgh: H. M. General Register House, 1878–1908.

Secular Lyrics of the XIVth and XVth Centuries. Ed. Rossell Hope Robbins. Oxford: Clarendon Press, 1952.

Sir Gawain and the Green Knight. Ed. J. R. R. Tolkien and E. V. Gordon. 1925. Second ed. Rev. Norman Davis. Oxford: Clarendon Press, 1979.

Tilley, Morris Palmer. *A Dictionary of the Proverbs in England in the Sixteenth and Seventeenth Centuries: A Collection of the Proverbs Found in English Literature and the Dictionaries of the Period*. Ann Arbor: University of Michigan Press, 1950.

Whiting, Bartlett Jere, with Helen Wescott Whiting. *Proverbs, Sentences, and Proverbial Phrases from English Writings Mainly before 1500*. Cambridge, MA: Belknap Press of Harvard University Press, 1968.

Selected Secondary Works

Aitken, Adam J., Matthew P. McDiarmid, and Derick S. Thomson, eds. *Bards and Makars: Scottish Language and Literature: Medieval and Renaissance*. Glasgow: University of Glasgow Press, 1977.

Bawcutt, Priscilla. "Aspects of Dunbar's Imagery." In *Chaucer and Middle English Studies in Honour of Rossell Hope Robbins*. Ed. Beryl Rowland. Kent, OH: Kent State University Press, 1974. Pp. 190–200.

———. "The Text and Interpretation of Dunbar." *Medium Ævum* 50 (1981), 88–100.

———. "Elrich Fantasyis in Dunbar and Other Poets." In McClure and Spiller, 1989. Pp. 162–78.

———. *Dunbar the Makar*. Oxford: Clarendon Press, 1992.

Baxter, J. W. *William Dunbar: A Biographical Study*. Edinburgh: Oliver and Boyd, 1952.

Bloomfield, Morton W. *The Seven Deadly Sins: An Introduction to the History of a Religious Concept, with Special Reference to Medieval English Literature*. East Lansing: Michigan State College Press, 1952; rpt. 1967.

Breeze, Andrew. "Middle English *Tod* 'Fox': Old Irish *Taid* 'Thief.'" *Scottish Language* 13 (1994), 51–53.

———. "A Celtic Etymology for *Maggle* 'to Spoil' in Dunbar and Gavin Douglas." *American Notes and Queries* 11.2 (1998), 12–13.

Burness, Edwina. "Dunbar and the Nature of Bawdy." In McClure and Spiller, 1989. Pp. 209–20.

Cowan, Ian Borthwick. *The Medieval Church in Scotland*. Ed. James Kirk. Edinburgh: Scottish Academic Press, 1995.

Introduction

Craigie, William A., Sir. "The Scottish Alliterative Poems." *Proceedings of the British Academy* 28 (1942), 217–36.

Cruttwell, Patrick. "Two Scots Poets." In *The Age of Chaucer*. Ed. Boris Ford. London: Penguin, 1954. Pp. 175–87.

Curtius, Ernst Robert. *European Literature and the Latin Middle Ages*. Trans. Willard R. Trask. London: Routledge and K. Paul, 1953.

Drexler, R. D. "Dunbar's 'Lament for the Makaris' and the Dance of Death Tradition." *Studies in Scottish Literature* 13 (1978), 144–58.

Eade, J. C. *The Forgotten Sky: A Guide to Astrology in English Literature*. Oxford: Clarendon Press, 1984.

Ebin, Lois A. "The Theme of Poetry in Dunbar's 'Goldyn Targe.'" *Chaucer Review* 7 (1972), 147–59.

Emmerson, Richard Kenneth. *Antichrist in the Middle Ages: A Study of Medieval Apocalypticism, Art, and Literature*. Manchester: Manchester University Press, 1981.

Evans, Deanna Delmar. "Ambivalent Artifice in Dunbar's *The Thrissill and the Rois*." *Studies in Scottish Literature* 22 (1987), 95–105.

———. "Donald Oure and Bernard Stewart: Responding to a Villain and a Hero in William Dunbar's Poetry." *Proceedings of the Medieval Association of the Midwest* 1 (1991), 117–30.

Ewan, Elizabeth. *Townlife in Fourteenth-Century Scotland*. Edinburgh: Edinburgh University Press, 1990.

Fox, Denton. "Dunbar's *The Golden Targe*." *English Literary History* 26 (1959), 311–34.

———. "The Chronology of William Dunbar." *Philological Quarterly* 39 (1960), 413–25.

———. "The Scottish Chaucerians." In *Chaucer and Chaucerians: Critical Studies in Middle English Literature*. Ed. D. S. Brewer. London: Thomas Nelson and Sons, 1966. Pp. 164–200.

———. "Manuscripts and Prints of Scots Poetry in the Sixteenth Century." In Aitken, McDiarmid, and Thomson, 1977. Pp. 156–71.

19

The Works of William Dunbar

———. "Middle Scots Poets and Patrons." In *English Court Culture in the Later Middle Ages*. Ed. V. J. Scattergood and J. W. Sherborne. London: Duckworth, 1983. Pp. 109–27.

Fradenburg, Louise. *City, Marriage, Tournament: Arts of Rule in Late Medieval Scotland.* Madison: University of Wisconsin Press, 1991. [See Ch. 10, "Spectacle and Chivalry in Late Medieval Scotland," pp. 172–91.]

Gray, Douglas. "William Dunbar." In *Authors of the Middle Ages: English Writers of the Late Middle Ages*. Vol. 3. Ed. M. C. Seymour, et al. Aldershot, UK: Variorum, 1996. Pp. 179–94.

Harrison, David V. "The 'Woefull Prisonnere' in Dunbar's 'Golden Targe.'" *Studies in Scottish Literature* 22 (1987), 173–82.

Hasler, Antony J. "William Dunbar: The Elusive Subject." In McClure and Spiller, 1989. Pp. 194–208.

Hope, A. D. *A Midsummer Eve's Dream: Variations on a Theme by William Dunbar*. Edinburgh: Oliver and Boyd, 1971.

Hyde, I. "Poetic Imagery: A Point of Comparison between Henryson and Dunbar." *Studies in Scottish Literature* 2 (1964–65), 183–97.

———. "Primary Sources and Associations of Dunbar's Aureate Imagery." *Modern Language Review* 51 (1956), 481–92.

Jack, R. D. S. "Dunbar and Lydgate." *Studies in Scottish Literature* 8 (1970–71), 215–27.

———, ed. and intro. *The History of Scottish Literature I: Origins to 1660 (Mediaeval and Renaissance)*. Gen. ed. Cairns Craig. Aberdeen: Aberdeen University Press, 1988.

Jung, Annette. "William Dunbar and the Morris Dancers." In McClure and Spiller, 1989. Pp. 221–43.

King, Pamela. "Dunbar's 'The Golden Targe': A Chaucerian Masque." *Studies in Scottish Literature* 19 (1984), 115–31.

Kinsley, James. "The Tretis of the Tua Mariit Wemen and the Wedo." *Medium Ævum* 23 (1954), 31–35.

Kratzmann, Gregory. *Anglo-Scottish Literary Relations, 1430–1550*. Cambridge, UK: Cambridge University Press, 1980.

Lampe, David. "'Flyting no Reason hath': The Inverted Rhetoric of Abuse." In *The Early Renaissance*. Ed. Aldo S. Bernardo. Binghamton, NY: Center for Medieval and Early Renaissance Studies, 1978. Pp. 101–20.

Lawton, David. "Dullness and the Fifteenth Century." *English Literary History* 54 (1987), 761–99.

Lewis, C. S. *The Allegory of Love: A Study in Medieval Tradition*. Oxford: Clarendon Press, 1936.

———. *English Literature in the Sixteen Century, excluding Drama*. Oxford: Clarendon Press, 1954. [See "The Close of the Middle Ages in Scotland," pp. 66–119.]

Leyerle, John. "The Two Voices of William Dunbar." *University of Toronto Quarterly* 31 (1962), 316–38.

Lyall, Roderick J. "Moral Allegory in Dunbar's 'Golden Targe.'" *Studies in Scottish Literature* 11 (1973), 47–65.

———. "Politics and Poetry in Fifteenth and Sixteenth Century Scotland." *Scottish Literary Journal* 3.2 (1976), 5–29.

———. "Complaint, Satire and Invective in Middle Scots Literature." In *Church, Politics and Society: Scotland 1408–1929*. Ed. Norman MacDougall. Edinburgh: John Donald, 1983. Pp. 44–64.

McClure, J. Derrick, and Michael R. G. Spiller, eds. *Bryght Lanternis: Essays on the Language and Literature of Medieval and Renaissance Scotland*. Aberdeen: Aberdeen University Press, 1989.

MacDonald, A. A. "Poetry, Politics, and Reformation Censorship in Sixteenth-Century Scotland." *English Studies* 64 (1983), 410–21.

———. "Alliterative Poetry and Its Context: The Case of William Dunbar." In *Loyal Letters: Studies in Mediæval Alliterative Poetry & Prose*. Ed. L. A. J. R. Houwen and A. A. MacDonald. Mediaevalia Groningana 15. Groningen: Egbert Forsten, 1994. Pp. 261–79.

MacDonald, A. A, Michael Lynch, and Ian B. Cowan, eds. *The Renaissance in Scotland: Studies in Literature, Religion, History and Culture Offered to John Durkhan*. Leiden: E. J. Brill, 1994.

MacDonald, Roderick. "A Dictionary Ramble." *Scottish Language* 13 (1994), 84–85.

MacDougall, Norman. *Church, Politics and Society: Scotland 1408–1929*. Edinburgh: John Donald, 1983.

———. *James IV*. Edinburgh: John Donald, 1989.

McKenna, Steven R. "Drama and Invective: Traditions in Dunbar's 'Fasternis Evin in Hell.'" *Studies in Scottish Literature* 24 (1989), 129–41.

Mackie, R. L. *King James IV of Scotland: A Brief Survey of His Life and Times*. Edinburgh: Oliver and Boyd, 1958.

McNeil, Peter G. B., and Hector L. MacQueen, eds. *Atlas of Scottish History to 1707*. Edinburgh: The Scottish Medievalists and Department of Geography, University of Edinburgh, 1996.

MacQueen, Hector L. *Common Law and Feudal Society in Medieval Scotland*. Edinburgh: Edinburgh University Press, 1993.

MacQueen, John. *Ballattis of Luve*. Edinburgh: Edinburgh University Press, 1970.

Nichols, P. H. "William Dunbar as a Scottish Lydgatian." *Publications of the Modern Language Association* 46 (1931), 214–24.

Nicholson, Ranald. *Scotland: The Later Middle Ages*. Edinburgh: Oliver and Boyd, 1978.

Norman, Joanne S. "Sources for the Grotesque in William Dunbar's 'Dance of the Sevin Deidly Synnis.'" *Scottish Studies* 29 (1989), 55–75.

———. "William Dunbar: Grand Rhetoriqueur." In McClure and Spiller, 1989. Pp. 179–95.

Pearcy, Roy. "The Genre of Dunbar's *Tretis of the Tua Mariit Wemen and the Wedo*." *Speculum* 55 (1980), 58–74.

Introduction

Reiss, Edmund. *William Dunbar*. Boston: Twayne Publishers, 1979.

Ridley, Florence H. "Middle Scots Writers." In *A Manual of the Writings in Middle English, 1050–1500*. Vol 4. Ed. A. E. Hartung. New Haven: Connecticut Academy of Arts and Sciences, 1973. Pp. 961–1060, 1123–1284.

———. "The Treatment of Animals in the Poetry of Henryson and Dunbar." *Chaucer Review* 24 (1990), 356–66.

Robbins, Mary E. "Carnival at Court and Dunbar in the Underworld." In *History, Literature, and Music in Scotland 700–1560*. Ed. R. Andrew McDonald. Toronto: University of Toronto Press, 2002. Pp. 144–62.

Robichaud, Paul. "'Titteir Quhat I Sould Wryt': 'The Flyting of Dunbar and Kennedy' and Scots Oral Culture." *Scottish Literary Journal* 25.2 (1998), 9–16.

Robinson, Christine M. "More than One Meaning in *The Flyting of Dunbar and Kennedy*." *Neuphilologische Mitteilungen* 99 (1998), 275–83.

Ross, Ian Simpson. *William Dunbar*. Leiden: E. J. Brill, 1981.

Roth, Elizabeth. "Criticism and Taste: Readings of Dunbar's *Tretis*." *Scottish Literary Journal* Supplement 15 (1981), 57–90.

Scheps, Walter. "*The Goldyn Targe*: Dunbar's Comic Psychomachia." *Papers on Language and Literature* 11 (1975), 339–56.

———, and J. A. Looney. *Middle Scots Poets: A Reference Guide to James I, Robert Henryson, William Dunbar, and Gavin Douglas*. Boston: G. K. Hall, 1986.

Scott, Tom. *Dunbar: A Critical Exposition of the Poems*. Edinburgh: Oliver and Boyd, 1966.

Shaffer, Pamela K. "Parallel Structure in Dunbar's 'Surrexit Dominus de Sepulchro.'" *Scottish Language* 13 (1994), 54–60.

Shire, Helena Mennie. *The Thrissil, the Rois and the Flour-de-lys: A Sample-Book of State Poems and Love-Songs Showing Affinities between Scotland, England and France in the Sixteenth and Seventeenth Centuries*. Cambridge, UK: The Ninth of May, 1962.

Shuffelton, Frank. "An Imperial Flower: Dunbar's *The Golden Targe* and the Court Life of James IV of Scotland." *Studies in Philology* 72 (1975), 193–207.

Spearing, A. C. *Medieval Dream-Poetry*. Cambridge, UK: Cambridge University Press, 1976.

————. *Medieval to Renaissance in English Poetry*. Cambridge, UK: Cambridge University Press, 1985.

Swart, Judith. "On Re-reading William Dunbar." In *Chaucer and Middle English Studies in Honour of Rossell Hope Robbins*. Ed. Beryl Rowland. Kent, OH: Kent State University Press, 1974. Pp. 201–09.

Szittya, Penn R. *The Antifraternal Tradition in Medieval Literature*. Princeton: Princeton University Press, 1986.

Tentler, Thomas N. *Sin and Confession on the Eve of the Reformation*. Princeton: Princeton University Press, 1977.

Tilley, E. Allen. "The Meaning of Dunbar's 'The Golden Targe.'" *Studies in Scottish Literature* 10 (1973), 220–31.

Ting, Jenny. "A Reappraisal of William Dunbar's *Dregy*." *Scottish Literary Journal* 14.1 (1987), 19–36.

Welsford, Enid. *The Court Masque: A Study in the Relationship between Poetry & the Revels*. Cambridge, UK: Cambridge University Press, 1927.

Wormald, Jenny. *Court, Kirk and Community: Scotland, 1470–1625*. London: E. Arnold, 1981.

Ziolkowski, Jan. "Avatars of Ugliness in Medieval Literature." *Modern Language Review* 79 (1984), 1–20.

The Works of William Dunbar

1. *On the Nativity of Christ*
  [*Et nobis puer natus est*]

Rorate, celi, desuper!	*Drop down dew, you heavens, from above*
Hevins distill your balmy schouris,	*heavens let fall; fragrant showers*
For now is rissin the brycht day ster	
Fro the ros Mary, flour of flouris.	*rose; flower*
5 The cleir sone quhome no clud devouris,	*sun/son whom no cloud*
Surminting Phebus in the est	*Surpassing*
Is cumin of His hevinly touris;	*from; tower*
Et nobis puer natus est.	*And for us a boy was born*
Archangellis, angellis, and dompnationis,	*dominations*
10 Tronis, potestatis, and marteiris seir,	*Thrones, powers; martyrs many*
And all ye hevinly operationis,	
Ster, planeit, firmament, and speir,	*sphere*
Fyre, erd, air, and watter cleir,	*earth*
To Him gife loving, most and lest,	*the greatest and the least (i.e., everyone)*
15 That come into so meik maneir;	*[He] who has come; meek*
Et nobis puer natus est.	
Synnaris be glaid and pennance do,	*Sinners*
And thank your Makar hairtfully,	*full-heartedly*
For He that ye mycht nocht cum to,	*not*
20 To yow is cumin full humly,	*humbly*
Your saulis with His blud to by,	*buy*
And lous yow of the feindis arrest,	*free; fiend's*
And only of His awin mercy;	*own*
Pro nobis puer natus est.	*For us . . .*
25 All clergy do to him inclyne,	*learned people*
And bow unto that barne benyng,	*child gracious*
And do your observance devyne	

To Him that is of kingis King;
Ensence His altar, reid and sing   *read*
30 In haly kirk, with mynd degest,   *holy church; sober*
Him honouring attour all thing,   *above*
Qui nobis puer natus est.   *Who . . .*

Celestiall fowlis in the are,   *birds; air*
Sing with your nottis upoun hicht;   *notes; high*
35 In firthis and in forrestis fair   *woods*
Be myrthfull now at all your mycht,   *joyful now with*
For passit is your dully nycht.   *dismal night*
Aurora hes the cluddis perst,   *Daybreak; clouds pierced*
The son is rissin with glaidsum lycht,   *joyful*
40 *Et nobis puer natus est.*

Now spring up, flouris, fra the rute,   *root*
Revert yow upwart naturaly,
In honour of the blissit frute   *fruit*
That rais up fro the rose Mary.   *arose*
45 Lay out your levis lustely,   *Spread; leaves*
Fro deid tak lyfe now at the lest   *death; last*
In wirschip of that Prince wirthy,   *worthy*
Qui nobis puer natus est.

Syng, hevin imperiall, most of hicht,   *height*
50 Regions of air mak armony;
All fische in flud and foull of flicht   *fishes; flood; fowls; flight*
Be myrthfull and mak melody.
All *Gloria in excelsis* cry —   *Glory in the highest*
Hevin, erd, se, man, bird, and best —   *earth, sea; beast*
55 He that is crownit abone the sky   *above*
Pro nobis puer natus est.

2. *Of the Passion of Christ*

Amang thir freiris, within ane cloister,   *these friars*
I enterit in ane oritorie,
And knelit doun with ane *Pater Noster*   *Our Father*

26

Poem 2: Of the Passion of Christ

Befoir the michtie King of Glorie, — *mighty*

5 Haveing His Passioun in memorie;

Syn to His mother I did inclyne, — *Then*

Hir halsing with ane *gaude flore*; — *hailing; rejoice in the flower (see note)*

And sudandlie I sleipit syne. — *then*

Methocht Judas with mony ane Jow — *a Jew*

10 Tuik blissit Jesu, our Salvatour, — *Savior*

And schot Him furth with mony ane schow, — *hurled; shove*

With schamefull wourdis of dishonour,

And lyk ane theif or ane tratour

Thay leid that hevinlie Prince most hie — *led; high*

15 With manassing attour messour, — *menacing beyond measure*

O mankynd, for the luif of thee. — *love*

Falslie condamnit befoir ane juge — *condemned; judge*

Thay spittit in His visage fayr;

And as lyounis with awfull ruge, — *lions; roaring*

20 In yre thay hurlit Him heir and thair, — *anger; violently threw; here*

And gaif Him mony buffat sair — *blows sore*

That it wes sorow for to se. — *see*

Of all His claythis thay tirvit Him bair, — *clothes; stripped*

O mankynd, for the luif of thee.

25 Thay terandis, to revenge thair tein, — *Those villains; anger*

For scorne thai cled Him into quhyt, — *clothed; white*

And hid His blythfull glorious ene — *eyes*

To se quham angellis had delyt; — *see which*

Dispituouslie syn did Him smyt — *Cruelly then; smite*

30 Saying, "Gif sone of God Thow be, — *If*

Quha straik Thee now, Thow tell us tyt?" — *Who struck; at once*

O mankynd, for the luif of thee.

In tene thay tirvit Him agane, — *pain; stripped*

And till ane pillar thai Him band; — *to; bound*

35 Quhill blude birst out at everie vane, — *While*

Thay scurgit Him bayth fut and hand; — *both foot*

At everie straik ran furth ane strand — *stroke; stream*

Quhilk mycht have ransonit warldis thre; — *Which; ransomed*

27

He baid in stour quhill He mycht stand,   *endured the conflict*
40   O mankynd, for the luif of thee.

Nixt all in purpyr thay Him cled,   *purple; clad*
And syne with thornis scharp and kene   *then*
His saikles blude agane thay sched,   *innocent; shed*
Persing His heid with pykis grene;   *Piercing; thorns fresh*
45   Unneis with lyf He micht sustene   *Scarcely*
That croune on thrungin with crueltie,   *thrust on*
Quhill flude of blude blindit His ene,   *eyes*
O mankynd, for the luif of thee.

Ane croce that wes bayth large and lang   *A cross; both*
50   To beir thay gaif this blissit Lord;   *bear they gave*
Syn fullelie, as theif to hang,   *Then foully; [a] thief*
Thay harlit Him furth with raip and corde;   *hurled; rope*
With bluid and sweit was all deflorde   *sweat; disfigured*
His face, the fude of angellis fre;   *food; noble*
55   His feit with stanis was revin and scorde,   *feet by stones; torn; cut*
O mankynd, for the luif of thee.

Agane thay tirvit Him bak and syd,   *stripped*
Als brim as ony baris woid;   *fierce; mad boars*
The clayth that claif to His cleir hyd   *cloth; cleaved; bright skin*
60   Thay raif away with ruggis rude,   *tore; rips harsh*
Quhill fersly followit flesche and blude   *While fiercely went with it*
That it was pietie for to se.
Na kynd of torment He ganestude,   *All varieties; withstood*
O mankynd, for the luif of thee.

65   On to the Crose of breid and lenth   *breadth*
To gar His lymmis langar wax,   *make; limbs grow longer (i.e., hyperextend)*
Thay straitit Him with all thair strenth,   *stretched; strength*
Quhill to the Rude thay gart Him rax,   *Rood (Cross); made; stretch*
Syn tyit Him on with greit irne takkis;   *Then tied; iron clasps*
70   And Him all nakit on the Tre
Thay raissit on loft be houris sax,   *at the sixth hour*
O mankynd, for the luif of thee.

Poem 2: Of the Passion of Christ

	Quhen He was bendit so on breid,	*stretched; in breadth*
	Quhill all His vanis brist and brak,	*sinews burst*
75	To gar His cruell pane exceid	*make; pain increase*
	Thay leit Him fall doun with ane swak	*crash*
	Quhill cors and corps and all did crak.	*flesh; body; crack*
	Agane thay rasit Him on hie,	*high*
	Reddie may turmentis for to mak,	*Ready*
80	O mankynd, for the luif of thee.	

	Betuix tuo theiffis the spreit He gaif	*Between two thieves; spirit; gave up*
	Onto the Fader most of micht.	*Unto; might*
	The erde did trimmill, the stanis claif,	*earth; tremble; stones split*
	The sone obscurit of his licht,	*sun*
85	The day wox dirk as ony nicht,	*dark*
	Deid bodies rais in the cité.	*Dead; rose*
	Goddis deir Sone all thus was dicht,	*treated*
	O mankynd, for the luif of thee.	

	In weir that He wes yit on lyf,	*fear; alive*
90	Thay rane ane rude speir in His syde	*rough*
	And did His precious body ryff,	*tear*
	Quhill blude and watter did furth glyde.	*While*
	Thus Jesus with His woundis wyde	
	As martir sufferit for to de	*die*
95	And tholit to be crucifyid,	*suffered*
	O mankynd, for the luif of thee.	

	Methocht Compassioun, vode of feiris,	*void of manners*
	Than straik at me with mony ane stound,	*Then struck; a wound*
	And soir Contritioun, bathit in teiris,	*sore; bathed; tears*
100	My visage all in watter drownit;	*countenance*
	And Reuth into my eir ay rounde,	*Pity; ear ever whispered*
	"For schame, allace, behald, man, how	*alas*
	Beft is with mony ane bludy wound	*Beaten*
	Thy blissit Salvatour Jesu!"	

105	Than rudelie come Remembrance	*harshly comes*
	Ay rugging me withouttin rest,	*Ever pulling*
	Quhilk Crose and nalis, scharp scurge and lance	*Which Cross; nails*

	And bludy crowne befoir me kest;	*cast*
	Than Pane with passioun me opprest,	*Pain*
110	And evir did Petie on me pow,	*Pity; pull*
	Saying, "Behald how Jowis hes drest	*Jews have treated*
	Thy blissit Salvatour, Chryst Jesu!"	
	With greiting glaid be than come Grace	*greeting*
	With wourdis sweit saying to me,	*words sweet*
115	"Ordane for Him ane resting place,	*Prepare*
	That is so werie wrocht for thee:	*weary made*
	The Lord within thir dayis thre	*these*
	Sall law undir thy lyntell bow;	*Shall low*
	And in thy hous sall herbrit be	*sheltered*
120	Thy blissit Salvatour, Chryst Jesu."	
	Than swyth Contritioun wes on steir,	*at once; in a stir*
	And did eftir Confessioun ryn;	*run*
	And Conscience me accusit heir	*here*
	And kest out mony cankerit syn;	*cast; corrupting sins*
125	To rys Repentence did begin	*arise*
	And out at the gettis did schow.	*gates; shove*
	Pennance did walk the hous within,	
	Byding our Salvitour, Chryst Jesu.	*Awaiting*
	Grace become gyd and governour,	*guide*
130	To keip the hous in sicker stait	*a secure condition*
	Ay reddie till our Salvatour,	*ready for*
	Quhill that He come, air or lait;	*When; early or late*
	Repentence ay with cheikis wait	*cheeks wet*
	No pane nor pennence did eschew	*avoid*
135	The hous within evir to debait,	*(i.e., the soul); defend*
	Onlie for luif of sweit Jesu.	*Only*
	For grit terrour of Chrystis deid	*great; death*
	The erde did trymmill quhair I lay,	*earth trembled where*
	Quhairthrow I waiknit in that steid	*Through which I awakened; place*
140	With spreit halflingis in effray.	*spirit creatures; alarm*
	Than wrayt I all without delay,	*wrote; everything*
	Richt heir as I have schawin to yow,	*shown*

Poem 3: On the Resurrection of Christ

Quhat me befell on Gud Fryday   *What*
Befoir the Crose of sweit Jesu.

3. *On the Resurrection of Christ*
[*Surrexit Dominus de sepulchro*]

Done is a battell on the dragon blak,
Our campioun Chryst confountit hes his force;   *champion; has*
The gettis of Hell ar brokin with a crak,   *gates*
The signe triumphall rasit is of the Croce,   *raised; Cross*
5   The divillis trymmillis with hiddous voce,   *devils tremble; hideous voices*
The saulis ar borrowit and to the blis can go,   *redeemed*
Chryst with His blud our ransonis dois indoce: *has repaid*
Surrexit Dominus de sepulchro.   *The Lord has arisen from the grave (Luke 24:34)*

Dungin is the deidly dragon Lucifer,   *Defeated*
10   The crewall serpent with the mortall stang,
The auld kene tegir with his teith on char,   *fierce tiger; teeth ajar (i.e., bared)*
Quhilk in a wait hes lyne for us so lang,   *Who has lain in wait (ambush)*
Thinking to grip us in his clowis strang;   *claws*
The merciful Lord wald nocht that it wer so,   *did not wish*
15   He maid him for to felye of that fang: *caused him to fail; prey*
Surrexit Dominus de sepulchro.

He for our saik that sufferit to be slane,   *sake*
And lyk a lamb in sacrifice wes dicht,   *prepared*
Is lyk a lyone rissin up agane,   *lion*
20   And as a gyane raxit Him on hicht;   *giant raised Himself aloft*
Sprungin is Aurora, radius and bricht,   *Dawn, radiant*
On loft is gone the glorius Appollo,   *Aloft has; Sun*
The blisfull day depairtit fro the nycht: *has been separated from*
Surrexit Dominus de sepulchro.

25   The grit Victour agane is rissin on hicht   *great; again; high*
That for our querrell to the deth wes woundit;
The sone that wox all paill now schynis bricht,   *sun*
And dirknes clerit, our fayth is now refoundit.   *has cleared; re-established*
The knell of mercy fra the hevin is soundit,

30	The Cristin ar deliverit of thair wo,	*Christians*
	The Jowis and thair errour ar confoundit:	*Jews*
	Surrexit Dominus de sepulchro.	
	The fo is chasit, the battell is done ceis,	*foe is put to flight; over*
	The presone brokin, the jevellouris fleit and flemit;	*prison; jailers fled; banished*
35	The weir is gon, confermit is the peis,	*war; over; peace*
	The fetteris lowsit and the dungeoun temit,	*loosened; emptied*
	The ransoun maid, the presoneris redemit,	*ransom made; redeemed*
	The feild is win, ourcumin is the fo,	*field is won, overcome*
	Dispulit of the tresur that he yemit:	*Despoiled; guarded*
40	*Surrexit Dominus de sepulchro.*	

4. *A Ballad of Our Lady*
    [*Ave Maria, gracia plena*]

	Hale, sterne superne, hale in eterne,	*Hail, heavenly star; eternity*
	In Godis sicht to schyne!	*God's sight*
	Lucerne in derne for to discerne	*Lantern; darkness to be seen*
	Be glory and grace devyne;	*Through*
5	Hodiern, modern, sempitern,	*Today, now, [and] forever*
	Angelicall regyne!	*queen*
	Our tern inferne for to dispern,	*infernal darkness; disperse*
	Helpe, rialest rosyne.	*most royal rose*
	Ave Maria, gracia plena!	*Hail Mary, full of grace*
10	Haile, fresche floure femynyne!	
	Yerne us guberne, virgin matern,	*Swiftly guide us; maternal*
	Of reuth baith rute and ryne.	*pity (ruth) both root; rind*
	Haile, yhyng, benyng, fresche flurising!	*young, gentle; flourishing*
	Haile, Alphais habitakle!	*Alpha's (God's) habitation*
15	Thy dyng ofspring maid us to syng	*worthy; made*
	Befor His tabernakle.	
	All thing maling we doune thring	*malign; throw*
	Be sicht of His signakle,	*By; sign (i.e., the Cross)*
	Quhilk King us bring unto His ryng	*kingdom*
20	Fro dethis dirk umbrakle.	*death's shadowy place*
	Ave Maria, gracia plena!	

32

Poem 4: A Ballad of Our Lady

Haile, moder and maide but makle!	*without stain*
Bricht syng, gladyng our languissing	*sign, making glad*
Be micht of thi mirakle.	*By [the] power*
25 Haile, bricht be sicht in Hevyn on hicht!	*by sight; high*
Haile, day sterne orientale!	*star in the east*
Our licht most richt in clud of nycht	
Our dirknes for to scale.	*scatter*
Hale, wicht in ficht, puttar to flicht	*strong*
30 Of fendis in battale!	
Haile, plicht but sicht! Hale, mekle of mycht!	*anchor unseen; great*
Haile, glorius Virgin, hale!	
Ave Maria, gracia plena!	
Haile, gentill nychttingale!	*nightingale*
35 Way stricht, cler dicht, to wilsome wicht	*straight; prepared; erring ones*
That irke bene in travale.	*weary are*
Hale, qwene serene! Hale, most amene!	*pleasant*
Haile, hevinlie hie emprys!	*high*
Haile, schene unseyne with carnale eyne!	*fair [one] unseen with physical eyes*
40 Haile, ros of Paradys!	
Haile, clene bedene ay till conteyne!	*pure complete; continue*
Haile, fair fresche flour delyce!	*fleur-de-lis*
Haile, grene daseyne! Hale, fro the splene,	*living daisy; from the heart*
Of Jhesu genitrice!	*mother*
45 *Ave Maria, gracia plena!*	
Thow baire the Prince of Prys;	*gave birth to; Great Wealth*
Our teyne to meyne and ga betweyne	*pain; relieve*
As humile oratrice.	*humble intercessor*
Hale, more decore than of before,	*beautiful*
50 And swetar be sic sevyne,	*sweeter by seven times*
Our glore forlore for to restore	*lost*
Sen thow art qwene of Hevyn!	*Since*
Memore of sore, stern in aurore,	*Reminder; pain, star; [the] dawn*
Lovit with angellis stevyne;	*voice*
55 Implore, adore, thow indeflore,	*pray; undefiled*
To mak our oddis evyne.	*odds even*
Ave Maria, gracia plena!	

With lovingis lowde ellevyn.   *praises loud eleven*
Quhill store and hore my youth devore,   *While pains; age; devour*
60   Thy name I sall ay nevyne.   *always name (declare)*

Empryce of prys, imperatrice,   *Empress; imperatrix*
   Bricht polist precious stane;   *stone*
Victrice of vyce, hie genitrice   *Victress; high mother*
   Of Jhesu, Lord Soverayne:
65   Our wys pavys fro enemys   *wise shield*
   Agane the Feyndis trayne;   *Against the Fiend's deceits*
Oratrice, mediatrice, salvatrice,   *Intercessor; savior*
   To God gret suffragane!   *helper*
    Ave Maria, gracia plena!
70   Haile, sterne meridiane!   *midday*
Spyce, flour delice of Paradys   *fleur-de-lis*
   That baire the gloryus grayne.   *carried; seed*

Imperiall wall, place palestrall,   *palatial*
   Of peirles pulcritud;   *peerless beauty*
75   Tryumphale hall, hie trone regall   *throne*
   Of Godis celsitud;   *majesty*
Hospitall riall, the Lord of all   *Royal hospice*
   Thy closet did include;   *enclose*
Bricht ball cristall, ros virginall,
80   Fulfillit of angell fude.   *Filled with; food*
    Ave Maria, gracia plena!
   Thy birth has with His blude
Fra fall mortal originall
   Us raunsound on the Rude.   *ransomed; Cross*

5. *In Praise of Women*

Now of wemen this I say for me,
Of erthly thingis nane may bettir be.   *earthly; none*
Thay suld haif wirschep and grit honoring   *should; worship; great*
Of men aboif all uthir erthly thing.   *From; above all other*
5   Rycht grit dishonour upoun himself he takkis   *takes*
In word or deid quhaevir wemen lakkis,   *deed whoever; disparages*

Sen that of wemen cumin all ar we;	*Since; come (born)*
Wemen ar wemen and sa will end and de.	*die*
Wo wirth the fruct wald put the tre to nocht,	*Ill betide*
10 And wo wirth him rycht so that sayis ocht	*anything (aught)*
Of womanheid that may be ony lak,	*womanliness; lack*
Or sic grit schame upone him for to tak.	*such*
Thay us consaif with pane, and be thame fed	*conceive; by*
Within thair breistis thair we be boun to bed;	*breasts where; are*
15 Grit pane and wo and murnyng mervellus	*pain; sorrow*
Into thair birth thay suffir sair for us;	*In; child-bearing; greatly*
Than meit and drynk to feid us get we nane	*food; feed; none*
Bot that we sowk out of thair breistis bane.	*what; suck; bone*
Thay ar the confort that we all haif heir —	*have here*
20 Thair may no man be till us half so deir;	*There; to; dear*
Thay ar our verry nest of nurissing.	*true; nurturing*
In lak of thame quha can say ony thing,	*blame; who does*
That fowll his nest he fylis, and for thy	*bird; fouls; therefore*
Exylit he suld be of all gud cumpany;	*Exiled*
25 Thair suld na wyis man gif audience	*wise; listen (lit., give audience)*
To sic ane without intelligence.	*such a one*
Chryst to His fader He had nocht ane man;	*not a*
Se quhat wirschep wemen suld haif than.	*See what; then*
That Sone is Lord, that Sone is King of Kingis,	
30 In Hevin and erth His majestie ay ringis.	
Sen scho hes borne Him in hir halines,	*Since; holiness*
And He is well and grund of all gudnes,	*[the] well; foundation; goodness*
All wemen of us suld haif honoring,	
Service and luve, aboif all uthir thing.	*above*

6. *The Manner of Going to Confession*

O synfull man, thir ar the fourty dayis	*these are*
That every man sulde wilfull pennence dre.	*should; endure*
Oure Lorde Jhesu, as haly writ sayis,	*holy*
Fastit Himself, oure exampill to be.	*Fasted*
5 Sen sic ane mychty king and lorde as He	*Since such a*
To fast and pray was so obedient,	
We synfull folk sulde be more deligent.	*should*

I reid thee, man, of thi transgressioun,   *advise*
With all thi hert that thou be penitent.   *heart*
10   Thow schrive thee clene and mak confessioun,
And se thairto that thou be deligent,   *see*
With all thi synnes into thi mynde presente,
That every syn be theselfe be schawin,   *by yourself be shown*
To thyne confessour it ma be kend and knawin.   *may be acknowledged*

15   Apon thi body gif thou hes ane wounde   *if; have any*
That caussis thee gret panis for to feill,   *feel*
Thair is no leiche ma mak thee haill and sounde   *doctor [who] may; healthy*
Quhill it be sene and clengit every deill;   *Until; seen; cleansed; bit*
Rycht sua thi schrift, bot it be schawin weill,   *Likewise; confession, unless; revealed*
20   Thow art not abill remissioun for to get   *able*
Wittandlie, and thou ane syn forget.   *Consciously, if; any*

Of tuenty wonddis and ane be left unhelit,   *wounds if one; unhealed*
Quhat avalis the leiching of the laif?   *What avails; curing; rest*
Rycht sua thi schrift, and thair be ouch conselit,   *Likewise; if; anything concealed*
25   It avalis not thi sely saule to saif,   *blessed soul; save*
Nor yit of God remissioun for to have.
Of syn gif thou wald have deliverance,   *if; would*
Thow sulde it tell with all the circumstance.   *should*

Se that thi confessour be wys and discreit,   *Make sure; is*
30   Than can thee discharge of every doute and weir,   *Then; doubt; fear*
And power hes of thi synnes compleit.   *have*
Gif thou cannot schaw furth thi synnes perqueir,   *perfectly*
And he be blinde and cannot at thee speir,   *spear (i.e., probe)*
Thow ma rycht weill in thi mynde consydder   *may*
35   Than ane blynde man is led furth be aneuther.   *a; another*

And sa I halde that ye ar baith begylde: *hold; beguiled*
He cannot speir nor thou cannot him tell   *ask*
Quhen nor how thi conscience thou hes fylde.   *When; fouled (defiled)*
Thairfor I reid that thou excuse thisell,   *thyself*
40   And rype thi mynde how everything befell —   *search*
The tyme, the place, and how and in quhat wys,   *fashion*
Sa that thi confessioun ma thi synnes pryce.   *may; account for*

36

Avys thee weill or thou cum to the preist   *Interrogate yourself; before*
Of all thi synnes, and namelie of the maist,   *especially; greatest*
45   That thai be reddy prentit in thi breist;   *clearly; heart*
Thow sulde not cum to schryfe thee in haist   *haste*
And syne sit doun abasit as ane beist: *then; thoughtless; beast*
With humyll hert and sad contrycioun
Thow suld cum to thine confessioun.

50   With thine awin mouth thi synnes thou suld tell;   *own*
Bot sit and heir the preist hes not ado.   *hear [so that] the priest has no difficulty*
Quha kennes thi synnes better na thisell?   *Who knows; than yourself*
Thairfor I reid thee, tak gude tent thairto;   *advise; heed*
Thow knawis best quhair bindis thee thi scho;   *where pinches; shoe*
55   Thairfor be wys afor or thou thair cum,   *before; there*
That thou schaw furth thi synnes, all and sum.   *show; one and all*

Quhair seldin compt is tane and hes a hevy charge,   *seldom reckoning; taken; burden*
And syne is rekles in his governance   *then is careless*
And on his conscience he takis all to large,   *too much*
60   And on the end hes no rememberance —   *in*
That man is abill to fall ane gret mischance.   *able; befall; misfortune*
The synfull man that all the yeir oursettis   *neglects*
Fra Pasche to Pasche, rycht mony a thing forgettis.   *Easter*

I reid thee, man, quhill thou art stark and young,   *advise; while; strong*
65   With pith and strenth into thi yeris grene,
Quhill thou art abill baith in mynde and toung,   *tongue*
Repent thee, man, and kepe thi conscience clen.
Till byde till age is mony perrell sene: *To wait until; peril*
Small merit is of synnes for to irke   *bemoan*
70   Quhen thou art ald and ma na wrangis wyrke.   *wrong deeds do*

7. *The Table of Confession*

To Thee, O marcifull Salviour myn, Jhesus,
My King, my Lord, and my Redemer sueit,   *sweet*
Befor Thy bludy figour dolorus   *pitiful*
I schryve me cleyne, with humile spreit and meike,   *spirit; meek*

5	That ever I did unto this hour compleit,	
	Baith in word, in wark, and in entent.	
	Falling on face full law befor Thy feit,	*low; feet*
	I cry Thee marcy and laser to repent.	*an opportunity (leisure)*

	To Thee, my meik sueit Salviour, I me schrife,	*sweet; confess*
10	And dois me in Thy marcy maist excelling,	*surpassing*
	Of the wrang spending of my wittis fyve —	*five wits*
	In hering, seing, tuiching, gusting, smelling —	*hearing; tasting*
	Ganestanding, greving, offending, and rebelling	*Opposing, vexing*
	Aganis my lord God omnipotent;	
15	With teris of sorrow fra myn ene distelling,	*tears; eyes falling*
	I cry Thee marcy and laser to repent.	

	I, wrachit synnar, vile and full of vice,	*wretched sinner*
	Of the sevin deidly synnis dois me schrif:	
	Of prid, invy, of ire, and covatice,	
20	Of lichory, gluttony, with sleuth ay till ourdrife,[1]	
	Exercing vicis ever in all my life,	*Practicing*
	For quhilk, allace, I servit to be schent.	*alas; deserve; punished*
	Rew on me, Jhesu, for Thy woundis five;	*Take pity*
	I cry Thee marcy and laser to repent.	

25	I schrif me, Lord, that I abusit have	*neglected*
	The sevin deidis of marcy corporall:	*deeds; physical*
	The hungry meit, nor thristy drink I gaif,	*food; gave*
	Vesyit the seik, nor redemit the thrall,	*Visited; sick; freed; captive*
	Herberit the wilsum, nor nakit cled at all,	*Sheltered; stranger; clothed the naked*
30	Nor yit the deid to bery tuke I tent.	*dead; took; heed*
	Thow that put marcy abone Thi werkis all,	*above*
	I cry Thee marcy and laser to repent.	

	In the sevin deidis of marcy spirituall:	
	To the ignorant nocht gaif I my teching,	*I did not give*
35	Synneris correctioun, nor distitud consall,	
	Nor unto wofull wrachis conforting,	*wretches*

---

[1] *Of lechery, gluttony, with sloth always to be overcome*

	Nor unto saulis support of my preching,	*souls*
	Nor wes to ask forgevinnes pacient,	
	Nor to forgif my nychtburis offending:	*neighbor's*
40	I cry Thee marcy and laser to repent.	
	Lord, I have done full littill reverence	*very little*
	Unto the sacramentis sevin of gret renoun:	
	To that hie Eucarist moist of exellence,	*high Eucharist (i.e., Holy Communion)*
	Baptasing, Pennence, and Confirmacioun,	
45	Matremony, Ordour, and Extreme uncioun.	*Ordination*
	Heirof sa fer as I wes necligent,	*Of this*
	With hert contrit and teris falling doun,	*tears*
	I cry Thee marcy and laser to repent.	
	Thy ten conmandmentis: a God for to honour,	*of*
50	Nocht tane in vane, na manslaar to be,	*Not taken; murderer*
	Fader and moder to worschip at all houre,	
	To be no theif, the haly day to uphie,	*uphold*
	Nychtburis to luf, fals witnes for to fle,	*flee*
	To leif adultré, to covat no manis rent:	*avoid*
55	In all thir, Lord, culpabill knaw I me.	*these*
	I cry Thee marcy and laser ro repent.	
	In the twelf artickillis of the treuth: a God to trow —	*in; believe*
	The Fader that all wrocht and comprehendit,	*made; created*
	And in His only Sone, blissit Jhesu,	
60	Of Mary borne, on Croce deid, and discendit,	*Cross died; descended*
	The thrid day rais, to the Faderis rycht hand ascendit,	*rose; right*
	Of quik and ded to cum and hald jugement:	*living; dead; hold*
	Into thir pointis, O Lord, quhare I have offendit,	*Unto these*
	I cry Thee marcy and lasere to repent.	
65	I trow into the blissit Haly Spreit,	*I believe in; Spirit*
	And in the Kirk, to do as it commandis,	
	And in the Day of Dome that we sall ris compleit	*Judgment; rise complete*
	And tak oure flesche agane, baith feit and handis,	
	All to be saif into the stait of grace that standis.	*saved; state*
70	Plane I revoik in thir quhair I myswent	*Fully; repent; these where*

39

Befoir Thee, Juge and Lord of sey and landis: *sea*
I cry Thee marcy and laser to repent.

I synnit, Lord, nocht being strang as wall   *not*
In hope, faith, and fervent cherité,
75   Nocht with the fair foure vertuis cardinall   *Not; Virtues*
Agins vicis sure anarmyng me: *vices securely arming*
With fortitud, prudence, and temporance, thir thre,   *these*
With Justice ever in word, werk, and in entent:
To Thee, Crist Jesu, casting up myn ee,   *eyes*
80   I cry Thee marcy and laser to repent.

In the sevin commandis of the Kirk, that is to say,
Thy teind to pay, and cursing to eschew,   *tithe; avoid*
To keipe the festuall and the fasting day,   *festival*
The Mes on Sonday, the parroche kirk persew,   *Mass; parish; [to] attend*
85   To proper curat to mak confessioun trew,
Anis in the yer to tak the sacrament: *Once*
Into thir pointis quhair I have offendit, sair I rew.   *these; sorely I regret*
I cry Thee marcy and laser to repent.

Of syn also into the Haly Spreit,   *unto*
90   Of schrift postponit, of syn aganis natour,   *confession; nature*
Of incontricioun, of confessour undiscreit,   *undiscerning*
Of ressait synfull of my Salviour,   *receiving sinfully the Sacrament*
Of undone pennence and satisfactioun sure,
Of the sevin giftis the Haly Gaist me sent,
95   Of *Pater Noster* and sevin peticionis pure: *Our Father*
I cry Thee marcy and laser to repent.

Nocht thankand Thee of gratitud and grace   *thanking*
That Thou me wrocht and bocht me with Thi ded;   *made; bought; death*
Of this schort tyme remembring nocht the space,
100   The Hevinnis blis, the Hellis hiddous feid,   *hate*
But mor trespas, my synnis to remeid,   *greater; remedy*
Concluding never all throu myn entent,   *Resolving*
Quhois blud on Rude for me ran reid,   *Whose blood; Cross*
I cry Thee marcy and laser to repent.

105 I knaw me vicius, Lord, and rycht culpabill
In aithis, swering, lessingis, and blasflemyng,   *oaths; lying*
Of frustrat speiking in court, in kirk, in tabill,   *needless; at meals*
In word, in will, in wantones expremyng,   *speaking*
Prising myself and evill my nychtburis demyng;   *judging*
110 And so in idilnes my dais I have myspent:
To Thee wes rent on Rude for my redeming,   *[who] was*
I cry Thee marcy and laser to repent.

I have synnit in discimilit thochtis joly,   *feigned*
Up to the Hevin extollit in myn entencioun
115 In hie exaltit arrogance and folly,   *high*
Imprudence, derisioun, scorne, and vilipencioun,   *vilification*
Presumpcioun, inobedience, and contempcioun,   *contempt*
In fals vanglore and deidis necligent:
O Thow that deit for my redempcioun,   *died*
120 I cry Thee marcy and laser to repent.

I have synnit also in reif and in opprecioun,   *theft*
In wrangus gudis taking and posceding   *wrongful goods; seizing*
Contrar gud ressoun, conscience, and discrecioun,   *Against*
In prodigall spending but reuth of pure folkis neding,   *without pity on poor*
125 In foule descepcioun, in fals invencionis bredyng,   *deception; tales devising*
To conqueir honour, tresour, land, or rent,   *gain*
In fleschely lust abone messour exceding: *beyond moderation*
I cry Thee marcy and laser to repent.

Of mynd dissimilit, Lord, I me confes,   *deceitful*
130 Of feid under ane freindlie continance,   *hatred; countenance*
Of parsiall juging and perverst wilfulnes,   *biased; perverse*
Of flattering wordis for finyng of substance,   *gaining*
Of fals seling for wrang deliverance   *attesting; decisions*
At Counsall, Sessioun, and at Perliament:
135 Of everilk gilt and wicket governance   *every sin*
I cry Thee marcy and laser to repent.

I schrif me of all cursit cumpany
In all tyme witting and unwiting me;   *known; unknown to me*
Of cryminall caus and deid of fellony,   *deed*

140	Of ded or slauchter culpabill knaw I me,
	Of tiranny, or vengabill cruelté,
	In ony wise, deid, counsall, or consent:
	O deir Jhesu that for me deit on Tre,
	I cry Thee marcy and laser to repent.

death; murder blameworthy

deed

died

145	Thoucht I have nocht Thi precius feit to kis
	As had the Magdalyn quhen scho did marcy craife,
	I sall, as scho, weipe teris for my mys,
	And every morrow seik Thee at Thi graife,
	That seis my hert; as Thou hir forgaife,
150	Thairfor forgife me as synner penitent.
	Thy precius body in honour I ressave;
	I cry Thee Marcy and laser to repent.

not; feet

when; pray for

shall; weep tears; sins

grave

says

receive

	Thow mak me, Jhesu, unto Thee to remember.
	I ask Thy passioun in me so to abound
155	Quhill nocht in me unmannyit be a member,
	Bot felling wo with Thee of every wound.
	At every straik mak throu my hart a stound
	That ever did strenye Thi fair flesche innocent,
	Sa at na part be of my body sound:
160	I cry Thee marcy and laser to repent.

Although; uninjured

feeling

stroke; a pain

stain

So that no

	Of all thir synnis that I heir expreme,
	And hes foryet, to Thee, Lord, I me schrife,
	Appelling fra Thy justice court extreme
	Unto Thi court of marcy exultive;
165	Thou mak my schip in blissit port arrive
	That sailis heir in stormes violent,
	And saife me, Jhesu, for Thy woundis five:
	I cry Thee marcy and laser to repent.

these; express

[others I] have forgotten; confess

Appealing

sails here

save

8. *All Earthly Joy Returns to Pain*

Of Lentren in the first mornyng,

Airly as did the day up spring,

Lent

Early

42

Poem 8: All Earthly Joy Returns to Pain

Thus sang ane bird with voce upplane: *a; voice quite clear*
"All erdly joy returnis in pane.   *earthly; turns into pain*

5   "O man, haif mynd that thow mon pas;   *must pass on*
Remembir that thow art bot as   *ash*
And sall in as return agane: *shall to ash*
All erdly joy returnis in pane.

"Haif mynd that eild ay followis yowth;   *Have; old age always*
10   Deth followis lyfe with gaipand mowth,   *gaping*
Devoring fruct and flowring grane: *fruit; grain*
All erdly joy returnis in pane.

"Welth, warldly gloir, and riche array   *glory*
Ar all bot thornis laid in thy way,
15   Ourcoverd with flouris laid in ane trane: *Covered over; as a trap*
All erdly joy returnis in pane

"Come nevir yit May so fresche and grene
Bot Januar come als wod and kene;   *[just] as wild; sharp*
Wes nevir sic drowth bot anis come rane: *such a drought; once [again]; rain*
20   All erdly joy returnis in pane.

"Evirmair unto this warldis joy
As nerrest air succeidis noy;   *closest heir follows distress*
Thairfoir, quhen joy ma nocht remane,   *when; may not remain*
His verry air succeidis pane.   *true heir*

25   "Heir helth returnis in seiknes,   *Here; turns into*
And mirth returnis in havines,   *heaviness*
Toun in desert, forrest in plane: *into; plain*
All erdly joy returnis in pane.

"Fredome returnis in wrechitnes,   *Generosity turns into poverty*
30   And trewth returnis in dowbilnes   *duplicity*
With fenyeit wirdis to mak men fane: *pretended words; glad*
All erdly joy returnis in pane.

"Vertew returnis into vyce,
And honour into avaryce;
35   With cuvatyce is consciens slane: *covetousness*
All erdly joy returnis in pane.

"Sen erdly joy abydis nevir,   *Since; is impermanent*
Wirk for the joy that lestis evir;   *lasts forever*
For uder joy is all bot vane: *other*
40   All erdly joy returnis in pane."

9. *Of Man's Mortality*
    [*Quod tu in cinerem revertis*]

Memento, homo, quod cinis es: *Remember, man, that you are ashes*
Think, man, thow art bot erd and as;   *but earth and ash*
Lang heir to dwell nathing thow pres,   *here; avails*
For as thow come sa sall thow pas.   *so shall you pass*
5   Lyk as ane schaddow in ane glas   *a mirror*
Hyne glydis all thy tyme that heir is;   *Away glides*
Think, thocht thy bodye ware of bras,   *though; were made*
Quod tu in cinerem reverteris.   *That you will return to ash*

Worthye Hector and Hercules,
10   Forcye Achill and strong Sampsone,   *Powerful*
Alexander of grit nobilnes,
Meik David and fair Absolone   *Modest*
Hes playit thair pairtis, and all are gone   *Have*
At will of God that all thing steiris: *things guides*
15   Think, man, exceptioun thair is none,   *there*
Sed tu in cinerem reverteris.   *But you will return to ashes*

Thocht now thow be maist glaid of cheir,   *Though*
Fairest and plesandest of port,   *demeanor*
Yit may thow be within ane yeir
20   Ane ugsum, uglye tramort.   *loathsome; decaying corpse*
And sen thow knawis thy tyme is schort   *since*
And in all houre thy lyfe in weir is,   *doubt*

Think, man, amang all uthir sport,	*pleasures*
Quod tu in cinerem reverteris.	

25	Thy lustye bewté and thy youth	*fair beauty*
	Sall feid as dois the somer flouris;	*Shall fade*
	Syne sall thee swallow with his mouth	*Then*
	The dragone death that all devouris.	
	No castell sall thee keip, nor touris,	*save*
30	Bot he sall seik thee with thy feiris.	*But; companions*
	Thairfore remembir at all houris	
	Quod tu in cinerem reverteris.	

	Thocht all this warld thow did posseid,	*Though; had possessed*
	Nocht eftir death thow sall posses,	*Nothing*
35	Nor with thee tak bot thy guid deid	*good deeds*
	Quhen thow dois fro this warld thee dres.	*go*
	So speid thee, man, and thee confes	*hurry*
	With humill hart and sobir teiris,	*tears*
	And sadlye in thy hart inpres	*soberly*
40	*Quod tu in cinerem reverteris.*	

	Thocht thow be taklit nevir so sure,	*Though; rigged*
	Thow sall in deathis port arryve,	*shall; death's*
	Quhair nocht for tempest may indure	*Where nothing*
	Bot ferslye all to speiris dryve.	*fiercely; fragments drive*
45	Thy Ransonner with woundis fyve	
	Mak thy plycht anker and thy steiris	*Makes; main anchor; rudder*
	To hald thy saule with Him on lyve,	*keep; in [eternal] life*
	Cum tu in cinerem reverteris.	*When you return to ashes*

10. *An Orison*

	Salviour, suppois my sensualité	*Savior, even if*
	Subject to syn hes maid my saule of sys,	*Obedient to sin; made; at times*
	Sum spark of lycht and spiritualité	*Some; light*
	Walkynnis my witt, and ressoun biddis me rys.	*Awakens my mind*
5	My corrupt conscience askis, clips, and cryis	*corrupted; begs, grasps*
	First grace, syne space for to amend my mys,	*then time; sins*

Substance with honour, doing none suppryis,   *Wealth; harm to no one*
Freyndis, prosperité, heir peax, syne Hevynis blys.[1]

11. *Of the World's Vanity*
   [*Vanitas vanitatum et omnia vanitas*]

O wreche, be war, this warld will wend thee fro,   *wretch; turn [away] from you*
Quhilk hes begylit mony greit estait.   *Which; beguiled; estates*
Turne to thy freynd, beleif nocht in thy fo.   *friend, believe not*
Sen thow mon go, be grathing to thy gait;   *Since; must; preparing for; journey*
5   Remeid in tyme and rew nocht all to lait;   *Redress; repent not too late*
Provyd thy place, for thow away man pas   *Ready; abode; must pass*
Out of this vaill of trubbill and dissait: *vale of trouble; deceit*
Vanitas vanitatum et omnia vanitas.   *Vanity of vanities and all is vanity*

Walk furth, pilgrame, quhill thow hes dayis licht,
10   Dres fra desert, draw to thy duelling place;   *Go; dwelling*
Speid home, for quhy anone cummis the nicht   *Hurry; because soon*
Quhilk dois thee follow with ane ythand chaise.   *constant pursuit*
Bend up thy saill and win thy port of grace,   *Draw*
For and the deith ourtak thee in trespas,   *if death; sin*
15   Than may thow say thir wourdis with "allace":   *Then; these; "alas"*
Vanitas vanitatum et omnia vanitas.

Heir nocht abydis, heir standis nothing stabill.   *Here nought remains*
This fals warld ay flittis to and fro: *always wavers*
Now day up bricht, now nycht als blak as sabill,
20   Now eb, now flude, now freynd, now cruell fo,   *ebb; flood; friend*
Now glaid, now said, now weill, now into wo,   *sad*
Now cled in gold, dissolvit now in as.   *clothed; ash*
So dois this warld transitorie go:
Vanitas vanitatum et omnia vanitas.

---

[1] *Friends, prosperity, here peace, then Heaven's bliss*

12. *Of Life*

Quhat is this lyfe bot ane straucht way to deid,	*What; straight path; death*
Quhilk hes a tyme to pas and nane to duell,	*Which; go; none; stay*
A slyding quheill us lent to seik remeid,	*turning wheel; seek a remedy*
A fre chois gevin to Paradice or Hell,	
A pray to deid, quhome vane is to repell,	*victim; death, who impossible*
A schoirt torment for infineit glaidnes,	*infinite*
Als schort ane joy for lestand hevynes.	*As short a joy; lasting grief*

13. *Of the Changes of Life*

I seik about this warld unstabille	*seek*
To find ane sentence convenabille,	*meaning convincing*
Bot I can nocht in all my wit	*not; understanding*
Sa trew ane sentence fynd of it,	*So*
As say, it is dessaveabille.	*Except to say; untrustworthy*

For yisterday I did declair	*observe*
Quhow that the seasoun soft and fair	*How*
Com in als fresche as pako fedder;	*Came; peacock feather*
This day it stangis lyk ane edder,	*stings; adder*
Concluding all in my contrair.	*Ending all to the contrary*

Yisterday fair up sprang the flouris;	
This day thai ar all slane with schouris,	*slain; showers (hail)*
And fowllis in forrest that sang cleir	*birds*
Now walkis with a drery cheir,	*dreary mood*
Full caild ar baith thair beddis and bouris.	*cold; bowers*

So nixt to symmer wyntir bene,	*next; is*
Nixt efter confort, cairis kene,	*cares sharp*
Nixt dirk mednycht the mirthefull morrow,	*midnight; cheerful*
Nixt efter joy aye cumis sorrow.	*always comes*
So is this warld and ay hes bene.	*always has been*

14. *The Lament for the Makars*
   [*Timor mortis conturbat me*]

	I that in heill wes and gladnes	*health*
	Am trublit now with gret seiknes	*troubled; sickness*
	And feblit with infermité:	*weakened*
	Timor mortis conturbat me.	*The fear of death distresses me*

5	Our plesance heir is all vane glory,	*joy here*
	This fals warld is bot transitory,	
	The flesche is brukle, the Fend is sle:	*fragile; Fiend; sly*
	Timor mortis conturbat me.	

	The stait of man dois change and vary,	*condition*
10	Now sound, now seik, now blith, now sary,	*sick; sad*
	Now dansand mery, now like to dee:	*dancing; die*
	Timor mortis conturbat me.	

	No stait in erd heir standis sickir;	*on earth; secure*
	As with the wynd wavis the wickir	*willow*
15	Wavis this warldis vanité:	
	Timor mortis conturbat me.	

	Onto the ded gois all estatis,	*Unto death*
	Princis, prelotis, and potestatis,	*rulers*
	Baith riche and pur of al degré:	*poor; ranks*
20	*Timor mortis conturbat me.*	

	He takis the knychtis into field	*knights; [the] field*
	Anarmyt undir helme and scheild,	*Unarmed*
	Victour he is at all mellé:	*conflicts*
	Timor mortis conturbat me.	

25	That strang unmercifull tyrand	*tyrant*
	Takis on the moderis breist sowkand	*mother's; sucking*
	The bab full of benignité:	*babe*
	Timor mortis conturbat me.	

	He takis the campion in the stour,	*champion; battle*
30	The capitane closit in the tour,	*enclosed; tower*
	The lady in bour full of bewté:	*bower*
	Timor mortis conturbat me.	

	He sparis no lord for his piscence,	*strength*
	Na clerk for his intelligence;	*Nor*
35	His awfull strak may no man fle:	*blow*
	Timor mortis conturbat me.	

	Art magicianis and astrologgis,	*astrologers*
	Rethoris, logicianis, and theologgis,	*Rhetoricians*
	Thame helpis no conclusionis sle:	*wise*
40	*Timor mortis conturbat me.*	

	In medicyne the most practicianis,	*best*
	Lechis, surrigianis, and phisicianis,	
	Thameself fra ded may not supplé:	
	Timor mortis conturbat me.	

45	I se that makaris amang the laif	*see; rest*
	Playis heir ther pageant, syne gois to graif;	*here; then go; grave*
	Sparit is nought ther faculté:	
	Timor mortis conturbat me.	

	He hes done petuously devour	*has sadly devoured*
50	The noble Chaucer, of makaris flour,	*the flower of poets*
	The monk of Bery, and Gower, all thre:	*Bury St. Edmunds (i.e., Lydgate)*
	Timor mortis conturbat me.	

	The gud Syr Hew of Eglintoun,	*good*
	And eik Heryot and Wyntoun	*also*
55	He hes tane out of this cuntré:	*taken from*
	Timor mortis conturbat me.	

	That scorpion fell has done infek	*cruel; poisoned*
	Maister Johne Clerk and James Afflek	
	Fra balat making and trigidé:	*balade; tragedy*
60	*Timor mortis conturbat me.*	

Holland and Barbour he has berevit;   *taken away*
Allace, that he nought with us levit   *Alas; left*
Schir Mungo Lokert of the Le:
Timor mortis conturbat me.

65   Clerk of Tranent eik he has tane
That maid the anteris of Gawane;   *made; adventures*
Schir Gilbert Hay endit has he:
Timor mortis conturbat me.

He has Blind Hary and Sandy Traill
70   Slaine with his schour of mortall haill,   *shower*
Quhilk Patrik Johnestoun myght nought fle: *Which*
Timor mortis conturbat me.

He has reft Merseir his endite   *ended; composing*
That did in luf so lifly write,   *of love so lively*
75   So schort, so quyk, of sentence hie: *vivid; meaning high*
Timor mortis conturbat me.

He has tane Roull of Aberdene
And gentill Roull of Corstorphin —
Two bettir fallowis did no man se: *see*
80   *Timor mortis conturbat me.*

In Dumfermelyne he hes done roune   *had whispered speech*
With Maister Robert Henrisoun.
Schir Johne the Ros enbrast has he: *embraced*
Timor mortis conturbat me.

85   And he has now tane, last of aw,   *taken; all*
Gud gentill Stobo and Quintyne Schaw,
Of quham all wichtis has peté: *whom; men; pity*
Timor mortis conturbat me.

Gud Maister Walter Kennedy
90   In poynt of dede lyis veraly —   *On the brink of death truly lies*
Gret reuth it wer that so suld be: *pity; should*
Timor mortis conturbat me.

50

Sen he has all my brether tane,   *Since; taken*
He will naught lat me lif alane;   *not let me live alone*
95   On forse I man his nyxt pray be: *Perforce; must; next prey*
Timor mortis conturbat me.

Sen for the ded remeid is none,   *Since; death remedy*
Best is that we for dede dispone,   *prepare*
Eftir our deid that lif may we: *death*
100 *Timor mortis conturbat me.*

15. *A Meditation in Winter*

Into thir dirk and drublie dayis   *these dark; overcast*
Quhone sabill all the hevin arrayis   *When darkness; heaven*
With mystie vapouris, cluddis, and skyis,   *clouds*
Nature all curage me denyis   *pleasure*
5   Of sangis, ballattis, and of playis.   *songs, poems*

Quhone that the nycht dois lenthin houris   *When; lengthen*
With wind, with haill, and havy schouris,
My dule spreit dois lurk for schoir;   *sad spirit; cower*
My hairt for langour dois forloir   *heart; sadness becomes forlorn*
10 For laik of Symmer with his flouris.   *lack; Summer*

I walk, I turne, sleip may I nocht,   *not*
I vexit am with havie thocht.   *heavy*
This warld all ovir I cast about,   *think*
And ay the mair I am in dout,
15 The mair that I remeid have socht.   *remedy; sought*

I am assayit on everie syde.   *assailed*
Despair sayis ay, "In tyme provyde   *soon*
And get sumthing quhairon to leif,   *on which to live*
Or with grit trouble and mischeif
20 Thow sall into this court abyd."   *shall*

Than Patience sayis, "Be not agast;
Hald Hoip and Treuthe within thee fast,   *Keep Hope*

And lat Fortoun wirk furthe hir rage,   *her desires*
Quhome that no rasoun may assuage   *Whom; reason; prevent*
25 Quhill that hir glas be run and past."   *Until; hourglass*

And Prudence in my eir sayis ay,   *ear*
"Quhy wald thow hald that will away?   *Why would; hold that which*
Or craif that thow may have no space,   *crave; length of time*
Thow tending to aneuther place,
30 A journay going everie day?"

And than sayis Age, "My freind, cum neir,   *then; Old Age*
And be not strange, I thee requeir: *aloof*
Cum, brodir, by the hand me tak.
Remember thow hes compt to mak   *has [a] reckoning*
35 Of all thi tyme thow spendit heir."   *here*

Syne Deid castis upe his gettis wyd   *Then Death; gates wide*
Saying, "Thir oppin sall thee abyd;   *These open; await*
Albeid that thow wer never sa stout,   *Although; bold*
Undir this lyntall sall thow lowt —   *lintel; bow down*
40 Thair is nane uther way besyde."

For feir of this all day I drowp.   *droop*
No gold in kist nor wyne in cowp,   *chest; cup*
No ladeis bewtie nor luiffis blys   *lady's beauty; love's*
May lat me to remember this,   *stop me from thinking*
45 How glaid that ever I dyne or sowp.   *However well; dine; sup*

Yit quhone the nycht begynnis to schort,   *when*
It dois my spreit sum pairt confort   *spirit*
Of thocht oppressit with the schowris.
Cum, lustie Symmer, with thi flowris,   *joyful*
50 That I may leif in sum disport.   *live; enjoyment*

16. *None May Assure in This World*

Quhome to sall I complene my wo   *To whom shall*
And kyth my kairis, on or mo?   *voice my cares, one; more*

52

Poem 16: None May Assure in This World

I knaw nocht amang riche nor pure   *not; poor*
Quha is my freynd, quha is my fo,   *Who*
5   For in this warld may none assure.   *no one be certain*

Lord, how sall I my dayis dispone?   *dispose (use)*
For lang service rewarde is none,
And schort my lyfe may heir indure,   *here*
And lossit is my tyme bygone: *lost; gone by*
10 Into this warld may none assure.

Oft falsett rydis with ane rowt   *Often falsehood rides; a retinue*
Quhen trewth gois on his fute abowt,   *When; foot*
And lak of spending dois him spur;   *money; prod*
Thus quhat to do I am in dowt: *what; doubt*
15 Into this warld may none assure.

Nane heir bot riche men hes renoun,   *here only*
And bot pure men ar pluckit doun,   *only poor; pulled*
And nane bot just men tholis injure;   *suffers*
Sa wit is blindit and ressoun: *Thus wit and reason are blind*
20 Into this warld may none assure.

Vertew the court hes done dispyis;   *has scorned*
Ane rebald to renoun dois ryis,   *A rascal; rise*
And cairlis of nobillis hes the cure,   *peasants from; receive offices*
And bumbardis brukis the benifyis: *laggards enjoy; benefices*
25 Into this warld may none assure.

All gentrice and nobilité   *gentility*
Ar passit out of he degré;   *high*
On fredome is laid foirfaltour;   *generosity; forfeiture*
In princis is thair no pety: *princes is there no compassion*
30 For in this warld may none assure.

Is non so armit into plait   *in armor plate*
That can fra truble him debait;   *defend*
May no man lang in welth indure   *remain*
For wo that evir lyis at the wait:
35 Into this warld may none assure.

Flattry weiris ane furrit goun,   *wears; furred*
And Falsett with the lordis dois roun,   *Falsehood; whisper*
And Trewthe standis barrit at the dure,   *barred outside the door*
And exul is Honour of the toun: *exiled; from*
40   Into this warld may none assure.

Fra everilk mowth fair wirdis proceidis;   *From every; words*
In every hairt disceptioun breidis;   *breeds*
Fra everylk e gois lukis demure,   *eye; looks inviting*
Bot fra the handis gois few gud deidis: *good deeds*
45   Into this warld may none assure.

Toungis now ar maid of quhyte quhaill bone,   *Tongues; made; white whale*
And hairtis ar maid of hard flynt stone,   *hearts*
And ene ar maid of blew asure,   *eyes are made; azure*
And handis of adamant laith to dispone: *are unwilling; give away*
50   Into this warld may none assure.

Yit hairt with hand and body all
Mon anser Deth quhen he dois call   *Must answer*
To compt befoir the Juge future;   *make account*
Sen all ar deid or than de sall,   *Since; dead or else shall die*
55   Quha suld into this warld assure?

Nothing bot deth this schortly cravis,   *soon*
Quhair Fortoun evir as fo dissavis   *deceives*
With freyndly smylingis of ane hure,   *whore*
Quhais fals behechtis as wind hyne wavis: *Whose; promises; ever varies*
60   Into this warld may none assure.

O, quha sall weild the wrang possessioun,   *who shall bear; wrongful*
Or the gold gatherit with oppressioun,   *by*
Quhen the angell blawis his bugill sture,   *bugle loud*
Quhilk unrestorit helpis no confessioun?   *Which unreturned*
65   Into this warld may none assure.

Quhat help is thair in lordschippis sevin,
Quhen na hous is bot Hell and Hevin,
Palice of licht or pitt obscure,

	Quhair youlis ar hard with horreble stevin?	*Where yells; heard; voices*
70	Into this warld may none assure.	

	Ubi ardentes anime,	
	Semper dicentes sunt, Ve Ve![1]	
	Sall cry "allace" that wemen thame bure,	*Shall; alas; them bore*
	O quante sunt iste tenebre!	*Oh how great is that darkness!*
75	Into this warld may none assure.	

	Than quho sall wirk for warldis wrak	*worldly goods*
	Quhen flude and fyre sall our it frak,	*flood; over; sweep*
	And frely fruster feild and fure	*destroy field; furrow*
	With tempest kene and hiddous crak?	*crack of thunder*
80	Into this warld may none assure.	

	Lord, sen in tyme sa sone to cum	*since; so*
	De terra surrectourus sum,	*I shall rise from the earth*
	Rewarde me with non erdly cure —	*earthly office*
	Tu regni da imperium:	*Grant me power of your kingdom*
85	Into this warld may non assure.	

17. *Best to Be Blithe*

	Full oft I mus and hes in thocht	*Quite often I ponder; have*
	How this fals warld is ay on flocht,	*always in flux*
	Quhair nothing ferme is nor degest;	*Where; firm; settled*
	And quhen I haif my mynd all socht,	*have; searched*
5	For to be blyth me think it best.	*cheerful*

	This warld evir dois flicht and vary;	*flutter*
	Fortoun sa fast hir quheill dois cary,	*wheel*
	Na tyme bot turne can it tak rest,	
	For quhois fals change suld none be sary;	*whose; should*
10	For to be blyth me thynk it best.	

---

[1] Lines 71–72: *Where burning souls / Are always crying, Woe Woe!*

	Wald man considdir in mynd rycht weill,	*Would*
	Or Fortoun on him turn hir quheill,	*wheel*
	That erdly honour may nocht lest,	*earthly; not last*
	His fall les panefull he suld feill;	*should feel*
15	For to be blyth me think it best.	

	Quha with this warld dois warsill and stryfe,	*Who; wrestle*
	And dois his dayis in dolour dryfe,	*worry spend*
	Thocht he in lordschip be possest,	*Though*
	He levis bot ane wrechit lyfe;	*lives*
20	For to be blyth me think it best.	

	Of wardlis gud and grit riches,	*worldly goods; great*
	Quhat fruct hes man but mirines?	*fruit; without merriness*
	Thocht he this warld had eist and west,	
	All wer povertie but glaidnes;	*without*
25	For to be blyth me thynk it best.	

	Quho suld for tynsall drowp or de	*Who should; depravation droop or die*
	For thyng that is bot vanitie,	
	Sen to the lyfe that evir dois lest	*Since*
	Heir is bot twynklyng of ane ee?	*eye*
30	For to be blyth me think it best.	

	Had I for warldis unkyndnes	
	In hairt tane ony havines,	*taken*
	Or fro my plesans bene opprest,	
	I had bene deid lang syne, dowtles;	*since, doubtless*
35	For to be blyth me think it best.	

	How evir this warld do change and vary,	
	Lat us in hairt nevirmoir be sary,	*nevermore; sorry*
	Bot evir be reddy and addrest	*prepared*
	To pas out of this frawdfull fary;	*false vision*
40	For to be blyth me think it best.	

18. *Of Content*

Quho thinkis that he hes sufficence	*Who; has enough*
Of gudis hes no indigence,	*goods; shortage*
Thocht he have nowder land nor rent,	*Though; neither*
Grit mycht nor hie magnificence,	*high*
He hes anewch that is content.	*enough*
Quho had all riches unto Ynd	*Who; India*
And wer not satefeit in mynd,	*satisfied*
With povertie I hald him schent —	*think him punished*
Of covatyce sic is the kynd.	*such; nature*
He hes anewch that is content.	
Thairfor I pray yow, bredir deir,	*brother*
Not to delyt in daynteis seir;	*luxuries many*
Thank God of it is to thee sent,	*for what is*
And of it glaidlie mak gud cheir.	
Anewch he hes that is content.	
Defy the warld, feynyeit and fals,	*Repudiate; deceitful; false*
Withe gall in hart and hunyit hals;	*bitterness; heart; honeyed throat*
Quha maist it servis maist sall repent:	*Who most; shall*
Of quhais subchettis sour is the sals.	*whose second serving; sauce*
He hes anewch that is content.	
Giff thow hes mycht, be gentill and fre,	*If; might; noble; generous*
And gif thow standis in povertie,	
Of thine awin will to it consent,	*own*
And riches sall returne to thee.	
He hes aneuch that is content.	
And ye and I, my bredir all,	*If; brothers*
That in this lyfe hes lordschip small,	*has little property*
Lat langour not in us imprent;	*misery; be imprinted*
Gif we not clym, we tak no fall.	*If; climb*
He hes aneuch that is content.	

	For quho in warld moist covatus is	*covetous*
	In warld is purast man, iwis,	*poorest; indeed*
	And moist nedy of his intent;	*needy of mind*
	For of all gudis nothing he hes,	*Despite; [his] goods*
35	That of nothing can be content.	

19. *Without Gladness No Treasure Avails*

	Be mery, man, and tak nocht fer in mynd	*merry; far in mind (i.e., do not dwell on it)*
	The wavering of this wrechit vale of sorrow.	*fluctuations*
	To God be hummle and to thi frend be kyind,	*humble*
	And with thi nichtbour glaidlie len and borow —	*lend*
5	His chance this nycht, it may be thine tomorow.	*opportunity*
	Be mery, man, for any aventure,	
	For be wismen it has bene said afforow:	*before*
	Without glaidnes avalis no tresure.	*avails*

	Mak gude cheir of it God thee sendis,	*Enjoy; what*
10	For warldis wrak but weilfar nocht avalis;	*worldly good without cheerfulness*
	Nothing is thine sauf onlie that thow spendis —	*save only what*
	The ramanent of all thow brukis with balis.	*possesses; misery*
	Seik to solace quhen saidnes thee assalis;	*delight*
	Thy lyfe in dolour ma nocht lang indure,	*sadness may; survive*
15	Quharfor of confurt set up all thi salis:	*Therefore; sails*
	Without glaidnes avalis no tresure.	

	Follow pece, flie trubill and debait,	*peace, flee conflict; argument*
	With famous folkis hald thi cumpany.	*respected*
	Be cheritable and hummle of estait,	*humble*
20	For warldis honour lestis bot ane cry.	*lasts*
	For truble in erd tak no malancholy.	*on earth*
	Be rich in patiens, gife thoue in gudis be pur.	*goods; poor*
	Quha levis mery, he levis michtely:	*Who lives happily; mightily*
	Without glaidnes avalis no tresur.	

25	Thow seis the wrechis set with sorow and care	*see; wretches*
	To gaddir gudis all thar liffis spaice;	*their*
	And quhen thar baggis ar full thar self ar bar	*themselves are bare*

And of thar riches bot the keping hes, *guarding have*

Quhill uthiris cum to spend it that hes grace, *While others*

30 Quhilk of the wynning no labour hed na cur. *had nor concern*

Tak thow example and spend with mirrines:

Without glaidnes avalis no tresure.

Thocht all the wrak that evir hed levand wicht *Though; wealth; living person*

War onlie thine, no mor thi part dois fall *Was only; more; share; belong*

35 Bot met and clacht, and of the laif ane sicht, *food; clothing; rest a glimpse*

Yet to the Juge thow sall mak compt of all. *account*

Ane raknyng richt cummis of ane ragment small; *A reckoning; short list*

Be just and joyus and do to none injur,

And treuth sall mak thee strang as ony wall:

40 Without glaidnes avalis no tresure.

20. *His Own Enemy*

He that hes gold and grit riches *has; great*

And may be into mirrynes, *cheerfulness*

And dois glaidnes fra him expell

And levis into wrechitnes, *lives in*

5 He wirkis sorrow to himsell. *brings; upon himself*

He that may be but sturt or stryfe *without quarrel*

And leif ane lusty plesand lyfe, *lives a carefree pleasing*

And syne with mariege dois him mell *then; marriage; himself involve*

And bindis him with ane wicket wyfe, *to; wicked*

10 He wirkis sorrow to himsell.

He that hes for his awin genyie *own arrow*

Ane plesand prop, but mank or menyie, *target, without flaw; blemish*

And schuttis syne at ane uncow schell, *shoots then; unfamiliar target*

And is forfairn with the fleis of Spenyie, *done in; fleas of Spain*

15 He wirkis sorrow to himsell.

And he that with gud lyfe and trewth,

But varians or uder slewth, *Without discord or other vice*

Dois evirmair with ane maister dwell,

59

20   That nevir of him will haif no rewth,   *on; have no pity*
         He wirkis sorrow to himsell.

         Now all this tyme lat us be mirry,
         And sett nocht by this warld a chirry,   *value not; cherry*
         Now quhill thair is gude wyne to sell,   *while; good; buy*
         He that dois on dry breid wirry,   *does; bread gnaw*
25   I gif him to the Devill of Hell!   *give*

21. *Spend Thine Own Goods*
     [*Thyne awin gude spend quhill thow hes space*]

         Man, sen thy lyfe is ay in weir,   *since; always in doubt*
         And deid is evir drawand neir,   *death; drawing*
         The tyme unsicker and the place,   *uncertain*
         Thyne awin gude spend quhill thow hes space.   *own good; while; [a] chance*

5   Gif it be thyne, thyself it usis;   *If*
         Gif it be nocht, thee it refusis —   *If it be not [used], it deserts you*
         Aneuthir of it the proffeit hes: *Another*
         Thyne awin gud spend quhill thow hes spais.

         Thow may today haif gude to spend
10   And hestely to morne fra it wend   *from [you] it goes*
         And leif aneuthir thy baggis to brais: *leaves; money-bags to embrace*
         Thyne awin gud spend quhill thow hes space.

         Quhill thow hes space, se thow dispone   *While; time, see that you dispose*
         That for thy geir, quhen thow art gone,   *goods, when*
15   No wicht aneuder slay nor chace: *person another; pursue*
         Thyne awin gud spend quhill thow hes space.

         Sum all his dayis dryvis our in vane,   *Someone; spends in vain*
         Ay gadderand geir with sorrow and pane,   *Always gathering possessions*
         And nevir is glaid at Yule nor Pais: *Easter*
20   Thyne awin gud spend quhill thow hes space.

Syne cumis aneuder glaid of his sorrow,   *Then comes another*
That for him prayit nowdir evin nor morrow,   *neither*
And fangis it all with mirrynais: *takes; cheerfulness*
Thyne awin gud spend quhill thow hes space.

25   Sum grit gud gadderis and ay it spairis,   *saves*
And eftir him thair cumis yung airis   *heirs*
That his auld thrift settis on ane es: *ace*
Thyne awin gud spend quill thow hes space.

It is all thyne that thow heir spendis,   *[will] spend*
30   And nocht all that on thee dependis,   *not; those that*
Bot his to spend it that hes grace: *the opportunity*
Thyne awin gud spend quhill thow hes spais.

Trest nocht aneuthir will do thee to   *Trust not*
It that thyself wald nevir do,   *What; would*
35   For gife thow dois, strenge is thy cace: *if; hard; situation*
Thyne awin gud spend quhill thow hes space.

Luke how the bairne dois to the muder,   *Look; child; mother*
And tak example be nane udder   *by none other*
That it nocht eftir be thy cace: *not; case*
40   Thyne awin gud spend quhill thow hes space.

22. *Of Covetise*
    [*And all for caus of cuvetice*]

Fredome, honour, and nobilnes,   *Generosity*
Meid, manheid, mirth, and gentilnes,   *Reward, courage; gentility*
Ar now in cowrt reput as vyce,   *court considered*
And all for caus of cuvetice.   *because*

5   All weilfair, welth, and wantones   *good-cheer, well-being; playfulness*
Ar chengit into wretchitnes,   *misery*
And play is sett at littill price,   *delight*
And all for caus of covetyce.

	Halking, hunting, and swift hors rynning	*Hawking*
10	Ar chengit all in wrangus wynnyng;	*changed; wrongful gaining*
	Thair is no play bot cartis and dyce,	*cards; dice*
	And all for caus of covetyce.	

	Honorable houshaldis ar all laid doun.	*decayed*
	Ane laird hes with him bot a loun	*lord; rascal*
15	That leidis him eftir his devyce,	*leads; design*
	And all for caus of covetyce.	

	In burghis, to landwart and to sie,	*cities; at sea (i.e., everywhere)*
	Quhair was plesour and grit plentie,	*Where*
	Vennesoun, wyld fowill, wyne, and spyce,	*Venison; fowl*
20	Ar now decayid thruch covetyce.	

	Husbandis that grangis had full grete,	*Farmers who farms*
	Cattell and corne to sell and ete,	
	Hes now no beist bot cattis and myce,	*beasts except*
	And all thruch caus of covettyce.	*because*

25	Honest yemen in every toun,	*yeomen*
	War wont to weir baith reid and broun,	*Who used; wear; red*
	Ar now arrayit in raggis with lyce,	
	And all for caus of covetyce.	

	And lairdis in silk harlis to the heill,	*[that] trails; heel*
30	For quhilk thair tennents sald somer meill	*sold summer meal*
	And leivis on rutis undir the ryce,	*live; roots [from] under the bushes*
	And all for caus of covetyce.	

	Quha that dois deidis of petie	*Who; deeds; mercy*
	And leivis in pece and cheretie	*lives; peace*
35	Is haldin a fule, and that full nyce,	*held; fool; stupid*
	And all for caus of covetyce.	

	And quha can reive uthir menis rowmis	*take; property*
	And upoun peur men gadderis sowmis	*poor; collect accounts*
	Is now ane active man, and wyice,	*wise*
40	And all for caus of covetyce.	

Poem 23: Of Deeming

Man, pleis thy Makar and be mirry,	*please; Maker*
And sett not by this warld a chirry.	*do not value; cherry*
Wirk for the place of Paradyce,	
For thairin ringis na covettyce.	*reigns*

23. *Of Deeming*

	Musing allone this hinder nicht	*the other night*
	Of mirry day quhen gone was licht,	
	Within ane garth undir a tre,	*garden*
	I hard ane voce that said on hicht,	*heard; voice; high*
5	"May na man now undemit be.	*no; unjudged*
	"For thocht I be ane crownit king,	*though*
	Yit sall I not eschew deming.	*avoid judgment*
	Sum callis me guid, sum sayis thai lie,	*good*
	Sum cravis of God to end my ring,	*reign*
10	So sall I not undemit be.	
	"Be I ane lord and not lord lyk,	
	Than every pelour and purspyk	*robber; pickpurse*
	Sayis, 'Land war bettir warit on me.'	*were; used*
	Thocht he dow not to leid a tyk,	*Though; does nothing; control a puppy*
15	Yit can he not lat deming be.	*refrain from criticizing*
	"Be I ane lady fresche and fair,	
	With gentillmen makand repair,	*making visits*
	Than will thay say, baith scho and he,	
	That I am jaipit, lait and air.	*deceived (japed), late and early*
20	Thus sall I not undemit be.	
	"Be I ane courtman or ane knycht,	
	Honestly cled, that cumis me richt,	*as properly suits me*
	Ane prydfull man than call thay me.	*then*
	Bot God send thame a widdy wicht	*them; withy (i.e., rope) strong*
25	That cannot lat sic demyng be.	*such*

"Be I bot littill of stature,
Thay call me catyve createure,   *[a] wretched*
And be I grit of quantetie,   *great*
Thay call me monstrowis of nature.
30   Thus can I not undemit be.

"And be I ornat in my speiche,   *speech*
Than Towsy sayis I am sa streiche,   *proper*
I speik not lyk thair hous menyie.   *servants*
Suppois hir mowth misteris a leiche,   *Even if; requires; doctor*
35   Yit can I not undemit be.

"Bot wist thir folkis that uthir demis   *knew these; others judge*
How that thair sawis to uthir semis,   *sayings; seem*
Thair vicious wordis and vanité,
Thair tratling tungis that all furth temis,   *chattering; empties*
40   Sum tyme wald lat thair demying be.

"War nocht the mater wald grow mair   *Were it not that*
To wirk vengeance on ane demair,   *judger*
But dout I wald cause mony de   *Without [a] doubt; [to] die*
And mony catif end in cair,   *many [a] wretch*
45   Or sum tyme lat thair deming be.   *(I.e., before they stopped their judging)*

"Gude James the Ferd, our nobill king,   *Fourth*
Quhen that he was of yeiris ying   *years young*
In sentens said full subtillie,   *[a] statement*
'Do weill, and sett not by demying,   *do not be concerned with censure*
50   For no man sall undemit be.'"   *unjudged*

And so I sall, with Goddis grace,
Keip His command into that cace,   *in; regard*
Beseiking ay the Trinitie   *Beseeching*
In hevin that I may haif ane place —
55   For thair sall no man demit be.

24. *How Should I Conduct Myself*
   [*Lord God, how sould I governe me*]

How sould I rewill me or in quhat wys	*should; rule myself; what fashion*
I wald sum wyse man wald devys,	*wish; would inform me*
Sen I can leif in no degré	*Since; live not at all*
Bot sum my maneris will dispys:	*Without someone deriding my manners*
5 Lord God, how sould I governe me?	
Giff I be lustye, galland, and blythe,	*If; lively; cheerful*
Than will thai say on me full swythe,	*immediately*
"Yon man, out of his mynd is he,	
Or sum hes done him confort kythe":	*has given him comfort (sex?)*
10 Lord God, how sould I governe me?	
Giff I be sorrowfull and sad,	
Than will thai say that I am mad;	
I do bot drowpe as I wald de,	*droop; as [if] I would die*
So will thai deyme, bayth man and lad:	*deem (judge); man and lad (i.e., everyone)*
15 Lord God, how sall I governe me?	
Giff I be lustie in myne array,	
Than lufe I paramoris, say thai,	*Then they say I love amorously*
Or in my mynd is proud and he,	*high*
Or ellis I haif it sum wrang way:	*somehow gone wrong*
20 Lord God, how sall I governe me?	
And gif I be not wele besene,	*pleasingly attired*
Than twa and twa sayis thame betwene,	
"Evill gydit is yon man, pardé —	*Ill-behaved; by God*
Be his clething it may be sene":	*By*
25 Lord God, how sould I governe me?	
Gif I be sene in court our lang,	*too long*
Than will thai quhispir thame amang,	*whisper*
My freindis ar not worthe ane fle	*a fly*
That I sa lang but gwerdon gang:	*without reward go*
30 Lord God, how sould I governe me?	

In court rewaird gif purches I,   *if I receive*
Than have thai malice and invy
And secreitlie on me thai lie
And dois me sklandir privaly:
35   Lord God, how sould I governe me?

How sould my gyding be devysit?   *conduct be prescribed*
Giff I spend litle I am dispysit;
Be I courtas, nobill, and fre,
A prodigall man than am I prysit   *considered*
40   Lord God, how sould I governe me?

Sen all is jugit, bayth gud and ill,   *Since everyone is judged*
And no mannis toung I may had still,   *hold*
To do the best my mynd sal be.   *shall be*
Lat everie man say quhat he will,
45   The gratious God mot governe me.   *must*

25. *Rule of Oneself*
      [*He rewllis weill that weill himself can gyd*]

To dwell in court, my freind, gife that thow list,   *if; wish*
For gift of fortoun invy thow no degré.   *not at all*
Behold and heir, and lat thy tung tak rest —   *Watch; listen*
In mekle speiche is pairt of vanitie;   *much speech*
5   And for no malyce preis thee nevir to lie.   *force*
Als trubill nevir thyself, sone, be no tyd   *Also; at no time*
Uthiris to reiwll that will not rewlit be: *Others to govern*
He rewlis weill that weill himself can gyd.   *well; guide*

Be war quhome to thy counsale thow discure,   *wary to whom; disclose*
10   For trewth dwellis nocht ay for that trewth appeiris.
Put not thyne honour into aventeure —   *at risk*
Ane freind may be thy fo, as fortoun steiris.   *goes*
In cumpany cheis honorable feiris,   *choose; companions*
And fra vyle folkis draw thee far on syd.   *away*

66

| 15 | The Psalme sayis, *Cum sancto sanctus eiris*:[1] | |
| | He rewlis weill that weill himself can gyd. | |

	Haif pacience thocht thow no lordschip posseid,	*Have; though you; possess*
	For hie vertew may stand in law estait.	*high; low*
	Be thow content, of mair thow hes no neid;	*more*
20	And be thow nocht, desyre sall mak debait	*If you are not; strife*
	Evirmoir, till Deth say to thee than "Chakmait!"	*Death says; then "Checkmate!"*
	Thocht all war thyne this warld within so wyd,	*Though; were*
	Quha can resist the serpent of dispyt?	*Who; animosity*
	He rewlis weill that weill himself can gyd.	

25	Fle frome the fallowschip of sic as ar defamit,	*Flee; such; disgraced*
	And fra all fals tungis fulfild with flattry,	
	Als fra all schrewis, or ellis thow art eschamit.	*Also; will be shamed*
	Sic art thow callit as is thy cumpany.	*Such*
	Fle parrellus taillis foundit of invy.	*Flee perilous tales based on*
30	With wilfull men, son, argown thow no tyd,	*argue; at no time*
	Quhome no ressone may seis nor pacify:	*Whom; stop*
	He rewlis weill that weill himself can gyd.	

	And be thow not ane roundar in the nuke,	*whisperer; nook*
	For gif thow be, men will hald thee suspect.	*if*
35	Be nocht in countenance ane skornar, nor by luke,	*not; face; look*
	Bot dowt siclyk sall stryk thee in the neck.	*Without [a] doubt in such a way*
	Be war also to counsall or coreck	*wary*
	Him that extold hes far himself in pryd,	*elevated*
	Quhair parrell is but proffeit or effect:	*Where peril; without worth*
40	He rewlis weill that weill himself can gyd.	

	And sen thow seyis mony thingis variand,	*since; sees; changing*
	With all thy hart treit bissines and cure.	*welcome diligence; responsibility*
	Hald God thy freind, evir stabill be Him stand;	*firm by*
	He will thee confort in all misaventeur.	*adversity*
45	And be no wayis dispytfull to the peure,	*not at all scornful; poor*
	Nor to no man do wrang at ony tyd.	*time*

---

[1] *"With the holy, holy you shall be"* (Psalm 17:26 in the Vulgate)

Quhoso dois this, sickir I yow asseure,   *certainly*
He rewlis weill that sa weill him can gyd.

26. *Discretion in Asking*
   [*In asking sowld discretioun be*]

Of every asking followis nocht   *not*
Rewaird, bot gif sum caus war wrocht;   *unless; produced*
And quhair caus is, men weill ma sie,   *where; well may see*
And quhair nane is, it wil be thocht: *none*
5   In asking sowld discretioun be.   *should*

Ane fule, thocht he haif cause or nane,   *A fool, though*
Cryis ay, "Gif me," into a rane;   *always; in a rant*
And he that dronis ay as ane bee   *drones (buzzes)*
Sowld haif ane heirar dull as stane.   *a hearer (listener)*
10   In asking sowld discretioun be.

Sum askis mair than he deservis,   *more*
Sum askis far les than he servis,
Sum schames to ask (as braidis of me)   *are ashamed; as applies to me*
And all withowt reward he stervis.   *dies*
15   In asking sowld discretioun be.

To ask but service hurtis gud fame,   *without [doing]*
To ask for service is not to blame,
To serve and leif in beggartie   *live*
To man and maistir is baith schame.
20   In asking sowld discretion be.

He that dois all his best servyis
May spill it all with crakkis and cryis,   *waste; boasts; shouts*
Be fowll inoportunitie.   *By foul begging (importuning)*
Few wordis may serve the wyis.   *wise*
25   In asking sowld discretioun be.

Nocht neidfull is men sowld be dum,   *should be silent*
Nathing is gottin but wordis sum;   *without; some*

Nocht sped but diligence we se,   *speed*
For nathing it allane will cum.
30   In asking sowld discretioun be.

Asking wald haif convenient place,   *requires*
Convenient tyme, lasar, and space,   *leisure*
But haist, or preis of grit menyie,   *Without haste; press of great company*
But hairt abasit, but toung rekles.   *heart dismayed; tongue careless*
35   In asking sowld discretioun be.

Sum micht haif "Ye" with littill cure,   *effort*
That hes oft "Nay" with grit labour;
All for that tyme not byd can he,   *wait*
He tynis baith eirand and honour.   *loses both errand; honor*
40   In asking sowld discretioun be.

Suppois the servand be lang unquit,   *unrewarded*
The lord sumtyme rewaird will it.
Gife he dois not, quhat remedy?   *If; what*
To fecht with Fortoun is no wit: *fight; not wise*
45   In asking descretioun be.

27. *Discretion in Giving*
     [*In geving sowld discretioun be*]

To speik of gift or almous deidis: *alms deeds*
Sum gevis for mereit and for meidis,   *rewards*
Sum, warldly honour to uphie,   *exalt*
Gevis to thame that nothing neidis.   *needs*
5   In geving sowld discretioun be.

Sum gevis for pryd and glory vane,
Sum gevis with grugeing and with pane,   *complaining; pain*
Sum gevis, in practik, for supplé,   *help*
Sum gevis for twyis als gud agane.   *twice as good*
10   In geving sowld discretioun be.

Sum gevis for thank and sum for threit,   *threat*
Sum gevis money and sum gevis meit,   *food*
Sum gevis wordis fair and sle,   *subtle*
Giftis fra sum ma na man treit.   *may; entreat*
15   In giving sowld discretioun be.

Sum is for gift sa lang requyrd,
Quhill that the crevar be so tyrd   *petitioner*
That, or the gift deliverit be,   *before*
The thank is frustrat and expyrd.   *useless*
20   In geving sowld discretioun be.

Sum gevis to littill full wretchitly,   *too*
That his giftis ar not set by,   *worth anything*
And for a huidpyk haldin is he   *miser held*
That all the warld cryis on him, "Fy!"
25   In geving sowld discretioun be.

Sum in his geving is so large   *free*
That all ourlaidin is his berge.   *overladen; barge*
Than vyce and prodigalité   *Then*
Thairof his honour dois dischairge.   *dissipate*
30   In geving sowld discretioun be.

Sum to the riche gevis geir   *goods*
That micht his giftis weill forbeir;
And thocht the peur for falt sowld de,   *though; poor; lack should die*
His cry nocht enteris in his eir.   *ear*
35   In geving sowld discretioun be.

Sum givis to strangeris with faces new,
That yisterday fra Flanderis flew,   *rushed*
And to awld servandis list not se,   *servants wishes; see*
War thay nevir of sa grit vertew.   *Were*
40   In geving sowld discretioun be.

Sum gevis to thame can ask and plenyie,   *complain*
Sum gevis to thame can flattir and fenyie,   *feign*
Sum gevis to men of honestie

70

	And haldis all janglaris at disdenyie.	*chatterers in disdain*
45	In geving sowld discretioun be.	

Sum gettis giftis and riche arrayis,
To sweir all that his maister sayis,
Thocht all the contrair weill knawis he —   *Though*
Ar mony sic now in thir dayis.   *[There] are many such; these*
50 In geving sowld discretioun be.

Sum gevis gudmen for thair thewis,   *virtues*
Sum gevis to trumpouris and to schrewis,   *triflers; villains*
Sum gevis to knaiffis awtoritie,   *knaves authority*
Bot in thair office gude fundin few is.
55 In geving sowld discretioun be.

Sum givis parrochynnis full wyd,   *parishes; wide*
Kirkis of Sanct Barnard and Sanct Bryd,   *Churches*
To teiche, to rewill, and to ouirsie,   *teach; rule; oversee*
That hes na wit thamselffe to gyd.   *guide*
60 In geving sowld discretioun be.

28. *Discretion in Taking*
  [*In taking sowld discretioun be*]

Eftir geving I speik of taking,
Bot littill of ony gud forsaiking.
Sum takkis our littill awtoritie,   *Some; too little authority*
And sum our mekle, and that is glaiking.   *too much; folly*
5 In taking sowld discretioun be.

The clerkis takis beneficis with brawlis,   *noisy disputes*
Sum of Sanct Petir and sum of Sanct Pawlis.
Tak he the rentis, no cair hes he,
Suppois the divill tak all thair sawlis.   *Although; devil; souls*
10 In taking sowld discretioun be.

Barronis takis fra the tennentis peure   *tenants poor*
All fruct that growis on the feure,   *furrow*

	In mailis and gersomes rasit ouirhie,	*rents and fees raised too high*
	And garris thame beg fra dur to dure.	*makes; door*
15	In taking sowld discretioun be.	

	Sum takis uthir mens takkis	*other; goods*
	And on the peure oppressioun makkis,	
	And nevir remembris that he mon die	*must*
	Quhill that the gallowis gar him rax.	*Until; make; stretch*
20	In taking sowld discretioun be.	

	Sum takis be sie and sum be land,	*by sea*
	And nevir fra taking can hald thair hand	
	Quhill he be tit up to ane tre;	*Until; tied*
	And syne thay gar him undirstand	*then; make*
25	In taking sowld discretioun be.	

	Sum wald tak all his nychbouris geir.	*goods*
	Had he of man als littill feir	*fear*
	As he hes dreid that God him see,	*dread*
	To tak than sowld he nevir forbeir.	
30	In taking sowld discretioun be.	

	Sum wald tak all this warldis breid,	*bread*
	And yit not satisfeit of thair neid,	*satisfy*
	Throw hairt unsatiable and gredie.	*insatiable; greedy*
	Sum wald tak littill and can not speid.	*thrive*
35	In taking sowld discretioun be.	

	Grit men for taking and oppressioun	
	Ar sett full famous at the Sessioun,	*Court of Justice*
	And peur takaris ar hangit hie,	*high*
	Schamit forevir and thair successioun.	*Shamed; descendants*
40	In taking sowld discretioun be.	

29. *Dunbar at Oxford*
    [*Ane peralous seiknes is vane prosperité*]

To speik of science, craft, or sapience,	*knowledge, skill, or wisdom*
Of vertew, morall cunnyng, or doctryne,	*precepts; dogma*
Of jure, of wisdome, or intelligence,	*law*
Of every study, lair, or disciplyne —	*subject*
5 All is bot tynt or reddy for to tyne,	*lost; be lost*
Nocht using it as it suld usit be,	*Not; should*
The craft excersing, considering nocht the fyne.	*not; result*
Ane peralous seiknes is vane prosperité.	*A perilous sickness; empty*

The curius probatcioun logicall,	*subtle logical proof*
10 The eloquence of ornat rethorye,	*rhetoric*
The naturall science filosophicall,	
The dirk apirance of astronomy,	*dark*
The theologgis sermon, the fablis of poetrye —	*theologian's*
Without guid lyff, all in the selfe dois de,	*does die*
15 As Mayis flouris dois in September drye.	
Ane peralows lyff is vane prosperité.	

Quhairfoir, ye clerkis grytast of constance,	*Wherefore; steadfastness*
Fullest off science and of knaleging,	
To us be mirrouris in yowr governance,	
20 And in owr dirknes be lampis in schining,	
Or thane in frustar is yowr lang lerning;	*then; vain*
Gyff to yowr sawis your deidis contrar be,	*If; teachings; deeds*
Yowr maist accusar is your awin cuning.	*greatest; intelligence*
Ane peralows seiknes is vane prosperitie.	

30. *The Thistle and the Rose*

Quhen Merche wes with variand windis past,	*When March; varying*
And Appryll had with hir silver schouris	*April; showers*
Tane leif at Nature with ane orient blast,	*Departed from; eastern*
And lusty May, that muddir is of flouris,	*joyful; mother*
5 Had maid the birdis to begyn thair houris	*made*

Amang the tendir odouris reid and quhyt,	*scents [of flowers] red and white*
Quhois armony to heir it wes delyt,	*Whose harmony; hear*
In bed at morrow sleiping as I lay,	
Me thocht Aurora with hir cristall ene	*eyes*
10 In at the window lukit by the day	
And halsit me, with visage paill and grene,	*greeted; pale; fresh*
On quhois hand a lark sang fro the splene:	*whose; heart*
"Awalk, luvaris, out of your slomering;	*Awaken, lovers; slumbering*
Se how the lusty morrow dois up spring!"	*See; merry*
15 Me thocht fresche May befoir my bed upstude	
In weid depaynt of mony divers hew,	*raiment*
Sobir, benyng, and full of mansuetude,	*Calm, gracious; gentleness*
In brycht atteir of flouris forgit new,	*attire; newly formed*
Hevinly of color, quhyt, reid, broun, and blew,	*white; red*
20 Balmit in dew and gilt with Phebus bemys	*Anointed with; gilded; beams*
Quhill all the hous illumynit of hir lemys.	*While; [was] illuminated by; rays*
"Slugird," scho said, "Awalk annone, for schame,	*Sluggard; Awake right away*
And in my honour sumthing thow go wryt;	*write*
The lork hes done the mirry day proclame	*lark*
25 To rais up luvaris with confort and delyt,	*lovers*
Yit nocht incress thy curage to indyt,	*[has] not increased; desire; compose*
Quhois hairt sumtyme hes glaid and blisfull bene	*Whose heart*
Sangis to mak undir the levis grene."	*Songs; leaves*
"Quhairto," quod I, "Sall I uprys at morrow,	*Why; Shall*
30 For in this May few birdis herd I sing?	*heard*
Thai haif moir caus to weip and plane thair sorrow,	*more; weep; express*
Thy air it is nocht holsum nor benyng;	*not wholesome; pleasant*
Lord Eolus dois in thy sessone ring;	*reign*
So busteous ar the blastis of his horne,	*harsh are*
35 Amang thy bewis to walk I haif forborne."	*boughs*
With that this lady sobirly did smyll	*gently*
And said, "Uprys and do thy observance;	
Thow did promyt in Mayis lusty quhyle	*promise; May's joyous time*
For to discryve the ros of most plesance.	*describe; rose; delight*

40	Go se the birdis how thay sing and dance,	*see*
	Illumynit our with orient skyis brycht	*[all] over*
	Annamyllit richely with new asur lycht."	*Adorned; blue*
	Quhen this wes said depairtit scho, this quene,	*departed*
	And enterit in a lusty gairding gent.	*merry garden fine*
45	And than, me thocht, sa listely besene	*then; thus well-arrayed*
	In serk and mantill, full haistely I went	*shirt; cloak*
	Into this garth, most dulce and redolent	*garden; sweet*
	Of herb and flour and tendir plantis sueit	*sweet*
	And grene levis doing of dew doun fleit.	*dripping; dropped*
50	The purpour sone with tendir bemys reid	*purple sun*
	In orient bricht as angell did appeir,	
	Throw goldin skyis putting up his heid,	*Through; head*
	Quhois gilt tressis schone so wondir cleir	*Whose*
	That all the world tuke confort, fer and neir,	*took*
55	To luke upone his fresche and blisfull face,	
	Doing all sable fro the hevynnis chace.	*Chasing; darkness; heavens*
	And as the blisfull soune of cherarchy,	*just like; sound; [heavenly] hierarchies*
	The fowlis song throw confort of the licht;	*birds sang; light*
	The birdis did with oppin vocis cry,	
60	"O luvaris fo, away thow dully nycht,	*lovers' foe*
	And welcum day that confortis every wicht;	*person*
	Haill May, haill Flora, haill Aurora schene!	
	Haill princes Natur, haill Venus luvis quene!"	*princess; love's queen*
	Dame Nature gaif ane inhibitioun thair	*gave; injunction*
65	To fers Neptunus and Eolus the bawld	*fierce; bold*
	Nocht to perturb the wattir nor the air,	*Not*
	And that no schouris scharp nor blastis cawld	*sharp; cold*
	Effray suld flouris nor fowlis on the fold;	*Alarm should; birds; earth*
	Scho bad eik Juno, goddas of the sky,	*bade also*
70	That scho the hevin suld keip amene and dry.	*pleasant*
	Scho ordand eik that every bird and beist	*ordained also; beast*
	Befoir hir hienes suld annone compeir,	*highness should; appear*
	And every flour of vertew, most and leist,	*virtue; least*

75

  And every herb be feild, fer and neir, *of the field*
75 As thay had wont in May fro yeir to yeir *were used to do; year*
  To hir thair makar to mak obediens, *obeisance*
  Full law inclynnand with all dew reverens. *low bowing; due reverence*

  With that annone scho send the swyfte ro *sent; deer*
  To bring in beistis of all conditioun; *animals*
80 The restles swallow commandit scho also
  To seche all fowll of small and greit renown; *birds*
  And to gar flouris compeir of all fassoun, *make; appear; varieties*
  Full craftely conjurit scho the yarrow,
  Quhilk did furth swirk als swift as ony arrow. *dart as*

85 All present wer in twynkling of ane e, *eye*
  Baith beist and bird and flour, befoir the quene.
  And first the lyone, gretast of degré, *lion, highest of rank*
  Was callid thair, and he most fair to sene, *there; see*
  With a full hardy contenance and kene,
90 Befoir Dame Natur come and did inclyne, *came; bow down*
  With visage bawld and curage leonyne.

  This awfull beist full terrible wes of cheir, *wondrous; dreadful; mien*
  Persing of luke and stout of countenance, *Piercing of look*
  Rycht strong of corpis, of fassoun fair but feir, *body; face; fierce*
95 Lusty of schaip, lycht of deliverance, *Lovely; agile; movement*
  Reid of his cullour as is the ruby glance; *Red; color; ruby's glint*
  On feild of gold he stude full mychtely *stood; mightily*
  With flour delycis sirculit lustely. *fleur-de-lis encircled gaily*

  This lady liftit up his cluvis cleir, *paws fair*
100 And leit him listly lene upone hir kne; *let; deftly lean*
  And crownit him with dyademe full deir, *costly*
  Of radyous stonis most ryall for to se, *radiant; royal; see*
  Saying, "The king of beistis mak I thee, *beasts*
  And the chief protector in the woddis and schawis. *woods; copses*
105 Onto thi leigis go furth, and keip the lawis. *Unto; subjects*

  "Exerce justice with mercy and conscience, *Exercise*
  And lat no small beist suffir skaith na skornis *harm nor scorn*

	Of greit beistis that bene of moir piscence.	*are; greater strength*
	Do law elyk to aipis and unicornis,	*Apply the law equally; apes*
110	And lat no bowgle with his busteous hornis	*wild ox; rough*
	The meik pluch ox oppres for all his pryd,	*meek plow; oppress*
	Bot in the yok go peciable him besyd."	*yoke; peaceably*
	Quhen this was said, with noyis and soun of joy	*noise*
	All kynd of beistis into thair degré	*kinds; beasts according to rank*
115	At onis cryit lawd, "*Vive le roy!*"	*loudly, "Long live the King!"*
	And till his feit fell with humilité,	*at*
	And all thay maid him homege and fewté;	*they all made homage to him; fealty*
	And he did thame ressaif with princely laitis,	*receive; behavior*
	Quhois noble yre is *parcere prostratis*.[1]	*Whose; wrath*
120	Syne crownit scho the Egle, king of fowlis,	*Then crowned; birds*
	And as steill dertis scherpit scho his pennis,	*steel darts sharpened; feathers*
	And bawd him be als just to awppis and owlis	*bade; as; curlews*
	As unto pacokkis, papingais, or crennis,	*peacocks, parrots, or cranes*
	And mak a law for wycht fowlis and for wrennis,	*strong; wrens*
125	And lat no fowll of ravyne do efferay,	*bird of prey frighten*
	Nor devoir birdis bot his awin pray.	*devour; except; prey*
	Than callit scho all flouris that grew on feild,	
	Discirnyng all thair fassionis and effeiris;	*Distinguishing; kinds; manners*
	Upone the awfull Thrissill scho beheld	*dreadful Thistle; looked*
130	And saw him kepit with a busche of speiris.	*guarded by; spears*
	Concedring him so able for the weiris,	*Considering; wars*
	A radius croun of rubeis scho him gaif	*radiant; rubies; gave*
	And said, "In feild go furth and fend the laif.	*defend the rest*
	"And sen thow art a king, thow be discreit;	*since; discreet*
135	Herb without vertew hald nocht of sic pryce	*Plant; not; such value*
	As herb of vertew and of odor sueit;	*fragrance sweet*
	And lat no nettill vyle and full of vyce	*let*
	Hir fallow to the gudly flour delyce,	*be equal to; fleur-de-lis*

---

[1] *to show mercy to the downtrodden*

	Nor latt no wyld weid full of churlichenes	*let; weed; coarseness*
140	Compair hir till the lilleis nobilnes;	*Compare; to; lily's*

	"Nor hald non udir flour in sic denty	*Nor hold any other; such regard*
	As the fresche Ros of cullour reid and quhyt;	*Rose; color*
	For gife thow dois, hurt is thyne honesty,	*if*
	Conciddering that no flour is so perfyt,	
145	So full of vertew, plesans, and delyt,	
	So full of blisfull angelik bewty,	
	Imperiall birth, honour, and dignité."	

	Than to the Ros scho turnyt hir visage	*Then; face*
	And said, "O lusty dochtir most benyng,	*lovely daughter; gracious*
150	Aboif the lilly illustare of lynnage,	*Above; illustrious; family*
	Fro the stok ryell rysing fresche and ying,	*royal stock; young*
	But ony spot or macull doing spring,	*Without; blemish having sprung*
	Cum, blowme of joy, with jemis to be cround,	*Come, bloom; gems*
	For our the laif thy bewty is renownd."	*over the rest*

155	A coistly croun with clarefeid stonis brycht	*clarified*
	This cumly quene did on hir heid inclois,	*comely*
	Quhill all the land illumynit of the licht;	*Which; by the light*
	Quhairfoir me thocht all flouris did rejos,	*Whereat; thought; rejoice*
	Crying attonis, "Haill be thow richest Ros,	*at once*
160	Haill hairbis empryce, haill freschest quene of flouris!	*herbs' empress*
	To thee be glory and honour at all houris!"	

	Thane all the birdis song with voce on hicht,	*sang; high*
	Quhois mirthfull soun wes mervelus to heir.	*Whose; sound; hear*
	The mavys song, "Haill, Rois most riche and richt,	*song-thrush sang; true*
165	That dois up flureis undir Phebus speir;	*flourish; sphere*
	Haill plant of yowth, haill princes dochtir deir;	*prince's daughter dear*
	Haill blosome breking out of the blud royall,	*blood*
	Quhois pretius vertew is imperiall!"	*Whose*

	The merle scho sang, "Haill, Rois of most delyt,	
170	Haill of all flouris quene and soverane!"	
	The lark scho song, "Haill, Rois both reid and quhyt,	*red; white*
	Most plesand flour of michty cullouris twane!"	*pleasing; colors two*

78

The nychtingaill song, "Haill, Naturis suffragene,   *protégé*
In bewty, nurtour, and every nobilnes,   *nurture; nobility*
175   In riche array, renown, and gentilnes!"

The commoun voce uprais of birdis small   *uprose*
Apone this wys: "O blissit be the hour   *In this manner*
That thow wes chosin to be our principall;
Welcome to be our princes of honour,   *princess*
180   Our perle, our plesans, and our paramour,   *pearl; delight; beloved*
Our peax, our play, our plane felicité: *peace; delight; true happiness*
Chryst thee conserf frome all adversité!"   *preserve*

Than all the birdis song with sic a schout   *Then; sang; such*
That I annone awoilk quhair that I lay,   *awoke where*
185   And with a braid I turnyt me about   *jerk*
To se this court, bot all wer went away.   *but*
Than up I lenyt, halflingis in affrey,   *rose, halfway in alarm*
And thus I wret, as ye haif hard toforrow,   *wrote; heard before*
Of lusty May upone the nynt morrow.   *ninth morning*

31. *To Princess Margaret*
    [*Welcum of Scotlond to be quene*]

Now fayre, fayrest of every fayre,   *beautiful one*
Princes most plesant and preclare,   *Princess; delightful; illustrious*
The lustyest one alyve that byne: *most cheerful; is*
Welcum of Scotlond to be quene!

5   Younge tender plant of pulcritud   *beauty*
Descendyd of imperyalle blode,
Fresche fragrant floure of fayrehede shene: *loveliness bright*
Welcum of Scotlond to be quene!

Swet lusty lusum lady clere,   *joyful lovely*
10   Most myghty kyngis dochter dere,   *king's daughter*
Borne of a princes most serene: *princess*
Welcum of Scotlond to be quene!

Welcum the rose bothe rede and whyte,
Welcum the floure of our delyte,
15   Oure spreit rejoysyng frome the sone beme: *spirit gladdening by; sun beam*
Welcum of Scotlond to be quene!
Welcum of Scotlonde to be quene!

32. *To Princess Margaret*
    [*Gladethe, thoue queyne of Scottis regioun*]

Gladethe, thoue queyne of Scottis regioun,   *Rejoice; queen*
Ying tendir plaunt of plesand pulcritude,   *Young; pleasing*
Fresche flour of youthe, new germyng to burgeoun,   *germinating*
Our perle of price, our princes fair and gud,   *pearl; princess*
5   Our charbunkle chosin of hye imperiale blud,   *high*
Our rois riale most reverent under croune,   *rose royal*
Joy be and grace onto thi selcitud: *majesty*
Gladethe, thoue queyne of Scottis regioun.

O hye triumphing peradis of joy,   *high; paradise*
10   Lodsteir and lamp of every lustines;   *Lode star; delight*
Of port surmounting Pollexen of Troy,   *In manner surpassing*
Dochtir to Pallas in angillik brichtnes,
Mastres of nurtur and of nobilnes,   *Mistress*
Of fresch depictour princes and patroun,   *painting*
15   O hevin in erthe of ferlifull suetnes: *wondrous sweetness*
Gladethe, thoue queyne of Scottis regioune.

Of thi fair fegour Natur micht rejoys   *figure*
That so thee kervit withe all hir curiys slicht.   *carved; subtle art*
Sche has thee maid this verray wairldis chois,   *made*
20   Schawing one thee hir craftis and hir micht,   *on*
To se quhow fair sche couthe depant a wicht,   *see how; could depict a person*
Quhow gud, how noble of all condicioun,   *good*
Quhow womanly in every mannis sicht:
Gladethe, thoue queyne of Scottis regioun.

25   Rois red and quhit, resplendent of colour,   *Rose; white*
New of thi knop at morrow fresche atyrit   *bud; attired*

One stalk yet grene, O yong and tendir flour   *On*
That with thi luff has ale this regioun firit,   *love; inspired*
Gret Gode us graunt that we have long desirit —   *what*
30   A plaunt to spring of thi successioun,   *from*
Syne witht ale grace His spreit to be inspirit: *Then; spirit*
Gladethe, thoue queyne of Scottis regioun.

O precius Margreit, pleasand, cleir and quhit,   *white*
Moir blitht and bricht na is the beriale schene,   *More; than; beryl bright*
35   Moir deir na is the diamaunt of delit,   *precious than*
Moir semly na is the sapheir one to seyne,   *to look on*
Moir gudely eik na is the emerant greyne,   *also; emerald green*
Moir riche na is the ruby of renowne,
Fair gem of joy, Margreit, of thee I meyne: *mean*
40   Gladethe, thoue queyne of Scottis regioun.

33. *To Aberdeen*
    [*Be blyth and blisfull, burgh of Aberdein*]

Blyth Aberdeane, thow beriall of all tounis,   *beryl (i.e., gem)*
The lamp of bewtie, bountie, and blythnes,   *beauty*
Unto the heaven upheyt thy renoun is,   *uplifted*
Of vertew, wisdome, and of worthines;   *virtue*
5   He nottit is thy name of nobilnes.   *Highly celebrated*
Into the cuming of oure lustie quein,   *delightful queen*
The wall of welth, guid cheir, and mirrines: *well*
Be blyth and blisfull, burgh of Aberdein.

And first hir mett the burges of the toun,   *her; burgesses*
10   Richelie arrayit, as become thame to be,
Of quhom they cheset four men of renoun   *chose*
In gounes of velvot, young, abill, and lustie,
To beir the paill of velves cramase   *bear; canopy; velvet crimson cloth*
Abone hir heid, as the custome hes bein.   *Above; head*
15   Gryt was the sound of the artelyie: *artillery*
Be blyth and blisfull, burgh of Aberdein.

Ane fair processioun mett hir at the port,   *gateway*
In a cap of gold and silk full pleasantlie,   *cape*
Syne at hir entrie with many fair disport   *Then; delights*
20   Ressaveit hir on streittis lustilie;   *Received; streets joyfully*
Quhair first the salutatioun honorabilly   *Where*
Of the sweitt Virgin guidlie mycht be seine,   *goodly; seen*
The sound of menstraillis blawing to the sky:
Be blyth and blisfull, burgh of Aberdein.

25   And syne thow gart the orient kingis thrie   *then; made*
Offer to Chryst with benyng reverence
Gold, sence, and mir with all humilitie   *incense*
Schawand Him king with most magnificence;   *Showing*
Syne quhow the angill, with sword of violence, *Then how; angel*
30   Furth of the joy of Paradice putt clein   *from; entirely*
Adame and Ev for innobedience: *disobedience*
Be blyth and blisfull, burcht of Aberdein.   *town (burgh)*

And syne the Bruce, that evir was bold in stour,   *then; battle*
Thow gart as roy cum rydand under croun,   *made; king; riding*
35   Richt awfull, strang, and large of portratour, *awesome; appearance*
As nobill, dreidfull, michtie campioun.   *mighty champion*
The royall Stewartis syne, of great renoun,   *then*
Thow gart upspring, with branches new and greine, *made*
Sa gloriouslie quhill glaidid all the toun: *while cheered*
40   Be blyth and blisfull, burcht of Aberdein.

Syne come thair four and tuentie madinis ying, *Then came; maidens young*
All claid in greine, of mervelous bewtie,
With hair detressit, as threidis of gold did hing, *untressed; hang*
With quhyt hattis all browderit rycht bravelie,   *embroidered*
45   Playand on timberallis and singand rycht sweitlie.
That seimlie sort in ordour weill besein   *seemly group; order*
Did meit the quein, hir halsand reverentlie: *approach; greeting*
Be blyth and blisfull, burcht of Aberdein.

The streittis war all hung with tapestrie;   *streets were*
50   Great was the pres of peopill dwelt about,
And pleasant padgeanes playit prattelie.   *prettily*

The legeis all did to thair lady loutt,   *lieges; bow down*
Quha was convoyed with ane royall routt   *Who; company*
Of gryt barrounes and lustie ladyis schene.   *great; bright*
55 "Welcum, our quein!" the commones gaif ane schout: *commons gave*
Be blyth and blisfull, burcht of Aberdein.

At hir cuming great was the mirth and joy,
For at thair croce aboundantlie rane wyne.   *cross*
Untill hir ludgeing the toun did hir convoy;   *lodging*
60 Hir for to treit thai sett thair haill ingyne.   *entertain; whole intent*
Ane riche present thai did till hir propyne,   *to; present*
Ane costlie coup that large thing wald contene,   *cup*
Coverit and full of cunyeitt gold rycht fyne: *coined*
Be blyth and blisfull, burcht of Aberdein.

65 O potent princes, pleasant and preclair,   *princess; illustrious*
Great caus thow hes to thank this nobill toun,
That for to do thee honnour did not spair
Thair geir, riches, substance, and persoun,   *goods*
Thee to ressave on maist fair fasoun.   *receive in; fashion*
70 Thee for to pleis thai socht all way and mein.   *ways; means*
Thairfoir sa lang as quein thow beiris croun,   *bears*
Be thankfull to this burcht of Aberdein.

34. *To the Queen*
    [*Devoyd languor and leif in lustines*]

O lusty flour of yowth, benyng and bricht,   *lovely; gracious*
Fresch blome of bewty, blythfull, brycht and schene,   *bloom; joyful*
Fair lufsum lady, gentill and discret,   *lovable*
Yung brekand blosum yit on the stalkis grene,   *Young budding*
5 Delytsum lilly, lusty for to be sene: *Delightful; joyful*
Be glaid in hairt and expell havines.   *sorrow*
Bair of blis, that evir so blyth hes bene,   *Bare; merry*
Devoyd langour and leif in lustiness.   *Expel sadness; live; joy*

Brycht sterne at morrow that dois the nycht hyn chace,   *Bright star; hence chase*
10 Of luvis lychtsum day the lyfe and gyd,   *bright; guide*

Lat no dirk clud absent fro us thy face,   *dark cloud*
Nor lat no sable frome us thy bewty hyd,   *darkness; hide*
That hes no confort quhair that we go or ryd,   *have; where; ride*
Bot to behald the beme of thi brychtnes;   *Except; beam*
15   Baneis all baill and into blis abyd,   *Banish; sorrow*
Devoyd languor and leif in lustines.

Art thow plesand, lusty, yoing, and fair,   *You are delightful*
Full of all vertew and gud conditioun,   *character*
Rycht nobill of blud, rycht wyis and debonair,   *Very; blood; wise*
20   Honorable, gentill, and faythfull of renoun,   *by reputation*
Liberall, lufsum, and lusty of persoun.   *lovable; joyful*
Quhy suld thow than lat sadnes thee oppres?   *Why; then let*
In hairt be blyth and lay all dolour doun,   *heart; sorrow*
Devoyd languor and leif in lustines.

25   I me commend with all humilitie   *offer myself*
Unto thi bewty blisfull and bening,   *gracious*
To quhome I am and sall ay servand be   *whom; shall always*
With steidfast hairt and faythfull trew mening   *intentions*
Unto the deid without depairting.   *death*
30   For quhais saik I sall my pen addres,   *whose; shall*
Sangis to mak for thy reconforting,
That thow may leif in joy and lustines.

O fair sweit blossum, now in bewty flouris,
Unfaidit bayth of cullour and vertew,   *Unfaded; color*
35   Thy nobill lord that deid hes done devoir,   *death; devoured*
Faid nocht with weping thy vissage fair of hew.   *Fade not*
O lufsum lusty lady, wyse and trew,
Cast out all cair and comfort do incres.
Exyll all sichand, on thy servand rew.   *sighing; take pity*
40   Devoyd languor and lef in lustines.

35. *Eulogy to Bernard Stewart, Lord of Aubigny*
   [*Withe glorie and honour*]

	Renownit, ryall, right reverend, and serene,	*royal*
	Lord hie tryumphing in wirschip and valoure,	*high*
	Fro kyngis downe most Cristin knight and kene,	*Christian; fierce*
	Most wyse, most valyand, moste laureat hie victour,	*valiant*
5	Onto the sterris upheyt is thyne honour.	*stars raised*
	In Scotland welcum be thyne excellence	
	To king, queyne, lord, clerk, knight, and servatour,	
	Withe glorie and honour, lawde and reverence.	*praise*
	Welcum, in stour most strong, incomparable knight,	*battle*
10	The fame of armys and floure of vassalage,	
	Welcum, in were moste worthi, wyse, and wight,	*war; able*
	Welcum, the soun of Mars of moste curage,	*son; courage*
	Welcum, moste lusti branche of our linnage,	
	In every realme oure scheild and our defence,	
15	Welcum, our tendir blude of hie parage,	*blood; rank*
	With glorie and honour, lawde and reverence.	
	Welcum, in were the secund Julius,	*war*
	The prince of knightheyd and flour of chevalry,	
	Welcum, most valyeant and victorius,	
20	Welcum, invincible victour moste wourthy,	
	Welcum, our Scottis chiftane most dughti,	*doughty (strong)*
	Wyth sowne of clarioun, organe, song, and sence.	*sound; incense*
	To thee atonis, lord, "Welcum!" all we cry,	*at once*
	With glorie and honour, lawde and reverence.	
25	Welcum, oure indeficient adjutorie,	*unfailing helper*
	That evir our naceoun helpit in thare neyd,	*nation; their need*
	That never saw Scot yit indigent nor sory	*sorrowful*
	Bot thou did hym suport with thi gud deid.	*good deeds*
	Welcum, therfor, abufe all livand leyd,	*above every living person*
30	Withe us to live and to maik recidence,	
	Quhilk never sall sunye for thi saik to bleid,	*Who; hesitate; sake; bleed*
	To quham be honour, lawde, and reverence.	

Is none of Scotland borne fathfull and kynde
Bot he of naturall inclinacioune
35 Dois favour thee withe all his hert and mynde,
Withe fervent, tendir, trew intencioun,
And wald of inwart hie effectioun   *would; high*
But dreyd of danger de in thi defence,   *Without dread; die*
Or dethe or schame war done to thi persoun,   *Before (Ere); were*
40 To quham be honour, lawde, and reverence.

Welcum, thow knight moste fortunable in feild,
Welcum, in armis moste aunterus and able   *adventurous*
Undir the soun that beris helme or scheild,   *sun*
Welcum, thow campioun in feght unourcumable,   *invincible*
45 Welcum, most dughti, digne, and honorable,   *doughty, worthy*
And moist of lawde and hie magnificence
Nixt undir kingis to stand incomparable,
To quham be honour, lawde, and reverence.   *whom*

Throw Scotland, Ingland, France, and Lumbardy   *Through*
50 Fleys on weyng thi fame and thi renoune,   *Flies; wing*
And our all cuntreis undirnethe the sky   *over; countries*
And our all strandis fro the sterris doune.   *over; streams*
In every province, land, and regioune,
Proclamit is thi name of excellence
55 In every ceté, village, and in toune,
Withe glorie and honour, lawd and reverence.

O feyrse Achill in furius hie curage,   *fierce; high*
O strong invincible Hector undir scheild,
O vailyeant Arthur in knyghtli vassalage,   *prowess*
60 Agamenon in governance of feild,
Bold Henniball in batall to do beild,   *be courageous*
Julius in jupert, in wisdom and expence,   *audacity*
Most fortunate chiftane bothe in yhouth and eild,   *old age*
To thee be honour, lawde, and reverence.

65 At parlament thow suld be hye renownit,   *should; highly*
That did so mony victoryse opteyn.   *obtain*
Thi cristall helme withe lawry suld be crownyt,   *laurel*

     And in thi hand a branche of olyve greyn.

     The sueird of conquis and of knyghtheid keyn   *sword; keen*

70   Be borne suld highe before thee in presence,

     To represent sic man as thou has beyn,   *such*

     With glorie and honour, lawde and reverence.

     Hie furius Mars, the god armipotent,   *High*

     Rong in the hevin at thyne nativité.   *Rang*

75   Saturnus doune withe fyry eyn did blent   *down; fiery eye; look*

     Throw bludy visar men manasing to gar de.   *Through; threatening; make die*

     On thee fresche Venus keist hir amourouse e,   *cast; eye*

     On thee Marcurius furtheyet his eloquence.   *poured out*

     Fortuna maior did turn hir face on thee,   *Good Fortune*

80   Wyth glorie and honour, lawde and reverence.

     Prynce of fredom and flour of gentilnes,

     Sweyrd of knightheid and choise of chevalry,   *Sword; the best*

     This tyme I lefe, for grete prolixitnes,   *leave off (i.e., stop)*

     To tell quhat feildis thow wan in Pikkardy,   *fields*

85   In France, in Bertan, in Naplis and Lumbardy,   *Britain*

     As I think eftir withe all my diligence,

     Or thow departe, at lengthe for to discry,   *Before (Ere); describe*

     With glorie and honour, lawd and reverence.

     B in thi name betaknis batalrus,   *betokens warlike*

90   A able in feild, R right renoune most hie,

     N nobilnes, and A for aunterus,   *adventurous*

     R ryall blude, for dughtines is D,   *doughtiness*

     V valyeantnes, S for strenewité: *vigorousness*

     Quhoise knyghtli name so schynyng in clemencé   *Whose*

95   For wourthines in gold suld writtin be,

     With glorie and honour, lawd and reverence.

36. *Elegy for Bernard Stewart, Lord of Aubigny*
   [*Sen he is gon, the flour of chevalrie*]

     Illuster Lodovick, of France most Cristin king,   *Christian*

     Thow may complain with sighis lamentable

The death of Bernard Stewart, nobill and ding, *worthy*
In deid of armes most anterous and abill, *deeds; adventurous*
5   Most mychti, wyse, worthie, and confortable *comforting*
Thy men of weir to governe and to gy. *war; guide*
For him, allace, now may thow weir the sabill, *wear*
Sen he is gon, the flour of chevelrie. *Since*

Complaine sould everie noble valiant knycht
10   The death of him that douchtie was in deid, *doughty; deeds*
That many ane fo in feild hes put to flight, *a foe; has*
In weris wicht be wisdome and manheid. *wars strong by*
To the Turkas sey all land did his name dreid, *Turkish sea*
Quhois force all France in fame did magnifie. *Whose*
15   Of so hie price sall nane his place posseid, *high; shall none; possess*
For he is gon, the flour of chevilrie.

O duilfull death, O dragon dolorous! *doleful*
Quhy hes thow done so dulfullie devoir *Why; duty*
The prince of knychtheid, nobill and chevilrous,
20   The witt of weiris, of armes and honour, *best of commanders*
The crop of curage, the strenth of armes in stour, *paragon; battle*
The fame of France, the fame of Lumbardy,
The chois of chiftanes, most awfull in airmour, *choicest; awesome*
The charbuckell, cheif of every chevelrie?

25   Pray now for him all that him loveit heir, *here*
And for his saull mak intercessioun *soul*
Unto the Lord that hes him bocht so deir, *bought*
To gif him mercie and remissioun.
And namelie, we of Scottis natioun,
30   Intill his lyff quhome most he did affy, *During; serve*
Forgett we nevir into our orisoun *prayer*
To pray for him, the flour of chavelrie.

37. *To the King*
   [*In hansill of this guid New Yeir*]

My prince in God, gif thee guid grace,   *give*
Joy, glaidnes, confort, and solace,
Play, pleasance, myrth, and mirrie cheir   *Merriment*
In hansill of this guid New Yeir.   *As a gift for*

5   God gif to thee ane blissed chance,   *give; fortune*
       And of all vertew aboundance,
       And grace ay for to perseveir   *ever*
       In hansill of this guid New Yeir.

       God give thee guid prosperitie,
10   Fair fortoun and felicitie,   *fortune*
       Evirmair in earth quhill thow ar heir,   *while*
       In hansell of this guid New Yeir.

       The heavinlie Lord His help thee send
       Thy realme to reull and to defend,
15   In peace and justice it to steir,   *guide*
       In hansell of this guid New Yeir.

       God gif thee blis quharevir thow bownes,   *give; wherever you dwell*
       And send thee many Fraunce crownes,   *French*
       Hie liberall heart, and handis not sweir,   *Extremely; reluctant*
20   In hansell of this guid New Yeir.

38. *To the King*
   [*God gif ye war Johne Thomsounis man*]

Schir, for your grace bayth nicht and day   *both*
Richt hartlie on my kneis I pray   *knees*
With all devotioun that I can:
God gif ye war Johne Thomsounis man!   *God grant that you were (see note)*

5   For war it so, than weill war me.   *were; then well were*
       But benefice I wald nocht be,   *Without*

89

My hard fortoun wer endit than: *then*
God gif ye war Johne Thomsounis man!

Than wald sum reuth within yow rest   *would; pity*
10   For saik of hir, fairest and best   *sake; her*
In Bartane sen hir tyme began: *Britain since*
God gif ye war Johne Thomsounis man.

For it micht hurt in no degré
That on so fair and gude as sche   *one*
15   Throw hir vertew sic wirschip wan   *Through; such; won*
Als yow to mak Johne Thomsounis man.   *As*

I wald gif all that ever I have   *give*
To that conditioun, sa God me saif,   *end; save*
That ye had vowit to the swan   *vowed*
20   Ane yeir to be Johne Thomsounis man.   *One year*

The mersy of that sweit meik Rose   *meek*
Suld soft yow, Thirsill, I suppois,   *Thistle*
Quhois pykis throw me so reuthles ran: *Whose thorns through; pitiless*
God gif ye war Johne Thomounis man!

25   My advocat, bayth fair and sweit,
The hale rejosing of my spreit,   *whole; spirit*
Wald speid into my erand than,   *hasten unto; then*
And ye war anis Johne Thomsounis man.   *If; once*

Ever quhen I think yow harde or dour   *stubborn*
30   Or mercyles in my succour,   *support*
Than pray I God and sweit Sanct An,   *Saint Anne*
Gif that ye war Johne Thomsounis man.

39. *To the King*
   [*My panefull purs so priclis me*]

Sanct Salvatour, send silver sorrow!   *Holy Savior*
It grevis me both evin and morrow,   *grieves*

90

Chasing fra me all cheritie. — *charity*
It makis me all blythnes to borrow, — *causes; joy; lose*
5 My panefull purs so priclis me. — *purse; prickles (torments)*

Quhen I wald blythlie ballattis breif, — *When; cheerfully poems write*
Langour thairto givis me no leif. — *leave (permission)*
War nocht gud howp my hart uphie, — *hope; sustain*
My verry corpis for cair wald cleif, — *body; cleave (tear apart)*
10 My panefull purs so prikillis me.

Quhen I sett me to sing or dance,
Or go to plesand pastance, — *pleasing pastimes*
Than pansing of penuritie — *Then thinking on poverty*
Revis that fra my remembrance, — *Takes; thoughts*
15 My panefull purs so prikillis me.

Quhen men that hes pursis in tone — *have purses; tune (i.e., that "clink")*
Pasis to drynk or to disjone, — *eat*
Than mon I keip ane gravetie — *Then must; sober face*
And say that I will fast quhill none, — *till noon*
20 My panefull purs so priclis me.

My purs is maid of sic ane skyn — *made; such*
Thair will na cors byd it within — — *coin remain*
Fra it as fra the Feynd thay fle! — *From; Fiend*
Quhaevir tyne, quhaevir win, — *Whoever loses*
25 My panefull purs so priclis me.

Had I ane man of ony natioun
Culd mak on it ane conjuratioun — *[Who] could; spell*
To gar silver ay in it be, — *make; always*
The Devill suld haif no dominatioun
30 With pyne to gar it prickill me. — *pain; make*

I haif inquyrit in mony a place — *have asked*
For help and confort in this cace, — *case*
And all men sayis, my lord, that ye
Can best remeid for this malice — *remedy; evil*
35 That with sic panis prickillis me. — *such pain torments*

40. *To the King*
   [*Schir, at this feist of benefice*]

	Schir, at this feist of benefice	*feast where benefices are given*
	Think that small partis makis grit service,	
	And equale distributioun	
	Makis thame content that hes ressoun,	*them*
5	And quha hes nane ar plesit na wyis.	*who; none; not at all*
	Schir, quhiddir is it mereit mair?	*which; merited more*
	To gif him drink that thristis sair,	*give; sorely*
	Or fill a fow man quhill he birst,	*full; until*
	And lat his fallow de a thrist,	*fellow die of*
10	Quhilk wyne to drynk als worthie war?	*Which; just as; was*
	It is no glaid collatioun	*light evening meal*
	Quhair ane makis myrrie, aneuther lukis doun,	*Where; another looks*
	Ane thristis, aneuther playis cop out.	*empties the cup*
	Lat anis the cop ga round about,	*once*
15	And wyn the covanis banesoun.	*win; coveted benison*

41. *To the King*
   [*Of benefice, sir, at everie feist*]

	Of benefice, sir, at everie feist,	*feast*
	Quha monyast hes makis maist requeist.	*Who has most makes the most requests*
	Get thai not all, thai think ye wrang thame.	
	Ay is the ovirword of the geist,	*Always; refrain; song*
5	Giff thame the pelffe to pairt among thame.	*Give; pelf (riches); themselves*
	Sum swelleis swan, sum swelleis duke,	*eat (swallows) swan; duck*
	And I stand fastand in a nuke	*fasting; nook*
	Quhill the effect of all thai fang thame.[1]	
	Bot Lord! how petewouslie I luke	*piteously; look*
10	Quhone all the pelfe thai pairt amang thame.	*When*

---

[1] *While the most valuable effects they grab for themselves*

	Of sic hie feistis of sanctis in glorie,	*At such high feasts; saints*
	Baithe of commoun and propir storie,	*Both*
	Quhair lairdis war patronis, oft I sang thame	*lords were; [to] them*
	Charitas, pro Dei amore;	*Charity, for the love of God*
15	And yit I gat na thing amang thame.	

	This blynd warld ever so payis his dett,	*its debt*
	Riche befoir pure spraidis ay thair nett —	*poor; always*
	To fische al watiris dois belang thame.	
	Quha nathing hes can nathing gett,	
20	Bot ay as syphir sett amang thame.	*cipher (a zero)*

	Swa thai the kirk have in thair cure,	*So long as; charge*
	Thai fors bot litill how it fure,	*care; fares*
	Nor of the buikis or bellis quha rang thame.	*books*
	Thai pans not of the prochin pure,	*care; parish poor*
25	Hed thai the pelfe to pairt amang thame.	

	So warryit is this warldis rent	*valued; goods*
	That nane thairof can be content,	
	Of deathe quhill that the dragoun stang thame.	*until*
	Quha maist hes than sall maist repent,	
30	With largest compt to pairt amang thame.	*reckoning*

42. *A Dream*

	This hinder nycht, halff sleiping as I lay,	*The other night*
	Me thocht my chalmer in ane new aray	*chamber*
	Was all depent with many divers hew	*adorned; hues*
	Of all the nobill storyis, ald and new,	
5	Sen oure first father formed was of clay.	*Since; (i.e., Adam)*

	Me thocht the lift all bricht with lampis lycht,	*air; light of lamps*
	And thairin enterrit many lustie wicht,	*lively folks*
	Sum young, sum old, in sindry wyse arayit.	*sundry fashion attired*
	Sum sang, sum danceit, on instrumentis sum playit,	
10	Sum maid disportis with hartis glaid and lycht.	*diversions*
	Thane thocht I thus, "This is an felloun phary,	*great marvel (illusion)*

Or ellis my witt rycht woundrouslie dois varie.   *waver*
This seimes to me ane guidlie companie,   *seems; goodly*
And gif it be ane feindlie fantasie,   *if; fiendish*
15   Defend me, Jhesu and his moder Marie!"   *Protect*

Thair pleasant sang, nor yett thair pleasant toun,   *song; music*
Nor yett thair joy, did to my heart redoun.   *penetrate*
Me thocht the drerie damiesall Distres,   *dismal*
And eik hir sorie sister Hivines,   *also; sorrowful; Depression (Heaviness)*
20   Sad as the leid in baid lay me abone.   *Heavy; lead; bed; above (i.e., upon)*

And Langour satt up at my beddis heid.
With instrument full lamentable and deid   *sad*
Scho playit sangis so duilfull to heir,   *doleful; hear*
Me thocht ane houre seimeit ay ane yeir;   *like*
25   Hir hew was wan and wallowed as the leid.   *hue; gray; faded; lead*

Thane com the ladyis danceing in ane trece,   *dance*
And Nobilnes befoir thame come ane space,
Saying withe cheir, bening and womanly,   *benign*
"I se ane heir in bed oppressit ly.   *see one here; afflicted*
30   My sisteris, go and help to gett him grace."   *relief*

With that anon did start out of a dance
Twa sisteris callit Confort and Pleasance,   *Delight*
And with twa harpis did begin to sing.
Bot I thairof mycht tak na rejoseing,
35   My heavines opprest me with sic mischance.   *such misery*

Thay saw that I not glader wox of cheir,   *waxed (became); mood*
And thairof had thai winder all, but weir,   *wonder; without [a] doubt*
And said ane lady that Persaveing hecht,   *Insight was called*
"Of hevines he fiellis sic a wecht   *feels such; weight*
40   Your melody he pleisis not till heir.   *does not enjoy hearing*

"Scho and Distres hir sister dois him greve."   *vex*
Quod Nobilnes, "Quhow sall he thame eschew?"   *How; avoid*
Thane spak Discretioun, ane lady richt bening,   *gracious*

Poem 42: A Dream

	"Wirk eftir me and I sall gar him sing,	*shall cause*
45	And lang or nicht gar Langar tak hir leve."	*before night make*

	And then said Witt, "Gif thai work not be thee,	*If; by*
	But onie dout thai sall not work be me."	*Without any doubt*
	Discretioun said, "I knaw his malady.	
	The strok he feillis of melancholie,	*feels*
50	And, Nobilnes, his lecheing lyis in thee.	*healing lies*

	"Or evir this wicht at heart be haill and feir,	*Before; man; healthy; fair*
	Both thow and I most in the court appeir,	*must*
	For he hes lang maid service thair in vane.	
	With sum rewaird we mane him quyt againe,	*must; repay*
55	Now in the honour of this guid New Yeir."	

	"Weill worth thee, sister," said Considerance,	*Well may you succeed*
	And I sall help for to mantene the dance."	
	Thane spak ane wicht callit Blind Effectioun:	*person*
	"I sall befoir yow be with myne electioun;	*in my official function*
60	Of all the court I have the governance."	

	Thane spak ane constant wycht callit Ressoun,	
	And said, "I grant yow hes beine lord a sessioun	*has been*
	In distributioun, bot now the tyme is gone.	
	Now I may all distribute myne alone.	*by myself only*
65	Thy wrangous deidis did evir mane enschesoun.	*unjust deeds; every man injure*

	"For tyme war now that this mane had sumthing,	
	That lange hes bene ane servand to the king,	
	And all his tyme nevir flatter couthe nor faine,	*could; pretend*
	Bot humblie into ballat wyse complaine	*in wise songs*
70	And patientlie indure his tormenting.	

	"I counsall him be mirrie and jocound.	*cheerful*
	Be Nobilnes his help mon first be found."	*By; must*
	"Weill spokin, Ressoun my brother," quoth Discretioun;	
	"To sett on dies with lordis at the Cessioun	*sit; dais*
75	Into this realme yow war worth mony ane pound."	*were*

Thane spak anone Inoportunitie: *Importuner*
"Ye sall not gar him speid without me,   *make; succeed*
For I stand ay befoir the kingis face.   *always*
I sall him deiff or ellis myself mak hace,   *deafen; else; hoarse*
80   Bot gif that I befoir him servit be.   *Unless*

"Ane besy askar soonner sall he speid   *diligent suppliant; succeed*
Na sall twa besy servandis out of dreid,   *Than; without a doubt*
And he that askis not tynes bot his word,   *loses [nothing]; words*
Bot for to tyne lang service is no bourd,   *waste; joke*
85   Yett thocht I nevir to do sic folie deid."   *such [a] foolish deed*

Thane com anon ane callit Schir Johne Kirkpakar,   *Church-gatherer*
Of many cures ane michtie undertaker.   *pastoral charges*
Quod he, "I am possest in kirkis sevin,   *in possession of*
And yitt I think thai grow sall till ellevin   *eleven*
90   Or he be servit in ane, yone ballet maker.   *Before; yon ballad*

And then Schir Bet-the-Kirk, "Sa mot I thryff,   *Destroy-the-Church, "So might I thrive*
I haif of busie servandis foure or fyve,   *have*
And all direct unto sindrie steidis,   *destined; farmsteads*
Ay still awaitting upoun kirkmenes deidis,   *churchmen's deaths*
95   Fra quham sum tithingis will I heir belyff."   *hear of soon*

Quod Ressoun than, "The ballance gois unevin   *uneven*
That thow, allece, to serff hes kirkis sevin,   *alas*
And sevin als worth kirk not haifand ane.   *as worth [a] church; having*
With gredines I sie this world ourgane,   *see; overrun*
100   And sufficience dwellis not bot in Heavin."   *satisfaction; not but (i.e., only)*

"I have not wyt thairof," quod Temperance,   *blame*
"For thocht I hald him evinlie the ballance   *though*
And but ane cuir full micht till him wey,   *weigh*
Yett will he tak aneuther and gar it suey.   *another; cause; sway*
105   Quha best can rewll wald maist have governance."

Patience to me, "My freind," said, "Mak guid cheir,
And on the prince depend with humelie feir.   *humble bearing*
For I full weill dois knaw his nobill intent: *well do*

96

He wald not, for ane bischopperikis rent,	*bishopric's income*
110 That yow war unrewairdit half ane yeir."	*were*

Than as an fary thai to duir did frak,	*Then like a vision; door; rush*
And schot ane gone that did so ruidlie rak	*a gun; rudely roar*
Quhill all the aird did raird the ranebow under.	*earth; resound; rainbow*
On Leith sandis me thocht scho brak in sounder,	*broke*
115 And I anon did walkin with the crak.	*soon wakened; noise*

43. *The Headache*

My heid did yak yester nicht,	*ache*
This day to mak that I na micht.	*compose verse; might not*
So sair the magryme dois me menyie,	*painfully; migraine; disable*
Perseing my brow as ony ganyie,	*Piercing; arrow*
5 That scant I luik may on the licht.	*scarcely; look*

And now, schir, laitlie eftir mes	*shortly; mass*
To dyt thocht I begowthe to dres,	*write though I tried to begin*
The sentence lay full evill till find,	*words; hard to*
Unsleipit in my heid behind,	*Drowsy*
10 Dullit in dulnes and distres.	*Dulled by heaviness*

Full oft at morrow I upryse	
Quhen that my curage sleipeing lyis.	*spirit*
For mirth, for menstrallie and play,	
For din nor danceing nor deray,	*revelry*
15 It will not walkin me no wise.	*awaken in me at all*

44. *To the King*
[*For to considder is ane pane*]

This waverand warldis wretchidnes,	*unsteady*
The failyeand and frutles bissines,	*failing; activities*
The mispent tyme, the service vane,	
For to considder is ane pane.	*reflect on; painful*

5	The slydand joy, the glaidnes schort,	*elusive (sliding)*
	The feynyeid luif, the fals confort,	*pretended*
	The sweit abayd, the slichtfull trane,	*delay; subtle share*
	For to considder is ane pane.	

	The sugurit mouthis with myndis thairfra,	*sugared words; thoughts otherwise*
10	The figurit speiche with faceis tua,	*ornate; faces two*
	The plesand toungis with hartis unplane,	*contrary*
	For to considder is ane pane.	

	The labour lost and liell service,	*loyal*
	The lang availl on humill wyse,	*in humble fashion*
15	And the lytill rewarde agane,	
	For to considder is ane pane.	

	Nocht, I say, all be this cuntré,	*Not; only in; country*
	France, Ingland, Ireland, Almanie,	
	Bot als be Italie and Spane,	*also in*
20	Quhilk to considder is ane pane.	

	The change of warld fro weill to wo,	
	The honourable use is all ago	
	In hall and bour, in burgh and plane,	*bower; city; plain*
	For to considder is ane pane.	

25	Beleif dois liep, traist dois nocht tarie,	*does leap [away], trust*
	Office dois flit and courtis dois vary,	
	Purpos dois change as wynd or rane,	*Intention*
	Quhilk to considder is ane pane.	

	Gud rewle is banist our the bordour	*Good rule; banished over*
30	And rangat ringis but ony ordour	*riot prevails without any order*
	With reird of rebaldis and of swane,	*noise; ribalds; workers*
	Quhilk to considder is ane pane.	

	The pepill so wickit ar of feiris,	*wickedly are treated by the friars*
	The frutles erde all witnes beiris,	*earth; bears*
35	The ayr infectit and prophane,	
	Quhilk to considder is ane pane.	

Poem 44: To the King

The temporale stait to gryp and gather,	*worldly estate to grasp; hoard*
The sone disheris wald the father	*son would disinherit (dispossess)*
And as ane dyvour wald him demane,	*devourer; deal with*
40 Quhilk to considder is ane pane.	
Kirkmen so halie ar and gude	
That on thair conscience, rowme and rude,	*large; rough*
May turne aucht oxin and ane wane,	*several oxen; wain (wagon)*
Quhilk to considder is ane pane.	
45 I knaw nocht how the Kirk is gydit,	*guided*
Bot beneficis ar nocht leill devydit.	*fairly divided*
Sum men hes sevin and I nocht ane,	*not one*
Quhilk to considder is ane pane.	
And sum unworthy to browk ane stall	*own*
50 Wald clym to be ane cardinall —	*climb*
Ane bischoprik may nocht him gane,	*not; gain*
Quhilk to considder is ane pane.	
Unwourthy I, amang the laif,	*remainder*
Ane kirk dois craif and nane can have.	*crave*
55 Sum with ane thraif playis passage plane,[1]	
Quhilk to considder is ane pane.	
It cumis be king, it cumis be quene,	*comes from*
Bot ay sic space is us betwene	*such*
That nane can schut it with ane flane,	*cross; arrow*
60 Quhilk to considder is ane pane.	
It micht have cuming in schortar quhyll	*come in shorter time*
Fra Calyecot and the New Fund Yle,	*Calcutta; New Found Isle*
The partis of transmeridiane,	
Quhilk to considder is ane pane.	

---

[1] *Some with a large number [of churches] play dice*

65   It micht be this, had it bein kynd,
    Cuming out of the desertis of Ynde[1]
    Our all the grit se oceane,   *Over; great sea*
    Quhilk to considder is ane pane

    It micht have cuming out of all ayrtis —   *directions (points of the compass)*
70   Fra Paris and the orient partis,   *eastern lands (i.e., Asia)*
    And fra the ylis of Aphrycane,   *isles; Africa*
    Quhilk to consydder is ane pane.

    It is so lang in cuming me till,   *to*
    I dreid that it be quyt gane will,   *quite gone astray*
75   Or bakwart it is turnit agane,   *Before*
    Quhilk to considder is ane pane.

    Upon the heid of it is hecht   *head; promised*
    Bayth unicornis and crownis of wecht.   *weight*
    Quhen it dois cum, all men dois frane,   *ask*
80   Quhilk to considder is ane pane.

    I wait it is for me provydit,   *know*
    Bot sa done tyrsum it is to byd it,   *But; tiresome; await*
    It breikis my hairt and birstis my brane,   *bursts; brain*
    Quhilk to considder is ane pane.

85   Greit abbais grayth I nill to gather   *abbeys wish I not*
    Bot ane kirk scant coverit with hadder,   *hardly; heather*
    For I of lytill wald be fane,   *fain (happy)*
    Quhilk to considder is ane pane.

    And for my curis in sindrie place,   *charges; various*
90   With help, schir, of your nobill grace,
    My sillie saule sall never be slane,   *innocent soul; slain*
    Na for sic syn to suffer pane.   *Nor; such*

---

[1] Lines 65–66: *It might by this [time], had it been [according to] the natural order of things, / Coming out of (all the way from) the deserts of India*

	Experience dois me so inspyr,	*inspire*
	Of this fals failyeand warld I tyre,	*failing*
95	That evermore flytis lyk ane phane,	*flits; phantom*
	Quhilk to considder is ane pane.	

	The foremest hoip yit that I have	*highest hope*
	In all this warld, sa God me save,	
	Is in your grace, bayth crop and grayne,	*both blossom; fruit*
100	Quhilk is ane lessing of my pane.	*lessening*

45. *Against the Solicitors at Court*

	Be divers wyis and operatiounes	*By various ways*
	Men makis in court thair solistationes:	
	Sum be service and diligence,	*Some by*
	Sum be continuall residence.	
5	Sum one his substance dois abyd	*on; lives*
	Quhill fortoune do for him provyd.	*Until; does*
	Sum singis, sum dances, sum tellis storyis,	
	Sum lait at evin bringis in the Moryis.	*late at night; Morris dance*
	Sum flirdis, sum fenyeis, and sum flatteris,	*jests; pretends*
10	Sum playis the fuill and all owt clatteris.	*fool; constantly chatters*
	Sum man, musand be the waw,	*musing by the wall*
	Luikis as he mycht nocht do with aw.	*not belong with the others*
	Sum standis in a nuk and rownes.	*nook and whisper*
	For covetyce aneuthair neir swownes.	*nearly*
15	Sum beris as he wald ga wud	*acts as [if]; go mad*
	For hait desyr of wardis gud.	*hot; worldly goods*
	Sum at the Mes leves all devocione	*Mass*
	And besy labouris for premocione.	*promotion*
	Sum hes thair advocattis in chalmir	*chamber*
20	And takis thameselff thairoff no glawmir.	*bring on themselves no slander*
	My sempillnes, amang the laiff,	*others*
	Wait of na way, sa God me saiff,	*Knows of; save*
	Bot with ane hummble cheir and face	
	Refferis me to the kyngis grace.	*Recommends*
25	Methink his gracious countenance	*face*
	In ryches is my sufficiance.	

46. *To the King*
   [*Schir, ye have mony servitouris*]

	Schir, ye have mony servitouris	
	And officiaris of dyvers curis:	*functions*
	Kirkmen, courtmen, and craftismen fyne,	
	Doctouris in jure and medicyne,	*law*
5	Divinouris, rethoris, and philosophouris,	*Theologians, rhetoricians*
	Astrologis, artistis, and oratouris,	
	Men of armes and vailyeand knychtis	*valiant*
	And mony uther gudlie wichtis,	*goodly men*
	Musicianis, menstralis, and mirrie singaris,	
10	Chevalouris, cawandaris, and flingaris,	*entertainers; dancers*
	Cunyouris, carvouris, and carpentaris,	*Coiners, carvers*
	Beildaris of barkis and ballingaris,	*Builders; ships; boats*
	Masounis lyand upon the land	*Masons resting*
	And schipwrichtis hewand upone the strand,	*cutting; shore*
15	Glasing wrichtis, goldsmythis, and lapidaris,	*Glass workers; jewelers*
	Pryntouris, payntouris, and potingaris —	*Printers, painters; apothecaries*
	And all of thair craft cunning	*skillful*
	And all at anis lawboring,	*once*
	Quhilk pleisand ar and honorable	*pleasing*
20	And to your hienes profitable	*highness*
	And richt convenient for to be	*fitting*
	With your hie regale majestie,	
	Deserving of your grace most ding	*worthy*
	Bayth thank, rewarde, and cherissing.	
25	And thocht that I amang the laif	*though; rest*
	Unworthy be ane place to have	
	Or in thair nummer to be tald,	*number; counted*
	Als lang in mynd my work sall hald,	*shall be remembered*
	Als haill in everie circumstance,	*whole (i.e., perfect); respect*
30	In forme, in mater, and substance,	
	But wering or consumptioun,	*Without eroding*
	Roust, canker, or corruptioun	*Rust, disease*
	As ony of thair werkis all,	
	Suppois that my rewarde be small.	*Although*

35	Bot ye sa gracious ar and meik	*so; are; humble*
	That on your hienes followis eik	*after; highness; also*
	Aneuthir sort more miserabill	
	Thocht thai be nocht sa profitable:	*Though*
	Fenyeouris, fleichouris, and flatteraris,	*Fakes, coaxers*
40	Cryaris, craikaris, and clatteraris,	*Loudmouths, boasters; gossipers*
	Soukaris, groukaris, gledaris, gunnaris,	*Parasites, complainers, yes-men*
	Monsouris of France (gud clarat cunnaris),	*Gentlemen; wine experts*
	Inopportoun askaris of Yrland kynd,	*Importuning beggars; Ireland*
	And meit revaris lyk out of mynd,	*food thieves*
45	Scaffaris and scamleris in the nuke,	*Spongers; parasites; corner*
	And hall huntaris of draik and duik,	*drake; duck*
	Thrimlaris and thristaris as thai war woid,	*Jostlers; thrusters; were mad*
	Kokenis, and kennis na man of gude,	*Rogues; knows*
	Schulderaris and schovaris that hes no schame	*Pushers; shovers*
50	And to no cunning that can clame,	
	And can non uthir craft nor curis	*know; skill*
	Bot to mak thrang, schir, in your duris,	*throng; doors*
	And rusche in quhair thay counsale heir	*where*
	And will at na man nurtir leyr;	*breeding learn*
55	In quintiscence eik, ingynouris joly	*also, alchemists*
	That far can multiplie in folie —	
	Fantastik fulis, bayth fals and gredy,	*fools*
	Of toung untrew and hand evill diedie.	*given to*
	Few dar of all this last additioun	
60	Cum in Tolbuyth without remissioun.	*Tolbooth*
	And thocht this nobill cunning sort —	
	Quhom of befoir I did report —	
	Rewardit be, it war bot ressoun;	
	Thairat suld no man mak enchessoun.	*Therefore; objection*
65	Bot quhen the uther fulis nyce	*fools ignorant*
	That feistit at Cokelbeis gryce	*feasted; suckling pig*
	Ar all rewardit, and nocht I,	
	Than on this fals warld I cry "Fy!"	*Then*
	My hart neir bristis than for teyne,	*bursts then; pain*
70	Quhilk may nocht suffer nor sustene	
	So grit abusioun for to se	*abuse; see*
	Daylie in court befoir myn e.	*eye*

	And yit more panence wald I have,	*penance*
	Had I rewarde amang the laif.	*rest*
75	It wald me sumthing satisfie	
	And les of my malancolie,	*lessen*
	And gar me mony falt ourse	*cause; faults [to] overlook (ignore)*
	That now is brayd befoir myn e.	*broad (i.e., evident); eye*
	My mind so fer is set to flyt	*scold*
80	That of nocht ellis I can endyt.	*write*
	For owther man my hart tobreik,	*either must; burst*
	Or with my pen I man me wreik	*must; be avenged*
	And sen the tane most nedis be —	*since the one; needs*
	Into malancolie to de,	*die*
85	Or lat the vennim ische all out —	*let; venom flow*
	Be war anone, for it will spout,	
	Gif that the tryackill cum nocht tyt	*If; medicine; soon*
	To swage the swalme of my dispyt.	*assuage; swelling; anger*

47. *To the King*
   [*Complane I wald*]

	Complane I wald, wist I quhome till,	*would, knew I to whom*
	Or unto quhome darett my bill:	*[to] direct; letter*
	Quhidder to God that all thing steiris,	*Whether; steers (directs)*
	All thing seis, and all thing heiris,	*sees; hears*
5	And all thing wrocht in dayis seveyne,	*made*
	Or till His Moder, Quein of Heveyne,	
	Or unto wardlie prince heir downe	*worldly prince down here [on earth]*
	That dois for justice weir a crownne —	
	Of wrangis and of gryt injuris	*great*
10	That nobillis in thar dayis induris,	
	And men of vertew and cuning,	*knowledge*
	Of wit and wysdome in gydding,	*guiding*
	That nocht cane in this cowrt conquys	*nothing can; win over*
	For lawté, luiff, nor lang servys.	*loyalty, love*
15	Bot fowll jow-jowrdane-hedit jevellis,	*foul Jew-piss-pot-headed ruffians*
	Cowkin kenseis and culroun kevellis,	*Be-shitten knaves; rascal rogues*
	Stuffettis, strekouris, and stafische strummellis,	*Lackeys; unruly bumblers (?)*
	Wyld haschbaldis, haggarbaldis, and hummellis,	*[obscure phrases]*

Poem 47: To the King

	Druncartis, dysouris, dyvowris, drevellis,	*Drunkards, dicers, debtors, worthless lads*
20	Misgydit memberis of the Devellis,	
	Mismad mandragis of mastis strynd,	*Mis-made mandrakes; mastiff race*
	Crawdones, couhirttis, and theiffis of kynd,	*Traitors, cowards; born thieves*
	Blait-mouit bladyeanes with bledder cheikis	*Loose-mouthed blowhards; puffy-cheeks*
	Clubfacet clucanes with clutit breikis,	*yokels; patched breeches*
25	Chuff midding churllis, cuming of cart fillaris	*Dung heap churls, sired by; fillers*
	Gryt glaschewe-hedit gorge-millaris,	*jug-headed gluttons (?)*
	Evill horrible monsteris, fals and fowll.	*foul*
	Sum causles clekis till him ane cowll,	*clutches; hood*
	Ane gryt convent fra syne to tys,	*after that; entice*
30	And he himselff exampill of vys,	*vice*
	Enterand for geir and no devocioun.	*material goods*
	The Devill is glaid of his promocioun.	
	Sum ramyis ane rokkat fra the roy	*begs; bishop's vestment; king*
	And dois ane dastart destroy,	*coward*
35	And sum that gaittis ane personage	*parsonage*
	Thinkis it a present for a page,	
	And on no wayis content is he	*in*
	"My lord" quhill that he callit be.	
	Bot quhow is he content or nocht	*whether*
40	(Deme ye abowt into yowr thocht)	*Judge*
	The lerit sone of erll or lord	*learned*
	Upone this ruffie to remord,	*ruffian to reflect*
	That with ald castingis hes him cled,	*cast-off apparel*
	His erandis for to ryne and red	*run; arrange*
45	(And he is maister native borne	
	And all his eldaris him beforne,	
	And mekle mair cuning be sic thre	*much more intelligent*
	Hes to posseid ane dignité),	
	Saying his odius ignorance	*Testing (assaying)*
50	Panting ane prelottis countenance,	*Displaying (lit., painting)*
	Sa far above him set at tabell	
	That wont was for to muk the stabell —	
	Ane pykthank in a prelottis clais	*flatterer; clothes*
	With his wavill feit and wirrok tais,	*twisted feet; calloused toes*
55	With hoppir hippis and henches narrow	*flabby hips; skinny thighs*
	And bausy handis to beir a barrow;	*clumsy (greasy?)*

With lut schulderis and luttard bak   *bowed; crooked*
Quhilk Natur maid to beir a pak;   *pack (peddler's bundle)*
With gredy mynd and glaschane gane,   *oily (?) face*
60   Mell-hedit lyk ane mortar stane,   *Block-headed*
Fenyeing the feris of ane lord   *Counterfeiting; bearing*
(And he ane strumbell, I stand ford)   *beast (?); guarantee*
And he evirmoir as he dois rys,   *rise*
Nobles of bluid he dois dispys,   *despise*
65   And helpis for to hald thame downe
That thay rys never to his renowne.

Thairfoir, O prince maist honorable,
Be in this meter merciabill,   *matter merciful*
And to thy auld servandis haff e,   *have [an] eye*
70   That lang hes lipinit into thee.   *trusted*
Gif I be ane of tha mysell,   *If; those myself*
Throw all regiones hes bein hard tell,   *heard*
Of quhilk my wrytting witnes beris.
And yete thy danger ay me deris.   *reluctance; hurts*
75   Bot efter danger cumis grace,
As hes bein herd in mony plece.

48. *To the King*
    [*Exces of thocht dois me mischeif*]

Schir, yit remember as befoir
How that my youthe is done forloir   *has been entirely spent*
In your service with pane and greiff.   *pain*
Gud conscience cryis reward thairfoir.   *Good*
5   Exces of thocht dois me mischeif.   *harm*

Your clarkis ar servid all aboute,   *fed*
And I do lyke ane rid halk schout   *a red hawk*
To cum to lure that hes na leif,   *permission*
Quhair my plumis begynnis to mowt.   *Although my feathers; molt*
10   Exces of thocht dois me mischeiff.

Poem 48: *To the King*

Forget is ay the falcounis kynd, — *Forgotten; always; breed (race)*
Bot ever the myttell is hard in mynd; — *inferior raptor; firmly remembered*
Quhone the gled dois the peirtrikis preiff, — *When; kite; partridge eat*
The gentill goishalk gois undynd. — *goshawk; undined (unfed)*
15 Exces of thocht dois me mischeiff.

The pyat withe the pairtie cote — *magpie; parti-colored coat*
Feynyeis to sing the nychtingale note, — *Pretends*
Bot scho cannot the corchet cleiff — *high notes cleave (trill?)*
For hasknes of hir carleche throte. — *huskiness; churlish*
20 Exces of thocht dois me mischeiff.

Ay fairast feddiris hes farrest foulis. — *feathers; farthest [away] birds*
Suppois thai have na sang bot yowlis, — *Although*
In sylver caiges thai sit at cheif; — *in places of honor*
Kynd native nestis dois clek bot owlis. — *hold only owls*
25 Exces of thocht dois me mischeiff.

O gentill egill, how may this be — — *eagle*
Quhilk of all foulis dois heast fle — — *Which; highest fly*
Your leggis, quhy do ye not releif — *lieges; relieve*
And chirreis thame eftir thair degré? — *cherish*
30 Exces of thocht dois me mischeiff.

Quhone servit is all uther man, — *When; men*
Gentill and sempill of everie clan — — *Nobles and commoners*
Kyne of Rauf Colyard and Johnne the Reif — — *(I.e., the likes of); Reeve*
Nothing I gett nor conqueis can. — *acquire*
35 Exces of thocht dois me mischeif.

Thocht I in courte be maid refuse — *Though; turned down*
And have few vertewis for to ruse, — *virtues; boast about*
Yit am I cum of Adame and Eve
And fane wald leif as utheris dois. — *fain; live as others do*
40 Exces of thocht dois me mischeif.

Or I suld leif in sic mischance, — *Before; live; such misfortune*
Giff it to God war na grevance, — *If; were*
To be ane pykthank I wald preif, — *sycophant; prove*

107

For thai in warld wantis na plesance. *lack*
45 Exces of thocht dois me mischeif.

In sum pairt of myselffe I pleinye *complain*
Quhone utheris dois flattir and feynye; *When; pretend*
Allace, I can bot ballattis breif. *poems write*
Sic barnheid leidis my brydill reynye: *Such childishness leads my bridle reins*
50 Exces of thocht dois me mischeiff.

I grant my service is bot lycht. *admit; of little value*
Thairfoir, of meryce and not of rycht *mercy*
I ask you, schir, no man to greiff, *grieve*
Sum medecyne gif that ye mycht. *medicine (relief) if; might*
55 Exces of thocht dois me mischeiff.

Nane can remeid my maledie *cure; illness*
Sa weill as ye, schir, veralie. *truly*
With ane benefice ye may preiff, *prove*
And gif I mend not haistalie, *if*
60 Exces of thocht lat me mischeif.

I wes in youthe on nureice kne *nurse's*
Cald "dandillie, bischop, dandillie." *Called*
And quhone that age now dois me greif *when*
A sempill vicar I cannot be.
65 Exces of thocht dois me mischeif.

Jok that wes wont to keip the stirkis *Jock; young bulls*
Can now draw him ane cleik of kirkis *receive; fistful*
With ane fals cairt into his sleif *card up his sleeve*
Worthe all my ballattis under the byrkis. *poems; birches*
70 Exces of thocht dois me mischeif.

Twa curis or thre hes uplandis Michell *ecclesiastical livings*
With dispensationis in ane knitchell, *papal licenses; bundle*
Thocht he fra nolt had new tane leif. *Though; cattle; taken life*
He playis with totum and I with nychell. *everything; nothing*
75 Exces of thocht dois me mischeiff.

108

	How sould I leif, and I not landit,	*live; landed*
	Nor yit withe benefice am blandit?	*consoled*
	I say not, schir, yow to repreiff,	*reprove*
	Bot doutles I go rycht neirhand it.	*come very close to it*
80	Exces of thocht dois me mischeiff.	

	As saule into Purgatorie,	
	Leifand in pane with hoip of glorie,	*Living; hope*
	So is myselffe, ye may beleiff,	
	In hoip, schir, of your adjutorie.	*hope; help*
85	Exces of thocht dois me mischeiff.	

49. *To the King*
   [*That I suld be ane Yowllis yald*]

	Schir, lat it never in toune be tald	*said*
	That I suld be ane Yowllis yald.[1]	

	Suppois I war ane ald jaid aver,	*Even if I were a worn-out cart-horse (jade)*
	Schott furth our clewch to squische the clever,	*Sent; over hillside; crop; clover*
5	And hed the strenthis of all Strenever,	*had; strength of*
	I wald at Youll be housit and stald:	*Yule; stalled*
	Schir, lat it never in toune be tald	
	That I suld be ane Yowllis yald.	

	I am ane auld hors, as ye knaw,	
10	That ever in duill dois drug and draw.	*pain does drag*
	Gryt court hors puttis me fra the staw,	*Great; horses put*
	To fang the fog be firthe and fald.	*take; by wood; field*
	Schir, lat it never in toune be tald	
	That I suld be ane Yowllis yald.	

15	I heff run lang furth in the feild	*have*
	On pastouris that ar plane and peld.	*plain; bare*
	I mycht be now tein in for eild,	*taken; age*

---

[1] *That I should be a Yuletide nag (i.e., a horse put out to pasture/a "holiday" horse too old to work)*

My bekis ar spruning, he and bald.   *teeth; protruding, high and bold*
Schir, lat it never in toune be tald
20   That I suld be ane Yowllis yald.

My maine is turned into quhyt,   *mane; white*
And thairof ye heff all the wyt.   *already know*
Quhen uthair hors hed brane to byt,   *other horses had bran to eat*
I gat bot gris, grype giff I wald.   *only grass; if*
25   Schir, lat it never in towne be tald
That I suld be ane Yowllis yald.

I was never dautit into stabell.   *pampered*
My lyff hes bein so miserabell,
My hyd to offer I am abell   *hide*
30   For evill schoud strae that I reiv wald.   *pitiful straw; tear would*
Schir, lat it never in towne be tald
That I suld be ane Yowllis yald.

And yett, suppois my thrift be thyne,   *although; prosperity; meager*
Gif that I die your aucht within   *If; property*
35   Lat nevir the soutteris have my skin,   *cobblers*
With uglie gumes to be gnawin.   *gums*
Schir, lat it nevir in toun be tald
That I sould be ane Yuillis yald.

The court hes done my curage cuill   *made; courage cool*
40   And maid me ane forriddin muill.   *overworked mule*
Yett to weir trapperis at the Yuill,   *trappings; Yule*
I wald be spurrit at everie spald.   *limb*
Schir, lett it nevir in toun be tald
That I sould be ane Yuillis yald.

45   Now lufferis cummis with larges lowd.   *lovers come; great generosity*
Quhy sould not palfrayis thane be prowd,   *Why*
Quhen gillettis wil be schomd and schroud   *mares; adorned; covered*
That riddin ar baith with lord and lawd?   *by nobles; commoners*
Schir, lett it nevir in toun be tald
50   That I sould be ane Yuillis yald.

Quhen I was young and into ply — *in good condition*
And wald cast gammaldis to the sky, — *gambols (i.e., kick up my heels)*
I had beine bocht in realmes by, — *bought; lands nearby*
Had I consentit to be sauld. — *sold*
55 Schir, lett it nevir in toun be tauld
That I sould be ane Yuillis yald.

With gentill hors quhen I wald knyp, — *noble; nibble*
Thane is thair laid on me ane quhip. — *whip*
To colleveris than man I skip — *coal-horses; must; go*
60 That scabbit ar, hes cruik and cald. — *scabby are, bowed (lame); cold*
Schir, lett it nevir in toun be tald
That I sould be ane Yuillis yald.

Thocht in the stall I be not clappit, — *Though; pampered*
As cursouris that in silk beine trappit, — *coursers; are dressed*
65 With ane new hous I wald be happit — *cloth; covered*
Aganis this Crysthinmes for the cald. — *Christmas*
Schir, lett it nevir in toun be tald
That I sould be ane Yuillis yald.

Respontio Regis — *The King's Response*

Efter our wrettingis, thesaurer, — *directions, treasurer*
70 Tak in this gray hors, auld Dumbar,
Quhilk in my aucht with service trew — *Who; possession*
In lyart changeit is his hew. — *Unto gray has changed; hue*
Gar hows him new aganis this Yuill — *Prepare for him a covering*
And busk him lyk ane bischopis muill, — *dress himself; mule*
75 For with my hand I have indost — *endorsed*
To pay quhatevir his trappouris cost. — *trappings*

50. *Of People Hard to Please*

Four maner of folkis ar evill to pleis. — *difficult to please*
Ane is that riches hes and eis, — *One; has wealth and ease*
Gold, silver, cattell, cornis, and ky, — *property (chattel), grain; cattle (kine)*
And wald have part fra utheris by. — *from others nearby*

5   Aneuther is of land and rent   *Another; income*
    So great ane lord and ane potent   *mighty*
    That he may nother rewll nor gy,   *neither rule nor guide*
    Yet he wald have fra utheris by.

    Ane is that hes of nobill bluid   *Another; has*
10   Ane lusty lady, fair and guid,   *A lovely*
    Boith verteous, wyse, and womanly,
    And yett wald have aneuther by.

    Aneuther dois so dourlie drink,   *heavily*
    And aill and wyne within him sink,   *ale*
15   Quhill in his wame no roume be dry,   *That; womb (belly); space*
    Bot he wald have fra utheris by.

    In earth no wicht I can perseav   *On; person*
    Of guid so great aboundance have,   *goods*
    Nor in this world so welthful wy,   *wealthy a person*
20   Bot he wald have frome utheris by.

    Bot yitt of all this gold and guid   *goods*
    Or uthir cunyie, to concluid,   *other [kinds of] wealth*
    Quhaevir it have, it is not I.
    It gois frome me to utheris by.

25   And nemlie at this Chrystis Mes,   *especially; Christmas*
    Quharevir Schir Gold maid his regres.   *Whenever; has made his return*
    Of him I will na larges cry,   *gifts cry out for*
    He yeid fra me till utheris by.   *turned*

    Of him I will na larges cry,
30   He yeid fra me till utheris by.

51. *The Antichrist*

    Lucina schyning in silence of the nycht,   *The moon*
    The hevyn all being full of sterris bricht,   *stars*
    To bed I went, bot thair I tuke no rest.

Poem 51: The Antichrist

	With havie thocht so sair I wes opprest	*sorely*
5	That sair I langit eftir the dayis licht.	*greatly I longed for*
	Of Fortoun I complenit havalie	*heavily*
	That scho to me stude so contrariouslie,	*stood so opposed*
	And at the last, quhone I had turnit oft,	*when*
	For werynes on me a slumer soft	*slumber*
10	Come with a dreming and a fantasie.	
	Me thocht Dame Fortoun with a fremmit cheir	*angry look*
	Stude me beforne, and said on this maneir:	*in*
	"Thow suffir me to wirk gif thow do weill,	*if; do well (i.e., be wise)*
	And preis thee not to stryve aganis my quheill,	*urge; wheel*
15	Quhilk everie wardlie thing dois turne and steir.	*worldly; guide*
	"Full mony ane I set upone the heycht,	*[a] one; height*
	And makis mony full law doun to lycht.	*low; fall*
	Upone my stagis or that thow do ascend,	*steps before*
	Traist wele thi trouble is neir at ane end,	*Trust*
20	Seing thir takynnis; quhairfoir thow mark thame richt.	*these omens; carefully*
	"Thy trublit gaist sall never be degest,	*spirit; calm*
	Nor thow into no benefice possest,	*in possession of a church living*
	Quhill that ane abbot him cleythe in eirnis pennys	*Until; clothe; eagle's feathers*
	And fle up in the air amang the crennys,	*cranes*
25	And as a falcoun fair fro eist to west.	*travels*
	"He sall ascend as ane horrible griphoun.	*griffin*
	Him meit sall in the air ane scho dragoun.	*shall meet; female*
	Thir terribill monsturis sall togiddir thrist,	*These; monsters; mate (thrust)*
	And in the cluddis get the Antechrist,	*clouds beget*
30	Quhill all the air infect of thair poysoun.	*While; poison*
	"Undir Saturnus fyrie regioun	*fiery*
	Symon Magus sall meit him, and Mahoun,	
	And Merleyn at the mune sall him be bydand,	*moon; awaiting*
	And Jonet the Wedo on a busum hame rydand,	*broom stick riding home*
35	Of wytchis with ane wondrus garesoun.	*witches; wondrous troop*

113

"And syne thai sall discend with reik and fyre, *then; smoke*
And preiche in eird the Antechristis impyre; *preach on earth; empire*
And than it sal be neir the warldis end."
With that this ladie did schortlie fra me wend. *quickly*
40 Sleipand and walkand wes frustrat my desyre. *Sleeping and waking (i.e., entirely)*

Quhone I awoyk, my dreme it wes so nyce, *ridiculous*
Fra everie wicht I hid it as a vyce, *person*
Quhill I hard tell be mony suthfast wy, *Until I heard; truthful person*
Fle wald ane abbot up into the sky *Fly would*
45 And all his feddrem maid wes at devyce. *feathers; with skill*

Within my hert confort I tuke full sone.
"Adew," quod I, "My drerie dayis ar done. *unhappy; over*
Full weill I wist to me wald never cum thrift *prosperity*
Quhill that twa munis wer first sene in the lift, *Until; moons; sky (firmament)*
50 Or quhill ane abbot flew abone the moyne." *until; above; moon*

52. *To the Lord Treasurer*
  [*Welcome, my awin lord thesaurair*]

I thocht lang quhill sum lord come hame,[1]
Fra quhome faine kyndnes I wald clame. *desired kindness I would claim*
His name of confort I will declair:
Welcome, my awin lord thesaurair! *own lord treasurer*

5 Befoir all rink of this regioun, *Above all men*
Under our roy of most renoun, *king*
Of all my mycht, thocht it war mair, *With; though (even if)*
Welcom, my awin lord thesaurair!

Your nobill payment I did assay, *hoped to obtain*
10 And ye hecht sone, without delay, *promised*
Againe in Edinburgh till repair: *to return*
Welcom, my awin lord thesaurair!

---

[1] *I was anxious until a certain lord (the Lord Treasurer) came home*

114

Ye keipit tryst so winder weill,   *kept [your] promise wondrously well*
I hald yow trew as ony steill.   *steel*
15 Neidis nane your payment till dispair: *No one needs; to despair [of receiving]*
Welcom, my awin lord thesaurair!

Yett in a pairt I was agast,   *somewhat; afraid*
Or ye the narrest way had past   *Before (until); shortest; traveled*
Fra toun of Stirling to the air.   *circuit court*
20 Welcom, my awin lord thesaurair!

Thane had my dyt beine all in duill,   *Then; poetry been entirely sad*
Had I my wage wantit quhill Yuill,   *lacked until Yule*
Quhair now I sing with heart onsair: *joyful*
Welcum, my awin lord thesaurair!

25 Welcum, my benefice and my rent,   *income*
And all the lyflett to me lent,   *livelihood; given*
Welcum, my pensioun most preclair: *splendid*
Welcum, my awin lord thesaurair!

Welcum als heartlie as I can,   *sincerely*
30 My awin dear maister, to your man,
And to your servand singulair: *personal servant*
Welcum, my awin lord thesaurair!

53. *To the Lords of Chalker*

My Lordis of Chalker, pleis yow to heir   *Exchequer, [if] it pleases you*
My coumpt, I sall it mak yow cleir   *reckoning; clear to you*
But ony circumstance or sonyie;   *Without any excuses or delays*
For left is nether corce nor cunyie   *neither large coins nor small*
5 Of all that I tuik in the yeir.   *received*

For rekkyning of my rentis and roumes   *properties*
Yie neid not for to tyre your thowmes,   *You; tire your thumbs (i.e., bother)*
Na for to gar your countaris clink,   *Nor to make; counters*
Na paper for to spend nor ink,
10 In the ressaveing of my soumes.   *calculating; sums*

	I tuik fra my lord thesaurair	*took (received); treasurer*
	Ane soume of money for to wair.	*A sum; use*
	I cannot tell yow how it is spendit,	
	Bot weill I waitt that it is endit,	*know; gone*
15	And that me think ane coumpte our sair.	*a painful account*
	I trowit, the tyme quhen that I tuik it,	*believed; received*
	That lang in burgh I sould have bruikit.	*enjoyed it*
	Now the remanes ar eith to turs —	*easy to assemble*
	I have na preiff heir bot my purs,	*proof; purse*
20	Quhilk wald not lie and it war luikit.	*if it were examined*

54. *A Ballad of the Friar of Tungland*

	As yung Aurora with cristall haile	*i.e, Dawn; halo (dew drops)*
	In orient schew hir visage paile,	*In the east; pale face*
	A swevyng swyth did me assaile	*vision quickly*
	Of sonis of Sathanis seid.	*About the sons of Satan's seed*
5	Me thocht a Turk of Tartary	
	Come throw the boundis of Barbary	*Had crossed the border from Barbary*
	And lay forloppin in Lumbardy	*in exile*
	Full lang in waithman weid.	*an outlaw's clothing*
	Fra baptasing for to eschew,	*avoid*
10	Thair a religious man he slew	
	And cled him in his abeit new,	*himself; habit*
	For he couth wryte and reid.	*knew how to; read*
	Quhen kend was his dissimulance	*When known; imposture*
	And all his cursit govirnance,	*conduct*
15	For feir he fled and come in France,	*fear*
	With littill of Lumbard leid.	*language*
	To be a leiche he fenyt him thair,	*physician he pretended*
	Quhilk mony a man micht rew evirmair,	*regret*
	For he left nowthir seik nor sair	*neither [the] sick nor [the] sorrowful*
20	Unslane or he hyne yeid.	*Unslain before he hence went*
	Vane organis he full clenely carvit.	*Jugular veins; slit*
	Quhen of his straik so mony starvit,	*surgery; died*

Dreid he had gottin that he desarvit,   *Afraid*

  He fled away gud speid.   *quickly*

25   In Scotland than the narrest way   *then; shortest*

     He come his cunnyng till assay.   *skills to exhibit*

     To sum man thair it was no play,   *some men*

       The preving of his sciens.   *testing*

     In pottingry he wrocht grit pyne,   *pharmacy he caused great pain*

30   He murdreist mony in medecyne.   *murdered many in [the guise of] medicine*

     The Jow was of a grit engyne,   *Infidel (lit., Jew); great ingenuity*

       And generit was of gyans.   *descended from giants*

     In leichecraft he was homecyd.   *healing; [a] murderer*

     He wald haif, for a nycht to byd,   *one night's attendance*

35   A haiknay and the hurt manis hyd,   *horse; hide (i.e., the patient's skin)*

       So meikle he was of myance.   *So high were his fees*

     His yrnis was rude as ony rawchtir.   *iron instruments were rough; rafter*

     Quhair he leit blude it was no lawchtir.   *let blood; laughing matter*

     Full mony instrument for slawchtir   *slaughter*

40   Was in his gardevyance.   *trunk*

     He cowth gif cure for laxatyve   *could give; diarrhea*

     To gar a wicht hors want his lyve.   *make a strong horse die*

     Quhaevir assay wald, man or wyve,   *Whoever would try*

       Thair hippis yeid hiddy giddy.   *Their hips would shiver and shake*

45   His practikis nevir war put to preif

     Bot suddane deid or grit mischeif.   *Without sudden death*

     He had purgatioun to mak a theif

       To dee withowt a widdy.   *withy (hangman's noose)*

     Unto no Mes pressit this prelat   *Mass hurried*

50   For sound of sacring bell nor skellat.   *handbell*

     As blaksmyth bruikit was his pallatt   *blackened; face*

       For battering at the study.   *hammering; anvil*

     Thocht he come hame a new maid channoun,   *Though; newly-made canon*

     He had dispensit with matynnis channoun.   *the canonical service of matins*

55   On him come nowther stole nor fannoun   *neither stole nor maniple*

       For smowking of the smydy.   *smoking; smithy*

	Me thocht seir fassonis he assailyeit	*many methods; attempted*
	To mak the quintessance, and failyeit.	*failed*
	And quhen he saw that nocht availyeit,	*nothing worked*
60	A fedrem on he tuke,	*coat of feathers*
	And schupe in Turky for to fle.	*prepared to fly to Turkey*
	And quhen that he did mont on he,	*mount on high*
	All fowill ferleit quhat he sowld be,	*[the] birds wondered; could*
	That evir did on him luke.	*look*
65	Sum held he had bene Dedalus,	*believed*
	Sum the Menatair marvelus,	*Minotaur*
	Sum Martis blaksmyth, Vulcanus,	*Mars'*
	And sum Saturnus kuke.	*Saturn's cook*
	And evir the tuschettis at him tuggit,	*lapwings; pecked*
70	The rukis him rent, the ravynis him druggit,	*rooks tore at him, ravens tugged at him*
	The hudit crawis his hair furth ruggit,	*hooded crows; pulled*
	The hevin he micht not bruke.	*enjoy*
	The myttane and Sanct Martynis fowle	*lesser birds of prey*
	Wend he had bene the hornit howle,	*Thought; horned owl*
75	Thay set aupone him with a yowle	*screech*
	And gaif him dynt for dynt.	*gave him blow for blow*
	The golk, the gormaw, and the gled	*cuckoo; cormorant; kite*
	Beft him with buffettis quhill he bled,	*Beat; until*
	The sparhalk to the spring him sped	
80	Als fers as fyre of flynt,	*fierce*
	The tarsall gaif him tug for tug,	*tercel (male hawk)*
	A stanchell hang in ilka lug,	*kestrel hung on each ear*
	The pyot furth his pennis did rug,	*magpie; feathers; seize*
	The stork straik ay but stynt,	*struck without ceasing*
85	The bissart, bissy but rebuik,	*buzzard, acting without rebuke*
	Scho was so cleverus of hir cluik	*piercing with her claws*
	His bawis he micht not langer bruik,	*balls (testicles); use*
	Scho held thame at ane hint.	*in a grip*
	Thik was the clud of kayis and crawis,	*Thick; cloud; daws and crows*
90	Of marleyonis, mittanis, and of mawis,	*merlins, gulls*

	That bikkrit at his berd with blawis,	*pecked*
	In battell him abowt.	
	Thay nybbillit him with noyis and cry,	*noise*
	The rerd of thame rais to the sky,	*din; rose*
95	And evir he cryit on Fortoun, "Fy!"	
	His lyfe was into dowt.	*at risk*
	The ja him skrippit with a skryke	*jay; shriek*
	And skornit him, as it was lyk.	*scorned; as was its wont*
	The egill strong at him did stryke	*eagle*
100	And rawcht him mony a rowt.	*gave; blow*
	For feir uncunnandly he cawkit,	*uncouthly he defecated*
	Quhill all his pennis war drownd and drawkit.	*Until; feathers; drenched*
	He maid a hundreth nolt all hawkit	*cattle; besmirched*
	Beneth him with a spout.	
105	He schewre his feddreme that was schene,	*shed; feather coat; bright*
	And slippit out of it full clene,	
	And in a myre up to the ene	*bog; eyes*
	Amang the glar did glyd.	*mud; slide*
	The fowlis all at the fedrem dang	*birds; feathers; pecked*
110	As at a monster thame amang,	
	Quhill all the pennis of it owtsprang	
	In till the air full wyde.	
	And he lay at the plunge evirmair,	*immersed*
	Sa lang as any ravin did rair.	*raven; cry*
115	The crawis him socht with cryis of cair	
	In every schaw besyde.	*copse*
	Had he reveild bene to the ruikis,	*revealed; rooks*
	Thay had him revin all with thair cluikis.	*torn; claws*
	Thre dayis in dub amang the dukis	*pond; ducks*
120	He did with dirt him hyde.	
	The air was dirkit with the fowlis	*darkened by*
	That come with yawmeris and yowlis,	
	With skryking, skrymming, and with scowlis,	*shrieking, screaming; scowls*
	To tak him in the tyde.	
125	I walknit with the noyis and schowte,	*awakened; shouts*

119

So hiddowis beir was me abowte.   *Such [a] hideous din*
Sensyne I curs that cankerit rowte,   *Since then; malicious crowd*
    Quhairevir I go or ryde.   *Wherever*

55. *Sir Thomas Norny*

Now lythis of ane gentill knycht,   *listen [to the tale of]*
Schir Thomas Norny, wys and wycht   *brave*
    And full of chevelry,   *knightly virtue*
Quhais father was ane giand keyne,   *Whose; giant bold*
His mother was ane farie queyne,   *fairy queen*
    Gottin be sossery.   *by sorcery*

5

Ane fairar knycht nor he was ane   *A finer*
On ground may nothair ryd nor gane,   *earth; nowhere ride or go*
    Na beire buklar nor brand;   *Nor bear a shield nor sword*
Or comin in this court, but dreid,   *Before coming; to be sure*
He did full mony valyeant deid   *deeds*
    In Rois and Murray land.   *Ross and Moray*

10

Full mony catherein hes he chaist,   *robber; chased*
And cummerid mony Helland gaist   *pursued; Highland ghosts*
    Amang thay dully glennis.   *the gloomy glens*
Of the Glen Quhettane twenti scoir   *Clan Chattan; score*
He drawe as oxin him befoir —   *drove*
    This deid thocht na man kennis.   *deed though; knows*

15

At feastis and brydallis upaland   *in the uplands*
He wan the gre and the garland,   *won the prize*
    Dansit non so on deis.   *Danced no one; dais (platform)*
He hes att werslings bein ane hunder,   *wrestlings; hundred*
Yet lay his body never at under —
    He knawis giff this be leis.   *if this is a lie*

20

Was never wyld Robein under bewch   *Robin [Hood]; boughs*
Nor yet Roger of Clekniskleuch
    So bauld a berne as he;   *bold a man*
Gy of Gysburne, na Allan Bell,

25

Na Simonis sonnes of Quhynfell
30   At schot war never so slie.   *archery; skilled*

This anterous knycht, quharever he went,   *adventurous; wherever*
    At justing and at tornament   *jousting*
        Evermor he wan the gre;   *won the prize*
    Was never of halff so gryt renowne   *half*
35 Schir Bevis the knycht of Southe Hamptowne —
        I schrew him giff I le.   *I curse him if I lie*

Thairfoir Quenetyne was bot a lurdane   *rascal*
    That callid him ane full plum jurdane,   *a brim-full pisspot*
        This wyse and worthie knycht.
40 He callit him fowlar than a full,   *more foul; fool*
    He said he was ane licherous bull
        That croynd baith day and nycht.   *bellowed*

He wald heff maid him Curris kneff.   *would have made; helper*
    I pray God better his honour saiff   *save*
45   Na to be lychtleit sua.   *Than; so insulted*
    Yet this far furth I dar him prais: *to this extent*
    He fyld never sadell in his dais,   *befouled; days*
        And Curry befyld twa.   *Whereas; defiled two*

Quhairfoir ever at Pesche and Yull   *Therefore; Easter and Yule*
50 I cry him lord of evere full   *every fool*
        That in this regeone dwellis;
    And verralie that war gryt rycht,   *a great truth*
    For of ane hy renowned knycht,   *high*
        He wantis nothing bot bellis.   *lacks; but bells*

56. *A Dance in the Queen's Chamber*
    [*A merrear daunce mycht na man see*]

Sir Jhon Sinclair begowthe to dance,   *began*
For he was new cum owt of France.   *newly come from*
For ony thing that he do mycht
The an futt yeid ay onrycht   *one foot always went awry*

121

5	And to the tother wald nocht gree.	*with the other would not agree*
	Quod an, "Tak up the quenis knycht!"	*Said one, "Remove . . ."*
	A mirrear dance mycht na man see.	*merrier*
	Than cam in maistir Robert Schau —	
	He leuket as he culd lern tham a,	*looked like he could teach them all*
10	Bot ay his an futt did waver.	
	He stackeret lyk an strummall awer	*staggered; clumsy pack-horse*
	That hopschackellt war aboin the kne.	*hobbled was above*
	To seik fra Sterling to Stranawer,	
	A mirrear daunce mycht na man see.	
15	Than cam in the maister almaser,	*almoner*
	An hommiltye-jommeltye juffler.	*humilty-jumilty shuffler*
	Lyk a stirk stackarand in the ry,	*bullock crashing about*
	His hippis gaff mony hoddous cry.	*rear-end gave many horrible noises*
	John Bute the fule said, "Wa es me,	*fool; Woe is me*
20	He is bedirtin, fye, fy!"	*has befouled himself*
	A mirrear dance mycht na man se.	
	Than cam in Dunbar the mackar —	*poet*
	On all the flure thair was nan frackar —	*none more daring*
	And thair he dancet the dirrye dantoun.	*dirty boogie (?)*
25	He hoppet lyk a pillie wanton,	*randy cock*
	For luff of Musgraeffe, men tellis me.	*love*
	He trippet quhill he tint his panton.	*danced until he lost his slipper*
	A mirrear dance mycht na man see.	
	Than cam in Maesteres Musgraeffe —	*Mistress Musgrave*
30	Schou mycht heff lernit all the laeffe.	*She; taught; rest*
	Quhen I schau hir sa trimlye dance,	*saw; neatly*
	Hir guid convoy and contenance,	*goodly bearing*
	Than for hir saek I wissitt to be	*sake I wished*
	The grytast erle or duk in France.	*greatest*
35	A mirrear dance mycht na man see.	
	Than cam in dame Dounteboir —	
	God waett gif that schou louket sowr.	*God knows if she looked sour*
	Schou maid sic morgeownis with hir hippis,	*made such grotesque movements*

For lachtter nain mycht hald thair lippis. *laughter none*
40 Quhen schou was danceand bisselye,
An blast of wind son fra hir slippis.
A mirrear dance mycht na man se.

Quhen thair was cum in fyve or sax, *six*
The quenis Dog begowth to rax, *began to stretch*
45 And of his band he maid a bred *off his leash; leap*
And to the dancing soin he him med. *he soon made his way*
Quhou mastevlyk abowt yeid he! *How like a mastiff; went*
He stinckett lyk a tyk, sum saed. *stank like a mongrel pup*
A mirrear dance mycht na man see.

57. Of James Dog
[*Madame, ye heff a dangerous dog*]

The wardraipper of Venus boure, *wardrobe-keeper; Venus' bower*
To giff a doublett he is als doure *give; reluctant*
As it war of ane futt syd frog: *full-length frock*
Madame, ye heff a dangerous dog. *have*

5 Quhen that I schawe to him your markis, *marks [of authorization]*
He turnis to me again and barkis
As he war wirriand ane hog: *As [if] he were nipping at*
Madame, ye heff a dangerous dog.

Quhen that I schawe to him your wrytin, *written [approvals]*
10 He girnis that I am red for bytin — *snarls; fearful of being bitten*
I wald he had ane havye clog: *wish; a heavy restraint*
Madame, ye heff an dangerous dog.

Quhen that I speik till him freindlyk,
He barkis lyk an middling tyk *dunghill mongrel*
15 War chassand cattell throu a bog: *[That] was chasing*
Madam, ye heff a dangerous dog.

He is ane mastive, mekle of mycht, *mastiff, great*
To keip your wardroippe over nycht

123

Fra the grytt sowdan Gog Magog: *great sultan*
20   Madam, ye heff a dangerous dog.

He is ouer mekle to be your messan.   *too large; lap dog*
Madam, I red you, get a less an.   *advise; smaller one*
His gang garris all your chalmeris schog.   *causes your whole chamber to shake*
Madam, ye heff a dangerous dog.

58. *Of the Aforesaid James Dog*
     [*He is na dog, he is a lam*]

O gracious Princes, guid and fair,   *Princess*
Do weill to James, your wardraipair,   *Treat well; wardrobe-keeper*
Quhais faythfull bruder maist freind I am: *brother most friendly*
He is na dog, he is a lam.   *lamb*

5   Thocht I in ballet did with him bourde,   *Though; poem; jest*
In malice spack I nevir an woord,   *spoke*
Bot all, my dame, to do you gam: *to amuse you*
He is na dog, he is a lam.

Your hienes can nocht gett ane meter   *highness; one more able*
10 To keip your wardrope, nor discreter
To rewle your robbis and dres the sam: *care for the same*
He is na dog, he is a lam.

The wyff that he had in his innis,   *place of dwelling*
That with the taingis wald braek his schinnis,   *fire tongs*
15 I wald schou drownet war in a dam: *mill pond*
He is na dog, he is a lam.

The wyff that wald him kuckald mak,   *make [a] cuckold of him*
I wald schou war, bayth syd and back,   *I wish she were, in all ways*
Weill batteret with ane barrou tram: *beaten; barrow handle*
20 He is na dog, he is an lam.

He hes sa weill doin me obey
In till all thing, thairfoir I pray   *wherefore*

124

That nevir dolour mak him dram: sorrow; sad
He is na dog, he is a lam.

59. *Epitaph for Donald Oure*

In vice most vicius he excellis
That with the vice of tressone mellis.   deals
  Thocht he remissioun   Though he pardon
  Haif for prodissioun,   Has [received] for [his] treachery
5   Schame and susspissioun
  Ay with him dwellis.   Ever

And he evir odious as ane owle,
The falt so filthy is and fowle: fault
  Horrible to natour   nature
10 Is ane tratour,
  As feind in fratour   fiend; abbey dining hall
  Undir a cowle.   monk's hooded robe

Quha is a tratour or ane theif   Whoever
Upoun himselff turnis the mischeif.   returns the harm
15 His frawdfull wylis   deceitful wiles
  Himself begylis,
  As in the Ilis   Western Isles
  Is now a preiff.   evident

The fell, strong tratour, Donald Owyr,   cruel, guilty
20 Mair falsett hes nor udir fowyr,   falsehood has than any four others
  Round ylis and seyis   isles and seas
  In his suppleis,   Upon his supporters (?)
  On gallow treis   the gallows
  Now he dois glowir.   does stare

25 Falsett no feit hes nor deffence   Falsehood has no feet [to stand on]
  Be power, practik, nor puscence.   By means of; cunning; armed force
  Thocht it fra licht
  Be smord with slicht,   hidden

	God schawis the richt	
30	With soir vengence.	*extreme*
	Of the fals fox dissimulatour	
	Kynd hes all reffar, theiff, and tratour:	*Nature; robber*
	Eftir respyt	
	To wirk dispyt	*To engage in malicious acts*
35	Moir appetyt	*Greater*
	He hes of natour.	*by nature*
	War the fox tane a thowsand fawd	*Were; captured a thousand times*
	And grace him gevin als oft for frawd,	
	War he on plane	*[If he] were on the plain*
40	All war in vane,	*would be in vain*
	Frome hennis agane	*hens*
	Micht non him hawd.	*hold*
	The murtherer ay murthour mais,	*murder commits*
	And evir quhill he be slane he slais.	*always until he be slain he slays*
45	Wyvis thus makis mokkis,	*engage in scornful speech*
	Spynnand on rokkis:	*[While] spinning on their distaffs*
	Ay rynnis the fox	*Ever runs*
	Quhill he fute hais.	*While he has feet*

60. *A Complaint against Mure*

	Schir, I complane of injuris:	
	A refing sonne of rakyng Muris	*thieving son of roving Moors*
	Hes magellit my making throw his malis	*mangled; poetry; malice*
	And present it into yowr palis.	*presented it in your palace*
5	Bot sen he ples with me to pleid,	*since he wishes; debate*
	I sall him knawin mak hyne to Calis,	*make known from here to Calais*
	Bot giff yowr henes it remeid.	*Unless your highness redresses it*
	That fulle dismemberit hes my meter	*fool*
	And poysonid it with strang salpeter,	
10	With rycht defamous speiche of lordis,	*very insulting*
	Quhilk with my collouris all discordis,	*poetic devices*

Poem 61: Sweet Rose of Virtue

Quhois crewall slander servis ded,   *deserves the death penalty*
And in my name all leis recordis.   *lies*
Your grace beseik I of remeid.   *I beg for redress*

15   He has indorsit myn indyting   *written on top of my poetry*
With versis of his awin hand wryting,
Quhairin baithe sclander is and tressoun.
Of ane wod fuill far owt of seasoun,   *Like a crazy fool; out*
He wantis nocht bot a rowndit heid,   *lacks only a close-cropped head*
20   For he has tynt baith wit and ressoun.   *lost*
Your grace beseik I of remeid.

Punes him for his deid culpabile,   *Punish*
Or gar deliver him a babile   *make him carry a bauble*
That Cuddy Rug, the Drumfres fuill,   *[So] that; Dumfries fool*
25   May him resave agane this Yuill,   *welcome in preparation for; Yule*
All roundit into yallow and reid,   *attired*
That ladis may bait hym lyk a buill —   *youths; bull*
For that to me war sum remeid.

61. *Sweet Rose of Virtue*

Sweit rois of vertew and of gentilnes,
Delytsum lyllie of everie lustynes,   *Delightful; loveliness*
Richest in bontie and in bewtie cleir   *goodness; beauty*
And everie vertew that is deir,
5   Except onlie that ye are mercyles.

Into your garthe this day I did persew.   *private garden; enter*
Thair saw I flowris that fresche wer of hew,   *hue (color)*
Baithe quhyte and rid, moist lusty wer to seyne,   *white and red, most pleasant*
And halsum herbis upone stalkis grene,   *flourishing*
10   Yit leif nor flour fynd could I nane of rew.   *leaf; none of rue*

I dout that Merche with his caild blastis keyne   *fear*
Hes slane this gentill herbe that I of mene,   *of which I speak*
Quhois petewous deithe dois to my hart sic pane   *such pain*

127

| | That I wald mak to plant his rute agane, | *root* |
| 15 | So that confortand his levis unto me bene. | *comforting; might be* |

62. *Beauty and the Prisoner*

	Sen that I am a presoneir	*Since*
	Till hir that farest is and best,	*To; fairest*
	I me commend fra yeir till yeir	*myself entrust*
	Intill hir bandoun for to rest.	*power; remain*
5	I govit on that gudliest:	*gazed; goodliest one*
	So lang to luk I tuk laseir,	*[my] leisure*
	Quhill I wes tane withouttin test	*Until; captured without physical contact*
	And led furth as a presoneir.	

	Hir Sweit Having and Fresche Bewté	*Attractive Manner*
10	Hes wondit me but swerd or lance.	*wounded; without sword*
	With thame to go commandit me	
	Ontill the Castell of Pennance.	
	I said, "Is this your govirnance,	*custom*
	To tak men for thair luking heir?"	*seize; looking here*
15	Fresche Bewty said, "Ya, schir, perchance	*Yes; by chance*
	Ye be my ladeis presoneir."	

	Thai had me bundin to the get	*brought me bound to the gate*
	Quhair Strangenes had bene portar ay,	*Disdain; [the] porter ever*
	And in deliverit me thairat	
20	And in thir termis can thai say:	*these words did they say*
	"Do wait and lat him nocht away."	*Make him stay; not escape*
	Quo Strangenes unto the porteir,	*Said*
	"Ontill my lady, I dar lay,	*Unto; assert*
	Ye be to pure a presoneir."	*too poor*

25	Thai kest me in a deip dungeoun	*cast*
	And fetterit me but lok or cheyne.	*without lock or chain*
	The capitane, hecht Comparesone,	*called*
	To luke on me he thocht greit deyne.	*[a] great insult*
	Thocht I wes wo I durst nocht pleyne,	*Although I was sad I dared not complain*
30	For he had fetterit mony a feir.	*many a worthy adversary*

128

Poem 62: Beauty and the Prisoner

With petous voce thus cuth I sene,   *could I say*
"Wo is a wofull presoneir."

Langour wes weche upoun the wall,   *Indifference; watchman*
That nevir sleipit bot evir wouke.
35 Scorne wes bourdour in the hall   *jester*
And oft on me his babill schuke,   *bauble shook*
Lukand with mony a dengerous luke.   *hostile look*
"Quhat is he yone that methis us neir?   *observes (?)*
Ye be to townage, be this buke,   *too townish (bourgeois); book*
40 To be my ladeis presoneir."

Gud Houp rownit in my eir   *Good Hope whispered; ear*
And bad me baldlie breve a bill;   *boldly write a letter*
With Lawlines he suld it beir,   *Humility; should it carry*
With Fair Service send it hir till.
45 I wouk and wret hir all my will.   *awakened and wrote to her; desire*
Fair Service fur withouttin feir,   *went without fear*
Sayand till hir with wirdis still,   *soft words*
"Haif pety of your presoneir."   *"Have pity on"*

Than Lawlines to Petie went   *Pity*
50 And said till hir in termis schort,   *brief*
"Lat we yone presoneir be schent,   *[If] we allow; [to] be destroyed*
Will no man do to us support.   *[Then] no man will support us*
Gar lay ane sege unto yone fort."   *Let us make a siege*
Than Petie said, "I sall appeir."   *appear [there, too]*
55 Thocht sayis, "I hecht, coim I ourthort,   *pledge, I come across*
I houp to lows the presoneir."   *hope to release*

Than to battell thai war arreyit all   *arranged*
And ay the vawart kepit Thocht.   *always in the vanguard remained*
Lust bur the benner to the wall,   *Desire bore the banner*
60 And Bissines the grit gyn brocht.   *Vigor the great siege engine brought*
Skorne cryis out, sayis, "Wald ye ocht?"   *What do you want?*
Lust sayis, "We wald haif entré heir."   *have entry here*
Comparisone sayis, "That is for nocht.   *[all] for nought*
Ye will nocht wyn the presoneir."

65	Thai thairin schup for to defend,	*prepared*
	And thai thairfurth sailyeit ane hour.	*assailed*
	Than Bissines the grit gyn bend,	*great siege engine drew*
	Straik doun the top of the foir tour.	*foretower*
	Comparisone began to lour	*grovel*
70	And cryit furth, "I yow requeir	*I request of you*
	Soft and fair and do favour,	*favorable treatment (?)*
	And tak to yow the presoneir."	*[will] bring to you*
	Thai fyrit the gettis deliverly	*set fire to the gates immediately*
	With faggottis wer grit and huge,	*bundles of sticks [that] were*
75	And Strangenes, quhair that he did ly,	*where he lay*
	Wes brint into the porter luge.	*burned in the porter's lodge*
	Lustely thay lakit bot a juge,	*Vigorously they fought without a judge*
	Sik straikis and stychling wes on steir.[1]	
	The semeliest wes maid assege,	*The seemliest [one] was [now] besieged*
80	To quhome that he wes presoneir.	
	Throucht Skornes nos thai put a prik,	*Through Scorn's nose; stab wound*
	This he wes banist and gat a blek.	*Thus he was banished; scar*
	Comparisone wes erdit quik,	*quickly put to earth (i.e., killed)*
	And Langour lap and brak his nek.	*leaped and broke his neck*
85	Thai sailyeit fast, all the fek.	*fled; remainder*
	Lust chasit my ladeis chalmirleir;	*chased; chambermaid*
	Gud Fame wes drownit in a sek:	*drowned in a sack*
	Thus ransonit thai the presoneir.	*freed*
	Fra Sklandir hard Lust had undone	*After Slander heard; defeated*
90	His ennemeis, he him aganis	
	Assemblit ane semely sort full sone	*band*
	And rais and rowttit all the planis.	*rose up and rode all over the plains*
	His cusing in the court remanis,	*cousin*
	Bot jalous folkis and geangleiris	*scandalmongers*
95	And fals Invy, that nothing lanis,	*conceals*
	Blew out on Luvis presoneir.	*Blabbed about*

---

[1] *Such strikings and strugglings were on [the] stair*

	Syne Matremony, that nobill king,	*Then*
	Was grevit and gadderit ane grit ost,	*annoyed; great host*
	And all enermit, without lesing,	*entirely armed, without falsehood (i.e., assuredly)*
100	Chest Sklander to the west se cost.	*Chased; sea coast*
	Than wes he and his linege lost,	*Then*
	And Matremony, withouttin weir,	*without [a] doubt*
	The band of freindschip hes indost	*endorsed*
	Betuix Bewty and the presoneir.	

105	Be that of eild wes Gud Famis air	*By then of age was Good Fame's heir*
	And cumyne to continuatioun,	*had come into [his] inheritance*
	And to the court maid his repair	*brought himself*
	Quhair Matremony than woir the crowne.	*wore*
	He gat ane confirmatioun,	
110	All that his modir aucht but weir,	*mother possessed without doubt*
	And baid still, as it wes resone,	*And still abides, as is proper*
	With Bewty and the presoneir.	

63. *To a Lady*

	My hartis tresure and swete assured fo,	*heart's; undoubted foe*
	The finale endar of my lyfe forever,	
	The creuell brekar of my hart in tuo,	
	To go to deathe this I deservit never.	*thusly*
5	O man slayar, quhill saule and life dissever,	*which; separate*
	Stynt of your slauchtir, allace, your man am I,	*Cease; slaughter*
	A thousand tymes that dois yow mercy cry.	

	Have mercie, luif, have mercie, ladie bricht.	*love*
	Quhat have I wrocht aganis your womanheid	*done; womanliness*
10	That ye suld murdir me, a saikles wicht,	*should; an innocent man*
	Trespassing never to yow in word nor deid?	*deed*
	That ye consent thairto, O God forbid!	
	Leif creuelté and saif your man, for schame,	*Leave; save*
	Or throucht the warld quyte losit is your name.	*throughout; quite injured*

15	My deathe chasis my lyfe so besalie	*vigorously*
	That wery is my goist to fle so fast.	*weary; spirit*

131

Sic deidlie dwawmes so mischeifaislie   *Such deadly swoons; harmfully*
Ane hundrithe tymes hes my hairt ovirpast.   *experienced*
Me think my spreit rynnis away full gast,   *spirit runs; aghast*
20   Beseikand grace on kneis yow befoir,   *Beseeching; knees*
Or that your man be lost for evermoir.   *Before*

Behald my wod, intollerabill pane,   *wild, intolerable pain*
Forevermoir quhilk sal be my dampnage.   *which shall be my injury*
Quhy undir traist your man thus have ye slane?   *Why under [your] safe-keeping*
25   Lo, deithe is in my breist with furious rage,   *death*
Quhilk may no balme nor tryacle assuage   *ointment; medicine*
Bot your mercie, for laik of quhilk I de.   *Without; for lack of which I die*
Allace, quhair is your womanlie petie?   *pity*

Behald my deidlie passioun dolorous,
30   Behald my hiddous hew and wo, allace.   *hue (color)*
Behald my mayne and murning mervalous,   *grief; mourning*
Withe sorrowfull teris falling frome my face.   *tears*
Rewthe, luif, is nocht, helpe ye not in this cace,   *Pity; useless, [if] you help not*
For how sould ony gentill hart indure   *should*
35   To se this sycht on ony creature?   *see*

Quhyte dov, quhair is your sobir humilnes?   *White dove; humility*
Swete gentill turtour, quhair is your peté went?   *turtle dove*
Quhair is your rewthe, the frute of nobilnes,   *compassion; fruit*
Of womanheid the tresour and the rent?   *wealth*
40   Mercie is never put out of meik intent,   *absent from gentle thoughts*
Nor out of gentill hart is fundin petie,
Sen mercyles may no weycht nobill be.   *Since; person*

Into my mynd I sall you mercye cry
Quhone that my toung sall faill me to speik,   *When; to speak for me*
45   And quhill that Nature me my sycht deny,   *while; sight*
And quhill my ene for pane incluse and steik,   *eyes; close up and shut*
And quhill the dethe my hart in soundir breik,   *asunder breaks*
And quhill my mynd may think and toung may steir —   *until; move*
And syne, fair weill, my hartis lady deir!   *And then, farewell*

64. *Good Counsel for Lovers*
[*Be secreit, trewe, incressing of your name*]

Be ye ane luvar, think ye nocht ye suld	*If you are a lover; not; should*
Be weill advysit in your governing?	*behavior*
Be ye nocht sa, it will on yow be tauld.	*If you are not; about you be said*
Be war thairwith for dreid of misdemying.	*fear of false judgment*
Be nocht a wreche nor skerche in your spending,	*miser nor stingy*
Be layth alway to do amis or schame,	*loath*
Be rewlit rycht and keip this doctring:	*ruled rightly*
Be secreit, trew, incressing of your name.	

5

Be ye ane lear, that is werst of all.	*liar*
Be ye ane tratlar, that I hald als evill.	*tattle-tell*
Be ye ane janglar and ye fra vertew fall.	*scandal-monger*
Be nevirmair onto thir vicis thrall.	*to these vices [a] slave*
Be now and ay the maistir of your will,	
Be nevir he that lesing sall proclame,	*falsehood*
Be nocht of langage quhair ye suld be still:	*be not a talker when*
Be secreit, trew, incressing of your name.	

10

15

Be nocht abasit for no wicket tung,	*dismayed because of wicked tongues*
Be nocht sa set, as I haif said yow heir,	*disposed; have told you before*
Be nocht sa lerge unto thir sawis sung,	*so free in spouting these wise sayings*
Be nocht our prowd, thinkand ye haif no peir.	*overly proud; have no equal*
Be ye so wyis that uderis at yow leir,	*others from you learn*
Be nevir he to sklander nor defame.	
Be of your lufe no prechour as a freir:	*proclaimer like a friar*
Be secreit, trew, incressing of your name.	

20

65. *The Golden Targe*

Ryght as the stern of day begouth to schyne,	*star; began*
Quhen gone to bed war Vesper and Lucyne,	*were the evening star and moon*
I raise and by a rosere did me rest.	*arose; a rose bush; recline*
Up sprang the goldyn candill matutyne	*of the morning*
With clere depurit bemes cristallyne	*purified beams*
Glading the mery foulis in thair nest.	*birds*

5

133

Or Phebus was in purpur cape revest   *Before; purple; clothed*
Up raise the lark, the hevyns menstrale fyne,
In May intill a morow myrthfullest.   *upon a most mirthful morn*

10 Full angel-like thir birdis sang thair houris   *these*
Within thair courtyns grene into thair bouris   *Behind; curtains*
Apparalit quhite and rede wyth blomes suete;   *blossoms sweet*
Anamalit was the felde wyth all colouris.   *Enameled; field*
The perly droppis schuke in silvir schouris,   *showers*
15 Quhill all in balme did branch and levis flete.   *balm (i.e., dewdrops); flow*
To part fra Phebus did Aurora grete —   *weep*
Hir cristall teris I saw hyng on the flouris,
Quhilk he for lufe all drank up wyth his hete.

For mirth of May wyth skippis and wyth hoppis
20 The birdis sang upon the tender croppis   *plants*
With curiouse note, as Venus chapell clerkis.   *artful notes*
The rosis yong, new spreding of thair knopis,   *buds*
War powderit brycht with hevinly beriall droppis   *Were*
Throu bemes rede birnyng as ruby sperkis.   *glowing*
25 The skyes rang for schoutying of the larkis,   *resounded*
The purpur hevyn, ourscailit in silvir sloppis,   *overlaid; streaks*
Ourgilt the treis branchis, lef, and barkis.   *Gilded*

Doun throu the ryce a ryvir ran wyth stremys   *glade*
So lustily agayn thai lykand lemys   *lovely; those pleasing gleams*
30 That all the lake as lamp did leme of licht,   *lake (i.e., water); shine*
Quhilk schadowit all about wyth twynkling glemis.   *shown*
The bewis bathit war in secund bemys   *boughs*
Throu the reflex of Phebus visage brycht.   *reflection; face*
On every syde the hegies raise on hicht,   *hedges; up high*
35 The bank was grene, the bruke was full of bremys,   *brook; breams (carp)*
The stanneris clere as stern in frosty nycht.   *pebbles; stars*

The cristall air, the sapher firmament,   *sapphire*
The ruby skyes of the orient,
Kest beriall bemes on emerant bewis grene.   *Cast; boughs*
40 The rosy garth, depaynt and redolent,   *garden, decorated and fragrant*
With purpur, azure, gold, and goulis gent   *red*

134

Arayed was by Dame Flora, the quene,
So nobily that joy was for to sene
The roch agayn the rivir resplendent,   *cliff*
45   As low enlumynit all the leves schene.   *flame illuminated*

Quhat throu the mery foulys armony   *Because of; harmony*
And throu the ryveris soun rycht ran me by,   *river's sound*
On Florais mantill I slepit as I lay;
Quhare sone into my dremes fantasy
50   I saw approch agayn the orient sky   *against; eastern*
A saill als quhite as blossum upon spray,   *as white*
Wyth merse of gold brycht as the stern of day,   *top-castle; star*
Quhilk tendit to the land full lustily,   *moved toward; eagerly*
As falcoun swift desyrouse of hir pray.

55   And hard on burd unto the blomyt medis   *close beside the flowery meadow*
Amang the grene rispis and the redis   *sedge and the reeds*
Arrivit sche; quhar fro anon thare landis   *from which there disembarked*
Ane hundreth ladyes, lusty into wedis,   *attired in lovely clothing*
Als fresch as flouris that in May up spredis,
60   In kirtillis grene, withoutyn kell or bandis.   *garments; caps or headbands*
Thair brycht hairis hang gleting on the strandis   *hung shining; strands*
In tressis clere, wyppit wyth goldyn thredis,   *tied*
With pappis quhite and mydlis small as wandis.   *white breasts*

Discrive I wald, bot quho coud wele endyte   *would; who; fully tell*
65   How all the feldis wyth thai lilies quhite   *those*
Depaynt war brycht, quhilk to the hevyn did glete?   *shine*
Noucht thou, Omer, als fair as thou coud wryte,   *Not; Homer*
For all thine ornate stilis so perfyte.
Nor yit thou, Tullius, quhois lippis swete   *Marcus Tullius Cicero*
70   Of rethorike did into termes flete.   *abound*
Your aureate tongis both bene all to lyte   *too insufficient*
For to compile that paradise complete.   *portray*

Thare saw I Nature and Venus, quene and quene,   *queen*
The fresch Aurora and Lady Flora schene,   *bright*
75   Juno, Appollo, and Proserpyna,
Dyane, the goddesse chaste of woddis grene,

My Lady Cleo, that help of makaris bene,   *poets is*
Thetes, Pallas, and prudent Minerva,
Fair feynit Fortune, and lemand Lucina.   *dissembling; gleaming*
80   Thir mychti quenis in crounis mycht be sene   *These*
Wyth bemys blith, bricht as Lucifera.   *joyous beams*

Thare saw I May, of myrthfull monethis quene,
Betuix Aprile and June hir sistir schene,   *her sisters bright*
Within the gardyng walking up and doun,
85   Quham of the foulis gladdith all bedene.   *greatly*
Scho was full tender in hir yeris grene.   *in her green youthfulness*
Thare saw I Nature present hir a goun
Rich to behald and nobil of renoun,   *worth*
Of eviry hew under the hevin that bene,   *color; exists*
90   Depaynt and broud be gude proporcioun.   *Decorated and embroidered*

Full lustily thir ladyes all in fere   *joyously; all together*
Enterit within this park of most plesere,
Quhare that I lay ourhelit wyth levis ronk.   *covered by thick leaves*
The mery foulis blisfullest of chere
95   Salust Nature, me thoucht, on thair manere;   *Welcomed*
And eviry blome on branch and eke on bonk   *also on bank*
Opnyt and spred thair balmy levis donk,   *Opened; dewy leaves*
Full low enclynyng to thair quene so clere   *bowing*
Quham of thair noble norising thay thonk.   *nourishing*

100   Syne to Dame Flora on the samyn wyse   *Then; same manner*
Thay saluse and thay thank a thousand syse,   *greeted; times*
And to Dame Venus, lufis mychti quene,   *love's*
Thay sang ballettis in lufe, as was the gyse,   *songs of love; fashion*
With amourouse notis lusty to devise
105   As thay that had lufe in thair hertis grene.   *green (i.e., fresh)*
Thair hony throtis opnyt fro the splene   *heart*
With werblis suete did perse the hevinly skyes,   *warblings sweet; pierce*
Quhill loud resownyt the firmament serene.   *While loudly resounded*

Aneothir court thare saw I consequent   *following*
110   Cupide the king, wyth bow in hand ybent
And dredefull arowis grundyn scharp and square.

Thare saw I Mars the god armypotent,   *warlike*
Aufull and sterne, strong and corpolent.   *muscular*
Thare saw I crabbit Saturn, ald and haire —   *ill-tempered; hoary*
115   His luke was lyke for to perturb the aire.   *glance*
Thare was Mercurius, wise and eloquent,
Of rethorike that fand the flouris faire.   *founded the flowers (i.e., ornaments)*

Thare was the god of gardingis, Priapus,   *gardens*
Thare was the god of wildernes, Phanus,
120   And Janus, god of entree delytable.   *delightful entry*
Thare was the god of fludis, Neptunus,   *[the] seas*
Thare was the god of wyndis, Eolus,
With variand luke rycht lyke a lord unstable.   *changeable looks*
Thare was Bacus, the gladder of the table,
125   There was Pluto, the elrich incubus,   *elfish*
In cloke of grene — his court usit no sable —   *black*

And eviry one of thir in grene arayit.   *them; arrayed*
On harp or lute full merily thai playit,
And sang ballettis with michty notis clere.
130   Ladyes to dance full sobirly assayit,   *performed*
Endlang the lusty ryvir so thai mayit   *Along*
Thair observance rycht hevynly was to here.   *hear*
Than crap I throu the levis and drew nere   *crept*
Quhare that I was rycht sudaynly affrayt,   *frightened*
135   All throu a luke quhilk I have boucht full dere.

And schortly for to speke, be lufis quene   *by love's*
I was aspyit. Scho bad hir archearis kene   *archers*
Go me arrest, and thay no tyme delayit.
Than ladyes fair lete fall thair mantillis grene,
140   With bowis big in tressit hairis schene   *strong bows of braided hair*
All sudaynly thay had a felde arayit.   *battle formation assumed*
And yit rycht gretly was I noucht affrayit,   *afraid*
The party was so plesand for to sene.   *pleasing to look upon*
A wonder lusty bikkir me assayit.   *wondrous assault assailed me*

145   And first of all with bow in hand ybent
Come Dame Beautee, rycht as scho wald me schent.   *destroy*

137

Syne folowit all hir dameselis yfere,   *Then; together*
With mony diverse aufull instrument.
Unto the pres Fair Having wyth hir went,
150 Fyne Portrature, Plesance, and Lusty Chere.
Than come Resoun with schelde of gold so clere;
In plate and maille as Mars armypotent,   *like war-like Mars*
Defendit me that nobil chevallere.   *knight*

Syne tender Youth come wyth hir virgyns ying,   *Then; young*
155 Grene Innocence, and schamefull Abaising,   *shy Bashfulness*
And quaking Drede wyth humble obedience.   *trembling Timidness*
The goldyn targe harmyt thay nothing.   *they harmed not at all*
Curage in thame was noucht begonne to spring,   *was not yet present*
Full sore thay dred to done a violence.   *do a violent deed*
160 Suete Womanhede I saw cum in presence —
Of artilye a warld sche did in bring,   *artillery; world (i.e., a large amount)*
Servit wyth ladyes full of reverence.

Sche led wyth hir Nurture and Lawlynes,   *Humility*
Contenence, Pacience, Gude Fame, and Stedfastnes,   *Purity*
165 Discrecioun, Gentrise, and Considerance,   *Gentility; Thoughtfulness*
Levefull Company, and Honest Besynes,   *Companionship; Activities*
Benigne Luke, Mylde Chere, and Sobirnes:
All thir bure ganyeis to do me grevance.   *All these bore weapons*
Bot Reson bure the targe wyth sik constance,   *held the shield; such*
170 Thair scharp assayes mycht do no dures   *attacks; harm*
To me, for all thair aufull ordynance.   *military might*

Unto the pres persewit Hie Degree: *pursued High Rank*
Hir folowit ay Estate and Dignitee,   *Position and Respect*
Comparisoun, Honour, and Noble Array,
175 Will, Wantonnes, Renoun, and Libertee,   *Desire*
Richesse, Fredome, and eke Nobilitee.   *Generosity*
Wit ye thay did thair baner hye display.
A cloud of arowis as hayle schour lousit thay,   *hail shower they loosed*
And schot quhill wastit was thair artilye,   *until used up*
180 Syne went abak reboytit of thair pray.   *Then; deprived*

138

Quhen Venus had persavit this rebute,   *repulse*
Dissymilance scho bad go mak persute   *ordered; pursuit*
At all powere to perse the goldyn targe;   *With; pierce*
And scho, that was of doubilnes the rute,   *the root of deceitfulness*
185   Askit hir choise of archeris in refute.   *for protection*
Venus the best bad hir go wale at large.   *choose at will*
Scho tuke Presence, plicht anker of the barge,   *[the] main anchor*
And Fair Callyng, that wele a flayn coud schute,   *arrow*
And Cherising for to complete hir charge.

190   Dame Hamelynes scho tuke in company,   *Familiarity*
That hardy was and hende in archery,   *skillful*
And broucht Dame Beautee to the felde agayn
With all the choise of Venus chevalry.   *choicest of Venus' knights*
Thay come and bikkerit unabaisitly —   *attacked unabashedly*
195   The schour of arowis rappit on as rayn.   *fell like rain*
Perilouse Presence, that mony syre has slayn,   *many [a] man*
The bataill broucht on bordour hard us by.   *on the field close by*
The salt was all the sarar, suth to sayn.   *assault; more fierce, truth*

Thik was the schote of grundyn dartis kene,
200   Bot Resoun, with the scheld of gold so schene,
Warly defendit quhosoevir assayit.
The aufull stoure he manly did sustene,   *awful attack; endure*
Quhill Presence kest a pulder in his ene;   *Until; cast; powder; eyes*
And than as drunkyn man he all forvayit.   *mis-went*
205   Quhen he was blynd, the fule wyth him thay playit   *the fool*
And banyst hym amang the bewis grene.   *banished; boughs*
That sory sicht me sudaynly affrayit.

Than was I woundit to the deth wele nere,
And yoldyn as a wofull prisonnere   *taken*
210   To Lady Beautee in a moment space.
Me thoucht scho semyt lustiar of chere   *more lively in manner*
(Efter that Resoun tynt had his eyne clere)   *had lost*
Than of before, and lufliare of face.   *lovelier*
Quhy was thou blyndit, Resoun, quhi, allace?   *Why*
215   And gert ane hell my paradise appere,   *made*
And mercy seme quhare that I fand no grace.   *found*

Dissymulance was besy me to sile,   *assail*
And Fair Calling did oft apon me smyle,
And Cherising me fed wyth wordis fair.
220 New Acquyntance enbracit me a quhile
And favouryt me, quhill men mycht go a myle,
Syne tuke hir leve, I saw hir nevirmare.   *Then*
Than saw I Dangere toward me repair.   *approach*
I coud eschew hir presence be no wyle,   *could avoid; by no means*
225 On syde scho lukit wyth ane fremyt fare.   *in a disdainful manner*

And at the last Departing coud hir dresse,   *presented herself*
And me delyverit unto Hevynnesse
For to remayne, and scho in cure me tuke.   *control*
Be this the lord of wyndis with wodenes,   *And then; fierceness*
230 God Eolus, his bugill blew I gesse,
That with the blast the levis all toschuke.   *leaves all shook*
And sudaynly in the space of a luke   *glance*
All was hyne went — thare was bot wildernes,   *gone*
Thare was no more bot birdis, bank, and bruke.

235 In twynklyng of ane eye to schip thai went,
And swyth up saile unto the top thai stent,   *quickly; spread*
And with swift course atour the flude thai frak.   *upon the sea they fled*
Thai fyrit gunnis with powder violent   *fired guns*
Till that the reke raise to the firmament.   *smoke rose*
240 The rochis all resownyt wyth the rak,   *cliffs; racket*
For rede it semyt that the raynbow brak.   *Because of the din*
Wyth spirit affrayde apon my fete I sprent   *feet I leapt*
Amang the clewis, so carefull was the crak.   *crags; terrible*

And as I did awake of my sweving,   *from my dream*
245 The joyfull birdis merily did syng
For myrth of Phebus tender bemes schene.
Suete war the vapouris, soft the morowing,   *were the mists*
Halesum the vale depaynt wyth flouris ying,   *Freshly [was]*
The air attemperit, sobir, and amene.   *temperate; mild; pleasant*
250 In quhite and rede was all the felde besene
Throu Naturis nobil fresch anamalyng   *enameling*
In mirthfull May, of eviry moneth quene.

140

Poem 66: The Merle and the Nightingale

O reverend Chaucere, rose of rethoris all,	*rhetoricians*
As in oure tong ane flour imperiall	*tongue*
255 That raise in Britane, evir quho redis rycht,	
Thou beris of makaris the tryumph riall,	*bear of poets; royal*
Thy fresch anamalit termes celicall	*celestial*
This mater coud illumynit haue full brycht.	*illuminated*
Was thou noucht of oure Inglisch all the lycht,	*English*
260 Surmounting eviry tong terrestriall,	*Surpassing*
Alls fer as Mayes morow dois mydnycht?	

O morall Gower and Ludgate laureate,	*eloquent*
Your sugurit lippis and tongis aureate	*sugared lips; golden*
Bene to oure eris cause of grete delyte.	*Are; ears; delight*
265 Your angel mouthis most mellifluate	
Oure rude langage has clere illumynate,	*clearly illuminated*
And fair ourgilt oure spech that imperfyte	*gilded*
Stude or your goldyn pennis schupe to write.	*Stood before*
This ile before was bare and desolate	*isle*
270 Of rethorike or lusty fresch endyte.	*poetry*

Thou lytill quair, be evir obedient,	*book*
Humble, subject, and symple of entent	*modest*
Before the face of eviry connyng wicht.	*skillful person*
I knaw quhat thou of rethorike hes spent.	*expended*
275 Of all hir lusty rosis redolent	*roses fragrant*
Is non into thy gerland sett on hicht.	
Eschame tharof and draw thee out of sicht.	*Be shame-faced*
Rude is thy wede, disteynit, bare, and rent;	*clothing; stained; torn*
Wele aucht thou be aferit of the licht.	*ought; afraid*

66. The Merle and the Nightingale

In May as that Aurora did upspring	*the Dawn*
With cristall ene chasing the cluddis sable,	*eyes; the dark clouds*
I hard a merle with mirry notis sing	*heard*
A sang of lufe with voce rycht confortable,	*pleasing*
5 Agane the orient bemis amiable	*In response to; beams*
Upone a blisfull brenche of lawry grene.	*laurel*

This wes hir sentens sueit and delectable: *saying sweet*
"A lusty lyfe in luves service bene." *joyful*

Undir this brench ran doun a revir bricht
10 Of balmy liquour cristallyne of hew *water*
Agane the hevinly aisur skyis licht, *Reflecting*
Quhair did upone the tother syd persew *other side spoke*
A nychtingall with suggurit notis new, *sweet notes*
Quhois angell fedderis as the pacok schone. *Whose angelic feathers*
15 This wes hir song and of a sentens trew:
"All luve is lost bot upone God allone."

With notis glaid and glorius armony *harmony*
This joyfull merle so salust scho the day *greets*
Quhill rong the widdis of hir melody, *While the woods rang (reverberated)*
20 Saying, "Awalk, ye luvaris, o this May! *lovers*
Lo, fresche Flora hes flurest every spray
As Natur hes hir taucht, the noble quene.
The feild bene clothit in a new array:
A lusty lyfe in luvis service bene."

25 Nevir suetar noys wes hard with levand man *was heard by living man*
Na maid this mirry gentill nychtingaill. *Than made*
Hir sound went with the rever as it ran
Outthrow the fresche and flureist lusty vaill. *blooming*
"O merle," quod scho, "O fule, stynt of thy taill, *fool, cease*
30 For in thy song gud sentens is thair none, *meaning*
For boith is tynt the tyme and the travaill *lost*
Of every luve bot upone God allone."

"Seis," quod the merle, "thy preching, nychtingale! *Cease*
Sall folk thair yewth spend into holines?
35 Of yung sanctis growis auld feyndis, but faill. *without fail*
Fy, ypocreit in yeiris tendirnes, *hypocrite; youth*
Agane the law of kynd thow gois expres *Against; nature you speak*
That crukit aige makis on with yewth serene, *crooked age should agree*
Quhome Natur of conditionis maid dyvers: *Nature made of diverse traits*
40 A lusty lyfe in luves service bene."

The nychtingaill said, "Fule, remembir thee   *Fool (or Fowl)*
That both in yewth and eild and every hour   *old age*
The luve of God most deir to man suld be,
That Him of nocht wrocht lyk His awin figour   *from nothing made*
45   And deit Himself, fro deid him to succour.   *died; death; save*
O, quhithir wes kythit thair, trew lufe or none?   *which was shown there*
He is most trew and steidfast paramour:
All luve is lost bot upone him allone."

The merle said, "Quhy put God so grit bewté   *Why did God put such great beauty*
50   In ladeis with sic womanly having,   *such femininity*
Bot gife He wald that thay suld luvit be?   *Unless; wished*
To luve eik Natur gaif thame inclynnyng,   *also*
And He, of Natur that wirker wes and king,   *creator*
Wald nothing frustir put nor lat be sene   *worthless*
55   Into his creature of His awin making:
A lusty lyfe in luves service bene."

The nychtingall said, "Nocht to that behufe   *Not; purpose*
Put God sic bewty in a ladeis face
That scho suld haif the thank thairfoir, or Lufe,
60   Bot He, the wirker, that put in hir sic grace
Of bewty, bontie, riches, tyme or space,   *whenever or wherever*
And every gudnes that bene to cum or gone,   *is to come or has been*
The thank redoundis to Him in every place: *credit belongs*
All luve is lost bot upone God allone."

65   "O nychtingall, it wer a story nyce   *foolish tale*
That luve suld nocht depend on cherité;
And gife that vertew contrair be to vyce,   *if*
Than lufe mon be a vertew, as thinkis me,   *must*
For ay to lufe invy mone contrair be.
70   God bad eik lufe thy nychtbour fro the splene,   *also; heart*
And quho than ladeis suetar nychbouris be?   *sweeter*
A lusty lyfe in lufes service bene."

The nychtingaill said, "Bird, quhy dois thow raif?   *rave*
Ane man may in his lady tak sic delyt
75   Him to forget that hir sic bewtie gaif,

And for his hevin rassaif hir cullour quhyt.   *take her white color (i.e., lovely skin)*
Hir goldin tressit hairis redomyt,   *resplendent*
Lyk to Appollois bemis thocht thay schone,   *beams though*
Suld nocht him blind fro lufe that is perfyt:
80   All lufe is lost bot upone God allone."

The merle said, "Lufe is caus of honour ay,
Luve makis cowardis manheid to purchas,   *obtain*
Luve makis knychtis hardy at assey,   *during battle*
Luve makis wrechis full of lergenes,   *misers; generosity*
85   Luve makis sueir folkis full of bissines,   *lazy folks; activity*
Luve makis sluggirdis fresche and weill besene,   *sluggards attractive*
Luve changis vyce in vertewis nobilnes.
A lusty lyfe in luvis service bene."

The nychtingaill said, "Trew is the contrary!
90   Sic frustir luve it blindis men so far   *Such worthless*
Into thair myndis it makis thame to vary.
In fals vane glory thai so drunkin ar,
Thair wit is went, of wo thai ar nocht war
Quhill that all wirchip away be fro thame gone —
95   Fame, guddis, and strenth — quhairfoir weill say I dar,
All luve is lost bot upone God allone."

Than said the merle, "Myn errour I confes.
This frustir luve all is bot vanité.
Blind ignorance me gaif sic hardines
100 To argone so agane the varité.   *argue; the truth*
Quhairfoir I counsall every man that he
With lufe nocht in the Feindis net be tone,   *Fiend's; taken*
Bot luve the Luve that did for his lufe de.   *die*
All lufe is lost bot upone God allone."

105 Than sang thay both with vocis lowd and cleir.
The merle sang, "Man, lufe God that hes thee wrocht."   *made*
The nychtingall sang, "Man, lufe the lord most deir
That thee and all this warld hes maid of nocht."   *made from nothing*
The merle said, "Luve Him that thy lufe hes socht   *sought*
110 Fra hevin to erd and heir tuk flesche and bone."   *earth*

144

Poem 67: Love's Inconstancy

The nychtingall sang, "And with His deid thee bocht.	*bought (redeemed)*
All luve is lost bot upone Him allone."	
Thane flaw thir birdis our the bewis schene,	*these; over; bright boughs*
Singing of lufe amang the levis small,	
115 Quhois ythand pleid into my thocht is grene,	*Whose sustained dispute*
Bothe sleping, walking, in rest and in travall.	*waking*
Me to reconfort most it dois availl,	*comfort*
Agane for lufe quhen lufe I can find none,	
To think how song this merle and nychtingaill:	
120 All lufe is lost bot upone God allone.	

67. *Love's Inconstancy*

Quha will behald of luve the chance	*[Let] whoever wishes behold*
With sueit dissavyng countenance,	*sweet deceiving*
In quhais fair dissimulance	*whose; dissembling*
May none assure;	*have trust*
5 Quhilk is begun with inconstance	*Which; inconstancy*
And endis nocht but variance.	*[with] nothing but inconstancy*
Scho haldis with continuance	*steadfastness*
No serviture.	*service*
Discretioun and considerance	
10 Ar both out of hir govirnance,	*control*
Quhairfoir of it the schort plesance	
May nocht indure.	
Scho is so new of acquentance,	*friendships*
The auld gais fra remembrance.	*old goes*
15 Thus I gife our the observans	*abandon*
Of luvis cure.	*labor*
It is ane pount of ignorance	*sign*
To lufe in sic distemperance,	*such disarray*
Sen tyme mispendit may avance	*Since; misused; profit*
20 No creature.	
In luve to keip allegance,	
It war als nys an ordinance	*were as foolish an order*

145

As quha wald bid ane deid man dance   *ask a dead man to dance*
  In sepulture.   *[the] tomb*

68. *True Love*
  [*And trew luve rysis fro the splene*]

Now cumis aige quhair yewth hes bene,   *comes old age where youth*
And trew luve rysis fro the splene.   *arises from the heart*

Now culit is Dame Venus brand,   *cooled; torch*
Trew luvis fyre is ay kindilland,   *always burning*
5   And I begyn to undirstand
In feynit luve quhat foly bene.   *false love what folly [there] is*
  Now cumis aige quhair yewth hes bene,
And trew luve rysis fro the splene.

Quhill Venus fyre be deid and cauld,   *When; is dead and cold*
10   Trew luvis fyre nevir birnis bauld.   *burns boldly*
So as the ta lufe waxis auld,   *one [kind of] love grows*
The tothir dois incres moir kene.   *other; more keenly*
Now cumis aige quhair yewth hes bene,
And trew lufe rysis fro the splene.

15   No man hes curege for to wryte   *[the] ability*
Quhat plesans is in lufe perfyte,   *perfect love*
That hes in fenyeit lufe delyt —   *Who delights in false love*
Thair kyndnes is so contrair clene.   *Their natures are opposite*
Now cumis aige quhair yewth hes bene,
20   And trew lufe rysis fro the splene.

Full weill is him that may imprent   *Well-off; impress upon*
Or onywayis his hairt consent   *in any way*
To turne to trew luve his intent
And still the quarrell to sustene.   *conflict to withstand*
25   Now cumis aige quhair yewth hes bene,
And trew lufe rysis fro the splene.

Poem 68: True Love

	I haif experience by mysell,	*have; myself*
	In luvis court anis did I dwell;	*once*
	Bot quhair I of a joy cowth tell,	*whereof I one joy could tell*
30	I culd of truble tell fyftene.	
	Now cumis aige quhair yewth hes bene,	
	And trew lufe rysis fro the splene.	

	Befoir quhair that I wes in dreid,	*uncertainty*
	Now haif I confort for to speid;	*succeed*
35	Quhair I had maugré to my meid,	*ill-will as my reward*
	I trest rewaird and thankis betuene.	*expect [to receive] reward; also*
	Now cumis aige quhair yewth hes bene,	
	And trew lufe rysis fro the splene.	

	Quhair lufe wes wont me to displeis,	
40	Now find I into lufe grit eis;	*great ease*
	Quhair I had denger and diseis,	*disdain and pain*
	My breist all confort dois contene.	
	Now cumis aige quhair yewth hes bene,	
	And trew lufe rysis fro the splene.	

45	Quhair I wes hurt with jelosy	
	And wald no luver wer bot I,	*wished there were no lover but me*
	Now quhair I lufe I wald all wy	*wish all men*
	Als weill as I luvit, I wene.	*[Were] loved as well as I*
	Now cumis aige quhair yewth hes bene,	
50	And trew lufe rysis fro the splene.	

	Befoir quhair I durst nocht for schame	
	My lufe discure nor tell hir name,	*disclose*
	Now think I wirschep wer and fame	*were*
	To all the warld that it war sene.	*were seen*
55	Now cumis aige quhair yewth hes bene,	
	And trew lufe rysis fro the splene.	

	Befoir no wicht I did complene,	
	So did hir denger me derene;	*aloofness me derange*
	And now I sett nocht by a bene	*not the value of a bean*
60	Hir bewty nor hir twa fair ene.	*eyes*

Now cumis aige quhair yewth hes bene,
And trew lufe rysis fro the splene.

I haif a luve farar of face,   *fairer*
Quhome in no denger may haif place,   *In whom no disdain*
65   Quhilk will me guerdoun gif and grace,   *Who; give reward and grace*
And mercy ay quhen I me mene.   *lament*
Now cumis aige quhair yewth hes bene,
And trew lufe rysis fro the splene.

Unquyt I do nothing nor sane,   *Unrepaid; say*
70   Nor wairis a luvis thocht in vane.   *expends*
I sal be als weill luvit agane,   *shall be as well loved in return*
Thair may no jangler me prevene.   *gossiper; injure*
Now cumis aige quhair yewth hes bene,
And trew luve rysis fro the splene.

75   Ane lufe so fare, so gud, so sueit,   *sweet*
So riche, so rewthfull, and discreit,   *merciful; wise*
And for the kynd of man so meit,   *nature; fitting*
Nevirmoir sal be nor yit hes bene.
Now cumis aige quhair yewth hes bene
80   And trew lufe rysis fro the splene.

Is none sa trew a luve as He
That for trew lufe of us did de.   *die*
He suld be luffit agane, think me,   *loved*
That wald sa fane our luve obtene.   *joyfully*
85   Now cumis aige quhair yewth hes bene,
And trew lufe rysis fro the splene.

Is non but grace of God, iwis,   *[There] is no one; indeed*
That can in yewth considdir this.
This fals dissavand warldis blis   *deceiving*
90   So gydis man in flouris grene.   *guides; (i.e, during his youth)*
Now cumis aige quhair yewth hes bene,
And trew luve rysis fro the splene.

69. *A Wooing in Dunfermline*
    [*And that me thocht ane ferly cace*]

This hindir nycht in Dumfermeling	*The other night*
To me was tawld ane windir thing:	*told; wondrous*
That lait ane tod wes with ane lame	*recently a fox; lamb*
And with hir playit and maid gud game,	*flirted*
5 Syne till his breist did hir imbrace	*Then*
And wald haif riddin hir lyk ane rame —	*mounted; ram*
And that me thocht ane ferly cace.	*an astonishing thing*
He braisit hir bony body sweit	*embraced her lovely*
And halsit hir with fordir feit,	*held; front feet*
10 Syne schuk his taill with quhinge and yelp,	*Then shook; whining*
And todlit with hir lyk ane quhelp;	*played; puppy*
Syne lowrit on growfe and askit grace,	*crouched down flat*
And ay the lame cryd, "Lady, help!" —	*all the while*
And that me thocht ane ferly cace.	
15 The tod wes nowder lene nor skowry.	*neither lean; scruffy*
He wes ane lusty reid haird lowry,	*red-haired sly creature*
Ane lang taild beist and grit with all.	*large everywhere*
The silly lame wes all to small	*innocent lamb/penis; too*
To sic ane tribbill to hald ane bace.	*treble; bass*
20 Scho fled him nocht, fair mot hir fall —	*well may she prosper*
And that me thocht ane ferly cace.	
The tod wes reid, the lame wes quhyte,	*red; white*
Scho wes ane morsall of delyte —	
He lovit na yowis, auld, tuch, and sklender.	*ewes; tough; skinny*
25 Becaus this lame wes yung and tender,	
He ran upoun hir with a race,	*rush*
And scho schup nevir for till defend hir —	*tried not at all to*
And that me thocht ane ferly cace.	
He grippit hir abowt the west	*waist*
30 And handlit hir as he had hest.	*haste*
This innocent that nevir trespast	*had transgressed*
Tuke hert that scho wes handlit fast,	*Was pleased*

	And lute him kis hir lusty face.	*let; lovely*
	His girnand gamis hir nocht agast —	*grinding fangs she did not fear*
35	And that me thocht ane ferly cace.	
	He held hir till him be the hals	*neck*
	And spak full fair, thocht he wes fals,	*though*
	Syne said and swoir to hir be God	*Then; swore; by*
	That he suld nocht tuich hir prenecod.	*touch her pincushion*
40	The silly thing trowd him, allace,	*naive; believed*
	The lame gaif creddence to the tod —	*gave*
	And that me thocht ane ferly cace.	
	I will no lesingis put in vers,	*falsehoods*
	Lyk as thir jangleris dois rehers,	*these gossipers*
45	Bot be quhat maner thay war mard.	*injured*
	Quhen licht wes owt and durris wes bard	*doors were barred*
	I wait nocht gif he gaif hir grace,	*if he showed her mercy*
	Bot all the hollis wes stoppit hard —	*holes were*
	And that me thocht ane ferly cace.	
50	Quhen men dois fleit in joy maist far,	*float*
	Sone cumis wo or thay be war.	*Soon comes; before*
	Quhen carpand wer thir two most crows,	*talking; these; intimately*
	The wolf he ombesett the hous	*surrounded*
	Upoun the tod to mak ane chace.	*chase*
55	The lamb than cheipit lyk a mows —	*squeaked; mouse*
	And that me thocht ane ferly cace.	
	Throw hiddowis yowling of the wowf	*Through hideous*
	This wylie tod plat doun on growf,	*crawled on the ground*
	And in the silly lambis skin	
60	He crap als far as he micht win	*crept; get*
	And hid him thair ane weill lang space.	*very long time*
	The yowis besyd thay maid na din —	*ewes nearby*
	And that me thocht ane ferly cace.	
	Quhen of the tod wes hard no peip,	*heard no peep*
65	The wowf went all had bene on sleip;	*wolf thought; asleep*
	And quhill the bell had strikkin ten,	*when; struck*

Poem 70: To the Queen

	The wowf hes drest him to his den,	*went*
	Protestand for the secound place.	*Claiming*
	And this report I with my pen,	
70	How at Dumfermling fell the cace.	

70. *To the Queen*
    [*Madam, your men said*]

	Madam, your men said thai wald ryd	*intended to ride*
	And latt this Fasterennis Evin ouer slyd,	*let; slip by*
	Bott than thair wyffis cam furth in flockis	*But then; wives*
	And baid tham betteis soin abyd	*better now to remain*
5	Att haem, and lib tham of the pockis.	*home; cure themselves of the pox*

	Nou propois thai, sen ye dwell still,	*since you remain here*
	Of Venus feest to fang an fill,	*Of Venus' feast to take your fill*
	Bott in the fedle preiff thai na cockis.	*field tested they no [fighting] cocks*
	For till heff riddin hed bein les ill,	
10	Nor latt thair wyffis breid the pockis.[1]	

	Sum of your men sic curage hed,	*such sexual desire had*
	Dam Venus fyre sa hard tham sted,	*beset*
	Thai brak up durris and raeff up lockis	*doors; tore up*
	To get ane pamphelet on a pled	*wench in a plaid (?)*
15	That thai mycht lib tham of the pockis.	*have sex with them*

	Sum that war ryatous as rammis	*were eager as rams*
	Ar nou maid tame lyk ony lammis,	*any lambs*
	And settin down lyk sarye crockis,	*brought low; old ewes*
	And hes forsaekin all sic gammis	*such games*
20	That men callis libbin of the pockis.	

| | Sum thocht thamselffis stark lyk gyandis | *strong like giants* |
| | Ar nou maid waek lyk willing wandis | *made weak; pliant wands* |

---

[1] Lines 9–10: *For to have ridden away would have been less humiliating / Than to have allowed their wives to have been infected with the pox*

	With schinnis scharp and small lyk rockis,	*thin like distaffs*
	And gottin thair bak in bayth thair handis	*holding their backs*
25	For ouer offt libbin of the pockis.	*excessive*

	I saw coclinkis me besyd	*prostitutes*
	The young men to thair howses gyd	*guide*
	Had bettir lugget in the stockis.	*lodged*
	Sum fra the bordell wald nocht byd	*brothel; stay away*
30	Quhill that thai gatt the Spanyie pockis.	*Until they got the Spanish Pox*

	Thairfoir, all young men, I you pray,	
	Keip you fra harlottis nycht and day —	
	Thai sall repent quhai with tham yockis —	*whoever; yokes*
	And be war with that perrellous play	*of that perilous play*
35	That men callis libbin of the pockis.	

71. *Of a Black Moor*
   [*My ladye with the mekle lippis*]

	Lang heff I maed of ladyes quhytt,	*Long have I written; white*
	Nou of an blak I will indytt	*write*
	That landet furth of the last schippis.	*recent ships*
	Quhou fain wald I descryve perfytt	*How happily would*
5	My ladye with the mekle lippis.	*huge lips*

	Quhou schou is tute mowitt lyk an aep,	*large-mouthed like an ape*
	And lyk a gangarall onto graep,	*toad to grab onto*
	And quhou hir schort catt nois up skippis,	*cat nose turns up*
	And quhou schou schynes lyk ony saep,	*shines like any soap*
10	My ladye with the mekle lippis.	

	Quhen schou is claid in reche apparrall,	
	Schou blinkis als brycht as an tar barrell.	*gleams*
	Quhen schou was born the son tholit clippis,	*sun suffered an eclipse*
	The nycht be fain faucht in hir querrell —	*night; fought*
15	My ladye with the mekle lippis.	

Quhai for hir saek with speir and scheld		*Whoever; sake*
Preiffis maest mychtellye in the feld,		*Proves*
Sall kis and withe hir go in grippis,		*embrace*
And fra thyne furth hir luff sall weld —		*from thenceforth*
20	My ladye with the mekle lippis.	
And quhai in fedle receaves schaem		*who; field; shame*
And tynis thair his knychtlie naem,		*loses; name*
Sall cum behind and kis hir hippis		*hips*
And nevir to uther confort claem,		*claim*
25	My ladye with the mekle lippis.	

72. *In a Secret Place*
  [*Ye brek my hart, my bony ane*]

	In secreit place this hyndir nycht	*the other night*
	I hard ane beyrne say till ane bricht:	*heard a young man say to a lady*
	"My huny, my hart, my hoip, my heill,	*honey; hope; happiness*
	I have bene lang your luifar leill	*devoted lover*
5	And can of yow get confort nane.	
	How lang will ye with danger deill?	*treat me with disdain*
	Ye brek my hart, my bony ane."	*pretty one*
	His bony beird wes kemmit and croppit,	*beard; combed; clipped*
	Bot all with cale it wes bedroppit,	*broth; besplattered*
10	And he wes townysche, peirt, and gukit.	*townish, bold; foolish*
	He clappit fast, he kist and chukkit	*embraced; kissed; fondled*
	As with the glaikis he wer ouirgane.	*foolish desires; overcome*
	Yit be his feirris he wald have fukkit —	*behavior; fucked her*
	"Ye brek my hart, my bony ane."	
15	Quod he: "My hairt, sweit as the hunye,	*sweet as honey*
	Sen that I borne wes of my mynnye,	*Since; mommy*
	I never wowit weycht bot yow.	*wooed anyone*
	My wambe is of your luif sa fow	*belly; so full*
	That as ane gaist I glour and grane.	*ghost I stare; groan*
20	I trymble sa, ye will not trow,	*believe*
	Ye brek my hart, my bony ane."	

"Tehe!" quod scho, and gaif ane gawfe. — *gave a guffaw*
"Be still, my tuchan and my calfe, — *tactile object*
My new spanit howffing fra the sowk, — *weanling lamb*
25   And all the blythnes of my bowk. — *delight of my body*
My sweit swanking, saif yow allane — *fellow*
Na leyd I luiffit all this owk: — *lad I loved; week*
Full leif is me yowr graceles gane." — *Very dear to me is; ugly mug*

Quod he: "My claver and my curldodie, — *clover; wild flower*
30   My huny soppis, my sweit possodie, — *honey-soaked bread; spiced drink*
Be not oure bosteous to your billie, — *too rough; lover*
Be warme hairtit and not evill wille. — *ill-willed*
Your heylis, quhyt as quhalis bane, — *heels, white as whale's bone*
Garris ryis on loft my quhillelille: — *Makes rise aloft my willy-lilly*
35   Ye brek my hart, my bony ane."

Quod scho: "My clype, my unspaynit gyane, — *clumsy fellow; unweaned giant*
With moderis mylk yit in your mychane, — *tummy*
My belly huddrun, my swete hurle bawsy, — *belly-cover; impetuous fellow*
My huny gukkis, my slawsy gawsy, — *sweet fool; plump fellow (?)*
40   Your musing waild perse ane harte of stane.
Tak gud confort, my grit-heidit slawsy: — *big-headed fellow*
Full leif is me your graceles gane."

Quod he: "My kid, my capirculyoun, — *wood grouse (?)*
My bony baib with the ruch brylyoun, — *babe; rough pudendum (?)*
45   My tendir gyrle, my wallie gowdye, — *girlie; pretty flower (?)*
My tyrlie myrlie, my crowdie mowdie, — *female genitalia*
Quhone that oure mouthis dois meit at ane,
My stang dois storkyn with your towdie: — *stake stiffens; buttocks*
Ye brek my hairt, my bony ane." — *pretty one*

50   Quod scho: "Now tak me by the hand,
Welcum, my golk of Marie land, — *fool from faerie land (?)*
My chirrie and my maikles munyoun, — *cherry; matchless darling*
My sowklar sweit as ony unyoun, — *suckler; onion*
My strumill stirk yit new to spane. — *stumbling bullock; being weaned*
55   I am applyit to your opunyoun: — *agreeable to your suit*
I luif rycht weill your graceles gane." — *face*

Poem 73: These Fair Ladies That Repair to Court

He gaiff to hir ane apill rubye.   *ruby-red apple*
Quod scho, "Gramercye, my sweit cowhubye!"   *sweet fool*
And thai tway to ane play began
60   Quhilk men dois call the dery dan,   *(i.e., the dance of love)*
Quhill that thair myrthis met baythe in ane.   *joys*
"Wo is me," quod scho, "Quhair will ye, man?   *Where will you [go]*
Best now I luif that graceles gane."

73. *These Fair Ladies That Repair to Court*

Thir ladeis fair that maks repair   *These; are present*
   And in the courte ar kend,   *well-known*
Thre dayis thair thai will do mair   *more*
   Ane mater for to end
5   Than thair gud men will do in ten
   For ony craift thai can.   *skill they have*
So weill thai ken quhat tyme and quhen   *know*
   Thair meynis thai sould mak than.   *complaints*

Withe litill noy thai can convoy   *difficulty; conduct*
10   A mater finalie,   *decisively*
Yit myld and moy thai keip it coy   *modest; quiet*
   On evynnis quyetlie.   *evenings*
Thai do no mys, bot gif thai kys   *wrong; if; kiss*
   And kepis collatioun,   *[a] tête-à-tête*
15   Quhat rak of this? The mater is   *Why does it matter; business*
   Brocht to conclusioun.

Ye may wit weill thai have grit feill   *know well; ability*
   A mater to solist.   *solicit (entreat)*
Traist as the steill, syne never a deill   *True as steel*
20   Quhone thai cum hame is myst.   *missed*
Thir lairdis ar, me think, rycht far   *These lords*
   Sic ladeis behaldin to
That sa weill dar go to the bar   *bar (i.e., the judge's railing)*
   Quhone thair is ocht ado.   *When; something to be done*

25	Thairfoir, I rid, gif ye have pleid	*advise, if you have [a] case*
	Or mater in to pley,	*to litigate*
	To mak remeid send in your steid	*To have success*
	Your ladeis grathit up gay.	*decked out gaily*
	Thai can defend, evin to the end,	
30	Ane mater furthe expres.	
	Suppois thai spend, it is onkend	*Although; unknown*
	Thair geir is not the les.	*wealth/sexual apparatus*

	In quyet place and thai have space	*if*
	Within les nor twa houris,	
35	Thai can, percace, purchas sic grace	*perchance, achieve such success*
	At the compositouris,	*From the compositors*
	Thair compositioun, without suspitioun,	
	Thair finalie is endit	*conclusively is ended*
	With expeditioun and full remissioun	*settlement*
40	And selis thairto appendit.	*seals; attached*

	All haill almoist thai mak the coist	*wholly; cost*
	With sobir recompence.	
	Rycht litle loist thai get indoist	*endorsed*
	All haill thair evidens.	*wholly*
45	Sic ladyis wyis ar all to pryis,	*Such; wise; [be] prized*
	To say the verité,	*truth*
	Sic can devyis and none supprys	*Such [ladies]; devise; damage*
	Thame throw thair honesté.	

74. *Tidings from the Session*

	Ane murelandis man of uplandis mak	*moorland; highland kind*
	At hame thus to his nychtbour spak:	*home; neighbor*
	"Quhat tythingis, gossope, peace or weir?"	*tidings, friend; war*
	The uther roundit in his eir:	*whispered*
5	"I tell yow this, undir confessioun.	
	Bot laitlie lychtit of my meir,	*lately alighted from my mare*
	I come of Edinburch fra the Sessioun."	

Poem 74: Tidings from the Session

"Quhat tythingis herd ye thair, I pray yow?"
The tuther ansuerit, "I sall say yow,
10 Keip this in secreit, gentill brudir —
Is no man thair trowis ane udir. *trusts another*
A commoun doar of transgressioun *wrong-doer*
Of innocent folkis prevenis a fuider: *takes advantage of many*
Sic tythandis hard I at the Sessioun.

15 "Sum withe his fallow rownys him to pleis *whispers [to] him pleasing things*
That wald for anger byt of his neis. *bite off his nose*
His fa sum be the oxtar ledis. *foe one man by the arm leads*
Sum pattiris with his mouthe on beidis *One mutters; in prayer*
That hes his mynd all on oppressioun. *harmful actions*
20 Sum bekis full laich and schawis bair heidis *bows; low; bare heads*
Wald luke full heich war not the Sessioun. *act quite haughty were he not [at]*

"Sum bydand law layis land in wed, *One whose case is pending; in mortgage*
Sum superspendit gois to his bed, *One who is bankrupt*
Sum spedis for he in court hes meynis, *succeeds because; friends*
25 Of parcialité sum complenis, *Of favoritism*
How feid and favour fleymis discretioun. *disliking and liking corrupts*
Sum speikis full fair and falslie feynis: *dissembles*
Sic tythandis herd I at the Sessioun. *Such*

Sum castis summondis and sum exceppis, *rejects summons; objects*
30 Sum standis besyd and skayld law keppis, *has [a] little legal knowledge*
Sum is contineuit, sum wynnis, sum tynis, *receives a continuance; loses*
Sum makis thame myrre at the wynis, *merry with wine*
And sum putt out of his possessioun, *loses his property*
Sum hyrreit and on credence dynis: *is impoverished; lives on credit*
35 Sic tythingis hard I at the Sessioun.

"Sum sweiris and sum forsaikis God, *swears to; forsakes*
Sum in ane lamb skyn is a tod, *fox*
Sum on his toung his kyndnes tursis, *carries*
Sum kervis throittis, and sum cuttis pursis. *carves throats; cuts purses*
40 To gallows sum gais with processioun, *goes*
Sum sanis the Sait, and sum thame cursis: *blesses the Court*
Sic tythingis herd I at the Sessioun.

"Religious men of dyvers places   *from various communities*
Cumis thair to wow and se fair faces.   *Come there to woo*
45   Baith Carmeletis and Coirdeleiris   *Franciscans*
Cumis thair to gener and get freirris,   *generate; recruit friars*
As is the use of thair professioun.   *custom*
The youngar at the elder leiris: *from the older learns*
Sic tythingis herd I at the Sessioun.

50   "Thair cumis young monkis of het complexioun,   *hot*
Of devoit mynd, lufe, and affectioun,   *devout; love*
And in the courte thair proud flesche dantis,   *subdues*
Full fadirlyk with pechis and pantis.   *fatherly; gasps*
Thai ar so humill of intercessioun,   *humble*
55   All mercyfull women thair errand grantis:
Sic tythingis hard I at the Sessioun."

75. *To the Merchants of Edinburgh*

Quhy will ye, merchantis of renoun,   *Why; high standing*
Lat Edinburgh, your nobill toun,   *Allow*
For laik of reformatioun   *lack of improvement*
The commone proffeitt tyine and fame?   *good injure and defame (abuse)*
5   Think ye not schame   *Are you not ashamed*
That onie uther regioun   *any other*
Sall with dishonour hurt your name?   *Might with insult tarnish*

May nane pas throw your principall gaittis   *pass through; gates*
For stink of haddockis and of scattis,   *skates (fish)*
10   For cryis of carlingis and debaittis,   *old women; arguments*
For feusum flyttinis of defame.   *foul hurling of insults*
        Think ye not schame,
Befoir strangeris of all estaittis   *social ranks*
That sic dishonour hurt your name?

15   Your Stinkand Stull that standis dirk   *Stinking Passageway; dark*
Haldis the lycht fra your parroche kirk.   *Blocks; parish church*
Your foirstairis makis your housis mirk   *forestairs; dark*

Lyk na cuntray bot heir at hame.   *no country*
   Think ye not schame,

20   Sa litill polesie to work,   *So few improvements to make*

   In hurt and sklander of your name?

At your Hie Croce quhar gold and silk   *High Cross where*

Sould be, thair is bot crudis and milk,   *Should; curds*

And at your Trone bot cokill and wilk,   *the public weighing beam; shellfish*

25   Pansches, pudingis of Jok and Jame.   *Tripe, haggis*

   Think ye not schame,

Sen as the world sayis that ilk,   *Since the world says the same*

In hurt and sclander of your name?

Your commone menstrallis hes no tone   *minstrels; tunes (songs)*

30   Bot "Now the day dawis" and "Into Joun."   *dawns; June*

Cunningar men man serve Sanct Cloun   *More skillful; must; St. Clown (?)*

And nevir to uther craftis clame.   *lay claim*

   Think ye not schame,

To hald sic mowaris on the moyne,   *keep such mockers at the moon*

35   In hurt and sclander of your name?

Tailyouris, soutteris, and craftis vyll   *Tailors, cobblers; vile*

The fairest of your streitis dois fyll,   *defile*

And merchantis at the Stinkand Styll   *Stinking Passageway*

Ar hamperit in ane honycame.   *crammed into a honeycomb*

40   Think ye not schame

That ye have nether witt nor wyll   *neither wit nor will*

To win yourselff ane bettir name?

Your burgh of beggeris is ane nest,   *beggars*

To schout thai swentyouris will not rest.   *those scoundrels*

45   All honest folk they do molest,

Sa piteuslie thai cry and rame.   *clamor*

   Think ye not schame,

That for the poore hes nothing drest,   *been provided*

In hurt and sclander of your name?

50   Your proffeit daylie dois incres,

Your godlie workis, les and les.   *virtuous deeds*

Through streittis nane may mak progres
For cry of cruikit, blind, and lame. *crippled*
   Think ye not schame,
55   That ye sic substance dois posses, *such*
And will not win ane bettir name?

Sen for the Court and the Sessioun, *Since to*
The great repair of this regioun *attendance*
Is in your burgh, thairfoir be boun *ready*
60   To mend all faultis that ar to blame,
   And eschew schame. *avoid*
Gif thai pas to aneuther toun, *If they (the Court and Session) are moved to*
Ye will decay and your great name. *be diminished*

Thairfoir strangeris and leigis treit, *lieges (subjects) welcome*
65   Tak not ouer mekill for thair meit, *Do not overcharge for their food*
And gar your merchandis be discreit. *make; reasonable*
That na extortiounes be, proclame *To prevent extortions, denounce*
   All fraud and schame. *shameful conduct*
Keip ordour and poore nighbouris beit, *assist*
70   That ye may gett ane bettir name.

Singular proffeit so dois yow blind, *Personal gain*
The common proffeit gois behind. *general welfare*
I pray that Lord remeid to fynd *[a] remedy*
That deit into Jerusalem, *died in*
75   And gar yow schame, *cause*
That sumtyme ressoun may yow bind, *govern*
For to restor to yow guid name. *restore*

76. *How Dunbar Was Desired to Be a Friar*

This nycht befoir the dawing cleir *Last night; dawn*
Me thocht Sanct Francis did to me appeir *Saint*
With ane religious abbeit in his hand *habit*
And said, "In this go cleith thee my servand. *clothe; [as] my servant*
5   Reffus the warld, for thow mon be a freir." *Renounce; must*

Poem 76: How Dunbar Was Desired to Be a Friar

With him and with his abbeit bayth I skarrit	*By; was startled*
Lyk to ane man that with a gaist wes marrit.	*ghost was frightened*
Me thocht on bed he layid it me abone,	*laid it over me*
Bot on the flure delyverly and sone	*floor quickly*
10 I lap thairfra and nevir wald cum nar it.	*leaped; come near*
Quoth he, "Quhy skarris thow with this holy weid?	*Why scares; garment*
Cleith thee thairin, for weir it thow most neid.	*Clothe; wear*
Thow that hes lang done Venus lawis teiche	*taught Venus' laws*
Sall now be freir and in this abbeit preiche.	*habit*
15 Delay it nocht, it mon be done but dreid."	*must; without [a] doubt*
Quod I, "Sanct Francis, loving be thee till,	
And thankit mot thow be of thy gude will	*thanked must; for*
To me, that of thy clathis ar so kynd,	*generous*
Bot thame to weir it nevir come in my mynd.	
20 Sweit confessour, thow tak it nocht in ill.	
"In haly legendis haif I hard allevin	*have I heard indeed*
Ma sanctis of bischoppis nor freiris, be sic sevin.	*More saints than; by seven*
Of full few freiris that hes bene sanctis I reid;	*very; have read*
Quhairfoir ga bring to me ane bischopis weid,	*Therefore; gown*
25 Gife evir thow wald my sawle gaid unto Hevin."	*If; soul went*
"My brethir oft hes maid thee supplicationis	*brethren; to you*
Be epistillis, sermonis, and relationis	*letters; reports*
To tak the abyte, bot thow did postpone.	*habit*
But forder proces cum on thairfoir annone,	*Without further delay*
30 All sircumstance put by and excusationis."	*evasions put aside; excuses*
"Gif evir my fortoun wes to be a freir,	*If*
The dait thairof is past full mony a yeir;	*date (time); year*
For into every lusty toun and place	*lively; manor house*
Of all Yngland, frome Berwick to Kalice,	*Calais*
35 I haif into thy habeit maid gud cheir.	*gone cheerfully*
"In freiris weid full fairly haif I fleichit.	*flattered*
In it I haif in pulpet gon and preichit	
In Derntoun kirk and eik in Canterberry;	*also*

In it I past at Dover our the ferry — *over*
40 Throw Piccardy, and thair the peple teichit. — *there; taught*

"Als lang as I did beir the freiris style, — *friar's title*
In me, God wait, wes mony wrink and wyle. — *knows; trick*
In me wes falset with every wicht to flatter, — *falsehood; person*
Quhilk mycht be flemit with na haly watter. — *cleansed*
45 I wes ay reddy all men to begyle." — *always*

This freir that did Sanct Francis thair appeir,
Ane fieind he wes in liknes of ane freir. — *fiend*
He vaneist away with stynk and fyrie smowk.
With him, me thocht, all the hous end he towk, — *wall*
50 And I awoik as wy that wes in weir. — *awoke as one who was perturbed*

77. The Dance of the Seven Deadly Sins

Of Februar the fyiftene nycht — *In; fifteenth night*
Full lang befoir the dayis lycht
   I lay in till a trance,
And than I saw baith Hevin and Hell.
5 Me thocht amangis the feyndis fell — *cruel fiends*
   Mahoun gart cry ane dance — *Muhammad (i.e., Satan) proclaimed*
Of schrewis that wer nevir schrevin — *sinners that were unconfessed*
Aganis the feist of Fasternis Evin — *In preparation for the feast of Fastern's Eve*
   To mak thair observance.
10 He bad gallandis ga graith a gyis — *ordered gallants to go and prepare a masquerade*
And kast up gamountis in the skyis — *throw up wild cavortings*
   That last came out of France. — *recently came from*

"Lat se," quod he, "now, quha begynnis?" — *who shall begin*
With that the fowll Sevin Deidly Synnis — *foul Seven Deadly Sins*
15   Begowth to leip at anis. — *Began to leap at once*
And first of all in dance wes Pryd, — *Pride*
With hair wyld bak and bonet on syd, — *spread across his back (?)*
   Lyk to mak waistie wanis. — *cause wasted dwellings*
And round abowt him as a quheill — *like a wheel*
20 Hang all in rumpillis to the heill — *Hung all in pleats to the heels*

Poem 77: The Dance of the Seven Deadly Sins

His kethat for the nanis.	*His surcoat (?) for the occasion*
Mony prowd trumpour with him trippit,	*trumpeters (i.e., musicians); danced*
Throw skaldand fyre ay as thay skippit	*Through burning fire*
Thay gyrnd with hiddous granis.	*growled; groans*

25 Heilie harlottis on hawtane wyis	*Proud rogues in haughty fashion*
Come in with mony sindrie gyis,	*sundry costumes*
Bot yit luche nevir Mahoun	*But yet the Devil never laughed*
Quhill preistis come in with bair schevin nekkis —	*Until priests; bare shaven necks*
Than all the feyndis lewche and maid gekkis,	*Then; laughed and made gestures*
30 Blak Belly and Bawsy Broun.	*(i.e., two of the demons)*

Than Yre come in with sturt and stryfe,	*Wrath; quarreling and strife*
His hand wes ay upoun his knyfe,	
He brandeist lyk a beir.	*made gestures like a bear*
Bostaris, braggaris, and barganeris	*Boasters, braggarts, and arguers*
35 Eftir him passit into pairis,	
All bodin in feir of weir.	*All equipped in anticipation of war*
In jakkis and stryppis and bonettis of steill,	*padded jerkins; metal splints; helmets*
Thair leggis wer chenyeit to the heill,	*legs were chained at the heels*
Frawart wes thair affeir.	*Hostile was their demeanor*
40 Sum upoun udir with brandis beft,	*others; swords beat*
Sum jaggit uthiris to the heft	*stabbed others; haft*
With knyvis that scherp cowd scheir.	*knives that sharply could slice*

Nixt in the dance followit Invy,	*Envy*
Fild full of feid and fellony,	*hatred and cruelty*
45 Hid malyce and dispyte.	*Hidden; resentment*
For pryvie hatrent that tratour trymlit.	*secret hatred; trembled*
Him followit mony freik dissymlit	*deceitful men*
With fenyeit wirdis quhyte,	*false white words*
And flattereris into menis facis,	
50 And bakbyttaris in secreit places	*back-biters (i.e., slanderers)*
To ley that had delyte,	*lie*
And rownaris of fals lesingis —	*whisperers; lies*
Allace, that courtis of noble kingis	*Alas*
Of thame can nevir be quyte.	*free*

163

55	Nixt him in dans come Cuvatyce,	*dance; Covetise*
	Rute of all evill and grund of vyce,	*Root; [the] foundation of vice*
	That nevir cowd be content.	*could*
	Catyvis, wrechis, and ockeraris,	*Villains, misers, and usurers*
	Hudpykis, hurdaris, and gadderaris	*Skinflints, hoarders, and gatherers*
60	All with that warlo went.	*evil being*
	Out of thair throttis thay schot on udder	*spewed on the others*
	Hett moltin gold, me thocht a fudder,	*Hot molten; a cartload*
	As fyreflawcht maist fervent.	*Like a lightning flash most intense*
	Ay as thay tomit thame of schot,	*emptied themselves of shot*
65	Feyndis fild thame new up to the thrott	*Fiends filled; throat*
	With gold of all kin prent.	*every kind stamped [into coins]*
	Syne Sweirnes, at the secound bidding,	*Then Sloth*
	Come lyk a sow out of a midding,	*dungheap*
	Full slepy wes his grunyie.	*grunting*
70	Mony sweir, bumbard-belly huddroun,	*lazy, fat-bellied idlers*
	Mony slute daw and slepy duddroun	*sluttish slatterns; sleepy slovens*
	Him servit ay with sounyie.	*reluctance*
	He drew thame furth in till a chenyie,	*into a set of chains*
	And Belliall with brydill renyie	*bridle reins*
75	Evir lascht thame on the lunyie.	*lashed them; loins*
	In dance thay war so slaw of feit,	*slow of foot*
	Thay gaif thame in the fyre a heit	
	And maid thame quicker of counyie.	*dance*
	Than Lichery, that lathly cors,	*Lechery; loathsome creature*
80	Come berand lyk a bagit hors,	*Came moving like a pregnant horse*
	And Lythenes did him leid.	*Wantonness; lead*
	Thair wes with him ane ugly sort	*assortment*
	And mony stynkand fowll tramort	*stinking foul corpses*
	That had in syn bene deid.	*had died in sin*
85	Quhen thay wer entrit in the dance,	
	Thay wer full strenge of countenance	*strange in facial appearance*
	Lyk turkas birnand reid.	*Like a smith's tongs burning red*
	All led thay uthir by the tersis.	*genitals*
	Suppois thay fycket with thair ersis,	*Although they fidgeted with their arses*
90	It mycht be na remeid.	*It could not be helped*

	Than the fowll monstir Glutteny,	*foul monster Gluttony*
	Of wame unsasiable and gredy,	*belly insatiable*
	To dance he did him dres.	*make ready*
	Him followit mony fowll drunckart	*drunkards*
95	With can and collep, cop and quart,	*tankard, cup*
	In surffet and exces.	
	Full mony a waistles wallydrag	*waistless slob*
	With wamis unweildable did furth wag	*flabby bellies*
	In creische that did incres.	*creases [of fat]*
100	"Drynk!" ay thay cryit, with mony a gaip.	*gaping mouth*
	The feyndis gaif thame hait leid to laip,	*gave them hot lead to lap*
	Thair lovery wes na les.	*allowance was no less*
	Na menstrallis playit to thame, but dowt,	*without [a] doubt*
	For glemen thair wer haldin owt	*entertainers; held out*
105	Be day and eik by nycht,	*also*
	Except a menstrall that slew a man,	
	Swa till his heretage he wan	*heritage he won*
	And entirt be "breif of richt."	*was entered by "brief of right"*
	Than cryd Mahoun for a Heleand padyane.	*the Devil; Highland pageant*
110	Syne ran a feynd to feche Makfadyane	*Then; fetch Macfaydyane*
	Far northwart in a nuke.	*nook*
	Be he the correnoch had done schout	*By [the time] he had shouted the summons*
	Erschemen so gadderit him abowt,	*Highlanders (Gaelic folk); gathered*
	In Hell grit rowme thay tuke.	
115	Thae tarmegantis, with tag and tatter,	*Those fiends, in rags and tatters*
	Full lowd in Ersche begowth to clatter	*in Gaelic began*
	And rowp lyk revin and ruke.	*croaked like ravens and rooks*
	The Devill sa devit wes with thair yell	*so deafened*
	That in the depest pot of Hell	*pit*
120	He smorit thame with smuke.	*smothered*
	Nixt that a turnament wes tryid	*attempted*
	That lang befoir in Hell wes cryid	*announced*
	In presens of Mahoun,	*(i.e., Satan)*
	Betuix a telyour and ane sowtar,	*Between a tailor and a shoemaker*
125	A pricklous and ane hobbell clowttar,	*louse-stabber; a boot-mender*
	The barres wes maid boun.	*lists were made ready*

The tailyeour baith with speir and scheild
Convoyit wes unto the feild
   With mony lymmar loun   *rascally rogues*
130 Of seme-byttaris and beist knapparis,   *seam-biters; basting thread snappers*
Of stomok-steillaris and clayth-takkaris —   *stomach-steelers; cloth-tackers*
   A graceles garisoun.   *set of defenders*

His baner born wes him befoir   *carried*
Quhairin wes clowttis ane hundreth scoir,   *Wherein were pieces of cloth*
135   Ilkane of divers hew,   *Each one of different color*
And all stowin out of sindry webbis.   *stolen from various larger cloths*
For quhill the Greik Sie fillis and ebbis,   *For while the Greek Sea ebbs and flows*
   Telyouris will nevir be trew.
The tailyour on the barrowis blent,   *lists gazed*
140 Allais, he tynt all hardyment,   *Alas, he lost all courage*
   For feir he chaingit hew.   *fear he blanched*
Mahoun come furth and maid him knycht —
Na ferly thocht his hart wes licht   *No wonder though his heart was light*
   That to sic honor grew.   *such; received*

145 The tailyeour hecht hely befoir Mahoun   *pledged strongly*
That he suld ding the sowtar doun,   *knock the cobbler down*
   Thocht he wer strang as mast.   *strong as [a ship's] mast*
Bot quhen he on the barrowis blenkit   *lists gazed*
The telyouris curage a littill schrenkit,   *shrank*
150   His hairt did all ourcast.   *turn gray*
And quhen he saw the sowtar cum   *shoemaker approach*
Of all sic wirdis he wes full dum,   *such words*
   So soir he wes agast.   *afraid*
For he in hart tuke sic a scunner   *took such a fright*
155 Ane rak of fartis lyk ony thunner   *A series; thunder*
   Went fra him, blast for blast.

The sowtar to the feild him drest,   *shoemaker; readied*
He wes convoyid out of the west
   As ane defender stout.
160 Suppois he had na lusty varlot,   *Even though; noble attendant*
He had full mony lowsy harlott   *lice-ridden rogues*
   Round rynnand him aboute.   *running*

His baner wes of barkit hyd   *tanned hide*
Quhairin Sanct Girnega did glyd
165   Befoir that rebald rowt.   *rascally rabble*
Full sowttarlyk he wes of laitis,   *cobbler-like; in manner*
For ay betuix the harnes plaitis
   The uly birsit out.   *oil burst out*

Quhen on the talyeour he did luke,
170 His hairt a littill dwamyng tuke.   *faintness took*
   Uneis he mycht upsitt.   *Scarcely*
Into his stommok wes sic ane steir   *Within; such a stirring*
Of all his dennar quhilk cost him deir,   *dinner; dearly*
   His breist held never a bitt.
175 To comfort him or he raid forder,   *before he rode farther*
The devill of knychtheid gaif him order,   *of knighthood gave*
   For stynk than he did spitt.
And he about the devillis nek
Did spew agane ane quart of blek,   *blacking*
180   Thus knychtly he him quitt.   *repaid*

Than fourty tymis the feynd cryd, "Fy!"
The sowtar rycht effeiritly   *cobbler; fearfully*
   Unto the feild he socht.   *sought*
Quhen thay wer servit of thair speiris,   *equipped with their spears*
185 Folk had ane feill be thair effeiris,   *sense of their fear*
   Thair hairtis wer baith on flocht.   *hearts; a-flutter*
Thay spurrit thair hors on adir syd,   *toward the other side*
Syne thay attour the grund cowd glyd
   Than tham togidder brocht.
190 The tailyeour was nocht weill sittin,   *not at all well seated*
He left his sadall all beschittin
   And to the grund he socht.

His birnes brak and maid ane brattill,   *armor; clatter*
The sowtaris hors start with the rattill   *was startled; racket*
195   And round about cowd reill.   *did cavort*
The beist, that frayit wes rycht evill,   *badly frightened*
Ran with the sowtar to the Devill,
   And he rewardit him weill.

Sumthing frome him the feynd eschewit,   *avoided*
200 He wend agane to bene bespewit,   *expected; vomited upon*
    So stern he wes in steill.   *valiant; in armor*
He thocht he wald agane debait him.   *defend himself*
He turnd his ers and all bedret him   *arse; befouled*
    Quyte our from nek till heill.   *All over from the neck to the heels*

205 He lowsit it of with sic a reird   *fired it off with such a roar*
Baith hors and man he straik till eird,
    He fartit with sic ane feir.   *farted in such a fashion*
"Now haif I quitt thee," quod Mahoun.   *repaid*
The new maid knycht lay into swoun
210   And did all armes forswer.   *renounce*
The Devill gart thame to dungeoun dryve   *sent them to the dungeon*
And thame of knychtheid cold depryve,   *did strip*
    Dischairgeing thame of weir,   *Banning them from warfare*
And maid thame harlottis bayth forevir,   *lowlifes*
215 Quhilk still to keip thay had fer levir   *to remain they greatly preferred*
    Nor ony armes beir.

I had mair of thair werkis writtin   *I would have more; deeds*
Had nocht the sowtar bene beschittin
    With Belliallis ers unblist.
220 Bot that sa gud ane bourd me thocht,   *so good a jest*
Sic solace to my hairt it rocht,   *Such joy; made*
    For lawchtir neir I brist,   *laughing I nearly burst*
Quhairthrow I walknit of my trance.   *Through which I awakened*
To put this in rememberance   *(i.e., to record this tale)*
225   Mycht no man me resist,   *prevent*
To dyte how all this thing befell   *relate*
Befoir Mahoun, the air of Hell.   *lord (heir)*
    Schirris, trow it gif ye list!   *Sirs, believe it if you choose*

78. *Of the Tailors and the Shoemakers*
    [*Telyouris and sowtaris, blist be ye*]

Betuix twell houris and ellevin,   *(i.e., about midnight)*
I dremed ane angell came fra hevin

Poem 78: Of the Tailors and the Shoemakers

With plesand stevin sayand on hie: *pleasing voice saying on high*
"Telyouris and sowtaris, blist be ye.   *Tailors and shoemakers*

5   "In Hevin hie ordand is your place   *Heaven high ordained*
     Aboif all sanctis in grit solace,   *Above all saints in great joy*
     Nixt God grittest in dignitie:
     Tailyouis and sowtaris, blist be ye.

     "The caus to yow is nocht unkend;   *not unknown*
10   That God mismakkis, ye do amend   *That which God mis-makes*
     Be craft and grit agilitie: *By; great skill*
     Tailyouris and sowtaris, blist be ye.

     "Sowtaris, with schone weill maid and meit   *shoes; fitting*
     Ye mend the faltis of ill maid feit,   *flaws; ill-made feet*
15   Quhairfoir to Hevin your saulis will fle: *Therefore; souls will fly*
     Telyouris and sowtaris, blist be ye.

     "Is nocht in all this fair a flyrok   *fair (i.e., world); deformed person*
     That hes upoun his feit a wyrok,   *a corn*
     Knowll tais nor mowlis in no degrie,   *Arthritic toes nor chilblains*
20   Bot ye can hyd tham, blist be ye.   *hide*

     "And ye tailyouris, with weil maid clais   *clothes*
     Can mend the werst maid man that gais   *goes*
     And mak him semely for to se:
     Telyouris and sowtaris, blist be ye.

25   "Thocht God mak ane misfassonit swayne,   *Though; mis-fashioned fellow*
     Ye can him all schaip new agane   *shape*
     And fassoun him bettir be sic thre: *fashion; by three times*
     Telyouris and sowtaris, blist be ye.

     "Thocht a man haif a brokin bak,
30   Haif he a gud telyour, quhattrak,   *[If] he has a good tailor, so what*
     That can it cuver with craftis slie: *cover with [his] subtle skill*
     Telyouris and sowtaris, blist be ye.

"Of God grit kyndnes may ye clame   *From; claim*
That helpis His peple fra cruke and lame,   *deformity and lameness*
35   Supportand faltis with your supplé: *Curing flaws; assistance*
Tailyouris and sowtaris, blist be ye.

"In erd ye kyth sic mirakillis heir,   *On earth you work such miracles here*
In hevin ye sal be sanctis full cleir,
Thocht ye be knavis in this cuntré: *Even though you are servants*
40   Telyouris and sowataris, blist ye be."

79. *The Devil's Inquest*
    [*Renunce thy God and cum to me*]

This nycht in my sleip I wes agast,   *distressed*
Me thocht the Devill wes tempand fast   *tempting*
The peple with aithis of crewaltie,   *violent oaths*
Sayand, as throw the mercat he past,   *through the market*
5   "Renunce thy God and cum to me."

Me thocht as he went throw the way   *through*
Ane preist sweirit be God verey   *priest swore by the true God*
Quhilk at the alter ressavit he.   *Which he received at the altar*
"Thow art my clerk," the Devill can say,   *cleric; did say*
10   "Renunce thy God and cum to me."

Than swoir ane courtyour mekle of pryd   *courtier great of pride*
Be Chrystis windis, bludy and wyd,   *By Christ's wounds*
And be His harmes wes rent on Tre.   *arms [who] was torn on the Cross*
Than spak the Devill hard him besyd,   *close beside him*
15   "Renunce thy God and cum to me."

Ane merchand his geir as he did sell   *goods*
Renuncit his pairt of Hevin and Hell.
The Devill said, "Welcum mot thow be,   *may*
Thow sal be merchand for mysell.   *shall be; for me*
20   Renunce thy God and cum to me."

Poem 79: The Devil's Inquest

Ane goldsmyth said, "The gold is sa fyne	*pure*
That all the workmanschip I tyne —	*lose*
The Feind ressaif me gif I le."	*take me if I lie*
"Think on," quod the Devill, "that thow art myne.	*Reflect on [the fact]*
25 Renunce thy God and cum to me."	
Ane tailyour said, "In all this toun	*tailor*
Be thair ane better weilmaid goun,	*well-made*
I gif me to the Feynd all fre."	*give myself*
"Gramercy, telyour," said Mahoun,	*Great thanks; (i.e., the Devil)*
30 "Renunce thy God and cum to me."	
Ane sowttar said, "In gud effek,	*shoemaker; In truth*
Nor I be hangit be the nek	*May I; by the neck*
Gife bettir butis of ledder ma be."	*If better boots of leather may be*
"Fy!" quod the Feynd, "thow sairis of blek.	*smell of blacking*
35 Ga clenge thee clene and cum to me."	*cleanse; clean*
Ane baxstar sayd, "I forsaik God	*baker*
And all His werkis, evin and od,	*(i.e., completely)*
Gif fairar stuff neidis to be."	*If better provisions are required*
The Dyvill luche and on him cowth nod,	*laughed; did look*
40 "Renunce thy God and cum to me."	
Ane fleschour swoir be the sacrament	*butcher*
And be Chrystis blud maist innocent,	
Nevir fatter flesch saw man with e.	*meat; eye*
The Devill said, "Hald on thy intent;	*Retain those thoughts*
45 Renunce thy God and cum to me."	
The maltman sais, "I God forsaik,	*malt-maker says*
And that the Devill of Hell me taik	
Gif ony bettir malt may be,	*If*
And of this kill I haif inlaik."	*kiln I have [any] deficiency*
50 "Renunce thy God and cum to me."	
Ane browstar swoir, "The malt wes ill,	*brewer*
Bath reid and reikit on the kill	*discolored and smoke-tainted in the kiln*
That it will be na aill for me.	*produce no ale*

Ane boll will nocht sex gallonis fill."   *One measure [of that malt]; six gallons make*
55   "Renunce thy God and cum to me."

The smyth swoir, "Be rude and raip,   *By cross and rope*
In till a gallowis mot I gaip   *Upon; may I gape*
Gif I ten dayis wan pennyis thre,   *If; won three pennies*
For with that craft I can nocht thraip."   *contend*
60   "Renunce thy God and cum to me."

Ane menstrall said, "The Feind me ryfe   *pierce*
Gif I do ocht bot drynk and swyfe."   *anything except drink and copulate*
The Devill said, "Hardly mot it be —   *Thus must it be*
Exers that craft in all thy lyfe.   *Practice*
65   Renunce thy God and cum to me."

Ane dysour said with wirdis of stryfe   *dicer; words of anger*
The Devill mot stik him with a knyfe
Bot he kest up fair syisis thre.   *Unless he fairly threw three sixes*
The Devill said, "Endit is thy lyfe;
70   Renunce thy God and cum to me."

Ane theif said, "God, that evir I chaip,   *escape*
Nor ane stark widdy gar me gaip   *a strong withy (rope) makes me gape*
Bot I in Hell for geir wald be."   *Hell's possessions*
The Devill said, "Welcum in a raip;   *to a rope*
75   Renunce thy God and cum to me."

The fische wyffis flett and swoir with granis   *fish sellers scolded; groans*
And to the Feind, saule, flesch, and banis   *bones*
Thay gaif thame with ane schowt on hie.   *loud shout*
The Devill said, "Welcum all att anis;   *at once*
80   Renunce thy god and cum to me."

Me thocht the devillis als blak as pik   *pitch*
Solistand wer as beis thik,   *Entreating were as thick as bees*
Ay tempand folk with wayis sle,   *Always; sly methods*
Rownand to Robene and to Dik,   *Whispering*
85   "Renunce thy God and cum to me."

172

80. *Master Andro Kennedy's Testament*

     I Maister Andro Kennedy   *Master Andrew*
     Curro quando sum vocatus.   *I run when I am called*
     Gottin with sum incuby   *Begotten by some demon*
     Or with sum freir *infatuatus,*   *by a lusty friar*
5   In faith I can nought tell redly   *readily*
     Unde aut ubi fui natus.   *By whom or where I was conceived*
     Bot in treuth I trow trewly   *believe*
     Quod sum dyabolus incarnatus.   *That I am a fiend in human form*

     Cum nichill sit cercius morte   *Since nothing is more certain than death*
10   We mon all de, man, that is done.   *must all die; a certainty*
     Nescimus quando vel qua sorte   *We do not know when or by what chance*
     Na Blind Allane wait of the mone.   *No [more than]; knows of the moon*
     Ego pacior in pectore,   *Therefore I suffer in my breast*
     This night I myght not sleip a wink.
15   *Licet eger in corpore,*   *[Although] I lie sick in body*
     Yit wald my mouth be wet with drink.

     Nunc condo testamentum meum.   *Now I make my testament*
     I leiff my saull forevirmare,
     Per omnipotentem Deum,   *By almighty God*
20   Into my lordis wyne cellar,
     Semper ibi ad remanendum   *Always to remain there*
     Quhill Domisday, without dissever, *Until the Day of Judgment; departing*
     Bonum vinum ad bibendum   *Good wine to drink*
     With sueit Cuthbert that luffit me nevir.   *sweet; loved*

25   *Ipse est dulcis ad amandum.*   *He is sweet for loving*
     He wald oft ban me in his breith,   *curse me with his words*
     Det michi modo ad potandum,   *Let him just give me something to drink*
     And I forgif him laith and wraith,   *hatred and wrath*
     Quia in cellario cum cervisia   *Since in the cellar with beer*
30   I had lever lye, baith air and lait,   *I would rather lie, both early and late*
     Nudus solus in camesia   *Naked except for my shirt*
     Na in my lordis bed of stait.   *Than*

	A barell bung ay at my bosum,	*stopper always*
	Of warldis gud I bad na mair.	*desire*
35	*Corpus meum ebriosum*	*My drunken body*
	I leif onto the toune of Air,	*town of Ayr*
	In a draf mydding forevir and ay,	*dunghill*
	Ut ibi sepeliri queam,	*So that I may be buried there*
	Quhar drink and draff may ilka day	*Where; dregs; every*
40	Be cassyne *super faciem meam.*	*Be thrown over my face*
	I leif my hert that nevir wes sicir	*leave; constant*
	Sed semper variabile,	*But was always fickle*
	That nevirmare wald flow nor flicir	*always would waver or flicker*
	Consorti meo Jacobe.	*Toward my companion Jacob*
45	Thought I wald bynd it with a wicir	*Even though I would; wicker*
	Verum deum renui.	*I denied the true God*
	Bot and I hecht to teme a bicker	*But if I promised to empty a cup*
	Hoc pactum semper tenui.	*This promise I always kept*
	Syne leif I the best aucht I bocht	*best thing I own*
50	(*Quod es Latinum propter "caupe"*)	*Which is Latin for "caupe" (see note)*
	To hede of kyn; bot I wait nought	*(i.e., the head of the family); know not*
	Quis est ille, than I schrew my scawpe.	*Who he is, than I would curse my scalp*
	I callit my lord my heid, but hiddill,	*without concealment*
	Sed nulli alii hoc dixerunt.	*But no others said this*
55	We weir als sib as seve and riddill,	*were as related as sieve and strainer*
	In una silva que creverunt.	*That grew in one forest*
	Omnia mea solacia	*All my pleasures*
	(Thai wer bot lesingis, all and ane)	*false things*
	Cum omni fraude et fallacia	*With every fraud and deceit*
60	I leif the maister of Sanct Antane,	*leave to the master of St. Anthony's*
	Willelmo Gray, sine gratia,	*without gratitude*
	Myne awne deir cusing, as I wene,	*cousin, as I think*
	Qui nunquam fabricat mendatia	*Who never makes up lies*
	Bot quhen the holyne growis grene.	*Except when the holly is green*
65	My fenyening and my fals wynyng	*deceit; dishonest profits*
	Relinquo falsis fratribus,	*I leave to the false friars*
	For that is Goddis awne bidding:	

174

Poem 80: Master Andro Kennedy's Testament

	Dispersit, dedit pauperibus.	*He distributed, he gave to the poor*
	For menis saulis thai say thai sing,	
70	*Mencientes pro muneribus.*	*Lying [in exchange] for gifts*
	Now God gif thaim ane evill ending	
	Pro suis pravis operibus.	*For their wicked deeds*
	To Jok Fule my foly fre	*Jock Fool; foolishness freely*
	Lego post corpus sepultum.	*I bequeath after my body is buried*
75	In faith, I am mair fule than he,	
	Licet ostendit bonum vultum.	*Although he shows a good face*
	Of corne and catall, gold and fe	*livestock; goods*
	Ipse habet walde multum,	*He himself has a great deal*
	And yit he bleris my lordis e	*eye*
80	*Fingendo eum fore stultum.*	*By pretending to be a fool*
	To master Johne Clerk syne	*next*
	Do et lego intime	*I do give and bequeath secretly*
	Goddis malisone and myne.	*curse*
	Ipse est causa mortis mee.	*He himself is the cause of my death*
85	War I a dog and he a swyne	
	Multi mirantur super me,	*Many might wonder at me*
	Bot I suld ger that lurdane quhryne	*make that villain squeal*
	Scribendo dentes sine de.	*By writing teeth without a "d" (?)*
	Residuum omnium bonorum	*The remainder of all my goods*
90	For to dispone my lord sall haif,	*dispose*
	Cum tutela puerorum —	*With the wardship of my children*
	Ade, Kytte, and all the laif.	*rest*
	In faith, I will na langar raif.	*rant*
	Pro sepultura ordino	*I will arrange for my burial*
95	On the new gys, sa God me saif,	*In the new fashion*
	Non sicut more solito.	*Not after the usual custom*
	In die mee sepulture	*On the day of my burial*
	I will nane haif bot our aune gyng,	*own gang*
	Et duos rusticos de rure	*And two country peasants*
100	Berand a barell on a styng,	*Carrying; pole*
	Drynkand and playand cop out evin,	*chug-a-lugging*
	Sicut ego met solebam.	*As I myself was accustomed to do*

175

Singand and gretand with hie stevin,   *weeping with high voices*
Potum meum cum fletu miscebam.   *I mixed my drinking with tears*

105   I will na preistis for me sing   *desire no priests*
      Dies illa, dies ire,   *That day, the day of wrath*
      Na yit na bellis for me ring,
      Sicut semper solet fieri,   *As is always the custom to be done*
      Bot a bag pipe to play a spryng   *tune*
110   *Et unum* ail wosp *ante me*;   *And one ale wisp before me*
      Instayd of baneris for to bring
      Quatuor lagenas cervisie,   *Four flagons of beer*
      Within the graif to set sic thing   *grave*
      In modum Crucis juxta me,   *In the manner of the Cross next to me*
115   To fle the fendis, than hardely sing
      De terra plasmasti me.   *Out of earth thou hast made me*

81. *Dunbar's Dirge*

      We that ar heir in hevynnis glorie   *here (i.e., Edinburgh)*
      To you that ar in purgatorie
      Commendis us on hartlie wys —   *in a hearty manner*
      I mene we folk of paradys   *mean*
5   In Edinburgh with all merynes —
      To yow at Striveling in distres,   *Stirling*
      Quhair nowdir plesour nor delyt is,   *neither*
      For pietie this epistell wrytis.   *Out of pity; letter writes*
      O ye heremytis and ankirsadillis   *anchorites*
10   That takkis your pennance at your tabillis
      And eitis no meit restorative   *eat no meat*
      Nor drinkis no wyne confortative
      Nor aill, bot that is thin and small,   *ale, except what is thin*
      With few coursis into your hall,
15   But cumpany of lordis and knychtis   *Without [the] fellowship of*
      Or ony uther gudlie wychtis,   *excellent people*
      Solitar walking your alone,   *Walking alone by yourself*
      Seing nothing bot stok and stone;   *stumps and stones*
      Out of your panefull purgatorie
20   To bring yow to the blys and glorie

Poem 81: Dunbar's Dirge

Of Edinburcht, the myrrie town,
We sall begin ane cairfull sown,   *shall begin a sorrowful song*
Ane dirige devoit and meik,   *A dirge devout and mild*
The Lord of blys doing beseik   *beseeching*
25   Yow to delyver out of your noy   *discomfort*
And bring yow sone to Edinburgh joy,
For to be merye amangis us.
The dirige begynnis thus:

Lectio prima   *First reading*

The Fader, the Sone, the Holie Gaist,
30   The blissit Marie, virgen chaist,   *blessed Mary*
Of angellis all the ordour nyne,   *nine orders*
And all the hevinlie court divyne
Sone bring yow fra the pyne and wo   *from the pain and woe*
Of Striveling, everie court manis foo,   *Stirling*
35   Agane to Edinburchtis joy and blys,
Quhair wirschip, welthe, and weilfair is,   *Where honor; prosperity*
Play, plesance eik, and honestie.   *Entertainment, pleasure also, and honor*
Say ye amen, for chirritie.   *charity (i.e., love)*
     Tu autem, Domine.   *Do Thou, oh Lord [have mercy on us]*

Responsio   *Response*

40   Tak consolatioun in your payne,
In tribulatioun tak consolatioun,
Out of vexatioun cum hame agayne,
Tak consolatioun in your payne.
Iube, Domine, etc.   *Give, oh Lord [Thy blessing]*
45   Out of distres of Stirling town
To Edinburgh blys God mak you bown.   *ready*

Lectio secunda   *Second reading*

Patriarchis, prophetis, apostillis deir,   *beloved*
Confessouris, virgynis, and martyris cleir,   *Saints; shining martyrs*
And all the saitt celestiall,   *celestial assembly*
50   Devoitlie we upone thame call   *Devoutly*

177

	That sone out of your paynis fell	*cruel pains*
	Ye may in hevin heir with us duell	*here*
	To eit swan, cran, peirtrik, and pluver,	*eat; partridge; plover*
	And everie fische that swowmis in rever;	*swims*
55	To drink withe us the new fresche wyne	
	That grew apone the revar of Ryne,	*Rhine river*
	Fresche fragrant claretis out of France,	
	Of Angeo and of Orliance,	*Anjou; Orleans*
	With mony ane cours of grit daynté.	*great delicacy*
60	Say ye amen, for chirrité.	
	Tu autem, Domine.	

Responsio

	God and Sanct Geill heir yow convoy,	*St. Giles bring you here*
	Baythe sone and weill, God and Sanct Geill,	*soon and safely*
	To sonce and seill, solace and joy,	*abundance and prosperity*
65	God and Sanct Geill heir yow convoy.	
	Iube, Domine.	

	Out of Stirling paynis fell	*cruel pains*
	In Edinburgh joy sone mot ye dwell.	*may*

Lectio tertia   *Third reading*

	We pray to all the sanctis in Hevin	*saints*
70	That ar abuif the sternis sevin,	*are above the seven spheres*
	Yow to delyver out of your pennance,	
	That ye may sone play, sing, and dance	
	And into Edinburgh mak gud cheir	
	Quhair welthe and weilfair is, but weir.	*without [a] doubt*
75	And I that dois your paynis discryve	*describe*
	Thinkis for to visie you belyve,	*see you soon*
	Nocht in desert with yow to duell,	*Not in [a] desert*
	Bot as the angell Gabriell	
	Dois go betweyne fra Hevynis glorie	
80	To thame that ar in Purgatorie,	
	And in thair tribulatioun	
	To gif thame consolatioun,	*give them*

Poem 81: Dunbar's Dirge

	And schaw thame quhone thair pane is past	*show them when*
	Thay sall to Hevin cum at the last,	*shall*
85	And how nane servis to have sweitnes	*no one deserves; sweetness*
	That never taistit bittirnes.	*tasted*
	And thairfoir how sould ye considdir	
	Of Edinburgh blys quhone ye cum hiddir,	*come hither*
	Bot gif ye taistit had befoir	*Unless*
90	Of Stirling toun the paynis soir?	*sore pains*
	And thairfoir tak in patience	
	Your pennance and your abstinence,	
	And ye sall cum or Yule begyn	*before*
	Into the blys that we ar in,	
95	Quhilk grant the glorious Trinité.	
	Say ye amen, for chirrité.	
	Tu autem, Domine.	

Responsio

	Cum hame and duell no mair in Stirling,	
	Fra hyddows hell cum hame and duell,	*From hideous*
100	Quhair fische to sell is nane bot spyrling,	*Where; spurlings*
	Cum hame and duell na mair in Stirling.	
	Iube, Domine.	

Et ne nos inducas in tentationem de Stirling
Sed libera nos a malo eiusdem.

105	*Requiem Edinburgi dona eis, Domine,*
	Et lux ipsius luceat eis.
	A porta tristitiae de Stirling
	Erue, Domine, animas et corpora eorum.
	Credo gustare vinum Edinburgi
110	*In villa viventium.*
	Requiescant statim in Edinburgo. Amen.

Domine, exaudi orationem meam
Et clamor meus ad te veniat.
Oremus.

115   *Deus qui iustos et corde humiles ex eorum tribulatione*
       liberare dignatus es: libera famulos tuos apud villam
       de Stirling versantes a penis et tristitiis eiusdem, et ad
       Edinburgi gaudia feliciter perducas. Amen.[1]

82. *The Twa Cummars*
       [*This lang Lentrin it makis me lene*]

       Richt arely one Ask Wedinsday   *Quite early on Ash Wednesday*
       Drinkande the wyne sat cummaris tua.   *two gossips*
       The tane couthe to the tothir complene,   *one did to the other*
       Granand ande suppand couth sche say: *Groaning and sipping*
5   "This lang Lentrin it makis me lene."   *Lenten season; lean*

       One couch befor the fyir sche sat.   *On [a] couch*
       God wait gif sche was gret and fat,   *God knows if*
       Yet to be feble sche did hir fene,   *pretend*
       Ay sche said, "Cummar, lat preif of that: *let's prove [the truth] of that*
10   This lang Lentrin makis me lene."

       "My fair suet cummar," quod the tothir,   *sweet friend (gossip)*
       "Ye tak that megirnes of your modir.   *inherit your slenderness from your mother*
       Ale wyne to tast sche wald disdene   *All wine; disdain*
       Bot malwasy, and nay drink uthir: *Except Malmsey; never*
15   This lang Lentryn it makis me lene."

       "Cummar, be glaid baith evin and morrow,
       The gud quharevere ye beg or borrow.[2]

---

[1] Lines 103–18: *And do not lead us into the temptation of Stirling, / But deliver us from its evil. / Give them the peace of Edinburgh, Lord, / And let its light shine upon them. / From Stirling's gate of sadness, / Lord, bring forth their souls and bodies. / I believe I shall taste the wine of Edinburgh / In the city of the living. / May they shortly be at rest in Edinburgh. Amen. / Lord, hear my prayer, / And let my cry come to Thee. / Let us pray. / God, who deigns to free the just and the humble of heart from their tribulations, release Thy servants dwelling in the town of Stirling from all its pain and sorrows, and bring them joyfully to the bliss of Edinburgh. Amen.*

[2] *For the good things in life, wherever you get them*

Poem 83: The Flyting of Dunbar and Kennedy

Fra our lang fasting youe refrene *you must refrain*
And lat your husband dre the sorrow. *endure*
20   This lang Lentryn it makis me lene."

"Your counsaile, commar, is gud," quod scho.
"Ale is to tene him that I do; *All I do is cause him to suffer*
In bed he is nocht wortht ane bane. *not worth a bean*
File anis the glas and drink me to: *Fill [at] once*
25   This lang Lentryn it makis me lene."

Of wyne out of ane chopin stoip *half-pint stoup*
Thai drank tua quartis, bot soip and soip, *sip after sip*
Of droucht sic axis did thame strene, *Of thirst such an excess; afflict*
Be thane to mend thai hed gud hoip, *By which to compensate they had high hopes*
30   That lang Lentrin suld nocht mak thaim lene.

83. *The Flyting of Dunbar and Kennedy*

"Schir Johine the Ros, ane thing thair is compild *has been written*
In generale be Kennedy and Quinting, *In general [terms] by*
Quhilk hes thameself aboif the sternis styld. *above the stars exalted*
Bot had thay maid of mannace ony mynting *If they had made; any threat*
5   In speciall, sic stryfe sould rys but stynting; *should arise without end*
Howbeit with bost thair breistis wer als bendit *Although with pride; swollen*
As Lucifer that fra the hevin discendit, *fell from heaven*
Hell sould nocht hyd thair harnis fra harmis hynting. *heads from receiving harms*

The erd sould trymbill, the firmament sould schaik, *earth; heavens; shake*
10   And all the air in vennaum suddane stink, *venom suddenly*
And all the divillis of Hell for redour quaik, *fear quake*
To heir quhat I suld wryt with pen and ynk; *hear what*
For and I flyt, sum sege for schame sould sink, *if I debate, some man*
The se sould birn, the mone sould thoill ecclippis, *sea; burn; moon; suffer*
15   Rochis sould ryfe, the warld sould hald no grippis, *Rocks would crumble; fall apart*
Sa loud of cair the commoun bell sould clynk. *loud of warning; ring*

Bot wondir laith wer I to be ane baird. *very loath were; bard*
Flyting to use richt gritly I eschame, *To engage in flyting; am ashamed*

181

	For it is nowthir wynnyng nor rewaird,	*In it is neither*
20	Bot tinsale baith of honour and of fame,	*worthless trappings*
	Incres of sorrow, sklander, and evill name.	
	Yit mycht thay be sa bald in thair bakbytting	*slanderous remarks*
	To gar me ryme and rais the feynd with flytting	*cause me to rhyme*
	And throw all cuntreis and kinrikis thame proclame."	*countries; kingdoms*

Quod Dumbar to Kennedy

25	"Dirtin Dumbar, quhome on blawis thow thy boist,	*Beshitten*
	Pretendand thee to wryte sic skaldit skrowis,	*scabrous scrolls*
	Ramowd rebald, thow fall doun att the roist	*Foul-mouthed rascal; banquet*
	My laureat lettres at thee and I lowis.	*worthy writings; if I loosed*
	Mandrag mymmerkin, maid maister bot in mows,	*Mandrake dwarf; in scorn*
30	Thrys scheild trumpir with ane threidbair goun,	*Thrice-exposed trickster*
	Say '*Deo mercy*' or I cry thee doun,	*'Mercy to God' before*
	And leif thy ryming, rebald, and thy rowis.	*cease; rascal; rolls*

	"Dreid, dirtfast dearch, that thow hes dissobeyit	*besmirched dwarf*
	My cousing Quintene and my commissar.	*cousin; deputy*
35	Fantastik fule, trest weill thow sal be fleyit.	*fool, trust; put to flight*
	Ignorant elf, aip, owll irregular,	*ape, misshapen owl*
	Skaldit skaitbird and commoun skamelar,	*Scabby scavenger; sponger*
	Wanfukkit funling that Natour maid ane yrle,	*Misconceived foundling; dwarf*
	Baith Johine the Ros and thow sall squeill and skirle	*shriek*
40	And evir I heir ocht of your making mair.	*If; hear anything more; poetry*

	"Heir I put sylence to thee in all pairtis.	*command; in all regions*
	Obey and ceis the play that thow pretendis,	*cease the game*
	Waik walidrag and werlot of the cairtis;	*Weak wastrel and cart-varlet*
	Se sone thow mak my commissar amendis,	*See [that] you soon; assistant*
45	And lat him lay sax leichis on thy lendis	*six leeches on your loins*
	Meikly in recompansing of thi scorne,	*Meekly as recompense*
	Or thow sall ban the tyme that thow wes borne:	*curse*
	For Kennedy to thee this cedull sendis."	*document*

Quod Kennedy to Dumbar

Juge in the nixt quha gat the war

182

  "Iersche brybour baird, vyle beggar with thy brattis,   *Gaelic vagabond; rags*

50 Cuntbittin crawdoun Kennedy, coward of kynd,   *Impotent craven; by nature*

  Evill-farit and dryit as Denseman on the rattis,   *Ill-treated; dried; Danishman; wheel*

  Lyk as the gleddis had on thy gulesnowt dynd,   *kites had dined on your nose (see note)*

  Mismaid monstour, ilk mone owt of thy mynd,   *Misshapen; like a lunatic*

  Renunce, rebald, thy rymyng, thow bot royis.   *raves*

55 Thy trechour tung hes tane ane Heland strynd,   *has assumed a Highland manner*

  Ane Lawland ers wald mak a bettir noyis.   *A Lowland arse would*

  "Revin raggit ruke, and full of rebaldrie,   *Torn ragged rook*

  Skitterand scorpioun, scauld in scurrilitie,   *Befouling; scold*

  I se the haltane in thy harlotrie   *haughtiness*

60 And into uthir science nothing slie,   *learning not at all skilled*

  Of every vertew voyd, as men may sie.   *see*

  Quytclame clergie and cleik to thee ane club,   *Renounce learning; snatch*

  Ane baird blasphemar in brybrie ay to be,   *A blasphemous bard; beggary*

  For wit and woisdome ane wisp fra thee may rub.   *a wisp [of straw]*

65 "Thow speiris, dastard, gif I dar with thee fecht.   *ask, villain, if; fight*

  Ye, Dagone dowbart, thairof haif thow no dowt.   *Yes, vile Dagon dimwit; doubt*

  Quhairevir we meit, thairto my hand I hecht,   *meet; pledge*

  To red thy rebald rymyng with a rowt.   *get rid of; blow*

  Throw all Bretane it sal be blawin owt,   *Throughout Britain; announced*

70 How that thow, poysonit pelour, gat thy paikis.   *envenomed thief; got whipped*

  With ane doig leich I schepe to gar thee schowt   *dog leash I intend to make you shout*

  And nowther to thee tak knyfe, swerd, nor aix.   *neither*

  "Thow crop and rute of tratouris tressonable,   *(i.e., extreme example)*

  The fathir and moder of morthour and mischeif,   *murder and wrongdoing*

75 Dissaitfull tyrand with serpentis tung unstable,   *Deceitful tyrant*

  Cukcald, cradoun cowart, and commoun thief,   *Cuckold, craven coward*

  Thow purpest for to undo our lordis cheif   *attempted*

  In Paislay with ane poysone that wes fell,   *poison; deadly*

  For quhilk, brybour, yit sall thow thoill a breif.   *vagabond; be summoned*

80 Pelour, on thee I sall it preif mysell.   *Robber; prove myself*

  "Thocht I wald lie, thy frawart phisnomy   *(I.e., even if I'm lying); vile body*

  Dois manifest thy malice to all men.   *reveal your maliciousness*

  Fy, tratour theif, fy, glengoir loun, fy, fy!   *syphilitic ruffian*

	Fy, feyndly front far fowlar than ane fen,	*fiendish face; fouler; midden*
85	My freyindis thow reprovit with thy pen.	*friends; accused*
	Thow leis, tratour, quhilk I sall on thee preif,	*lie; prove*
	Suppois thy heid war armit tymis ten,	*Even if; head; ten times*
	Thow sall recry it, or thy croun sall cleif.	*retract; head shall be split*

"Or thow durst move thy mynd malitius,   *Before you dared speak; malicious*
90   Thow saw the saill abone my heid up draw.   *sail above; was raised*
Bot Eolus, full woid, and Neptunus,   *quite fierce*
Mirk and moneles us met with wind and waw,   *Dark and moonless; wave*
And mony hundreth myll hyne cowd us blaw,   *miles hence did us blow*
By Holland, Seland, Yetland, and Northway coist,   *Zeeland, Shetland; Norway*
95   In sey desert quhair we wer famist aw.   *[the] wild sea; all famished*
Yit come I hame, fals baird, to lay thy boist.   *to put an end to*

"Thow callis thee rethore with thy goldin lippis.   *yourself a rhetorician*
Na, glowrand gaipand fule, thow art begyld.   *staring gaping fool; deceived*
Thow art bot gluntoch, with thy giltin hippis,   *knobby-kneed (?); kilted hips (?)*
100   That for thy lounry mony a leisch hes fyld.   *villainy; lash has received*
Wan-visaged widdefow, out of thy wit gane wyld,   *Dark-faced corpse*
Laithly and lowsy, als lauchtane as ane leik,   *lice-ridden; loathsome; leek*
Sen thow with wirschep wald sa fane be styld,   *Since; would so happily; styled*
Haill, soverane senyeour, thy bawis hingis throw thy breik.[1]

105   "Forworthin fule, of all the warld reffuse,   *Deformed fool; rejected*
Quhat ferly is thocht thow rejoys to flyte?   *What a marvel it is*
Sic eloquence as thay in Erschry use,   *Gaelic-speaking areas*
In sic is sett thy thraward appetyte.   *perverse*
Thow hes full littill feill of fair indyte.   *sense of good writing*
110   I tak on me ane pair of Lowthiane hippis   *I suggest that; Lothian*
Sall fairar Inglis mak and mair parfyte   *Shall; English*
Than thow can blabbar with thy Carrik lippis.   *(i.e., Ayrshire)*

"Bettir thow ganis to leid ane doig to skomer,   *are suited; dog to poop*
Pynit pykpuris pelour, than with thy maister pingill.   *Starved thief; strive*
115   Thow lay full prydles in the peis this somer   *peas; summer*

---

[1] *Hail, sovereign lord, your balls hang out through your breeches*

	And fane at evin for to bring hame a single,	*small bundle*
	Syne rubb it at aneuther auld wyvis ingle.	*hearth*
	Bot now in winter for purteth thow art traikit,	*poverty; wasted*
	Thow hes na breik to latt thy bellokis gyngill,	*breeches; testicles jingle*
120	Beg thee ane bratt, for baird, thow sall go naikit.	*cloak*

	"Lene, larbar loungeour, lowsy in lisk and longe,[1]	
	Fy, skolderit skyn, thow art bot skyre and skrumple:	*sunburned; creased; wrinkled*
	For he that rostit Lawrance had thy grunye,	*roasted St. Lawrence; snout*
	And he that hid Sanct Johnis ene with ane wimple,	*eyes*
125	And he that dang Sanct Augustyne with ane rumple	*struck; fish tail*
	Thy fowll front had, and he that Bartilmo flaid.	*foul face; St. Bartholomew*
	The gallowis gaipis eftir thy graceles gruntill,	*nose*
	As thow wald for ane haggeis, hungry gled.	*haggis; kite*

	"Cummerwarld crawdoun, na man comptis thee ane kers.[2]	
130	Sueir swappit swanky, swynekeper ay for swaittis,	*Lazy drunken lout; beer*
	Thy commissar, Quintyne, biddis thee cum kis his ers.	*assistant; arse*
	He luvis nocht sic ane forlane loun of laittis,	*useless uncouth fool*
	He sayis thow skaffis and beggis mair beir and aitis	*scrounge; beg; beer and oats*
	Nor ony cripill in Karrik land abowt.	*Than; Carrick*
135	Uther pure beggaris and thow for wage debaittis,	*poor*
	Decrepit karlingis on Kennedy cryis owt.	*old women*

	"Mater annwche I haif, I bid not fenyie,	*enough; I need not pretend*
	Thocht thow, fowll trumpour, thus upoun me leid.	*vile trickster; have lied*
	Corrupt carioun, he sall I cry my senyie.	*loudly; my war-cry*
140	Thinkis thow nocht how thow come in grit neid,	*Have you forgotten*
	Greitand in Galloway lyk to ane gallow breid,	*Weeping; gallows bred*
	Ramand and rolpand, beggand koy and ox.	*Yelling and croaking; cow*
	I saw thee thair into thy wathemanis weid,	*poacher's garb*
	Quhilk wes nocht worth ane pair of auld gray sox.	

145	"Ersch katherene, with thy polk breik and rilling,	*Gaelic robber; bag; shoes*
	Thow and thy quene as gredy gleddis ye gang	*wench like greedy kites you travel*

---

[1] *Lean, impotent lay-about, louse-ridden in groin and loin*

[2] *Useless coward, no one accounts you [to be worth] a piece of cress*

	With polkis to mylne and beggis baith meill and schilling.	*bags to mill; husks*
	Thair is bot lys and lang nailis yow amang,	*lice*
	Fowll heggirbald, for henis thus will ye hang.	*hedgebreaking thief (?); hens*
150	Thow hes ane perrellus face to play with lambis.	*scary*
	Ane thowsand kiddis, wer thay in faldis full strang,	*young goats; pens (folds)*
	Thy lymmair luke wald fle thame and thair damis.	*awful gaze; scare; mothers*
	"Intill ane glen thow hes, owt of repair,	
	Ane laithly luge that wes the lippir menis.	*loathly lodge; lepers*
155	With thee ane sowtaris wyfe of blis als bair,	*cobbler's*
	And lyk twa stalkaris steilis in cokis and henis.	*steal cocks and hens*
	Thow plukkis the pultré and scho pullis of the penis.	*poultry; she pulls off; feathers*
	All Karrik cryis, 'God gif this dowsy be drownd!'	*God grant; slut to be*
	And quhen thow heiris ane guse cry in the glenis,	*a goose; glens*
160	Thow thinkis it swetar than sacryne bell of sound.	*sacred*
	"Thow Lazarus, thow laithly lene tramort,	*lean corpse*
	To all the warld thow may example be,	
	To luk upoun thy gryslie, peteous port;	*grisly, pitiful face*
	For hiddowis, haw, and holkit is thyne ee,	*dark, and hollow; eye*
165	Thy cheikbane bair and blaiknit is thy ble.	*cheekbones; darkened; complexion*
	Thy choip, thy choll garris men for to leif chest;	*jaw; jowls cause; live chastely*
	Thy gane, it garris us think that we mon de.	*face; reminds us that we must die*
	I conjure thee, thow hungert Heland gaist.	*summon; famished Highland ghost*
	"The larbar linkis of thy lang lenye craig,	*feeble bones; lean neck*
170	Thy pure pynit thrott, peilit and owt of ply,	*skinny; pealed and crooked*
	Thy skolderit skin, hewd lyk ane saffrone bag,	*sunburnt; colored; yellow*
	Garris men dispyt thar flesche, thow spreit of Gy.	*Makes; despise their; ghost of Gy*
	Fy, feyndly front, fy, tykis face, fy, fy!	*fiendish face; cur's*
	Ay loungand lyk ane loikman on ane ledder	*waiting; hangman; ladder*
175	With hingit luik, ay wallowand upone wry,	*hanged look; moving crookedly*
	Lyk to ane stark theif glowrand in ane tedder.	*staring; noose*
	"Nyse nagus nipcaik with thy schulderis narrow,	*Foolish stingy cheapskate (miser)*
	Thow lukis lowsy, loun of lounis aw,	*look lice-ridden, fool of all fools*
	Hard hurcheoun hirpland, hippit as ane harrow,	*hobbling hedgehog, [with] hips*
180	Thy rigbane rattillis and thy ribbis on raw,	*backbone; [show] in rows*
	Thy hanchis hirklis with hukebanis harth and haw,	*hipbones rough and coarse*

Thy laithly lymis ar lene as ony treis.   *loathly limbs; trees*
Obey, theif baird, or I sall brek thy gaw.   *spirit*
Fowll carrybald, cry mercy on thy kneis.   *monster; knees*

185   "Thow pure, pynhippit, ugly averill   *pitiful, thin-hipped; nag*
With hurkland banis holkand throw thy hyd,   *moving bones poking through*
Reistit and crynit as hangit man on hill,   *Dried and shriveled*
And oft beswakkit with ane ourhie tyd   *drenched; high tide*
Quhilk brewis mekle barret to thy bryd.   *causes much distress; bride*
190   Hir cair is all to clenge thy cabroch howis,   *cleanse; scraggy hocks*
Quhair thow lyis sawsy in saphron, bak and syd,   *lie coated in yellow*
Powderit with prymros, savrand all with clowis.   *scented; cloves*

"Forworthin wirling, I warne thee, it is wittin   *Misshapen wretch (?); known*
How, skyttand skarth, thow hes the hurle behind.   *befouled monster; diarrhea*
195   Wan wraiglane wasp, ma wormis hes thow beschittin   *wriggling; more*
Nor thair is gers on grund or leif on lind.   *Than there is grass on ground; leaf on tree*
Thocht thow did first sic foly to me fynd,   *such filth attribute to me*
Thow sall agane with ma witnes than I.   *more witnesses*
Thy gulsoch gane dois on thy bak it bind,   *jaundiced face proves it*
200   Thy hostand hippis lattis nevir thy hos go dry.   *spewing hips; hose*

"Thow held the burch lang with ane borrowit goun   *remained in the burgh*
And ane caprowsy barkit all with sweit,   *garment darkened by sweat*
And quhen the laidis saw thee sa lyk a loun,   *lads; rascal*
Thay bickerit thee with mony bae and bleit.   *heckled; baa and bleat*
205   Now upaland thow leivis on rubbit quheit,   *live on rubbed wheat*
Oft for ane caus thy burdclaith neidis no spredding   *tablecloth*
For thow hes nowthir for to drink nor eit,   *nothing*
Bot lyk ane berdles baird that had no bedding.   *beardless bard*

"Strait Gibbonis air, that nevir ourstred ane hors,   *heir; rode upon*
210   Bla, berfute berne, in bair tyme wes thow borne.   *Bluish, barefoot man; bleak*
Thow bringis the Carrik clay to Edinburgh Cors,   *Cross*
Upoun thy botingis hobland, hard as horne.   *hobbling boots*
Stra wispis hingis owt quhair that the wattis ar worne.   *welts*
Cum thow agane to skar us with thy strais,   *scare; straws*
215   We sall gar scale our sculis all thee to scorne   *dismiss; schools*
And stane thee up the calsay quhair thow gais.   *stone; street; goes*

"Of Edinburch the boyis as beis owt thrawis   *boys like bees; throng*
And cryis owt, 'Hay, heir cumis our awin queir clerk!'   *strange*
Than fleis thow lyk ane howlat chest with crawis   *owlet chased by crows*
220 Quhill all the bichis at thy botingis dois bark.   *dogs; skin-boots*
Than carlingis cryis, 'Keip curches in the merk —
Our gallowis gaipis — lo, quhair ane greceles gais!'[1]
Aneuthir sayis, 'I se him want ane sark —   *shirt*
I reid yow, cummer, tak in your lynning clais.'   *advise; friend; linens*

225 "Than rynis thow doun the gait with gild of boyis   *road; cries*
And all the toun tykis hingand in thy heilis.   *dogs clinging to; heels*
Of laidis and lownis thair rysis sic ane noyis   *lads and wastrels*
Quhill runsyis rynis away with cairt and quheilis   *horses run; wheels*
And cager aviris castis bayth coillis and creilis   *horses; coals; baskets*
230 For rerd of thee and rattling of thy butis.   *clamor; boots*
Fische wyvis cryis 'Fy!' and castis doun skillis and skeilis,   *baskets; tubs*
Sum claschis thee, sum cloddis thee on the cutis.   *strikes; pelts; ankles*

"Loun lyk Mahoun, be boun me till obey,   *Fiendish rascal; prepared*
Theif, or in greif mischeif sall thee betyd.
235 Cry grace, tykis-face, or I thee chece and fley,   *dog-face, before I chase you and skin*
Oule, rare and yowle, I sall defowll thy pryd,   *Owl, roar and howl*
Peilit gled, baith fed and bred of bichis syd   *Plucked kite; from a dog*
And lyk ane tyk, purspyk, quhat man settis by thee!   *cur, pickpurse; values you*
Forflittin, countbittin, beschittin, barkit hyd,
240 Clym ledder, fyle tedder, foule edder, I defy thee![2]

"Mauch muttoun, byt buttoun, peilit gluttoun, air to Hilhous,
Rank beggar, ostir dregar, flay fleggar in the flet.[3]
Chittirlilling, ruch rilling, lik schilling in the milhous,

---

[1] Lines 221–22: *Then old women cry, "Keep your kerchiefs (finery) hidden (in the dark) — / Our gallows gape (i.e., are empty) — lo, where an ill-favored loser lurks (goes)!"*

[2] Lines 239–40: *Outdone in flytting, poxed (cunt-bitten/impotent/infected by venereal disease), filthy (beshitten), scruffy (hardened skin), / Ladder-climber (i.e., one about to be executed), one who befouls the hangman's noose, loathsome (vile, plague-infected) adder, I defy you*

[3] Lines 241–42: *Maggoty sheep, nipple-biter, naked glutton, heir to a sheepshed (?), / Nasty-smelling beggar, oyster dredger, flea infestation in the hall*

Baird rehator, theif of nator, fals tratour, feyindis gett,[1]

245   Filling of tauch, rak sauch — cry crauch, thow art oursett!

Muttoun dryver, girnall ryver, yadswyvar, fowll fell thee![2]

Herretyk, lunatyk, purspyk, carlingis pet,   *old woman's fart*

Rottin crok, dirtin dok — cry cok, or I sall quell thee!"   *ewe, befouled arse; kill*

                 Quod Dumbar to Kennedy

"Dathane, deivillis sone, and dragone dispitous,   *Dathan; cruel*

250   Abironis birth and bred with Beliall,   *Abiron's child*

Wod werwoif, worme, and scorpion vennemous,   *Insane werewolf, reptile*

Lucifers laid, fowll feyindis face infernall,   *lad*

Sodomyt syphareit fra sanctis celestiall,   *separated from celestial saints*

Put I nocht sylence to thee, schiphird knaif?   *shepherd's knave*

255   And thow of new begynis to ryme and raif.   *anew; rhyme and rave*

Thow sal be maid blait, bleir eit bestiall.   *meek (sheep-like), bleary-eyed beast*

"How thy forbear is come I haif a feill: *forebear was born; notion*

At Cokburnispeth, the writ makis me war,   *Cockburnspath; aware*

Generit betuix ane scho-beir and a deill,   *Engendered by a she-bear; devil*

260   Sa wes he callit Dewlbeir and nocht Dumbar.   *Devil-bear*

This Dewlbeir, generit on a meir of Mar,   *mare of Mar*

Wes Corspatrik, erle of Merche, and be illusioun.   *Patrick, Earl of March; by*

The first that evir put Scotland to confusioun

Wes that fals tratour, hardely say I dar.   *boldly I dare to say*

265   "Quhen Bruce and Balioll differit for the croun,   *disputed*

Scottis lordis could nocht obey Inglis lawis.   *English laws*

This Corspatrik betrasit Berwik toun   *betrayed*

And slew sevin thousand Scottismen within thay wawis.   *those walls*

The battall syne of Spottismuir he gart caus,   *afterward; caused*

270   And come with Edwart Langschankis to the field   *Edward Longshanks*

Quhair twelf thowsand trew Scottismen wer keild   *Where*

And Wallace chest, as the carnicle schawis.   *chased; chronicle*

---

[1] Lines 243–44: *Pig guts, ill-made shoe, chaff-licker in the millhouse, / Villainous "poet," born thief, false traitor, spawn of a fiend*

[2] Lines 245–46: *Tallow-stuffing, stretched sack (i.e., gallows bird) — epitome of defeat (cry "beaten"), you are overcome! / Mutton driver, grain thief, mare humper, evil befall you*

"Scottis lordis chiftanis he gart hald and chessone   *held and accused*
In firmance fast quhill all the feild wes done,   *custody*
275   Within Dumbar, that auld spelunk of tressoun.   *den*
Sa Inglis tykis in Scottland wes abone.   *dogs; were in charge*
Than spulyeit thay the haly stane of Scone,   *stole; holy stone*
The croce of Halyrudhous, and uthir jowellis.   *cross; other jewels*
He birnis in Hell — body, banis, and bowellis —   *burns; bones*
280   This Corspatrik that Scotland hes undone.

"Wallace gart cry ane counsale into Pert   *summoned; Perth*
And callit Corspatrik tratour be his style.   *by his title*
That dampnit dragone drew him in disert   *damned; approached; desert*
And sayd he kend bot Wallace, king in Kyle.   *knew only*
285   Out of Dumbar that theif he maid exyle   *exiled*
Unto Edward and Inglis grund agane.
Tigiris, serpentis, and taidis will remane   *tigers; toads; remain*
In Dumbar wallis, todis, wolffis, and beistis wyle.   *foxes; wily beasts*

"Na fowlis of effect amangis tha binkis   *birds of value; those mounds*
290   Biggis nor abydis, for nothing that may be.   *Builds or dwells*
Thay stanis of tressone as the bruntstane stinkis.   *Those stones; brimstone*
Dewlbeiris moder, cassin in by the se   *Devil-bear's mother, cast; sea*
The wariet apill of the forbiddin tre   *accursed apple*
That Adame eit quhen he tint Parradyce,   *ate when he lost Paradise*
295   Scho eit, invennomit lyk a cokkatryce,   *She ate, poisonous*
Syne merreit with the divill for dignité.   *Then married*

"Yit of new tressone I can tell thee tailis   *tales*
That cumis on nycht in visioun in my sleip: *come at night*
Archebauld Dumbar betrasd the hous of Hailis   *betrayed*
300   Becaus the yung lord had Dumbar to keip;   *protect*
Pretendand throw that to thair rowmis to creip,   *Pretending through; rooms*
Rycht crewaly his castell he persewit,   *cruelly; attacked*
Brocht him furth boundin and the place reskewit,   *recovered*
Sett him in fetteris in ane dungeoun deip.

305   "It war aganis bayth natur and gud ressoun   *was against*
That Dewlbeiris bairnis wer trew to God or man,   *Devil-bear's children*
Quhilkis wer baith gottin, borne, and bred with tressoun,   *begotten*

Belgebubbis oyis and curst Corspatrikis clan.   *Beelzebub's offspring*
Thow wes prestyt and ordanit be Sathan   *made a priest; ordained by*
310 For to be borne to do thy kin defame   *disgrace*
And gar me schaw thy antecessouris schame.   *cause me to show*
Thy kin that leivis may wary thee and ban.   *lives; curse*

"Sen thow on me thus, lymmer, leis and trattillis,   *rascal, lies; chatters*
And fyndis sentence foundit of invy,   *invent statements stemming from envy*
315 Thy elderis banis ilk nycht rysis and rattillis: *banished elders each; cry*
Apon thy cors vengeance, vengeance thay cry —   *body*
Thow art the cause thay may not rest nor ly.
Thow sais for thame few psaltris, psalmis, or credis   *say*
Bot geris me tell thair trentalis of mysdedis   *make; trental masses*
320 And thair ald sin wyth new schame certify.

"Insensuate sow, cesse, false Eustase air,   *Unfeeling sow, cease; heir*
And knaw, kene scald, I hald of Alathya,   *bold liar; hold with*
And cause me not the cause lang to declare   *long list*
Of thy curst kyn, Deulber and his allya.   *Devil-bear; allies*
325 Cum to the Croce on kneis and mak a crya,   *Cross; knees; public statement*
Confesse thy crime, hald Kenydy the king,
And wyth ane hauthorne scurge thyself and dyng.   *strike*
Thus dree thy penaunce wyth *deliquisti quia*.   *suffer; because you have sinned*

"Pas to my commissare and be confest,   *deputy; confessed*
330 Cour before him on kneis and cum in will,   *Cower; be humble*
And syne ger Stobo for thy lyf protest.   *then make*
Renounce thy rymis, bath ban and birn thy bill,[1]
Heve to the hevyn thy handis ande hald thee still.   *Raise*
Do thou not thus, bogane, thou sal be brynt   *If you do not do this, fellow; burnt*
335 Wyth pik, fire, ter, gun puldre, and lynt   *pitch; tar; flax*
On Arthuris Sete or on ane hyar hyll.   *Arthur's Seat; higher hill*

"I perambalit of Pernaso the montayn,   *walked upon; mountain*
Enspirit wyth Mercury fra his goldyn spere,   *Inspired by; sphere*
And dulcely drank of eloquence the fontayne   *sweetly; fountain*

---

[1] *Retract your poems, both ban and burn thy letter.*

340 Quhen it was purifit wyth frost and flowit clere.
     And thou come, fule, in Marche or Februere   *fool*
     Thare till a pule and drank the padok rod   *pool; toad spawn*
     That gerris the ryme into thy termes glod   *makes; gluey figures (?)*
     And blaberis that noyis mennis eris to here.   *blabs what annoys men's ears*

345 "Thou lufis nane Irische, elf, I understand,   *You have no love for Gaelic*
     Bot it suld be all trew Scottis mennis lede.   *language*
     It was the gud langage of this land
     And Scota it causit to multiply and sprede   *Scota (a woman)*
     Quhill Corspatrik, that we of tresoun rede,   *Until; speak*
350 Thy forefader, maid Irisch and Irisch men thin,
     Throu his tresoun broght Inglise rumplis in.   *English rumps (fish tails)*
     Sa wald thyself, mycht thou to him succede.

     "Ignorant fule, into thy mowis and mokis   *fool; foolery and mocking*
     It may be verifyit that thy wit is thin;
355 Quhare thou writis 'Densmen dryit apon the rattis,' *Danes dried upon the wheel*
     Densmen of Denmark ar of the kingis kyn.
     The wit thou suld have had was castin in
     Evyn at thyne ers bakwart wyth a staf slong.   *Totally; arse; sling staff*
     Herefore, false harlot hursone, hald thy tong,   *Therefore; whoreson*
360 Deulbere, thou devis the devill thyne eme wyth dyn. *deafens; uncle; noise*

     "Quhareas thou said that I stall hennis and lammys, *Whereas; stole hens; lambs*
     I latt thee witt I have land, store, and stakkis.   *know; stores, and stacks*
     Thou wald be fayn to gnaw, lad, wyth thy gammys   *happy; jaws*
     Under my burd smoch banis behynd doggis bakkis.   *table smashed bones (?)*
365 Thou has a tome purs, I have stedis and takkis;   *empty; farms and holdings*
     Thou tynt cultur, I have cultur and pleuch.   *lack [a] plowshare; the whole plow*
     For substance and gere thou has a wedy teuch   *property; hangman's noose*
     On Mount Falcoun about thy crag to rax.   *neck to stretch*

     "And yit Mount Falcoun gallowis is our fair   *too good*
370 For to be fylde wyth sik a fruteles face.   *defiled by such a worthless*
     Cum hame and hyng on oure gallowis of Aire —   *hang*
     To erd thee undir it I sall purchas grace;   *bury; permission*
     To ete thy flesch the doggis sall have na space,

192

The ravyns sall ryve nathing bot thy tong rutis.[1]

375   For thou sik malice of thy maister mutis,   *mutters*
        It is wele sett that thou sik barat brace.   *fitting; such agony embrace*

        "Small fynance amang thy frendis thou beggit
        To stanch the storm wyth haly muldis thou loste.   *calm; holy ashes*
        Thou sailit to get a dowcare for to dreg it,   *tried; diver; dredge*
380   It lyis closit in a clout on Seland cost.   *lies enclosed; cloth; coast*
        Sik reule gerris thee be servit wyth cald rost   *conduct caused; cold roast*
        And sitt unsoupit oft beyond the sey   *unfed; sea*
        Criant "*caritas*," at duris, "*amore Dei*,"[2]
        Barefut, brekeles, and all in duddis updost.   *pantsless; tattered clothes*

385   "Deulbere has not ado wyth a Dunbar.   *nothing to do*
        The erlis of Murray bure that surname ryght,   *earls; bore; properly*
        That evyr trew to the king and constant ware,
        And of that kyn come Dunbar of Westfelde knyght.
        That successione is hardy, wyse, and wicht   *brave*
390   And has nathing ado now wyth the Devile.
        Bot Deulbere is thy kyn and kennis thee wele
        And has in Hell for thee a chaumir dicht.   *chamber readied*

        "Cursit croapand craw, I sall ger crop thy tong   *Cursed croaking crow; snip*
        And thou sall cry *cor mundum* on thy kneis.   *clean heart; knees*
395   Duerch, I sall dyng thee quhill thou dryte and dong,   *Dwarf; hit; until; poop*
        And thou sal lik thy lippis and suere thou leis.   *lick; swear; lies*
        I sall degrade thee, graceles, of thy greis,   *take from you, villain; degrees*
        Scaile thee for scorne and shere thee of thy scule,   *Strip; remove; learning*
        Ger round thy hede, transforme thee till a fule,   *Shave around; fool*
400   And syne for tresone trone thee to the treis.   *tie you to the gallows (?)*

        "Raw-mowit ribald, renegate rehatour,   *Foul-mouthed ruffian, villainous renegade*
        My linage and forebearis war ay lele.   *were always loyal*
        It cumis of kynde to thee to be a traytoure,   *comes naturally for*
        To ryde on nycht, to rug, to reve and stele.   *grab; take*

---

[1] *The ravens shall tear nothing except your tongue's roots (i.e., throat)*

[2] *Crying "charity," at doors, "by the love of God"*

405   Quhare thou puttis poysoun to me, I appelle[1]
        Thee in that part — preve it, pelour, wyth thy persone!   *prove it, thief*
        Clame not to clergy, I defy thee, gersone.   *benefit of clergy; fellow*
        Thou sall by it dere wyth me, duerche, and thou dele.[2]

        "In Ingland, oule, suld be thyne habitacione.   *owl*
410   Homage to Edward Langschankis maid thy kyn,   *made*
        In Dunbar thai ressavit hym, the false nacione: *people*
        Thay suld be exilde Scotland, mare and myn.   *exiled [from]; each and all*
        A stark gallowis, a wedy, and a pyn   *rope; peg*
        The hede poynt of thyne elderis armes ar,   *coat of arms are*
415   Wryttyn abone in poesi: "Hang Dunbar,   *above in verse*
        Quarter and draw, and mak that surname thin!"   *few in number*

        "I am the kingis blude, his trew speciall clerk
        That nevir yit ymaginit hym offense,   *imagined offending him*
        Constant in myn allegeance, word, and werk,
420   Onely dependand on his excellence,
        Traistand to have of his magnificence   *Trusting*
        Guerdoun, reward, and benefice bedene   *Recompense; benefice wholly*
        Quhen that the ravyns sal ryve out bath thine ene   *peck; eyes*
        And on the rattis sal be thy residence.   *wheel of execution*

425   "Fra Etrike Forest furthward to Drumfrese   *Ettrick Forest; Dumfries*
        Thou beggit wyth a pardoun in all kirkis   *churches*
        Collapis, cruddis, mele, grotis, grisis, and geis,   *Meat, curds, meal, grain, herbs; geese*
        And onder nycht quhile stall thou staggis and stirkis.   *at night stole; livestock*
        Because that Scotland of thy begging irkis,   *grows weary*
430   Thou scapis in France to be a knycht of the felde;   *escape into*
        Thou has thy clamschellis and thy burdoun kelde —   *clamshells; staff*
        Unhonest wayis all, wolroun, that thou wirkis.   *rascal (?)*

        "Thou may not pas Mount Barnard for wilde bestis,   *beasts*
        Nor wyn throu Mount Scarpre for the snawe;
435   Mount Nycholas, Mount Godart — thare arestis   *captures*

---

[1] *Whereas you accuse me of poisoning, I charge*

[2] *You shall buy it dearly, dwarf, if you deal with me*

194

	Brigantis sik bois and blyndis thame wyth a blawe.	*Robbers such lads [as you]; blow*
	In Parise wyth the maister buriawe	*Paris; hangman*
	Abyde, and be his prentice nere the bank,	*apprentice near*
	And help to hang the pece for half a frank,	*each one*
440	And at the last thyself sall thole the lawe.	*suffer*
	"Haltane harlot, the devill have gude thou hais!	*Haughty rogue; have the goods*
	For fault of puissance, pelour, thou mon pak thee.	*lack of money, thief; flee*
	Thou drank thy thrift, sald and wedsett thy clais.	*earnings, sold; pawned; clothes*
	Thare is na lorde that will in service tak thee.	
445	A pak of flaskynnis fynance for to mak thee	*flea-skins*
	Thou sall ressave in Danskyn, of my tailye;	*Danzig; reckoning*
	With *De profundis* fend thee, and that failye,[1]	
	And I sall send the blak devill for to bak thee.	*support*
	"Into the Katryne thou maid a foule cahute,	*Katherine (a ship); made a foul cabin*
450	For thou bedrate hir doun fra starn to stere.	*befouled her from stem to stern*
	Apon hir sydis was sene thou coud schute —	*did "shoot" (excrete)*
	Thy dirt clevis till hir towis this twenty yere.	*excrement adheres; ropes*
	The firmament na firth was nevir cler	*sky nor estuary*
	Quhill thou, Deulbere, devillis birth, was on the see.	*spawn; sea*
455	The saulis had sonkyn throu the syn of thee	*souls*
	War not the peple maid sa grete prayere.	*Had not*
	"Quhen that the schip was saynit and undir saile,	*signed (blessed)*
	Foul brow, in holl thou preposit for to pas.	*face; ship's hold; intended*
	Thou schot and was not sekir of thy tayle,	*vomited; firmer of your behind*
460	Beschate the stere, the compas, and the glas.	*Befouled the helm*
	The skippar bad ger land thee at the Bas.	*ordered you off at Bass Rock*
	Thou spewit and kest out mony a lathly lomp	*cast out; loathly lump*
	Fastar than all the marynaris coud pomp,	*mariners could pump*
	And now thy wame is wers than evir it was.	*belly*
465	"Had thai bene prouvait sa of schote of gune	*provided*
	By men of were, but perile thay had past.	*war, without equal; surpassed*
	As thou was louse and redy of thy bune,	*loose; rear-end*

---

[1] *With "Out of the depths" defend yourself, and [if] that fails*

	Thay mycht have tane the collum at the last,	*captured the ship (?)*
	For thou wald cuk a cartfull at a cast.	*excrete*
470	Thare is na schip that wil thee now ressave,	*receive*
	Thou fylde faster than fyftenesum mycht lawe,	*defiled; fifteen; clean up*
	And myrit thaym wyth thy muk to the myd-mast.	*soiled; muck; mid-mast*

	"Throu Ingland, thef, and tak thee to thy fute,	*[Go] through England; feet*
	And boun with thee to have a false botwand.	*prepare; riding-crop (?)*
475	A horse marschall thou call thee at the mute	*law-court*
	And with that craft convoy thee throu the land.	
	Be nathing argh, tak ferily on hand.	*not hesitant, go briskly*
	Happyn thou to be hangit in Northumbir,	*If it happens that you are hanged*
	Than all thy kyn ar wele quyte of thy cumbir,	*Then; kin will be well rid; encumbrance*
480	And that mon be thy dome, I undirstand.	*must be your fate*

	"Hye souverane lorde, lat nevir this synfull sot	*fool*
	Do schame fra hame unto your nacion!	*at home*
	Lat nevir nane sik ane be callit a Scot,	*such [a] one*
	A rottyn crok, louse of the dok, thare doun!	*diseased ewe, loose of the bowels*
485	Fra honest folk devoide this lathly lown	*cast out this loathsome rascal*
	In sum desert quhare thare is na repaire;	*from which there is no escape*
	For fylyng and infecking of the aire,	*defiling and infecting*
	Cary this cankerit corrupt carioun.	*Take away*

	"Thou was consavit in the grete eclips,	*conceived during*
490	A monstir maid be god Mercurius,	*by*
	Na hald agayn, na hoo is at thy hips.	*Nor held; no halt*
	Infortunate, false, and furius,	*Ill-fortuned; violent*
	Evill-schryvin, wanthryvin, not clene na curius,	*Unforgiven, undergrown; nor skilled*
	A myten full of flyting, flyrdom like,	*A quarrelsome dwarf, an object of scorn*
495	A crabbit, scabbit, evill facit messan tyke,	*crabby, scabby, ugly lapdog*
	A schit but wit, schir and injurius.	*A shit without wit, vacant (?); harmful*

	"Greit in the glaykis, gude maister Gilliam gukkis,	*trickery; William the fool*
	Our imperfyte in poetry or in prose.	*Overly flawed*
	All clocis undir cloud of nycht thou cukkis.	*Enclosed; defecates*
500	Rymis thou of me, of rethory the rose?	*Do you write about me; rhetoric*
	Lunatike lymare luschbald, louse thy hose	*Crazy drunken fool (?), loose*
	That I may touch thy tone wyth tribulation	*bottom; affliction*

	In recompensing of thy conspiration,	*conspiracy*
	Or turse thee out of Scotland — tak thy chose!	*take yourself*
505	"Ane benefice quha wald gyve sic ane beste	*who would give to such a beast*
	Bot gif it war to gyngill Judas bellis?	*Unless; jingle Judas' bells*
	Tak thee a fidill or a floyte, and geste!	*flute; play*
	Undought, thou art ordanyt to not ellis.	*worthless fellow; nothing else*
	Thy cloutit cloke, thy skryp, and thy clamschellis	*patched; pilgrim's wallet*
510	Cleke on thy cors, and fare on into France,	*Put on thy body; go*
	And cum thou nevir agayn but a mischance.	*without misfortune*
	The Fend fare wyth thee forthward our the fellis.	*The Devil; over the hills*
	"Cankrit Caym, tryit trowane Tutivillus,	*Poisonous Cain; truant fiend*
	Marmaidyn, mymerken, monstir of all men,	*Mermaid, dwarf*
515	I sall ger bake thee to the lard of Hillhouse	*have you baked for the lord*
	To suelly thee in stede of a pullit hen.	*swallow; plucked*
	Fowmart, fasert, fostirit in filth and fen,	*Polecat, coward; midden*
	Foule fond, flend fule, apon thy phisnom fy!	*Vile fool; face*
	Thy dok of dirt drepis and will nevir dry,	*arse drips with excrement*
520	To tume thy tone it has tyrit carlingis ten.	*scrub your bottom; tired out ten old women*
	"Conspiratour, cursit cocatrice, hell caa,	*hellish jackdaw*
	Turk trumpour, traitour, tyran intemperate,	*Fiendish deceiver (Infidel)*
	Thou irefull attircop, Pilate *apostata*,	*angry spider; misbeliever*
	Judas, Jow, juglour, Lollard laureate,	*Jew, conjurer, chief heretic*
525	Sarazene, Symonyte provit, pagane pronunciate,	*Saracen, Simonite; declared pagan*
	Machomete, manesuorne, bugrist abhominabile,	*Devil, perjurer, buggerer*
	Devill, dampnit dog, sodomyte insatiable,	
	With Gog and Magog grete glorificate.	*worshiper of demons*
	"Nero thy nevow, Golyas thy grantsire,	*descendant, Goliath*
530	Pharao thy fader, Egiptia thy dame,	*father; mother*
	Deulbere, thir ar the causis that I conspire.	*these are charges I allege*
	Termygantis tempise thee, and Vaspasius thine eme,	*Fiends incite; uncle*
	Belzebub, thy full brothir, will clame	*claim*
	To be thyne air, and Cayphas thy sectour,	*heir; executor*
535	Pluto thy hede of kyn and protectour,	*head of family*
	To Hell to lede thee on lycht day and leme.	*by daylight or by torchlight*

197

"Herode thyne othir eme, and grete Egeas,   *uncle*
Marciane, Machomete, and Maxencius,
Thy trew kynnismen Antenor and Eneas,   *kinsmen*
540   Throp thy nere nece, and austern Olibrius,   *niece; stern*
Puttidew, Baal, and Eyobulus —
Thir fendis ar the flour of thy four branchis,   *These fiends are*
Sterand the potis of Hell and nevir stanchis.   *Stirring; ceases*
Dout not, Deulbere, *tu es dyabolas*!   *Doubt; you are a devil!*

545   "Deulbere, thy spere of were but feir thou yelde —[1]
Hangit, mangit, edir-stangit, strynde *stultorum* — *silly, adder-stung; offspring of fools*
To me, maist hie Kenydie, and flee the felde.   *high*
Prikkit, wickit, conwickit lamp *Lollardorum*,   *Stabbed; convicted lamp of Lollards*
Defamyt, blamyt, schamyt *primas paganorum*,   *first of pagans*
550   Out, out, I schout, apon that snowt that snevillis!   *snivels*
Tale tellare, rebellare, induellar wyth the devillis,
Spynk, sink wyth stynk *ad Tertera Termagorum*."   *to the hell of the Termagi (devils)*
                    Quod Kennedy to Dumbar

        Juge ye now heir quha gat the war

84. *The Tretis of the Tua Mariit Wemen and the Wedo*

Apon the Midsummer Evin, mirriest of nichtis,   *Midsummer's Eve*
I muvit furth allane in meid as midnicht wes past   *[a] meadow*
Besyd ane gudlie grein garth full of gay flouris,   *enclosed garden*
Hegeit of ane huge hicht with hawthorne treis   *Hedged; height*
5   Quhairon ane bird on ane bransche so birst out hir notis   *Where; notes*
That never ane blythfullar bird was on the beuche hard.   *happier; bough heard*
Quhat throw the sugarat sound of hir sang glaid   *Because of; sweet*
And throw the savour sanative of the sueit flouris,   *wholesome fragrance*
I drew in derne to the dyk to dirkin efter mirthis.   *in secret; wall; seek*
10   The dew donkit the daill and dynnit the feulis.   *moistened; the birds sang*
I hard under ane holyn hevinlie grein hewit   *heard; holly; hued*
Ane hie speiche at my hand with hautand wourdis.   *lofty conversation; haughty*

---

[1] *Devil-bear, your spear of war doubtless you must yield (i.e., you are defeated)*

With that in haist to the hege so hard I inthrang   *Then; into the hedge; thrust*
That I was heildit with hawthorne and with heynd leveis.   *hidden; pleasant*
15   Throw pykis of the plet thorne I presandlie luikit   *spikes; woven; looked*
Gif ony persoun wald approche within that plesand garding.

I saw thre gay ladeis sit in ane grein arbeir   *green (fresh)*
All grathit into garlandis of fresche gudlie flouris.   *bedecked with garlands*
So glitterit as the gold wer thair glorius gilt tressis[1]
20   Quhill all the gressis did gleme of the glaid hewis.
Kemmit war thair clier hair and curiouslie sched   *Combed; artfully arranged*
Attour thair schulderis doun schyre schyning full bricht   *Above; clearly*
With curches cassin thair abone of kirsp cleir and thin.   *kerchiefs cast above; gauze*
Thair mantillis grein war as the gres that grew in May sessoun,   *season*
25   Fetrit with thair quhyt fingaris about thair fair sydis.   *Held by; white fingers*
Of ferlifull fyne favour war thair faceis meik,   *wondrously lovely; gentle*
All full of flurist fairheid as flouris in June —   *flourishing beauty*
Quhyt, seimlie, and soft as the sweit lillies   *White, lovely*
Now upspred upon spray as new spynist rose,   *opened*
30   Arrayit ryallie about with mony riche wardour   *royally; greenery*
That Nature full nobillie annamalit with flouris,   *adorned*
Of alkin hewis under hevin that ony heynd knew,   *every color; person*
Fragrant, all full of fresche odour fynest of smell.
Ane cumlie tabil coverit wes befoir tha clier ladeis   *those bright*
35   With ryalle cowpis apon rawis full of ryche wynis.   *cups in rows*
And of thir fair wlonkes tua weddit war with lordis,   *these lovely ladies*
Ane was ane wedow, iwis, wantoun of laitis.   *indeed, merry in manner*
And as thai talk at the tabill of mony taill sindry,   *of various things*
Thay wauchtit at the wicht wyne and waris out wourdis,   *quaffed; poured*
40   And syn thai spak more spedelie and sparit no matiris.   *vigorously*

"Bewrie," said the wedo, "ye woddit wemen ying,   *Reveal; wedded; young*
Quhat mirth ye fand in maryage sen ye war menis wyffis.
Reveill gif ye rewit that rakles conditioun,   *if; regretted; reckless*
Or gif that ever ye luffit leyd upone lyf mair   *loved another man more*
45   Nor thame that ye your fayth hes festinit forever,   *Than the one that*
Or gif ye think, had ye chois, that ye wald cheis better.   *choice; choose*

---

[1] *So glittered like gold wire their glorious gilt tresses*

Think ye it nocht ane blist band that bindis so fast — *blessed bond*
That none undo it a deill may bot the deith ane?" — *a bit; except death alone*

Than spak ane lusty belyf with lustie effeiris: — *lovely lady soon; lively manner*
50   "It that ye call the blist band that bindis so fast
Is bair of blis and bailfull and greit barrat wirkis. — *painful; trouble produces*
Ye speir, had I fre chois, gif I wald cheis bettir — — *You ask*
Chenyeis ay ar to eschew and changeis ar sueit. — *Chains; changes; sweet*
Sic cursit chance till eschew, had I my chois anis, — *Such cursed fortune; once*
55   Out of the cheinyeis of ane churle I chaip suld forevir. — *escape*
God, gif matrimony wer made to mell for ane yeir! — *God, if [only]; last; year*
It war bot merrens to be mair bot gif our myndis pleisit. — *[a] vexation; unless*
It is agane the law of luf, of kynd, and of nature — *against; nature*
Togidder hartis to strene that stryveis with uther. — *hearts to constrain*
60   Birdis hes ane better law na bernis be meikill, — *than man by far*
That ilk yeir, with new joy, joyis ane maik, — *each year; enjoy a mate*
And fangis thame ane fresche feyr, unfulyeit and constant, — *take; mate, unworn*
And lattis thair fulyeit feiris flie quhair thai pleis. — *used up companions*
Cryst, gif sic ane consuetude war in this kith haldin, — *custom was; land held*
65   Than weill war us wemen that evir we war born!
We suld have feiris as fresche to fang quhen us likit, — *companions; embrace*
And gif all larbaris thair leveis quhen thai lak curage.[1]
Myself suld be full semlie in silkis arrayit,
Gymp, jolie, and gent, richt joyus and gent. — *Graceful; elegant*
70   I suld at fairis be found new faceis to se,
At playis and at preichingis and pilgrimages greit,
To schaw my renone royaly quhair preis was of folk, — *high repute; press*
To manifest my makdome to multitude of pepill — *display my loveliness*
And blaw my bewtie on breid quhair bernis war mony[2]
75   That I micht cheis and be chosin and change quhen me lykit.
Than suld I waill ane full weill our all the wyd realme — *choose; [from] over*
That suld my womanheid weild the lang winter nicht, — *enjoy*
And quhen I gottin had ane grome, ganest of uther, — *fellow, better than the others*
Yaip and ying, in the yok ane yeir for to draw, — *Eager and young; yoke one year*
80   Fra I had preveit his pitht the first plesand moneth, — *After; tested his virility*

---

[1] *And give all impotent men their walking papers when they lack heartiness (potency)*

[2] *And proclaim my beauty abroad where men were numerous*

Than suld I cast me to keik in kirk and in markat   *apply myself to look about*
And all the cuntré about, kyngis court and uther,
Quhair I ane galland micht get aganis the nixt yeir   *handsome suitor*
For to perfurneis furth the werk quhen failyeit the tother —   *perform; used up*
85   A forky fure, ay furthwart, and forsy in draucht,[1]
Nother febill nor fant nor fulyeit in labour,   *exhausted by*
Bot als fresche of his forme as flouris in May.   *shape*
For all the fruit suld I fang, thocht he the flour burgeoun.[2]

    "I have ane wallidrag, ane worme, ane auld wobat carle,[3]
90   A waistit wolroun na worth bot wourdis to clatter,   *used up swine worth nothing*
Ane bumbart, ane dronbee, ane bag full of flewme,   *An idler; phlegm*
Ane scabbit skarth, ane scorpioun, ane scutarde behind.[4]
To se him scart his awin skyn grit scunner I think.   *scratch; disgust I feel*
Quhen kissis me that carybald, than kyndillis all my sorow.   *monster*
95   As birs of ane brym bair his berd is als stif,   *bristles; fierce boar*
Bot soft and soupill as the silk is his sary lume.   *sorry instrument*
He may weill to the syn assent, bot sakles is his deidis.   *harmless*
With gor his tua grym ene ar gladderit all about   *rheum; eyes*
And gorgeit lyk tua gutaris that war with glar stoppit.   *clogged; gutters; slime*
100 Bot quhen that glowrand gaist grippis me about,   *glowering incubus*
Than think I hiddowus Mahowne hes me in armes.   *(i.e., Lucifer)*
Thair ma na sanyne me save fra that auld Sathane,   *There may no sign*
For thocht I croce me all cleine fra the croun doun,   *cross myself entirely*
He wil my corse all beclip and clap to his breist.   *body embrace and hold*
105 Quhen schaiffyn is that ald schaik with a scharp rasour,   *shaven; fellow*
He schowis on me his schevill mouth and schendis my lippis,[5]
And with his hard hurcheone scyn sa heklis he my chekis   *hedgehog skin; scratches*
That as a glemand gleyd glowis my chaftis.   *burning coal; jaws*
I schrenk for the scharp stound bot schout dar I nought   *cower; sharp pain*
110 For schore of that auld schrew, schame him betide.   *fear*

---

[1] *A vigorous furrower, always up front, and forceful in plowing*

[2] *For all the fruit that I should seize, though he [made] the flower bloom*

[3] *I have [as husband] a useless slob, a worm, an old hairy caterpillar*

[4] *A scabby cormorant, a scorpion, a befouled behind*

[5] *He shoves on me his shovel-mouth and befouls my lips*

The luf blenkis of that bogill fra his blerde ene — *love-looks; goblin; bleary eyes*

As Belzebub had on me blent, abasit my spreit. — *As [if]; looked, depressed*

And quhen the smy on me smyrkis with his smake smolet — *wretch; vile smile (?)*

He fepillis like a farcy aver that flyrit on a gillot.[1]

115 Quhen that the sound of his saw sinkis in my eris, — *voice sinks into my ears*

Than ay renewis my noy or he be neir cumand. — *annoyance before he comes near*

Quhen I heir nemmyt his name, than mak I nyne crocis — *named; nine crosses*

To keip me fra the cummerans of that carll mangit — *annoyance; crazy fellow*

That full of eldnyng is and anger and all evill thewis. — *jealousy; habits*

120 I dar nought luke to my luf for that lene gib. — *lean tom-cat*

He is sa full of jelusy and engyne fals, — *evil designs*

Ever ymagynyng in mynd materis of evill,

Compasand and castand cacis a thousand — *Imagining and devising situations*

How he sall tak me with a trawe at trist of aneothir. — *trick (?)*

125 I dar nought keik to the knaip that the cop fillis — *glance at the lad; cup*

For eldnyng of that ald schrew that ever on evill thynkis, — *jealousy*

For he is waistit and worne fra Venus werkis

And may nought beit worght a bene in bed of my mystirs.

He trowis that young folk I yerne yeild, for he gane is,[2]

130 Bot I may yuke all this yer or his yerd help. — *itch; year before his rod helps*

Ay quhen that caribald carll wald clym on my wambe, — *monster; climb*

Than am I dangerus and daine and dour of my will. — *standoffish; haughty*

Yit leit I nevir that larbar my leggis ga betuene — *impotent fool*

To fyle my flesche na fummyll me without a fee gret; — *defile; fumble*

135 And thoght his pen purly me payis in bed, — *though his penis poorly*

His purse pays richely in recompense efter.

For or he clym on my corse, that carybald forlane, — *before; useless beast*

I have condition of a curche of kersp all ther fynest, — *require a kerchief of sheer fabric*

A goun of engranyt claight right gaily furrit, — *gown of scarlet-dyed cloth; fur-trimmed*

140 A ring with a ryall stane or other riche jowell,

Or rest of his rousty raid, thoght he wer rede wod. — *clumsy attack; furious with anger*

For all the buddis of Johne Blunt, quhen he abone clymis, — *bribes; climbs on top*

Me think the baid deir aboucht, sa bawch ar his werkis.[3]

---

[1] *He extends his lip like a sick old nag leering at a filly*

[2] Lines 128–29: *And may not satisfy my needs in bed worth a bean. / He thinks I yearn eagerly for young folk, since he is senile*

[3] *I think the delay dearly bought, so feeble are his works*

And thus I sell him solace thoght I it sour think.

145 Fra sic a syre God yow saif, my sueit sisteris deir!" *such a man*

Quhen that the semely had said hir sentence to end, *lovely [lady]*
Than all thai leuch apon loft with latis full mery *laughed loudly; behavior*
And raucht the cop round about full of riche wynis, *passed*
And ralyeit lang or thai wald rest with ryatus speche. *jested; before*

150 The wedo to the tothir wlonk warpit thir wordis: *lady spoke these words*
"Now, fair sister, fallis yow but fenying to tell, *it falls [to] you without deceit*
Sen man ferst with matrimony yow menskit in kirk, *Since; honored*
How haif ye farne — be your faith, confese us the treuth! — *have you fared*
That band to blise or to ban, quhilk yow best thinkis; *bond; pain*
155 Or how ye like lif to leid into lell spousage? *to lead in loyal marriage*
And syne myself ye exem on the samyn wise, *then myself you may examine*
And I sall say furth the suth, dissymyland no word." *truth, faking*

The plesand said, "I protest, the treuth gif I schaw, *lovely [lady]; if I reveal*
That of your toungis ye be traist." The tothir twa grantit. *trustworthy*
160 With that sprang up hir spreit be a span hechar. *spirit; higher*
"To speik," quod scho, "I sall nought spar, ther is no spy neir.
I sall a ragment reveil fra rute of my hert, *list; root*
A roust that is sa rankild quhill risis my stomok. *rancor so bitter; swells*
Now sall the byle all out brist that beild has so lang. *burst; built up*
165 For it to beir on my breist wes berdin our hevy. *burden too great*
I sall the venome devoid with a vent large *pour forth; discharge*
And me assuage of the swalme that suellit wes gret. *swelling*

"My husband wes a hur maister, the hugeast in erd. *whoremaster; on earth*
Tharfor I hait him with my hert, sa help me our Lord. *hate*
170 He is a young man ryght yaip, bot nought in youth flouris, *active*
For he is fadit full far and feblit of strenth.
He wes as flurising fresche within this few yeris,
Bot he is falyeid full far and fulyeid in labour. *enfeebled; exhausted*
He has bene lychour so lang quhill lost is his natur, *lecher; until*
175 His lume is waxit larbar and lyis into swoune. *sexual instrument; useless*
Wes never sugeorne wer set na on that snaill tyrit, *rest; tired slug*
For efter sevin oulkis rest it will nought rap anys. *weeks; tap once*
He has bene waistit apon wemen or he me wif chesit, *before; [for] wife chose*

	And in adultré in my tyme I haif him tane oft.	*caught often*
180	And yit he is als brankand with bonet on syde,	*prancing*
	And blenkand to the brichtest that in the burght duellis,	*glancing*
	Alse curtly of his clething and kemmyng of his haris	*courtly; combing*
	As he that is mare valyeand in Venus chalmer.	*more valiant*
	He semis to be sumthing worth, that syphyr in bour,	*cipher in the bedroom*
185	He lukis as he wald luffit be, thoght he be litill of valour.	
	He dois as dotit dog that damys on all bussis	*foolish; pees; bushes*
	And liftis his leg apon loft thoght he nought list pische.	*need to piss*
	He has a luke without lust and lif without curage.	*sexual desire*
	He has a forme without force and fesson but vertu,[1]	
190	And fair wordis but effect, all fruster of dedis.	*worthless of deeds*
	He is for ladyis in luf a right lusty schadow,	*shadow (i.e., fake)*
	Bot into derne at the deid he sal be drup fundin.	*in the dark; deed; droopy be found*
	He ralis and makes repet with ryatus wordis,	*jokes; noise; jovial*
	Ay rusing him of his radis and rageing in chalmer.	*Ever boasting; prowess*
195	Bot God wait quhat I think quhen he so thra spekis	*knows; boldly*
	And how it settis him so syde to sege of sic materis.[2]	
	Bot gif himself of sum evin myght ane say amang thaim:	*some evening*
	Bot he nought ane is bot nane of naturis possessoris.	
	Scho that has ane auld man nought all is begylit —	*is not entirely deceived*
200	He is at Venus werkis na war na he semys.	*no worse than he appears*
	I wend I josit a gem and I haif geit gottin;	*thought I enjoyed; jet*
	He had the glemyng of gold and wes bot glase fundin.	*found to be glass*
	Thought men be ferse, wele I fynd, fra falye ther curage,	*fierce; afterwards fails*
	Thar is bot eldnyng and anger ther hertis within.	*jealousy*
205	Ye speik of berdis on bewch — of blise may thai sing,	*birds on [a] bough*
	That on Sanct Valentynis day ar vacandis ilk yer.	*are free [to mate] each year*
	Hed I that plesand prevelege to part quhen me likit,	
	To change and ay to cheise agane, than chastité adew!	
	Than suld I haif a fresch feir to fang in myn armys;	*mate to embrace*
210	To hald a freke quhill he faynt may foly be calit.	*man; is weak*
	Apone sic materis I mus at mydnyght full oft	*muse*
	And murnys so in my mynd I murdris myselfin.	*mourn*
	Than ly I walkand for wa and walteris about,	*waking for woe; toss*

---

[1] *He has a body without strength and appearance without energy*

[2] *And how it suits him so widely to boast of such matters*

Poem 84: The Tretis of the Tua Mariit Wemen and the Wedo

	Wariand oft my wekit kyn that me away cast,	*Cursing; my wicked kin*
215	To sic a craudoune but curage that knyt my cler bewté,[1]	
	And ther so mony kene knyghtis this kenrik within.	*bold; realm*
	Than think I on a semelyar, the suth for to tell,	*handsomer [one]*
	Na is our syre be sic sevin; with that I syth oft.	*Than; by seven times*
	Than he ful tenderly dois turne to me his tume person,	*flaccid (empty)*
220	And with a yoldin yerd dois yolk me in armys	*pliant rod; hold*
	And sais, 'My soverane sueit thing, quhy sleip ye no betir?	
	Me think ther haldis yow a hete, as ye sum harme alyt.'	*fever; suffered*
	Quod I, 'My hony, hald abak and handill me nought sair,	
	A hache is happinnit hastely at my hert rut.'	*An ache; heart's root*
225	With that I seme for to swoune thought I na swerf tak,	*do not faint*
	And thus beswik I that swane with my sueit wordis.	*deceive; that man*
	I cast on him a crabit e quhen cleir day is cummyn,	*crabby look*
	And lettis it is a luf blenk quhen he about glemys.	*let on; love look; glances*
	I turne it in a tender luke that I in tene warit	*glance what I in anger feel*
230	And him behaldis hamely with hertly smyling.	*kindly*

	"I wald a tender peronall that myght na put thole,	*young girl; not wish to suffer*
	That hatit men with hard geir for hurting of flesch,	*instruments*
	Had my gud man to hir gest, for I dar God suer,	*good man (i.e., lover); swear*
	Scho suld not stert for his straik a stray breid of erd.[2]	
235	And syne I wald that ilk band that ye so blist call	
	Had bund him so to that bryght quhill his bak werkit;	*young lady till his back ached*
	And I wer in a beid broght with berne that me likit,	*bed; [a] man*
	I trow that bird of my blis suld a bourd want."	*girl; would not be amused*

	Onone quhen this amyable had endit hir speche,	*Then when; pleasant [woman]*
240	Loud lauchand the laif allowit hir mekle.[3]	
	Thir gay wiffis maid gam amang the grene leiffis,	*These*
	Thai drank and did away dule under derne bewis,	*sorrow; secret boughs*
	Thai swapit of the sueit wyne, thai swan quhit of hewis,[4]	
	Bot all the pertlyar in plane thai put out ther vocis.	*more boldly in complaint*

---

[1] *To such a coward without desire who possessed my splendid beauty*

[2] *She should not flinch at his stroke a straw's breadth of earth*

[3] *Laughing loudly the others commended her greatly*

[4] *They quaffed the sweet wine, those swan-white ladies*

245   Than said the weido: "Iwis, ther is no way othir.
       Now tydis me for to talk, my taill it is nixt.   *it befalls; tale; next*
       God my spreit now inspir and my speche quykkin,   *spirit; enliven*
       And send me sentence to say substantious and noble,   *wisdom; weighty*
       Sa that my preching may pers your perverst hertis   *pierce; wicked*
250   And mak yow mekar to men in maneris and conditiounis.

       "I schaw yow, sister, in schrift I wes a schrew ever,   *assure you, sisters; truth*
       Bot I wes schene in my schrowd and schew me innocent;   *lovely in my clothing*
       And thought I dour wes and dane, dispitois and bald,   *though I disdainful; haughty*
       I wes dissymblit suttelly in a sanctis liknes.   *subtly; saints*
255   I semyt sober and sueit and sempill without fraud,
       Bot I couth sexty dissaif that suttillar wer haldin.   *could sixty deceive; more subtle*
       Unto my lesson ye lyth and leir at me wit,   *listen and learn*
       Gif you nought list be forleit with losingeris untrew.[1]
       Be constant in your governance and counterfeit gud maneris,   *behavior*
260   Thought ye be kene, inconstant, and cruell of mynd.   *Though; bold*
       Thought ye as tygris be terne, be tretable in luf,   *ferocious; compliant*
       And be as turtoris in your talk, thought ye haif talis brukill. *doves; frail sexual parts*
       Be dragonis baitht and dovis ay in double forme,   *both*
       And quhen it nedis yow, onone note baith ther stranthis.   *then practice; strengths*
265   Be amyable with humble face as angellis apperand,
       And with a terrebill tail be stangand as edderis.   *stinging as adders*
       Be of your luke like innocentis, thoght ye haif evill myndis.
       Be courtly ay in clething and costly arrayit —
       That hurtis yow nought worth a hen, yowr husband pays for all.

270   "Twa husbandis haif I had, thai held me baith deir.
       Thought I dispytit thaim agane, thai spyt it na thing.   *despised; spied*
       Ane wes a hair hogeart that hostit out flewme.   *hoary fellow; coughed up phlegm*
       I hatit him like a hund thought I it hid prevé.   *dog; secretly*
       With kissing and with clapping I gert the carill fon;   *made the fellow fawn*
275   Weil couth I claw his cruke bak and kemm his kewt noddill,
       And with a bukky in my cheik bo on him behind,

---

[1] *If you do not wish to be abandoned to faithless deceivers*

Poem 84: The Tretis of the Tua Mariit Wemen and the Wedo

And with a bek gang about and bler his ald e,[1]
And with a kyind contynance kys his crynd chekis,   *winkled cheeks*
Into my mynd makand mokis at that mad fader,   *making scornful faces*
280   Trovand me with trew lufe to treit him so fair.   *Trusting*
This cought I do without dule and na dises tak,   *could; pain; discomfort*
Bot ay be mery in my mynd and myrthfull of cher.   *disposition*

"I had a lufsummar leid my lust for to slokyn   *more lovable lad; slake*
That couth be secrete and sure and ay saif my honour,
285   And sew bot at certane tymes and in sicir placis.   *engage; safe*
Ay quhen the ald did me anger with akword wordis,
Apon the galland for to goif it gladit me agane.   *gaze*
I had sic wit that for wo weipit I litill,   *such; wept*
Bot leit the sueit ay the sour to gud sesone bring.
290   Quhen that the chuf wald me chid with girnand chaftis,   *boor; snarling jaws*
I wald him chuk, cheik and chyn, and cheris him so mekill   *kiss, cheek and chin*
That his cheif chymys he had chevist to my sone,   *chief manor house; bequeathed*
Suppos the churll wes gane chaist or the child wes gottin.   *Although; impotent before*
As wis woman ay I wrought and not as wod fule,   *crazy fool*
295   For mar with wylis I wan na wichtnes of handis.   *more; won than strength*

"Syne maryt I a merchand myghti of gudis.   *Then married; goods*
He wes a man of myd eld and of mene statur,   *middle age; medium*
Bot we na fallowis wer in frendschip or blud,
In fredome na furth bering, na fairnes of persoune —[2]
300   Quhilk ay the fule did forget for febilnes of knawlege.
Bot I sa oft thoght him on quhill angrit his hert,   *reminded him, which*
And quhilum I put furtht my voce and peddir him callit.   *sometimes; peddler*
I wald ryght tuichandly talk be I wes tuyse maryit,   *sharply; because; twice*
For endit wes my innocence with my ald husband.
305   I wes apperand to be pert within perfit eild: *mature age*
Sa sais the curat of our kirk that knew me full ying.   *says*
He is our famous to be fals, that fair worthy prelot.   *too respectable*

---

[1] Lines 275–77: *Well could I scratch his crooked back and comb his cropped head, / And with puffed out cheeks make a face at him from behind, / And with a look of respect turn about and blear his old eye*

[2] Lines 298–99: *But we were not equals in friendship nor in descent, / Nor generosity nor conduct, nor personal beauty*

I sal be laith to lat him le quhill I may luke furtht.   *tell lies; look around*

I gert the buthman obey — ther wes no bute ellis —   *made the shopkeeper; remedy*

310   He maid me ryght hie reverens fra he my rycht knew,   *after; just deserts*

For, thocht I say it myself, the severance wes mekle   *difference; great*

Betuix his bastard blude and my birth noble.

That page wes never of sic price for to presome anys[1]

Unto my persone to be peir, had peté nought grantit.   *equal*

315   Bot mercy into womanheid is a mekle vertu,

For never bot in a gentill hert is generit ony ruth.   *never except (i.e., always); pity*

I held ay grene into his mynd that I of grace tuk him,   *always fresh*

And that he couth ken himself I curtasly him lerit.   *recognize; taught*

He durst not sit anys my summondis, for or the secund charge[2]

320   He wes ay redy for to ryn, so rad he wes for blame.   *run; afraid*

Bot ay my will wes the war of womanly natur: *desire; the worst*

The mair he loutit for my luf, the les of him I rakit,   *fawned; cared for*

And eik — this is a ferly thing — or I him faith gaif   *also; wondrous; before*

I had sic favour to that freke and feid syne forever.   *man; hated afterward*

325   Quhen I the cure had all clene and him ourcummyn haill,   *control; overcome wholly*

I crew abone that craudone as cok that wer victour.   *crowed over; coward*

Quhen I him saw subjeit and sett at myn bydding,   *submissive*

Than I him lichtlyit as a lowne and lathit his maneris.   *despised; rascal; hated*

Than woxe I sa unmerciable to martir him I thought,   *grew*

330   For as a best I broddit him to all boyis laubour.   *beast; goaded*

I wald haif riddin him to Rome with raip in his heid   *rope; head*

Wer not ruffill of my renoune and rumour of pepill.[3]

And yit hatrent I hid within my hert all,   *hatred; entirely*

Bot quhilis it hepit so huge quhill it behud out.   *But sometimes; until it was forced out*

335   Yit tuk I nevir the wosp clene out of my wyde throte   *plug*

Quhill I oucht wantit of my will or quhat I wald desir.   *While I anything lacked*

Bot quhen I severit had that syre of substance in erd

And gottin his biggingis to my barne and hie burrow landis,   *buildings; child*

Than with a stew stert out the stoppell of my hals   *stink jerked; stopper from my throat*

340   That he all stunyst throu the stound as of a stele wappin.   *was stunned; shock; weapon*

Than wald I efter lang first sa fane haif bene wrokin   *afterwards; gladly; avenged*

---

[1] *That lower-class person was never of such worth as to presume ever*

[2] *He dared not once disregard my summons, for before a second command*

[3] *If not for the injury to my reputation and the people's disapproval*

	That I to flyte wes als fers as a fell dragoun.	*scold; cruel*
	I had for flattering of that fule fenyeit so lang,	*fool pretended*
	Mi evidentis of heritagis or thai wer all selit,	*lineage documents; sealed*
345	My breist that wes gret beild bowdyn wes sa huge	*was so greatly swollen*
	That neir my baret out birst or the band makin.	
	Bot quhen my billis and my bauchles wes all braid selit,[1]	
	I wald na langar beir on bridill bot braid up my heid.	*endure; tossed*
	Thar myght na molet mak me moy na hald my mouth in.	*bridle bit; meek*
350	I gert the renyeis rak and rif into sondir,	*made the reins rip and tear*
	I maid that wif carll to werk all womenis werkis	*effeminate fellow to perform*
	And laid all manly materis and mensk in this eird.	*[I] conducted; dignity; earth*
	Than said I to my cummaris in counsall about,	*gossips*
	'Se how I cabeld yone cout with a kene brydill.	*tied; colt*
355	The cappill that the crelis kest in the caf mydding	*horse; baskets cast; dungheap*
	Sa curtasly the cart drawis and kennis na plungeing,	
	He is nought skeich na yit sker na scippis nought on syd.'	*spirited; skittish; skips*
	And thus the scorne and the scaith scapit he nothir.	*humiliation escaped*
	"He wes no glaidsum gest for a gay lady,	*cheerful lover*
360	Tharfor I gat him a gam that ganyt him bettir.	*made him a game; suited*
	He wes a gret goldit man and of gudis riche;	*i.e., wealthy*
	I leit him be my lumbart to lous me all misteris,	*banker; free me of need*
	And he wes fane for to fang fra me that fair office	*happy to take*
	And thoght my favoris to fynd throw his feill giftis.	*receive; many gifts*
365	He grathit me in a gay silk and gudly arrayis,	*dressed*
	In gownis of engranyt claight and gret goldin chenyeis,	*dyed cloth; chains*
	In ringis ryally set with riche ruby stonis,	
	Quhill hely raise my renoune amang the rude peple.	*Which greatly raised*
	Bot I full craftely did keip thai courtly wedis	*those fancy dresses*
370	Quhill efter dede of that drupe that docht nought in chalmir.[2]	
	Thought he of all my clathis maid cost and expense,	
	Aneothir sall the worschip haif that weildis me eftir.	*possesses*
	And thoght I likit him bot litill, yit for luf of othris	
	I wald me prunya plesandly in precius wedis	*preen myself*

---

[1] Lines 346–47: *That my anger nearly erupted before the contract was established. / But when my legal documents and formal reproaches were all fully sealed*

[2] *Until after the death of that drooper who was useless in bed*

375   That luffaris myght apon me luke and ying lusty gallandis
        That I held more in daynté and derer be ful mekill   *delight; dearer by far*
        Ne him that dressit me so dink — full dotit wes his heyd!   *Than; finely*
        Quhen he wes heryit out of hand to hie up my honoris,   *plundered; raise*
        And payntit me as pako, proudest of fedderis,   *peacock; feathers*
380   I him miskennyt, be Crist, and cukkald him maid.   *ignored; cuckold*
        I him forleit as a lad and lathlyit him mekle —   *abandoned; despised*
        I thoght myself a papingay and him a plukit herle.   *parrot; plucked heron*
        All thus enforsit he his fa and fortifyit in strenth   *Thus strengthened; foe*
        And maid a stalwart staff to strik himselfe doune.   *sturdy*

385   "Bot of ane bowrd into bed I sall yow breif yit: *trick; tell*
        Quhen he ane hal year wes hanyt and him behuffit rage,[1]
        And I wes laith to be loppin with sic a lob avoir,   *mounted by such a clumsy old horse*
        Alse lang as he wes on loft I lukit on him never   *aroused*
        Na leit never enter in my thoght that he my thing persit;   *"thing" penetrated*
390   Bot ay in mynd aneothir man ymagynit that I haid,
        Or ellis had I never mery bene at that myrthles raid.   *ride*
        Quhen I that grome geldit had of gudis and of natur,   *castrated fellow*
        Me thoght him gracelese on to goif, sa me God help.   *ugly to look at*
        Quhen he had warit all on me his welth and his substance,   *spent*
395   Me thoght his wit wes all went away with the laif.   *rest*
        And so I did him dispise; I spittit quhen I saw
        That superspendit evill spreit spulyeit of all vertu.   *used up; deprived*
        For weill ye wait, wiffis, that he that wantis riches   *wives; lacks*
        And valyeandnes in Venus play is ful vile haldin.   *valiance; held*
400   Full fruster is his fresch array and fairnes of persoune,   *worthless*
        All is bot frutlese his effeir and falyeis at the upwith.   *implement; failure at climax*
        I buskit up my barnis like baronis sonnies   *dressed my children*
        And maid bot fulis of the fry of his first wif.   *fools; spawn*
        I banyst fra my boundis his brethir ilkane,   *banished; lands; brethren each one*
405   His frendis as my fais I heid at feid evir.   *foes; feud*
        Be this ye beleif may, I luffit nought himself,   *By*
        For never I likit a leid that langit till his blude.   *person who belonged*
        And yit thir wismen, thai wait that all wiffis evill   *these wisemen; know*
        Ar kend with ther conditionis and knawin with the samin.   *Are known by these actions*

---

[1] *When he a whole year was curbed and needed sexual passion*

410	"Deid is now that dyvour and dollin in erd.	*debtor; buried in earth*
	With him deit all my dule and my drery thoghtis.	*died; sorrow*
	Now done is my dolly nyght, my day is upsprungin.	*mournful*
	Adew, dolour, adew, my daynté now begynis.	*pleasure*
	Now am I a wedow, iwise, and weill am at ese.	*certainly*
415	I weip as I wer woful, bot wel is me for ever.	*weep as [if]*
	I busk as I wer bailfull, bot blith is my hert.	*dress as if I were in mourning*
	My mouth it makis murnyng and my mynd lauchis.	*laughs*
	My clokis thai ar caerfull in colour of sabill,	*mournful*
	Bot courtly and ryght curyus my corse is ther undir.	*beautiful; body*
420	I drup with a ded luke in my dule habit,	*droop; sad; mournful*
	As with manis daill I had done for dayis of my lif.[1]	

	"Quhen that I go to the kirk cled in cair weid,	*(i.e., widow's clothing)*
	As foxe in a lambis fleise fenye I my cheir.	*I fake my mood*
	Than lay I furght my bright buke on breid on my kne	*forth; book open*
425	With mony lusty letter ellummynit with gold,	*illuminated*
	And drawis my clok forthwart our my face quhit	*over; white*
	That I may spy unaspyit a space me beside.	
	Full oft I blenk by my buke and blynis of devotion	*glance from; cease*
	To se quhat berne is best brand or bredest in schulderis	
430	Or forgeit is maist forcely to furnyse a bancat[2]	
	In Venus chalmer valyeandly withoutin vane ruse.	*vain boast*
	And as the new mone all pale oppressit with change	*moon*
	Kythis quhilis her cleir face throw cluddis of sable,	*Shows awhile; through*
	So keik I throw my clokis and castis kynd lukis	*peek; looks*
435	To knychtis and to cleirkis and cortly personis.	
	Quhen frendis of my husbandis behaldis me on fer,	*behold me from afar*
	I haif a watter spunge for wa within my wyde clokis,	*sponge for woe*
	Than wring I it full wylely and wetis my chekis.	*cleverly*
	With that watteris myn ene and welteris doune teris.	*eyes; flows*
440	Than say thai all that sittis about, 'Se ye nought, allace,	
	Yone lustlese led, so lelely scho luffit hir husband.	*joyless person; loyally*
	Yone is a peté to enprent in a princis hert,	*sorrow*

---

[1] *As if with man's sexual dealings I were done for the rest of my life*

[2] Lines 429–30: *To see what man is best brawned or broadest in shoulders / Or forged is most strongly to provide a [sexual] banquet*

That sic a perle of plesance suld yone pane dre.' *pearl of delight; experience such pain*
I sane me as I war ane sanct and semys ane angell, *I cross myself; saint*
445 At langage of lichory I leit as I war crabit. *lechery I pretend to be angry*
I sith without sair hert or seiknes in body, *sigh*
According to my sable weid I mon haif sad maneris, *I must have*
Or thai will se all the suth — for certis we wemen, *certainly*
We set us all for the syght to syle men of treuth.[1]
450 We dule for na evill deid, sa it be derne haldin. *suffer; deed; held secret*

    "Wise wemen has wayis and wonderfull gydingis *ways [of acting]*
With gret engyne to bejaip ther jolyus husbandis, *stratagems; fool*
And quyetly with sic craft convoyis our materis *achieve our ends*
That under Crist no creatur kennis of our doingis. *under Christ (i.e., on earth); knows*
455 Bot folk a cury may miscuke that knawlege wantis *dish; mis-cook*
And has na colouris for to cover ther awne kindly fautis, *devices; faults*
As dois thir damysellis for derne dotit lufe *secret foolish love*
That dogonis haldis in dainté and delis with thaim so lang *worthless men*
Quhill al the cuntré knaw ther kyndnes and faith.
460 Faith has a fair name bot falsheid faris beittir —
Fy on hir that can nought feyne her fame for to saif! *pretend; good name*
Yit am I wise in sic werk and wes all my tyme.
Thoght I want wit in warldlynes I wylis haif in luf, *wiles have*
As ony happy woman has that is of hie blude. *high blood*
465 Hutit be the halok lase a hunder yeir of eild! *Shamed be the foolish lass*
I have ane secrete servand, rycht sobir of his toung,
That me supportis of sic nedis quhen I a syne mak. *such; sign make*
Thoght he be sympill to the sicht, he has a tong sickir; *sight; reliable*
Full mony semelyar sege wer service dois mak. *man worse*
470 Thoght I haif cair under cloke the cleir day quhill nyght, *until*
Yit haif I solace under serk quhill the sone ryse — *chemise*
Yit am I haldin a haly wif our all the haill schyre.
I am sa peteouse to the pur quhen ther person is mony.[2]
In passing of pilgrymage I pride me full mekle —
475 Mair for the prese of peple na ony pardon wynyng. *praise; than [for] any*

---

[1] *We present ourselves in such a way as to deceive men of the truth*

[2] *I am so piteous to the poor when there are many people*

"Bot yit me think the best bourd quhen baronis and knychtis   *trick*

And othir bachilleris blith, blumyng in youth,   *blooming*

And all my luffaris lele my luging persewis,   *loyal lovers my home frequent*

And fyllis me wyne wantonly with weilfair and joy.   *pours; playfully; happiness*

480   Sum rownis and sum ralyeis and sum redis ballatis,   *whisper; joke; read poems*

Sum raiffis furght rudly with riatus speche,   *rave wildly; riotous*

Sum plenis and sum prayis, sum prasis mi bewté,   *complain; praise*

Sum kissis me, sum clappis me, sum kyndnes me proferis,   *embrace; affection*

Sum kerffis to me curtasli, sum me the cop giffis,   *carves [choice pieces]; cup offers*

485   Sum stalwardly steppis ben with a stout curage   *inside*

And a stif standand thing staiffis in mi neiff,   *thrusts; fist*

And mony blenkis ben our that but full fer sittis,[1]

That mai for the thik thrang nought thrif as thai wald.   *not succeed*

Bot with my fair calling I comfort thaim all: *warm welcome*

490   For he that sittis me nixt, I nip on his finger;

I serf him on the tothir syde on the samin fasson;   *same fashion*

And he that behind me sittis I hard on him lene;   *lean*

And him befor, with my fut fast on his I stramp;   *foot hard; stamp*

And to the bernis far, but sueit blenkis I cast.   *men far off, only*

495   To every man in speciall speke I sum wordis,

So wisly and so womanly quhill warmys ther hertis.   *which*

Thar is no liffand leid so law of degré   *living lad so low*

That sall me luf unluffit, I am so loik hertit.   *warm-hearted*

And gif his lust so be lent into my lyre quhit   *if; desire; given; white skin*

500   That he be lost or with me lak, his lif sall not danger.   *if he does not have me*

I am so mercifull in mynd and menys all wichtis,   *take pity on all men*

My sely saull sal be saif quhen Sabot all jugis.   *innocent soul; (i.e., God); judges*

Ladyis, leir thir lessonis and be no lassis fundin.   *girls proved*

This is the legeand of my lif, thought Latyne it be nane."   *Latin*

505   Quhen endit had hir ornat speche this eloquent wedow,

Lowd thai lewch all the laif and loffit hir mekle,   *laughed; others; loved*

And said thai suld exampill tak of her soverane teching

And wirk efter hir wordis, that woman wes so prudent.

Than culit thai ther mouthis with confortable drinkis   *cooled*

510   And carpit full cummerlik with cop going round.   *spoke quite intimately; cup*

---

[1] *And many glance inside who sit far on the outside*

Thus draif thai our that deir nyght with danceis full noble — *passed*
Quhill that the day did up daw and dew donkit flouris. — *Until; dawned; bathed*
The morow myld wes and meik the mavis did sing, — *mild; blackbirds*
And all remuffit the myst and the meid smellit. — *gone was; meadow [was] fragrant*

515 Silver schouris doune schuke as the schene cristall, — *bright crystal*
And berdis shoutit in schaw with ther schill notis. — *birds sang; wood*
The goldin glitterand gleme so gladit ther hertis,
Thai maid a glorius gle amang the grene bewis. — *music; boughs*
The soft sowch of the swyr and soune of the stremys, — *murmuring; vale*

520 The sueit savour of the sward and singing of foulis — *flowers*
Myght confort ony creatur of the kyn of Adam
And kindill agane his curage thoght it wer cald sloknyt. — *quenched*
Than rais thir ryall rosis in ther riche wedis — *these royal roses; garments*
And rakit hame to ther rest throw the rise blumys. — *went home; blooming bushes*

525 And I all prevély past to a plesand arber, — *privately; garden*
And with my pen did report ther pastance most mery. — *pastime*

Ye auditoris most honorable that eris has gevin — *ear has given*
Onto this uncouth aventur quhilk airly me happinnit, — *strange; which early*
Of thir thre wanton wiffis that I haif writtin heir,

530 Quhilk wald ye waill to your wif gif ye suld wed one? — *choose for; if*

214

Explanatory Notes

Abbreviations

Ar	Arundel MS	Mc	Mackenzie, *Poems of William Dunbar* (1932; rev. 1960)
As	Asloan MS		
B	Bannatyne MS	*MED*	*Middle English Dictionary*
BD	Bannatyne Draft MS	*MEL*	*Middle English Lyrics*, ed. Luria and Hoffman
Bw	Bawcutt, *Poems of William Dunbar* (1998), 2 vols.		
		MF	Maitland Folio MS
CM	Chapman and Myllar Print	*OED*	*Oxford English Dictionary*
CT	*Canterbury Tales*	*PF*	*Parliament of Fowls*
DOST	*Dictionary of the Older Scottish Tongue.*	R	Reidpeth MS
		RP	The so-called Rouen Print
HF	*House of Fame*	*RR*	*Roman de la Rose*
IMEV	Brown and Robbins, *Index of Middle English Verse*	*SGGK*	*Sir Gawain and the Green Knight*
K	Kinsley, *William Dunbar: Poems* (1957)	*TA*	*Accounts of the Lord High Treasurer of Scotland*
LGW	*Legend of Good Women*	*TC*	*Troilus and Criseyde*

1. *On the Nativity of Christ* [*Et nobis puer natus est*]

Dunbar's hymn on the birth of Christ is often considered one of the finest expressions of sheer joy in English literature. In what is sometimes referred to as the *Jubilate omnia* theme, the voices of all Creation blend together in celebration of this most special occasion, Christ's Nativity. The Latin phrase with which the poem begins, and the second Latin phrase that provides the refrain for each stanza, both derive from messianic passages in Isaias; they were incorporated in the liturgy for Advent services and were also used for the Feast of the Annunciation. The image of the dew dropping from Heaven was commonly associated in the Middle Ages with the Incarnation and is frequently found in hymns in the Adoration of the Virgin tradition. (Compare the "dew in Aprille" [line 15] of the Marian lyric "I syng of a Maiden" — *MEL*, p. 170.) While the poem focuses primarily on Christ's Nativity, it also contains many traditional images and symbols that occur in literary and visual depictions of the Annunciation and the Incarnation. Seven 8-line stanzas rhyming *ababbcbC*, the refrain in Latin. Found in B only. Mc79, K1, Bw58.

1–2   Verse 2 is the English paraphrase of the Latin in verse 1, which comes from Isaias 45:8, the Introit for the fourth Sunday in Advent.

3–7   Here the birth of Christ is treated as if a new sun has arisen, a daystar so bright that no clouds can hide it and not even the old sun, Phoebus Apollo, can rival it. (Compare Apocalypse 22:16 where Jesus is called "the bright and morning star.") This new sun, which has come down from His heavenly tower, is born of the Virgin Mary, the flower of flowers and the rose of Paradise. Compare "A Ballad of Our Lady" (Poem 4), line 26, where the phrase "day sterne" is used to describe Mary.

8   *Et nobis puer natus est.* The Latin phrase from Isaias 9:6 commonly appears as a refrain in nativity carols as well as the Christmas Mass Introit.

9–10   There are nine groups of angels comprising the heavenly hierarchy, and five of them are mentioned here: archangels, angels, dominations, thrones, and powers (the four not mentioned are seraphim, cherubim, virtues, and principalities). The *marteris seir* ("martyrs many," line 10) probably refers to the 144,000 of Apocalypse 14 who have merited a place for themselves in Heaven prior to the general Last Judgment.

9–16   Beginning with the denizens of Heaven, the movement in this stanza is downward from the angels and martyred saints, to the operations of the cosmos — the stars, planets, spheres, and the heavenly vault — and then to the realm of Nature existing beneath the moon and composed of the elements fire, earth, air, water. These verses probably suggest that the birth of Christ has brought about a great cosmic harmony, and as a result, all of creation rejoices.

12   *firmament.* The heavenly vault generally, though possibly the eighth sphere of the fixed stars.

17–24   In this stanza the focus shifts to sinful man, whose redemption is made possible by Christ's birth, death, and resurrection. Lines 19–20 reveal that because sinners were not able to come to Christ, Christ has humbly volunteered to come to them.

25–32   Now the poet turns more specifically to members of the clergy, who are urged to fulfill their responsibilities and to honor this occasion with reverence and ceremony.

28   *of kingis King*. From Apocalypse 19:16. Compare "In Praise of Women" (Poem 5), line 29.

33–56   The final three stanzas return to the *Jubilate omnia* theme introduced earlier, as the birds, the flowers, and then all of creation unite in singing *Gloria in excelsis*.

38–39   In "On the Resurrection of Christ" (Poem 3), lines 21–23, Christ is also depicted as the glorious dawn or daybreak that dispells the darkness of night. This image also recalls Isaias 9:2 ("the people that walk in darkness shall see a bright light"), a verse read by Christian exegetes as an allusion to the Harrowing of Hell.

43–44   The image of Jesus as the blessed fruit of Mary would have been familiar from the angelic salutation of the Annunciation (Luke 1:28, 42): *Ave Maria, gratia plena; dominus tecum: benedicta tu in mulieribus, et benedicus fructus ventris tui Jesus* ("Hail Mary, full of grace, the Lord is with thee; blessed art thou among women and blessed is the fruit of thy womb, Jesus").

47   *Prince*. Compare Isaias 9:6 ("the prince of peace").

49–51   The regions of the universe treated in stanzas 2 and 3 — the heavens, the area of the cosmos between Heaven and earth, and the earthly realm itself — are again shown to be three distinctive places that unite in celebrating the Lord's coming.

49   *hevin imperiall*. The highest heaven of all and God's dwelling place. Compare Douglas, *The Palis of Honoure*, line 1878, and Lindsay, *Dreme*, lines 383 and 514–18.

51   *fische . . . foull*. A common juxtaposition indicative of scope. Compare the thirteenth-century song "Foweles in the frith / þe fisses in þe flod" — *MEL*, p. 7.

53   *Gloria in excelsis*. "Glory in the highest"; these are the initial words of the *Gloria* in the Mass, reflecting the angels' words to the shepherds in Luke 2:14.

2. *Of the Passion of Christ*

One of Dunbar's several dream-vision poems, "Of the Passion of Christ" is a Good Friday meditation that offers a vivid account of the events surrounding Christ's Passion. In addition to depicting the terrible agony experienced by Christ both before and during the Crucifixion, the poem also reminds sinful man of the spiritual preparations he must make in preparing a resting place for Christ in his heart. After the initial stanza, in which the narrator falls asleep in the oratory of a friary, the next eleven stanzas (lines 9–96) focus on the horrific events themselves; among the grisly details depicted are several that are absent from the gospel accounts but that are often seen in the visual arts and in literary works such as the mystery plays. The next sub-section comprises five stanzas depicting the narrator's emotional responses, which are reflected in a series of personified figures (representing the narrator's own internal feelings) who vigorously accost him and ultimately purify him, making him a fit receptacle for God's grace. In the final stanza the narrator awakens and immediately records his visionary experience. Hasler comments on the meditative patterns that foreground the cultural construction of subjectivity as the poem establishes connections *between* language and desire: "The subject observing the Passion becomes a series of metamorphoses of allegorical spaces; the engaged witness is transformed into a stage for a *psychomachia*, to emerge finally as a house fit for Christ to enter" (p. 197). Eighteen 8-line stanzas rhyming *ababbcbc* in MF; As contains only twelve stanzas. Mc80, K3, Bw1.

3–4   *And knelit doun with ane Pater Noster / Befoir the michtie King of Glorie.* I.e., he kneels down and recites the Lord's Prayer before an image of Christ; for the phrase *King of Glory*, see Psalm 24:7–10 in the Vulgate. Compare "The Table of Confession" (Poem 7), lines 1–3.

7   *gaude flore.* He sings the popular Latin hymn *Gaude flore virginali*, which concerns the seven heavenly joys of the Virgin. In my gloss I have followed the ME poet's translation of "Gaude virgo, Mater Christi": "Glade us, maiden, moder milde." See *Middle English Marian Lyrics*, ed. Karen Saupe (Kalamazoo, MI: Medieval Institute Publications, 1998), Poem 87, line 1 (p. 162).

16   *O mankynd, for the luif of thee.* This line, which becomes the refrain for this 11-stanza sub-group, recalls line 49 in Lydgate's *Cristes Passioun*: "Al this was doon, O man, for love of the!" (p. 218).

19   *ruge.* According to *DOST*, the word primarily means "to tug," esp. violently, and is often used in conjunction with the feeding habits of beasts that *ruge* (i.e., "rend") their food, a meaning utilized in lines 60 and 106. A secondary, nominal meaning of the word is "roaring," for which *DOST* lists only this line as a source. It is likely that Dunbar has both meanings in mind here, an implication that further emphasizes the terrible violence perpetrated on Christ.

26   *For scorne thai cled Him into quhyt.* That Jesus was garbed in white as a mark of scorn reflects the Latin phrase *vesta alba* in the Vulgate text of Luke 23:11.

29   *Dispituouslie syn did Him smyt.* Luke 22:64.

38   *warldis thre.* Three is a number indicative of a totality, thus "all worlds"; see Vincent Hopper, *Medieval Number Symbolism* (New York: Columbia University Press, 1938), pp. 4–5, and Aristotle's *De Caelo* 1.1. Augustine, in *De Libro Arbitro* 2.11.126, implies a formulation whereby the three worlds of air, land, and sea are equivalent to the "everywhere" that would perish were it not for God's numbering of Creation.

54   *His face, the fude of angellis fre.* The reference recalls line 28, which had mentioned the delight angels took in looking upon His eyes; in both cases the references emphasize the vileness of what is taking place. The phrase may ultimately derive from the Latin phrase *panis angelorum* ("the bread of angels") in Psalm 77:25 in the Vulgate. Compare *IMEV* 1715, where Jesus is called "the faire aungels fode" (line 33) and "aungels brede" (line 44).

59–62   *The clayth that claif to His cleir hyd . . . That it was pietie for to se.* This gruesome detail is not found in the canonical scriptures but does occur in other literary accounts, including the cycle plays (see Rosemary Woolf's discussion, *The English Religious Lyric in the Middle Ages* [Oxford: Clarendon Press, 1968], pp. 226–27).

71   *be houris sax.* Possibly "for six hours," though more likely "at the sixth hour" (John 19:14).

74–76   *Quhill all His vanis brist and brak . . . Thay leit Him fall doun with ane swak.* Christ's tormentors allow the Cross to fall to intensify His suffering; this is a traditional feature rather than a scriptural one.

81   *Betuix tuo theiffis the spreit He gaif.* Luke 23:46.

83–85   *The erde did trimmill . . . The day wox dirk as ony nicht.* Luke 23:45.

86   *Deid bodies rais in the cité.* Matthew 27:52–53.

89–92   *weir that He wes yit on lyf . . . blude and watter did furth glyde.* John 19:34.

97–136   In this 5-stanza sub-group (which introduces a new refrain line), the vision shifts from focusing on the events of the Passion to focusing on the narrator's emotional response to them. The device of having a series of allegorical personifications interact directly with the narrator is one that Dunbar uses in many poems. The afflictions visited upon him by Compassion, Contrition, Ruth, Remembrance, Pain, and Pity show how genuine and how painful is his response to Christ's suffering. Unlike the others, Grace treats him kindly and urges him to prepare a final resting place for Christ.

104   *Thy blissit Salvatour Jesu.* The new refrain reflects the dreamer's acceptance of Jesus as his "blessed Savior," one of the most important of the traditional names for Jesus.

106   *rugging.* The verbal echo of lines 19 and 60 deftly recalls both the buffeting and scourging of Christ, a literal example of the act of Remembrance and thereby of the experience of the dreamer.

109   *passioun.* Once again, Dunbar utilizes a verbal echo, this time of line 5, to provide a concrete example of the experience of the dreamer. The dream is situated by reflection upon the Passion, and it is the pain of that Passion — graphically revealed in the dream vision itself — that causes the dreamer such pain and moves him, at last, to Pity and Grace.

115–19   The final resting place that Grace urges the narrator to prepare for Christ is not a tomb or sepulcher but rather a home — presumably a spiritual home within the heart or body of the true Christian (compare 2 Corinthians 5:1). This metaphor is continued in the next two stanzas.

117   *dayis thre.* The three days between the dreamer's witnessing of the Passion and the Christ's return into his soul parallels the three days between Christ's death on Good Friday and His resurrection on Easter Sunday (Luke 24:7). It is also likely meant to recall the three worlds ransomed by Christ's Passion (line 38).

119   *in thy hous sall herbrit be.* For the body as the soul's dwelling place, see 2 Corinthians 5:1. This medieval commonplace provides the allegorical framework for works such as *King Hart*.

121–28   Here Contrition, Confession, Conscience, and Repentance cleanse the dwelling and open its gates so that Penance can enter, all in anticipation of the Savior's arrival. In the following stanza Grace becomes the dwelling's caretaker.

123   *Conscience me accusit heir.* Conscience plays a vital role at the Last Judgment; see 2 Corinthians 1:12 and *King Hart*, line 572.

131–132   Being spiritually prepared for the Lord's arrival is the message of such parables as "The Good Steward" in Matthew 24 and "The Wise and Foolish Virgins" in Matthew 25.

138–39   The earthquake which awakes the narrator recalls the shaking of the earth at the moment of Christ's death in the gospel accounts (e.g., Matthew 27:51, compare line 83); here, of course, it also provides the device by which the narrator's visionary experience is brought to an end.

140   *With spreit halflingis in effray.* The line may reflect the state of emotional turmoil in which the narrator awakens, while also suggesting that the spirit creatures who have appeared to him are fleeing in all directions. Compare line 187 of "The Thistle and the Rose" (Poem 30).

3. *On the Resurrection of Christ* [*Surrexit Dominus de sepulchro*]

The third of Dunbar's hymn-like poems depicts Christ's great triumph over Satan and his minions in the Harrowing of Hell and celebrates His Resurrection on Easter Sunday morning. Here the poet creates a striking collage of traditional images and ideas associated with the time immediately following the Crucifixion. Virtually every commentator on the poem has been in awe of the compelling rhythmic power of Dunbar's verses; C. S. Lewis called it "speech of unanswerable and thundering greatness" (1954, p. 96). Contributing to the thundering effect of the verses is Dunbar's frequent use of alliteration and especially the end-stopped quality of every line in the poem. It seems quite possible that the poem was composed for choral singing, though we have no evidence that that actually occurred. The Latin refrain is a versicle for the Mass for Easter Sunday.

    The poem contains a total of forty lines, arranged in five 8-line stanzas, and it is possible that the numbers 5, 8, and 40, numbers rich in biblical associations and symbolism, were selected to enhance the themes of the Resurrection. In regard to structure, the first and last stanzas of the poem summarize the overall events; the second stanza focuses on images of Satan and his malice; the third focuses on images of Christ and His victory over Satan; and the fourth stanza emphasizes the glorious consequences of Christ's Resurrection. See Pamela K. Shaffer, pp. 54–60, for a detailed analysis of the poem's symmetrical architecture. The rhyme scheme — *ababbcbC* — is that of Dunbar's other hymns. B only. Mc81, K4, Bw10.

1   *dragon blak.* The dragon symbolizes Satan several times in Apocalypse, particularly in the War in Heaven. See Apocalypse 12:7–9, 12:17, and 20:2.

2   *Our campioun Chyrst.* The heroic actions of Christ following His death on the Cross provide the subject for numerous literary works throughout the Middle Ages. The English mystery play cycles include a Harrowing of Hell play, and there are vivid descriptive accounts in poems such as the Middle English debate poem *Death and Liffe.* The principal source for all of these materials is the apocryphal Gospel of Nicodemus. The scriptural basis for the Harrowing of Hell is very slight, occurring only in 1 Peter 3:18–20 and 4:6.

3   *The gettis of Hell ar brokin with a crak.* The breaking open of the gates of Hell is a common element in the Harrowing of Hell; it occurs in Nicodemus 18, and may derive ultimately from Psalm 23:7 in the Vulgate.

4   *The signe triumphall rasit is of the Croce.* Depictions of Christ — both visual and literary — carrying the Cross as a battle standard were medieval commonplaces.

6   *The saulis ar borrowit and to the blis can go.* The redeemed souls that now can go to bliss are those of the Old Testament patriarchs, who were condemned to Hell as a consequence of Adam's sin. Compare the Middle English lyric "Adam lay i-bounden" (*MEL,* p. 147).

7   *indoce.* Literally, "endorse"; the metaphor is a financial one in which Christ has repaid Man's ransom by endorsing the promissory note with His own blood.

8   *Surrexit Dominus de sepulchro.* Compare Luke 24:34.

9   *the deidly dragon Lucifer.* Satan is not depicted as a serpent in Genesis 3 alone, but also in Apocalypse 12:9, where he is called "the ancient serpent . . . the deceiver of the whole world." For the name Lucifer ("light-bearer"), compare Isaias 14:12.

11–15   The tiger, like the dragon and the serpent, was also a common symbol of the devil in the Middle Ages. This cruel beast who lies in wait for his prey will be thwarted by the lion, the resurrected Christ of line 19.

Explanatory Notes to Poem 3

18   *lyk a lamb in sacrifice*. Christ is depicted as a lamb in many passages of Scripture: e.g., Isaias 53:7, Acts 8:32, 1 Peter 1:19, and throughout Apocalypse.

19   *lyk a lyone rissin up agane*. In Apocalypse 5:5 Christ is called the Lion of Judah; and commonly in medieval bestiary literature the lion was a symbol of Resurrection — this was because a lion cub was said to be brought to life on the third day after its birth when its father licked it into shape and breathed into its face.

20   *as a gyane raxit Him on hicht*. Probably an allusion to the exultant giant in Psalm 18:6 in the Vulgate; but the story of Samson carrying off the gates of Gaza (Judges 16:3) may also be pertinent. In any case, it is a powerful and arresting image. See *Biblia Pauperum*, plate 1 (p. 43), which juxtaposes Samson carrying the gates with the Resurrection.

21–23   Christ is the bringer of radiant light — He is the dawn, the sun, and the day that vanquishes the night. Compare "On the Nativity of Christ" (Poem 1), lines 36–40.

27–28   The allusion in these verses is to the darkness that occurs during the Crucifixion (Luke 23:44–45).

29   *The knell of mercy*. This refers to the ringing of the church bells on Easter Sunday morning, emblematic of the triumph of the Resurrection. Compare *Piers Plowman*, B.18.428.

33–39   This final descriptive summary returns us to the initial stanza of the poem. Here the rhythm of each line is intensified by the yoking of pairs of related items: "The foe is chased, the battle is done / The prison broken, the jailers fled," etc.

35   *weir*. "War" is the obvious gloss, though there may also be connotations of *weir* n. 2: "uncertainty, doubt, and confusion"; and *weir* n. 3: "a bog, or slough, swamp," which are common metaphors of Hell (n.b., Bunyan's "slough of despond" from *Pilgrim's Progress*).

39   This verse takes us back to the first verse of the poem, telling us once more that the terrible black dragon that had guarded his hoard for so long has been vanquished and his treasure taken away. Thus the poem concludes with an image of Christ as a heroic dragon-slayer.

4. *A Ballad of Our Lady* [*Ave Maria, gracia plena*]

Dunbar's poem in praise of the Virgin is highly traditional and yet also quite unusual. It draws heavily upon the great store of traditional images associated with the Virgin in numerous Adoration of the Virgin poems, images that are derived not only from the scriptures but also from the liturgy, biblical commentaries, sermons, and Latin hymns. Most of these images are familiar to students of medieval literature — e.g., Mary as the bright heavenly star, Mary as the rose of Paradise, Mary as the fleur-de-lis, Mary as both mother and maiden, Mary as intercessor for sinful man. Others are probably less familiar — Mary as a shield and as a strong warrior, Mary as an unseen anchor, and Mary having been fed with angel food.

At the same time, Dunbar's penchant for experimentation and innovation is greatly evident in this poem. For example, in each of the 12-line stanzas the Latin refrain occurs not in the final verse but in the ninth verse; and in each of these stanzas, aside from the Latin refrain, the end rhyme is achieved with just two rhyming sounds. Even more remarkable is the fact that in each *a* verse in the rhyme scheme internal rhyme occurs in triplets, while in each *b* verse there is alliteration. Aureate diction also occurs throughout the poem, and Dunbar often seems to be inventing words or adapting them directly from Latin phraseology — e.g., "regyne" (line 6) from *regina*, "rosyne" (line 8) from *rosa*. The end result of this profusion of devices is a jewel-like creation, though one, it is probably safe to say, that does not suit the taste of every modern reader. The poem survives only in As. Seven 12-line stanzas rhyming *abababa bCbab*. Mc82, K2, Bw16.

1   *Hale.* Echoes of the angelic salutation to Mary, recorded in Luke 1:28 and 42, reverberate throughout the poem both in English and in the Latin *Ave maria, gracia plena!* of the refrain.

1–12   The dominant image in the first stanza is of Mary as a heavenly beacon who disperses the darkness and serves as our guide. Very often in poems on the Virgin she is called the *stella maris*, "the star of the sea," though that particular image does not occur in Dunbar's poem. Dunbar returns to the image of Mary as a heavenly star in lines 25–28.

5   *Hodiern, modern, sempitern.* "For this day, for this age, for all eternity"; compare Hebrews 13:8.

6   *Angelicall regyne.* The Virgin was often thought of as the queen of Heaven and the queen of angels; students of ME literature will be familiar with this idea from the anonymous ME poem *Pearl.* Compare Kennedy's *Passioun of Crist*, line 123.

8–10   The association of flowers with the Virgin — especially roses and lilies — probably derives from the imagery of the Canticle of Canticles 2:1–2.

9   *Ave Maria, gracia plena.* See Luke 1:28.

11   *virgin matern.* The phrase reflects the Virgin's paradoxical status as both maiden and mother.

14   *Alphais habitakle.* The reference is to the physical Incarnation of Christ in Mary; she has become His "dwelling." For *Alphais,* compare "I am the Alpha and the Omega" — Apocalypse 1:8 and 22:13.

16   *His tabernakle.* This is a common image for the Virgin's womb; compare Kennedy's *Passioun,* line 28: "The Haly Gaist schane in hir tabernkill."

22   *but makle.* "Without blemish," i.e., immaculate; in the ME lyric "I sing of a maiden" (*MEL,* p. 170) the Virgin is similarly said to be "makeles" (line 2).

26   *day sterne.* A phrase more often applied to Christ than to Mary, as in "On the Nativity of Christ" (Poem 1), line 23.

29–30   *puttar to flicht / Offendis in battale.* This striking image of Mary as strong in fight is fairly unusual in adoration poems; nevertheless, the Virgin is sometimes so portrayed in Miracle of the Virgin narratives and in various works in the visual arts.

31   *plicht.* Although Mary is not called the *stella maris* in this poem, her frequent association with maritime metaphors is reflected in her image as an anchor, a traditional symbol of hope for medieval Christians.

34   *gentill nychttingale.* The nightingale, though often associated with amorous love in medieval literature, could also be associated with Christian love. Lydgate refers to Mary as a nightingale in *Ballade of Reverence of Our Lady* (line 80, p. 258); and in Dunbar's own "The Merle and the Nightingale" (Poem 66), the nightingale speaks in favor of loving God.

39   *schene unseyne with carnale eyne.* This image of Mary as a beauteous one who is unseen by human eyes, which contrasts strongly with the many references to her as a radiant heavenly beacon, accords with the image of Mary as an unseen anchor in line 31.

40   *ros of Paradys*. The rose of Paradise is also the *rosa sine spina*, the "rose without a thorn," a phrase commonly applied to the Virgin in poems of adoration. In medieval tradition, prior to the Fall the rose was unfading and thornless.

42   *flour delyce*. The fleur-de-lis, a variety of lily, often used to symbolize Mary's royalty and her sexual purity, a tradition arising from biblical commentaries on Canticle of Canticles 2:2.

43   *grene daseyne*. "Green daisy" — "green" perhaps in the sense of "fresh." The daisy, a variety of sunflower, was a common symbol of truth and fidelity in the Middle Ages, and in its whiteness and perfect circularity was associated the pearl. The Latin word *margarita* may be used to refer to either the daisy or the pearl.

47–48   Mary as intercessor or mediator is one of her most familiar and important roles. *Oratice* (line 48) means "orator" or "speaker" and is just one of the several terms Dunbar creates by applying the feminizing suffix *-ice*.

51   *Our glore forlore for to restore*. Mary, as the second Eve, restores our lost glory by undoing Eve's deed, which results in a greater good than would have otherwise been; this is perhaps an oblique allusion to the paradox of the Fortunate Fall.

56   *To mak our oddis evyne*. The phrase apparently refers to Mary's help in "evening up the odds" for sinners at the time of the Last Judgment when their souls are being weighed in the balance. There may also be a hint in this stanza that Mary will help to "even the odds" by producing a fortunate roll of the dice, suggested by the references to seven and eleven in lines 50 and 58.

59   *Quhill store and hore my youth devore*. "While pain and age devours my youth" — the only personal reference in the entire poem.

65   *Our wys pavys fro enemys*. In regard to Mary as our "shield," it is interesting to note that Sir Gawain has the image of the Virgin painted on the inside of his shield in *SGGK* (lines 648–50).

73   *Imperiall wall*. Kinsley interprets *wall* to mean "well" (or fountain), and Mary as a "well" or "wellspring" is certainly a common image in Marian poetry. But the central figure that runs through lines 73–78 is of Mary as a magnificent habitation suitable for enclosing Christ. Thus *wall* may actually refer to the "outer wall" or

"rampart" which surrounds the palace, the hall, the hospice, and the private chamber ("closet" [line 78]) — all of which are itemized in the ensuing verses.

74   *peirles pulcritud.* Compare Douglas, *The Palis of Honoure*, line 1414.

79   *Bricht ball cristall.* Crystal was often used as a symbol of the Virgin's purity, though the image of the Virgin as a crystal ball was not so common. Here, though, it creates a compelling sense not only of her purity but also of her physical perfection, making her the perfect house in which to enclose the Lord.

80   *angell fude.* Compare "Of the Passion of Christ" (Poem 2), line 54 and note.

82–84   The final verses of the poem emphasize the crucial importance of the Virgin in the ransoming of fallen man by Christ on the Cross.

5. *In Praise of Women*

Because this poem in praise of women contrasts so strongly with the negative attitude toward women reflected in many of Dunbar's poems, some commentators have wondered whether "Now of wemen" should be assigned to him at all, or whether his praise of women might actually be ironic. While neither of those suggestions can be entirely discounted, they seem unlikely. Indeed, just as the previous poem is a genuine celebration of the Virgin Mary in particular, this poem appears to be a genuine celebration of women generally; and the two poems are directly connected by the fact that the Virgin is here presented as the supreme example of womanhood.

While "In Praise of Women" is a celebration of all women, what it especially praises is mothers and motherhood and the most glorious mother of all, the Virgin mother. (If Mother's Day had been celebrated in the sixteenth century, one could imagine this poem as having been written for that occasion.) Beginning with verse 14, the emphasis in what follows is on the pain and suffering that mothers experience for the sake of their children — in conception and pregnancy, in giving birth, and in nursing and child-rearing. And as the poet points out in his final verses, although Christ did not have a human father, He had a human mother who bore Him in perfect holiness. For that reason, he suggests, women should be honored above all things. A ME poem containing many of the same sentiments is the Vernon MS poem "Of Women cometh this Worldes Weal" (*IMEV* 1596; see *Religious Lyrics of the XIVth Century*, ed. Brown, pp. 174–77). This is Dunbar's only poem in iambic pentameter couplets. B and MF. Mc45, K72, Bw40.

4–6   Here the speaker denounces men who disparage women — which was certainly a common medieval phenomenon — by saying that a man who dishonors women only dishonors himself. Lines 22–26 repeat this sentiment in even stronger terms.

7–8   *Sen that of wemen cumin all ar we; / Wemen ar wemen and sa will end and de*. It is not entirely clear how these lines relate to each other, or what is intended by line 8. But what seems to be stressed is the commonality of men and women — women give birth to all people, men and women alike; and women are merely flesh and blood and thus subject to death, just as are men. Bawcutt believes there may be a visual play on words in *wemen*, with its possible suggestion of *we men* (Bw 2.373).

13   *consaif with pane*. This phrase probably refers to the pain of childbirth rather than conception, though it is also possible that it refers to the physical discomforts experienced by women during pregnancy.

22–24   "Whoever says anything against them, he fouls his own nest and should be exiled from good company." Although the unnatural act of fouling one's own nest is proverbial (Whiting B306), these lines directly recall issues raised in the ME bird debates the *Owl and the Nightingale* and the *Thrush and the Nightingale*. In the *O&N* the nightingale accuses the owl of being such a bird. The *T&N* concludes with the thrush, who has been disparaging women, being bested by the nightingale — whose trump card is Virgin Mary. The final result is that the thrush is exiled from the land.

27–30   The final argument in support of women stems from the fact that Christ had a human mother but no human father. At this point one might expect the poem to pursue the Adoration of the Virgin theme, but it does not. This has led some commentators to suspect that the poem has been abridged in order to satisfy post-Reformation religious sentiments.

29   *King of Kingis*. Compare "On the Nativity of Christ" (Poem 1), line 28; and Apocalypse 19:16.

6. *The Manner of Going to Confession*

"The Manner of Going to Confession" is one of Dunbar's several religious poems that focus on the Lenten season. Its particular concern is with the Christian's spiritual preparation for confession, and it is therefore one of the only poems we have in which we see the poet fulfilling one of his clerical responsibilities. The tone of the poem is sober and fatherly, gently admonishing its hearers to be mindful of the sins they must reveal to their priest. The forty days of Lent, the period from Ash Wednesday to Easter Sunday, was a time for penitence and reflection on one's spiritual condition, all in anticipation of receiving the Holy Eucharist at mass on Easter Sunday. One curious side note in the poem is the speaker's admonition (in lines 29–35) to select one's confessor with care, comments that imply a criticism of some of his fellow clergymen. The main emphasis in the poem, though, is on the importance of searching one's conscience thoroughly, uncovering every sin, and then fully reporting those sins in confession. Ten 7-line rhyme royal stanzas rhyming *ababbcc*. Ar only. Mc84, K5, Bw41.

1	*fourty dayis*. The forty days of Lent, from Ash Wednesday to Easter Sunday. Compare Henryson's *Fables*, lines 320 and 2120. Forty is used to signify a period of trial in the Bible: it measures the time Moses spent on the mountain (Exodus 24:18), Elijah traveled before his vision in the cave (3 Kings 19:8), Ninevah was given to repent (Jonas 3:4), the spies were in the land (Numbers 13:26), and, of course, the time Jesus spent in the wilderness (Matthew 4:2, Mark 1:13, Luke 4:2).
2	*wilfull*. "Willing," i.e., voluntary; a valid confession must be freely offered and not compelled.
3–6	The reference is to Jesus' forty-day fast in the wilderness. See Matthew 4:1–2.
8–14	The first requirement in preparation for confession, as these verses suggest, is a truly penitent heart.
13	*That every syn be theselfe be schawin*. This verse seems to indicate that each sin must be separately revealed.
15–28	This pair of stanzas develops an analogy between physical ailments and spiritual ailments. A person can be neither physically whole nor spiritually whole unless all ailments have been addressed. The confessor is a person's spiritual physician.
28	*Thow sulde it tell with all the circumstance*. The full circumstances surrounding a particular sin should also be recounted.
29	*discreit*. "Discerning"; the confessor must be able to distinguish, for example, between the lesser sins (venial sins) and greater sins (mortal sins). Compare "The Table of Confession" (Poem 7), line 91.

29–36 The speaker here urges his listeners to choose their confessors wisely. If they do not, it becomes a case of the blind leading the blind.

35 *ane blynde man is led furth be aneuther.* "The blind leading the blind" is a popular medieval proverb (Whiting B350), originating in Matthew 15:14. Pieter Bruegel the Elder has a striking painting illustrating this proverb (*The Parable of the Blind Leading the Blind*, 1568). Compare *Piers Plowman*, B.12.180–86, and "Als I lay in a winteris nyt" (*IMEV* 351), lines 375–76.

48 *contrycioun.* On contrition as the first step toward penance, followed by confession of mouth, see Chaucer's Parson's Tale (*CT* X[I]106–315).

50–56 Here, finally, the sinner is advised to confess with his "own mouth" all of his sins, which he knows far better than anyone else.

54 *Thow knawis best quhair bindis thee thi scho.* Proverbial (Whiting S266).

57–63 Medieval Christians were required to go to confession at least once a year, a ruling that was established at the Lateran Council of 1215. The advice offered here is that they take stock of their spiritual situations far more frequently.

60 *And on the end hes no rememberance.* I.e., "And on the end [of life] gives no thought."

64–70 The advice offered in this final stanza is that we should be mindful of our moral conditions while we are still young, for there is great danger in putting it off until old age has come upon us. Compare Ecclesiastes 12:1.

7. *The Table of Confession*

This comprehensive enumeration of the sins probably served as a guide to confession for members of the laity, but it may also reflect the poet's own heartfelt contrition. Like the previous poem, it seems to give us a glimpse of Dunbar in his role as professional cleric; and also like the previous poem, it was probably written expressly for the Lenten season. Unlike "The Manner of Going to Confession," however, in which the speaking voice is admonitory and directed at the sinner, here the voice is that of the sinner himself.

  The poem reads like a primer in medieval Christian doctrine, with stanzas devoted to the five senses, the seven deadly sins, the seven deeds of corporal mercy, the seven deeds of spiritual mercy, the seven sacraments, the ten commandments, the twelve articles of faith, the seven virtues, and so on. But, as Bawcutt observes, the poem "is more than a dry tabulation of sins, and is suffused with emotion, particularly in the refrain and the final prayers" (Bw 2.485). "The Table of Confession" survives in four MS texts, three of which have been altered, probably to make them more palatable to Protestantism; the text here printed is from BL MS Arundel 285, a pre-Reformation devotional book once belonging to the Howard family. Twenty-one 8-line stanzas rhyming *ababbcbC*. Mc83, K6, Bw83.

1–8   This introductory stanza depicts the state of mind the humble and genuinely penitent sinner should be in as he approaches confession.

3   *Befor Thy bludy figour dolorus*. The speaker is presumably kneeling before an image of the Crucifixion, as in lines 3–5 of "Of the Passion of Christ" (Poem 2).

6   *in word, in wark, and in entent*. I.e., "In word, deed, and thought," a phrase from the General Confession.

8   *I cry Thee marcy and laser to repent*. I.e., "I beg of you mercy and a chance to repent"; compare Henryson's *Fables*, lines 775–76, and *The Wallace* 9.275–76.

9   *I me schrife*. The dative of agency construction, with the recipient of the action as subject, heightens the idea that shrift is an act performed on oneself.

11   *my wittis fyve*. The five wits, which are the five physical senses, are often mentioned in manuals on confession. The failure to control them leads to sins of the flesh. In *SGGK* they are one of the five fives symbolized by the pentangle on Sir Gawain's shield; Gawain is said to be faultless in his control of them (line 640), which the story largely bears out.

17–24 Here the speaker expresses his regret for exercising (*Exercing*, line 21) the seven deadly sins. The sins are listed in lines 19–20, beginning with pride, envy, wrath, and covetousness — the sins of the spirit. Then come lust, gluttony, and sloth — the sins of the flesh (although sloth may also be a spiritual sin). Compare their depiction in lines 13–102 of "The Dance of the Seven Deadly Sins" (Poem 77).

23   *Thy woundis five*. The five wounds of Christ (two in the hands, two in the feet, and one in the side) became a commonplace in medieval devotional literature. They are also one of the fives represented by the pentangle on Gawain's shield (*SGGK*, lines 642–43).

25–32   The seven deeds of corporal mercy derive from Matthew 25:35–36: "I was hungry
          and you gave me food, I was thirsty and you gave me drink . . . ."

33–40   The seven deeds of spiritual mercy are correcting the sinner (line 35), teaching the
          ignorant (line 34), counseling the doubter (line 35), comforting the sorrowful (line
          36), bearing wrongs with patience (line 38), forgiving others their offenses (line 39),
          and praying for the souls of the living and the dead (line 37).

43   *hie Eucarist moist of exellence.* The first — and "most of excellence" — of the
          seven sacraments is Holy Communion; the serving of the Eucharist on Easter
          Sunday is the culminating act of the entire Lenten season. The other sacraments are
          Baptism, Penance, Confirmation, Holy Matrimony, Ordination, and Extreme
          Unction.

49–56   The ten commandments are presented twice in the Old Testament, in Exodus
          20:1–17 and in Deuteronomy 5:6–21.

57–72   The twelve articles of faith listed in this stanza are familiar to many Christians as
          the Apostles' Creed.

73–80   The seven virtues consist of the three theological virtues — hope, faith, and charity
          — and the four cardinal virtues — fortitude, prudence, temperance, and justice. For
          the Christian virtues compare 1 Corinthians 13:13 and Galatians 5:5–6.

76   *Agins vicis sure anarmyng me.* "Against the sins arming myself securely"; compare
          Ephesians 6:13–17.

81–88   The seven commands of the Church enumerated in this stanza are tithing, avoiding
          cursing, observing fast days, hearing mass, attending the parish church, making
          one's confession, and receiving communion once a year at Easter.

89–96   This stanza surveys the sins against the Holy Spirit, which St. Mark warns against
          in Mark 3:28–30. Compare Chaucer's Parson's Tale (*CT* X[I]692–95).

90   *syn aganis natour.* Presumably, this refers to "unnatural" sex acts; compare Romans
          1:26–27.

91   *of confessour undiscreit.* As he did in line 29 of the previous poem and in line 85 of this poem, Dunbar again emphasizes the importance of selecting one's confessor wisely.

92   *ressait synfull of my Salviour.* I.e., receiving the Eucharist while still in a state of sinfulness.

94   The seven gifts of the Holy Spirit originate in Isaias 11:2–3.

95   *Pater Noster.* The Lord's Prayer, from Matthew 6:9–13, which includes a series of seven clauses called the seven petitions.

105–44   These stanzas offer a lengthy catalogue of more particular offenses — especially sins of word, thought, and deed — in contrast to the more standard violations of Christian doctrine previously described.

105–12   This stanza focuses on varieties of the sin of evil speaking.

113–20   This stanza focuses on varieties of the sin of evil thinking.

121–28   This stanza depicts varieties of sinful deeds, especially improper actions concerning money and property.

129–36   Here the focus shifts to the speaker's sins involving duplicity, hypocrisy, and deceit.

134   *Counsall.* The King's Council, his chief group of advisors.

           Sessioun. The Court of Sessions, the supreme civil court of Scotland, a parliamentary court that sat at various times in various places after 1425. See *DOST Ses(s)io(u)n(e), ii.* In "Tidings from the Session" (Poem 74), Dunbar affiliates the Session with Edinburgh. See also "Dunbar at Oxford" (Poem 28), line 37, and "To the Merchants of Edinburgh" (Poem 75), line 57.

140   *culpabill knaw I me.* In contrast to the previous stanzas, the speaker now acknowledges sins he knows he is capable of committing — sins that lodge in his heart — even though he has not actually committed them.

145–52   In this stanza the speaker likens himself to Mary Magdalene, whose sins Christ forgave. The model for the penitent sinner, she became the object of a popular cult in the Middle Ages. She was one of the witnesses to the Crucifixion and was among the first to see the risen Christ on Easter morning; she was also traditionally identified with the unnamed woman who washed Christ's feet with her tears in Luke 7:37–50. In Luke 8:2, Jesus cast seven demons out of her, traditionally seen as the seven deadly sins. See the Digby play of *Mary Magdalene* for a late medieval confluence of Magdalene traditions on penance and redemption.

153–60   Here the speaker, though physically unharmed, expresses his desire to share with Christ the full experience of His Passion on the Cross. Compare "Of the Passion of Christ" (Poem 2), lines 97–112.

163–64   Using a judicial metaphor, the speaker expresses his desire for his case to be heard, not in the Lord's court of extreme justice, but in His court of surpassing mercy; it is Christ's death and resurrection that makes such a request possible.

165–66   Although it is a medieval commonplace, the figure of the soul as a ship striving to reach safe harbor is a poignant one. Compare "Of Man's Mortality" (Poem 9), lines 41–44, and "Of the World's Vanity" (Poem 11), line 13.

8. *All Earthly Joy Returns to Pain*

There is no neat dividing line between Dunbar's religious poems and his moral poems, as this poem illustrates, for while it clearly belongs to the poet's series of Lenten poems — it is written specifically for Ash Wednesday — it also shares with his moral poems a fundamental concern with human mortality and earthly mutability. Dunbar has several poems in which the narrator tells us what he has overheard; in this case it is the "words" of a bird's song, a fairly common device in medieval poetry (Chaucer had used it in *The Complaint of Mars*, for example). It seems likely that the poem's forty lines are intended to provide a parallel to the forty days of Lent. The verse form of the poem is the French *kyrielle*, a quatrain rhyming *aabB*; Dunbar was fond of this form, employing it about a dozen times. B and MF (which omits lines 17–20). Mc71, K59, Bw49.

4   *All erdly joy returnis in pane.* The sentiment expressed in the refrain is a medieval commonplace. Compare Chaucer's "evere the latter ende of joye is wo" (*CT* VII[B^2]3205); compare also Henryson's *Praise of Age*, line 26. Whiting cites several early proverbs that express this same idea (J58–61).

Explanatory Notes to Poem 8

5–7   These verses reflect passages of Scripture such as Genesis 3:19 and Ecclesiastes 3:20 and 12:17, which provided the basis for the Ash Wednesday liturgy.

10   *Deth followis lyfe with gaipand mowth.* Hellmouth is commonly represented in medieval drama by the mouth of the Leviathan. Sometimes it was represented on maps as a place far in the west, opposite Eden, which was said to be in the east.

15   *flouris laid in ane trane.* Compare Henryson's *Fables*, line 1856.

17–18   January and May were traditional opposites in the Middle Ages; compare Chaucer's Merchant's Tale, and *The Kingis Quair*, line 765.

19   *Wes nevir sic drowth bot anis come rane.* The image of the rain coming after a period of drought might seem more like joy following woe than the other way round, although in a damp, cold northern climate dry spells might be highly valued; in any case, the saying is proverbial (Whiting D417).

21–24   Although the literal meaning of these verses is problematic, the general sense seems to be that it is a joyful thing when a person has a true heir who can succeed him after the painful experience of his death. The refrain line here deviates from the refrain used in the other stanzas.

29–36   The sentiments expressed in these two stanzas are often found in satiric poems in the tradition of the "complaint against the times."

37–40   In several of Dunbar's moral poems there is a slight shift in thought at the very end, as there is here. It is as if he is saying, "Since this is the way things are, let us endeavor to achieve a joy that will never end" — the joy of salvation.

9. *Of Man's Mortality* [*Quod tu in cinerem revertis*]

This highly conventional poem on the *memento mori* theme also belongs to the poet's series of Lenten poems. Both the opening Latin verse and the Latin refrain are derived from the Ash Wednesday service as reflected in the Sarum Missal. Blending the motif of the fallen heroes (one variety of *ubi sunt*) with the motif depicting what we shall soon become (the *ubi erunt* theme), the speaker admonishes his readers or hearers to "speed thee, man, and thee confess," for you shall soon return to ashes. Once again, the central concern in this poem is with penitence, contrition, and confession. Six 8-line stanzas rhyming *ababbcbC*. B and MF (where it is anonymous). Mc74, K61, Bw32.

1–2   The Latin opening, as well as the Latin refrain, reflects the words spoken by the priest on Ash Wednesday as he touches a worshiper's forehead with ashes: "Man, remember that you are dust and to dust you will return." Verse 2 contains an English paraphrase of the Latin. These phrases derive from Genesis 3:19 — "dust thou art and unto dust thou shall return." The Latin phrasing of lines 1 and 8 is that of the Sarum Liturgy used in Scotland (Bw 2.360).

3   *Lang heir to dwell nathing thow pres*. Bawcutt translates the line: "Strive in no way to remain here long" (Bw 2.360).

4–6   Compare Job 14:2, "Who cometh forth like a flower, and is destroyed, and fleeth as a shadow"; and Job 8:9, "for we are but of yesterday and are ignorant that our days upon earth are but a shadow." Compare also Whiting B511.

9–16   The theme of the fallen heroes is often used to illustrate human mortality and impermanence, and this is a fairly standard group of such figures. They are usually selected to show that whatever outstanding qualities people may possess — strength, wisdom, power, or beauty — those things have no value when death arrives, for all people go the way of all flesh.

11   *Alexander*. As Bawcutt points out, Alexander the Great "had particular popularity in Scotland (the name was given to three kings)" (Bw 2.360). Like Hector of Troy, he was one of the Nine Worthies.

13   *playit thair pairtis*. "Fulfilled their roles" on the great stage of life. Compare "The Lament for the Makars" (Poem 14), line 46.

17–32   This pair of stanzas reflects the *ubi sunt* theme, graphically depicting the physical dissolution that lies ahead for every person.

27–28   For Death as a dragon, compare "Elegy for Bernard Stewart, Lord of Aubigny" (Poem 36), lines 17–18, and "To the King" (Poem 41), line 28.

29–30   These verses bring to mind the conclusion of Ingmar Bergman's classic film *The Seventh Seal*, when Death comes for the knight and his companions who have taken shelter within the knight's castle.

33–36   Regardless of the extent of a person's worldly goods, only one's good deeds have value after death; this idea, which stems from Apocalypse 14:13, is at the heart of the ME morality play *Everyman*. Compare "A Meditation in Winter" (Poem 15), line 44.

37–39   The admonition to go quickly to confession is the basic message of the poem.

41–48   The extended metaphor contained in these verses describes the sinner as a tempest-tossed ship that is inevitably driven into Death's harbor; only his Ransomer with His five wounds can save the sinner by providing an anchor and a rudder that will steer the ship to the haven of eternal life. Dunbar also uses this figure in line 13 of "Of the World's Vanity" (Poem 11).

45   The five wounds are the five wounds of Christ on the Cross; Christ is the Ransomer because He ransomed humankind from sin and death by paying with His own life. Compare "The Table of Confession" (Poem 7), line 23.

46   The anchor as a symbol of hope derives from Hebrews 6:19. The rudder (*steiris*) as a symbol of divine guidance is seen in Chaucer's Man of Law's Tale (*CT* II[B¹]833).

10. *An Orison*

In this short, simple devotional poem the speaker acknowledges that his sensuality has sometimes lured his soul into sin, but he rejoices in the spark of "light and spirituality" that has awakened his mind and has allowed him to rise up in new awareness. He begs for God's grace and a chance to make amends for his sins, in the hope that he can achieve peace and prosperity in this life and afterward attain the bliss of Heaven. This gentle, heartfelt poem anticipates the poetry of George Herbert in the seventeenth century. Bawcutt suggests that the poem may be an extract from a longer poem, which was a common practice in the sixteenth century (Bw 2.421). R and MF. One 8-line stanza rhyming *ababbcbc*. Mc78, K7, Bw60.

1   *sensualité*. I.e., the pursuit and indulgence in physical, sensual pleasures.

4   *witt*. Wit is the intellectual faculty that relates to knowledge and understanding, while *ressoun* ("reason") often relates more to one's ability to make sound moral decisions. As Bawcutt points out, "in *King Hart* Reason and Wit arrive in each other's company (line 578)" (Bw 2.422).

6–8   Kinsley calls attention to the similarity between these verses and a passage in the Scottish Book of Common Prayer: "May the almighty and merciful Lord grant unto you pardon and remission of all your sins, time for true repentance, amendment of life, and the grace and comfort of the Holy Spirit" (K, p. 241n7, 6–8). The request for time to repent and atone for one's sins is also reflected in the refrain line of "The Table of Confession" (Poem 7) in the phrase "laser to repent" ("the time to repent").

11. *Of the World's Vanity* [*Vanitas vanitatum et omnia vanitas*]

This is one of Dunbar's most conventional poems on the theme of worldly impermanence; as in several others, the voice of the preacher urges its hearers to be spiritually prepared for the journey they will soon take. Although it does not mention confession specifically, that appears to be its implicit message. While "Of the World's Vanity" consists largely of moral commonplaces, the poem is enhanced by its rhetorical flair and its effective use of poetic devices. Three 8-line stanzas rhyming *ababbcbC*. MF only. Mc75, K60, Bw42.

1   *O wreche, be war.* As Reiss points out (p. 128), this phrase is typical of a small group of Dunbar's poems in which the speaking voice is that of a moralizing preacher speaking to "everyman."

2   *mony greit estait.* I.e., many people of high rank and great achievement.

3   *freynd . . . fo.* While "friend" and "foe" may be taken literally, it is surely figurative as well — i.e., Christ and Satan.

5   *Remeid in tyme and rew nocht all to lait.* This is one of the verses (along with line 12) in which the need for repentance, contrition, and confession are most strongly implied.

6   *Provyd thy place.* The "place" that needs to be readied is our heavenly abode, not our earthly habitation. Compare Psalm 83:5 in the Vulgate — "Blessed are they that dwell in thy house, O Lord."

7   *Out of this vaill of trubbill and dissait.* The image of this earthly life as a "vale of trouble," a medieval commonplace, derives from Psalm 83:7 in the Vulgate. Compare Henryson's *Thre Deid Pollis*, line 2, and Lindsay's *Monarche*, line 5077.

8   *Vanitas vanitatum et omnia vanitas*. The well-known refrain is taken from Ecclesiastes 1:2.

9   *Walk furth, pilgrame, quhill thow hes dayis licht*. Hebrews 11:13–15 provides the scriptural basis for viewing life as a spiritual pilgrimage to God. Dunbar's phrase "Walk furth, pilgrame" seems to echo line 18 from Chaucer's lyric "Truth": "Forth, pilgrim, forth! Forth, beste, out of thy stal!"

10   *desert*. I.e., the wasteland of this world.

13   *Bend up thy saill and win thy port of grace*. This nautical metaphor is similar to what occurs in "Of Man's Mortality" (Poem 9), lines 41–47. Bawcutt points out that the phrase "port of grace" was used for "New Haven and Burntisland, two small harbours on the Firth of Forth," and may therfore have had "a special piquancy for Scottish readers" (Bw 2.376).

17–18   N.b., echoes of instability and change in Chaucer's "Lak of Stedfastness."

17–24   Several of the verses in this stanza alliterate, and internal rhyme occurs in line 22. Especially striking is the rhetorical pattern in lines 19–22; here the first and fourth lines consist of a balanced pair of antithetical "now" phrases, while the two verses within them each contain four "now" phrases arranged in contrasting pairs. Compare uses of alliteration and internal rhyme in "An Orison" (Poem 10).

12. *Of Life*

This short homiletic poem provides a succinct analysis of life as offering a choice between Heaven and Hell: we can choose short torment and receive unending bliss, or we can choose short-lived joy and receive lasting sorrow. What is unstated but clearly implied is the fact that we make this choice by how we live our lives. It is possible that this single rhyme royal stanza (*ababbcc*) is an excerpt from a longer poem. MF and B (where it is anonymous). Mc76, K57, Bw51.

1   *Quhat is this lyfe*. This recalls the opening phrase of Arcite's death speech in Chaucer's Knight's Tale: "What is this world? What asketh men to have?" (*CT* I[A]2777). The notion of life as a *way to deid* ("a road to death") is a medieval commonplace and is also reflected in The Knight's Tale in Egeus' comment that "This world nys but a thurghfare ful of wo" (*CT* I[A]2847).

3   *A slyding quheill.* The image of the sliding wheel is allied to the medieval concept of Dame Fortune and her wheel. It brings to mind instances in which figures such as the Nine Worthies are placed upon Fortune's wheel and then dashed to their destruction when she spins it; e.g., the ME *Alliterative Morte Arthure*, lines 3388–90.

5   *A pray to deid, quhome vane is to repell.* The image of man as death's prey also occurs in line 95 of "The Lament for the Makars" (Poem 14).

13. *Of the Changes of Life*

One of Dunbar's several poems on the topic of earthly mutability, "Of the Changes of Life" focuses especially on the changes in the weather and the seasons as reflective of the impermanence of life in this world. Life's basic pattern, the poet suggests once again, is the alternation of joy and woe. But here, in contrast to poems such as "All Earthly Joy Returns to Pain" (Poem 8), there is no positive upturn at the end, and no admonition to work to achieve a life of permanence in the life to come. Four 5-line stanzas rhyming *aabba*. Two texts are preserved in MF, and one in R (copied from the first in MF). Mc66, K58, Bw20.

6–15   In both stanzas the poet establishes the contrast between *yisterday* (lines 6 and 11), when the weather was soft and fair and the flowers were springing, and *This day* (lines 9 and 12), when the weather stings like an adder and the flowers are all slain. This may simply imply the natural turning of the seasons with winter following summer, or it may suggest the unexpectedness of life, with winter making an untimely reappearance in spring.

8–9   The juxtaposed images of the peacock feather and the adder's sting may reflect (and reverse) a traditional piece of Scottish weather lore: "When March comes in with an adder's head, it goes out with a peacock's tail" (Bw 2.333), which is similar to the American expression, "In like a lion and out like a lamb."

14   *walkis.* May mean "awakens" rather than "walks" or "moves."

16–19   This pairing of items — summer/winter, comfort/care, midnight/morrow, joy/sorrow — often occurs in mutability poems. The third juxtaposition in line 18 (midnight/morrow), reverses the pattern of something negative following something positive. This may be an intentional variation; or it may simply result from the requirements of the rhyme scheme.

14. *The Lament for the Makars* [*Timor mortis conturbat me*]

"The Lament for the Makars" is a poignant tribute to the poet's fellow poets as well as a general meditation on human mortality in the *memento mori* tradition. The Latin refrain — *Timor mortis conturbat me* — which originates in the response to the seventh lesson in the Office of the Dead, a service read daily by medieval clerics such as Dunbar — became a familiar phrase in the later Middle Ages. It occurs as the refrain in other poems and was often inscribed on tombs. Structurally, the poem consists of two major sections. The first is the speaker's general meditation on the plight of all mankind, and the second is his more specific meditation on the mortality of the great poets, a fellowship to which he himself belongs. The poem may obliquely reflect the late medieval tradition of the *danse macabre*, the Dance of Death, although that association is never made explicit. Scholars debate whether the somber tone of the poem — and the reference to the speaker being "sick" — implies a late date of composition. But the simple fact that all but one of the poets named in the catalogue of *makaris* are now deceased — poets who in some cases were still alive in the first decade of the sixteenth century — justifies the suggestion that this is a fairly late poem.

Two aspects of the poem especially impress this reader. The first is the way the poem creates a sense of Death closing in on the speaker, coming ever nearer and nearer. It does this by first depicting all the general classes of humanity — rulers, nobles, high churchmen, the rich and the poor, the powerful and the weak, the scholar, the theologian, the physician — and then focusing directly on poets — first on the great English poets and then on the Scottish poets. Finally Death turns his attention to Dunbar's closest contemporaries; now, in fact, he is on the verge of taking the last of them, "good Master Walter Kennedy" (lines 89–90). Death's next victim will be the poet himself. Also impressive is the variety of images and metaphors used to depict Death's taking of the poets. It devours Chaucer and Gower; poisons Master John Clerk and James Afflek like a cruel scorpion; kills Blind Hary and Sandy Traill with a shower of mortal hail; and ensnares Robert Henryson and Sir John Ross with the intimacy of a lover's embrace.

But despite the somberness of the poem overall, it is important to note that this poem, like many of Dunbar's poems on the mutability theme, ends on a positive note, emphasizing that life in this world should be viewed as a preparation for the life to come. The length of the poem, 100 lines, may be intended to create a sense of completion and finality. And while it may well be just a coincidence, it is worth noting that the poem contains twenty-five stanzas, which is also the number of *makaris* listed in the catalogue of poets, with the speaker being the twenty-fifth. Twenty-five 4-line stanzas rhyming *aabB* (the Old French *kyrielle*). B, MF, and RP. Mc7, K62, Bw21.

1–44   The first eleven stanzas, essentially the first half of the poem, offer a fairly traditional treatment of the mutability theme. The opening stanza, in which the speaker's own condition is described, provides the point of departure for his meditation on death. Stanzas 2–4 discuss human and worldly mutability in quite general terms, while stanza 5 shifts the focus to more specific groups within society. Stanzas 6 to 11 focus on individuals in highly impressive occupations; despite their great abilities, however, they are completely powerless in the face of Death.

2   *gret seiknes*. Most commentators suspect the phrase refers to the poet's actual ill health. Reiss suggests that it should be taken symbolically (pp. 229–30).

3   *And feblit with infermité*. Although the poem touches in earnest upon a wide range of themes pertaining to death, A. A. MacDonald suggests that "if the poem were to be read aloud at the court, it would without doubt lend itself to ironic presentation: 'Dunbar at death's door' could easily be another of the protean poet's poses." He might be "deeply concerned at the fact of human mortality, even at the very moment of employing this subject in a profoundly comic poem." Dunbar's actual death was still nearly a decade away when he wrote the poem, perhaps as "a parody of the cliché-ridden and vapid rhetoric all too common in such complaints of love" ("Alliterative Poetry," pp. 277–78).

4   *Timor mortis conturbat me*. From the seventh lesson of the Office of the Dead. See headnote, above.

5–11   Nicolaisen juxtaposes the repetitive syntax in lines 5 and 6, with the half lines of line 7 and 11, the stress patterning of line 9, the chopped-up quadrupartite line 10, and the later refrain's classic structural division of the sentence into its ultimate constituents (i.e., *Timor mortis conturbat me*) to exemplify the metrical, syntactic, grammatical, in short the linguistic virtuosity of Dunbar, whose understanding of sentence and line makes him "the Hopkins of his age" (Nicolaisen, "Line and Sentence in Dunbar's Poetry," in Aitken, pp. 61–71, esp. pp. 63–69).

6–7   The World, the Flesh, and the Devil are man's three traditional foes. Compare *Als I lay in a winteris nyt* (*IMEV* 351), lines 377–432, possibly derived from St. Bernard's "De tribus inimicis hominis, carne, mundo, et diabolo"; compare also *IMEV* 2865.

10–11   Dunbar uses similar sets of opposing pairs elsewhere, e.g., in "Of the World's Vanity" (Poem 11), lines 19–22. The phrase about "dancing merrily" in line 11 depicts a fleeting moment of joy in this life and is not an allusion to the Dance of Death.

13   *stait.* Perhaps Dunbar is using this word in both of its senses, "state" (condition) and "estate" (social position).

17–19 Here Death is the Great Leveler, taking all humankind without regard to power, status, or wealth.

21–44 The listing of the specific occupations that fall prey to Death recalls the *vado mori* ("I go to death") motif encountered in several ME poems in which individual representatives of estates or occupations testify to their "going to death." Compare, for example, "I wend to deeth, knight stith in stour . . . / . . . I wende to deeth, clerk ful of skile" (*IMEV* 1387: "I Wende to dede a kyng y-was").

37–39 Grouped together here are various practitioners and possessors of arcane knowledge, people whose vast learning avails them not at all when Death arrives.

41–43 The allusion is to Luke 4:23, "Physician, heal thyself." Compare Whiting L170.

45–48 This stanza provides the transition into the second half of the poem, with its focus on the *makars* or poets.

46   *Playis heir ther pageant, syne gois to graif.* "Perform here their parts in life's pageant, then go to the grave." Compare line 13 in "Of Man's Morality" (Poem 9). The "life's a stage" metaphor was common long before Shakespeare. Compare Whiting P5.

49–52 Here Dunbar celebrates his greatest predecessors among the English poets. Line 50 contains his famous homage to Chaucer, whom he describes as *of makaris flour* — the flower of all poets in the English language (line 50). *The monk of Bery* in line 51 is John Lydgate (1370–1449), a Benedictine monk in the monastery at Bury St. Edmunds and the most prolific English poet of the fifteenth century. *Gower*, line 51, is John Gower (c. 1330–1408), Chaucer's contemporary and the author of *Confessio Amantis*, among other notable works.

53–92 Now Dunbar begins his roll call of the deceased Scottish poets. A few of them are well-known as poets, but several of them, to the extent that they can be identified at all, are not known for having been poets, though presumably they were. Nothing is known about some of them. See explanatory notes, below, for details.

53–54   Of the first three Scottish poets mentioned, *Heryot* is completely unknown. Sir Hugh Eglintoun, who died in the 1470s, was the brother-in-law of Robert II; he is not known as a poet unless he is the "Huchown of the Awle Ryale" for whom Wyntoun provides a list of works. *Wyntoun* is Andrew Wyntoun, the prior of Lockleven and author of a long verse chronicle, *Oryginale Chronkil of Scotland*.

55   *this cuntré*. I.e., Scotland, as distinct from England.

57   *scorpion*. The agent of the "sting of Death"; compare 1 Corinthians 15:55.

58   *Johne Clerk* may be the author of the several poems in the B MS attributed to "Clerk," though that is only a supposition. The "Johne Clerk" mentioned in line 81 of "Master Andro Kennedy's Testament" (Poem 80) is thought to be a different John Clerk. *James Afflek* (or perhaps Auchinleck?) has not been identified.

59   *trigidé*. Not a "tragedy" in the narrower sense but rather a sad and moving narrative; compare Henryson's *Testament of Cresseid*, line 4, and Chaucer's *TC* V.1786. Compare also the definition of the term offered by Chaucer's Monk (*CT* VII[B]1973–77).

61   *Holland* is Sir Richard Holland, an important fifteenth-century Scottish cleric and author of the allegorical animal fable *Buke of the Howlat*. *Barbour* is John Barbour (d. 1395), author of the life of Sir Robert the Bruce, *The Actes and Life of Robert Brus*.

63   *Schir Mungo Lokert of the Le* has not been positively identified, although the Lockharts of the Lee were a prominent family in Lanarkshire.

65–66   *Clerk of Tranent* is the second "Clerk" in the list, but no more is known about him than is known about *Johne Clerk*. Tranent is a small town located between Edinburgh and Haddinton. If the phrase *anteris of Gawane* is a title rather than a description, it is the only specific work mentioned in the catalogue. Several MS copies of a ME romance called *The Awntyrs off Arthur* survive in a northern dialect of English and Sir Gawain is the central character. Perhaps also pertinent is the Middle Scots romance *Gologras and Gawain*, which is written in the same strange form as *Awntyrs*. See Thomas Hahn, ed., *Sir Gawain: Eleven Romances and Tales* (Kalamazoo, MI: Medieval Institute Publications, 1995).

67   *Schir Gilbert Hay*. The fifteenth-century cleric Sir Gilbert Hay was primarily a translator of prose works but also translated the poem *The Buik of Alexander*. He lived much of his life in France and was Charles VII's chamberlain.

69   *Sandy Traill* has not been identified, but *Blind Hary* has long been considered the author of *The Wallace — The Actis and Deidis of Schir William Wallace* — even though his name is not mentioned in the single surviving manuscript of the poem.

70   *Slaine with his schour of mortall haill*. Showers of mortal hail were sometimes used as God's instruments of death in the Old Testament, e.g., Exodus 9:23–25 and Joshua 10:11.

71   The poem "The Thre Deid Polis," usually attributed to Robert Henryson, is assigned to *Patrik Johinstoun* in B. It is known that Johnston was an actor and a producer of dramatic entertainments, in addition to being a notary and a landowner who received revenues from Crown lands in West Lothian (Bw 2.336).

73–75   These verses offer the fullest praise in the catalogue, and *Merseir* is the only deceased poet to receive an entire stanza. Several poems in B are ascribed to him, but he is otherwise unknown, although Lindsay includes a "Merser" in a list of poets in *Papyngo* (line 19).

75   *So schort, so quyk, of sentence hie*. This verse echoes a line from Chaucer's description of the Clerk of Oxenford, whose speech was "short and quyk and ful of hy sentence" (*CT* I[A]306).

77–78   Neither of these *Roulls* have been identified, though one of them may be the author of *The Cursing of Sr Iohine Rowlis* in B, which Bawcutt describes as "a blackly comic poem" (Bw 2.336).

81–82   *Robert Henrisoun*. Dunbar's famous older contemporary and the author of the *Testament of Cresseid*, the *Fables*, and *Orpheus and Eurydice*. He was often called "the schoolmaster of Dunfermline," an important royal and monastic town; he did not live beyond 1505. See the METS edition of his works, ed. Robert Kindrick and Kristie A. Bixby (Kalamazoo, MI: Medieval Institute Publications, 1997).

83   The identity of *Schir Johne the Ros* remains uncertain, though he is almost certainly the same person mentioned in the opening line of Dunbar's famous *Flyting* with

Kennedy (Poem 83), and probably a very close friend of Dunbar's. None of his poems survive.

86   *Stobo* is John Reid, a very notable clergyman who had served in the secretary's office under James II, James III, and James IV. He is mentioned in line 331 in the *Flyting* with Kennedy (Poem 83). He died in July of 1505.

        Quintyne Schaw is the author of one poem in MF; he was still alive in 1504, when there is a record of his receiving a royal pension. He is possibly the same person as the *Quinting* that Dunbar links with Kennedy in line 2 of the *Flyting* (Poem 83).

89–91   *Walter Kennedy*, Dunbar's opponent in the *Flyting*, is the one poet in his catalogue who has not yet succumbed to death; but Dunbar's great sorrow at Kennedy's imminent demise is poignantly reflected in line 91. Bawcutt points out, however, that he did not actually die until 1518 (Bw 2.337).

93   *brether.* I.e., brother-poets.

94   *lat me lif alane.* Although the line could mean "leave my life alone," it is more likely to mean "let me live alone"; this sets up a parallel with line 99, where Dunbar hopes that all may live together after death. The latter reading could also be extended to the idea that a man, perhaps especially a poet, cannot truly live in solitude.

97   *Sen for the ded remeid is none.* Proverbial; compare Whiting D78.

98   *Best is that we for dede dispone.* Preparing for death would involve attending to worldly concerns such as making a will, but perhaps more importantly, attending to spiritual concerns, "so that after our death we may live" (line 99).

15. *A Meditation in Winter*

In contrast to most of Dunbar's general meditations on earthly instability and human mortality, "A Meditation in Winter" focuses on the bitter winter weather that creates for the poet an oppressive sense of melancholy, a spiritual malaise that is akin to the emotional state reflected in several of Dunbar's petitions. Here those feelings are caused by the long nights and the dark, wintry days that prevent him from taking pleasure in songs, poems, or plays (line 5) — which probably includes his inability to take pleasure in the *writing* of songs, poems, and plays. In his petition poems the remedy the poet needs is some tangible reward, but here it is simply the coming of spring. Commentators agree that this is one of Dunbar's finest poems. Ross calls it "the gem" of Dunbar's moral poems (p. 157), and Ridley calls it a "beautiful meditation" (p. 1010). Ten 5-line stanzas rhyming *aabba*. MF contains both a complete version and an incomplete version; R contains only lines 1–22. Mc10, K69, Bw26.

1–10   With these verses compare the well-known Harley lyric "Wynter wakenth al my care" (*Mel*, pp. 13–14).

2   *sabill*. The heraldic term for "black," but also customarily described the color of clothing worn by mourners.

4   *Nature all curage me denyis*. The meaning of the term *curage* differs widely in ME texts, depending on the particular context in which it occurs. Here the meaning may be "Nature denies me any pleasure in songs," or perhaps "Nature deprives me of any desire to compose songs."

6   *nycht dois lenthin houris*. If one follows ecclesiastical time, whereby the daylight and nighttime hours are 12, in winter the nighttime hours are long; in summer short.

11–15   These verses recall the opening lines of Chaucer's *Book of the Duchess* in which the narrator describes his similar condition.

17   The personified figures who address the narrator are similar to the ones found in several of Dunbar's petitions and satires. Despair expresses his frustrated attempts to achieve at court the material rewards he believes he deserves; this is the central topic of Dunbar's petition poems.

21–30   Patience and Prudence provide the kind of advice that Lady Philosophy offers Boethius in *The Consolation of Philosophy* — that Fortune does not accord with reason and that earthly rewards are simply false felicities that do not last.

26   *Prudence* is an especially high form of wisdom. Compare Henryson's *Fables*, lines 1757–59, and Chaucer's Tale of Melibee (*CT* VII[B^2]1869–72). Prudence as a cardinal virtue equates with discernment and right reason.

31–40   The benign-seeming words of welcome of Old Age and Death are terrifying in their understated gentleness, as the following stanza makes clear. The little vision is sometimes thought to imply that the poet has now entered old age (and thus that this is one of his later poems). But this *petit rêve* of what lies in store holds true for all, whether youth or eld.

34–35   Making a final reckoning or accounting after death was a common feature in homiletic literature about death and is a central element in the ME morality play *Everyman*. Compare Romans 14:12.

36   *Deid castis upe his gettis wyd.* For a biblical reference to the gates of Hell, compare Job 38:17.

39   *this lyntall.* The grave is depicted in numerous works — poems, plays, sermons — as a low, narrow, windowless house.

46   *Yit quhone* — "yet when" — introduces "the turn" or the about face that turns this stanza (not unlike that of an Elizabethan sonnet) toward a note of hopefulness, on which the poem ends.

48   *schowris* refers back to the literal "schouris" of line 7, but also metaphorically to the speaker's frame of mind.

49   *Cum, lustie Symmer, with thi flowris.* This verse recalls the joyous welcome the birds sing to summer near the end of Chaucer's *PF*: "Now welcome, somor, with thy sonne softe" (line 680). Compare also *The Kingis Quair*, line 235.

16. *None May Assure in this World*

Because it reflects the characteristics of several poetic types — the moral poem, the petition, the complaint against the times, and the courtly satire — "None May Assure in this World" illustrates the difficulty in neatly categorizing many of Dunbar's poems. Clearly, though, the poem reflects the poet's devout religious feelings, and, because it incorporates several Latin verses of liturgical origin in its final stanzas, it also reflects the poet's clerical status. Much of the material in the poem about the unfairness and uncertainty of life is familiar — the difficulty in distinguishing friend from foe, falsehood flourishing while truth goes unrewarded, the poor suffering at the hands of the rich, and so on. Yet there are also moments of remarkable freshness, as in the striking group of interconnected metaphors in lines 46–55. All in all, this is one of Dunbar's most intriguing moral poems. Seventeen 5-line stanzas rhyming *aabaB*. B, MF, and R. Mc21, K63, Bw54.

1–50   This initial section of the poem, with its catalogue of social ills, is essentially a complaint against the present time. The emphasis in these stanzas is on the lack of fairness that prevails in the world. In the second section of the poem, which is introduced in line 51 with the word "yet," the focus shifts away from present evils to a consideration of future events — especially death and judgment — and these stanzas are filled with apocalyptic images and overtones.

6–9   These verses suggest the feelings of an aggrieved petitioner. Whether *Lord* in line 6 refers to his earthly lord or his heavenly Lord is somewhat ambiguous. There is no ambiguity, however, about which lord is addressed in line 81.

18   *And nane bot just men tholis injure.* Ironically, it is the just who are treated unjustly.

23–24   Similar sentiments about the undeserving being rewarded with important secular and religious offices are reflected in Dunbar's petition poems.

26–30   In this stanza the speaker suggests that noble qualities are no longer found in members of the nobility. In line 28 *fredome*, the noble virtue of generosity, has been replaced by an insistence upon *foirfaltour*, forfeiture, which indicates legal proceedings (probably involving confiscation of land) against those unable to pay.

36–40   Court flatterers are listened to and rewarded while truth-speakers are excluded. Compare Isaias 59:14.

44   *fra the handis gois few gud deidis.* Compare "Of Man's Mortality" (Poem 9), line 35.

46–49   These lines present conventional images in an unconventional fashion. The "white whale bone" of line 46 — a reference to the ivory tusk of the narwhal — is often used to describe the loveliness of a lady's complexion, and "azure blue" (line 48) commonly describes a lady's eyes. Here "flint stone" and "adamant" (lines 47, 49) convey a sense of hardness, coldness, and unfeelingness. "Azure" in line 48 refers more to the stone lapis lazuli than to the color, already described in the word *blew*. Adamant was a legendary stone of extreme hardness; it would be difficult to pry open hands of adamant.

51–55   This stanza, which initiates the second section of the poem, is linked to the previous stanza by the physical images of the body — "heart, hand, and body all" — which now must face death and a final accounting before the Judge. (Compare 2 Corinthians 5:10).

55   *Quha suld into this warld assure.* This is the only variation on the refrain line in the poem, a device Dunbar uses elsewhere. It presents the first in a series of rhetorical questions that occur in these final stanzas.

57–59   For other depictions of Fortune as an alluring whore, compare Barbour's *Bruce* 13.636–38, and *The Kingis Quair*, lines 1124–25.

63   *the angell blawis his bugill sture.* This is "the last trump" mentioned in several apocalyptic passages of Scripture — e.g., 1 Corinthians 15:52, 1 Thessalonians 4:15, and Apocalypse 11:15.

66   *Quhat help is thair in lordschippis sevin.* Compare Proverbs 11:4: "Riches profit not in the day of wrath."

71–72   This verse is based on a passage from the liturgy for the Office of the Dead. Compare also Matthew 6:23.

73   *Sall cry "allace" that wemen thame bure.* Compare Job 3:3: "Let the day perish wherein I was born."

74   *O quante sunt iste tenebre.* Compare Matthew 6:23.

76–79   These apocalyptic verses stem from passages of Scripture such as Apocalypse 8:8 and 11:19. They also exhibit the heaviest use of alliteration in the poem, climaxing with the running alliteration of lines 77–78 and the four alliterating words of line 78.

17. *Best to Be Blithe*

Contrasting with Dunbar's bleaker moralities is a small group of poems informed by Boethian philosophy and possibly influenced by such Chaucerian works as "Truth" and The Knight's Tale. In these poems the speaker, while fully observing the falseness of the world, seeks consolation in being cheerful in the face of adversity and in being content with his lot. But the optimistic face the speaker is trying to put on in this poem — "For to be blythe me think it best" — seems to be just that, and the poem actually reflects a strong sense of personal pain, most notably in the next-to-last stanza. Eight 5-line stanzas rhyming *aabaB*, with the *b* rhyme continuing through all stanzas. B, MF (which lacks lines 16–20), and R. Mc69, K64, Bw14.

1–5   The poem begins in much the same vein as several of the preceding poems, with the speaker musing on the falseness and impermanence of life in this world. But what is different here is his expressed desire to enjoy life in this world anyway; he does not view life as a vale of tears that must be endured, though he does make one brief mention of the everlasting life that is to come (line 28).

5   *For to be blyth me think it best*. Bawcutt suggests that the refrain sounds proverbial (Bw 2.319). Compare also Henryson's *Fables*, line 521: "Be blyith in baill, for that is best remeid."

6–15   These verses concerning Fortune and her wheel reflect common sentiments in medieval literature that derive from Boethius' *Consolation of Philosophy*. The poet's point is that by not placing one's heart in the gifts of Fortune, or by recognizing their impermanence, the inevitable fall that occurs when Fortune turns her wheel will be less painful (line 14).

26   *tynsall*. Bawcutt glosses the word to mean "loss, deprivation," and she may be correct (Bw 2.319). But in this context a more specific meaning seems likely. Kinsley argues that the poet literally means "tinsel," a fabric with golden threads woven through it, a distant relative of what we call tinsel today. If that is so, Dunbar is using the term to symbolize things that appear attractive but have no real lasting value.

28–29   Medieval writers commonly used the phrase "The twinkling of an eye" to reflect the brevity of life; its origin is 1 Corinthians 15:52 — "In a moment, in the twinkling of an eye, at the last trumpet"; compare Whiting T547.

31–34   These poignant, personal-sounding verses indicate that the only thing that prevented the speaker from being destroyed by the world's unkindness was his conviction that it is best "for to be blithe."

39   His characterization of life in this world as a *frawdfull fary* — a "deceitful dream" — is certainly a powerful indictment of it, and one wonders how successful he has been in his brave attempt to remain cheerful.

18. *Of Content*

This poem has much in common with Dunbar's other poems on Boethian themes; the benefits of being content are also endorsed by Paul in Phillippians 4:1 and 11, and in 1 Timothy 6:6–8. Ridley suggests that these poems "would seem to reflect Dunbar's reaction to the failure of his petitions" (1973, p. 1041), a notion worth considering; Ross observes that "the general note struck by the poem is that of Proverbs" (p. 134); and Bawcutt notes the similarity to the *moralitas* in Henryson's fable of *The Two Mice* (1992, p. 142). Dunbar's hortatory or "preaching voice" is often in evidence, as illustrated by line 11: "Thairfor I pray yow, bredir deir . . ." Seven 5-line stanzas rhyming *abaB*. R and MF (differing significantly). Mc70, K66, Bw53.

5   *He hes anewch that is content.* The refrain line reflects a common medieval proverb (Whiting E120).

6   *unto Ynd.* "As far as India"; India was considered to be a rich and exotic realm.

6–10   This stanza, which reverses the sentiments of first stanza, touches on covetousness, a topic treated more fully in another of Dunbar's moral poems — "Of Covetise" (Poem 22).

11   *bredir.* "Brother," i.e., "fellow human."

13   *Thank God of it is to thee sent.* Compare Chaucer's Boethian ballad "Truth: Balade de Bon Conseyl," especially lines 2 and 19. Compare also "Without Gladness No Treasure Avails" (Poem 19), line 9, and the refrain in Henryson's "The Abbey Walk."

17   *Withe gall in hart and hunyit hals.* I.e., "with a malicious heart and a honey-speaking mouth"; this is a common proverbial saying on the theme of hypocrisy and deceit (compare Whiting G12 and H433).

18   *Quha maist it servis.* "Who most it serves"; the "it" refers to the world of line 16.

19   *subchettis.* The reading in R is *subcharges.* In either case, the meaning probably is something like "second servings" or "extra dishes"; it is clear from the context that eating to excess proves bitter.

21   *Giff thow hes mycht.* In light of Dunbar's many petition poems, it is easy to see in a verse such as this one an indirect appeal to the king for his support.

29   *Gif we not clym, we tak no fall.* This verse expresses another common proverb; compare Whiting C295 and C296.

31–33   Also proverbial; compare Whiting C489 and 494.

19. *Without Gladness No Treasure Avails*

This is another of Dunbar's moral poems that reflects Boethian themes. While it expresses many of the same general ideas as the others, here the emphasis is on being merry (rather than on just being content) and on enjoying what life has to offer. Although the mood of the poem is not fully that of the *carpe diem* poem, it leans in that direction, reflecting Dunbar's conviction that comedy can play an important role in providing consolation. Bawcutt points out that several similar pieces in Scottish poetry, the most distinguished of which is Henryson's fable of *The Two Mice* (Bw 2.301). Five 8-line stanzas rhyming *ababbcbc*. Aberdeen Minute Book, B, and MF. Mc73, K65, Bw6.

1   *man.* Several of Dunbar's moral poems address "man" and admonishing him to be mindful of the speaker's advice. Henryson does much the same in the *Moralitates* applied to his *Fables*.

3–6   A spirit of charity and generosity flows through the entire poem. Here, in contrast to Polonius' advice to Laertes, the hearer is urged to be both a borrower and a lender, for the help he gives his neighbor now may be returned to him later. Compare Proverbs 3:28.

5   *His chance this nycht, it may be thine tomorow.* Proverbial; compare Whiting T405 and T349; also Ecclesiasticus 38:23.

11–12   In these verses stress is placed on using and enjoying whatever one has, not on storing it away in a miserly fashion. This is a central theme in Dunbar's "Spend Thine Own Goods" (Poem 21).

14   *Thy lyfe in dolour ma nocht lang indure.* The idea that a person cannot long survive in such a depressed state of mind is also expressed in line 34 of Dunbar's "Best to Be Blithe" (Poem 17).

20   *bot ane cry*. No longer than the duration of a shout, i.e., a short time.

23   *Quha levis mery, he levis michtely*. Proverbial; compare Whiting M131.

28–30   As was indicated in line 12, great misery attends the hoarding of goods; and here there is the additional point that others will soon come along and use them up anyway.

33–37   Only the basic necessities of food and clothing really matter; but if you do happen to possess great wealth, you will only enjoy it fleetingly, and you will still be held accountable for it. A more favorable final reckoning will come from a shorter list of possessions.

39   *treuth sall mak thee strang as ony wall*. "Strong as any wall" is proverbial; compare Whiting W14–18.

20. *His Own Enemy*

This is one of Dunbar's more controversial moral poems, if in fact it *is* one. At first glance the poem seems straightforward enough, advising its hearers to be cheerful and to enjoy what they are fortunate enough to possess. To do otherwise, the refrain suggests, is to bring sorrow upon oneself. Yet there is a sardonic quality to this poem that sets it apart from Dunbar's other moral poems; and the third stanza, surprisingly, seems to be informed by a bawdy double entendre. The final stanza also has a flippant quality not usually seen in Dunbar's moral poems. Five 5-line stanzas rhyming *aabab*, with much alliteration. B and MF (where it is anonymous). Mc2, K70 [*Ane werkis Sorrow to him sell*], Bw17 .

1–5   In several of Dunbar's moral poems the speaker urges his hearers to be content with whatever they have, however little; here it is the inverse — use fully what you have, however much.

6–10   This stanza reflects sentiments found in many ME poems that satirize the evils of marriage. In most instances these anti-marriage poems also contain statements about the wickedness of women, as in line 9.

11–15   The figure developed in this stanza apparently concerns the danger of shooting one's arrow at an unfamiliar target rather than the customary one; but the phrases and images are rife with sexual innuendo. The speaker's warning against illicit sex, though, has little to do with morality; it has more to do with avoiding the unpleasant physical consequences of venereal disease. Archery was a favorite pastime at the Scottish court, and the king often participated along with his courtiers (Bw 2.325).

12   *prop.* "Target"; *DOST* cites it as a current figure in Scots for a sexual mark. N.b. "gengie" ("arrow") in line 11. The Wife of Bath makes a similar joke in her send-up of St. Paul: "The dart is set up for virginitee; / Cacche whoso may, who renneth best lat see" (*CT* III[D]75–76) where "dart" (prize) becomes dart (arrow) and virginity the target (prop). The allusion is to 1 Corinthians 9:24.

13   *schuttis.* "Shoot/have sex" (Burness, p. 211).

13   *uncow schell.* "A strange target"; but *schell* may also mean "shell," which may imply the female sex organs. As Kinsley points out, in folklore "the correspondence between the cowrie shell and the female pudendum is a familiar theme" (K, p. 362).

14   *fleis of Spenyie.* Literally "fleas of Spain," but probably meaning syphilis. Bawcutt quotes the Glasgow surgeon, Peter Lowe: "Amongst the Frenchmen, it is called the Spanishe sicknesse, in England the great pocks, in Scotland the Spanish Fleas, and that for two causes, the one because it began first amangst the Spanyards; the other because when the infection spreadeth . . . it is like unto red spots called flea-bitings" (Bw 2.326).

16–20   Considering the sentiments expressed in so many of Dunbar's petition poems, this stanza may offer a comment on his own situation, in which case his pitiless master would be the king.

25   *I gif him to the Devill of Hell.* Rather than the expected final refrain, the poet gives us something with a little more punch.

21. *Spend Thine Own Goods* [*Thyne awin gude spend quhill thow hes space*]

This poem has had its doubters and detractors — those who doubt Dunbar's authorship, and those who question the poem's worth. Scott calls it "the worst poem Dunbar wrote" (p. 258), and Mackenzie believes it is "scarcely congruous with Dunbar's usual utterances" (Mc, p. 223). While it is attributed to Dunbar in B, it is not in MF, and many commentators such as Bawcutt have noted its "several clumsy passages" (p. 144). What may be most important to observe about this poem, though, is its repudiation of miserliness; for what the speaker is advocating is the judicious use of one's own goods while it is still possible, that is, while you are still alive. His comments on the future misuse of one's goods and on the callous attitudes of one's heirs and relatives may seem rather cynical, but many other medieval works reflect the same sentiments. Ten quatrains rhyming *aabB*. B and MF (where it is anonymous). Mc72, K67, Bw31.

1–3	Many ME lyrics on death and mutability comment on the certainty of death and the uncertainty of when it will arrive; compare the ME lyric, "Wanne I thenke thinges thre" (*IMEV* 3969).
4	*Thyne awin gude spend quhill thow hes space.* The refrain accords with a common ME saying; compare Whiting M59.
9–10	*today . . . to morne.* I.e., today (while you are alive) . . . tomorrow (when you are dead).
13–15	As Bawcutt suggests (Bw 2.144), these lines may advise drawing up a will to prevent future strife among heirs.
17–19	These verses satirize the hoarder or the miser (much like the figure of Winner in the ME debate *Winner and Waster*), the person who spends all his time gathering but then never expends what he has gathered at joyful celebrations.
21–23	These lines comment on ungrateful heirs who care only about their own good fortune and who do not care at all about the eternal welfare of the one who has died.
27	*settis on ane es.* "Sets on an ace," i.e., "places a very low value on"; an ace is the one on a die. *Thre Prestis of Peblis*, lines 176–248, offers a full account of the wasteful extravagance of one's heirs.
33–35	I.e., "Do not assume that others will not do to you what you would never do to them; if you do, you'll learn the hard way" — a bitter comment on human nature.
37	*the bairne dois to the muder.* Children turning against their parents — filial ingratitude — long predates Shakespeare's *King Lear*. Compare also Ecclesiasticus 3:18, which cautions against angering your mother.

22. *Of Covetise* [*And all for caus of cuvetice*]

This poem reflects the medieval tradition of complaints against the times, and it also has much in common with Dunbar's poems satirizing the court. The first ten stanzas offer a long list of societal ills, all of which stem from the sin of covetousness. The final stanza presents the speaker's conclusion: please your Maker, be merry, do not care about the world, and work to attain a place in Paradise, where there is no covetousness. Kinsley suggests that the poem was probably written after the Battle of Flodden in 1513, when Scottish society was thrown into great turmoil (K, p. 360), but there is nothing in the poem that explicitly or specifically substantiates that notion. Eleven quatrains rhyming *aabB*. MF and B (where it is anonymous). Mc67, K68, Bw13.

1–3   The virtues listed in the first two lines — which the speaker says are now considered vices — were commonly assumed to be the natural attributes of the aristocratic class.

4   *all for caus of cuvetice*. Covetousness is the root of all evil — 1 Timothy 6:10; compare also Whiting C491.

9–11   The noble pastimes of hunting and hawking, he says, have now been abandoned in favor of gambling — especially for cards and dice; the more usual courtly games of chess and "tables" (backgammon) are not mentioned. Compare Lindsay's *Complaint*, line 83: "There was no play bot cardis and dyce."

29–31   The speaker is outraged by the social injustice of lords going about in long silk cloaks that trail to the ground while their tenants survive by eating roots.

33–35   In the first stanza it is pointed out that the noble virtues are held to be vices; now the Christian virtues also are held to be foolish. As the next stanza will point out, the man who is considered wise in these times is the one who is good at taking from others.

41–44   The advice offered in the final stanza is similar to that expressed elsewhere in Dunbar's moral poems; but in the face of all that has gone before in the poem, it sounds rather like a "hoe your own garden" consolation.

42   *And sett not by this warld a chirry*. As Bawcutt notes, "A cherry typifies something of small value" (Bw 2.318). Compare Whiting C184 and 187; compare also line 8

in the ME lyric "Farewell, this world": "This lyfe i see, is but a cherye feyre" (line 8, *MEL*, pp. 228–29).

44   *For thairin ringis na covettyce.* The altered refrain in the final stanza is a device Dunbar also uses in "How Should I Conduct Myself" (Poem 24) and in "Of Content" (Poem 18).

23. *Of Deeming*

Although attributed to "Stewarte" in MF, B assigns it to Dunbar, and most scholars have accepted that attribution. (Mackenzie, however, demurs.) The poem condemns the human failing of speaking ill of others, what in the Middle Ages was often called "backbiting," a common form of the sin of envy. After suggesting that no one is immune from vicious gossip, the speaker's anger at such behavior rises to near fever pitch (lines 41–45) when he expresses his desire to take vengeance on those who judge others, something he resists doing only because it would serve to make matters worse. Ultimately he accepts the wise advice of King James IV — to live virtuously and ignore malicious tongues. Perhaps implicit in the poem is the biblical admonition: "Judge not, that ye be not judged" (Matthew 7:1). Some commentators have seen in line 26 — "be I but little of stature" — and line 31 — "be I ornate in my speech" — references to the poet's personal characteristics. Eleven 5-line stanzas rhyming *aabaB*, with variations on the refrain. B, and two versions in MF (neither attributed to Dunbar). Mc8, K81, Bw33.

1–5   This stanza employs a common device to introduce the topic of the poem. The voice the narrator hears in line 4 — the voice of a moralizing preacher — is presumably the speaking voice throughout the poem until the final stanza, when the narrator's own voice resumes. Since no further mention is made of the voice the narrator hears, perhaps we can assume it is his inner thoughts he is listening to.

3   *Within ane garth undir a tre.* Compare line 1 in Henryson's *Praise of Age*: "Wythin a garth, under a red rosere," and lines 4–5 in *The Tretis of the Tua Mariit Wemen and the Wedo* (Poem 84).

6–35   These six stanzas suggest that no one remains unjudged, not king, nobleman, lady, courtier, knight, small man, huge man, or ornate speaker.

14   *Thocht he dow not to leid a tyk.* Compare *The Flyting of Dunbar and Kennedy* (Poem 83), line 114.

18   *scho and he.* "She and he," i.e., everyone, both men and women.

19   In this context *jaipit* probably implies "seduced"; presumably the gossipers are impugning the lady's moral behavior. The phrase *lait and air* — "late and early" — reverses the usual word order of this common expression for the sake of rhyme but still means "constantly."

24–25 "God send them a strong rope" with which to be hanged — sentiments elaborated on in lines 41–44.

26   "Be I but little of stature" may be a reference to the poet's small physical size, which is alluded to elsewhere in Dunbar's poetry and perhaps most directly in his *Flyting* with Kennedy (Poem 83), who repeatedly calls Dunbar a "dwarf."

32   The name *Towsy* is used to suggest a frowzy, sharp-tongued, peasant woman. Compare *Christis Kirk*, line 54.

34   *Suppois hir mowth misteris a leiche.* I.e., "despite the fact that her own speech is so fractured as to require surgery"; her speech, one might say, is uncouth.

46–47 These verses seem to indicate that King James IV, who was born in 1473, is no longer young; James was killed in battle at Flodden in 1513, but was obviously alive at the time the poem was written.

48–50 While the wisdom contained in verses 49–50 is attributed to King James IV, the verses actually paraphrase Matthew 7:1–2. Perhaps the poet means to flatter the king (as he does in some of his petitions); or perhaps there is some irony here, a device only rarely used by Dunbar.

51–55 The final sentiments are similar in a general way to what is expressed in several of Dunbar's more conventional moral poems, poems in which the poet expresses his belief that he will escape the unfairness of this life in the life to come.

24. *How Should I Conduct Myself* [*Lord God, how sould I governe me*]

Ridley aptly describes this poem as a companion piece to the preceding poem (1973, p. 1010), although the behavior the speaker here deplores is malicious speaking, which was commonly viewed as a sub-category of the sin of envy. Several other ME lyrics also deplore this vice (compare, e.g., *IMEV* 1633 and Lydgate's "A wicked tunge wille seye amys"), and Bawcutt is correct in suggesting that the poem "treats a didactic theme very common in the late Middle Ages" (Bw 2.326). Like several of Dunbar's poems in this general vein, the poem not only offers a negative critique of slanderous speech but also reflects the speaker's determination to ignore such behavior and to be governed (and judged) by God. MF, B, and R. There are significant differences between the MF and B texts; and each of them has virtues and each has flaws. Nine 5-line stanzas rhyming *aabaB*. Mc9, K82, Bw18.

9   *confort.* Kinsley suggests the implication here is that someone has given him strong drink; Bawcutt suggests (Bw 2.326) the implication is that he has been comforted by having received sexual favors; either could be right. Or perhaps people assume that his jaunty behavior stems from certain financial benefactions.

17   *paramoris.* This is an adverbial usage of the noun *paramour*; to love *paramoris* is to love sexually, perhaps illicitly.

28   *not worthe ane fle.* "Not worth a fly" is a proverbial phrase for something of little value. See Whiting F345. Compare Chaucer (*CT* V[F]1132; VII[B^2]172; VIII[G] 1150) and Henryson (*Fables*, lines 2054 and 2286).

41–45   The sentiments here expressed are similar to those in lines 49–55 of the previous poem.

25. *Rule of Oneself* [*He rewllis weill that weill himself can gyd*]

One of the most sententious of Dunbar's moralizing poems, "Rule of Oneself" provides advice, not about how to live life generally, but about how to survive the vagaries of life at court. Thus the speaker's words of advice to his "friend" (who is also referred to as his "son"), inevitably bring to mind Polonius' advice to Laertes, though there was an ancient tradition of works that offer similar counsel that long predated either Dunbar or Shakespeare. (See Bw 2.483.) While the poem conveys no sense that the speaker himself is being satirized, there can be no doubt that life at court is. Bawcutt observes that the poem "has had few admirers" (1992, p. 141), a circumstance not likely to change. Six 8-line stanzas rhyming *ababbcbC*. B only. Mc41, K77, Bw81.

1–2   The speaker's initial observation seems crucial — if you wish to dwell at court, do not desire the gifts of fortune. Although he does not explain himself here, he does later on: such gifts are "variand" (line 41), that is, constantly changing and untrustworthy. Compare Boethius, *Consolation of Philosophy*, II, prose 2.

3   *lat thy tung tak rest*. This is the first of many references in the poem to the importance of speaking in all of its varieties, including false-speaking and malicious-speaking; especially important is minding one's own tongue.

8   *He rewlis weill that weill himself can gyd*. Compare the refrain here and in lines 16, 24, 32, 40, and 48 with Chaucer's "Truth: Balade de Bon Conseyl": "Reule wel thyself that other folk canst rede" (line 6). Compare Whiting M414, R231, and G407.

9–16   This stanza focuses on the importance of choosing one's friends wisely, another topic treated throughout the poem.

15   *Cum sancto sanctus eiris*. See Psalm 17:26 in the Vulgate.

17–24   This advice on being content reflects the sentiments expressed in some of Dunbar's other moral poems — e.g., "Of Content" (Poem 18) — as well as elaborating upon the first two verses of the poem.

19   *Be thow content, of mair thow hes no neid*. Compare the refrain of "Of Content" (Poem 18).

21   *Chakmait*. "Checkmate," the word signifying the end of a chess match.

25–32   This stanza merges the themes of keeping good company with keeping well one's tongue.

33–40   These verses offer the most overt statement of the wisdom of following the expedient course — for if you do not, your behavior may bounce back at you and "strike you in the neck" (line 36). It becomes very clear that the principal object at court is self-preservation. The implications of these verses also recall the "moral message" contained in Chaucer's Manciple's Tale about the tale-telling crow.

33–34   Compare Ecclesiasticus 21:28: "The lips of the unwise will be telling foolish things: but the words of the wise shall be weighed in a balance."

35–36   Proverbial (Whiting S92).

41–48   Only in this final stanza does a Christian element appear — hold God for your friend, do not mistreat the poor, and wrong no man at any time.

26. *Discretion in Asking* [*In asking sowld discretioun be*]

This is the first in a series of three superficially similar poems: poems that share the same form, have similar refrains, and reflect a central concern with "discretion." In fact, though, they are quite distinctive pieces. This one is the least satirical of the three, the most optimistic, and has the most in common with Dunbar's moral poems, though its advice is of a decidedly worldly kind. In essence, it outlines the best ways to go about asking for deserved rewards. Overall the tone is quite hopeful, though the poem ends on a rather bleak note by pointing out that if this advice is unsuccessful, there is little to be done about it. This is one of Dunbar's moral poems that also has some affinities to his petition poems. Nine 5-line stanzas rhyming *aabaB*. B (two versions), MF (where it is anonymous), and R. Mc14, K78, Bw44.

1–4   To begin with, the speaker says, one must have good cause before asking; if there is no justification for reward, that will be perceived.

6–9   Do not be constantly asking, for it will dull the ears of your listeners. Compare Proverbs 30:15.

11–14   Some ask for more than they deserve, some for less, and some (like the speaker) are too shamefaced to ask, and thus they go unrewarded. This last comment seems to provide a link with Dunbar's petition poems. These sentiments also bring to mind the various groups of petitioners in Chaucer's *HF* (lines 1553–1867).

16–19   Do not ask without having served, and do not hesitate to ask for service. But to have served and still to live in poverty is shameful both to the master and the servant — another comment that reflects sentiments expressed in Dunbar's petition poems.

21–24   Similar to the advice in the second stanza, here the suggestion is, do not spoil your good works by constant importuning.

22   *May spill it all with crakkis and cryis.* Compare *King Hart*, line 903, and Lindsay's *Satyre*, line 2220.

24   *Few wordis may serve the wyis.* This is a well-known saying; compare Whiting W588.

26–27   *Nocht neidfull is men sowld be dum, / Nathing is gottin but wordis sum.* Compare Whiting M276: "Seldom gets a dumb man land."

29   *For nathing it allane will cum.* Compare Whiting N151: "Nothing has its being of nought."

31–32   *Asking wald haif convenient place, / Convenient tyme, lasar, and space.* Compare Proverbs 15:23 and Ecclesiastes 8:6.

36–39   Biding your time may result in a "yes," when pressing your suit may result in many "no"s.

38   *All for that tyme not byd can he.* Compare *The Kingis Quair*, line 926, and Whiting T303.

41–42   A lord will ultimately reward his servant, even if he has to go unrewarded for a long time — yet another comment that brings to mind Dunbar's petition poems.

27. *Discretion in Giving* [*In geving sowld discretioun be*]

The second in the interconnected sequence of poems on discretion in asking, giving, and taking, this one concerns such things as the reasons for which people give, the manners in which they give, and the attitudes with which they give. A good deal of attention is paid to the selfish motives of the givers and to the unworthy causes or individuals to which they give. Although giving alms and providing for the poor were important Christian responsibilities (compare lines 25–32 in "The Table of Confession" [Poem 7]), here the emphasis is on satirizing the vanity and foolishness of givers rather than applauding their charity. Twelve 5-line stanzas rhyming *aabaB*. B (two versions), MF, and R. Mc15, K79, Bw45.

1–5   The reasons for giving listed here seem noble until we discover at the end of line 4 that the recipients have little need of reward.

8–9   Both verses suggest that the giver is giving in the selfish hope of gaining more in return.

14   *Giftis fra sum ma na man treit.* The verse suggests that we are offered gifts by some people that we simply must not accept.

16–19   The too long overdue gift — or the "too little, too late" gift — expresses a sentiment found in many of Dunbar's petition poems. Compare Henryson's *Fables*, line 2269, and Whiting T45.

21–30   These two stanzas play off the miserly giver against the excessive giver, condemning both.

26–27   As Bawcutt observes, "The figure of the overladen boat or barge had various medieval applications (see Whiting B422 and S249). Here, it refers to an over-generous man, loaded with debts, who founders financially" (Bw 2.381).

31–40   This pair of stanzas expresses familiar sentiments in Dunbar's poetry, the first deploring the giving of gifts to those who do not need them while ignoring those who do, the second deploring the practice of rewarding strangers with fresh faces while ignoring familiar faces who have served long and well.

36–37   Dunbar is frequently aggrieved by the generosity of the court to foreign newcomers, while familiar longtime servers are ignored. Compare "To the King" (Poem 47), line 69.

41–44   Here the poet presents a contrasting pair within a single stanza, with a positive example of discretion in giving (one of the few in the poem) being used to counter-balance a negative one.

46–50   This stanza satirizes court flatterers and yes-men, of which "there are many such now in these days" (line 49), verses reminiscent of Chaucer's Nun's Priest's Tale (*CT* VII[B^2]3325–30).

56–60   The final stanza focuses on the giving of benefices and clerical offices to the undeserving or incompetent, which again brings to mind the central concern in many of Dunbar's petition poems.

57   *Sanct Barnard.* St. Bernard of Clairvaux, the great twelfth-century theologian and founder of the Cistercian monastic order.

          Sanct Bryd. St. Bride (a variant on the name St. Bridget), who was an Irish abbess in the sixth century; many Scottish churches are dedicated to her.

28. *Discretion in Taking* [*In taking sowld discretioun be*]

The third poem in this sequence offers the most overt social criticism, attacking those members of society that "take" from others through various immoral and illegal means. In contrast to the previous two poems, which offer some positive examples of "asking" and "giving," there is little here but selfish grasping. In fact, throughout much of the poem "taking" is merely a euphemism for stealing. Eight 5-line stanzas rhyming *aabaB*. B, MF, and R. Mc16, K80, Bw46.

1   *Eftir geving I speik of taking.* The first verse provides a direct link back to the previous poem. For the linkage between "giving" and "taking," compare Acts 20:35; compare also Whiting G93–94.

2   *Bot littill of ony gud forsaiking* is in fact an understatement, since the poet does not speak at all of anything that could be described as "good forsaking," that is, refusing to take what one should not take.

3–4   In typical fashion, Dunbar contrasts those who refuse to take enough authority with those who insist upon taking too much. Each extreme is folly.

6–15   In this pair of stanzas the satire is first against greedy clerics who take income from their ecclesiastical holdings while caring little for the spiritual welfare of their parishioners, and then against greedy barons who gouge their tenants — actions in both cases that are immoral rather than strictly illegal. As Bawcutt points out, "sympathy for the rural poor is rare in Dunbar, and recalls Henryson" (Bw 2.382). Compare Henryson's fable of the wolf and the lamb, *Fables*, lines 2728–62.

6   *The clerkis takis beneficis with brawlis.* Bawcutt notes that "Disputes between churchmen over rich benefices were common, and occasionally turned into pitched battles" (Bw 2.382).

13   *Mailis* and *gersomes*, terms often used together in legal documents, refer to the annual rents and payments tenants are charged by their overlords, payments in money or in kind; in this case those charges are so excessive that the tenants are forced to become beggars.

15   MF includes a stanza here that is not in B:

Thir merchandis takis unlesum win   *unlawful*
Quhilk makis thair pakkis oftymes full thin;

Be thair successioun ye may see
That ill won geir riches not the kin *goods enrich*
In taking suld discretioun be.

Mackenzie includes the stanza within his text. Bawcutt prints it in her notes.

16–30   In these three stanzas, in contrast to the previous two, the focus is on varieties of theft, illegal practices that may result in harsh punishments if the perpetrators are caught.

27–29   Here the moral consequences and the legal consequences of these actions are compared; it is too bad, the poet says, that people are more afraid of being found out by other men than they are of being found out by God.

31–35   These verses contrast the insatiably greedy (lines 31–33) with the person who takes so little that he cannot succeed (line 34), the only time in the poem the poet faults someone for *not* taking.

36–40   The final stanza comments on the great social injustice reflected by the fact that the powerful receive acclaim for their taking while the poor are cruelly punished and their families are shamed. Compare Lindsay's *Satyre*, lines 2657–68, and Whiting T68.

29. *Dunbar at Oxford* [*Ane peralous seiknes is vane prosperité*]

Although the colophon in the second version of the text in MF reads "Dunbar at Oxinfurde," there are no specifics in the poem to justify that association, nor is there any historical evidence that Dunbar was ever in Oxford, either as a visitor or a student. On the other hand, there is no doubt that the poem addresses learned scholars, reminding them that their wisdom is of little worth if they fail to live good lives — that moral wisdom surpasses all other wisdom. Whether or not it is "a rather dull piece," as Bawcutt suggests (1992, p. 151), she is certainly right in pointing out that it lacks local color. The poem's chief interest lies in the way it celebrates the intellectual achievements of scholars while exhorting them to maintain their moral grounding. MF (two slightly variant texts) and R. Three 8-line stanzas rhyming *ababbcbC*, with varying refrain. Mc53, K76, Bw82.

1–8   The opening stanza addresses intellectual achievements in a general way, as line 4 clearly suggests, referring to "every field of study, every subject, every discipline."

7   *the fyne*. "The end," probably meant in several senses — "the end result" of their endeavor, "the end of life," and the "end" they achieve after the end of life. Compare Chaucer's *TC* 5.1828–34. Compare also Ecclesiasticus 7:36 and Whiting E84.

8   *Ane peralous seiknes is vane prosperité*. Compare Henryson's *Fables*, line 291, and Whiting P420–23.

9–16   The second stanza addresses more directly the academic fields common to the medieval university. Logic (line 9) and rhetoric (line 10), along with grammar, are the verbal arts comprising the *trivium*. The mathematical arts of the *quadrivium* are suggested by astronomy (line 12) and natural science (line 11), the study of natural phenomena. Theology and literature (line 13) would be more specialized fields of study.

12   Bawcutt believes this line "suggests suspicion of the branch of astronomy now called astrology" (Bw 2.485).

17   Here the use of direct address creates the "preaching voice" often heard in Dunbar's moral poems.

19–20   Two of the most effective verses in the poem, they simultaneously praise scholars for being shining lamps in the darkness, while urging them to be mirrors to us — i.e., moral examples — in the way they govern their own lives. Compare 2 Kings (2 Samuel) 22:29.

20   *lampis*. I.e., sources of moral and intellectual illumination.

22   *Gyff to yowr sawis your deidis contrar be*. Compare Whiting W642.

30. *The Thistle and the Rose*

Dunbar's celebration of the impending marriage of James IV of Scotland to Princess Margaret Tudor of England was first given the title "The Thrissill and the Rose" by James Ramsay in his *Ever Green* (1724), by which it has been known ever since. Although the wedding did not take place until August of 1503, the poem was apparently composed for an earlier occasion, perhaps in May of that year, for the poet states near the end of the poem that he "wret . . . / Of lusty May upone the nynt morrow" (lines 188–89). It is possible that it was presented at a public ceremony marking the beginning of summer, as several scholars have suggested. Certainly the poem reflects well upon ambitions of court entertainment of the kind James IV adored. Louise Fradenburg puts the matter well: "The poem is spectacular; and while we have no external evidence to suggest that it was performed to the accompaniment of dancing, costume or 'machinery,' its poetics . . . are clearly those of the court masque — of shifting 'scenes,' visual astonishment, splendid 'discryving'" (p. 173).

The poem blends several genres and traditions. It is both an epithalamium and an elegant love vision in the French dream-vision tradition, and it pays particular homage to Chaucer's dream visions, especially *PF*. Along the way the poem incorporates many elements from classical myth, animal fable tradition, medieval natural histories and herbals, heraldry, Scottish folklore, Scripture, and the imagery of medieval lyrics in praise of the Virgin Mary. Seventy-seven 7-line stanzas rhyming *ababbcc* (rhyme royal). B only. Mc55, K50, Bw52.

1–7	This otherwise conventional description of spring — with its April showers, May flowers, and songbirds singing the divine hours — contains an unexpected reference to the *orient blast* (line 3), which is not the gentle west wind, Chaucer's "Zephirus . . . with his sweete breeth" (*CT* I[A]5). This reference is elaborated upon in lines 29–35, where the wind is identified as "Lord Eolus" (line 33), and again in lines 64–70; in Greek mythology, Aeolus is the king of the winds.
4	*And lusty May, that muddir is of flouris.* A probable echo of lines from Chaucer's *TC*: "In May, that moder is of monthes glade, / That fresshe floures, blew and white and rede, / Ben quike agayn, that wynter dede made" (*TC* 2.50–2*)*. Compare also Douglas, *The Palis of Honoure*, line 65.
5	*maid the birdis to begyn thair houris.* By the fifteenth century, the description of the birds' singing as the singing of the divine hours had become a commonplace, occurring in poem after poem.
8	*In bed at morrow sleiping as I lay.* Chaucer's dreamer in *The Book of the Duchess* is similarly "awakened" while lying in his bed at dawn in the month of May (lines 291 ff.).
9	Aurora's *cristall ene* refers to the morning dew, the tears the dawn-goddess sheds for her son Memnon, who was killed at Troy. Compare lines 1–2 of Dunbar's "The Merle and the Nightingale" (Poem 66) and the first line of Douglas' *The Palis of Honoure*.

11   *visage paill and grene.* Ross interprets the phrase as referring to the dreamer, whom he sees as a "typical Ovidian lover" (p. 242); it more likely refers to Aurora.

12   *On quhois hand a lark sang fro the splene.* The lark, Aurora's bird, is the traditional announcer of the dawn.

15–21   This description of the personified figure of May focuses on her wondrous raiment, which reflects the loveliest attributes of the month. Compare *The Golden Targe* (Poem 65), lines 82–90. Evans (1987) points out that May wears the Tudor colors — perhaps alluding to the May-January theme of Chaucer's Merchant's Tale (pp. 98–99).

22   Compare the opening verses of Robert Herrick's "Corinna's Going A-Maying."

23   May's command, that the narrator write something in her honor, is fulfilled by the poem itself, as he tells us in the final lines: "And thus I wret . . . / Of lusty May upone the nynt morrow" (lines 188–89).

26–35   The narrator's lack of desire to write songs, which May says has not always been the case, stems from the atypical May weather, which many readers have seen as reflecting his internal landscape — is he perhaps a forlorn lover? — rather than the actual weather. The effect, in any case, is to create a narrative persona similar to the narrators in Chaucer's dream poems. Compare Geffrey's apathy for learning in *HF* lines 994–95. Evans (1987) reads this stanza as Dunbar's evidence "that a court poet is sometimes encouraged to describe things more favorably than seems natural in a grumpy, early-morning mood" (p. 97). In addition, Evans suggests that throughout the poem, Dunbar — a poet who would have found it difficult *not* to satirize a marriage between "such discrepancies in age and sophistication" — alludes to the May-January theme in dealing with James and Margaret (pp. 98–99).

33   *Lord Eolus dois in thy sessone ring.* In Scottish tradition Aeolus takes on the characteristics of Boreas, the north wind (Bw 2.397). Compare Henryson's reference to his "blastis boreally" *Fables*, line 1693.

37   *Uprys and do thy observance.* Compare Chaucer's Knight's Tale: "The sesoun priketh every gentil herte / . . . And seith, 'Arys, and do thyn observaunce'" (*CT* I[A]1043–45*).

38–39   These verses seem to suggest that the poet had agreed to write a poem honoring Princess Margaret that would be performed on a particular occasion during the month of May.

44   *a lusty gairding gent*. The lovely garden that May enters, and into which the narrator sees himself go also, reflects the general medieval topos of the *locus amoenus;* its more specific literary model, however, is the garden of Nature in Chaucer's *PF*.

45–46   These verses in B (see textual notes) are clearly flawed, for the poet surely would not have repeated the phrases *full hestely* and *full haistely* in successive lines. Various emendations have been proposed. I suggest keeping the MS reading in line 46 and emending the phrase in line 45 to *sa listely*.

56   *Doing all sable fro the hevynnis chace*. Compare "The Merle and the Nightingale" (Poem 66), line 1–2.

62–63   The birds salute five personified ladies — May, Flora, Aurora, Nature, and Venus — but from this point on the focus is exclusively on the figure of Nature, as she presides over the activities in her garden.

64–70   Nature is God's "vicaire general" ("chief deputy"), as Chaucer puts it in The Physician's Tale (*CT* VI[C]20), and because she has control over the natural elements, she is able to instruct the lesser deities of water (Neptune), wind (Aeolus), and sky (Juno) to do her bidding. In Douglas' *The Palis of Honoure,* similarly, Aeolus and Neptune, along with "ald Saturne," are similarly excluded from Nature's garden (lines 49–52). Compare Lindsay's *Monarche*, line 185. Nature's injunction to Aeolus, Neptune, and Juno is a reminder that the marriage between Margaret and James is acting as a peace treaty after James supported Perkin Warbeck's rebellion against Henry VII in 1499. Evans (1987) says that "the presence of the Medieval literary goddess suggests that the English-Scottish marriage was prompted by Reason and blessed by God; consequently, the once inimical nations should flourish now in peace and harmony" (p. 101).

71–77   In Chaucer's *PF*, set on Valentine's Day, Nature assembles all the birds to select their mates for the coming year. Here Nature not only summons all the birds but also all the beasts and flowers, who come and do homage to her, their maker. Dunbar's other specific literary model for this portrayal of Nature is found in Richard Holland's *The Howlat,* where Nature also presides over an assembly of her creatures.

75   *As thay had wont in May fro yeir to yeir.* Compare Chaucer's *PF*, line 321.

76–77   These verses reflect the feudalistic practice of doing homage to one's superior (Bw 2.398). The staging of such practices became a principal court entertainment in James IV's reign. Few poets have been more skilled than Dunbar in celebrating (or mocking) the style of court pageantry. Enid Welsford, long ago, astutely observed that Dunbar saw "nature" through the "medium of courtly pageant; the artificiality of which his poetry has been accused is an artifice that strives, like the masque, to empower illusion to give evanescence an essence" (Fradenberg, p. 173, paraphrasing Welsford, p. 74).

78–84   Nature sends her three messengers to summon the three sets of living things. The first two messengers, the swift roe and the restless swallow, are understandable enough. The third messenger is the *yarrow*, or milfoil, a daisy-like flower which according to Kinsley was "said to be used by witches to give them speed on night rides" (K, p. 352); but it may have been selected simply because of the way this wild flower spreads so rapidly across the fields.

87   *first the lyone, gretast of degré.* The lion is the king of the beasts in animal fable tradition, bestiaries, and in other symbolic contexts, but he is also the central figure in the royal arms of Scotland and by this time had become the traditional emblem of the Scottish king. In the poem he is the first of the triumvirate of royal figures — Lion, Eagle, and Thistle — each of whom stands for James IV of Scotland.

93–102 Here Dunbar's flattery of James rests not just in representing the king as a regal lion, but "by making him an actual replica of the royal arms of Scotland," that is, crowned, on a field of gold, and surrounded by fleur-de-lis (Ridley, 1990, p. 357). Ridley's discussion engages many examples of Dunbar's use of animal and heraldic imagery in specific poems (Poems 3, 49, 54, and 84), commenting that he consistently turns "man into creature" (p. 359). But her essay is particularly useful in this context because it compares Dunbar's use of animal imagery to Robert Henryson's. Henryson's poetry, particularly his *Moral Fables*, uses animal imagery in a more general way than Dunbar. In Fable II, for example, the discussion between the country mouse and the town mouse over the former's coarse diet reveals more about the author's reading of bourgeois attitudes towards the poor than it does about one particular person (see lines 208–35, quoted in Ridley). Ridley argues that, whereas Dunbar's subjects are animalized to achieve a specific, self-related effect (e.g., humiliating Walter Kennedy or getting a Christmas bonus from the king),

271

Henryson's poetry takes place in an animalized world to effect social or moral change.

103–12   In this coronation ceremony in which Nature makes the lion king of the beasts, she instructs him to protect the people and uphold the laws, and to apply the laws equally to all and exercise justice with mercy.

110–12   These verses may imply that the king has a responsibility to make the Highlander — the *bowgle* ("wild ox," line 110) — and the Lowlander — the *meik pluch ox* ("the gentle plough ox," line 111) — work together in harmony.

117   *homege and fewté*. "Formal acknowledgement of allegiance by a vassal to his lord" (Bw 2.398).

119   *parcere prostratis*. "To show mercy to the downtrodden"; Dunbar is quoting a part of a well-known Latin maxim: *Parcere protratis scit nobilis ira leonis* ("the noble wrath of the lion knows how to spare those who are prostrated before him").

120–26   The eagle, the traditional king of the birds, receives far less attention than the lion and the thistle, the two more familiar symbols of Scottish royalty. But like the lion, the eagle is told to uphold justice for all birds, the weak (e.g., the wrens, line 124) as well as the strong. This second ceremony in the poem, Dunbar's "parliament of fowls," alludes, as Evans (1987) sees it, to the agreement between James and Henry to cease border warfare by not allowing the other country's criminals to take refuge over the border. Nature sharpens the eagle's feathers to make him a better law enforcer (pp. 102–03). In "To the King" (Poem 48), lines 26–29, King James is also depicted as an eagle who rules over his kingdom.

130   *a busche of speiris*. I.e., the many large thorns and prickly foliage that surround the flower of the spear thistle. The thistle had only recently been adopted as a royal emblem, and it symbolized the king's duty to protect his kingdom from invasion (Bw 2.399).

131–33   Here Nature refers to the king's responsibility to be the defender of his people and their leader in war.

134–47   Commentators agree that this lengthy passage urging the thistle to maintain a well-ordered garden is also meant as an admonition to King James against future sexual indiscretions. As Spearing observes, "James IV was a notorious womaniser, and it is known that in the very summer of his marriage he had left the court in order to renew acquaintance with an old flame" (p. 214).

138   *Hir fallow to.* "To be her equal," i.e., allow her to receive the same (sexual) favors.

138–40   The *gudly flour delyce*, the fleur-de-lis, which is either the lily or the iris. Perhaps both the iris and the lily (mentioned specifically in line 140) represent Princess Margaret, as the rose in the following stanza certainly does.

142   The "fresh rose of color red and white," the chief symbol in the poem for Princess Margaret, reflects that fact that she is the daughter of Elizabeth of York (the white rose) and Henry of Lancaster (the red rose). The Tudor rose, in which the white rose is enclosed within the red rose, combines the two.

144–54   Nature's great praise of the rose — of her virtue, beauty, and perfection — accords with descriptions of the rose found in medieval herbals and other works of natural history, where the rose is often exalted as the chief of all flowers. The phrases *Imperiall birth* (line 147) and *stok ryell* (line 151) allude once again to her royal parentage, and the phrase *Aboif the lilly* (line 150) may suggest not only the rose's superiority to the lily but the superiority of English royalty to French royalty, commonly symbolized by the lily.

153   *Cum, blowme of joy, with jemis to be cround.* This verse may echo Canticle of Canticles 4:8 — "Come . . . my spouse, . . . come: thou shalt be crowned from the top of Amana" — a verse usually associated in the Middle Ages with the Virgin Mary.

162–82   The narrator's dream concludes with the birds singing in praise of the rose; first there is a succession of individual birdsongs — by the mavis, the merle, the lark, and the nightingale — and then all the birds sing in unison. Ross describes this as "a secular *Salve Regina*" (p. 248), and it does contain many images commonly found in "Adoration of the Virgin" poetry.

180   *perle.* Probably a play on the name Margaret, whose Latin form is *margarita*, meaning "pearl."

183–89   The shouting of the birds similarly awakens Chaucer's dream-narrator in *PF*, lines 693–95. The specific date given here, the ninth morrow of May, is also the date Douglas gives for writing the Prologue to his *Eneados*. The ninth of May was the

273

Feast of the Translation of St. Nicholas, "sometimes regarded as the first day of summer" (Bawcutt, 1992, pp. 74–75), and thus may have provided an occasion for Scottish court revels. Chaucer had also given a specific date for the writing of his dream vision *HF*, in that case 10 December.

187   *Than up I lenyt, halflingis in affrey.* Compare line 140 in "Of the Passion of Christ" (Poem 2).

31. *To Princess Margaret* [*Welcum of Scotlond to be quene*]

This brief and possibly fragmentary lyric in praise of Princess Margaret is commonly attributed to Dunbar, though it is anonymous in its unique MS text, the appendix to BL Royal 58, an early sixteenth-century collection of English madrigals. Its style, diction, and imagery suggest Dunbar's authorship, and, if that is true, it is the only one of Dunbar's poems we can be certain was set to music. According to Ross: "This piece is set in the key of F major/D minor, and the last note of the first stanza in the tonic F. This fact and the range of the part suggest it is the bass of a madrigal. There is an interlude of instrumental music following the two stanzas presented in the manuscript, which is in keeping with the idea that the music formed part of a pageant" (p. 205). In addition to its praise of Margaret, the poem also celebrates her parents, the Tudor monarch Henry VII and his wife Elizabeth of York. Four 4-line stanzas rhyming *aabB*, with the refrain repeated twice in the final stanza. BL Royal MS 58. Mc89, K24. (Bawcutt excludes it from her edition.)

5   *Younge tender plant.* Margaret was thirteen at the time of her marriage to James in 1503. Compare line 2 in "To Princess Margaret" (Poem 32).

6   *Descendyd of imperyalle blode.* This verse pays tribute to Margaret's noble lineage, and is surely meant as a compliment to Henry VII.

10–11   Once again the poet compliments the English King Henry, this time along with his wife Elizabeth, *a princes most serene* (line 11).

13   The *rose bothe rede and whyte* is the Tudor rose, formed by the union of the red rose of Lancaster and the white rose of York. Compare lines 148–61 in "The Thistle and the Rose" (Poem 30).

15   *Oure spreit rejoysyng frome the sone beme.* A problematic line in both sound and sense; it has too many syllables and an imperfect rhyme; I have followed Kinsley in emending *seqete* to *spreit.*

32. *To Princess Margaret* [*Gladethe, thoue queyne of Scottis regioun*]

The text of this poem in praise of Margaret Tudor is found only in the Aberdeen Minute Book, where "*q dunbar*" is written beneath the final stanza, and most of the editors and commentators have accepted this ascription. The poem is a rather conventional panegyric in which the young queen — she was thirteen at the time of her marriage to James in 1503 — is portrayed as the epitome of beauty, goodness, and refinement. The poet especially uses two sets of comparisons in praising her. The first involves comparing her to various gemstones and plays upon the Latin word *margarita* (meaning "pearl"), the gem that surpasses all others. The second involves flower imagery, particularly emphasizing red and white roses, and plays upon Margaret Tudor's Lancastrian and Yorkist family lineage. The flower images are also associated with the desire clearly stated in the poem for "A plaunt to spring of thi successioun" (line 30), who would be an heir to continue the Scottish royal line. Since Margaret's first child was born in 1507, when she was seventeen, the poem was almost certainly written before that date. Five 8-line stanzas rhyming *ababbcbC.* Aberdeen Minute Book. Mc90, K31, Bw15.

2–3   *Ying tendir plaunt of plesand pulcritude, / Fresche flour of youthe, new germyng to burgeoun.* While these verses celebrate the freshness of Margaret's beauty, they also reflect the fact that she was very young when she married James. The use of alliteration, as in line 2, occurs frequently throughout the poem.

2   Compare line 5 in "To Princess Margaret" (Poem 31).

4–6   The paired images of "Our pearl of price" and "Our chosen ruby of high imperial blood" in lines 4–5 not only celebrate her beauty and value but reflect the white and red colors of the Tudor rose mentioned in line 6. The phrase "pearl of great price" originates in the biblical parable in Matthew 13:46.

5   *charbunkle.* The carbuncle, or ruby, which was believed to radiate light in the darkness, was often used by Scottish poets as an emblem of great perfection. Compare Douglas' praise of Virgil in *Eneados* 1.Prol.7.

10   *Lodsteir.* A lodestar is a guiding star such as the North Star.

11–12   Polyxena was the beautiful and accomplished daughter of Priam and Hecuba of Troy. Pallas is Pallas Athena, goddess of wisdom.

13   *Mastres of nurtur and of nobilnes*. This line praises her refined behavior. In *The Thre Prestis of Peblis*, peasants possess neither "nurtour nor nobilnes" (line 328).

17–24   *Natur* is the goddess Natura, the creator of all natural creatures. These verses recall the passage in Chaucer's Physician's Tale concerning Natura's creation of Virginia (*CT* VI[C]30–71).

29–31   Here the poet states explicitly the desire of the Scots for an heir to ensure the succession of the monarchy. Producing such an heir was "A queen's most important duty" (Bw 2.321).

33–39   Margaret, the "perle of price" (line 4) and *Fair gem of joy* (line 39), is here compared to the gemstones beryl, diamond, sapphire, emerald, and ruby; she embodies all of their finest qualities and even surpasses them in those qualities. Compare the ME lyrics *IMEV* 1394 ("Annot and John") and 752 ("A Lover's Farewell"), lines 89–96.

38   *Moir riche na is the ruby of renowne*. The ruby was often valued above all the other gemstones (compare Whiting R227); compare also Proverbs 31:10, where a virtuous woman is said to be more valuable than rubies.

33. *To Aberdeen* [*Be blyth and blisfull, burgh of Aberdein*]

One of Dunbar's most topical poems, "To Aberdeen" celebrates Queen Margaret's visit to the burgh in May of 1511. The poem describes the colorful pageantry surrounding the royal visit, appearing to be an eyewitness account, and is a paean not only to the queen but also to the burgh. The poem has nine stanzas, seven of which depict the city's joyous and elaborate welcome to the queen. Those seven stanzas are enclosed within a pair of stanzas that offer balanced apostrophes, with the opening stanza addressing "Blyth Aberdeane, thow beriall of all tounis, / The lamp of bewtie" (lines 1–2), and the final stanza addressing Margaret — "O potent princes, pleasant and preclair" (line 65). The poem's final stanza, though, rather than presenting a lavish eulogy to the queen, focuses more on the fact that she should be thankful to the citizens of this burgh, who have pulled out all the stops for her. As Fradenburg notes, the poem attests "the strongly visual character of much of [Dunbar's] writing and the court's

276

interest in pageants and entertainments" (p. 173). Nine 8-line stanzas rhyming *ababbcbC*. R only, with several lacunae. Mc64, K48, Bw8.

1   Beryl, the gemstone the poet associates with Aberdeen, was noted for its clarity and brightness; the eighth foundation of the New Jerusalem in Apocalypse (21:20) is entirely formed of beryl, and perhaps a comparison of the two cities is obliquely suggested.

1–5   Aberdeen was a royal burgh and an important North Sea port city. This eulogy to a city is not unique. Compare "London, thou art of townes A perse" (sometimes attributed to Dunbar) and Lindsay's *Papyngo*, lines 626–46.

7–8   Here the poet's praise shifts from the burgh to the queen, who is called the *wall of welth* (line 7), i.e., "the well-spring of prosperity," an image often associated with the Virgin Mary.

8   A burgh was a town with a royal charter; it enjoyed special laws and privileges.

9–24   The second and third stanzas describe the queen's ceremonial entry to the city and the first pageant presented for her entertainment. This pageant, fittingly, is the biblical story of the angel's salutation to Mary (Luke 1:28–38).

18   *cap.* Bawcutt suggests "cape; specifically cope, ecclesiastical vestment" (Bw 2.528).

25–31   The second pageant depicts the adoration of the Magi (Matthew 2:1–12), and the third the expulsion of Adam and Eve from Paradise (Genesis 3:23–4).

33–40   The queen next views a dramatic enactment depicting more recent Scottish historical figures, beginning with Robert Bruce and followed by figures in the family tree of Scottish kings of the Stewart line, probably ending with a depiction of James IV. This is partly conjectural, however, because the text has a lacuna in line 37.

33   *the Bruce.* Robert Bruce "reigned as Robert I (1306–29). His success in the war of Independence was celebrated by Barbour . . . , and he figures as a tenth hero in Scottish treatments of the Nine Worthies theme" (Bw 2.305). He is often viewed as the hero of the great Scottish victory over the English at Bannockburn in 1314.

41–48   There is a strongly Celtic flavor to the final entertainment described, in which twenty-four maidens clad in green sing, dance, and play small timbrels before the queen.

Their garb and the specific number of twenty-four suggests a company of lovely faerie maidens dancing in a meadow, as in The Wife of Bath's Tale (*CT* III[D]991–93). In Malory, the queen and her knights are similarly garbed all in green when they go a-maying (*Works*, p. 649).

45   The timbrel was a small percussion instrument (similar to the tambourine) often played by young women; see "timbre" in Henry Holland Carter, *A Dictionary of Middle English Musical Terms* (Bloomington: Indiana University Press, 1961), pp. 500–01.

49–56   This stanza depicts the common citizens of the town doing homage to their royal visitor.

57–64   Here the emphasis is on the city's generosity toward the queen, bestowing upon her the lavish gift of a large and costly cup filled with gold coins.

65–72   The emphasis in these verses is on the poet's expectation (or hope) that the queen will acknowledge the city's generosity with generosity of her own.

34. *To the Queen* [*Devoyd languor and leif in lustines*]

This poem is only found in B, where it is anonymous, and thus Dunbar's authorship remains conjectural. But several editors, including Laing and Kinsley, accept this attribution, largely on stylistic grounds. In addition to the uncertainty about the poem's authorship, it also is not certain to whom the poem is addressed. Laing suggested Queen Margaret who, when she was widowed by James' death at Flodden in 1513, was just twenty-four years old. If so, the poem surely would have had to be written before August of 1514, when Margaret married the earl of Angus. Regardless of these uncertainties, the poem is a tender and moving attempt on the part of a poet to comfort a grieving widow. Ross aptly describes it as a "graceful poem of praise, consolation, and proffer of service" (p. 98). Both the stanza form and the number of verses are identical to those used in "To Princess Margaret" (Poem 32). Five 8-line stanzas rhyming *ababbabC*. B only. Mc91, K49. (Does not appear in Bawcutt's edition.)

1–8   In contrast to the rose imagery used to describe Margaret in other poems, here the woman is described as a lily, which might be more appropriate for a woman who is no longer in her teens — and who is no longer so closely associated with her Tudor lineage? — and who is now a widow and perhaps also a queen. Furthermore, Dunbar does associate the lily and fleur-de-lis with Margaret in "The Thistle and the

Rose" (Poem 30), lines 138–40. In this stanza, as throughout the poem, there is a heavy use of alliteration.

8   *Devoyd langour and leif in lustiness*. Although each stanza ends with the poet urging the woman to be glad and to expel sorrow, the cause of her sorrow is not revealed until line 35 in the final stanza.

9–16   *Brycht sterne at morow*. Here the imagery shifts to "the bright star of the morning" and the poet's desire that no dark cloud will hide her face. Compare "A Ballad of Our Lady" (Poem 4), lines 25–28.

17–24 This stanza presents a catalogue of the woman's exemplary qualities, including praise for her noble lineage (line 19), which recalls the praise of Henry VII and Elizabeth of York found in "To Princess Margaret" (Poem 31).

25–32 Here the poet offers his service to the woman, whose servant he is, and for whom he offers to make songs for her *reconforting* (line 31).

35   Finally — and briefly — the poet reveals the cause of the woman's grief; it is fittingly brief, since the poem is not an elegy for the dead but a poignant expression of support for the living.

35. *Eulogy to Bernard Stewart, Lord of Aubigny* [*Withe glorie and honour*]

Among the most dateable of Dunbar's poems are the two written in praise of Bernard Stewart. The first is a eulogy celebrating Stewart's return to Scotland in May of 1508; the second is an elegy which was probably composed shortly after Stewart's death in June of that same year. Stewart was a famous French knight of Scottish ancestry who achieved international acclaim for his many feats of arms. He led the French contingent that fought in support of Henry Tudor at the Battle of Bosworth Field in 1485; he also served for a time as French ambassador to Scotland and was thus a familiar figure to the Scottish court. Indeed, he seems to embody personally the close ties between Scotland and France during the fifteenth and early sixteenth centuries. Bawcutt describes the poem as "a well-deserved tribute to a great soldier" (1992, p. 82). The poem may seem repetitious, but there is a skillful interweaving of three or four principal motifs, with the later stanzas often elaborating on what had been briefly suggested earlier. Twelve 8-line stanzas rhyming *ababbcbC*. CM and MF. Mc61, K35, Bw56. CM introduces the poem with the following heading (quoted in Bw 1.177):

The ballade of ane right noble victorious and myghty lord, Barnard Stewart, lord of Aubigny, erle of Beaumont Rober and Bonaffre, consaloure and chamerlane ordinare to the maist hee, maist excellent and maist crystyn prince Loys, king of France, knyght of his ordoure, capitane of the kepyng of his body, conquereur of Naplis and umquhile constable general of the same. Compilit be Maister Willyam Dumbar at the said lordis cumyng to Edinburghe in Scotland send in ane ryght excellent embassat fra the said maist crystin king to our maist souuerane lord and victorious prince, Iames the ferde kyng of Scottis.

1–8	The poem is highly rhetorical throughout; there is frequent use of classical devices such as anaphora, and there is also frequent use of alliteration, as in lines 1 and 3. In part, these elaborate rhetorical devices may strike readers, in Reiss' words, as "too full of hyberbole" (p. 47). If Dunbar's praise of Stewart seems over the top to a modern audience, we would do well to keep in mind Evans' argument that the highly aureate language in the poem serves a formal purpose in signifying responses to the audience and moving them to appreciate Stewart as a man highly worthy of their praise. These reader-response signals, says Evans, are marked both by rhetorical devices and by formal comparisons of Stewart to the Nine Worthies, the optimistic reading of his horoscope (unfortunately, an inaccurate once, since he died the next month), and by the climactic acrostic on his name at the end of the poem. See Evans (1991), pp. 123–24.
4	*laureat.* In this case referring to the laurel wreath bestowed upon a military victor; compare Chaucer's Knight's Tale (*CT* I[A]1027). Later in the Renaissance this gives rise to the concept of the poet laureate.
5	*Onto the sterris.* I.e., Stewart is exalted "unto the heavens" or "up to the skies."
7	*servatour.* The term is used here, as in "To the King" (Poem 46), to refer to members of the court who fulfill official functions. Dunbar considered himself to belong to this group.
8	*Withe glorie and honour, lawde and reverence.* Bw 2.408 notes that the refrain echoes the Palm Sunday processional hymn, *Gloria laus et honor tibi sit* ("glory, praise, and honor be unto you"). Compare Douglas, *The Palis of Honoure*, line 1063.
13	*moste lusti branche of our linnage.* The poet pays tribute to the fact that Bernard Stewart is of Scottish ancestry. (His grandfather was Sir John Stewart of Darnley, who began his French service in 1422 and later became a landholder in France.)

Throughout the poem the poet conveys a strong sense that all Scotland embraces Stewart as one of their own.

17   *secund Julius.* Julius Caesar, whom the Middle Ages regarded as a great military conqueror and who was included in the famous group of heroes known as the Nine Worthies; two more of them (Hector and Arthur) are mentioned in lines 57–64 when the poet returns to this theme. Compare the reference in Chaucer's *TC* 2.158 to Troilus as "Ector the secounde."

25–32   This stanza focuses on Stewart's personal kindness to the Scottish people, and may reflect real deeds performed during the time he was the French ambassador to Scotland. Or, it may refer to his concern for the well-being of Scottish merchants abroad.

41–48   This stanza reiterates what was already expressed in lines 17–24, in a kind of theme and variation device.

49–56   The idea first expressed in line 5 of Stewart's great fame, which ascends to the heavens, is here elaborated. For a discussion of this topos, see Curtius, pp. 160–62.

50   Fame was commonly portrayed as a swift, winged goddess; compare Chaucer's *TC* 4.659–61.

57–64   Just as he had been compared to Julius Caesar in line 17, here Stewart is likened to a group of the world's most worthy warriors and war leaders — Achilles, Hector, King Arthur, Agamemnon, Hannibal, and once again, Julius Caesar.

67   *Thi cristall helme withe lawry suld be crownyt.* Compare line 4, above, and Chaucer's Knight's Tale (*CT* I[A]1027).

68   The olive branch is the traditional sign of peace, an emblem used occasionally in envoys. Compare Douglas, *Eneados* 7.3.15–16, and Whiting O32.

73–80   At Stewart's birth, the poet suggests in this presumably imaginary horoscope, several of the planetary deities bestowed upon him their particular virtues — Mars gave him his fierceness, Mercury gave him his eloquence, etc. Kinsley proposes that *Fortuna maior* (line 79) was a group of stars marking out a particular geometric pattern; to be born under that sign would presage good fortune (K, p. 311). Bawcutt disagrees, suggesting instead that *Fortuna maior* is an astrological synonym for

Jupiter, a planet of positive influence (Bw 2.409). Chaucer used the device of creating a character's horoscope for the Wife of Bath (*CT* III[D]609–16) and for Hypermnesta in *LGW* (lines 2576–93). Compare also Lindsay, *Testament*, lines 64–91.

74   *Rong.* Bawcutt proposes (Bw 2.409) the gloss "reigned"; but perhaps it simply means "rang" or "resounded," for each of the planetary deities in this stanza is making a particular sign or action to bless Stewart's birth. In The Knight's Tale the sign Mars gives to Arcite also involves the ringing of his metal hauberk (*CT* I[A]2431–32).

83–87   Using the rhetorical device of *occupatio*, the poet tells us in short what he does not plan to tell us at greater length, Stewart's many military victories. He suggests in lines 86–87 that he intends to do this before Stewart departs again from Scotland; unfortunately, Stewart's death occurred scarcely over a month later.

85   *Bertan.* Britain; probably a reference to Stewart's service in command of a French force at Bosworth Field in 1485.

89–93   Within these verses the poet creates an acrostic, spelling out in its Latin form Steward's first name, BARNARDVS. Such acrostics were fairly common in eulogistic poetry.

94–95   Compare Lydgate's *Fall of Princes* 4.371 and Douglas, *Eneados* 12.Prol.309–10.

36. *Elegy for Bernard Stewart, Lord of Aubigny* [*Sen he is gon, the flour of chevalrie*]

Bernard Stewart arrived in Scotland in May of 1508, and within a few weeks he fell ill while traveling from Edinburgh to Sterling. Stewart wrote his will on 8 June and died on 11 June, and Dunbar's short, somber elegy was probably written shortly thereafter. The poem is addressed to Louis XII of France, and probably should be seen primarily as expressing the grief of the entire "Scottis natioun" (line 29) rather than Dunbar's own personal grief (Bawcutt, 1992, p. 87). It stands as a companion piece with Dunbar's eulogy to Stewart, with which it shares several phrases and a common stanza form. The catalogues of warriors and victories in the eulogy add to the moving injunction of the elegy, which turns loss into what Fradenburg calls an occasion: "The memorializing, the final theatrical manifestation, of a life ideally devoted to the risk of death, to an intentional relation with death. Though Stewart died of illness, his last antagonist, in Dunbar's poem, is the *dragon dolorous* [line 178] — a heroization of loss, the obverse of the grandeur of risk" (p. 178).The funeral lament became a distinct genre in late medieval poetry, especially on the continent but also in Scotland (see Bw 2.338). As Bawcutt notes, several fine examples "are embedded in larger works; in Henryson's *Orpheus*, 134–81; Hary, *Wallace*, XII, 1109–28 . . . and the verse on James I in Bower, *Scotichronicon*, XVI.38" (Bw 2.338). Four 8-line stanzas rhyming *ababbcbC*. R only. Mc62, K36, Bw23.

1	Bawcutt points out (1992, p. 87) that it was customary in medieval Europe to restrict the use of the epithet *most Cristin king* to the king of France, who at this time was Louis XII.
4	*In deid of armes most anterous and abill*. Compare line 42 in the previous poem.
7	*sabill*. Sable is the heraldic term for black, as well as the color traditionally associated with mourning. Compare line 284 in Chaucer's *Complaint of Mars*: "Now have ye cause to clothe yow in sable."
8	*the flour of chevelrie*. "The flower of chivalry" was a phrase often used for a knight who represented chivalric perfection; it occurs twice in Chaucer's Knight's Tale (*CT* I[A]982 and 3059), once to describe Theseus, and once in Theseus' tribute to the slain Arcite.
13	*To the Turkas sey all land did his name dreid*. Whereas in the previous poem Stewart's fame reaches up to the stars (line 5), here his reputation as a fearsome warrior reaches across a vast expanse of earthly terrain, all the way to the Turkish sea (i.e., the Black Sea), the point where Asia begins.
17	*O dragon dolorous*. Dunbar refers to death as a dragon in several other poems, e.g., "Of Man's Mortality" (Poem 9), line 28.
17–24	Evans (1991) sees the poem not just as an elegy, but as a presentation of Stewart's life as an *exemplum* of the perfect Christian knight and a guide for moral behavior. She agrees with Scott (p. 260) that the "moral conclusion" to the poem may be *vanitas vanitatum omnia vanitas*, as this is a common theme in Dunbar's poetry (p. 125). For example, see "Of the World's Vanity" (Poem 11). While Stewart's life is certainly a model for good behavior, it does not appear to be an example of vanity, only that all things pass. Dunbar is alluding to the common *ubi sunt* theme. Compare "When the turuf is thy tour" (*MEL*, p. 223). Dunbar seems to be comparing

Stewart's physical prowess to his earthly goods, and, in an interesting twist on *ubi sunt*, asks "why?" instead of "where?"

20   *The witt of weiris.* I.e., "the wisest of military commanders." Compare *Golagros and Gawain*, line 1137.

24   *charbuckell.* The carbuncle, or ruby, was a gem that represented great excellence; compare its use in Dunbar's eulogizing Princess/Queen Margaret ("To Princess Margaret" [Poem 31]), line 5.

25–32   These verses urge all the poem's hearers to pray for Stewart's soul; such admonitions were common in medieval laments for the dead; the greater the number of prayers on earth that are said for you (this is "intercessioun"), the shorter your time in Purgatory.

37. *To the King* [*In hansill of this guid New Yeir*]

In this "gay, fresh, hopeful" poem (Scott, p. 135) the poet presents his New Year's greeting to King James IV of Scotland. Although it is very brief, the poem does several things. Primarily, it expresses the speaker's wish that the king receive many blessings — "Joy, gladness, comfort, and solace" (line 2) and "prosperity, fair fortune, and felicity" (lines 9–10). Less obviously, the poem appears to be exhorting the king to pursue a virtuous path both in his private behavior (stanza 2) and in his ruling of Scotland (stanza 4). And finally, in the last stanza it tenders a request for the king to be liberal toward his faithful servers, which by implication includes the poet. It is reasonable, therefore, to consider the poem one of Dunbar's petitions, even though it contains no explicit request. Because its tone is light and cheerful and lacks any hint of cynicism, "To the King [In hansill of this guid New Yeir]" is commonly assumed to be one of Dunbar's earliest petitions, though that is only a guess. R only. Five 4-line stanzas rhyming *aabB*. Mc26, K18, Bw37.

4   A *hansill* was a gift given in honor of a special occasion, most frequently around the time of the New Year, and was a token of the giver's good wishes for the receiver. In the poem Dunbar expresses his desire for the king's good fortunes, and the poem itself is the poet's *hansill* to the king. Compare the giving of such gifts in Arthur's court in *SGGK*: "And sythen riche forthe runnen to reche hondeselle, / Yeghed yeres-giftes on high, yelde hem bi hond" (lines 66–67).

5   *ane blissed chance.* "A blessed good fortune"; i.e., good luck.

13–16   Among the king's most important responsibilities are protection of the realm and preservation of justice, duties which are emphasized in "The Thistle and the Rose" (Poem 30), lines 103–12.

18   *And send thee many Fraunce crownes*. The French crown, or *ecu*, was a gold coin highly valued in Scotland, though worth slightly less than the Scottish pound.

19   *handis not sweir*. "Hands not ungenerous"; this verse hints at the poet's own desire to receive a generous *hansill* from the king.

38. *To the King* [*God gif ye war Johne Thomsounis man*]

Like the previous poem, this petition also begins with the poet's prayer for the king's well-being. But it quickly modulates into something quite different — a comic plea for the poet's receipt of a benefice. The humor in the poem, which Bawcutt terms witty and "audacious" (1992, p. 109) and Ridley "rueful whimsy" (1973, p. 1013), stems from the desire expressed in the refrain: "God gif ye war Johne Thomsounis man." This essentially means, "I wish to God you were more under your wife's thumb." Apparently the poet has found a strong ally in Queen Margaret; but just as apparently, at least for the comic purposes of the poem, the king remains hard-hearted and merciless (lines 29–30) in his attitude toward the poet. The poem would have had to be written between 1503 (the date of the royal marriage) and 1513 (the date of the king's death), perhaps earlier in this period rather than later. Eight 4-line stanzas rhyming *aabB*. MF only. Mc18, K25, Bw63.

1   *Schir*. This is the form of address Dunbar uses for the king in several poems. It is formal and respectful, but by no means flowery, and usually connotes a seriousness of purpose.

6   *benefice*. An ecclesiastical office or living by which Dunbar could attain financial security. The poet's desire to receive such a benefice, and the king's reluctance to grant him one, is the central source of conflict throughout most of Dunbar's petition poems. Chaucer's Clerk of Oxenford has not yet attained a benefice, though in contrast to Dunbar he seems to have little interest in doing so (*CT* I[A]291–2).

9–16   These two stanzas (as are two later ones) are filled with compliments to the queen. It may be that he is flattering her in the hope that she will intervene on his behalf, though throughout his poetry one has the sense that Dunbar truly admired Margaret.

14   *fair and gude.* Dunbar also uses the phrase to describe Margaret in line 4 of "To Princess Margaret" (Poem 32) and in the opening verse of "Of the Aforesaid James Dog" (Poem 58).

19   *ye had vowit to the swan.* Dunbar is here having fun with the practice of offering a chivalric vow on a noble bird, a practice that is described in many romances and that was sometimes performed in real life. It apparently originates in Jacques de Longuyon's *Voeux du Paon* (c. 1310), in which vows are made upon the peacock.

21–23   The *Rose* (line 21) and the *Thirsill* (line 22) are references to Margaret and James. It is not clear whether we should take a verse such as 23 seriously, in which case the poet feels that he has been abused by the king, or whether it is all part of a comic pretense.

25   *My advocat, bayth fair and sweit.* Perhaps part of the joke, as this verse may suggest, involves a parody of a Christian's prayer to Mary to intercede on his behalf with God.

31   *sweit Sanct An.* Stories of St. Anne, the Virgin Mary's mother, were greatly revered throughout the Middle Ages. Although no mention of her is made in the New Testament, the Latin apocryphal Protoevangelium of James and, especially, the Gospel of Pseudo-Matthew provided details of Mary's birth and childhood that sustained many rewritings — the *De Nativitate Mariae*, the Franciscan *Meditationes Vitae Christi*, Mirk's *Festial*, and popular collections of saint's lives such as Jacobus de Voragine's *Legenda Aurea* and Bokenham's *Legendys*. The N-Town Cycle includes a sequence of Mary plays, the first two of which (plays 8 and 9) deal with Joachim and Anne and the marvelous conception of Mary, and her presentation at the Temple. Dunbar might have known the story from Lydgate's *Life of Our Lady*. Bawcutt suggests that Anne's "name was often used in asseverations, as here, to supply a rhyme. Compare Chaucer's Friar's Tale, *CT* III(D)1613: 'by the sweete Seinte Anne'; and Lindsay, *Satyre*, 878" (Bw 2.425).

39. *To the King* [*My panefull purs so priclis me*]

This wry, clever petition to the king focuses on the poet's financial hardship, hardship that causes him great mental and physical distress due to the lamentable emptiness of his purse. The poem brings to mind "The Complaint of Chaucer to His Purse," which also makes a direct appeal to the king for aid; Chaucer's poem, however, does not dwell at such length on the practical consequences of his penury, which is Dunbar's main concern through the first five stanzas of the poem. One of the charms of this petition is its ironic, or upside-down, quality. For example, the speaker begins by cursing silver, but it turns out that he is not cursing silver because silver is a bad thing (which in the medieval Christian frame of reference it probably *is*), he is cursing silver because it is the very thing he wants but lacks. And later in the poem, he says he wishes he could make a conjuration to put silver in his purse, since that would ward off the devil, who might be attracted to his empty purse (there is an old saying that "the devil dances in an empty purse"). But making magical conjurations would itself involve engaging in a demonic exercise; and a purse *full* of silver is much more likely to lead to a person's moral downfall than an empty one is, since money is the root of all evil. Seven 5-line stanzas rhyming *aabaB*. B only. Mc1, K19, Bw61.

1   *Sanct Salvatour, send silver sorrow.* "Holy Savior, accused be silver!" Several Scottish churches were dedicated to Saint Salvatour — a title commonly used for Christ — including the collegiate church at St. Andrews University, which Dunbar may have attended.

3   *cheritie.* Probably meant in both senses, i.e., in possession of a loving spirit, and having a desire to be generous to others.

4   *borrow.* Probably means "give away," i.e., no longer have.

5   *My panefull purs so priclis me.* His purse is painful because it is empty, and that emptiness, like an empty stomach, causes pain. The line may possibly contain sexual innuendo, as some commentators have suggested — i.e., the purse can also mean the scrotum — and there are other lines in the poem that invite similar speculations (e.g., lines 21–22). But such implications, if they are even there, do not seem much in keeping with what the poet is attempting. More interesting is the possibility that he is playing upon the penitential concept of "the mortification of the flesh" in a cleverly inverted fashion. Here pain is being inflicted upon his flesh — not by a hair shirt but by an empty purse!

6–7   The languor that prevents him from creating cheerful verse is probably related to the depressed state of mind that he describes at length in several other petition poems. Compare "A Dream" (Poem 42), lines 16–25, the entirety of "The Headache" (Poem 43), and "A Meditation in Winter" (Poem 15), lines 4–10.

16 *in tone.* "In tune," i.e., they clink with the sound of coins. Compare "The Complaint of Chaucer to His Purse," line 9, and the "blisful soun" (the clink of coins) that he misses.

17 *disjone.* Lit., "breakfast," from OF *desjeun*; but probably here it means simply "to eat." The word is needed for the rhyme.

22–23 *cors.* "Cross," referring to a coin with a cross stamped on one side; in these lines Dunbar is reversing the usual idea that the Cross (or making the sign of the Cross) frightens away the devil.

24 *Quhaevir tyne, quhaevir win.* "Whoever loses, whoever wins," i.e., "regardless" or "whatever the case."

26–29 A magic purse that is never empty brings to mind various folk tales, as well as stories such as Marie de France's *Lanval*, in which the title character's faerie lover gives him just such a purse.

33 The *lord* he is addressing is presumably his earthly king, not his heavenly Lord, though a double meaning is possible.

33–34 These verses may echo line 25 from "The Complaint of Chaucer to His Purse": "And ye, that mowen alle oure harmes amende."

34 *malice.* This word, too, may be meant in at least two senses — "harm" or "evil," but also perhaps "malaise" or "disease." The king is the speaker's physician who can undo his harm and cure his disease.

40. *To the King* [*Schir, at this feist of benefice*]

This is one of Dunbar's lighter, wittier, and fairly good-humored petition poems, yet there can be no doubt that the poet is serious in his desire to receive what he has been denied, a benefice from which he could derive a proper income. The Scottish king, the "Schir" of lines 1 and 5, had the authority to nominate members of the clergy to a variety of ecclesiastical offices, and the poem clearly reflects the poet's devout wish to receive such a nomination. The poem develops an extended metaphor in which the handing out of benefices is compared to a feast at which the guests should be served equal portions but are not — those who "thirst sorely" are allowed to die of thirst, while those who are already full get fed until they burst. The poem is a plea for fairness. Three 5-line stanzas rhyming *aabba*. MF contains two texts of the poem (MFb is used here), and R (based on MFa). Mc11, K41, Bw62.

1	*Schir.* This is the formal mode of address the poet normally uses in his petition poems when addressing James IV.

2   *Think that small partis makis grit service.* Proverbial; see Whiting S397.

7   The rightness of giving a drink to a thirsty man may also be a biblical allusion: "I was thirsty and you gave me drink" (Matthew 25:35).

11   *collatioun.* Dunbar is playing on the two meanings of the word: "an evening repast" and "the conferral of a benefice on a clerygman."

13   The phrase *playis cop out* suggests a drinking game in which the participants are trying to be the first one to swill the entire contents of the cup. Compare "Master Andro Kennedy's Testament" (Poem 80), line 101. See also Douglas, *Eneados* 1.11.91–92.

14   "Let [for] once the cup go around the table" — so that all may sip from it equally. A refrain in drinking songs. Compare Oxford drinking carol, "How, butler, How! / Bevis a towt!" where the refrain, "Fill the boll, jentill butler, and let the cup rowght," apparently refers to just such an appeal for drinking equity. See Greene, *Carols*, p. 254.

41. *To the King* [*Of benefice, sir, at everie feist*]

This petition poem is often paired with the previous one, with which it has a good deal in common. However, it is far more explicit in its condemnation of ecclesiastical greed and the way in which ecclesiastical appointments are made. The poem is twice the length of the preceding poem and is perhaps twice as harsh in tone. Here, though, the poet's criticisms are not directed at the king but at greedy churchmen who grab everything for themselves and still feel that they have not received enough. This is one of Dunbar's petitions that reflects a fairly strong note of self-pity. Six 5-line stanzas rhyming *aabaB*, with varying refrain. MF preserves two versions (MFb is here used), and R. Mc12, K40, Bw43.

1   *sir.* Dunbar's usual form of address for the king.

2   I.e., "Those who [already] have the most are the ones who make the most urgent requests [for more]." The word *monyast* is the superlative form of "many."

4   "Ever the refrain of the song is." The word *ovirword* ("the refrain") literally means the "over word," i.e., the phrase that is repeated over and over.

5   The image here is of a gang of thieves dividing their plunder ("parting the pelf") among themselves. Compare Lindsay's *Complaint*, line 198.

6–7   Returning to the feast metaphor, the poet says that some eat very fine food (swans), some eat quite respectable food (ducks), and some (like him) eat nothing at all. A fat roasted swan, the food of royalty, since all swans belong to the king, was the favorite food of Chaucer's gluttonous Monk (*CT* I[A]206).

11–12   Feasts celebrating saints days could be either "common," that is, a day celebrating a general category of saints (e.g., martyrs) or even all the saints (All Hallows); or they could be "proper," that is, a feast day celebrating a particular saint (e.g., 27 December, St. John's Day).

13   Dunbar indicates that he sang at such feasts, perhaps fulfilling his professional responsibilities as a cleric; or perhaps he sang as a court entertainer.

14–15   The irony of his singing "Charity, for the love of God" — for which he receives nothing — is readily apparent. Compare *The Flyting of Dunbar and Kennedy* (Poem 83), line 383.

16–20   In this stanza the metaphor shifts to fishing, with the rich ecclesiastics catching all the fish in their nets and leaving nothing for the poor. The metaphor is perhaps an ironic allusion to St. Peter as fisherman after the Resurrection catching so many fish that his nets are full (John 21), whereupon Jesus admonishes him three times to "Feed my lambs."

19   *Quha nathing hes can nathing gett.* This is probably a proverbial expression (compare Whiting N176 and Tilley N337); and it brings to mind King Lear's famous remark to Cordelia that "Nothing can come of nothing" (*King Lear* I.i.85).

20   *syphir.* A cipher or zero, which in itself had no value except as a placeholder; thus, such a person is essentially a nonentity.

21–25   These verses criticize wealthy churchmen for neglecting the everyday needs of local parish churches. It is possible, as Bawcutt suggests, that Dunbar is referring to the practice of influential cathedrals and abbeys assuming control over smaller churches and then failing to pay attention to their needs (Bw 2.377).

28   Dunbar refers to death as a dragon in several poems; compare "Elegy for Bernard Stewart, Lord of Aubigny" (Poem 36), line 17, and "Of Man's Mortality" (Poem 9), line 28.

29–30   These sentiments are similar to those found in some of Dunbar's moral poems, e.g., "None May Assure in This World" (Poem 16), lines 61–64, or "Without Gladness No Treasure Avails" (Poem 19), lines 33–35.

42. *A Dream*

Perhaps more than any other poem, "A Dream" reflects the wide range of devices and techniques Dunbar employed within his group of petition poems. Here, in his continued pursuit of ecclesiastical preferment (i.e., the receipt of a benefice), he draws upon the techniques of the medieval dream vision, techniques he uses very effectively in some of his courtly poems and in some of his comic poems. In the case of this poem, however, most commentators do not admire the result. Scott calls the poem "more of a curiosity than an achievement" (p. 154), and Kinsley bluntly declares it "not an artistic success" (K, p. 334); Reiss, on the other hand, calls it "one of Dunbar's most interesting poems" (p. 86). What is especially striking to this commentator is the poem's pervasive tone of cynicism and disillusionment in its depiction of court corruption, and also the poet's use of irony, a device Dunbar employs only occasionally. Twenty-three 5-line stanzas rhyming *aabba*. R only. Mc60, K51, Bw75.

1   *halff sleiping as I lay*. Medieval dream visions often begin with the narrator in a state midway between waking and sleeping; compare *The Cuckoo and the Nightingale*: "I fil in such a slombre and swow — / Nought al a-slepe, ne fulli wakyng" (lines 87–88), *Middle English Debate Poetry*, ed. Conlee, p. 255.

2–5   It is common in dream visions in the tradition of *RR* for the dreamer to discover that the walls of his chamber have been adorned with splendid frescoes. This occurs, for example, in Chaucer's *Book of the Duchess* (lines 321–34); *HF* (lines 119 ff.); and Lindsay's *Squire Meldrum* (lines 883–84).

11–15   The dreamer is uncertain whether this impressive company has come for friendly or fiendly purposes. There are many instances in medieval and Renaissance literature where visual displays are conjured up for diabolical purposes, e.g., Marlowe's *Dr. Faustus* and the ME *Disputation between a Christian and a Jew* (lines 149–258). Being unsure, the dreamer prays to Jesus and Mary to protect him.

16–20   The dreamer's predicament, we discover, is a sickness of spirit reminiscent of what Chaucer's dreamer initially experiences in *The Book of the Duchess*. Because he is beset by the personified figures of Distress, Heaviness (i.e., Depression), and Languor (in line 21), he finds no pleasure in the singing of this company.

20   *lay me abone.* "Lay above me," i.e., were pressing down upon me.

26   *in ane trece.* This phrase is usually glossed, "in a processional dance"; but perhaps the meaning is "in a trice" (in an instant), indicating the suddenness of their appearance.

26–57   The dancing ladies who attempt to address the dreamer's plight are the sister virtues of Nobleness, Comfort, Pleasance, Perceiving (i.e., Insight), Wit, and Consideration. Their efforts, however, fail.

27   *Nobilnes* is a virtue of particular importance to healing the dreamer; the reference is probably to the king.

48–50   Discretion suggests that the dreamer's illness stems from melancholy. She then points out that his remedy lies with Nobleness, which is an implied indictment of the court — perhaps of the king in particular — for failing to reward the dreamer according to his deserts.

53   The reference to the dreamer's "long service made in vain" suggests that this may be one of Dunbar's later petition poems.

55   *this guid New Yeir.* Distributing New Year's gifts to servants and members of the court was a common practice in the Middle Ages; compare *SGGK* lines 66–68. Dunbar's "To the King" (Poem 37), thought to be one of his earlier petitions, also reflects this practice. There is a good likelihood that both of these poems are in some sense New Year's poems.

58–60   *Blind Effectioun*. Volunteering to speak on the dreamer's behalf is the personified figure of Blind Affection — which might be translated as "Blind Favoritism" — a person kindly disposed, who enjoys an important standing at court.

60–72   Reason argues that the period of Blind Affection's influence at court is now over, and Reason proposes that the time has come for the dreamer — who has long served the king though he is no flatterer — to receive his proper deserts.

62   *sessioun*. See explanatory note to "Discretion in Taking" (Poem 28), line 37.

72   *Be Nobilnes his help mon first be found*. This verse (like line 50 earlier) once again indicates that the dreamer's cure resides with Nobleness.

74   The Lords of Session were members of the king's council who were appointed to hear civil complaints. Dunbar refers to them often; compare "The Table of Confession" (Poem 7), line 134; "Discretion in Taking" (Poem 28), line 37; "Tidings from the Session" (Poem 74), line 21; "To the Merchants of Edinburgh" (Poem 75), line 57.

76–85   *Inoportunitie* — meaning something like "persistent importuning" or "constant demanding" — belongs with "Blind Effectioun" (line 58) in the ranks of the court sycophants.

81–82   These verses indicate that the "besy askar" (line 81) is the one who succeeds, while deserving servants who do not ask are ignored — a clear case of squeaky wheels getting the grease. Similar sentiments are expressed in "Discretion in Asking" (Poem 26), especially lines 26–29.

83   *And he that askis not tynes bot his word*. Compare Chaucer's *TC* 5.798 and Whiting S614.

84   "But to waste long service is no joke" — this refers to the two busy servants in line 82 whose service goes unrewarded.

86   *Schir Johne Kirkpakar*. A clergyman with many churches crammed into his pack. Having many ecclesiastical holdings, he stands at the opposite extreme from the dreamer, who can lay claim to no churches at all. Clergymen, especially corrupt ones, were often pejoratively called "Sir John." Pluralism, the practice of having multiple church holdings, was widely deplored. Dunbar concurs.

293

90   In using the phrase *yon ballad maker*, Sir John Kirkpakar is heaping scorn on the narrator.

91–95   *Sir Bet-the-Kirk.* "Sir Beat-the-Church," or perhaps "Sir Best-the-Church." Although it is not entirely clear who he is, most commentators believe he is a secular figure who has been "besting" the church by snatching up ecclesiastical holdings for his own personal gain. Reason's comments in lines 96–100, though, indicate that this is merely another name for Sir John Kirkpakar.

96   *The ballance gois unevin.* The balanced scales being uneven clearly indicate the injustice of the situation.

100   *sufficience dwellis not bot in Heavin.* Reason is suggesting, rather pessimistically, that the only satisfaction the dreamer will ever receive will come in Heaven, not in this world — a sentiment expressed in some of Dunbar's moral poems.

102   *him.* "Him" may refer to the dreamer, though it seems more likely that it refers to the king and that lines 102–04 are commenting on the king's capriciousness rather than on the dreamer's dissatisfaction with what has been offered to him — since it appears that nothing has ever been offered to him. If this is the case, line 105 is ironic.

106–10   Patience's advice to the dreamer — to "make good cheer and depend on the prince" — seems cold comfort indeed.

109–10   In instances where a bishopric was vacant, the income generated by its holdings reverted to the king. But Patience asserts that the king would never intentionally delay the dreamer's preferment in order to reap such benefits for himself; perhaps Patience truly believes this, but the irony is inescapable.

111–15   The dreamer's vision is suddenly shattered by the firing of a great gun, which causes the earth to reverberate. Compare the conclusion to Dunbar's *The Golden Targe* (Poem 65). A variety of similar devices occur in other dream poems; compare Chaucer's *Book of the Duchess* (lines 1321–25), where the dreamer is awakened by the sound of a bell, and the ME *Parliament of the Three Ages* (lines 656–57), where the dreamer is awakened by the sounding of a bugle.

114   Leith was a port very close to Edinburgh where foreign goods, including guns, were brought into Scotland. Bawcutt observes that a large cannon was fired on Leith sands in July of 1506, in the king's presence (Bw 2.469).

43. *The Headache*

This is one of Dunbar's most personal poems and is a petition only in that it seems to be designed to evoke the sympathetic understanding of the person to whom it is addressed, presumably King James. The narrator's predicament is that he is experiencing an excruciating headache (the "magryme," or migraine, of line 3), and thus composing poetry is completely out of the question. The poem appears to be an apology for his inability to produce a poem, and may be Dunbar's explanation for his failure to fulfill a specific request. A central irony, of course, is that he has written a poem about the inability to write a poem. "The Headache" conveys a strong sense of reality and probably should be accepted as a literal description of a headache. It therefore stands in contrast to several other petitions where the speaker's dilemma is characterized more by psychological or spiritual torpor than by real physical suffering. The final stanza, however, which describes his "curage" (line 12) lying asleep even though he has physically arisen, may suggest that there is also a spiritual component to his distress. Three 5-line stanzas rhyming *aabba*. R only. Mc3, K21, Bw35.

4   *Perseing my brow as ony ganyie.* The image of an arrow piercing his brow bestows a palpable realness on the description.

6   *And now, schir.* Here, as in several of Dunbar's petition poems, the "sir" he is addressing is almost certainly the king. The poem does not make it clear why he is addressing the king, but probably because he has been unable to fulfill a specific request made of him, or a promise made by him. On the other hand, it may be that this is just a clever device for playing on the king's sympathy.

8   *sentence.* "The meaning" or "the heart of the matter," rather than the actual words. Compare "Of the Changes of Life" (Poem 13), lines 1–5.

9   *Unsleipit*, rather than meaning "unasleep" or "awake," literally means "un-slept," i.e., not having slept, or unrefreshed by sleep.

12   *curage.* Always a difficult word to translate in ME texts, here it seems to mean "spirit" or "mental faculties."

13–15   All of these things that fail to awaken the speaker's spirit — mirth, minstrelsy, play, din, dancing, and revelry — recall the personified company of entertainers who entered the dreamer's chamber in "A Dream" (Poem 42), lines 7–10, but who likewise failed to provide the narrator with any cheer.

44. *To the King* [*For to considder is ane pane*]

Although this poem clearly belongs among Dunbar's petitions, it blends elements from several lyric categories. Most of the first half of the poem intertwines general observations about worldly mutability with comments deploring the failure of people in authority to reward those who have given long service. Some of the sentiments reflected in these verses are also typically found in satires against the times. But, beginning in line 41, the poem focuses more specifically on ecclesiastical corruption; then, in line 47, we discover the speaker's particular grievance: some men possess seven benefices while he does not possess a single one! In lines 61–75 he compares his long wait for a benefice with that of a merchant who hopes for the safe arrival of a well-laden ship from far-distant lands. Finally, near the end of the poem, he addresses the king directly, beseeching his help (line 90). In the king, he says, lies his only hope help for a lessening of his pain (lines 96–100). This poem does not reflect the powerful sense of disillusionment seen in some of Dunbar's other petitions, but it begins to lean in that direction. Twenty-five 4-line stanzas rhyming *aabB*; this is the *kyrielle*, a form Dunbar employs in about a dozen poems. MF and R. Mc13, K39, Bw79.

5   *The slydand joy*. I.e., happiness that does not last — it slip-slides away; compare the phrase "a slyding quhiell" ("a slippery or turning wheel") in line 3 of "Of Life" (Poem 12). Compare also Chaucer's reference to alchemy in The Canon Yeoman's Tale as the "slidynge science" ("the elusive science"), *CT* VIII(G)732. The sequence of half line oppositions is tonally akin to the first stanza of *PF*, where "dredful joye . . . slit so yerne" (line 3).

6   *feynyeid luif*. "Pretended love"; Dunbar also uses this phrase in line 17 of "True Love" (Poem 68); variant forms of the word *feynyeid* occur frequently in his poems.

7   *sweit abayd*. Kinsley glosses this phrase as "adroit delay" and Bawcutt as "sweet waiting." I would suggest "pleasurable anticipation."

9–12   Similar sentiments occur in some of Dunbar's moralities; compare, for example, lines 41–50 in "None May Assure in This World" (Poem 16).

10   *faceis tua.* "Two faces"; hypocritical or deceitful people have long been considered two-faced; compare Whiting F12.

16–20   What he is criticizing, he claims, is not unique to Scotland but also occurs in all the major countries of Europe. Perhaps this is a ploy to suggest that the king is not the only one at whom he is pointing a finger.

21   This commonplace sentiment is also expressed in several of Dunbar's moral poems, e.g., "All Earthly Joy Returns to Pain" (Poem 8), lines 21–22, and "Of the Changes of Life" (Poem 13), line 17. Compare Whiting W132 and 133.

23   *In hall and bour, in burgh and plane.* This verse captures the all-pervasiveness of what the poet is describing — it is simply everywhere.

27   People are as changeable as the weather — or the wind and rain. Compare Chaucer's comments in The Clerk's Tale (*CT* IV[E] 995–98); and Whiting W289 and W295.

29   "Good Rule" often pertains to law and order; the border probably refers to the border-country separating England from Scotland, an area notorious for its lawlessness.

42–43   A clergyman with an overly broad conscience is one who is far too tolerant of sin. Compare Tilley W888.

47   *Sum men hes sevin and I nocht ane.* Compare "A Dream" (Poem 42), in which "Schir Johne Kirkpakar" is said to possess seven churches (lines 86–90).

49   *browk ane stall.* "Possess a stall" within a cathedral.

50–51   A bishopric is not good enough for him; he must be made a cardinal.

53   The speaker, considered unworthy, remains among those completely left out.

55   "Some play dicing games with a large number (of churches)"; the sense seems to be that some men who are rich in church holdings manage them frivolously. As Bawcutt points out (Bw 2.479), *passage* was the name of a dice game corresponding to French *passe-dix*.

57–83   The *It* in these verses is the benefice or church holding that the speaker so greatly desires.

62   *Calyecot* is Calicut (Calcutta), on the Malabar coast of southwest India; the *New Fund Yle* is either Newfoundland (discovered by Cabot in 1497) or another North American locale (i.e., on the other side of the globe).

63   *The partis of transmeridiane* may refer to recent discoveries in the southern hemisphere. Literally, *transmeridiane* would mean beyond the meridian, the dividing line in the Atlantic between the Old World and the New World.

69   *out of all ayrtis*. I.e., "from all points of the compass"; or, "from any direction you can think of."

70–71   Some have suggested that *Paris* (line 70) is an error for *Percia*. But more likely Paris equated with Europe, *orient partis* (line 70) with Asia, and *The ylis of Aphrycane* (line 71) with Africa, thus implying the threefold geographical division of the world. See Bw 2.450, note to lines 69–71.

71   Perhaps the "isles of Africa" are the Canary or Cape Verde Islands, which were well-known by the end of the fifteenth century.

78   In 1486 James III issued gold coins with a unicorn stamped on one side; "crowns of weight" would be crowns of the standard weight, not "light crowns."

81–82   Apparently provision has definitely been made for the poet to receive what he wants; but it is the interminable wait that he has trouble coping with.

83   The reference to the long wait "bursting his brain" brings to mind his migraine headache described in "The Headache" (Poem 43).

85–88   His desires, he suggests, are modest. He does not require a great abbey, merely a humble parish church roofed with heather.

86   Bawcutt notes that heather was sometimes used to cover the roofs of small country churches but never for wealthy abbeys (Bw 2.480).

89–91   Since he can never be accused of pluralism (possessing several ecclesiastical holdings at the same time), he suggests, facetiously, that his soul will certainly be better off because of it.

93–95   The poet returns once more to sentiments commonly expressed in his poems about earthly mutability. The key image here is of the world being as changeable as an ever-moving weather vane. Compare Whiting V5 and V6.

99   "Your grace" is an honorific title usually assigned to a high-ranking churchman, though here it is clearly directed at the king; perhaps the poet is playing on "grace" to mean "favor" as well as "mercy."

45. *Against the Solicitors at Court*

This poem, which is a petition only by implication, offers an overview of the strategies adopted by those at court who are soliciting royal patronage. Some of them, the poet says, make their case by performing true and diligent service, some by just hanging around, some by providing various kinds of entertainment, some by flirting, flattering, or pretense, and so on. As for the poet, he claims that he knows no other way to conduct himself except with humility; and, as far as he is concerned, the king's gracious countenance offers him riches enough. In Scott's view the poem provides a blatant "example of the guile [Dunbar] disclaims having. Certainly it is a study in, and example of, hypocrisy" (pp. 92–93). Such an appraisal may be harsh, but it is certainly true that in "Against the Solicitors at Court" Dunbar is employing the modesty topos, a device that he will move away from in what appear to be his later petitions. Twenty-six verses in octosyllabic couplets. MF contains two versions (MFa is used here), and R. Mc29, K20, Bw5.

2   *solistationes*. "Solicitations," here probably more in the sense of "making attempts to gain the royal attention" than in the sense of making formal petitions to the king.

3   In this single verse Dunbar briefly mentions those who truly merit the king's recognition; in the next poem, "To the King" (Poem 46), they receive much fuller attention.

4   *be continuall residence*. I.e., by their constant presence; they are court hangers-on.

5–6   These verses probably mean: "One on his own means survives, / Until fortune does for him provide." A second, though less likely, reading is: "A certain one preserves his own resources / While fortune (i.e., the court) provides for him."

7   "The Scottish court records list payments to singers, musicians, and entertainers of many kinds. . . . One singer brought 'a sang buke' for the king . . . [and] several story-tellers are named, such as 'Wallass that tellis the geistis to the king'" (Bw 2.300).

8   *the Moryis.* The Morris dance; the phrase apparently derives from "Moorish dance," a colorful spectacle involving outlandish music, dancing, and costuming that became a popular entertainment at the Scottish court. There are many references to it in court records, and one was organized by John Damian, the chief subject in "The Antichrist" (Poem 51) and "A Ballad of the Friar of Tungland" (Poem 54) (see Bw 2.301).

10   *Sum playis the fuill and all owt clatteris.* This verse may refer to an actual court fool — Dunbar mentions real fools elsewhere, most notably in lines 73–80 of "Master Andro Kennedy's Testament" (Poem 80) — or it may be figurative.

11–12   "One man, musing alone by the wall, / Looks like he wants nothing to do with all the rest." This man may be setting himself apart from the others in order to call attention to himself. Or perhaps the poet is referring to himself as an objective observer.

13   Whisperers are usually gossipers or backbiters. Compare "Rule of Oneself" (Poem 25), lines 33–34.

17–18   Some even turn holy occasions into occasions for self-promotion.

19–20   Some shamelessly have their own advocates working on their behalf within the king's inner circle. (In "To the King" [Poem 38], line 25, Dunbar calls the queen his "advocat.")

21–26   In these verses the poet calls attention to his own "simpleness" — his innocence, or lack of worldliness, or absence of guile. In contrast to the previous person, who has his own advocate to recommend him, all the poet has to recommend him is his "humble cheer and face."

25–26   The king's "gracious countenance" refers literally to his "face," but also to his "regal bearing" or "demeanor." There may also be an oblique biblical allusion in these verses to the light of God's countenance (compare Psalm 4:4–7 in the Vulgate).

46. *To the King* [*Schir, ye have mony servitouris*]

This poem is "one of the most subtle and carefully composed of Dunbar's petitions" (Bw 2.450) and a poem that must be considered one of the most artful in the Dunbar canon. As Spearing has observed, "After nearly five hundred years, this poem still has the power to move as well as to entertain" (1985, p. 205). It offers a rich and colorful depiction of various activities that occurred within the larger context of the Scottish royal court. The poem is organized into two major sections that offer lengthy catalogues of two contrasting groups of servitors. The first group (3–24) is composed entirely of true contributors, and all the members of this group have been appropriately rewarded. In the 10-line passage that follows, the poet flirts with the modesty topos, though his true feelings soon emerge — he not only believes that he belongs among this first group, he also believes that his poetry will endure as long as the accomplishments of any of them.

The poet then turns his attention to a second group of servitors, a group composed entirely of fakes, leeches, spongers, and flatterers. But what infuriates the poet is the fact that each of these contemptible folk has *also* been rewarded. Not only does the poet find himself excluded from the ranks of the first group, those who have been deservingly rewarded, but he has also been excluded from the ranks of the second group, those who have been *un*deservingly rewarded. In essence, he comprises a third category all by himself, that of the deserving but unrewarded person. At this point, in the section that begins at line 61, he can no longer contain his anger; ultimately, he says, either his heart must break, or he must take his pen and get revenge by letting "the venom issue all out" (line 85). In these final verses, the poet's anger seems real and considerable. Eighty-eight lines in iambic couplets. MF only. Mc17, K44, Bw67.

1–16   Here the speaker pays tribute to a long list of *servitouris* (line 1) and *officiaris* (line 2) who perform valuable, honorable service for the king and who are fully deserving of their rewards and the king's gratitude. They range from highly accomplished lawyers and physicians to more humble craftsmen and artisans. Norman (in McClure and Spiller, 1989) makes the shrewd observation that Dunbar in this passage "castigates the vice and folly of the court only to reveal his own willing complicity with that same corruption. It is as if the poet in playing various roles before and within the court exposes the ambiguities inherent in that experience" (p. 190).

3   *Kirkmen, courtmen, and craftismen fyne*. The ordering and grouping of individuals who serve the king has a rough logic, perhaps, moving downward through the social hierarchy, though many of the verses seem to be arranged more for their sounds than for the close connection of the individuals' functions. The group in this line is linked by "k" alliteration and that in line 6 by vowel alliteration; in lines 9 and 12 the alliteration does coincide with a unified grouping, but in lines 11 and 16 that is not the case.

5   *Divinouris* probably means "theologians" (i.e., doctors of divinity), not "practitioners in the art of divination," as has been suggested. Compare the similar word in Chaucer's Knight's Tale: "I nam no divinistre; / Of soules fynde I nat in this registre" (*CT* I[A]2811–12).

6   *artistis*. Here it probably means "scholars," men who have completed their study of the liberal arts.

7   *Men of armes*. Often called "men at arms," these are professional soldiers of lower social status than the knights they accompany.

8   The "many other goodly wights" probably refers to the lesser foot soldiers who would have accompanied the knights and men at arms of line 7, perhaps men such as Chaucer's Yeoman, who accompanied and served the Knight and the Squire.

9   There is a wealth of evidence, both from within Dunbar's poems and elsewhere, to show that James' court was greatly enlivened by musical entertainment.

10   *Chevalouris, cawandaris, and flingaris*. Since the poet has already mentioned valiant knights and other military figures, perhaps these terms refer to varieties of entertainers; the meaning of *cawandaris* is obscure, but *flingaris* normally means "dancers." Bawcutt suggests it may have a military sense: "hurlers of missiles" (Bw 2.451).

11   *Cunyouris*. "Coiners"; the king's mint was known as the *cunyehouse*. In this context, *carvouris* probably are "wood carvers."

12–14   *Beildaris of barkis . . . schipwrichtis*. In the early years of the sixteenth century James IV embarked on an extensive, costly program of shipbuilding; its finest product was a ship called the *Great Michael*. Completed in 1511, the *Great Michael* carried a crew of 300, along with 120 gunners and a thousand men of war. The phrase *barkis and ballingaris* (line 12) refers to sea-going ships of all varieties. Compare Douglas, *Eneados* 4.7.72.

13   *Masounis lyand upon the land*. This line alludes to James' massive program of castle building and rebuilding.

16   *Pryntouris*. If this term actually means "printers" rather than something like "stampers" or "impressors," then this line offers evidence for dating the poem, since the first printing press in Scotland was established in 1507 by Chepman and Myllar, whose first book actually appeared in April 1508. The poem, then, would have had to be written after this date.

25–34   The speaker's attitude toward his plight is initially stated with becoming modesty (lines 25–27); but then he reveals his belief (lines 28–32) that his works are just as perfect as any performed by the people previously mentioned; and by the end of this passage, his bitterness is undisguised. In the following section (lines 35–60), as the speaker presents a huge catalogue of "Aneuthir sort" (line 37) — the king's *un*deserving servitors who have also been rewarded — his bitterness intensifies. On the highly ornate, rhetorical idiom of Dunbar's court poetry here and in the two long lists of court functionaries see Norman (in McClure and Spiller, 1989), pp. 179–80: "The key to understanding Dunbar as 'makar' lies in his role as court poet. He is the only one of the important fifteenth-century Scots *poets* who was directly and solely dependent on the patronage of the court for his livelihood" (pp. 179–80).

28–33   Here Dunbar expresses the classical view, much reiterated in Renaissance poetry, that art has the power to endure despite the ravages of time.

39–49   Many of the terms in this catalogue of underserving servers are both highly colloquial and terribly insulting, and many of them are recorded nowhere else, making it difficult to be certain of their meanings. But one thing is certain — everyone included in this list is either a self-serving parasite or a hanger-on of one variety or another.

41   *gunnaris*. Perhaps these "gunners" are included among the "leeches" because of the great expense that gunnery practice required; or perhaps because most of them were

foreigners, like the figures mentioned in lines 42–43. "James IV's interest in artillery and fire arms is well known" (Bw 2.451).

42   *Monsouris*. He is probably using this French title sarcastically. The fact that they are experts in fine wines — good clarets — suggests their gluttony and drunkenness. Delicacy, the second daughter of Gluttony, according to John Gower, is a particular vice of nobles who "reconcile their taste for gluttony to all delights so that they can live delicately." In particular Gower describes Delicacy's wine cellar, which includes "vernage, malmsey, spiced claret" and "foaming wine" (John Gower, *Mirour de l'Omme*, trans. William Burton Wilson [East Lansing, MI: Colleagues Press, 1992], p. 108).

42–43   As these lines suggest, at James' court there were many foreigners (here French and Irish), something the poet seems to resent greatly.

44   *lyk out of mynd*. "As if out of their minds."

46   *hall huntaris*. Hunters who do their "hunting" in the dining hall, not in the fields.

48   *and kennis na man of gude*. "And who know no good of any man," i.e., have nothing good to say of anyone.

54–60   These verses reflect James' keen interest in alchemy and Dunbar's aversion to it, a topic also treated in Dunbar's poems on John Damian ("The Antichrist" [Poem 51] and "A Ballad of the Friar of Tungland" [Poem 54]).

60   In a Scottish burgh the Tolbooth served as a meeting place for the town council, as the seat of the burgh court, as a center for financial administration, as a prison or town jail, or simply as a place of security; see *DOST*. In some instances it even served as a school. In Edinburgh, the Tolbooth was on the High Street near St. Giles church.

65–66   These lines contain an allusion to the popular poem *Colkelbie Sow*, in which a gathering of fools feast upon a little pig called a *gryse*.

73   *panence*. "Penance"; but perhaps the sense of the line is that he would feel more "forgiving" or "tolerant" had he too been rewarded.

76   The poet's melancholy, mentioned here and again in line 84, is caused, according to medieval humor theory, by an excess of black bile. One remedy for it would be "to vent his spleen." His melancholy is also mentioned in line 49 of "A Dream" (Poem 42). Compare Pertelote's comments on "malencolie" in Chaucer's Nun's Priest's Tale (*CT* VII[B]2933–37).

82–88   In these verses, the poet seems to be casting himself in the role of the ancient Celtic bard, or satirist, whose words had the power to destroy the reputation of the person at whom they were directed.

87   The *tryackill*, the sweet medicine that can calm his heart, is of course the better treatment he wishes to receive from the king. Compare the Host's use of the word in Chaucer's Prologue to The Pardoner's Tale (*CT* VI[C]314)

47. *To the King* [*Complane I wald*]

"To the King [Complane I wald]" has much in common with "To the King [Schir, ye have mony servitouris]" (Poem 46), and, like the previous poem, it appears to be one of Dunbar's angriest petitions — at least on the face of it. But here the poet's sense of outrage and his use of vituperative language has become so extreme and exaggerated that the poem moves beyond the realm of serious satire and into the realm of comic invective, the realm of the *flyting*. Commentators have been especially intrigued by the colorful, and in some instances very obscure, set of abusive epithets the poet uses in his catalogue of rascals (lines 15–27). Ridley plausibly suggests that many of these terms may have been "neologisms, coined for the sake of verbal attack and highly suited for it because of the harsh, contemptuous effect they create even when their literal meaning is unknown — if it ever existed" (1973, p. 1014).

Following the catalogue of rogues are brief descriptions of three varieties of ecclesiastical abuses (lines 28–39) practiced by those scoundrels. There then follows a scathing portrait of a low-born cleric who lords it over members of the aristocracy (including the speaker, presumably) and who does all he can to see that they "never rise to his renown" (line 66). As Ross observes, this cleric's "crooked body betrays his crooked nature" (p. 144). Some critics have been incensed by the anti-egalitarian attitude Dunbar expresses in this poem, but others have defended him as being a man of his time who simply reflects the viewpoint of the class to which he was born. In any case, in the final ten lines the poet once again voices his plea to the king to "have an eye toward your old servant, who has long relied on you" (lines 69–70), verses perhaps suggesting that this is one of Dunbar's later petitions. Seventy-six verses in octosyllabic couplets. MF and R. Mc19, K45, Bw9.

1–8   The gentle, benign, almost devotional tone of the poem's opening verses is surely meant to provide a stark contrast with the stream of invective that soon follows.

6   The epithet "Queen of Heaven" is commonly used for the Virgin Mary. Compare "A Ballad of Our Lady" (Poem 4), lines 6, 38, and 61.

7–14   One of the king's most important responsibilities was to insure that justice was had by all. Dunbar refers to this fact elsewhere, especially in lines 106–26 of "The Thistle and the Rose" (Poem 30). Compare also "To the King" (Poem 37), line 15.

10–11   The nobles and men of virtue mentioned in these verses are people who have been slighted. They stand in contrast, in their virtue and in their unrewardedness, to the men listed in the ensuing catalogue.

15–27   Now the poet's string of abusive phrases pours forth — almost as a fulfillment of the poet's prediction in lines 85–86 of the previous poem, so that what we see here is an example of the poet "spouting" his venom. The precise meanings of some of these phrases are uncertain, but on the whole the passage reviles rustics and men at court who come from rural backgrounds, i.e., men of low birth and little cultural sophistication.

18   *haschbaldis, haggarbaldis . . . hummellis.* Bawcutt observes: "Obscure, but *DOST* (s.v. *luschbald*) notes the existence of a group of abusive words, employing the pejorative suffix *-bald*, and suggests their connection with verbs, such as *hasch*, *hag*, *lusch*, meaning 'strike, cut down.' *[H]ummellis*. Perhaps cattle. In later Scottish the word was used of polled domestic animals" (2.307n18).

28–38   The three varieties of unworthy clerics described in these verses are found among the same men just described; now we are given further elaboration of the vices they practice.

28–32   Some of the men just described snatch for themselves a cowl — that is, they wear a monk's habit — and soon they are in charge of a great convent, that is, they have risen to the position of abbot. (It is possible that one such figure is John Damian, the abbot of Tungland and the subject of two of Dunbar's most scathing poems, "The Antichrist" [Poem 51] and "A Ballad of the Friar of Tungland" [Poem 54].)

33–34   Some beg from the king a *rokkat* (line 33), i.e., a rochet (the white vestment of a bishop), which destroys a worthless person, i.e., which thus converts a nobody into a somebody.

35–38   Some who receive just an ordinary parsonage think it a gift that is greatly beneath them — a gift fit only for a page boy; they cannot be content until they have received the title of "my lord" — an honorific title used for prelates as well as for nobles.

39–40   "But whether he is content or not / Judge for yourself in your own mind." The answer, clearly, is that he is not content, not even when he has achieved the title of "my lord."

41–48   In these verses the poet expresses his outrage at the plight of impoverished young noblemen who are reduced to accepting castoff clothing and running errands for their far less worthy and capable "superiors."

45   *maister*. Here the term probably means a gentleman, a man of noble birth, rather than a university graduate.

47–48   "And has much more intelligence — by three times — to possess such a dignified office."

51–52   "Seated at table so far above the place / suitable for one who formerly mucked out the stable." The seats at a meal or banquet were assigned according to social rank. Compare *SGGK*, lines 72–73.

54–60   Now the poet additionally portrays his depraved clergyman as being physically grotesque, perhaps in the tradition of Chaucer's Summoner, or perhaps as a kind of male counterpart to the "loathly lady" of medieval romance. It is possible that the "pack" mentioned in line 58 does not refer to an actual pack but to the hump of a hunchbacked clergyman.

59   The term *glaschane* is obscure. Bawcutt suggests *glaschane gane* may mean something like "fish face" (Bw 2.308). My suggestion is that *glaschane* may mean "glowing" or "glassy" — indicating that his face has become shiny from excessive food and drink; Chaucer's portrait of the Monk comes to mind: "His heed was balled, that shoon as any glas, / And eek his face, as he hadde been enoynt" (*CT* I[A]198–99).

62   *strumbell*. A plodding farm horse (?); it is probably related to "strummellis" in line 17.

67   *O prince maist honorable*. The prince is King James, to whom he is making his petition; the phrase also recalls the "wardlie prince" he had mentioned in line 7.

69   *And to thy auld servandis haffe*. This verse recalls line 38 in "Discretion in Giving" (Poem 27): "And to awld servandis list not se."

73   The reference to his "writing" may refer to his poetry, or it may refer to other kinds of secretarial services he has performed as a clerk in the king's household.

74–76   With the terms *danger* (line 74) and *grace* (line 75), the poet is playing on the relationship of a lady and her suitor; the lady long displays her *danger* (her disdain or standoffishness) before finally taking pity on the lover and bestowing upon him her *grace*.

48. *To the King* [*Exces of thocht dois me mischeif*]

This petition poem has a good deal in common with the next poem, "To the King [That I suld be ane Yowllis yald]," especially in what it suggests about the poet's advancing years and in its comparison of the poet to an animal — in this case a bird, in that case a horse. It also offers suggestions (yet again) about Dunbar's attitude toward rustics and foreigners who have benefitted from the king's generosity (while he has not), and it may also offer important insights into the poet's relationship with the king. As Ridley observes, "The poem is interesting for what it suggests about Dunbar's early and lasting ecclesiastical ambitions, his attitudes toward low-born men, and his relations with James IV, which were either so intimate or so misguided that he felt he could reprove the King in most outspoken terms" (1973, p. 1015). Scott suggests that one of "the freshest things in the poem is the [poet's] honest self-analysis, self-revelation, and confession of state of mind" (p. 118). The bird metaphor, which is only sustained through the first six stanzas of the poem, draws upon heraldic imagery, animal fable tradition, and on specific works such as Chaucer's *Parliament of Fowls* and Dunbar's own "The Thistle and the Rose" (Poem 30). Dunbar surely selected the bird metaphor with James' passion for falconry in mind. Seventeen 5-line stanzas rhyming *aabaB*. MF, B, and R (which only preserves a fragment of the text). Mc20, K42, Bw68.

4   *Gud conscience.* It is the king's "good conscience" of course, not the speaker's, which should be crying out for the poet to be rewarded; and it is to the king's conscience that he is making his appeal.

5   *Exces of thocht dois me mischeif.* This refrain line is similar in sentiment to the refrain in "To the King" (Poem 44): "For to consider is ane pane." Both reflect the pain the speaker feels when he thinks about these things — something he cannot help doing.

6   *clarkis.* Probably minor scribes, not clergymen.

7–9   "And I, like a red hawk, do cry out / To come to the lure (but) I do not have permission, / Even though my feathers have begun to molt." Why like a *red* hawk? No one is sure. Kinsley wonders whether Dunbar may have had red hair (K, p. 319). If that is so, perhaps the reference to his beginning to molt implies that he has also begun to grow bald. In the next poem, he indicates that his hair has turned white (lines 21–22).

11   *falcounis kynd.* "The falcon's race," i.e., noble birds (as opposed to lesser ones).

12   *myttell.* This unidentified term seems to refer to a specific variety of lesser bird of prey; but perhaps it simply means "middle," referring generically to birds of middle rank, birds that would stand in contrast to truly noble high-ranking birds.

   hard in mynd. I.e., "firmly remembered"; that is, not forgotten or neglected, as the poet is.

13–14   The kite (*gled*, line 13) was considered a rapacious and cowardly bird that fed, ignobly, on carrion; the goshawk, though a relatively low-ranking falcon, was still a genuinely noble bird. In Chaucer's *PF* the goshawk is the first of the "egles of a lowere kynde" (line 332).

16–19   The magpie imitates the songs of other birds; but when it tries to mimic the song of the nightingale, it cannot begin to reproduce the actual song of the nightingale. Here the magpie symbolizes a plagiarizing or derivative poet, in contrast to a true artist, the nightingale. Perhaps Dunbar means to contrast himself with lesser poets at court. In "A Complaint against Mure" (Poem 60) he lodges a complaint against a man named Mure for stealing his verses.

21   *Ay fairast feddiris hes farrest foulis.* The earliest recorded example of a well-known proverb (Whiting F573).

21–23   It was often fashionable in late medieval courts to have exotic species of birds on public display; these verses, though, are clearly alluding to the favoritism shown to foreigners in James' court.

24   *Kynd native nestis.* These "natural, native nests" (of owls!) stand in sharp contrast to the silver cages of the exotic birds mentioned in the previous verse.

26   The *gentill egill* is of course the king; the eagle, a traditional symbol of kingship, is one of the three symbols Dunbar uses for the king in "The Thistle and the Rose" (Poem 30).

28–29   These verses contain one of Dunbar's most direct and audacious rebukes of the king.

33   *Kyne of.* I.e., "The likes of"; Rauf Colyard and Johnne the Reif represent commoners who have been elevated to noble status. Both names may be drawn from tales in which this occurs (compare *Ralph the Collier*, in *Three Middle English Charlemagne Romances*, ed. Alan Lupack [Kalamazoo, MI: Medieval Institute Publications, 1990], pp. 161–204).

36   Perhaps there is a play on words in *maid refuse* ("refused" or "turned down"), with the secondary meaning being "made into refuse," i.e., "treated like garbage."

38   This proverb (Whiting A37) usually occurs when the speaker is pleading for social equality; the irony here is that it is the person of high birth (Dunbar) who is pleading for equality with the commoner who has been elevated above him.

41–65   Autobiographical writing was not yet common in European writing. In England, Hoccleve, following tendencies in Chaucer (such passages as the Prologue to the *LGW*), had shown the way. These lines are among the most personal and self-revelatory verses in all of Dunbar's poetry.

48–49   "Alas, all I am able to do is write poems — such childishness controls my bridle's reins." This is, of course, mock humility; Dunbar has no doubts about the value of writing poetry.

54   For the figure of the king as the poet's physician, compare "To the King" (Poem 39), line 34, and "A Dream" (Poem 42), lines 49–50.

58–59   Here Dunbar makes a direct request for a benefice, which contrasts greatly with the indirect appeals he normally makes in his petitions.

61–64   The poet here reminisces about his early childhood. He says that as he was dandled on his nurse's knee she sang to him *dandillie, bischop, dandillie* (line 62). The implication is that from an early age it was expected of Dunbar that he would have a brilliant career in the church. But now that he is old, he has not even managed to become a simple vicar, a minor churchman who oversaw a parish church whose rector was non-resident.

66–75   These stanzas once again express the poet's sense of injury and injustice, that country rustics have come into possession of the things he wants but continues to lack.

66   *Jok.* Jock is a stock name for a man belonging to the lower class — a rustic.

68–69   Having a false card up your sleeve usually refers to cheating at cards; but here it may mean that not only does Jock openly possess far more than the poet, even the card he has tucked away has greater value than all the poet's poems.

71   *uplandis Michell* is similar to Jock, but perhaps the distinction between them is largely geographical — Jock being a Lowlander of low birth, while Michell comes from the Highlands.

72   *With dispensationis in ane knitchell.* Papal dispensations were often required in order for a churchman to hold several benefices at the same time.

74   *He playis with totum and I with nychell.* The reference here may be to a game involving a four-sided spinning toy; when the top stops spinning, the side resting on the ground will either show a T (for *totum*=all), or an N (for *nihil*=nothing).

78–79   Dunbar's sardonic wit is mischievously evident in his apophatic "excess of thought" (line 80): "I'm not saying this, sir, to criticize you, / But I very nearly am."

81–82   The comparison of himself to a soul in Purgatory awaiting God's assistance recalls the image of the interminable wait for his ship to arrive that Dunbar employs in "To the King" (Poem 44), lines 61–75.

49. *To the King* [*That I suld be ane Yowllis yald*]

In this poem Dunbar makes a specific but fairly modest request, asking the king for a new suit of clothes so that he may be suitably attired for Christmas. And judging from the *Respontio Regis* in lines 69–76, as well as from other external evidence (see *TA* iii, 181, 361), in this instance Dunbar's request was granted. In the metaphorical conceit that runs throughout the main body of the poem, the poet depicts himself as an old, exhausted workhorse relegated to the roughest pastures and considered unfit to be stabled next to "great court horses" such as palfreys (line 46) and coursers (line 64). As Bawcutt aptly observes, "The poem is striking for its balance of pathos and self-mockery, witty wordplay, and imaginative parallels between the hierarchies of men and horses" (Bw 2.447). The use of the "old horse" metaphor, along with the references to the horse's white mane (lines 21, 70, and 72), suggests that the poem is a late work. The poem has the form of a carol, the two-verse burden with which it begins providing the refrain for each stanza. The main body of the poem consists of eleven 6-line stanzas rhyming *aaabBB*; that is followed by the *Respontio Regis*, a single 8-line stanza in rhymed couplets. The text here printed combines the MF fragment with the text in R, following Kinsley's reconstruction. K43, Bw66. Not included in Mc.

1   *in toune*. I.e., "in public"; the speaker wants to avoid public humiliation.

2   *Yowllis yald*. *Yald* was a colloquial term for an old, worn-out horse, a "holiday" horse put out to pasture; apparently the term had come to be used to describe someone not properly dressed for the occasion, in this case the Yuletide. The word *yald* is related to the English word *jade* (see line 3), which also means a broken-down horse of little value, i.e., a nag.

3–6   These lines suggest that if he had been a worn-out workhorse from the wilds of the north, he would have been treated well — i.e., "housed and stalled" — revealing Dunbar's irritation at the king's beneficence toward Highlanders.

5   *Strenever*. Stranaver, located in northern Sutherland, is probably used to suggest a very remote and rugged place.

6   *housit*. Probably refers to the horse-cover placed over the horse's back rather than to the building containing the stables. That would make sense in the context of Dunbar's request for a suit of clothing. Compare its similar use in line 65.

9   *as ye knaw*. The phrase indicates the king's familiarity with Dunbar and his situation.

12   *To fang the fog*. The phrase probably refers to his having to feed on the rough, rank winter grass, although it may also suggest having nothing to feed on but damp air.

16   *On pastouris that ar plane and peld*. Bawcutt suggests that *pastouris* may refer to "the part of the horse's foot between the fetlock and the hoof" (Bw 2.448), in which case *peld* would mean "bare of hair or flesh."

17–18   Now that he is old and "long in the tooth," he says, he should be called in from his cold, bare pasturage. These verses may attest to Dunbar's advancing years, or they may just be part of a fiction he is creating.

22   *ye haff all the wyt*. I.e., "as you know full well," once more indicating that the king is personally acquainted with the speaker's situation.

30   *evill schoud strae*. The adjective *schoud* in the phrase is obscure, but the sense of the whole line is clear: "For the wretched straw that I would be given to eat."

36   *With uglie gumes to be gnawin*. Lit., "by ugly gums to be gnawed," if the word *gumes* means "gums"; perhaps this may be a figurative description of how cobblers would "chew on" the horse's hide.

41   See Douglas, *Eneados* 7.4.191–94 "for a description of richly embroidered horse-trappings" (Bw 2.449).

45   *Now lufferis cummis with larges lowd*. This line describes the ceremonial gift-giving of the holiday season, perhaps offering a real-life parallel to what is described fictionally in *SGGK*, lines 66–70. Bawcutt suggests that *lufferis* does not mean "lovers" but rather "liveries" (Bw 2.449), and that is quite possible.

47–48   This reference to mares that are ridden by both nobles and commoners may contain a humorous allusion to the king's sexual indiscretions.

53–54 These are intriguing verses. Do they suggest that in his younger days Dunbar had opportunities elsewhere (possibly abroad?) that he passed up in order to remain in the king's service?

64 "Coursers" are powerful war-horses — steeds or chargers. Compare *CT* I[A]2501.

65 *hous*. A cloth covering for a horse. See explanatory note to lines 3–6.

69–76 *Respontio Regis*. Scholars and critics disagree about whether these final lines were actually composed by the king. The relatively simple language and the basic couplet form of the "king's response" — which contrasts with the more sophisticated stanza form of what has preceded it — may be evidence that this truly is the king's response to Dunbar's petition. On the other hand, Dunbar might have written this response in such a way as to suggest that it is really the king's own work. Such effrontery might well have been part of the joke.

69 Among the duties of the king's treasurer was providing liveries for petitioners such as the speaker. The Lord Treasurer is also the person that the poet joyfully addresses in "To the Lord Treasurer" (Poem 52).

72 The term *lyart*, which means "silvery-gray," is commonly used to describe the color of horses, but was sometimes used to describe men's hair or beards.

74 Apparently it was common for high-ranking churchmen such as bishops to ride on mules, very often mules that were lavishly adorned. Compare Lindsay, *Papyngo*, lines 1050–52.

50. *Of People Hard to Please*

"Of People Hard to Please" is both a satiric poem and a moral poem (it bears an especially close relationship to "Of Covetise" [Poem 22]), but it is also one of Dunbar's most subtle petitions to the king. The central tactic here involves contrasting his own lack of wealth with the grasping of others who already enjoy great abundance; his own pride, though, prevents him from crying out for the largess he believes he deserves. This is the humility topos that also appears in poems such as "Against the Solicitors at Court" (Poem 45) and "To the King" (Poem 49). The four manner of men who "are evil to please" (who are never satisfied) are general types — rich men who want more riches; powerful landholders who want more land and power; men who seek sexual gratification outside of their marriages; and gluttons who can never get their fill of wine or ale. It is possible, however, that each of these men who are hard to please actually represents just a single man — the one man Dunbar finds it especially "hard to please" — King James IV. Barbed jokes directed at the king occur in several of Dunbar's petitions, and perhaps the king enjoyed hearing them as much as Dunbar enjoyed making them. Bawcutt suggests that the structure of the poem may be modeled upon Proverbs 30:15–16 (Bw 2.316). The poem is attributed to Dunbar only in R, but most of the editors and commentators accept his authorship. R and B (two versions, both defective). Seven 4-line stanzas rhyming *aabB*, and a concluding couplet. Mc23, K83, Bw12.

1–4   This stanza depicts the man of great wealth who desires still more.

4   *And wald have part fra utheris by.* The refrain line underscores this man's greedy desire to take some of what others have; in regard to the poet, the suggestion seems to be that the covetousness of men such as this is what keeps him from receiving his due.

5–8   In these verses the man who is not satisfied is a powerful landholder; he has a hard time managing what he already has, and yet he wants to have more.

7   *That he may nother rewll nor gy.* This verse may mean that this man is so mighty and powerful "That he may be neither ruled nor controlled" — he considers himself above the law. But it is more likely that it refers to his inability to rule or control the lands he already possesses.

9–12   This stanza is quite clear in its literal meaning. But given James' reputation for extramarital dalliances, and given the similarity of the phrases used to describe the nobleman's wife with those used elsewhere by Dunbar to describe Queen Margaret, it is likely that the king is one of the targets of the satire — perhaps the chief target.

17–20   This stanza provides a summation of the previous stanzas and also a transition into the more personal stanzas that follow.

22   The phrase *to concluid* often "signals the approaching end of a poem" (Bw 2.317). Compare Henryson, *Fables*, lines 394, 611, and 2970.

24   Here the meaning of the refrain is cleverly reversed. Now the flow of goods is not *from* the others nearby, but rather from the poet *to* the others nearby, who are presumably the very ones who in the previous stanzas were taking from the others nearby.

25–26   The poet's suggestion that he has been overlooked by "Sir Gold" in the handing out of gifts at Christmas brings to mind his plea in "To the King" (Poem 49) that he not be overlooked and that he be given clothing suitable for the occasion. "Sir Gold" may simply be a flippant way of alluding to the king; but perhaps there was actually a figure called Sir Gold who distributed the gifts to members of the court during a lavish public ceremony. Bawcutt suggests that the "personification is modelled on 'Sir Penny' . . . who often figures in medieval satiric verse" (Bw 2.317).

27   Bawcutt glosses *larges* here and in line 29 as "ceremonial distribution of gifts" (Bw 2.563). See explanatory note to lines 25–26.

29–30   The repetition of these verses is probably for the purpose of driving home his point with a final rhetorical flourish. It may also suggest that the poem was intended to be sung.

51. *The Antichrist*

This poem is one of a pair of Dunbar poems that ridicule a particular figure at the court of James IV — John Damian — a man who seems to represent almost everything the poet finds objectionable about the court. Damian was apparently a flamboyant figure (he did such things as organize Morris dancing) and a great favorite of the king, who not only appointed him to the position of abbot of Tongland (in Kirkcudbrightshire) but who also gave substantial financial support to his alchemical experiments. Damian was one of the many foreign courtiers (he was probably French or Italian) that Dunbar seems to have despised. But the most important thing about him in regard to Dunbar's poetry is his ill-fated attempt to fly from the battlements at Stirling Castle, an action that may have resulted in a broken leg (if, in fact, it actually happened).

The poem may be grouped with Dunbar's petitions because of the references in Dame Fortune's speech (lines 21 ff.) to the fact that the poet will never have a calm spirit or receive a benefice until an abbot dresses himself in eagle's feathers and flies up among the cranes. Since such a thing is unlikely ever to happen, it is equally unlikely that the poet will ever receive a benefice — a fine example of the medieval topos of *impossibilia*. The joke, however, is that an abbot *will* be foolhardy enough to try to fly, a fact in which the poet finds great comfort. Several of Dunbar's petitions satirize court figures who depended upon the king's generosity, and those poems may also contain thinly-veiled references to John Damian.

Also notable in this poem is its burlesque of prophetic and apocalyptic writings of the later Middle Ages, popular writings that were often attributed to figures such as Merlin or the "Scottish Merlin," Thomas of Erceldoun. The description of the griffin and the dragon copulating in mid-air and giving birth to the Antichrist (lines 26–30) parodies the kind of intentionally bizarre and obscure mumbo-jumbo found in such works. Ten 5-line stanzas rhyming *aabba*. MF, B, and R. Mc39, K53, Bw29.

1   *Lucina* is another name for Diana, the moon goddess.

4–5   The poet's heaviness of thought, as subsequent verses make clear, stems from his general lack of good fortune and his specific lack of a benefice.

10   Both Kinsley and Bawcutt have seen in the word *fantasie* "a hint that the dream may be delusive" (Bw 2.352); perhaps, though, it is meant to suggest that the dream will be filled with wondrous and fantastical occurrences.

11   Dame Fortune, the goddess Fortuna, is the traditional medieval emblem of worldly instability and uncertainty, symbolized by her ever-turning wheel. The poet's earlier complaints against her (lines 6–7) have provoked her anger against him, which is reflected in her *fremmit cheir*, the angry look on her face. For depictions of Fortune in Scottish literature, compare Barbour's *Bruce* 13.635–70 and *The Kingis Quair*, lines 1110–55.

13–14   These verses contain Dame Fortune's stern admonition to the poet to leave her alone and let her do her work.

16–18   These verses offer a traditional description of what happens to those who are placed upon Fortune's wheel.

19–20   Fortune tells the poet that the signs she is about to describe signify that his troubles are nearly over.

23–25   These verses obliquely allude to the episode in which John Damian attempted to fly from the walls of Sterling Castle. The poet will go on to suggest, in his satiric attack upon Damian, that he is the father of the Antichrist.

26   Like the cockatrice and basilisk, the griffin was a fabulous composite creature. It had the body of a lion and the head and wings of an eagle. According to bestiary lore, it was a vicious creature that would destroy any human it met, and it was sometimes believed to be the incarnation of Satan.

27–30   The "she-dragon" with which the griffin copulates in mid-air — thus begetting the Antichrist — is perhaps suggested by the Dragon mentioned in Apocalypse (12: 3–17 and 20:2–3). On diablerie in Dunbar see headnote to "The Dance of the Seven Deadly Sins" (Poem 77) and Bawcutt (1989), p. 165.

29   The Antichrist is the false prophet who will appear just before the Second Coming of Christ and who will attempt to lead believers astray. Although there are few scriptural references to such a figure (compare 1 John 2:18 and 4:3; and 2 John 7), it is often suggested that the second of the two beasts described in the thirteenth chapter of Apocalypse — the so-called Lamb-Beast — represents the Antichrist. In some medieval accounts of the birth of Merlin it is suggested that he was fathered by a demon in an attempt to place a satanic agent in the world who would function as a kind of Antichrist.

31   Saturn's *regioun* is the seventh sphere, the outermost sphere of the planets or "erratic stars." It is more often described as cold or frosty, not fiery, though Dunbar is right in associating Saturn with wondrous and often malevolent happenings, as Chaucer also does in The Knight's Tale (*CT* I[A]2443–69). Compare Henryson's *Orpheus*, line 191, and Lindsay's *Dreme*, line 378.

32   Simon Magus, mentioned in Acts 8:9–24, is an emblem of ecclesiastical greed (the sin of simony is named for him); but in the Middle Ages he was commonly portrayed as a sorcerer and as a man who attempted to fly up to Heaven but who failed.

   Mahoun in medieval texts is usually a reference to a devil worshiped as a false god, not a reference to the Islamic prophet Muhammad. In *Patience* (based upon the book of Jonah) he is one of the false gods the sailors pray to during the terrible storm at sea (lines 165–68).

33   *Merleyn at the mune.* Merlin's father, according to Geoffrey of Monmouth's account of Merlin's birth, is one of the incubus demons that inhabit the airy spaces between the earth and the moon.

34   "Janet the Widow" is probably just a generic name for a witch.

36   Smoke and fire, or fire and brimstone, are often associated with devils and with the apocalypse. Compare Apocalypse 9:18–19.

37–38   In Apocalypse 20:7–10, Satan and his supporters have a brief period of earthly triumph before being vanquished and cast into a lake of fire and brimstone forever.

39–40   Dame Fortune suddenly departs, leaving the dreamer completely frustrated in his desire to appease her.

41–43   The poet is too embarrassed by his ludicrous dream to even mention it to anybody until, incredibly, Dame Fortune's prophecy begins to come true.

49   Normally seeing two moons in the sky would be a portent of impending disaster; for the poet, ironically, it is an omen of good fortune, for now the impossible has actually happened.

52. *To the Lord Treasurer* [*Welcome, my awin lord thesaurair*]

This poem seems to indicate that the poet's desperate need of money has finally been satisfied. Indeed, line 25 seems to indicate that his long-sought-after benefice may have been obtained. Bawcutt suggests, however, that although the "tone sounds exultant, an underlying anxiety is present" (Bw 2.337). While the poem cannot be dated precisely, it was probably written after August 26, 1510, when Dunbar's annual pension was increased substantially. The lord treasurer, whom the poet so enthusiastically welcomes, was the official chiefly responsible for collecting and administrating Crown revenues. Eight 4-line stanzas rhyming *aabB*. R only. Mc24, K47, Bw22.

5   *rink.* "Men of rank" or "knights"; the word is borrowed from the specialized vocabulary of alliterative poetry; its more common spelling in ME alliterative poems such as *SGGK* and *Winner and Waster* is *renk*.

9–12   This stanza describes the promise the treasurer had made to him. The following stanza expresses the speaker's delight when this promise has been fulfilled.

17–20   This stanza reveals the anxiety and trepidation the poet was feeling until the promise had been kept. As Bawcutt notes, "delays in disbursements were common at most medieval courts, and it was often necessary to put pressure on the authorities, to speed up payment" (Bw 2.337).

18–19   "Before you came in the most direct way / From the town of Stirling to the courts of justice [in Edinburgh]." Apparently he is impressed and delighted at the treasurer's speedy journey, which has resulted in the timely paying of his pension.

19   *the air*. The justice ayres, or circuit courts, which were held in the spring and the fall of the year.

21–22   Pensions were paid in the spring at Whitsuntide (late May or early June, usually) and in the fall at Martinmas, November 11. If his fall payment had been delayed, he might have had to go until Christmas without it.

30–31   The poet addresses the lord treasurer as his "own dear master" and speaks humbly of himself as the lord treasurer's "man" and *servant singulair* (his "devoted servant," line 31).

53. *To the Lords of Chalker*

The lords of Chalker that the poet is fictitiously addressing are the lord auditors of the exchequer; they were responsible for making an annual audit of royal expenditures, which usually occurred during the summer between June and August. Although Dunbar's pension would not have come within their purview, he is having fun with the idea of having been called before them to make a formal reckoning — for he finds himself hard pressed to explain where all his funds have disappeared to! Ridley notes the poem's "combination of slight pomposity, down-to-earth urgency, and humor at the poet's own expense" (p. 1017). Four 5-line stanzas rhyming *aabba*. R only. Mc25, K46, Bw36.

4   *corce nor cunyie*. Lit., "cross nor cuigne"; these terms refer to two kinds of coins, with the *corce* probably being of greater value than the *cunyie*. The St. Andrew's cross was imprinted on one side of some Scottish coins.

6   *For rekkyning of my rentis and roumes*. The income he had received from rents and properties would be the auditors' major concern.

7   *tyre your thowmes*. To "tire one's thumbs" means to go to the trouble to do something; but in this case they do not need to.

8–10   They do not need to make their counters clink (referring to the metal disks used for counting), or need to waster paper or ink, in calculating his totals — since what he has left is zero.

54. *A Ballad of the Friar of Tungland*

This is the second Dunbar poem to satirize John Damian, the foreign-born physician and alchemist who was the abbot of Tungland (in Kirkcudbrightshire) from 1504 to 1509. But whereas "The Antichrist" (Poem 51) only briefly alludes to Damian's attempt to fly from the walls of Sterling Castle, here this ignominious event receives more than sixty lines of detailed description. And whereas "The Antichrist" appears to be primarily a lighthearted attempt to curry favor with the king, this poem seems designed to heap abuse upon a man for whom Dunbar must have felt great contempt.

In this dream vision, the poet first presents us with an outline — probably for the most part fictitious — of Damian's earlier life. In the lengthy opening stanza the poet characterizes Damian — whom he calls a "Turk of Tartary, a son of Satan's seed" (lines 4–5) — as a man who has continually managed to remain one step ahead of the law. Having had to flee from Europe, Damian turns up in Scotland where he continues to perform his nefarious deeds. In the next two stanzas Dunbar describes Damian's fraudulent medical practices, showing him to be not only a charlatan but also a murderer. In the second half of the poem, after Damian's alchemical experiments have proved failures, the poet focuses on Damian's final desperate act, his ill-fated attempt to fly from the battlements of Sterling Castle. In this section of the poem Dunbar presents an extended catalogue of the birds that viciously attack the airborne abbot (lines 69–118). And in the final phases of this description, the poet introduces a strong scatological element; for as this unnatural aviator becomes terrified by the birds' relentless attack, he defecates all over himself (lines 101–04). The poem is written in tail-rhyme stanzas rhyming *aaabcccb*; the *b* verses are in trimeter, the others in tetrameter; and the *b* rhyme is often carried over from one stanza to the next. B and As. Mc38, K54, Bw4.

1   Dream-vision poems are often set at dawn; that is also the case in Dunbar's "The Thistle and the Rose" (Poem 30), following the long-established tradition of the *RR*. What is puzzling about this verse, though, is the phrase *cristall haile*. Perhaps as Bawcutt suggests, *haile* means "dew-drops" rather than "hail," or it might mean "salutation" (Bw 2.297). But since Aurora's visage is appearing in the sky, perhaps "halo," or "glow" makes better sense for Aurora's aura in this context.

4   *sonis of Sathanis seid*. The reference is to beings such as Merlin, or perhaps the Antichrist, beings who were sired by incubus demons. In this case, of course, it

321

refers to John Damian. On diablerie in Dunbar see headnote to "The Dance of the Seven Deadly Sins" (Poem 77), below.

5   *Turk of Tartary*. Here Dunbar gives Damian an exotic and pagan origin.

7   *lay forloppin in Lumbardy*. The implication is that he is a fugitive from his native land.

11   *abeit new*. The phrase refers to the dress (i.e., the habit) of a religious order; thus because he can read and write (line 12), Damian is able to pretend that he belongs to an ecclesiastical order.

17   *To be a leiche he fenyt him thair*. After having fled from Lumbardy, Damian now pretends to be a medical man. Perhaps he had learned something of medical science at the university in Bologna, which at the time was a leading center for medical studies in Europe.

21   His ability to "skillfully slit throats" is meant sardonically.

23–24   Once again, Damian turns fugitive to avoid receiving his just deserts.

27   *it was no play*. I.e., it had serious consequences.

31   *The Jow*. Literally "the Jew," though here probably with the more general meaning of "the infidel" or "the unbeliever" — which is not to deny that the phrase contains an anti-Semitic slur. Bawcutt sees possible influence "by legends of the Wandering Jew . . . and of evil Jewish alchemists and doctors; one, Zedekiah, was credited with the power of flight and reassembling disembodied corpses" (Bw 2.298).

32   Monstrous creatures being the offspring of giants reflects the common medieval interpretation of Genesis 6:1–5 and Isaias 14:9. Compare *Crying of ane Play*, line 29, and Henryson's *Bludy Serk*, lines 25–32.

46   *suddane deid*. "Sudden death" was greatly feared by medieval Christians, who did not want to die unconfessed and unshriven; compare Henryson's *Fables*, lines 775–76.

49–50   Damian, the poet suggests, disdained the most holy observances; the *sacring bell* (line 50) would have been rung at the holiest moment in the mass, when the Eucharist was consecrated.

53–56   The abbey at Tungland, where Damian served as abbot, belonged to the order of Premonstratensian canons. Dunbar is playing on the two meanings of *channoun* in lines 53 and 54; and perhaps in using this term there is a sidelong glance in the direction of Chaucer's Canon's Yeoman's Tale, which concerns fraudulent and disreputable alchemists.

54   For an abbot not to attend the service of matins would be a serious breach of canon law.

55   He never donned ecclesiastical vestments such as the stole, which was worn around the priest's neck and shoulders, or the maniple, a strip of silk attached to the priest's wrist.

58   The *quintessance*, or fifth element, is here equated with the elixir or "touchstone," the material alchemists needed to create or discover in order to transmute base metals into precious ones. (Technically, the quintessence is "ether," the element in which all the heavens beyond the sphere of the moon are bathed; it is the fifth essence because it is an element other than earth, air, fire, and water.)

64–68   The birds are dumbfounded by this strange airborne creature: could he be Daedalus or the Minotaur or Vulcan or — the best guess of all — Saturn's cook? Daedalus is the famous craftsman of classical myth whose skillfully crafted wings led to the ill-fated flight of his son Icarus. The Minotaur was the monstrous half-man, half-bull creature on the isle of Crete; he was not a flier, but Icarus escaped from his Labyrinth by flying. Vulcan, the blacksmith to the gods (not just to Mars), is perhaps a candidate because Damian's besmirched clothing and blackened face give him the sluttish appearance of a blacksmith. Saturn's cook might have a similarly disreputable appearance (Saturn's sphere is the seventh sphere, the outermost sphere of the erratic stars.)

69   At this point the birds begin their attack. It might be suggested that Dunbar is anticipating film director Alfred Hitchcock by about five hundred years. A significant difference, however, is that in Hitchcock's film the birds' attack is presented as an aberration of nature, whereas here it is the winged figure of Damian

that is the aberration of nature. The birds' attack provides him with the final comeuppance he so richly deserves.

73   Neither the *myttane* nor the *Sanct Martynis fowle* have been positively identified. The former is thought to be a term for a lesser bird of prey; the latter may be the martin, so called because it begins its yearly migration around the time of Martinmas (11 November); other suggested identifications include the hen-harrier and the mergus, a diving, fish-eating bird. Bawcutt provides an intriguing explanation for this last possibility (Bw 2.299).

73–76   Dunbar is alluding to "the mobbing of the owl," when a large group of lesser birds gather together and harass the hated owl; this practice is also alluded to in the ME debate poem *The Owl and the Nightingale* (lines 1658–69).

77–105   Alliteration is used freely throughout the poem, but it is especially heavy between these lines.

83   *The pyot furth his pennis did rug.* "The magpie tugged at his feathers." It is possible, though, that *pennis* also carries a suggestion of "penis," which would be in keeping with the reference in line 86 to his "bawis" ("balls"). The poet's intention, in any case, is humiliation.

89   *Thik was the clud of kayis and crawis.* Compare Holland's *Howlat*, line 191.

97–98   Compare Holland's *Howlat*, line 61, and Chaucer's *PF*, line 346.

103   "He made a hundred cows all streaked." Dunbar is playing on the term *hawkit*, which was used to describe cattle with spotted or streaky hides. Here they are "streaked" because of Damian's massive loosing of excrement.

105–08   Damian slips out of his coat of feathers, falls, and lands in a bog, sinking up to his eyeballs.

113–24   Damian remains submerged in the mire (*at the plunge*, line 113) while the circling, squawking birds continue to search for him. *At the plunge*, in falconry, describes a technique of evasion used by diving birds.

115   How crows got their *cryis of cair*, their voices of woe, is the subject of Chaucer's Manciple's Tale. Compare also *PF*, line 363.

125–26   Employing a device found in many vision poems (e.g., the concluding stanzas of *PF*), the poet is suddenly awakened from his vision by a loud noise, which in this case is the yammering and clamoring of the birds.

55. *Sir Thomas Norny*

Dunbar's satiric exposé of Sir Thomas Norny, which is modeled on Chaucer's Sir Thopas, is a poem of mock praise for a court figure who, though he may not have actually been a court jester, seems to have made a great fool of himself at court. (A real court fool named Curry is mentioned in the poem, along with the suggestion that Norny has earned the right to be Curry's knave, his helper or tutee.) The comic effect in this poem, as in Sir Thopas, largely results from the incongruous juxtaposing of the chivalric with the unchivalric. Throughout the poem Norny's great feats of chivalry are celebrated, and yet the joke insinuated in the refrains of several stanzas is that he alone knows the truth about his allegedly glorious deeds. Scholars disagree about what Norny's actual status and position at court was, but it seems likely that he was a court braggart in the tradition of the *miles gloriosus*. Six-line stanzas rhyming *aabccb*, with the *b* verses in trimeter, the others in tetrameter — this is the basic stanza form of Chaucer's Tale of Sir Thopas. MF and R. Mc35, K27, Bw39.

1   *Now lythis*. This appeal for silence is the standard "minstrel-call" seen in the opening verse of Sir Thopas and in numerous popular romances and ballads.

4–6   These verses attest to the hero's noble lineage (compare Sir Thopas, *CT* VII[B²]718–23). In Norny's case, his parents are no less than a giant and a fairy queen. That he was begotten by sorcery recalls the conception of King Arthur, aided by the magic of Merlin.

12   Ross and Moray, located in the far north of Scotland, are probably meant to ironically suggest the "exotic" lands in which romance heroes perform their deeds of derring-do as they are bleak and remote. It may be, though, that Norny actually took part in some military excursions in those areas.

14   The phrase "Highland ghost" suggests the elusiveness of the Highlanders, whose ability to quickly disappear when pursued in their misty northern glens was legendary. Dunbar might also be taken to mean that the deeds of Norny are themselves phantom-like; they cannot be proved and border on being mere fantasy.

16   The Clan Chattan was a large and warlike group of the north that were allied together; one of the leading groups within this confederation of clans were the MacIntoshes. "It had a fierce, warlike reputation, and in 1430 murdered 'nearly the whole membership of Clan Cameron.' . . . Dunbar possibly recalls the clan's recent activities, such as a raid on Cromerty and Inverness in 1490, and the 1502 revolt . . . which threatened royal estates in Moray" (Bw 2.371).

17   As Bawcutt points out, "Norny turns the tables on the Highlanders, who were notorious as cattle-thieves" (Bw 2.371).

18   This is the first instance in which the poet hints that all these claims of heroic deeds might actually be lies.

19–21   His prowess at dancing must have really been something (we are told with a wink), since the Highlanders were renowned for their great skills at dancing. Perhaps part of the joke here, though, has to do with the uncouthness — from Dunbar's point of view — of the Highland fling.

22–23   Whether or not his Highland dancing is an ignoble activity, his wrestling clearly is, since wrestling was a lower-class sport more appropriate for someone such as Chaucer's Miller. Compare Sir Thopas, *CT* VII[B²]740.

25–30   These verses compare Norny to several heroes well-known from ballads and popular romances, including Robin Hood and Guy of Gisburn from the Robin Hood ballads. Roger of Clekniskleuch has never been identified, but Allan Bell is probably a mistake for Adam Bell, the hero of Child Ballad 116; or perhaps Allan Bell is a conflation of the names Alan Adale and Adam Bell. The sons of Simon of Whinfell have not been positively identified either, though the phrase occurs in line 381 of *Colkelbie Sow*, where it appears to be the title of a song. Archery, like wrestling, was not usually considered a chivalric activity, except for Sir Thopas, *CT* VII [B²]739, where Chaucer mocks the knight.

35   Bevis of Hampton was the hero of a popular medieval romance; it is one of the specific works that Chaucer burlesques in Sir Thopas, *CT* VII[B²]899.

37   The Quintin whose opinion the poet facetiously derides (facetiously, since he actually concurs with it), might be the man who serves as Kennedy's second in the *Flyting* (Poem 83), lines 2 and 34, though that is only a guess. It is also possible that

he may be the poet named Quintyne Scham who is mentioned in "The Lament for the Makars" (Poem 14), line 86.

38   The meaning of *plum* (adj.) is obscure. Perhaps it is related to the archaic American expression found in a sentence such as the following: "Sheriff, that man is plumb loco!" — meaning he is "completely insane."

43–48   Curry was a fool who is mentioned several times in court records between 1495 and 1506. He was apparently a fool "by nature" who had to have an attendant to look after him. See *TA* 2.529, 3.465.

46–48   I.e., "To this extent I dare to praise him: / He never once in his life befouled his saddle, / Whereas Curry befouled his twice" — some praise indeed!

49–50   Easter and Yule were two of the times during the year when great courtly festivities occurred. On these occasions, the poet suggests, Norny deserves to be treated as the king of fools, not just as a mere attendant to one.

54   Small bells were worn hanging down from the fool's costume. They are all that is needed to show Norny for the fool that he is.

56. *A Dance in the Queen's Chamber* [*A merrear daunce mycht na man see*]

This lighthearted, comic poem, which was possibly written for the queen's amusement, reflects the poet in one of his happiest moods, as he "burlesques the balletic abilities of the court" (Fradenburg, p. 174). He is both an observer of and a participant in the dance scene he describes, a scene in which members of the queen's retinue successively demonstrate their talents in tripping the light fantastic. There is a coarse element in some of the descriptions that is reminiscent of *fabliau*, but there is also a degree of tenderness and warm affection toward the elegant Mistress Musgrave, one of the queen's chief attendants. Dunbar's own dancing is frenzied and filled with sexual innuendo. Kinsley suggests that the awkward meter in several lines (e.g., 4, 10, 16–17) is intended to reflect the awkwardness of the dancers (K, p. 302), as they improvise talent where none exists. See Annette Jung in McClure and Spiller, pp. 221–43, on the Morris Dance trope here, and in "Against the Solicitors at Court" (Poem 45) and "The Dance of the Seven Deadly Sins" (Poem 77), as well as other Scots poems like *Peblis to the Play* and *Chrystis Kirk on the Grene*. Jung includes several drawings of Morris dancing at court or before ladies. Seven 7-line stanzas rhyming *aabbcbc*. MF and R. Mc32, K28, Bw70.

1–7	The first dancer is Sir John Sinclair, a well-known courtier during the reign of James IV. Because he is recently returned from France, the seat of high fashion, one would expect him to set a high standard for the dancers to follow. But he is so inept that someone rudely shouts out, "Take him away!"
8–14	The second dancer, Master Robert Shaw, is probably the court physician who had studied for several years at the University of Paris. He looks the part of a dancer, initially, but he too proves to be as clumsy as a hobbled cart-horse.
13	"From Sterling to Strathnaver" means "from one end of Scotland to the other."
15	The master almoner was responsible for distributing gifts to the poor. Throughout the reign of James IV the king's chief almoner was Sir Andrew McBrek; but he may not be the dancer in the third stanza, since the queen also had an almoner.
16	*hommiltye-jommeltye*. The phrase seems to be an invented reduplicating phrase, meaning something like "higgledy-piggledy" or "topsy-turvy."
18–20	These verses contain the first of the several vulgar jokes in the poem. There are many references in contemporary records to John Bute the Fool; one of them refers to him as "John of Bute," perhaps indicating his place of origin.
22–28	These verses depict Dunbar the Makar's dancing as bold and daring and almost frenzied, and they tell us that the dancer's performance has been inspired by his love of Mistress Musgrave. The *dirrye dantoun* in line 24 is apparently a specific kind of dance or dance step, though it has not been identified. However, the reference in line 60 of "In a Secret Place" (Poem 72) to the "dery dan" (there clearly referring to the act of sex) may offer a helpful suggestion. The word *pillie* in line 25 is a crude colloquial term for the male sex organ.
29–35	Putting all the other would-be dancers to shame is Mistress Musgrave, whose dancing is stylish and elegant. This woman, who is the object of the poet's admiration, is probably Agnes Musgrave, the wife of Sir John Musgrave, an important member of the queen's English entourage. There are many references to her in the account books, recording the gifts and clothing she often received. "Mistress" is a polite form of address for a married woman.

36–42   *Dame Dounteboir* (line 36) is probably a disparaging epithet rather than a surname, but those for whom the poem was intended would surely have known who the poet had in mind. Her dancing is treated more derisively than that of any of the others.

43–49   The "queen's dog," the figure depicted in this final stanza, is James Dog, the queen's wardrobe official who is the subject of the next two poems. Throughout this sequence of poems Dunbar puns on his name. He is referred to twice in these poems as a mastiff, which may indicate that he was a man of huge size.

47   Compare "Of James Dog" (Poem 57), line 17, where James Dog is also called a mastiff.

48   *He stinckett lyk a tyk, sum saed.* Compare Whiting H592.

57. *Of James Dog* [*Madame, ye heff a dangerous dog*]

This poem and the one that follows focus on the figure of James Dog, an officer of the queen's wardrobe who was the final member of her retinue to be described in the previous poem. There the poet ridiculed the man's dancing, and here he exposes the man's vicious, suspicious, and stingy nature; in the next poem, however, the poet completely recants — though it seems clear that his tongue is firmly in his cheek. While we cannot be certain that the previous poem was specifically addressed to the queen, in the case of this pair of poems concerning James Dog we can be. James Dog had been a groom in the king's wardrobe before passing into the service of the queen, where he became responsible for overseeing such things as the furnishings and tapestries in the queen's chamber, as well as the distribution of gifts and liveries to the members of her retinue. Records show that he continued in her service until 1527. The poet's canine imagery that runs through both poems sustains an obvious play on the man's name. Six 4-line stanzas rhyming *aabB*. MF and R. Mc33, K29, Bw72.

1   "Venus' bower" is obviously meant as a compliment to the queen.

2–3   These lines attest to James Dog's tightfistedness; the doublet which he refuses to give the poet is presumably the bone of contention here (so to speak). Because a doublet only reaches to the waist, it would cost much less than a long frock reaching all the way to a person's foot. *Frog* was the Scottish form of "frock." It was expansive enough to be worn over armor. Compare Barbour's *Bruce* 10.380–81.

4   Perhaps there is a play on the two meanings of *dangerous* — dangerous in the sense of being "a danger to others" and in the sense of being "hard to please" (i.e., stingy).

6–7   These verses contain the first of the canine images in the poem — here the image is of a barking dog that is "worrying" a hog.

17   The mastiff was frequently used as a guard dog; it is a large and unattractive dog, attributes the poet probably means to assign to James Dog. He is also called "mastiff-like" in "A Dance in the Queen's Chamber" (Poem 56), line 47.

19   *Gog Magog* became a traditional name for a fearsome pagan giant; this is probably not an allusion to the biblical figures Gog and Magog, or to the giant mentioned early in Geoffrey of Monmouth's *History of the Kings of Britain* (Thorpe, pp. 72–73). Bawcutt (Bw 2.464) cites Hay's *King Alexander*, where there is a strange oriental giant descended from *Gog Magog* found in a lists of *sowdanis*, lines 6049–67.

21–23   James Dog is so huge that when he walks the queen's whole chamber shakes; yes, he is much too large to be a lapdog!

23   Bawcutt compares *Crying of ane Play*, lines 37–38: "Gog Magog / ay quhen he dansit the warld wald schog" (Bw 2.464).

58. *Of the Aforesaid James Dog [He is na dog, he is a lam]*

Here the poet retracts — or appears to retract — the unflattering portrayal of James Dog offered in the previous poem. "He is no dog," he claims in the refrain to each stanza, "but a lamb." Perhaps the reason for this sudden about-face is that the queen was not amused by the previous poem. Or perhaps the poet received the doublet he had been seeking and so is now (facetiously) making amends. Or perhaps the joke here is more along the lines of the Manciple's remarks in the link into The Manciple's Tale in *The Canterbury Tales*, where the Manciple, after making a vicious verbal assault on the Cook, tries to make amends and claim that he was only kidding. In any case, it seems unlikely that the poet's opinion of James Dog has undergone a radical transformation. Six 4-line stanzas rhyming *aabB*. MF and R. Mc34, K30, Bw73.

1   The "gracious Princess" is Queen Margaret. Compare "To Princess Margaret" (Poem 32), line 4.

3   *maist friend.* Usually glossed as "most friendly," but possibly meaning "best friend" or "closest chum."

4   The vicious, dangerous dog of the previous poem is now said to be "as gentle as a lamb." That is a remarkable transformation and one that should make us suspicious of the poet's true intentions. Interestingly, Kinsley points out that there actually was a man at court named James Lam (K, p. 304), and so perhaps the poet is playing on the names of Mr. Dog and Mr. Lam, and perhaps on their contrastive personalities as well.

5–6   Compare the Manciple's remarks: "I wol nat wratthen hym, also moot I thryve! / That that I spak, I seyde it in my bourde" (*CT* IX[H]80–81).

9–11   Bawcutt suggests that "These lines sneeringly imply that Dog is performing tasks more fitted for a woman" (Bw 2.464).

13–20   This pair of stanzas concerning James Dog's relationship to his wife are highly insulting — they suggest that she physically abuses him and that she has made him a cuckold.

18   *syd and back.* This is an inclusive formula, meaning "all over."

19   *barrou tram.* One of the poles or handles used to carry a hand-barrow. Bawcutt notes that in *Christis Kirk*, lines 193–94, peasants used them as weapons (Bw 2.464).

21–22   These verses indicate that James Dog has complied with the poet's wish to receive a doublet, a desire that had been suggested in line 2 of the previous poem. But perhaps he did so only at the queen's insistence.

59. *Epitaph for Donald Oure*

Bawcutt points out that the subject of this poem is probably Donald Owyr (or Donald Dubh — in Gaelic meaning "Donald the Black"), a member of the Macdonalds, who as Lords of the Isles had maintained their virtual independence from Scotland until the reign of James IV (Bw 2.348–49). After the forfeiture of the Lordship of the Isles in 1493, Donald Owyr was held at court in the king's service. But he managed to escape in 1501, and he later led a major uprising of the western clans — including the Macdonalds, Camerons, MacLeans, and MacLeods —

against Scotland in 1503. Donald was eventually captured and imprisoned in Stirling Castle. He was not executed, however, as Dunbar appears to be urging in the poem. Indeed, he lived many more years and led yet another revolt against the crown in 1545. Although not all scholars accept this identification (e.g., Ross, p.183), the Highlander being reviled in this poem must have been a man of considerable prominence and Donald Owyr, who is specifically named in line 19, is the most likely candidate. For a fuller account of the Lordship of the Isles, see Jean Munro, "The Lordship of the Isles," in *The Middle Ages in the Highlands*, ed. Loraine Maclean (Inverness: Inverness Field Club, 1981), pp. 23–37. Kinsley points out that the form Dunbar uses for this poem is associated with satire (K, p. 309). Eight 6-line stanzas rhyming *aabbba* (a variant of the tail-rhyme stanza). BD, MF, and R. Mc36, K34, Bw27.

1–6   Bawcutt calls attention to the repeated use of sibilant sounds in these verses (Bw 2.349). Clearly there is an association between Oure and a hissing serpent.

7–8   In the Middle Ages the owl was often viewed not only as an especially ugly creature but also as an unnatural one, for of all the birds it was the only one to "foul its own nest" (compare the ME *The Owl and the Nightingale*, lines 625–58). Also, in one of the fables in the popular fourteenth-century work *Dialogus Creaturarum Moralizatus*, the owl leads an unsuccessful rebellion against the eagle, resulting in its banishment.

11–12   The figure of a dissembling fiend lurking in a monk's habit and eating alongside the brothers in the monastery *frater* is quite striking; perhaps anti-clerical satire is intended.

13–16   Compare the proverb cited near the end of Chaucer's Reeve's Tale: "A gylour shal hymself bigyled be" (*CT* I[A]4321); compare also Whiting T444 and G491, and Psalm 7:16 in the Vulgate.

19–24   The meaning of this stanza seems to be that Donald Owyr, by far the worst of the rebels, has been spared, though he must watch the executions of his lesser allies. Dunbar is apparently incensed at the fact that the chief culprit has been pardoned. Bw 2.350 offers the paraphrase: "Donald Owyr has more falsehood than any four of his supporters from around the isles and seas, [who] now grimace on high upon gibbets."

22   This is a problematic verse. Kinsley glosses *suppleis* as "punishment, torture," but Bawcutt argues for "allies, armed supporters" (Bw 2.350).

24   *Now he dois glowir*. The sense appears to be "Now he glowers" from the gallow tree (line 23). Though possibly "he" could mean "high," as in "A Ballad of the Friar of Tungland" (Poem 54), line 62.

31–48 Just as Dunbar had compared this villain earlier to the foulness of the owl, now he compares Owyr at even greater length to another beast well-known from animal fable tradition, the cunning, deceitful, thieving fox. In the *Fables* Henryson says that the fox, by nature, is "fenyeit, craftie and cawetous" (line 402). See Bw 2.350.

32   *reffar, theiff, and tratour*. "An inclusive phrase for malefactors; cf. the excommunication of 'common traitouris reyffaris theyffis' in the *St Andrews Forumulare*, I, 268" (Bw 2.350).

45–46 Apparently it is in the nature of women who are spinning at the distaff to engage in rude or scornful speech; compare the lyric tradition of the *chanson de mal mariée*.

47–48 See Whiting F592. The sense of this proverb is that a fox will always behave like a fox — it is the nature of the beast. Compare Henryson's witty "ay runnis the foxe, als lang as he feete hais," *Fables*, line 827.

60. *A Complaint against Mure*

Here the poet requests the king to redress an injury inflicted upon his poetry by a man named Mure, presumably a rival poet. Mure has not been identified, and once again it is difficult to know if he was a real person, if the poem reflects a real or an imagined situation, and if the great anger the poet expresses in the poem is real or pretended. However, the charge Dunbar makes against Mure — that the man has extracted lines from Dunbar's poetry and inserted them into his own — has a ring of truth about it. The poem certainly reflects the great pride Dunbar took in his own literary artistry, and may also provide some evidence about how poems were transmitted at this time. Four 7-line stanzas rhyming *aabbcbC*. MF and R. Mc5, K26, Bw64.

2   This verse casts aspersions upon Mure's family background by calling him the thieving offspring of a troop of roving vagabonds, or possibly, by suggesting that he is of Moorish descent, if the poet is playing on "Mure" and "Moor."

3–4   These verses indicate that Mure has "mangled" Dunbar's poetry — that is, hacked it up — and then presented it to the king. As Bawcutt points out, the word *magellit*

333

(line 3) commonly referred to the hacking up of corpses on the battlefield (Bw 2.426). Breeze (1998, pp. 12–13) suggests that Scots "maggle" may not be, as the *OED* describes, a derivation of "mangle" or "maul." Instead the word could come from early Welsh or Cumbric *maglu* meaning "to defile or spoil." Although "mangle" and "defile" are similar, the connotations of the latter meaning could carry a much stronger sense of shame, making Mure's actions that much more unbearable.

5–6   Apparently Mure denies Dunbar's charges or wishes to debate them. If so, Dunbar says, he will slander Mure from here to Calais, recalling the ancient Celtic tradition of the bardic satirist destroying a person's name. "From here to Calais" means from one end of Britain to the other. Compare "How Dunbar Was Desired to Be a Friar" (Poem 76), line 34.

8–9   These verses continue the figure of dismemberment from line 3 and add to it the image of poisoning. Saltpeter, potassium nitrate (a key ingredient in gunpowder), was foul-smelling and considered poisonous.

8   *fulle dismemberit hes my meter.* This verse recalls Chaucer's plea near the end of *TC* that "non myswrite the, / Ne the mysmetre for defaute of tonge" (5.1795–96). Compare also Douglas, *Eneados* 4.194, where he urges scribes not to "maggill nor mismetyr my ryme" (Bw 2.426).

10–13   These verses suggest the nature of the piece that Mure has "written," which apparently involves serious, possibly slanderous, attacks upon certain high-ranking figures. Dunbar objects to the slander and resents having his poetry adapted for such a purpose.

15–16   These verses indicate that what Mure has produced is a pastiche of Dunbar's verses and his own.

18–19   To be a fool out of season is to engage in foolery at the wrong time. And since Mure has been acting like a fool, he deserves to receive the close-cropped haircut appropriate to a fool.

23   *gar deliver him a babile.* One of the emblems of a fool is his carrying of a bauble, a round glass sphere.

23–27   In the *Flyting* (Poem 83), Kennedy suggests that such a punishment would be appropriate for Dunbar, lines 397–99.

24 The Dumfries fool named Cuddy Rug (more often, Cuddy Rig) was a real person who is mentioned several times in early historical records, "the last being 1512, when he is specifically termed a fool" (Bw 2.427).

26 Kinsley suggests that red and yellow were the colors of the royal livery (K, p. 300), but garments of those colors were commonly worn by court fools; Curry and John Bute, two of the fools at the court of James IV, wore coats and hose of those colors.

27 Apparently bull-baiting was a popular entertainment in Scotland at this time. Bawcutt compares *Christis Kirk*, line 211 (Bw 2.427).

61. *Sweet Rose of Virtue*

"Sweet Rose of Virtue" is a lovely, elegant poem in the *amour courtois* tradition. According to Scott it is "Dunbar's most perfect lyric, and one of the supreme lyrics in Scots and English. The three 5-line stanzas move with exquisite grace and smoothness of rhythm, no word, no syllable superfluous or misplaced, no phrase awkwardly turned, no image or thought jarring the mood" (pp. 57–58). Few readers, I think, would disagree. The speaker describes his lady in the imagery of a lovely flower-filled garden. But he laments the fact that this otherwise perfect person/place is lacking in just one essential virtue/plant — *rew* — playing on the two meanings of the word: "pity" and "a heavily scented medicinal plant with yellow flowers." Three 5-line stanzas rhyming *aabba*. MF only. Mc49, K8, Bw71.

1–4 Lilies and roses are conventional emblems of feminine beauty, and here they represent female virtue as well, perhaps because of their long association with the Virgin Mary. Compare *The Tretis of the Tua Mariit Wemen and the Wedo* (Poem 84), lines 28–29.

2 *of everie lustynes*. Dunbar uses this phrase in "To Princess Margaret" (Poem 32), line 10, to describe Princess Margaret.

5 *Except onlie that ye are mercyles*. In love lyrics in the *amour courtois* tradition the lady is normally depicted as being unfeeling and merciless in her attitude toward her suitor.

6–10 Here the speaker gazes upon her lovely face, which he describes metaphorically as a lovely garden (compare Campion's famous song, "There is a garden in her face"). He praises it for its freshness and beauty, yet no rue can he find therein.

8   *Baithe quhyte and rid.* In medieval idealizations of female beauty, white and red are the two colors most often used to describe a beautiful woman's face; they suggest that she possesses a "peaches and cream" complexion.

9   *And halsum herbis upone stalkis grene.* Compare "To Princess Margaret" (Poem 32), line 27, and Chaucer's Knight's Tale, *CT* I[A]1036.

10   *Rew* refers both to the human virtue of having pity or compassion and also to a variety of strongly-scented evergreen herb that in the Middle Ages was used for medicinal purposes, a fact the speaker may be alluding to in line 15.

62. *Beauty and the Prisoner*

This poem is written in imitation of the psychological love-allegory initiated in the Middle Ages by *RR*. Here the speaker, overcome by the sight of his lady's great beauty and her refined manners, finds himself completely in her thrall. As a result, he is taken to the Castle of Penance (i.e., of suffering); he is put in her dungeon by the personified figures of Strangeness and Comparison and guarded by Languor and Scorn, the court jester. But Good Hope, Lowliness (Humility), and Fair Service rally to his support, and then Pity and Thought, aided by Lust (Desire) and Diligence, manage to set him free. In the process the castle's defenders are vanquished. But also destroyed is the figure of Good Reputation, which allows Slander and Envy to mount a counterattack. It is short-lived, however, and King Matrimony quickly chases them off to the west coast. The heir of Good Reputation is then confirmed in his inheritance at court, where he remains with Beauty and the Prisoner. The poem shares many specific features with a number of poems in this tradition, but especially notable are its similarities to the homiletic allegory *King Hart*. A second distinctive feature, as Bawcutt points out, is "the ferocity of the exotic siege, described in a style reminiscent of Barbour's *Bruce*" (Bw 2.456). One other notable feature of the poem is that while the love affair briefly creates a scandal, it finally ends with marriage, which is uncharacteristic of most poems in the *amour courtois* tradition. The poem also contains some additional oddities and inconsistencies, possibly the result of transmission errors. Most commentators suspect that this is one of Dunbar's earliest works; there is also the possibility that it is not even by Dunbar, since it is only attributed to him in R, a MS containing only a partial text. See Josephine Bloomfield, "A Test of Attribution: William Dunbar's 'Bewty and the Presonair,'" *English Language Notes* 30 (1993) pp. 11–19, for the case against Dunbar's authorship. The general consensus, however, is that the poem is his. Fourteen 8-line stanzas rhyming *ababbaba* or *ababbcbc*; although there is not a refrain, each stanza ends with the word "presoneir." B (where it is anonymous), and R (where the text is fragmentary). Mc54, K9, Bw69.

1–8   This stanza and stanza 6 contain only two rhyme sounds; the others contain three.

5–14   In the larger tradition to which this poem belongs, a key element in falling in love is a sudden visual experience — love at first sight. In *RR* the Lover is shot in the eye by Cupid's arrows, which go immediately to his heart. In Chaucer's *TC*, it is Troilus' initial sight of Criseyde that leads him into the service of Love.

9   In the final verse in each of the last two stanzas, the lady herself is referred to as "Beauty." But at this point in the narrative *Fresche Bewté* is shown to be one of her two most important personified qualities, along with *Sweit Having*; it is the combined power of these qualities that wound the narrator and force him to go bound to the Castle of Penance. This minor inconsistency is also encountered in lines 15–16, where it is clear that *Fresche Bewté* is only one of the lady's attributes. *Fresche* is also applied to Beauty in *King Hart*, lines 199 and 251 (Bw 2.457).

12   Penance is used to describe the lover's suffering in other poems in this tradition; compare Charles of Orleans, *English Poems*, line 526, and *The Kingis Quair*, line 887 (Bw 2.457).

18   *Strangenes* is the equivalent of *Daunger*, who is the porter to the castle in *RR*. In both cases the words mean something like "aloofness" or "disdain." The lady in the courtly love tradition must be cold and distant until she is won over by the lover's long suffering and faithful service. Compare *King Hart*, line 304.

22   This verse appears to be flawed. Strangeness *is* the porter and so clearly would not be addressing the porter. Kinsley suggests that *unto* means "in the manner of," but that seems unlikely.

27–28   *Comparesone* (line 27) reflects the lady's initial assessment of the lover, as she notes how inferior he is in comparison to her other suitors.

32   *wofull presoneir*. Compare *The Golden Targe* (Poem 65), line 208.

33   One might expect *Langour* to be one of the lover's qualities (i.e., his dispirited state of mind), but here it seems to reflect the lady's attitude of complete indifference toward him. In *King Hart*, lines 261–62, where Langour is also a watchman, he serves the lover rather than the lady (Bw 2.457).

39   Scorn accuses the lover of being too uncourtly to be the lady's suitor. The phrase *be this buke* ("by this book") probably refers to swearing an oath on Holy Scripture. Bawcutt compares Charles of Orleans, *English Poems*, line 4152 (Bw 2.458).

41–48   Here the lover's own qualities serve him well in proving his worth to the lady. Good Hope reflects his optimistic attitude, Lowliness his humble disposition, and Fair Service his willingness to fulfill his lady's wishes. Good Hope occurs in *RR*, lines 2754–87; *The Kingis Quair*, lines 787–88; and Charles of Orleans, *English Poems*, lines 196–200 (Bw 2.458).

45   *I wouk*. He awoke? This is one of the poem's minor oddities, since we were never told that he was asleep.

49   Pity is the feminine quality most sympathetic toward the lover; compare *King Hart*, lines 339–50 (Bw 2.458).

49–56   Here the lover, through the actions of Lowliness, finds allies among the lady's qualities in the figures of Pity and Thought.

55–56   Thought (which probably refers to the lady's state of mind) has now decided to change sides and support the prisoner.

57–60   Thought, *Lust* ("Desire," line 59), and *Bissines* ("Vigor," or "Physical Vitality," line 60) now mount their attack upon the castle. Dunbar works within a tradition of *RR* as the Barons of Love assail the Lady's defenses. The device is popular with English as well as Scots writers, often with religious as well as courtly overtones.

65–80   "Stylistically this is Barbour's manner; cf. the siege of Berwick in *Bruce*, XVII, 445–66" (Bw 2.458).

68   In *King Hart*, the defeat of the foretower (guarding the castle's main entrance) indicates defeat (line 875).

69–72   The exact meaning of this passage is unclear, but Comparison is apparently surrendering and voluntarily offering up the prisoner, in hopes that he will be treated "soft and fair." But line 83 seems to indicate that his pleas for mercy went unanswered, for he is destroyed along with the lady's other negative qualities.

73–88   All those things that had thwarted the lover are now destroyed or removed.

79–80   These verses indicate that the tables have been turned — the lady by whom the lover had been imprisoned is now herself under siege.

81–82   Bawcutt observes that "Animals, such as buds, had pins or skewers set in their noses, by which they might be controlled" (Bw 2.459); but perhaps the point here is that Scorn has received a disfiguring wound (which will cause him to be scorned), in addition to being banished.

83   Comparison must be put to death so that the lover will have the lady's attention exclusively.

84   It is fitting that Langour, the watchman atop the castle wall (lines 33–34), leaps off the wall to his death.

86   *Lust chasit my ladeis chalmirleir*. There are possible sexual implications in this verse, and perhaps what is implied here contributes to the death of Good Fame (Reputation or Good Name) in the next verse. In *King Hart* the queen's *chalmarere* (chamber attendant) is Chastity (lines 303 and 416).

87   *Gud Fame*. Compare *The Golden Targe* (Poem 65), line 164, and *King Hart*, line 116.

89–96   Slander is clearly a member of a large clan and finds it easy to assemble an extensive group of sympathizers. Indeed, Slander's cousin (line 93) apparently remains at court even when the bulk of his followers are banished. Compare "The Dance of the Seven Deadly Sins" (Poem 77), lines 50–54.

101   Compare *King Hart*, line 221.

103   *band of freindschip*. Presumably the bond of matrimony.

105–12   In line 87 Good Fame had been drowned in a sack, but now Good Fame is fully restored through the figure of his heir who has recently come of age. Thus the reputations of the lady and the lover, though attacked by Slander, are now above reproach.

109   *confirmatioun*. "The action of confirming a grant, or inheritance" (Bw 2.459).

63. *To a Lady*

This courtly love lyric has often been viewed as one of Dunbar's parodies — Ross, for example, suggests that it "exaggerates wildly the plea of the lover for mercy, burlesquing . . . the conventions of the weeping, wan-visaged suitor" (p. 215). Nevertheless, while the poem is largely a pastiche of courtly love lyric clichés, it is very typical of a popular category of late medieval love poetry. Indeed, the sentiments it expresses are similar to those reflected in the pseudo-Chaucerian lyrics "Complaynt D'Amours" and "Merciles Beaute" (*Riverside Chaucer*, pp. 658–59). Nor are they very different from sentiments voiced by Palamon and Arcite in The Knight's Tale, Aurelius in The Franklin's Tale, or Troilus in *TC*. Many fifteenth- and sixteenth-century love poems were written in this mode, perhaps the most notable being the lyrics of Charles of Orleans. Seven rhyme royal stanzas rhyming *ababbcc*. MF only. Mc50, K12, Bw34.

1–2   These verses may contain echoes from The Knight's Tale (*CT* I[A]2775–76 and 2780), and the phrase "sweet foe" is also used by Troilus to describe Criseyde (*TC* 1.874). Such oxymorons are Petrarchan commonplaces.

6   The lover as the lady's feudal vassal, typified in French poetry devolving from Andreas Capellanus and *RR*, burgeons in English and Scots poetry of the late fourteenth and fifteenth centuries. Compare *TC* 1.427 and 5.939, and *The Kingis Quair*, line 435.

15–16   Compare *TC* 4.302–3.

24   *undir traist*. The phrase concerns the protection or safe-assurance a lord extends to his vassal. A breach of such a promise would be a serious infringement on a social and legal commitment.

28   Pity, Mercy, Ruth — these are the related qualities the lover hopes to find in his lady. Note that in the previous poem Pity plays a key role in persuading the lady to look more kindly upon her wooer, lines 49–56.

31   *mayne and morning*. "Grief and mourning." Compare Henryson's *Fables*, line 1555.

36–37   The turtledove in the Middle Ages symbolizes not only fidelity in love but also great feeling and compassion. The poet compliments the lady by making the comparison, but at the same time urges her to feel as warmly toward him as the female turtledove does toward her mate. Bawcutt suggests the poet intends a distinction between *dov* and *turtour* (Bw 2.365), but they appear to be synonyms.

41   This verse recalls a famous phrase used several times in *The Canterbury Tales*: "For pitee renneth soone in gentil herte" (I[A]1761; IV[E]1986; V[F]479). Compare also Whiting P243.

43–49   As the lover's death approaches, he continues to beg for her mercy in his mind, even when all his physical senses have been stilled. Lines 48 and 49 may imply that "unless my mind may think and tongue may move" once more — as a result of having received her mercy — then there is nothing more to say except "farewell, my heart's lady dear."

64. *Good Counsel for Lovers* [*Be secreit, trewe, incressing of your name*]

Rules prescribing how a lover should behave occur frequently in medieval works in the courtly tradition. Deriving ultimately from Ovid's *Ars Amatoria*, influential passages on this theme occur in such works as Andreas Capellanus' *De Amore*, *RR*, and Chaucer's *TC*. Of special importance are secrecy, fidelity, and the continual improvement of one's good name, along with the careful governance of one's own tongue while ignoring the wicked tongues of others. Three 8-line stanzas rhyming *ababbcbC*. B only. Mc68, K11, Bw7.

3–4   The lover is urged to behave discreetly so that he will not become the subject of malicious criticism or public condemnation.

5   A lover was expected to be generous and giving, not miserly. In *RR*, for example, Avarice is one of the personified vices depicted on the outside of the wall surrounding the Garden of Delight, indicating that stinginess must be excluded from affairs of the heart.

8   *secreit*. The great emphasis upon secrecy in medieval love poetry reflects the idea that the lovers' love would be profaned if it became a subject for idle gossip. In *The Kingis Quair*, "Secretee" is the handmaiden of Venus (line 675). Compare also Chaucer's *PF*, line 395, and *TC* 1.743–44.

9–16   This stanza focuses on the lover's verbal behavior: he must not be a liar, a teller of false tales, or a gossip, and he must not speak when he should keep quiet.

17   In *RR* the personified figure of Wicked Tongue (Malebouche) is one of the
        defenders of the Rose. Here the lover is advised to persevere, even in the face of
        "wicked tongues." Compare Whiting T401–03.

19   *Be nocht sa lerge unto thir sawis sung.* This is a difficult verse, but perhaps the
        sense is "Be not so free in repeating these rules," an interpretation that keeps with
        the secrecy of the refrain. Alternatively, it could read something like, "Be not so
        freely given to the spouting of proverbs," i.e., to sententiousness.

20   The lover should be humble, not proud. In "Beauty and the Prisoner" (Poem 62) one
        of the lover's most important virtues is "Lawlines" ("Humility").

21   The lover should set an example for others by behaving wisely.

22–23   "Do not defame others, and do not proclaim to others the glories of your own love."

65. *The Golden Targe*

Although Dunbar's *The Golden Targe* no longer holds the same interest to readers and editors
that it once did, the general consensus remains that the poem should be considered one of the
poet's major works. It is certainly one of Dunbar's most ambitious poems, and it is perhaps the
finest achievement among his courtly poems. Like "Beauty and the Prisoner" (Poem 62), it
stands directly in the tradition of *RR*. But in this case the assessment of romantic love it offers
is quite different, for the poem suggests that passionate love, which can only occur after the
overthrow of reason, is ultimately ephemeral and leads to sorrow and disillusionment. What
has especially impressed many of the poem's commentators, however, is not the poem's
narrative elements but rather its language. Ridley, for example, points out that "The poem is
one of the best examples of the aureate style, and despite its artificiality of diction and action
contains description which has been justifiably praised for its striking vividness" (1973, p.
1034). Although Denton Fox's suggestion that *The Golden Targe* is "a poem about poetry"
(1959, pp. 331–32) has not been widely accepted, there can be no doubt that the poem reflects
the poet's preoccupation with the aural and visual effects of words.

   Dunbar was above all a court poet, and as such his poetry, particularly *The Golden Targe*,
is informed by "the medium of Court pageantry" (Welsford, p. 74). His preoccupation with
visual and auditory effects points to the pageant tradition and setting in which he was writing
— the court of James IV, and the court's main source of visual and auditory entertainment.
James' love of pageantry is well attested, particularly by events such as the Tournament of the
Black Lady (see "Of a Black Moor" [Poem 71]) and the various revels staged for events such

as his wedding to Margaret Tudor (see "The Thistle and the Rose" [Poem 30]) and Bernard Stewart's entry into Edinburgh (see "Eulogy to Bernard Stewart, Lord of Aubigny" [Poem 35]). For a discussion of pageantry and revels at the court of James IV, see Fradenburg, pp. 172–77, especially pp. 173–74. The king's love of spectacle and ceremony went so far as to the tailoring of his own set of mumming robes and his firing of a cannon at the newly constructed *Great Michael* — a ceremonial gesture that resulted in damage done to the costly ship (see King, p. 117). When we read Dunbar's very visual and perhaps "over the top" description of "A saill als quhite as blossum upon spray, / Wyth merse of gold brycht as the stern of day" (lines 51–52), it may be that we are reading a description of a sail that is to be understood as an actual, visible spectacle, not as a cartoonish figure in a dream-landscape.

While *The Golden Targe* may not describe an actual court masque or pageant, Dunbar certainly alludes to that practice and uses the masque's conventions to comment on his contemporary society. King reads *The Golden Targe* as a kind of "anti-masque" that deliberately reverses the conventions of the "court of love," and in which the male narrator, assisted by other men, has to defend his reason against female assailants. Dunbar's allegorical personifications perform on the stage of our imagination: Presence fights dirty, blinding the narrator's reason with powder, after which both the order of nature and the narrator's compact with God threaten to disintegrate. When he wakes up from his dream-pageant, the natural world has returned to order, and all is well again. King writes, "The message of the allegory is a severe one, particularly in view of James IV's philandering habits: to allow Reason [in this poem uncharacteristically represented as a male] to be blinded by female sexuality can destroy harmony" (p. 127).

The stanza form is the one Chaucer had used in his unfinished *Anelida and Arcite*, a 9-line pentameter stanza containing just two rhyming sounds; the only other important poem written in this demanding stanza is Douglas' *The Palis of Honoure*. Several Scottish poets use it for lover's complaints set within poems, such as Henryson in *The Testament of Cresseid*, line 407–69. *The Golden Targe* is one of the six Dunbar poems included in the Chepman and Myllar printing of 1508. Thirty-one 9-line stanzas rhyming *aabaabbab*. CM, B, and MF. Mc56, K10, Bw59.

1–9   Few poets graft art with nature more craftily than Dunbar. The opening stanza offers a lovely description of dawn on a May morning that is as fresh as it is conventional. In Dunbar, conventions give life to nature. Bawcutt observes, "The poet's rising parallels that of the sun and the lark" (Bw 2.414); a kind of elaborated parallel to Chaucer's "Up roos the sonne, and up roos Emelye" (The Knight's Tale, *CT* I[A]2273). But, given the dynamics of Dunbar's craft, the effect is "up rose the poet and up rose all nature." Harrison, commenting on the elaborately decorative language in these first five stanzas, writes that "the first five stanzas with all their sensory appeals quite plausibly lull the narrator into a mood of easy surrender, though the thought of surrendering to a person rather than to the flowers and music of nature has not yet occurred to him" (p. 175). By the time Beauty approaches (line 145), this narrator has already been half-seduced by the sensuous world around him.

1   *stern of day*. The "star of day" is the sun, although in some poetic contexts the phrase is used for Venus. In his religious poems Dunbar uses it for Christ ("On the Nativity of Christ" [Poem 1], line 3) and the Virgin Mary ("A Ballad of Our Lady" [Poem 4], line 26).

2   *Vesper*, the evening star, and *Lucyne*, the moon — i.e., the heavenly bodies of the night — have departed as dawn approaches.

4   *goldyn candill matutyne*. The "golden candle of the morning," a metaphorical description of the sun, recalls Old English kennings such as *heofon-candel* and *daeg candel*; similar phrases, however, occur throughout ME poetry. The adjective *matutyne*, like the reference to *Vesper* in line 2, suggests the canonical hours of the day, a concept continued in the singing of the birds in the second and third stanzas.

7   Perhaps *Phebus* (the sun) being "clothed in a purple robe" suggests both his regal majesty and his role as ecclesiastical dignitary — since *cape* may be read either as "cape" or as "cope."

8   *Up raise the lark, the hevyns menstrale fyne*. Compare "The Thistle and the Rose" (Poem 30), lines 12–14.

10   *thir birdis sang thair houris*. The birds' singing is like the singing of the divine hours, which in this case would be the morning service of matins. Compare *The Book of the Duchess*, lines 291–320.

14–18   These verses describe the morning dew, Aurora's tears. She sheds her tears because she must leave Phebus, who in turn "drinks" them with his heat. These verses recall numerous passages from earlier poems, but compare especially Chaucer's *LGW*: "Tyl on a day, whan Phebus gan to cleere — / Aurora with the stremes of hire hete / Hadde dreyed up the dew of herbes wete" (lines 773–75), and The Knight's Tale (*CT* I[A]1493–96). Compare also line 10 of Dunbar's "The Thistle and the Rose" (Poem 30).

20   *the tender croppis*. Compare *CT* I(A)7.

26   *The purpur hevyn, ourscailit in silvir sloppis.* This is a problematic verse because we do not know the precise meanings of the terms *ourscailit* and *sloppis*. Bawcutt glosses *sloppis* as "patches," Mackenzie as "bands," and Kinsley as "small clouds." The general meaning seems to be that the purple heavens were suffused with silver streaks.

28–36   Depictions of beautiful May mornings, especially in dream-vision poetry, often include a river flowing through the scene; compare *Pearl* (lines 207–22), *Piers Plowman* B.Prol.5–10, and *Death and Life* (lines 26–29). This is also one of the most highly alliterated stanzas in the poem, perhaps to reflect the music of the river. This passage was imitated by Douglas in *The Palis of Honoure* (lines 40–42) and in *Eneados* 12.Prol.59–62.

36   "The small pebbles shone as brightly as stars on a frosty night." The phrase "as stars on a frosty night" is a common simile (Chaucer uses it to describe the Friar's eyes — *CT* I[A]267–68), but in this instance compare especially lines 113–16 in *Pearl*, which also liken the small stones gleaming in a river to stars that "Staren in welkyn in wynter nygt." Compare Whiting S673 and S685.

37–39   Here the glorious air and sky are compared metaphorically to gemstones: crystal, sapphire, ruby, beryl, and emerald.

40–41   The description of the garden employs the dignity of heraldic terms and colors to convey its artificial brilliance.

42   Flora is the goddess of flowers and springtime; she is also mentioned in line 62 of "The Thistle and the Rose" (Poem 30). In line 48 the speaker, lying on her mantle, falls asleep.

46–48   It is a convention in dream-vision poems for the narrator to fall asleep as a result of the singing of the birds, the music of the river, and the fragrance of the flowers. Compare *The Cuckoo and the Nightingale*, lines 81–90.

46–60   Fradenburg suggests that the account "might well be an idealization of a ship-pageant wheeled into the banqueting-hall and there discharging its burden of disguised ladies" (p. 75).

48   "Flora's mantle," on which the narrator falls asleep, is the flower-covered ground. Medieval poets frequently described the spring landscape as being clad in a flowery

garment; Bawcutt compares *Complaint of the Black Knight*, lines 1–2, and *Wallace* 9.147: "fresch Flora hir floury mantill spreid" (Bw 2.416).

50–54   The dreamer sees a ship rapidly approaching, with white sails and a golden *merse*, i.e., the top-castle, a raised structure surrounding the ship's mast.

54   This simile involving the falcon in pursuit of its prey may provide an ominous foreshadowing of what will later happen to the narrator (Bw 2.416).

55–63   One hundred lovely ladies, all dressed in green, emerge from the ship.

64–72   Dunbar here employs the "inexpressibility" topos (n.b., Curtius, pp. 159–62), claiming that no poet, not even Homer or Cicero, could do justice to such a sight. See Hasler on how the self-reflexive indescribability topos functions here: "There is no developed outer layer of narrative activity — no narrator . . . looking back with whatever degree of involvement on youthful folly — to which such lines can finally be referred" (p. 198).

71   Compare *CT* IV(E)1736–7.

73   Venus and Nature (and their two temples) are paired and strikingly contrasted in Chaucer's *PF*. The phrase "There saw I" is a descriptive formula used by Chaucer in The Knight's Tale (*CT* I[A]1995–2040) and *HF*, lines 1214–81.

73–90   The poet provides an elaborate catalogue of all the illustrious ladies who were there — including, curiously, Apollo (line 75).

75   Kinsley suggests that the phrase *Juno Appollo* is used to refer to Juno as a sky goddess, just as elsewhere the phrase *Phebus Apollo* is commonly used to refer to the sun (p. 250); if so, that would account for the presence of "Apollo" among these female figures. But, as Bawcutt points out, "mistakes over the sex of classical figures were not uncommon in medieval authors" (Bw 2.416). *Proserpyna* is Persephone, the spring-goddess abducted by Pluto while she was gathering flowers. She figures importantly in Chaucer's Merchant's Tale.

76   *Dyane, the goddesse chaste of woddis grene.* Compare Chaucer's Knight's Tale *CT* I[A]2297.

77   *Cleo.* Clio, the muse of history, is also invoked by Chaucer's narrator at the beginning of Book 2 of *TC* (2.8–11). Compare *The Kingis Quair*, line 128.

78   *Thetes* (Thetis) is goddess of the sea; *Pallas* (Pallas Athena) is the Greek goddess of wisdom and the counterpart of the Roman goddess Minerva; here, though, Athena and Minerva are treated as two distinct entities. Compare Gower, *Confessio Amantis* 5.1189–1220.

79   Perhaps the goddesses Fortuna and Lucina (the moon) are listed together because both of them are often changeable; the moon, because of its constantly changing face, was commonly used to symbolize impermanence.

81   *Lucifera* is a feminine form of Lucifer, the name often given to the evening star, Venus.

82–90   This stanza describes May and the beautiful gown that Nature bestows upon her. Nature's association with an elaborate gown stems from Alan of Lille's *The Plaint of Nature* (trans. James J. Sheridan, Mediaeval Sources in Translation 26 [Toronto: Pontifical Institute of Mediaeval Studies, 1980], p. 85). Compare Chaucer's *PF*, lines 316–18.

93   *Quhare that I lay ourhelit wyth levis ronk.* The dreamer reminds us of his presence. The ladies entering the garden, however, do not see him because he is hidden among the leaves. See A. C. Spearing, *The Medieval Poet as Voyeur: Looking and Listening in Medieval Love-narratives* (Cambridge, UK: Cambridge University Press, 1993).

94–99   First the birds and the flowers honor and celebrate Nature, their own special goddess. In the next stanza they similarly celebrate Flora and Venus.

94–95   Compare lines 71–77 in "The Thistle and the Rose" (Poem 30).

96–99   Compare lines 146–47 in *The Kingis Quair*.

109–26   Balancing the assemblage of female goddesses is a similar assemblage of male gods; they receive two stanzas rather than four.

110–11   In medieval texts Cupid, Venus' son, is normally depicted as a handsome youth, and in several Scottish texts he is also referred to as a king, as here. What is most notable about him in every case, however, is his bow and his sharp, *dredefull* arrows (line 111). Compare *The Kingis Quair*, lines 653–65. For a fuller discussion of Cupid in the Middle Ages, see Erwin Panofsky, *Studies in Iconography* (New York: Harper and Row, 1962), pp. 95–128.

112–17   These verses depict three of the planetary deities — Mars, Saturn, and Mercury — assigning to each of them some of their major attributes: to Mars, anger and power; to Saturn, old age and malice; to Mercury, wisdom and eloquence.

114–15   For more extensive depictions of Saturn, see The Knight's Tale, *CT* I[A]2443–69, and Henryson's *Testament of Cresseid*, lines 151–68.

116–17   For a fuller depiction of Mercury, see Henryson's *Testament*, lines 239–52.

118–20   Priapus is the god of gardens as well as an emblem of male sexual arousal; Faunus is the god of the open countryside. Both figures are closely associated with fertility. Janus is the god of gates and doorways; in Chaucer's *TC*, Pandarus prays to him as the "god of entree" (2.77), a phrase that may also carry sexual overtones.

120–26   Whereas Priapus, Faunus, and Janus are gods associated with the earth, Neptune is the god of the sea, Aeolus the chief god of the air, and Pluto the god of the underworld. Bacchus, *the gladder of the table* (line 124), is of course the god of wine.

125   Pluto, dressed in a cloak of green, is here portrayed as a kind of faerie king, similar to his depiction in the ME *Sir Orfeo* and Chaucer's Merchant's Tale. Green is a kind of natural camouflage that enhances his lurking (and dangerous) presence. This depiction may reflect the Celtic tradition of faerie abductions that occur in May — the season in which Pluto abducted Persephone. The color green can also be associated with inconstancy, envy, and agents of the devil. See D. W. Robertson, Jr., "Why the Devil Wears Green," *Modern Language Notes* 69 (1954), 470–72.

elrich. Etymology uncertain. The word first appears here and in Gavin Douglas, *The Palis of Honoure* and *Eneados* 6.Prol.118, etc., to denote some fantastic connection with the supernatural, the uncanny, weird, or spooky. Bawcutt (1989) notes that "early Scottish writers apply the term to 'browneis' and 'bogillis,' to Pluto and to the Cyclops and the 'weird sistiris,' to angels and also to elves (with whom some etymological link has been posited), to the faery queen and to the desolate places inhabited by ghosts and demons" (p. 112). The modern word is *eldritch*.

127   *And eviry one of thir in grene arayit.* Green apparel was often worn during festivities honoring May. In "The Knight of the Cart" episode in Malory, for example, Gwenyver orders the ten knights who go a-Maying with her "to all be clothed in gryne" (*Works*, p. 649); see also the courtly literary dress-up games in *The Floure and the Leafe*, where the royal heralds wear "Chapelets of greene" (line 222), the knights wear crowns of "laurer grene" (line 249), and the ladies choose knights "Clad in grene" (line 401). Compare Dunbar's poem "To Aberdeen" (Poem 33), where the twenty-four maidens who dance in honor of the queen's visit are likewise "All claid in greine" (line 42).

133–35   The narrator now draws near to get a better look; compare him to the lurking, curious "poet" in *The Tretis of the Tua Mariit Wemen and the Wedo* (Poem 84) in this instance. He pays a heavy price for his looking in that it causes him to fall in love at first sight.

136–44   In this stanza the narrator is discovered and "arrested," but, like many a would-be lover, he is neither displeased nor dismayed.

136   "Love's queen" — i.e., Venus.

139–41   The ladies suddenly reveal the bows that have been concealed beneath their cloaks.

145–207   In this group of stanzas the narrator comes under attack from a large company (Dame Beautee, Fair Having, Fyne Portrature, etc.) reflecting the lady's qualities. Some of these figures are very common in medieval love allegory, but others are not so common.

146–50   Fittingly, Beauty is the first quality by which the narrator is smitten, and she is quickly followed by her attendant qualities of Attractive Deportment, Fine Appearance, Delightful Nature, and Joyful Countenance.

151–53   As in *RR*, Reason attempts to protect the narrator from being overwhelmed by his amorous desires. In this case Reason equips him with a shield of gold — the Golden Targe. As Bawcutt observes, the shield of Pallas Athene, which is important in Gower's *Confessio Amantis* (1.390–435), is a likely influence (Bw 2.419).

156   Previous editors have viewed *humble obedience* as one of the figures who accompanies Youth. It seems more likely, though, that this phrase simply describes how Innocence, Bashfulness, and Timidity were deporting themselves; compare the

349

similar use of the phrase "full of reverence" in line 162 to describe the deportment of the ladies accompanying Sweet Womanhood.

174   Note that the figure of *Comparisoun* plays an important role in defending the lady in "Beauty and the Prisoner" (Poem 62).

175   *Will*, meaning "desire," is Cupid's daughter in Chaucer's *PF*, line 214.

177   *Wit ye thay did thair baner hye display.* Displaying their banner on high should probably be seen as a challenge to him to come forth and do battle openly. But he remains entirely passive, hiding behind the golden shield of reason.

181–85   Seeing that the battle tactics used thus far have failed, Venus decides to pursue a different line of attack, now shifting to the use of guile. Thus she makes Dissimulation her field general, giving her a free hand in her operations. What follows seems to imply an attempt at a physical seduction.

187   *Presence* seems to mean "Intimate Physical Proximity." The fact that she is called "the main anchor of the barge" implies that she is Venus' trump card. Note that in line 196 she is called "Perilouse Presence."

188–89   *Fair Callyng* (line 188) is "Fair Welcome" (the equivalent of *Bialacoil* in *RR*), and *Cherising* (line 189) is "Kind Treatment." In *The Kingis Quair* "Fair Calling" is said to be Venus' "uschere" (line 673).

190   *Hamelynes* means something like "Intimate Familiarity."

199–207   As in *RR*, Reason is finally vanquished and then banished, leaving the narrator completely vulnerable to amorous attack.

205–06   When Reason has been blinded, he is briefly tormented ("they played the fool with him") and then exiled to the forest wastes.

214–16   These are transitional verses that reflect the narrator's ambivalence toward what is happening to him, for without Reason a hell may seem to be a paradise and mercy may seem to exist where grace does not exist. Now that he has been brought into the snare, the narrator is soon to discover that his love for the lady is not requited.

217–25   *Dissymulance* and her companions, having completed their mission, now desert the narrator, leaving him to *Dangere* (i.e., "Standoffishness" or "Cool Disdain"). In *RR*, *Dangier* is the Rose's protector and the lover's chief impediment.

226–27   *Departing.* I.e., "Separation." Now the narrator has been rebuffed and dismissed, leading him to *Hevynesse*, "Depression."

229–34   The stormy weather, which completely destroys the beautiful garden, probably symbolizes, or parallels, the emotional torment the narrator is experiencing.

235–43   The entire company swiftly returns to the ship where they fire their great guns, causing a huge commotion. The great noise of the guns serves to bring the narrator's vision to its end. Compare Lindsay's *Dreme*, lines 1018–29. The frightening sound of rocks cracking among the cliffs at the din evokes the natural upheaval that occurred at the death of Christ (see Matthew 27:51). This evocation combined with the narrator's fear that the rainbow — God's covenant against catastrophic floods (Genesis 9:13–17) — will break suggests a kind of apocalyptic fear from the point of view of the narrator. For a very different reading of this artillery salute, see Pamela King, who sees the departing shots as Dunbar's nod to James IV, whose enjoyment of ceremonial artillery firing was legendary (pp. 117–18).

244–52   When he awakens from his vision, the narrator finds himself back in the same beautiful May setting with which the poem began. However, the joyous sense of reveling in sensuous nature is somewhat lessened, as the narrator finds *The air attemperit, sobir, and amene* (line 249). Having been assaulted, overcome, and depressed by the sensual world (both of Nature and Love), he resembles Amans in Book 8 of the *Confessio Amantis*, who, after being healed of love by Cupid and Venus, goes home sobered and centered, "Thenkende upon the bedis blake" (8.2959). While Gower devotes the end of his poem to prayer, Dunbar devotes his to rhetoric and the English literary tradition.

253–70   This pair of stanzas celebrates Dunbar's greatest predecessors among the English poets. Compare *The Kingis Quair*, lines 1373–79, and, for line 253, compare Douglas, *Eneados*, 1.Prol.342, and Lindsay, *Papyngo*, line 24. John Gower was Chaucer's contemporary and the author of the *Confessio Amantis*, among other important works. He is one of the two people to whom Chaucer dedicated *TC*, and it is there that he is first called "moral Gower" (5.1856). John Lydgate, the Monk of Bury, was a prolific English writer of the fifteenth century; his works include the *Siege of Thebes*, the *Fall of Princes*, and the *Troy Book*. Hasler notes "This vision

351

of literary 'Inglis' [see line 259] as a barbaric tongue civilized into eloquence by means of the rhetoric of Chaucer, Gower and Lydgate is . . . worth pondering" (p. 200); he goes on to compare Dunbar's "clere illuminate" with what Chaucer calls Petrarch's "Enlumyned . . . art" (Clerk's Prologue, *CT* IV[E]33–35), the point being that Dunbar's rhetorical artifice of aureation, like Chaucer's and Petrarch's, elevated "Inglis" to the level of a noble tongue.

259   *oure Inglisch*. English was the common language of both the English and the Lowland Scots.

271–78 The farewell to one's book became popular in late medieval poetry, but Dunbar is clearly modeling his own farewell upon Chaucer's famous farewell in *TC* (5.1786–92). The modesty topos is a standard element in such farewells. Compare Lydgate's *Complaint of the Black Knight*, lines 674–81, and *The Kingis Quair*, lines 1352–65.

272   Compare *TC* 5.1790: "But subgit be to alle poesye."

278   "Coarse is your clothing," a metaphorical description of his crude and unsophisticated language — a very self-effacing note upon which to end his poem. Compare Douglas' similarly self-deprecating comments in the envoi to *The Palis of Honoure*, lines 2161–69.

66. *The Merle and the Nightingale*

The one true debate poem in Dunbar's corpus, "The Merle and the Nightingale" belongs to the significant group of poems comprising the ME bird-debate tradition. These poems touch upon a variety of topics, but one of the most central ones concerns the values and/or dangers of loving women. In Sir John Clanvowe's *The Cuckoo and the Nightingale*, a poem that Dunbar almost certainly knew, the idealistic nightingale has the role of defending the value of women and the love of them. In this case, however, it is the merle who speaks in favor of loving women and the nightingale who, to the contrary, urges the loving of God. Whereas some of the other ME bird debates remain unresolved or at least somewhat ambiguous in their resolution, here the poem's final resolution is made quite clear — the human love celebrated in courtly poetry is nothing but "frustir" love (line 54), that is, worthless love. Indeed, by the end of the poem both birds see eye to eye and join together in singing the same song, that "all love is lost except but upon God alone." Fifteen 8-line stanzas rhyming *ababbcbc*, with alternating refrains. B and MF. Mc63, K16, Bw24.

1–2   Similar descriptions of the coming of dawn on a May morning occur in the opening verses of *The Golden Targe* (Poem 65), "The Thistle and the Rose" (Poem 30), and "A Ballad of the Friar of Tungland" (Poem 54). Aurora's eyes are "crystal" because they shine with her tears, i.e., the dew she drops.

3   *a merle with mirry notis sing.* The merle is the European blackbird; like most of the birds in the ME bird-debate poems, she is highly regarded for her springtime singing.

6   *Upone a blisfull brenche of lawry grene.* In several ME poems, birds that sing in praise of secular, amorous love are perched on branches of laurel; compare *The Floure and the Leafe* (line 109) and Lydgate's *The Churl and the Bird* (line 25).

8   *A lusty lyfe in luves service bene.* The refrain sung by the merle reflects the traditional sentiments of the "courtly lover." In this case, "love" probably refers both to the emotional experience of amorous love and to the personified figure of Cupid, the god of love. Note that the narrator in Chaucer's *TC* depicts himself not as a servant of love but as serving lovers who are in the service of the love: "For I, that God of Loves servantz serve" (1.15). In *The Kingis Quair* birds are also singing in "lufis service" (line 448).

9–12   This description of the river is similar to the one in *The Golden Targe* (Poem 65), lines 28–31, but here the fact that the birds are singing from opposites sides of the river carries an obvious symbolism, reflecting their earthly and heavenly points of view. Perhaps there is an allusion to the pure "river of water of life, clear as crystal" in Apocalypse 22:1.

14   *Quhois angell fedderis as the pacok schone.* The nightingale, in fact, is *not* noted for its physical attractiveness. But the verse seems to be an echo of line 356 in Chaucer's *PF*: "The pekok, with his aungels fetheres bryghte."

16   *All luve is lost bot upone God allone.* The nightingale's refrain, in contrast to the merle's, reflects the traditional Christian principle that love has no value unless it is a reflection of man's love of God.

20–23   Compare these sentiments with those sung by the lark in "The Thistle and the Rose" (Poem 30), lines 13–14. Here the merle has assumed the role traditionally assigned to the lark, of greeting the dawn and waking would-be lovers.

21   Flora, the goddess of flowers and plants, is one of the chief goddesses of the springtime and a principal assistant to the goddess Natura. She is celebrated in both *The Golden Targe* (Poem 65), lines 40–44, and "The Thistle and the Rose" (Poem 30), line 62.

29   *O fule.* "Oh, bird" (i.e., fowl), or "Oh, fool" — or perhaps both, although neither of the relatively polite birds in this poem is very much given to name-calling, in contrast to most of their predecessors in medieval bird-debate tradition. (Note in line 73 that the nightingale also addresses the merle as "Bird.") See also line 41.

31   *For boith is tynt the tyme and the travaill.* Proverbial; compare Whiting T442 and also Barbour, *Bruce* 7.45.

35   *Of yung sanctis growis auld feyndis, but faill.* Proverbial; compare Whiting S19 and also Lindsay's *Satyre*, lines 233–34.

36–39   In these verses the merle argues that according to the law of Nature, people in their youth should behave one way and people in old age another — but that the nightingale, in violation of the law of Nature, desires young people to behave like old ones.

41   *Fule* may mean either "fool" or "fowl," but judging by line 73's "Bird," probably the latter.

41–45   The nightingale responds by reminding the merle of the injunction found in Ecclesiastes 12:1 to "Remember thy Creator in the days of thy youth."

44   *That Him of nocht wrocht lyk His awin figour.* Genesis 1:26–27.

46   "Oh, what was demonstrated there, true love or none?" — a rhetorical question.

47   *He is most trew and steidfast paramour.* Compare Chaucer's *TC* 5.1845–48.

53   *And He, of Natur that wirker wes and king.* This is a medieval commonplace, that God is the Creator and that Nature is his chief deputy. See *PF* and The Physician's Tale (*CT* VI[C]19–28).

57–64   The nightingale readily acknowledges the many virtues that God has bestowed upon women; but we should praise God for doing that, not women. In other words, we should worship the Creator, not His creation.

65–72   With an ingenuity worthy of the Wife of Bath, here the merle interprets the biblical admonition to "love your neighbor" (Christ's second great commandment — Matthew 22:39 and Mark 12:31) as an open invitation to love the women who happen to live nearby.

81–87   Descriptions of the ennobling power of love are common; compare, e.g., lines 151–60 in *The Cuckoo and the Nightingale* and *TC* 1.1079–85.

89   *Trew is the contrary.* Compare *The Cuckoo and the Nightingale*, lines 166–67.

92   *fals vane glory.* Vainglory was usually considered to be one of the major sub-varieties of the sin of Pride; but it was also sometimes considered a separate sin of the spirit equal in seriousness to Pride.

97   *Myn errour I confes.* The merle's unexpected and rather tame capitulation recalls the Thrush's surrender to the nightingale in the ME bird-debate *The Thrush and the Nightingale*.

102   *the Feindis net.* There are several scriptural references to the devil's nets and snares (e.g., 1 Timothy 3:7 and 2 Timothy 2:26), and Henryson places a similar warning in a bird's mouth in *Fables*, lines 1843–45. Douglas applies this metaphor to love in *Eneados* 4.Prol.246.

103   "But love the Love (i.e., Christ) who, because of His love (for man), died." The wordplay on "love" surely derives from the biblical adage that "God is charity" (1 John 4:8, 16). Here Christ replaces Cupid as the true "God of Love."

105–12   The antiphonal singing of the two birds links the poem with many other fifteenth-century poems in which the singing of the birds is likened to religious observances; compare also lines 164–75 in "The Thistle and the Rose" (Poem 30).

118–20   The narrator finds comfort in knowing that when love fails him in this world, God's love will not fail him. These verses again express the sentiments found near the end of Chaucer's *TC* (5.1842–48).

67. *Love's Inconstancy*

Whereas *The Golden Targe* (Poem 65) may offer a subtle and oblique indictment of romantic love, this poem does so very directly. As Ross points out, the speaker simply asserts that "love is untrustworthy, inconstant, indiscriminate, inconsiderate, and her pleasure is brief to boot " (p. 216), which surely accounts for his determination to have nothing further to do with it. Ridley aptly describes the poem as "A polished little piece, whose quick, graceful rhythm with its turns is well adapted to the subject of fickleness" (p. 1031). The poem is written in tail-rhyme stanzas of tetrameter and dimeter lines; and only two rhyme sounds are used throughout the twenty-four verses of the poem. Three 8-line stanzas rhyming *aaabaaab*. B only. Mc51, K15, Bw50.

1   *Quha will behald of luve the chance.* I.e., "Let him who wishes consider the fortunes of love."

5–6   I.e., "Love begins with inconstancy / And it ends in nothing but variance." In other words, inconstancy is its major characteristic from beginning to end. *Variance* probably implies the desire to pursue new lovers, what Chaucer often terms *new-fangelnesse* — novelty.

7   In Henryson's *Garmont of Gud Ladies*, line 15, "continuance" is one of woman's personified virtues (Bw 2.394).

9–12   Discretion and consideration are two virtues that love has no control over, and therefore if they were to be found in an amorous relationship, they would not remain for long.

11–12   The short duration of love and the pleasures of love is a medieval commonplace; compare Whiting L524.

13–14   Love is quick to pursue new acquaintances and quick to abandon old ones. Compare Chaucer's *TC* 4.414–16, and Whiting L547.

15–16   These verses, which reveal the speaker's decision to "give over" love (i.e., abandon it), are the logical result of all of his previous observations.

17–24   The final stanza expresses his final evaluation of pursuing love — it is a foolish, ignorant enterprise in which there is nothing to be gained and much time to be lost.

19   *tyme mispendit*. Medieval moralists, including Chaucer's Host (*CT* II[B¹]18–32), disapprove of the wasting of time; compare also Henryson, *Ane Prayer for the Pest*, line 86: "For we repent all tyme mispent."

21–24   I.e., "It would be as foolish to expect love to maintain its allegiance as it would be to command a dead man to dance within his tomb." Perhaps the notion of ordering a dead man to dance is suggested by the *Danse Macabre*, the Dance of Death. But the main idea here is that of the *impossibilia* — it would be just as unlikely for love to remain steadfast as it would be for dead people to dance in the grave.

68. *True Love* [*And trew luve rysis fro the splene*]

This poem follows the preceding poem in the B MS, and like the preceding poem, it draws a sharp distinction between "feynit" love (line 6), the imperfect and short-lived love represented by Venus, and true love, the perfect spiritual love represented by Christ. Here the poet merges two related themes, the praise of old age and the aged lover's repudiation of physical love; this latter theme became very popular in late medieval and early Renaissance lyric poetry. In its larger structure the poem consists of three 5-stanzas groups. The first group lays out the central point, the second describes the narrator's own experiences when he himself was at the court of Love, and the third celebrates his new love, Christ (Reiss, p. 115). Fifteen 6-line stanzas, with 2-line burden, rhyming *aaabBB*. B only. Mc52, K17, Bw38.

1–2   The poem is written in the form of the carol; these initial verses provide the burden used to conclude each of the poem's fifteen stanzas. The phrase *fro the splene* (line 2) — meaning "from the heart" or "from deep within" — is often used by Dunbar. Compare Henryson's *Annunciation*, line 65.

3–4   Here, stated succinctly, is the poem's main theme — while Venus' torch has cooled, the fire of true love remains ever burning. For Venus' torch, compare the wedding feast of January and May in Chaucer's Merchant's Tale, where Venus is described as dancing with "hire fyrbrond in hire hand" (*CT* IV[E]1727–28). For the cooling of Venus' torch, compare Henryson, *Testament of Cresseid*, lines 29–30. See Burness, p. 216, on Dunbar's use of Venus tropes here and in "To the Queen" (Poem 70).

10   *Trew luvis fyre*. Although "trew luve" in the refrain (line 8) is akin to divine love that abides ever burning in the heart regardless of Venus, *Trew luvis fyre* apparently alludes to the passions of cupidinous love that wane as Venus' fire diminishes.

Perhaps *Trew luvis* should be considered a plural form as well as a genitive. Or, if the service of true love in this line and the refrain is the same, then *nevir* should be emended to *evir*, which is, perhaps, the simplest solution. Bawcutt, Mackenzie, and Kinsley read *nevir* without comment. Kinsley notes that saints' lives speak of the divine fire "that bald can byrne" (p. 276), the implication being that such is the love that precedes and also can replace Venus' fires and is always more reliable.

21–24   These difficult verses praise the person who instructs his heart to accept true love, thus transcending the ancient quarrel between physical love and spiritual love.

27–30   Love's court is the court of Venus and Cupid, which the speaker himself has experienced, and where he has learned that troubles outnumber joys by fifteen to one. The next five stanzas touch upon some of these troubles.

59   To "set not a bean" by something is to consider it worthless. This is a very common phrase in medieval texts. Compare *CT* I(A)3772 and II(B^1)93, and Whiting B82–92.

63–92   In the last five stanzas the speaker celebrates the love of Christ.

81–84   These verses are very reminiscent of lines 1842–48 in Book 5 of Chaucer's *TC*.

87–90   I.e., "No one in his youth can understand this, except through the grace of God, because this false, deceiving world exerts such great control over the young."

90   *in flouris grene*. Compare *King Hart*, line 705, and the refrain in Henryson's *Ressoning betwix Age and Yowth*: "O ʒouth, be glaid in to this flouris grene."

69. *A Wooing in Dunfermline* [*And that me thocht ane ferly cace*]

This comic tale of seduction reflects the characteristics of both the *fabliau* and the animal fable. Indeed, the cuckolding of the wolf by the fox is one the central stories in the Reynard the Fox cycle, an event also alluded to in the ME comic tale of the *Fox and the Wolf in the Well*. In all probability, the poem is actually a parody of the animal fable, perhaps intended to spoof the fables written by the Middle Scots poet Robert Henryson, who is closely associated with the town of Dunfermline, the place where this comic adventure is set. The descriptive rubric for the poem in B is the "Wowing of the King quhen he wes in Dumfermeling," which has led several commentators to surmise that the poem is a thinly veiled account of an amorous exploit involving James IV. But while there is abundant evidence elsewhere to indicate that

James was indeed a philanderer, there are few specifics in the poem to support that suggestion. The poem may allude to a real situation involving real people, but it is impossible to be sure. Ten 7-line stanzas rhyming *ababbcc*. B, MF, and a fragmentary text in R. Mc27, K37, Bw76.

1	*This hindir nycht.* This is a common formula meaning "once upon a time" or "just the other night." Dunbar uses it at the outset of a half dozen poems, several of which are dreams (compare Poems 42, 43, 72, 76, and 79).
1–2	Dunbar here employs the narrative device of claiming to retell a tale that he has recently heard; compare lines 30–31 in *SGGK*. The choice of Dunfermline for the setting may be to "localize" the action, but it inevitably brings to mind Robert Henryson, the author of a collection of animal fables, who lived at Dunfermline. Dunfermline was also the location of one of James IV's palaces, a fact that may be pertinent to the historical reading of the tale.
3–49	This large section of the poem presents a detailed account of the wily fox's wooing and seducing of the innocent lamb — all of which the speaker finds quite astonishing. There is a good deal of irony, however, in the narrator's feigned astonishment at the lamb's feigned innocence.
3	*lait.* Probably "lately," though possibly "late at night."
4	"And with her he played and made good game." The word "play" often occurs in ME in the phrase "to rage and play" (compare *CT* I[A]3274); it usually means overt flirtatiousness and may also imply sexual foreplay.
6	*riddin.* Compare *CT* VII(B)3167–69, verses spoken by Chauntecleer in the Nun's Priest's Tale.
8–14	The description of the fox's actions in this stanza are quite consistent with real canine behavior. Perhaps it is all undercut in line 13, however, when the lamb, maintaining a posture of innocence, calls upon the Virgin Mary to protect her.
11	The word *todlit* probably means "toyed with" (or possibly "tootled"?); but Dunbar may also be punning on the word *tod* ("fox").
12	*Syne lowrit on growfe and askit grace.* This is an accurate depiction of the "play bow" that one dog makes to another when it wishes to be friends.

13 *Lady, help*. The lamb, in crying for the Lady's protection, is momentarily playing hard to get, as is expected of her, even in a work that is more fabliau than romance; compare Alison's initial rebuff of Nicholas in The Miller's Tale (*CT* I[A]3284–86).

15–18 The brutishness of the fox is here emphasized, presumably to create a striking contrast with the smallness of the lamb. Aside from its red hair, this creature does not seem much like a fox; perhaps these verses are meant to flatter a certain person (James IV?) for his physique or virility.

16 *lowry*. The word may derive from the name *Lawrence*, the Scottish nickname for the fox which was first recorded in Henryson's *Fables*. In English and Continental tradition the fox is usually called *Reynard*, though Chaucer calls him "Russell" in The Nun's Priest's Tale (*CT* VII[B²]3334), which is the name of Reynard's youngest son in the Cycle.

18 *silly lame*. Pun on "innocent lamb" and "useless lome" (penis), which is too small.

19 *To sic ane tribbill to hald ane bace*. Literally, "For such a treble to hold a bass." Dunbar is playing on musical terminology, and at the same time creating a sexual double entendre. For *tribbill* Kinsley cites "treble/triple instrument"; but also, through wordplay, "such a male genitalia (the triple being penis and two testicles) to hold [mount, pin down] a base (female foundation)." See K, p. 313n19. Bawcutt (Bw 2.471) notes a comparative "bawdy use of musical terms" in Greene, *Carols*, 46.1. Compare also the Summoner's "stif burdoun" in *CT* I(A)673.

20 Here, and in lines 27, 34, 41, and 49, the lamb's behavior seems to surprise the wide-eyed (but rather voyeuristic) narrator.

23–25 Compare January's insistence upon having a young, tender wife in The Merchant's Tale — for "bet than old boef is the tendre veel" (*CT* IV[E]1420).

34 *girnand gamis*. Compare the descriptions of the wolf's "girnand teeth" in Henryson's *Fables*, line 2630.

36 *He held hir till him be the hals*. Compare Henryson's *Fables*, line 2699.

39 *prenecod*. A pincushion, used here as a euphemistic metaphor for a woman's genitalia. See *DOST*. Burness notes that Partridge, in his *Slang Dictionary*, has it as a term for "the female pudenda" from the seventeenth century onwards.

45   *Bot be quhat maner thay war mard.* A problematic verse. Does it refer to the harm done to those who are gossiped about, or to the fact that gossipers only harm themselves?

48   *Bot all the hollis wes stoppit hard.* The sexual double entendre is hardly subtle.

50–51   This traditional bit of moralizing provides a narrative transition. Compare Whiting J58.

55   *The lamb than cheipit lyk a mows.* The lamb squeaking like a mouse is probably her attempt to deceive the wolf into thinking that she has been the victim of the fox's unwelcomed advances — and thus the narrator's expression of surprise. But perhaps Kinsley is right, too, in seeing it as "an ambiguous cry" designed "to meet the expectations of both male lovers" (K, p. 313).

58–61   The fox hiding beneath a sheep's skin suggests that he has climbed into her closet or wardrobe and has hidden beneath her clothing. Dunbar may also be playing on the phrase "a wolf in sheep's clothing" — here a fox hiding beneath sheep's clothing to escape from a wolf! Bawcutt, however, notes that "the image here is peculiarly sinister, and implies — on one level of the fable — that the fox has killed the lamb" (Bw 2.471).

62   The other ewes who make no din appear to be the lamb's chambermaids. They also seem complicitous in their mistress' deception — yet another thing that causes wonderment in the narrator.

66   The phrase *the bell*, the reading in MF, is an emendation adopted by most editors, although Bawcutt retains the B reading of *the tod*, the implication being that the wolf visits the fox after the latter has had ten "scores."

68   *Protestand for the secound place.* The wolf (unknowingly) claims for himself "second place," because the fox has already claimed "first place" — that is, he has taken his pleasure with the lamb first.

70. *To the Queen* [*Madam, your men said*]

Variously described as tasteless, tactless, and puzzling, this comic-satiric poem has produced a great deal of critical commentary. The one thing about which the commentators agree is that they do not much like the poem — Scott, for example, declares that it is "not worth the energy spent on construing it, being an inferior and distasteful thing, though morally serious under the jocularity" (p. 165). The "Madam" addressed is generally assumed to be the queen, and although there is no evidence to prove that assumption, it seems likely, especially in light of what is stated in line 6.

The poem is set on Fastern Eve (or Shrove Tuesday), the day before the beginning of Lent. Fastern Eve provided a final occasion for reveling before the forty days of self-denial of the Lenten season. The poem is thus related to Dunbar's other poems set at this time of the year. A major difficulty in interpreting the poem stems from a number of words and phrases of uncertain meaning. Also difficult to unravel is the complex wordplay involving the term "pockis" ("pox"), a term that could be used to refer to various physical ailments in either people or animals, but one that also clearly implied syphilis. Central to the poem is the meaning of the phrase "libbin of the pockis," which may literally mean "to be cured of the pox," but which appears to be a colloquial expression referring to sexual intercourse. Seven 5-line stanzas rhyming *aabab*, with each stanza ending with the same word. MF and R. Mc31, K32, Bw30.

1   *Madam.* A respectful term of address for a woman of high rank. If the woman addressed is indeed the queen, the *men* would be those belonging to her household.

1–5   The opening stanza seems to indicate that the men wanted to set off on their travels without participating in the Fastern Eve festivities but that their wives persuaded them to stay. There may also be a sexual double entendre in the phrase *thai wald ryd* (line 1); compare line 6 of the previous poem: "And wald haif riddin hir lyk ane rame."

2   During the later Middle Ages in Europe, Fastern Eve, the final evening before the beginning of Lent, was a time of carnivalesque entertainments and often of un-bridled physical indulgence. "How Dunbar Was Desired to Be a Friar" (Poem 76) is also set on Fastern Eve and may describe a comic pageant presented at court.

3   Bawcutt suggests that *flockis* was "chiefly used of animals, and anticipates the farmyard imagery in [lines] 8, and 16–18" (Bw 2.355). Compare Chaucer's Host, who "was oure aller cok, / And gadrede us togidre alle in a flok" (*CT* I[A]823–24.)

4   The phrase *betteis soin* (or possibly *som*) remains obscure and may result from textual corruption; still, the meaning of the line seems clear: the wives have requested their husbands not to leave.

5   Later in the poem the phrase *lib tham of the pockis* means "to have sex with them"; no one is quite sure how the phrase came to have that meaning. Here, though, it may carry its literal meaning of "cure them of the pox," possibly referring to medical treatments but perhaps implying that the wives hope to prevent their husbands from having illicit sex; or, that if a man has the pox, the woman might take it from him.

6   The phrase *sen ye dwell still* suggests that the queen and her household were about to set off on a journey, perhaps on a round of royal visits.

7   For a similar use of "Venus' banquet," compare *The Tretis of the Tua Mariit Wemen and the Wedo* (Poem 84), lines 430–31.

8   Cockfighting was apparently a popular entertainment on Fastern Eve, but the imagery is used here to suggest the men's sexual inadequacy. Compare *The Tretis of the Tua Mariit Wemen and the Wedo* (Poem 84), line 326.

14   *pamphelet on a pled.* Bawcutt makes a plausible case for *pamphelet* meaning "a woman of easy virtue" and for *pleid* meaning "plaid" (Bw 2.356). But the meaning of the line remains conjectural. Kinsley glosses *pled* as "plea, excuse," perhaps implying "a compromised position."

16–18   The men who were "riotous as rams" have been become like tame lambs, or, even more humiliating, like old ewes.

21–25   This stanza continues the imagery of the men having been unmanned — in this case with images of physical decrepitude that are the result of a surfeit of sex.

22   The phrase *willing wandis* may mean "pliant wands" or it may "willow wands"; in either case it also alludes to the men's sexual inadequacies.

23   The description of the men's shins as "sharp (i.e., bony) and small (i.e., skinny) like a distaff" recalls the description of the long, lean legs of Chaucer's Reeve which were like a staff, with "no calf ysene" (*CT* I[A]591–92). Compare also *Christis Kirk*, line 39.

24   *And gottin thair bak in bayth thair handis.* This verse may mean that they are placing their hands on their aching backs, or more likely, that they have become so thin that a pair of hands can encircle their emaciated bodies.

363

30   The Spanish Pox is syphilis. As Bawcutt aptly observes, "Most European nations
       traced the origin of the disease to their neighbours" (Bw 2.357). See "His Own
       Enemy" (Poem 20), line 14, and the note to that line.

33   *Thai sall repent quhai with tham yockis.* Compare 1 Corinthians 6:16–18.

71. *Of a Black Moor* [*My ladye with the mekle lippis*]

One of Dunbar's more controversial works, this poem "has been interpreted both as a broad
but good-natured caricature and as a display of unusual cruelty and inhumanity" (Ridley, 1973,
p. 1023). Here the poet presents the anti-type to the traditional idealization of feminine beauty,
an anti-type also seen in the Loathly Lady of medieval romance, a figure with whom Dunbar's
depiction shares specific details — e.g., the huge mouth, the cat-like nose, the comparison to
a toad. As Bawcutt observes, it appears that "Much care was lavished on the poem, which has
vivid animal imagery, and is structured by *repetitio*" (Bw 2.351). It is known that Africans
were present in Scotland as early as 1504, several of them serving in the court of James IV as
musicians and entertainers. Perhaps pertinent here too are the Tournaments of the Black Lady
held in 1507 and 1508, which are described in Pitscottie's *Chronicles* (1.242–44) and in *The
Treasurer's Accounts* (*TA*, III, 258–94). During these tournaments, jousts and mock battles
were held, and "the focus of the rivalry of the jousters was a Black Lady, presumably one of
the 'Moris [Moorish] lasses' mentioned in the court records of the time" (Ross, p. 70). It is
possible, as Fradenburg suggests (p. 174), that the black lady that the poem "blazons" could
have been the Black Lady of the Tournament, whereby the savagery of the description becomes
part of the carnivalesque cruelties. Five 5-line stanzas rhyming *aabab*. MF and R. Mc37, K33,
Bw28.

1–2   Medieval poets commonly lavish praise upon the fair white complexions of the
       ladies they celebrate, often comparing their skin to the ivory of the narwhal ("as
       white as whale bone" is a common simile). Dark-complexioned women are also
       sometimes celebrated in medieval literature, though they are likely to belong to the
       lower social classes. The term *blak* in line 2 could be used for a woman of dark
       complexion; but as the poem develops, it becomes clear that the poet is describing
       an African.

5–6   Contrast Chaucer's Prioress, whose mouth is "ful smal, and therto softe and reed"
       (*CT* I[A]153). Bawcutt notes that "physiognomists considered large lips a sign of
       folly" (Bw 2.351).

6   *lyk an aep*. Europeans were familiar with the Barbary ape, which they considered ugly and grotesque. Symkyn's bald head in The Reeve's Tale is compared to that of an ape (*CT* I[A]3935).

8   Pug or snub noses were considered very ugly, an attitude Chaucer touches on in The Reeve's Tale with the "camus" noses of Symkyn the miller and his daughter (*CT* I[A]3934, 3974). In a matched pair of sarcastic love letters in MS Rawlinson Poet. 36, the lady compares her lover's nose to that of a hare or a cat, and he returns the compliment with interest, saying that her "camusyd nose, with nose-thryllys brode" could be used in church to quench tapers burning on the altar (see *Secular Lyrics*, ed. Robbins, pp. 219–22).

9   *And quhou schou schynes lyk ony saep*. Bawcutt points out that soap was chiefly used "for washing clothes rather than persons" and "was made from a mixture of tallow, fish-oil, and potash" (Bw 2.352).

12   The image of the "tar barrel" is probably meant as a comment both on her blackness and on her physical shape. A lady's very slender waist — reflected in a phrase like "her sides small" (i.e., narrow) — was the standard for admiration.

13   This verse may either suggest an explanation for the lady's blackness — she is black because she was born during an eclipse of the sun — or it may rudely suggest that at her birth the sun was so frightened that it hid itself. Compare *Crying of ane Play*, line 55.

14   Following up on the previous verse, the speaker suggests that the personified figure of the Night will gladly fight as her champion, implying that the figure of Day would want nothing to do with her. There may be wordplay on "night" and "knight," also. And this verse might also refer to participants in a court pageant involving a mock joust.

23–24   The loser's reward is that he must kiss her "hips." Absolon in The Miller's Tale is tricked into performing this humiliating act; and Chaucer's Host also alludes to it in his angry exchange with the Pardoner (*CT* VI[C]948). Compare the *Flyting* (Poem 83), line 131.

72. *In a Secret Place* [*Ye brek my hart, my bony ane*]

Medieval literature produced a wide variety of love-dialogues, including the *pastourelle*, a poem involving the attempted seduction of a rural maiden by a young courtier, and the *aube* or *aubade*, the dawn song of parting lovers. A third notable variety is the dialogue of the night visit, in which a young man tries to woo his love from beneath her window or in some other private place. Dunbar's poem belongs to this latter category, and like several other examples in this tradition, it provides a lower class counterpart to upper class wooing. The humor in Dunbar's poem arises primarily from the use of comic inversions, from the would-be courtly behavior of a pair of lovers who are decidedly uncourtly, and from the amorous endearments the lovers lavish upon each other, endearments rich in sexual double entendre and ludicrous incongruities. Ridley may be right in suspecting that some of the more obscure phrases spoken by the lovers are actually nonsense terms designed to create the effect of baby talk (1973, p. 1019). Bawcutt notes that this "genre was popular in sixteenth-century Scotland, and Bannatyne contains a number of examples, extremely varied in tone and treatment: these include Henryson's *Robene and Makyne*, and several anonymous pieces" (Bw 2.343). See Burness on poetic uses of bawdy language in Dunbar. The poem is attributed to Dunbar in MF, an attribution that most scholars have accepted, despite the fact that in B it is attributed to Clerk. Nine stanzas rhyming *aabbcbc*, with alternating refrain. MF, B, R, and Osborn. Mc28, K13, Bw25.

1–2   It is a common convention in medieval dialogues and debates for a third party to overhear the dialogue, which he then duly reports. Perhaps in this case, then, it was not such a "secret place" after all, if the narrator has been able to eavesdrop so readily.

2   The terms *beyrne* and *bricht* — "young man" and "attractive lady" — are commonly found among the stock vocabulary of alliterative poetry and usually imply a high degree of social standing — which will turn out not to be the case.

3–7   In these verses the young man makes the standard appeal of the courtly lover, beseeching his lady whom he has long served to show him some kindness. Through line 7 the poet has offered few hints that the poem will become a burlesque of *amour courtois*.

3   *My huny, my hart, my hoip, my heill.* Alliteration, which is especially noticeable in this verse, is just one of several sound devices often used in the poem. Compare *Hary's Wallace*, ed. McDiarmid, 11.569.

6   Her coldness toward him, her *danger*, suggests that she is the disdainful lady of courtly love tradition.

8   Compare the description of Absolon in Chaucer's Miller's Tale: "He kembeth his lokkes brode, and made hym gay" (*CT* I[A]3374).

8–14   The second stanza completely undercuts the initial impression created in the first stanza, as we discover that this young man is no more a true courtly lover than is Absolon in Chaucer's Miller's Tale.

10   The young wooer here is "tounish," no country bumpkin like Robene in Henryson's *Robene and Makyne*.

11–14   These verses recall Nicholas' "wooing" of Alisoun in The Miller's Tale (*CT* I[A]3276–87).

13   *fukkit*. The term means exactly what it says, and this is one of the earliest recorded occurrences of the word. There may be an earlier use of it in a collection of proverbs and sayings contained in MS Peniarth 356B of the National Library of Wales: "Wemen were wode and sweryne by the rode / That thay owyles fuc ne men / Men were wys and turnyd her geryes / And swuyud ham" (fol. 149v, lines 1–4). Compare "wanfukkit" in the *Flyting* (Poem 83), line 38.

15   *sweit as the hunye*. For the clichéd simile "sweet as the honey," compare Whiting H430.

16–17   Compare Diomede's similar, though more courtly, assertions to Criseyde in Chaucer's *TC* 5.155–8.

18–19   The images in these linked verses are intentionally incongruous.

22   This verse obviously echoes Alisoun's "'Tehee!' quod she" from The Miller's Tale (*CT* I[A]3740).

23   *tuchan*. Bawcutt suggests that a *tuchan* might be a stuffed calf-skin that was placed beside a cow to trick her into giving milk. Or, perhaps the term is a nominal form of *toudr*, meaning a tactile effect for whatever purpose. See OED *touch* sb.1.a.

26–27   She suggests that he is the only lover she has had for an entire week!

29   *claver . . . curldodie*. Compare the similar comparison of Alisoun to wild flowers in The Miller's Tale: "She was a prymerole, a piggesnye" (*CT* I[A]3268). Kinsley follows *DOST* and glosses *curldodie* as "ribwort plantain" or the wild scabiosa (K, p. 257), which, like the clover, is round-headed in bloom. This, according to Burness (p. 210), suggests the shape of the vulva, thereby enhancing collectively the obscene endearments of the first wife's fantasy.

30   *huny soppis*. "Honey sops," which was bread soaked in water and honey. Chaucer's Franklin prefers his "sop" soaked in wine (*CT* I[A]334).

31   *Be not oure bosteous to your billie*. Perhaps the joke here is that he is asking her not to be too rough with him, the reverse of what we might expect.

33–34   The comparison of a lady's white neck to the whiteness of whale bone (the ivory from the tusk of the narwhal) is a commonplace. See note to "Of a Black Moor" (Poem 71), lines 1–2. But Bawcutt is probably right in suggesting that *heylis* (line 33) means "heels," not "neck" (*hals*), thus creating a "greater comic incongruity" (Bw 2.345). It is her white heels, then, that cause his sexual arousal.

34   *quhillelille*. The term refers to his penis (compare "pillie" in line 25 of "A Dance in the Queen's Chamber" [Poem 56]). It is possible the word was made up for the occasion (and perhaps also to satisfy the rhyme scheme), but in the United States "willie" is still a common slang expression for the penis. The "lilly" element in this compound noun may allude to his lily-white penis, or it may allude to the fleur-de-lis, which sometimes carries phallic overtones. Burness notes the term in Lyndsay's *Ane Satyre of the Thrie Estaitis* (line 4372) where the sense is "an attack of sickness, a spasm," which makes a kind of sense here too (p. 214).

37   *mychane*. One of several unexplained words in the poem. The context suggests that it is a slang expression for some part of the body, perhaps the mouth or stomach.

38   *belly huddrun . . . hurle bawsy*. Neither of these expressions has been fully explained, though both are evidently terms of endearment. *Huddrun* is perhaps some form of "hood" or a woman's covering (see *DOST* on *hude*). In The Merchant's Tale Januarie's God sees Adam as being "belly-naked" and in kindness supplies him with Eve (*CT* IV[E]1326), apparently as a belly-cover, which seems to be the same way that the woman here looks upon her eager friend. *Bawsy* is perhaps a term of affection for a clumsy person with a big belly. See *DOST*.

39   *slawsy.* This word, which also occurs in line 41, is apparently a slang term meaning something like "fellow."

40   *Your musing waild perse ane harte of stane.* Compare Chaucer's *TC* 3.114 and Whiting H277.

43   Alisoun in The Miller's Tale is also compared to a kid (i.e., a young goat), *CT* I(A)3260. See Burness, pp. 212–14, on sexual associations with various animals.

44–48   *brylyoun.* The term is obscure, but Kinsley suggests "pudendum muliebre." It seems likely that most of the images in lines 44–46 refer directly or euphemistically to the female genitals. See Burness, p. 210, on *tirly mirly* (line 46) for female pudendum (compare eighteenth-century *tirly-whirly*), and *towdy* (line 48) for buttocks (n.b., "Towdy-fee," a fine for fornication). *Mowdy* (line 46) is a variant of the verb *mow* ("to copulate" — *DOST*).

48   *stang.* This term (meaning "stake" or "pole," or possibly "sting") refers to his penis.

51   *Welcum, my golk of Marie land.* This difficult verse is usually explained as an allusion to *King Berdok*, another comic wooing poem contained in B.

52–53   *chirrie . . . unyoun.* On food with sexual associations, see Burness, p. 214.

53   *my sowklar sweit.* See lines 23–24 for other suggestions of what Burness refers to as the sexuality of "mammary stimulation" (p. 214).

57   The *apill rubye* may refer to the actual gift of an apple, and Bawcutt may be right in suggesting that it is also "a humorous reference to ruby rings given as love tokens" (Bw 2.346). Compare Henryson's *Testament of Cresseid*, line 582, and Lindsay's *Squire Meldrum*, lines 1003–06. Chaucer's Troilus and Criseyde also exchange rings, but it is the brooch she gives him that contains a ruby (*TC* 3.1368–72). Still, one cannot help wondering whether it is also a euphemistic reference to his penis.

59–61   Here the lovers engage in the *dery dan* (line 60), which is clearly the dance of love where "both of their joys are met in one." A similar phrase, the "dirrye dantoun," occurs in line 24 of "A Dance in the Queen's Chamber" (Poem 56), where it is used to describe a sexually suggestive dance.

369

62–63   These final verses suggest that their amorous passions have been satisfied and that he is about to leave, thus prompting her expression of regret.

73. *These Fair Ladies That Repair to Court*

This comic-satiric poem celebrates, with tongue in cheek, the ability of women to further their husbands' legal interests by "soliciting" at court. The satire is aimed both at judicial corruption and at women who are willing to grant sexual favors for personal gain. Ridley's comments on the poem seem especially apt: "It has been claimed that Dunbar does not pun, but this graceful minuet seems to be built upon just such a device. The tripping meter serves to intensify the irony, for it results in a rather dainty movement, one appropriate to woman's refinement but here used to describe her prostitution" (1973, p. 1030). Six 8-line tail-rhyme stanzas rhyming *ababcdcd*. MF, B, and R. Mc48, K71, Bw74.

2   *courte ar kend*. The word *courte* may refer either to the royal court or to the court of justice; in this case it may refer to both. The word *kend* may mean both "well-known" and "known carnally."

5   *gud men*. "'Husbands,' and, ironically, 'good men'" (Bw 2.465).

14   *collatioun*. A light refreshment often taken in the evening, and the word came to suggest a private evening of amorous intimacy. Compare Henryson, *Testament of Cresseid*, line 418, and Lindsay, *Satyre*, lines 437–38.

17   *Ye may wit weill thai have grit feill*. Dunbar is no doubt punning on *feill*, which means "having a natural ability for something" but also implies its literal, physical meaning of "feel."

19   "True as the steel" is a clichéd simile; compare Whiting S707 and S709; here it is used ironically..

31–32   A sexual double entendre on the word *spend* (line 31) seems likely, since the implication is that what they are "spending" is not money.

32   *geir*. The terminology, meaning "'property/sexual apparatus' (K), controls a reading of the poem, and by focusing and fusing the themes of selling sex and legality, neatly satirises both women and jurisprudence" (Burness, pp. 211–12).

370

35–40   *Compositouris*. The legal officials responsible for drawing up the financial settlements for people whom the court had found guilty of various crimes. It is not surprising that they were often accused of taking bribes. Compare Lindsay, *Satyre*, lines 2660–64.

47–48   The sense is: "Such (ladies) can succeed, and no one can stop / Them, because of their honest reputations."

48   *honesté*. "Dunbar plays ironically on the word's various implications: honour, moral integrity; the more specific sense, chastity; and the mere outward show of such virtues" (Bw 2.466). Hamlet does much the same when he asks Ophelia if she is "honest" (*Hamlet* 3.1.102–06).

74. *Tidings from the Session*

This satiric commentary on the legal corruption rampant in Edinburgh is presented through the voice of a naïve, impressionable "moorland man." Having just returned to his rural home from the city, he offers his neighbor a rapid-fire catalogue of all the shocking goings-on at the Court of Session, concentrating primarily on the illegal or morally dubious actions of lawyers and their clients. Henryson's fable of *The Sheep and the Dog* provides a similar satiric exposé (*Fables*, lines 1146–1320). In the final stanzas he turns his attention to the equally corrupt practices of the clergy. Eight 7-line stanzas rhyming *aabbcbc*, with slightly varying refrain. MF, B, and R. Mc43, K74, Bw2.

1   Bawcutt suggests that this opening line conveys "scorn for the simple peasant" (Bw 2.282). That may be so, but it does not undermine the truthfulness or accuracy of what he is about to report; his naiveté is contrasted with the corruption of the city in a fashion reminiscent of the fable of the town mouse and the country mouse.

1–7   The poem begins dramatically with the newly-arrived countryman being accosted by his neighbor, who is eager to hear the news of the outside world. The countryman, who has just climbed down from his horse, is happy to comply.

3   *Quhat tythingis, gossope, peace or weir*. The neighbor's question turns out to be wonderfully ironic. He wants to know the answer to the big questions — whether there is "peace or war" — but what he will hear is that people are completely caught up in their own petty concerns.

371

5   *I tell yow this, undir confessioun.* The speaker makes it clear, here and in lines 8–9, that what he is telling his neighbor is said in confidence. His experience at the Session, apparently, has given him cause to be distrustful of his fellow man.

7   The Session was the highest judicial court in Scotland. The king's council constituted its membership, and it sat for lengthy sessions two or three times a year at the Tolbooth in Edinburgh.

13   *fuider.* Lit., "a cart load." The term was used colloquially to mean "a great many."

15–42   These four stanzas itemize the actions and activities of those who come to court. The word *sum* with which most of these verses begin means "one" or "a certain one" rather than "some," although it is also meant collectively — i.e., each *sum* represents a type of behavior practiced by many.

15–21   This stanza emphasizes the duplicity and hypocrisy that characterize the behavior of many people at court.

18   *pattiris.* The word literally means "patters," i.e., speaks rapidly; this verb apparently derives from the rapid, mechanical recitation of the *Pater Noster*, the Lord's Prayer.

          beidis. Literally, beads, i.e., the beads of the rosary; but it became a standard metonym for "prayers."

20–21   I.e., "One bows quite low and bares his head (in a show of false humility) whose demeanor would be quite haughty under other circumstances."

22   *Sum bydand law layis land in wed.* Some who are still waiting for their cases to be heard are forced to mortgage their own land in order to survive.

29   *exceppis.* Formulate objections.

30   *Sum standis besyd and skayld law keppis.* Some bystanders are able to glean small amounts of legal knowledge or terminology, which they presumably use in a pretentious, pseudo-learned fashion.

37   For the image of a "fox in sheep's clothing," compare lines 58–61 of "A Wooing in Dunfermline" (Poem 69).

38   I.e., his kindness is expressed in words but not in deeds.

41   *Sait*. Lit., "Seat," collectively meaning the seated members of the court.

43–56   Now the satire shifts to the orders of friars and monks who come to court, ostensibly for the purpose of recruiting new members, but Dunbar draws upon the familiar portrayal of the lecherousness of the monks and friars.

45   The Carmelites, or White Friars, were a contemplative order originally established on Mount Carmel in the Holy Land. The *Coirdeleiris* is another name for the Franciscans, or Grey Friars, originally founded by St. Francis of Assisi. They could be identified by the knotted ropes or cords tied around the waist of their robes.

48   "The younger ones learn from the example of the older ones" — here, ironically, they learn their bad habits.

50–51   *het complexioun*. The phrase may well suggest that the bodily humors of blood and choler were dominant features of the monk's personality. But what Dunbar appears to be doing in this pair of verses is juxtaposing the monk's contradictory qualities — his hot complexion and his devout mind — to create the kind of humorous non sequitur that Chaucer sometimes used. Compare, for example, Chaucer's statement in the General Prologue that the Monk was "A manly man, to been an abbot able" (I[A]167).

50–56   These final verses depicting the "young monks of hot complexion" are filled with sexual double entendre, much in the fashion of Chaucer's portrait of the Friar in the General Prologue to *The Canterbury Tales*.

52–53   "And in the court they subdue their proud flesh / In a fatherly fashion, with gasps and pants" — verses with an obvious double meaning.

54–55   More verses with an obvious double meaning — the monks' intercession is so gentle and gracious that women are readily disposed to give them what they want.

75. *To the Merchants of Edinburgh*

The poem is both a powerful satiric exposé of the many social and economic ills that beset Edinburgh and an exhortation to the wealthy merchants of the city, very likely the important burgesses who sit upon the burgh council, to remedy this shameful state of affairs. Bawcutt is surely correct in suggesting that Dunbar "appeals to their civic pride . . . , their self-interest . . . , and above all their moral sense" (Bw 2.404). The poem is especially memorable for its vivid and realistic portrayal of late medieval urban life. Eleven 7-line stanzas rhyming *aaabBab*; the fifth verse, which provides the internal refrain, is a dimeter (and thus similar to the *bob* in a *bob and wheel*); also, each stanza ends with the word *name*. It is an unusual stanza form and one not used elsewhere by Dunbar. R only. Mc44, K75, Bw55.

4   The "common profit" refers to the general well-being of all. It is the opposite of the "Singular proffeit" (an individual's self interest) mentioned in line 71. Compare Chaucer's *PF*, line 47, and *CT* IV[E]431 and 1194.

5–7   These verses convey the poet's appeal to their civic pride, a theme sounded throughout the poem.

8   *gaittis*. While often meaning "gates," the term may actually refer to the city's major streets rather than to its gateways.

9   *For stink of haddockis and of scattis*. The stink the poet mentions may not be caused by the fish alone. As Kinsley observes, "fishmongers and butchers threw their trimmings into the streets, which were piled high with middens on both sides" (K, p. 367).

12–14   Again the poet expresses his concern with what visitors to the city will think.

15–19   These verses create a vivid sense of the city's dark and gloomy streets, passage-ways, churches, and houses, a condition the poet believes is a disgrace.

15–16   There is uncertainty over the meaning of the *Stinkand Stull* (line 15), but it was probably a rank passageway that was crammed with stalls, not a school, as some have suggested. Whatever it was, it blocked the light to St. Giles parish church in the High Street.

17   *foirstairis*. Wooden staircases attached to the fronts of the multi-storied tenements.

22   The High Cross was the Mercat Cross, or market cross, located to the northeast of St. Giles Church. It was the symbolic center of the city "where proclamations were made and punishments meted out" (K, p. 367). A fragment of the medieval cross

still survives, which has been incoporated into a nineteenth-century building (Bw 2.405). Compare the *Flyting* [Poem 83], line 211).

24   *Trone.* The public weighing house. Every Scottish *burgh* had one, and it was always located in close proximity to the market cross; in Edinburgh it was at the corner of West Bow and Castle Hill.

          cokill and wilk. "Cockles and whelks."

25   *Jok.* Jock or Jack, a conventional name for a man of lowbirth. Compare "To the King" (Poem 48), line 66 and "Master Andro Kennedy's Testament" (Poem 80), line 73.

29–30   The minstrels maintained by the burgh are criticized for their limited and trite repertoire. *Now the day dawis* has been identified as a popular song of the time, but *Into Joun* remains unidentified (line 30). Compare Douglas, *Eneados* 13.Prol.182.

31–32   The meaning of these verses is uncertain. *Sanct Cloun* (line 31) may be the Irish saint St. Cluanus who was linked with eating and drinking; but it is also possible that the phrase simply refers to a mock saint. The general point, in any case, seems to be that truly talented musicians are given no real opportunities. Compare Lindsay, *Satyre*, lines 1371 and 4388.

34   *To hald sic mowaris on the moyne.* This line refers back to the inept minstrels in the hire of the city. Bawcutt suggests that the phrase refers to gallow birds, criminals left to hang on the gallows who "make faces" at the moon (Bw 2.406).

36   Dunbar's scornful opinion of tailors and shoemakers is more fully revealed and explored in "The Dance of the Seven Deadly Sins" (Poem 77).

38   *merchantis at the Stinkand Styll.* In the fifteenth century there was a tenement of several stories built along the north side of St. Giles which was "pierced by two passages, one of which was the notorious *Stinkand Styll* that led directly to the north door of the church" (Bw 2.406). Dunbar is not the only one to be offended by it.

43–46   City records comment on Edinburgh's "multitude of beggars" (Bw 2.406).

57   *Sessioun.* The important judicial court that Dunbar satirizes in "Tidings from the Session" (Poem 74).

71–72   Here the contrast and conflict between *Singular proffeit* (line 71) and *common proffeit* (line 72) is made explicit.

74   Jerusalem, the city of God, provided the model after which earthly cities should aspire.

76   "That at some time (in the future) you will be governed by reason."

77   In this verse there is a blank space in the manuscript; the emendation here supplied seems as likely as those supplied by others; see textual note to this line.

76. *How Dunbar Was Desired to Be a Friar*

This poem presents one of Dunbar's strongest indictments of the friars, in particular the Franciscans, and its negative critique is consistent with the anti-fraternal feelings he expresses elsewhere. The poem is cast in the form of a vision in which the dreamer has a supernatural visitation, in this case from a figure who appears to be St. Francis of Assisi but who is actually a fiend. The central symbol in the poem is the friar's habit, which the visitant tries to lay over the dreamer and which the dreamer leaps from his bed to avoid; this despised habit, clearly, is the tangible emblem of the falseness and hypocrisy the poet associates with the friars. Is it possible that Dunbar had once been a novice in the Franciscan order and that he decided not to enter the order? This is a question that scholars have hotly debated, with no consensus emerging. Most recent commentators, however, tend to view lines 33–45 as being in the tradition of the mock confession; that is, his description of his travels "in freiris weid" ("in a friar's habit," line 36) is actually a fiction and should not be viewed as providing evidence about the poet's life. Ten 5-line stanzas rhyming *aabba*. B, MF, and R. Mc4, K55, Bw77.

2   *Sanct Francis*. St. Francis of Assisi (c. 1181–1226) founded the first of the fraternal orders of the friars, and his order was dedicated to poverty and to ministering to the poor and sick. Dunbar is probably not satirizing St. Francis nor the ideals of this order, but rather the practices of his later followers. Many Franciscan houses were established in Scotland in the later Middle Ages.

2–5   In "Tidings from the Session" (Poem 74) the speaker describes how older friars attempt to recruit younger men for their orders (lines 43–48), and here a figure in the guise of St. Francis appears before the dreamer in the hope of recruiting him to the Franciscan Order. His admonition to the dreamer in line 5 to repudiate the world

376

probably reflects the vows of poverty and chastity that were sworn by members of the regular clergy.

8–10   The friar's habit which the "saint" tries to place over the dreamer terrifies him so much that he leaps away from it and "would never come near it." Dunbar may be playing upon the idea encountered in various tales and romances that if a mortal has physical contact with fiendish persons or objects it will lead to his damnation.

13   *Thow that hes lang done Venus lawis teiche.* This verse probably alludes to Dunbar's courtly poems, which may well have been among his earliest works.

15   *Delay it nocht, it mon be done but dreid.* Here, as in line 5 and lines 29–30, there is a strong degree of coercion in the "saint's" manner of address, which contrasts with the dreamer's meek politeness.

19   *Bot thame to weir it nevir come in my mynd.* The dreamer makes it clear in this verse that he has never entertained any intention of becoming a friar.

20   *Sweit confessour.* "Sweet confessor" is a both a deferential and a correct manner of addressing a saint such as St. Francis who was not a martyred saint. Bawcutt suggests that "It has a further point here, since the friars' right to hear confessions was much resented" (Bw 2.473).

21–24   The speaker denigrates the friars by suggesting that far more saints were produced by the secular clergy than by the regular clergy; this point of view is not surprising, since Dunbar was probably a member of the secular clergy. The speaker's desire to wear a bishop's robe rather than a friar's habit may also hint at Dunbar's long-standing desire for ecclesiastical preferment within the secular clergy.

26–27   These verses reflect the various means by which the friars might urge young men to join their ranks — through letters, sermons, and other written documents.

34   From "Berwick to Calais" symbolizes the geographical extremes of England, from Berwick on Tweed in the far north of England, to the small portion of French soil around Calais that England still controlled. Compare "A Complaint against Mure" (Poem 60), line 6.

38 *Derntoun kirk*. The collegiate church in the English town of Darlington, in the shire of Durham. It would have been a stopping point along the main pilgrimage route from the north of Britain to Canterbury.

44 *Quhilk mycht be flemit with na haly watter*. This claim is surely hyperbolic, since holy water had the power to drive out evil spirits. Indeed, the very mention of it may contribute to the apparition's sudden disappearance in the next stanza. Compare Whiting D208.

47 *Ane fieind he wes*. Bawcutt (1989) compares the passage (lines 46–48) to other fiend poems like "Diabolus et Virgo" and "The False Knight on the Road" (p. 171).

48–50 The thwarted fiend departs, but he does not go without leaving a certain amount of wrack and ruin in his wake, probably reflecting his displeasure. Fiends were often given to making dramatic exits. Compare, for example, the exit the fiend makes in Malory (*Works*, p. 500) after failing to seduce Percival during the Grait Quest. On diablerie in Dunbar see headnote to "The Dance of the Seven Deadly Sins" (Poem 77).

77. *The Dance of the Seven Deadly Sins*

Set on Fastern Eve, the last day before the beginning of the Lenten season, this is one of Dunbar's most carnivalesque poems. It is a comically grotesque dream vision in which the dreamer observes a pair of elaborate and hellish entertainments. The poem has two major sections of 108 lines each, separated by a brief comic interlude of twelve lines. In the first half of the poem, Mahoun (a conventional synonym for Satan) summons for his entertainment the personified figures of the Seven Deadly Sins; accompanied by their personal entourages (consisting of damned souls who practiced those particular sins), they perform an elaborate and rather gruesome dance. This section of the poem is informed by a wide variety of medieval materials that pertain to the seven deadly sins and graphically depict the torments inflicted on sinners in Hell. Fradenburg (pp. 173–74) comments on the poem's pageantry and notes that the poem presents the "specifically monarchial poetics of spectacularity" (p. 224) at which Dunbar excels. See also Welsford's remarks on the poem's revel qualities: "The ground of the poet's imagination is a wild mumming or morisco" (p. 75). Bawcutt (1989) classifies this poem, along with "The Antichrist" (Poem 51), "A Ballad of the Friar of Tungland" (Poem 54), "How Dunbar Was Desired to Be a Friar" (Poem 76), and "The Devil's Inquest" (Poem 79), as diablerie poems — "all bad dreams or nightmares" (p. 168). Noting, with C. S. Lewis (1954, p. 94), how often in Dunbar "the comic overlaps with the demonic and terrifying," Bawcutt

(1989) argues that Dunbar's treatment of the uncanny (*elrich*) differs from that of other Scots writers: "The *elrich* is harnessed and put to some purpose, though this is not always or primarily a moral one. . . . Dunbar's characteristic tone is not genial, but dark and sinister; we are told that God laughed 'his hairt sair' at Kittok's exploits, and also at the Highlander, but in Dunbar's poems the only laughter (apart from the poet's) is that of devils (*Festernis Evin in Hell*, 29 [the present poem], and *Renunce Thy God*, 39 ["The Devil's Inquest" — poem 79]). It is not faerie that predominates in his comic poems, but diablerie" (p. 165).

In the brief interlude that occupies the center of the poem, Mahoun now calls for a Highland pageant. But the great rabble of Gaelic speakers who appear make such a terrible racket that Mahoun consigns them to the deepest pit of Hell where they are smothered in smoke. This section is clearly intended to satirize Highlanders, but it also serves to introduce the lighter comic tone that prevails in the second half of the poem. As a third entertainment Satan calls for a tournament between a tailor and a shoemaker who have been elevated to knightly status for the occasion. Their "joust itself is broad excremental farce, with the tailor sliding from his saddle leaving it 'all beschittin' when he comes near the soutar, whose horse is so alarmed at the rattle of the armour that it carries its rider to the Devil. [The Devil] wants no more of the soutar's vomit, so he turns his backside on the new-made knight and befouls him from neck to heel, striking horse and rider to the earth with a tremendous fart" (Ross, p. 175). This section of the poem belongs to the same comic tradition that produced such works as Chaucer's *Sir Thopas* and the ME *Tournament of Totenham*, works that intentionally burlesque popular romance tradition. The poem contains twenty stanzas: eighteen are 12-line stanzas of the tail-rhyme variety rhyming *aabccbddbeeb*, and two are 6-line stanzas rhyming *aabccb*. Only B contains all three sections as a continuous sequence; MF contains two versions; R's text copies the first of the MF versions; As contains only the Tournament section. Mc57 and Mc58, K52A and K52B, Bw47.

1   *Of Februar the fyiftene nycht.* Scholars debate whether 15 February possesses symbolic significance or whether it is the date of an actual dream. If the latter, then it might be possible to date the composition of the poem, since Fastern Eve (or Shrove Tuesday) was the day before the beginning of Lent. In "The Thistle and the Rose" (Poem 30) the poet's dream vision is also linked to a specific date, in that case 9 May. In both poems, though, Dunbar may simply be imitating Chaucer, who had provided a specific date for his dream experience in *HF*, line 63.

2–3   This is the time of night that visionary experiences in dream poems often occur — just a few hours before dawn. The dreamer's trance-like state is the state of semi-consciousness in which literary visions usually occur.

4   Medieval literature abounds with visions of Heaven and Hell — from the masterpieces of Dante and the *Pearl*-poet, to comic and parodic pieces such as Chaucer's Prologue to The Summoner's Tale. Dunbar's poem is very much in the latter tradition. In this poem we hear nothing about Heaven but a great deal about Hell.

6   *Mahoun.* This shortened form of the name of the Muslim prophet Mohammad was often used to signify Satan or the Devil. Compare "The Antichrist" (Poem 51), line 32, and *The Tretiis of the Tua Mariit Wemen and the Widow* (Poem 84), line 101.

7   Although this is primarily a comic poem, it should be noted that the sinners in Hell who must join in the dance are people who died without being shriven, that is, while still in a state of sin because they were unconfessed. The Lenten season, which follows Shrove Tuesday, was the spiritual preparation for the act of confession, and this is the central point of Dunbar's several religious poems that focus on Lent. Compare "A Ballad of the Friar of Tungland" (Poem 54), line 46, and its accompanying note.

8   *Fasternis Evin.* Fastern Eve is synonymous with Shrove Tuesday, the final day of carnival before the beginning of Lent on Ash Wednesday. At the court of James IV, Fastern Eve was marked by celebrations involving dancing, masquerading, and mock jousting. Fradenburg notes that "the king had mumming robes made for himself, so we know that the court participated in its own disguisings as well as patronized professional and municipal entertainments" (p. 175).

10   *gallandis.* Dunbar refers to young men of the court as gallants, i.e., sycophants always up on the latest fashions. Yet also here he addresses his courtly audience with a warning — there is a very different kind of aristocracy in Hell. Mary E. Robbins writes, "The force of the poet's communication here lies in the social standing of his audience, who are shown in this poem that the trappings of nobility have meaning only for the short span of man's earthly existence. In the next world, the deadly sins become courtiers, and craftsmen can be dubbed knights" (p. 147).

      gyis. Lit., "guise" or "disguising" — i.e., a masquerade.

11–12   The latest mode of French dancing is also made fun of in the opening verses of "A Dance in the Queen's Chamber" (Poem 56).

14–15　Dunbar seems to be combining two traditions here: visions of Hell and Purgatory common to Dante's *Divine Comedy* and English works such as *The Vision of Tundale*, *St. Patrick's Purgatory*, *Ayenbite of Inwit*, etc.; and the *Danse Macabre* so popular in late medieval art as well as poetry. Traditionally the *Danse* has skeletons or fiends leading the procession, with people of various social stations, regardless of class, (i.e., those guilty of the seven deadly sins) being dragged along in the dance. For a discussion of the *Danse Macabre*, see Paul Binski, *Medieval Death: Ritual and Representation* (Ithaca, NY: Cornell University Press, 1996), pp. 153–59.

16　The first of the personified figures of the Seven Deadly Sins is Pride, the mortal sin that provides the foundation for all the others. Compare Ecclesiasticus 10:14–15: "The beginning of the pride of man is to fall off from God: Because his heart is departed from him that made him: for pride is the beginning of sin." Mary E. Robbins notes that the order of the dancing of the sins is Gregorian, namely: Pride, Wrath, Envy, Covetousness, Sloth, Lechery, and Gluttony (p. 148). For the most thorough discussion of the seven deadly sins see Bloomfield.

17　*With hair wyld bak and bonet on syd.* Editors debate the literal meaning of this line and whether the text should read *hair* or *bair*. The point of the verse, in any case, seems to be to describe the vanity Pride takes in his appearance by his wearing his bonnet at a tilt and by displaying his hair. Chaucer's Pardoner comes to mind, who rode "Dischevelee, save his cappe" (i.e., "with unbound hair") and whose hair "his shuldres overspradde" (*CT* I[A]683, 677–78). See also The Parson's Tale, *CT* X[I]410–15.

19–21　*kethat.* The precise meaning of the term is not known, but the context indicates that it is an elaborate or luxurious garment. These verses recall the long, wide sleeves of the coat worn by Chaucer's Squire (*CT* I[A]93) as depicted in the Ellesmere MS portrait.

22　*prowd trumpour.* The phrase might also suggest "blowhards" or "self-proclaimers" — those who blow their own horns — in addition to the literal meaning, "impostor" or "trickster."

25–30　This is one of the poem's two 6-line stanzas.

27　*But yit luche nevir Mahoun.* This line points out indirectly to the audience that poems in this carnivalesque tradition are supposed to be funny in a grotesque way.

381

One of the ways we learn not the emulate the Seven Deadly Sins is to *laugh* at their tomfoolery. Satan, however, seems to take himself and his ridiculous court all too seriously, indicating his excessive pride. See the headnote, above.

28–30   The appearance of priests within this company of the proud sinners greatly amuses the fiends, including the two who are named in line 30. The poet is probably inventing these names; note that he uses the obscure word *Bawsy* (line 30) in two other poems: "In a Secret Place" (Poem 72), line 38, and "To the King" (Poem 47), line 56. *Bawsy* is the name of a dog in Henryson's fable of the Cock and the Fox, *Fables*, line 546.

31–42   Wrath and his followers next join the dance; the emphasis in these verses is upon their weaponry and bellicosity.

33   *He brandeist lyk a beir.* The image suggests an enraged bear being constrained by chains; bear-baiting was a common entertainment at this time in England and Scotland.

37   *In jakkis and stryppis and bonettis of steill.* As Bawcutt notes, this seems to be a very current description of medieval armor (Bw 2.386).

38   *Thair leggis wer chenyeit to the heill.* This line probably means that they wore chains on their legs in order to constrain them, not that their legs were protected by chain mail, which the context might suggest.

43–54   In this depiction of Envy and his followers, the emphasis is upon a set of vices frequently practiced at court, as lines 53–54 directly state.

48   The phrase *wirdis quhyte* ("white words") means statements that are insincere; it survives in the expression "little white lies." Compare Henryson's *Fables*, line 601, and Chaucer's *TC* 3.901.

54–66   The fourth of the Seven Deadly Sins is Covetousness, which in line 55 is called the root of all evil — compare 1 Timothy 6:10: *Radix enim omnium malorum est cupiditas* ("For the desire of money is the root of all evils"). The most striking aspects of these verses is in the way the punishment fits the crime (lines 61–66).

59   *Hudpykis.* Kinsley and Mackenzie gloss the term as "miser." I have followed Bawcutt's "skinflint," having already glossed "wrechis" (line 58) as "miser."

61–66   Bawcutt observes that "Force-feeding with molten metal was one of the stock torments of hell . . . , but to swallow gold was peculiarly, and aptly, a punishment of the covetous" (Bw 2.386). Compare Henryson, *Orpheus*, line 330.

66   These avaricious sinners are repeatedly filled with the molten gold from every kind of coin they had sought to obtain during their lives.

67–78   Sloth enters fittingly in the manner of a sow, an animal traditionally associated with filth and laziness (see, for example, Chaucer's use of this image in his portrait of the Miller in *CT* I[A]556, and Whiting S541). Sloth appropriately arrives only *at the secound bidding* (line 67); as has become increasingly clear throughout the poem, the Seven Deadly Sins personified exemplify the sins they represent. This kind of allegory is common in medieval poetry — and reaches its hilarious high point in *Piers Plowman* B.5.385–87: "Thanne cam Sleuthe al bislabered with two slymy eighen. / 'I moste sitte to be shryven or ellis sholde I happe; / I may noght stonde ne stoupe ne withoute stool knele.'" During confession Sloth falls asleep and Repentance has to wake him up sharply. The cartoon-like comedy of these representations helps to present them as creatures to be laughed at and ridiculed, not imitated.

70   *belly huddroun.* Compare "In a Secret Place" (Poem 72), line 38.

74   Belial was believed to be the name of one of the devils, an assumption deriving from several passages of Scripture, especially 2 Corinthians 6:15: "And what concord hath Christ with Belial?" (Compare also Judges 19:22 and 1 Kings [1 Samuel] 2:12.) Milton similarly associates Belial with the sin of Sloth when he describes him as "Timorous and slothful" in *Paradise Lost* 2.117.

75   *lunyie.* The term means "loins" but here may refer to the "rump."

76   Bawcutt notes that in Dante's *Purgatorio*, canto 18, "the slothful are forced to run incessantly" (Bw 2.387).

78   *counyie.* Kinsley and Mackenzie note the obscurity of the term and leave it without gloss. *DOST* cites verb forms meaning "to take leave," or "have permission to leave." But such meanings do not illuminate the sense here. Bawcutt glosses the term as "dance," which I follow since it fits the context and suits well the "dance of the Seven Deadly Sins" topic.

79–90   Lechery and his followers come next. While this sin was more commonly symbolized by a goat than a horse, the horse could also symbolize unbridled lust (as in The Reeve's Tale, *CT* I[A]4080–81). Compare also Jeremias 5:8: "They are become as amorous horses and stallions: every one neighed after his neighbour's wife." Here, too, the punishment in lines 88–90 is designed to fit the crime.

84   The poet reiterates the point that these are people who died in a state of sinfulness.

86–87   Kinsley suggests that their strange red countenances imply that they are suffering from sexually-related skin diseases (p. 339). In any case, the lines recall the "fyr-reed cherubynnes face" of Chaucer's Summoner (*CT* I[A]624). Bawcutt notes that the simile in line 87 "evokes not merely colour but torment" (Bw 2.387).

91–102 The final sin is Gluttony and, as is often the case, the emphasis here is as much or more on excessive drinking as it is on overeating.

102   *lovery*. A "livery," an allotment of food and drink on which one could live.

103–08 In stark contrast to Heaven, Hell lacks music and musicians and is a place of cacophony and disharmony. The only exception is the occasional murderous minstrel who earns himself a place there.

107–08 Bawcutt suggests that there is "a legal joke" here in the phrase *breif of richt* (line 108), a writ by which property descended to its rightful heir (Bw 2.338). In this case the property the murderer rightfully deserves to inherit is Hell itself.

109–20 This stanza provides a transition from the first half of the poem, with its frightening dance of the Seven Deadly Sins and their attendants, to the second half of the poem, with its farcical jousting between a tailor and a shoemaker. As Dunbar does elsewhere, here he ridicules Highlanders and speakers of Gaelic.

110   *Makfadyane*. Likely to be a type-name for a Highlander, though it may carry certain historical resonances as well. In Blind Hary's *Wallace*, for example, the hero wages a campaign against a fictional traitor of this name (ed. McDiarmid, 7.626–868).

111   "Northward" is probably used to indicate that Macfaydyane is a Highlander, but perhaps also to suggest that he comes from the worst part of Hell; that is, since north is the Devil's direction, the northern part of Hell would be the most hellish of all. Compare *CT* III[D]1413, *Piers Plowman* C.1.110–21, and *Death and Life*, lines

384

142–50; compare also Jeremias 6:1: "for evil is seen out of the north, and a great destruction."

113–14   The joke here is that Hell seems to be teeming with these *Erschemen* — just as Hell in the Prologue to The Summoner's Tale is teeming with friars.

115   In ME works, "Termagant" is a name sometimes used for a Muslim deity believed to be one of Satan's minions. Here, used in the plural, it simply means "fiends" or "demons." Minor devils were customarily depicted as wearing ragged, tattered garb. Compare the *Flyting* (Poem 83), line 532, and Henryson's *Annunciation*, line 68.

116–20   These verses treat speakers of Gaelic derisively. In order to shut them up, the Devil has to smother them with smoke.

117   Bawcutt notes that the verb *rowp* was often used to describe the croaking of ravens. Compare Holland's *Howlat*, line 215, and Lindsay's *Papyngo*, line 661 (Bw 2.388).

119   "The deepest pit of Hell" is the bottomless pit of Apocalypse 20:3.

121–23   These lines, opening the second section of the poem, recall "every tail-rhyme romance one has ever encountered" (Mary E. Robbins, p. 149). Dunbar is highly conscious here of the genre he is attempting to undercut. Compare *Sir Perceval of Galles* and, especially, Chaucer's Tale of Sir Thopas.

125   *A pricklous and ane hobbell clowttar.* These are probably contemptuous terms for a tailor and a cobbler, though their literal meanings and their implications are debated; puns may be involved also.

127–32   The tailor, along with his "graceless" supporters, is now led to the tournament field.

130–31   These are the tailor's apprentices, each of whom specializes in a particular task (some of which are unclear).

133–36   The ludicrous battle standard that is carried before the tailor reflects both his trade and his dishonesty. Comic banners of this sort are also carried by peasants in *Colkebie Sow*, lines 330–32.

137–38   "For as long as the Greek Sea ebbs and flows, / Tailors will never be honest" — in other words, always. Gibes at dishonest tradesmen were common; compare Whiting

T13. "The Greek Sea" was a common medieval phrase for the Mediterranean Sea: e.g., see *CT* I(A)59; Hay's *King Alexander*, lines 1110 and 2607; and Gower's *Confessio Amantis* 1.145 and 3.2488.

142–44   In romances kings often bestowed knighthood upon aspiring young heroes just before their participation in a great tournament.

148–56   An arranged fight between a pair of cowards is a common comic device; Shakespeare uses it to good effect in *Twelfth Night* 3.4.

157–59   As Bawcutt notes, the shoemaker comes from the west because he is the designated defender in the joust. The challenger, in this case the tailor, approaches from the east (Bw 2.389). For the intricate rules for conducting such arranged combats in late medieval Scotland, see "The Order of Combats," a document executed under the direction of King James I of Scotland and based on Thomas of Woodstock's French "Order of Battel." Woodstock's text, along with an early translation of it into English, is provided in *The Black Book of the Admiralty*, ed. Travers Twiss, Rolls Series 55 (London: Longman, 1871; rpt. Lessing-Druckerei: Kraus Reprint, Ltd., 1965), 1.301–29. The text of the Scots "Order of Combats" can be found in George Neilson's *Trial by Combat* (New York: Macmillan & Co., 1891), pp. 261–72; for the specific details utilized here, see especially p. 263.

164   *Sanct Girnega*. The general view is that this is probably a mock-saint or perhaps the name of a devil. It is not the name of the patron saint of shoemakers, which was St. Crispin.

168   The *uly* that bursts out between the plates in the cobbler's harness is the blacking or cobbler's oil used in his trade.

169–80   Just as the Devil had knighted the tailor, now he knights the shoemaker. And just as the tailor's fear produced his "series of farts like thunder" (line 155), the shoemaker's fear leads him to vomit all over himself and the Devil as well.

193   This alliterating line recalls the stirring battle descriptions often found in ME alliterative works, such as the *Alliterative Morte Arthure* or *Perceval of Galles*.

198–208   This time the Devil anticipates the shoemaker's "spewing." He not only manages to avoid being hit, but he uses his own *ers* (line 203) to launch a counterattack, which effectively ends the tournament. Mary E. Robbins notes that, for a poem warning its readers about the dangers and torments of Hell, it seems "mild by medieval standards" (p. 145) when the most graphically described pain is the shoemaker's beshittening of himself. Certainly the Hell torments of a poem like the *Vision of Tundale* (see, for example, lines 762–73) are much more frightening than this mock tournament. However, Dunbar is specifically invoking this tradition simply by his subject matter.

211–16   The Devil now strips the two jousters of their knightly status, bars them from further participation in warfare, and returns them to their previous status — something they themselves prefer.

227   *air*. Perhaps literally "heir," i.e., the inheritor or owner, though a pun on meanings of "air" or "breath" or "wind," thus referring to the power and stench of his prodigious farting, is hard to deny.

228   *Schirris*. The speaker addressing his audience as "Sirs" reflects the device known as "the minstrel call"; it often occurs at the beginning and/or end of a sub-section in a popular romance. It might also suggest that the poem was publically performed during a Fastern Eve celebration.

78. *Of the Tailors and the Shoemakers* [*Telyouris and sowtaris, blist be ye*]

Here, with tongue in cheek, the poet retracts his highly uncomplimentary depiction of tailors and shoemakers in the jousting section of the previous poem. But this mock-commendation — which is essentially the same device he uses in the second of his two poems concerning James Dog ("Of the Aforesaid James Dog" [Poem 58]) — is obviously intended to extend the joke. In this case the narrator's dream vision turns from hellish concerns to heavenly ones, as an angel comes and announces to tailors and shoemakers that their place in Heaven will surpass the saints and be next to God Himself. They merit such an exalted position, he says, because they are the ones who correct God's mistakes. The poem is "notable for its irreverence, word-play . . . , and a kind of crazy logic that transforms rogues into saints" (Bw 2.391). Ten 4-line stanzas rhyming *aabB*. B and MF. Mc59, K52C, Bw48.

1   "Between twelve o'clock and eleven," i.e., in the middle of the night. The odd inversion of the hours may have been necessitated by the rhyme, but it also effectively serves to introduce the topsy-turvy "logic" that operates throughout the poem.

2–3   Compare Apocalypse 1:1.

4   *Telyouris and sowtaris, blist be ye.* Bawcutt suggests that the refrain "humorously recalls the Beatitudes" (Bw 2.392), especially Matthew 5:3. The word *blist* literally means "blessed"; but when used sarcastically, the word could also convey the opposite sense of "cursed" or "accursed."

5–8   This stanza is not found in the text of MF, perhaps because of its irreverence.

9   *The caus to yow is nocht unkend.* This verse implies that tailors and shoemakers are fully cognizant of the vitally important role they play in tidying up God's little mistakes.

11   *craft.* The word means "skill," but may also carry overtones of "craftiness."

17   *fair.* The word may refer to actual fairs held on particular saints days, though more likely it is used here as a metaphor for life in this world; compare "This world is nis but a chirie feire" in the lyric "Bi a wode as I gone ride," contained in the Vernon MS (*IMEV* 563, line 85). This is the only known occurrence of the word *flyrok*, and thus the context offers the main clue to its meaning — a person with deformed feet?

20   *Bot ye can hyd tham, blist be ye.* A central irony of the poem is reflected in this verse: the tailors and shoemakers do not actually correct any of these deformities, all they do is hide them. There seems to be an implication that what they are doing is covering up the truth.

31   *craftis slie.* The phrase effectively captures the double meaning the poet hints at throughout the poem — "skillful artistry" and "sly deceptions."

39   *knavis.* The word is also double in meaning — "servants" but also "rogues."

79. *The Devil's Inquest* [*Renunce thy God and cum to me*]

Two widely differing versions of this poem are extant, and editors agree that it is "likely that neither version represents a finished poem; there are inconsistencies and clumsinesses in both, and in both some stanzas may have been interpolated" (K, p. 348). Bawcutt prints both versions on opposing pages, thus facilitating a comparison of the two texts. The poem itself is a nightmarish dream vision in which the narrator observes the Devil as he moves through the daily marketplace inciting a variety of dishonest people to utter self-damning oaths. Kinsley takes the refrain "Renunce thy God and cum to me," to be the poem's title; Mackenzie calls it "The Devil's Inquest." Both titles make sense: the poem's lengthy catalogue of society begins with a priest and a courtier, but the major emphasis of the satire is on the lesser varieties of merchants and craftsmen, again including tailors and shoemakers, who loudly but falsely proclaim their honesty. The central motif here is the common belief that the swearing of false or blasphemous oaths jeopardizes the soul of the swearer. Thus the poem has some affinity to Chaucer's Friar's Tale and Pardoner's Tale. B; a substantially different version occurs in MF and R. Seventeen 5-line stanzas rhyming *aabaB*. Mc42, K56, Bw78.

1–2 These verses establish a dream-vision framework, but aside from the use of the phrase *Me thocht* in lines 2, 5, and 81, the dreamer has little significance, and there is no return to the opening frame at the end of the poem.

2–5 The Devil moves surreptitiously through the city marketplace, planting in the people a desire to utter "oaths of cruelty." This phrase reflects the common belief that when people swear on the body of Christ they reenact Christ's torments on the Cross. Compare, for example, the actions of the three tavern rioters in Chaucer's Pardoner's Tale, who "many a grisly ooth thanne han they sworn, / And Cristes blessed body they torente" (*CT* VI[C]708–09). There is probably the additional sense that their oaths will also lead to the cruelty they will experience in Hell as a result of having sworn such oaths.

5 *Renunce thy God and cum to me.* "The refrain inverts the baptismal renunciation of the devil and all his works" (Bw 2.475).

7–8 The priest, symbolizing hypocrisy, takes God's name in vain — thus violating one of the Ten Commandments — while at the same time he is receiving God (in the form of the Host) at the altar.

9 *"Thow art my clerk," the Devill can say.* See Bawcutt on the ties between this poem and the Book of Job. "The figure of the devil is at the heart of Dunbar's poem" (1989, p. 169). See headnote to "The Dance of the Seven Deadly Sins" (Poem 77) on Dunbar's diablerie.

11–13 The courtier represents the sin of pride. He swears by Christ's wounds and arms, two very common oaths. Compare *CT* VI(C)654.

17   "Relinquished his portion of Heaven or Hell," i.e., expressed his disbelief in the existence of an afterlife.

21–23   The goldsmith claims, falsely, that his materials are so expensive that he cannot turn a profit. His asseveration in line 23 is similar to that spoken by the summoner in The Friar's Tale: "the foule feend me fecche / If I th'excuse" (*CT* III[D]1610–11). Compare also Lindsay's *Satyre*, lines 4166–71.

29   *Mahoun*. A shortened form of "Mohammad," it was often used as a synonym for the Devil. Compare "The Antichrist" (Poem 51), line 32; "The Dance of the Seven Deadly Sins" (Poem 77), line 6; and *The Tretiis of the Tua Mariit Wemen and the Wedo* (Poem 84), line 101.

37   *evin and od*. "Even and odd," a common idiom meaning "everything."

41   *be the sacrament*. I.e., on Christ's body, the sacrament of Holy Communion. Compare Lindsay's *Satyre*, lines 652 and 1541.

46–49   The malt-maker, or maltster, prepared the malt which would then be used by the brewer; malt was normally made from barley in a process that involved steeping, germinating, and then drying in a kiln.

51–54   The brewer criticizes the quality of the malt in order to pay less for it. A *boll* (a standard measurement — line 54) of malt should normally produce about twelve gallons of ale.

56   *Be rude and raip*. It was common to swear by the Cross. The "rope" may refer to the scourge used to beat Christ or perhaps to the rope by which He was bound to the pillar.

61   Beginning with the minstrel, the social catalogue focuses on the more disreputable members of society.

66–69   Dicing and swearing are often closely linked; see Chaucer's Pardoner's Tale (*CT* VI[C]651–55). Compare also the phrase "false as dicers' oaths" in *Hamlet* 3.4.45.

71–74   The precise meaning of the thief's words are debated, but he seems to be swearing that if he can escape hanging now, he is willing to be possessed by Hell later. In line 74 the Devil seems to agree, welcoming the thief to his "rope."

76   Fishwives were notoriously noisy and argumentative. (Compare "To the Merchants of Edinburgh" [Poem 75], lines 10–11 and the *Flyting* [Poem 83], line 231.) Later the term "fishwife" came to stand for any coarse, abusive woman.

82   *Solistand wer as beis thik.* Compare the description in the Prologue to The Summoner's Tale: "Right so as bees out swarmen from an hyve, / Out of the develes ers ther gonne dryve / Twenty thousand freres on a route" (*CT* III[D]1693–95).

84   Robin and Dick — stock names for two everyday fellows — rather like "Tom, Dick, and Harry."

80. *Master Andro Kennedy's Testament*

The poem is a mock-testament in which the speaker, lying on the brink of death, proposes a final disposition for his possessions (stanzas 3–12) and then describes the funeral and burial he wishes to receive (stanzas 12–14). He consigns his soul to his lord's wine cellar; his body to the midden heap in Ayr; his unfaithful heart to his special friend (or his wife?); his most valued possession to the head of his clan (though he does not know who that would be); his false pleasures to the master of St. Anthony's; his false winnings to the friars; his folly to Jock Fool; and his curse and God's to John Clerk. His remaining goods, and the care of his children, he gives to his lord. The poem satirizes many things but chiefly the speaker himself, who makes no effort to conceal the fact that he is an incorrigible drunk.

It is not clear if *Andro Kennedy* was a real person or a made-up figure meant to satirize the Kennedys, a prominent family in the royal burgh of Ayr. Some scholars have argued that Andro Kennedy was a quack doctor much favored at court, but there is little external evidence to support that claim, and the evidence within the poem is not especially compelling. It is possible that the speaker is meant to be an Augustinian canon belonging to the monastic house of St. Anthony's in Leith (see lines 57–64). If so, the poem should be viewed primarily as a piece of anti-clerical satire about a drunken clergyman rather than as an attack upon the Kennedys. It is not certain how many of the people mentioned in the poem are real, though some of them (particularly the master of St. Anthony's) probably are.

The literary genre of the mock-testament was in much in vogue in France in the later Middle Ages (Villon's *Grand Testament* is a major example), and Scottish literature of the late fifteenth and early sixteenth century preserves several examples, including *King Hart*, Lindsay's *Testament of Papyngo* and *Testament of Squyer Meldrum*, and the anonymous *Duncan Laideus' Testament*. Fourteen 8-line stanzas, rhyming *abababab*, *ababcdcd*, or *ababacac*; the final stanza contains fourteen lines rhyming *ababacacacac*. RP, B, MF, and R. Mc40, K38, Bw19.

1–8   The speaker proudly offers a commentary on his dubious lineage. He considers himself to be a fiend incarnate, having been sired either by an incubus demon or by a lecherous friar, sentiments recalling the opening verses in The Wife of Bath's Tale (*CT* III[D]873–81). (If he were a foundling who had been raised in a monastic house, a common phenomenon in the Middle Ages, he would not be certain who had fathered him.)

2   The Latin tags interspersed throughout the text are both made up and drawn from specific sources, sometimes passages of Scripture; they are designed to lend a "serious" and "legalistic" coloration to this ludicrous performance. They reflect the kind of Latin that a rather unstudious cleric (such as Chaucer's Monk) might be able to produce.

3   *sum incuby*. An incubus was a demonic being who liked to seduce mortal women. Compare the description of the birth of Merlin in Geoffrey of Monmouth's *History of the Kings of Britain* (Thorpe, pp. 167–69). Compare also "The Antichrist" (Poem 51), lines 26–30, and *The Golden Targe* (Poem 65), line 125.

9–12   These are moralistic commonplaces. Blind Allan is probably not an actual person; and not knowing any more about something "than Blind Allan does of the moon" was probably a common colloquial expression. Compare Lindsay's *Beaton*, line 396.

15–16   Fittingly, given his alcoholic predilections, Andro Kennedy's dying wish is for his mouth to be wet with drink; he is much less concerned, apparently, with the administration of Last Rites. Bawcutt suggests the Latin phrase is a "flippant rewriting of the common formula to attest sanity: *eger corpore sanus tamen mente*, 'sick in body, but sound in mind'" (Bw 2.329).

17   At this point the speaker begins his actual testament, which continues until line 94.

18–24   The speaker consigns his soul to his lord's wine cellar, there to remain until the Day of Judgment. This obliquely touches upon an interesting point of medieval theology — the matter of where the soul resides until the body and soul are once again united for the final judgment. The speaker has his own unique ideas on this matter, at least as it pertains to himself.

20   *Into my lordis wyne cellar*. Perhaps this verse alludes to Canticle of Canticles 2:4.

24   Sweet Cuthbert has never been identified, and most commentators believe he is a taverner or a cellar-keeper. If the speaker is a member of a monastic house, then very likely Cuthbert would be the cellarer, the official in charge of overseeing the wine cellar. Cuthbert, the name of a celebrated northern British saint, whose shrine is at Durham, would be a fitting name for a monastic official. In Chaucer, the saint's name carries a derogatory sexual connotation (cut beard = have sex) as John swears to Simkin "by Seint Cuthbert" before swiving the Miller's wife in The Reeve's Tale (*CT* I[A]4127).

24–32   There is no love lost between the speaker and Cuthbert, since Cuthbert keeps a careful watch over the cellar and knows the kind of fellow Andro is.

32   *bed of stait*. The bed of a great lord or lady, which would be hung with costly, lavishly decorated fabrics.

33–40   He stipulates that he wants his body to be buried, not in a churchyard, but in the refuse heap outside the town of Ayr, where the leavings of food and drink might be thrown over his face.

36   Ayr, in the county of Ayrshire in the southwest of Scotland was, like Aberdeen, a royal burgh. The Kennedys were one of Ayr's most prominent families.

41–48   In the previous two stanzas Andro consigned his soul and his body to their final resting places, and here he consigns his heart. But who is his "consort Jacob" to whom he gives his faithless heart? Bawcutt suggests it is either his mistress or his wife (interpreting *Jacobe* as the dative form of *Jacoba*) (Bw 2.330). But if it is his wife, why would she not retain the guardianship of his children (lines 91–92)? Are they illegitimate? Perhaps Jacob is a monastic brother with whom Andro had (at least ostensibly) a close friendship.

49–56   The *best aucht* (line 49) is a person's most valuable possession, to be claimed by the head of one's family upon one's death. The problem here is that Andro does not know who that is, for the matter of his family origins, as the first stanza indicated, is quite murky.

46   Compare Jeremias 9:6.

50   The Latin here does not parse, but the sense seems to be a gloss on the lines before and after the phrase. *Caupe* refers to the Highland custom of paying tribute to one's

393

head of kin. Bawcutt notes that the practice "was abolished by Parliament in 1490, but persisted into the late sixteenth century" (Bw 2.330).

51–52   The sense is: "but I no more know / Who that is than I would put a curse on my own head."

53–56   The lord he openly claims as his earthly lord is presumably the head of the Kennedy family. He says that they are as alike as two similar kinds of sieves, or as two trees that grow in the same forest — but no one else shares his opinion (line 54). "Kennedy is the sort of person who boasts, without justification, of being related to great men" (Bw 2.330).

57–64   This stanza contains a direct attack upon "William, the master of St. Anthony's" — a man who never tells lies except when the holly is green! (Compare Whiting H417.) William Gray has not been identified, but it seems unlikely that so specific an identification would have been fabricated.

65–72   All of his falsity he leaves to the friars, who are portrayed as masters of deceit and hypocrisy. Dunbar's attitude toward the friars is consistently negative and hostile; compare especially "Tidings from the Session" (Poem 74), lines 45–49, and "How Dunbar Was Desired to Be a Friar" (Poem 76) in its entirety.

68   Compare Psalm 111:9 in the Vulgate.

73–80   *Jok Fule* (Jock Fool) receives Andro's foolishness, for Andro is a bigger fool than Jok. Indeed, *Jok Fule* is only pretending to be a fool, to his considerable profit. Dunbar may or may not have had a specific fool in mind. In The Miller's Tale Alison refers to Absolom as "Jakke fool" (*CT* I[A]3708).

79   I.e., "pulls the wool over my lord's eye."

81–88   John Clerk has not been identified; the term *master* (line 81) might refer either to his degree of education or to his clerical position. Compare "The Lament for the Makars" (Poem 14), line 58.

84   One wonders why this man is said to be the cause of Andro's death.

88   This is a much-debated line; perhaps it completes the dog and swine metaphor of the previous verses. The dog's teeth are writing all over the swine's body — writing

without stopping (i.e., without a fixed day — *sine de*), or without including a single "d" (*de*) in the text.

89–92   Everything else, including his children, will go into the care of his lord — who perhaps in this case is his immediate superior in the monastery, if the speaker belongs to one. His children pose an interesting problem. Very possibly *Ade* and *Kytte* and "all the others" are illegitimate. (*Ade* was a nickname for Adam, *Kytte* for Katherine.)

93–116   The funeral Andro desires is much more in keeping with the Celtic tradition of the wake than with normal Christian burial.

101   *playand cop out*. Playing "empty the cup" may or may not refer to a specific drinking game. Compare "To the King" (Poem 40), line 13.

104   Compare Psalm 101:10 in the Vulgate — "For I did eat ashes like bread, and mingled my drink with weeping."

106   This famous Latin phrase comes from the Office for the Dead.

110   The "ale wisp" is what in Chaucer is called "the bush" or the "ale stake." It is the small bundle of straw that is displayed when an alehouse is open for business.

116   This final Latin phrase, taken from the burial service, derives from Job 10:8–9. Compare also Psalm 118:73 in the Vulgate.

81. *Dunbar's Dirge*

This comic and parodic poem consists of two main sections. Lines 1–28 are an introductory letter in which the speaker urges the king and his courtiers to free themselves from the pain and purgatorial bleakness of Stirling and return to the heavenly bliss of Edinburgh. What then follows is Dunbar's "dirge," an elaborate parody of the Office of the Dead, used here to commemorate the released soul's journey to the joy and bliss of the divine court of Heaven. The poem is dominated by two themes. One is the comic comparison between the cities of Edinburgh and Stirling, with Stirling coming off much the worse. The other is the clever parody of religious ritual and the liturgy, a medieval literary tradition more frequently encountered among Latin works than vernacular ones. According to Bawcutt, "Dunbar simulates the striking threefold structure of Matins of the Dead, which in its full form consisted of three nocturnes, each of which contained three lessons and three psalms. He does not parody the lessons, drawn from the book of Job, but substitutes prayers of his own invention; he also devises three *responsiones*, whose metrical form recalls the *repetenda*, or repeated short phrases, common in responsories. The poem is also punctuated by the liturgical forumulae *Iube domine* and *Tu autem*" (Bw 2.490).

Commentators have offered a good deal of speculation about the poem's historical context. James IV made frequent visits to Stirling for a variety of reasons. It is well-known that James had a mistress in Stirling, but he also often made a Lenten retreat to the friary of the Observant Franciscans, a religious house that he himself had founded near Stirling. That might accord well with the poem's references to hermits and to the meagerness of the food and drink at Stirling. On the other hand, the reference to Yule in line 89 suggests that the season may be fall, not spring, which would link the poem more to the liturgical season of Advent than to Lent. The poem is primarily in octosyllabic couplets, with interspersed triolets. MF, B, and R. Mc30, K22, Bw84.

3   *Commendis us.* A formula commonly used at the beginning of letters, meaning "recommend ourselves," i.e., "we send greetings."

6   *Striveling.* An earlier spelling of Stirling; the rhyme sounds in lines 98–101 provide evidence for the pronunciation.

9–18   These verses may refer to the simple lives of the friars with whom the king is in residence; or they may be wholly ironic, alluding to the fact that the king is actually enjoying himself a great deal. One of the well-known reasons for his trips to Stirling was to visit his mistress Margaret Drummond.

18   *stok and stone.* Literally, "stumps and stones," but a common phrase, especially in Lydgate (see *Fall of Princes* lines 2834–35; *Resson and Sensualite*, line 6411, and various minor works), meaning lifeless things or desolate countryside; compare Henryson's *Orpheus*, line 179. See also *Pearl*, line 380, *Cleanness*, lines 1344, 1522, and 1720; *TC* 3.589, *Sir Orfeo*, line 332, and romances such as *Sir Firumbras*, line 201, and the *Avowying of Arthur*, line 187.

23   *dirige.* The first word of the opening antiphon at Matins for the Office of the Dead — *Dirige, Deus meus, in conspectu tuo viam meam* ("Direct, O God, my way in Your sight").

30   *blissit.* The "Blessed Virgin" is a common epithet for Mary.

31 The angels of Heaven were traditionally grouped into nine orders, beginning with the angels and archangels. Compare "On the Nativity of Christ" (Poem 1), lines 9–10, and the notes to those lines.

38 Pious phrases such as these are often found at the end of works as benedictions. Compare Lindsay's *Squire Meldrum*, line 1593, and *CT* I[A]174 and VII[B²]3320.

39 *Tu autem, Domine*. This abbreviation of the liturgical formula is from the daily service of Matins, as *Tu autem Domine miserere nobis*, "Do Thou, O Lord, have mercy on us," is the *Iube Domine* of line 44. See Bw 2.490 and 2.491n39, as well as Bawcutt (1992), pp. 200–01, for discussion of the liturgical formula, which would normally precede and follow each lesson.

47–48 This brief catalogue lists those ranking highest in Heaven. The patriarchs are the founding fathers of Israel from the book of Genesis, figures such as Abraham, Isaac, and Jacob; the prophets would include Old Testament figures such as Daniel, Isaias, and Jeremias. Line 48 reflects a threefold classification of saints into martyrs, confessors, and holy virgins.

58 Bawcutt notes that financial records show how popular the wines of Anjou were in Scotland (Bw 2.492).

62 The great parish church of Edinburgh was dedicated to St. Giles, making him an appropriate saint to invoke in the desire to bring the king back to the city. His September 1 feast day was celebrated with processions through the city. Bawcutt (Bw 2.492) notes: "St. Giles was believed to have special power in obtaining forgiveness for sinners, because of his successful intercession for Charlemagne" (see *The Golden Legend* 5.84–85).

70 *sternis sevin*. Here the phrase refers to the spheres of the seven moveable "stars" — the five visible planets and the sun and the moon. The saints in Heaven would dwell in the highest Heaven (the *coelum empyreum*), located above the seven spheres of the planets, the eighth sphere of the fixed stars (the zodiac), and the ninth sphere known as the *primum mobile*.

78 The Archangel Gabriel was traditionally viewed as God's primary messenger (compare Daniel 9:21 and Luke 1:19, 26).

85–90 Compare Chaucer's *TC* 1.638–39.

103–04   These verses parody some of the petitions contained in the *Pater Noster*, the Lord's Prayer.

112–13   This is the second verse of Psalm 101 in the Vulgate, which is found in some versions of the Office of the Dead (Bw 2.493).

82. *The Twa Cummars* [*This lang Lentrin it makis me lene*]

This poem belongs to a minor comic genre in which carousing women, with drink-loosed tongues, speak derisively about their husbands. John Skelton's *The Tunning of Elynor Rumming* and Dunbar's own *Tretis of the Tua Mariit Wemen and the Wedo* (Poem 84) are the two most famous examples, but several others survive from late medieval literature (compare *IMEV* 1362 and 1852). In the case of this poem, the satire is also directed at those who create flimsy excuses in order to avoid participating in the Lenten fast required of all Christians. The poem survives in four MS copies, the earliest being the one in the Aberdeen Minute Book. Six 5-line stanzas rhyming *aabaB*. Aberdeen, B, MF, and R. Mc46, K73, Bw57.

1–2   Ash Wednesday is the first day of the forty-day Lenten season that culminates on Easter Sunday. The joke is that the two gossips have begun to violate the Lenten fast within a few hours of its beginning. Although the drinking of wine was not totally forbidden during Lent (the eating of meat *was* forbidden), sobriety was the rule and abstinence the ideal.

2   *cummaris*. "Gossips" or "female confidants"; like the word "gossip," *cummar* originally meant "godmother" but soon came to mean "close female friend."

5   It has not taken long for her to begin complaining about "the long Lenten season" — since it has only just begun.

7–8   Although the woman is "great and fat," she contends that observing the rigors of Lent will surely endanger her health, given her enfeebled physical condition.

9   *lat preif of that*. I.e., "Just look at me — there's the proof." Compare Lindsay's *Satyre*, Proclamation, line 225.

13–14   Her mother's slenderness, her friend alleges, was due to her refined taste in wines — she restricted her drinking to the sweet, fortified wine called malmsey; it was an expensive, imported wine, the preference for people of style and estate. See the

Alliterative Morte Arthure, line 236, and *Sir Degrevaunt*, line 1431. Bawcutt notes that "the boozy gossips of Noah's wife in play 3 of *The Chester Miracle Cycle* likewise prefer Malmsey to cheaper wine" (Bw 2.411).

18–19   There are two jokes here. The first is her advice that she should refrain from fasting (in Lent one refrains *by* fasting); and the second is that her husband should bear the burden of her refraining from fasting, causing him to experience the pain that a person should experience themselves during Lent.

23   The women's disparagement of their husbands' sexual prowess is a basic feature of this comic genre. Compare also May's appraisal of January's sexual performance in The Merchant's Tale: "She preyseth nat his pleyyng worth a bene" (*CT* IV [E]1854). Compare Whiting B92.

24   Compare *The Debate of the Carpenter's Tools*, lines 229–32.

29   "By which to mend they had great hope" — by forcing themselves to do all this drinking, they have high hopes of alleviating their debilitating leanness.

30   As he often does, Dunbar slightly alters the final refrain, signaling the end of the poem.

83. *The Flyting of Dunbar and Kennedy*

If *The Tretis of the Tua Mariit Wemen and the Wedo* (Poem 84) is Dunbar's most sexually explicit poem, *The Flyting of Dunbar and Kennedy* is his most scatologically explicit poem, what one critic, Tom Scott, has amusingly called "the most repellent poem . . . in any language" (p. 175). In contrast to all the other poems in this volume, however, the *Flyting* cannot be attributed exclusively to Dunbar, for Walter Kennedy, one of Dunbar's contemporaries, probably composed 328 of the poem's 552 verses. It is possible, in fact, that the poem was intended as a public entertainment, perhaps one in which the two contesting poets actually performed their parts before the court of James IV. Modern critical response to the poem has varied widely. Some readers and critics find the *Flyting* offensive — as much for its social attitudes as for its scatology — but others consider it to be one of the great comic poems of the later Middle Ages. Somewhat surprising, perhaps, is the fact that although the poem contains much that is coarse and vulgar, it appears to have been very well received throughout the sixteenth century. It was one of a small number of Dunbar's poems to appear in an early printed text; its text appears in both B and MF, and it inspired several imitations from Dunbar's Scottish successors (see Bw 2.428).

The genre of the *Flyting* has been much discussed, and scholars cite a wide range of possible influences and literary precursors. The poem clearly shares some of the basic characteristics of the medieval debate poem in that it is a verbal sparring match in which each speaker tries to demonstrate the superiority of his views to those of his opponent. In this poem, however, the main point seems to be not so much for each contestant to demonstrate the superiority of his views as it is to demonstrate his superior talent at heaping comic abuse on the other while at the same time displaying his poetic virtuosity. It is possible, therefore, that the poem was a conscious attempt to revive the ancient Celtic tradition of a public "slanging contest" between court bards or satirists. In this respect, the poem provides "a striking example of how orality can shape a written text" (Robichaud, p. 10). Walter J. Ong comments on the agonistic nature of oral civilizations that so mark flytings.[1] Slanging contests are often mentioned in the early Irish and Welsh narratives; compare, for example, Taliesin's virtuoso performance at the court of Maelgwn Gwynedd in the Welsh "Tale of Taliesin" (*The Mabinogi and Other Welsh Tales*, trans. Patrick K. Ford [Los Angeles: University of California Press, 1977], pp. 171–77). Also see "The Verse Debate between Dafydd ap Gwilym and Gruffudd Gryg" for another "slanging contest" between two well-known Celtic poets.[2] The technique of the *Flyting* relies on the additive rather than the subordinate for its effect, piling on insult upon insult. To a modern reader the effect "may seem overwrought and excessive, but in a residually oral culture, overstatement is a virtue if it is more memorable than plain presentation of opinion" (Robichaud, p. 11). The "cumulative nastiness" is created largely though alliterative combinations of adjective noun phrases using many reduplicative rhyming insults, puns, scatology, name calling, and verbal sexual assault.[3] As to the accuracy or directed purpose of

---

[1] *Fighting for Life: Contest, Sexuality, and Consciousness* (Ithaca, NY: Cornell University Press, 1981), pp. 124–25. See also *Orality and Literacy: The Technologizing of the Word* (London: Routledge, 2002), pp. 43–44.

[2] *Dafydd ap Gwilym: The Poems*, trans. and commentary, Richard Morgan Loomis (Binghamton: Medieval and Renaissance Texts and Studies, 1982), pp. 263–76. The two poets take turns composing *cywydd* (one of the most popular verse forms in Welsh poetry) of seemingly minor obscenity compared to Dunbar; Dafydd, however, gets the last word in: "very great hatred, lord of terror, / Anus of a goose, withdraw from between me and the man" (p. 276). It is worth noting, perhaps, that, like Dunbar's tribute to Kennedy in "The Lament for the Makars" (Poem 14), Gruffudd also praised his former rival in his elegy "The Yew Tree above Dafydd's Grave" (Loomis, p. 288).

[3] Insult slinging is in general out of place in the deodorized confines of modern American life, though the tradition, celebrated in such Shakespearian moments as *1 Henry IV*'s battle of wits between Falstaff and Hal, does survive. For a modern comparable version of a poetic slanging contest, see Spielberg's

the abuse each poet shovels on the other, see Scott (p. 176), Baxter (p. 67), and Bawcutt (1992, p. 7). Robinson, following Bawcutt, explains the insults as caricatures of sorts — severely exaggerated but accurate enough to be recognizable (p. 275).

Dunbar's *Flyting* has a very simple structure. First there are two short sections in which the disputants exchange their initial challenges, and then there are two very lengthy sections in which each one takes a turn at reviling the other. In both cases Dunbar speaks first and Kennedy second, a pattern that would seem to give Kennedy something of an advantage. The opening verses in Dunbar's initial speech indicate that he is responding to something Kennedy and his colleague Quintin have previously said or written, but that may simply be a device by which to initiate the contest. The poem ends without any concluding materials other than the final rubric: "Juge ye now heir quha gat the war" — "Judge you now here who got the worst."

Walter Kennedy, Dunbar's opponent in the *Flyting*, was a member of a prominent Ayrshire family and a graduate of Glasgow University (1478). The Kennedy family's land holdings were primarily in Carrick (located in the southern part of Ayreshire) and in Galloway, areas which at this time were still primarily Gaelic-speaking. Kennedy had a wife and a son, so he was probably not a member of the priesthood, though he did come to hold important church positions at Douglas and at Glasgow. Like Dunbar he was also a poet, and Dunbar speaks affectionately of Kennedy in "Lament for the Makars" (Poem 14), lines 89–92, as do Douglas (*The Palis of Honoure*, line 923) and Lindsay (*Papyngo*, lines 15–16). Here, though, Dunbar portrays him as being a poor, raggedy, thieving Gaelic bard. Kennedy, on the other hand, portrays Dunbar as a dwarfish benefice-beggar belonging to a family with a long history of treachery to Scotland. Kennedy's vitriolic attack on Dunbar may allude to actual events in Dunbar's life, though the exaggerated nature of his scurrilous "exposé" requires scholars to be cautious in drawing any firm conclusions from Kennedy's remarks. For a fuller account of Kennedy and his family, see Bw 2.427.

One of the main points of the poem is to allow the two poets to display their poetic talents. Dunbar's verses tend to be wittier and tighter, perhaps, and to demonstrate his particular aptitude for clever wordplay. Kennedy's verses are more discursive and long-winded, and he seems intent on displaying his learnedness through the frequent use of literary allusions, some of which are quite obscure. Both poets end their performances with fairly similar grand finales, grand finales that in both cases contain a profusion of internal rhyme. But on the whole the styles and techniques of the two poets seem to differ fairly significantly, and there is little reason to accept Reiss' suggestion that Dunbar is actually the author of the entire poem (p. 55).

Hook, in which Peter Pan and his opponent verbally battle each other for social leadership. While this flyting does not include the scatological and sexual references (the film is directed toward a young audience), the point of the battle is the same — to heap insult after insult on the opponent and let the audience judge the winner. The film even occasionally shares some of the internal rhymes with Dunbar's *Flyting*, as when Peter crows "You rude, crude, lewd piece of pre-chewed food!"

The *Flyting* contains 552 verses in 8-line stanzas, rhyming *ababbcbc* or *ababbccb*; 224 verses are attributed to Dunbar, and 328 verses are attributed to Kennedy. The text here presented is a composite, following Bawcutt: Lines 1–315 are based upon B; lines 316–552 are based upon CM. Mc6, K23, Bw65.

1   *Schir Johine the Ros*. Dunbar is addressing Sir John the Ross, his close friend and
           possibly his sometime collaborator (compare Kennedy's remarks in lines 39–40);
           Ross is included among the poets whose deaths Dunbar mourns in "The Lament for
           the Makars" (Poem 14), line 83.

1–5   The poet claims to be responding to something (possibly a poem) written by
           Kennedy and Quintin in which they praise themselves at the expense of other poets.
           Little is known of Quintin, though he was probably Kennedy's kinsman and his
           collaborator. It is possible that he is the Quintyne Schaw included in the list of
           deceased poets in "The Lament for the Makars" (Poem 14), line 86. Bawcutt doubts
           that he is the same man as the "Quenetyne" mentioned in line 37 of "Sir Thomas
           Norny" (Poem 55).

1–24   The first three stanzas provide a context and a justification for the verbal warfare to
           come. In them Dunbar is apparently making a public pronouncement to Sir John
           Ross, his friend and kinsman, commenting on the general grievance he feels toward
           Kennedy and Quintin, who in their pride have elevated themselves to a status above
           the stars. Dunbar serves warning of what he might be forced to do if they were to
           speak negatively about him. Dunbar's threat provokes Kennedy to do just that —
           although one suspects that this was all done by pre-arrangement.

4–12   Bawcutt remarks on the mock apocalyptic tone which, though comic, is, nonethe-
           less, ominous. "No reader is disposed to laugh at the menacing figure of the devil
           in Dunbar's poem on the Resurrection" (1989, p. 165). Dunbar seems perpetually
           interested in the world of evil spirits and the uncertainty about their nature. N.b., the
           flying Abbot of Tungland or his references to Titivullus (Bawcutt, 1989, pp.
           165–68).

6–7   Dunbar compares Kennedy's pride to that which caused Lucifer's fall; compare
           Isaias 14:12–14. See Whiting L587 and Lindsay, *Monarche*, lines 867–85.

9–15   The poet uses generalized apocalyptic imagery to suggest the catastrophic con-
           sequences of what he might write; these images do not have specific biblical
           sources, but compare verses such as Isaias 13:10–13 and Apocalypse 8:7–12.

14   *The se sould birn, the mone sould thoill ecclippis.* Compare line 489; and compare also "Of a Black Moor" (Poem 71), line 13.

16   *Sa loud of cair the commoun bell sould clynk.* This refers to the alarm bell sounded to warn the public of an impending disaster such as might be caused by fire or armed threat; but the verse seems to be intentionally ludicrous — in light of all that he has just described.

17–24   Dunbar initially indicates his reluctance to take part in any bardic flyting contest (lines 17–21), probably to suggest his disdain toward such an unworthy and uncouth activity. He concedes, though, that he will participate if his opponents force him into it — thus placing the onus upon them. Compare Douglas, *Eneados* 1.Prol.153, and Lindsay, *Complaint*, line 31.

25–48   Kennedy's response, also in three stanzas, balances Dunbar's opening statement and serves to conclude the introductory section of the poem. Dunbar has challenged Kennedy to throw down the verbal gauntlet, and Kennedy does not hesitate to do so.

25–26   The sense is: "Beshitten Dunbar, against whom do you make your boast, / Claiming the right to write such scabby scrolls (i.e., writings)?"

29   *Mandrag mymmerkin.* I.e., "dwarfish creature resembling a man"; this is the first of Kennedy's numerous references to Dunbar's dwarf-like stature. The mandrake is a European herb whose forked root was thought to resemble the body of a man. Compare John Donne's "get with child a mandrake root" ("Song," line 2).

29–30   These verses contain the first of Kennedy's several mocking references to Dunbar's university education. Here he claims that Dunbar was given a master's degree only as a scornful joke.

30   *Thrys scheild.* "Thriced shilled" or "peeled"; i.e., often exposed. "The phrase is agricultural in origin" (Bw 2.431).

36   *Ignorant elf, aip, owll irregular.* This verse also ridicules Dunbar's physical appearance by likening him to an elf (a comment on his small stature) and to an ape and an owl (a comment on his ugliness).

37   *Skaldit skaitbird and commoun skamelar.* Compare *King Berdok*, lines 26–27.

38 *Wanfukkit funling that Natour maid ane yrle.* "A misbegotten foundling that Nature made a dwarf." The prefix *wan-* in the verb *wanfukkit* means "poorly" or "badly," and the second element in *wanfukkit* is the vulgar term it appears to be; compare "In a Secret Place" (Poem 72), line 13.

41–48 In the final stanza of his opening salvo, Kennedy urges Dunbar to stop the action he has initiated and to make recompense to Quintin for having slandered him. Otherwise, he says, Dunbar will rue the day he was born.

43 *walidrag.* The term, which can mean "undergrown," is one of Kennedy's many insulting references to Dunbar's small stature.

49 *Iersche brybour baird.* Before launching into a string of scurrilous invective, Dunbar first establishes Kennedy's professional identity — he is an Irish (i.e., Gaelic) "vagabond bard, a vile beggar in rags."

49–64 All of the verses in these rhymed stanzas are perfect examples of the alliterative long line of ME. See A. A. MacDonald, 1994.

49–248 In this group of twenty-five stanzas Dunbar takes his turn at heaping invective upon Kennedy. In doing so, he draws heavily upon the stereotyped figure of the dirty, impoverished, dishonest Highlander, and he depicts Kennedy as a Gaelic bard — an idle, begging wanderer considered by Lowlanders to be thoroughly disreputable. Dunbar's imagery in these verses is frequently drawn from rural farm life in order to portray Kennedy as a barefoot yokel.

50 *Cuntbittin.* Probably means "impotent," though possibly "cuckolded," "syphilitic," or "pussy-whipped."

51–52 *Denseman . . . gulesnowt dynd.* "A Danishman"; there are records of Danish pirates having been executed in Edinburgh upon the execution wheel, a brutal instrument of torture and execution. The bodies of the dead often remain tied to these wheels and were feasted upon by birds. (Compare lines 423–24.) Both Kinsley and Bawcutt gloss *gulesnowt* as "yellow nose" — suggesting perhaps "ghoulish"; or maybe they have in mind a (sea)gull's beak. But *gules* is also a heraldic term (here used ironically?) meaning "red," in which case a "red nose" might imply a drunk. The drunkenness of pirates is mythic — "yo ho ho and a bottle of rum," etc. Certainly a "Denseman" would not be noted for abstinence. Robinson, on the other hand, sees Kennedy's *gulesnowt* (ghoul-snout) as a deformity resembling symptoms of leprosy,

404

syphilis, or tuberculosis, since "erosion of the nasal septum" is an indication of any one of these diseases. "Of course," she adds, "he might just have had an ugly nose" (p. 278). Perhaps there is wordplay on *gleddis*, which could mean "glowing red coals" as well as "kites."

56   *Lawland ers wald mak a bettir noyis.* "Dunbar uses the pun on Erse [Gaelic] / arse to suggest that Lowland farting is more pleasant than Highland speech" (Robichaud, p. 12).

64   I.e., "a mere wisp of straw may wipe away your wit and wisdom." (Wisps of straw could be used as toilet paper.)

65   *Thow speiris, dastard, gif I dar with thee fecht.* Dunbar is apparently referring back to Kennedy's original challenge in lines 1–2.

66   *Dagone dowbart.* Here used to mean "monster," but stemming from Dagon, the name of the Philistine deity in 1 Kings (1 Samuel) 5:2–7; *dowbart* is an abusive term of obscure origin. *DOST* glosses the sense as "a dull or stupid person."

71–72   Dunbar says he will cause him to cry out by whipping him with a dog leash; more noble weapons — such as a knife, sword, or ax — would be neither necessary nor appropriate for a cur such as Kennedy.

73   *crop and rute.* Literally, "shoots and root," but meaning something in its entirety. Here it implies that he is both the cause and the result of treason and treachery. Compare Chaucer's *TC* 2.348.

76   The verse reiterates what Dunbar has already suggested about Kennedy in line 50.

77–80   Here Dunbar accuses Kennedy of attempting to poison "our lord's chief [or 'our chief lords'?] in Paisley," possibly an allusion to a specific event, though that remains uncertain. Kennedy appears to be rebutting this charge in lines 417–20.

81–82   Dunbar suggests that Kennedy's physical appearance offers a clear indication of his malicious nature. The pseudo-science of physiognomy, which maintained that a person's external body offers clues to one's own inner nature, remained popular in Scotland in the late Middle Ages.

83   *glengoir loun.* Bawcutt emends to *ganyelon,* reasoning that Ganelon, the arch-traitor
      of the *Song of Roland,* better accords with the accusations of treachery. But the
      reading of the MS seems to fit the specific context of this stanza better, where the
      emphasis is on Kennedy's ugliness and physical abnormality — his "frawart
      phisnomy" (line 81).

84   *fen.* "Midden" (dunghill), not "marsh"; compare line 517, and Henryson's *Fables,*
      line 111. Compare also Whiting F120.

85   Dunbar's grievances against Kennedy also include Kennedy's attacks upon
      Dunbar's friends.

89–90   Dunbar suggests that Kennedy delayed making his malicious allegations until Dun-
         bar was on shipboard, thus giving Dunbar no chance to respond to them.

90–96   The stormy voyage Dunbar mentions here was probably a real one, though scholars
         are unsure of the date and have discussed at length the geographical possibilities.
         This is probably the same voyage that Kennedy depicts so graphically (!) in lines
         449–72.

91   The allusions to the classical gods Aeolus and Neptune, who cause this tempest at
      sea, provide a heroic coloration to the ill-fated voyage. Bawcutt suggests that these
      verses recall, "imperfectly, an episode in *Aeneid* 1.81–141 where Aeolus shatters
      the ships of Aeneas and black clouds obliterate the sun" (Bw 2.433).

94   *Seland.* Perhaps Zealand, the island on which Copenhagen stands, though more
      likely it is the area of Holland called Zeeland; *Yetland* (in the MS *ȝetland*) may be
      either Jutland (in Denmark), or Shetland.

97   *Thow callis thee rethore with thy goldin lippis.* Compare Kennedy's reference to
      himself in line 500 as "of rhetory the rose."

99   *gluntoch, with thy giltin hippis.* "You are knobby-kneed with your kilted hips" (?);
      if *giltin* does mean "kilted" (i.e., "tucked up") here, as the context suggests, it would
      be one of the earliest occurrences of the term. There is probably wordplay, also, on
      "golden lips" and "gilded hips." William Neill, on the other hand, traces *gluntoch*
      to Gaelic *glum dubh,* "black-kneed," suggesting that it "refers to a man who wore
      no breeches [. . .] and in those unhygienic days black knees would be common" (as

cited by Roderick MacDonald, p. 84). Neill glosses *giltin* as "yellow," implying old and jaundiced. See line 104.

104   *thy bawis hingis throw thy breik.* Refers to the fact that the kilted Highlander commonly wore no undergarments.

106–12   In these verses Dunbar disparagingly suggests that "flyting" is an art form in which Gaelic poets or bards took particular delight.

112   *Carrik.* The southern district of Ayrshire; it remained primarily Gaelic-speaking until after Dunbar's time. It was "a lowly populated area of upland pasture" (Bw 2.434).

113   Taking a dog out to defecate was a task given to the lowest ranking servants. Compare *The Flyting betwixt Polwart and Montgomerie*, in *The Poems of Alexander Montgomerie*, ed. David Irving (Edinburgh: J. Ballantyne and Co., 1821), line 370.

115–20   Dunbar depicts Kennedy as a country peasant who did not bother to work hard during the summer and thus starves in the winter.

121   Dunbar frequently remarks on Kennedy's dirty, unkempt, and lice-ridden body.

123–26   Kennedy's ugly visage is here compared to that of the men who persecuted the saints. St. Lawrence was martyred in Rome by being roasted on a grid. In some accounts and visual depictions, John the Baptist was blindfolded before being beheaded. St. Augustine of Canterbury, according to an early legend, was struck by attackers who wielded fish tails. And St. Bartholomew was flayed alive before being crucified.

128   *haggeis.* Haggis — made from chopped entrails, spices, eggs, and milk that are cooked in a sheep's stomach — wasn't exclusively a Scottish dish at this time. Dunbar is disparaging it for being peasant's fare.

129   *na man comptis thee ane kers.* "No one values you worth a piece of cress." Compare Whiting C546.

131   *kis his ers.* Compare *Towneley Plays* 2.61 and *CT* VI(C)948.

141   *Greitand in Galloway lyk to ane gallow breid.* Note the wordplay on *Galloway* and *gallow*.

143   Compare "A Ballad of the Friar of Tungland" (Poem 54), line 8.

145   *Ersch katherene.* William Neill points out that "*katherene* is not a woman's name; rather, an alternate form of *cateran*, a Highland marauder or a band of them." (As cited by Roderick MacDonald, pp. 84–85.) But, Roderick MacDonald continues, "is it not possible that Kennedy's wife may in reality have been named Catherine, and that Dunbar was guilty of perpetrating a rather low-grade pun?" (p. 85). As Bawcutt observes, this verse "sums up Lowlanders' view of the Highlander" (Bw 2.435), carrying a tartan bag and wearing shoes of undressed hide.

         polk breik. Often said to be nether garments made from sacking (polk britches). But possibly a variant on *pol breac*, in Gaelic "a speckled purse." See Roderick MacDonald, p. 84.

148   "There is nothing except lice and long fingernails among (the two of) you" — another of Dunbar's barbs about Kennedy's lack of cleanliness.

149–52   Although *heggirbald* (line 149) is an obscure term, these verses involving the stealing of hens, lamb, and kids suggest the predatory habits of a fox or wolf.

150–52   Compare the effect of the Summoner's face in frightening children (*CT* I[A]628). Here Kennedy's ugly face frightens mother goats and their offspring.

153–60   In this stanza Dunbar directs his abuse at Kennedy's home — which he says was formerly used to house lepers — and at his wife. Robinson observes that Dunbar frequently connects Kennedy to lepers in both his insulting physical descriptions of his rival and in his implications that Kennedy is guilty of the sin of lust. These insinuations build up repeatedly until the overt reference to Lazarus in stanza 21, at which point it should be clear to the audience that Dunbar is accusing Kennedy of being a leper. Whether or not this accusation is accurate, what is important is the difference it reveals about the attitudes of insulting between medieval and modern culture. While Dunbar's references to Kennedy's numerous and chronic gastrointestinal problems are "delightfully shocking" to its medieval audience, they are perhaps (depending, of course, on the reader) more unpleasantly shocking to us. In contrast, the accusation of leprosy would be much more "vicious and damning" than revealing to an audience the fact that Kennedy's wife has to clean his beshitten rear end for him. See Robinson, pp. 275–82.

154   For medieval attitudes concerning leprosy, see the introduction to Denton Fox's edition of Henryson, pp. lxxxvii–xc, and also Peter Richards, *The Medieval Leper and His Northern Heirs* (Rochester, NY: D. S. Brewer, 2000).

155   *of blis als bair.* "Devoid of bliss"; compare Henryson, *Fables*, line 1701.

158   Bawcutt is probably right in suggesting that *dowsy* means "harlot" and refers to Kennedy's wife (Bw 2.435).

160   *scaryne bell.* A bell rung at the consecration of the Eucharist. Compare "A Ballad of the Friar of Tungland" (Poem 54), lines 49–50.

161–76 In this pair of stanzas Dunbar depicts Kennedy as a spirit that has returned from the grave — a parody of the "warning from beyond the grave" motif that occurs in penitential works such as Robert Henryson's poem "The Thre Deid Polis."

161   Dunbar's depiction of Kennedy as Lazarus draws upon both of the biblical figures of that name, the Lazarus whom Christ raised from death (John 11:17) and the leper who lay at the rich man's gate (Luke 16:20). It was common for these two figures to be conflated in the Middle Ages.

171   *ane saffrone bag.* Small bags containing saffron were often worn about the neck; the yellow spice was used medicinally as well as for cooking.

172   *spreit of Gy.* In a popular work composed by the Dominican friar Jean Gobi, Gy (or Guido) of Corvo was a tormented spirit who returned to earth to warn his wife by describing the horrors of Purgatory. For a ME version, see *The Gast of Gy*, in *Three Purgatory Poems*, ed. Edward Foster (Kalamazoo, MI: Medieval Institute Publications, 2004), pp. 15–107. A vernacular version of the story occurs in *Scotichronicon* 13.6–9. Compare Lindsay's *Dreme*, line 16, and *Crying of ane Play*, line 14.

177–92 These stanzas contain Dunbar's depiction of Kennedy as a tall, thin scarecrow of a man; they provide a sharp contrast to Kennedy's later depiction of Dunbar as a tiny dwarf of a man.

179 *Hard hurcheoun hirpland, hippit as ane harrow.* Compare Henryson's *Fables*, line 903.

184 *carrybald.* An obscure term of abuse; it also occurs in line 94 of *The Tretis of the Tua Mariit Wemen and the Wedo* (Poem 84).

185–92 The figurative description of Kennedy in this stanza is that of a bony, shriveled old horse caked with mud and wildflowers.

191–92 Bawcutt notes that the images in these verbs are culinary. "Kennedy lies in a saffron sauce . . . sprinkled with powder made from primroses, and scented with cloves" (Bw 2.437).

193–200 Here Dunbar briefly engages in excremental humor, something Kennedy does later in the poem to a much greater extent.

198 I.e., "You shall (receive it back) again from more witnesses than just me"; what is rebounding against Kennedy is his earlier description of Dunbar as "dirtin" and "dirtfast" in lines 25 and 33.

201–32 The emphasis in this group of stanzas is upon Kennedy's extreme rusticity, which makes him an object of scorn and comic amusement in the more sophisticated urban environs of Edinburgh.

205 "Now in the uplands you live on rubbed wheat"; rubbing wheat between one's hands was a very primitive method of extracting the grain.

209 The identity of Strait Gibbons is uncertain, though a man by that name received a payment in 1503 by royal command. He may have been a court entertainer, very possibly a clown.

209–10 Never having ridden a horse reflects on Kennedy's lack of knightly qualities as well as on his poverty.

211 Edinburgh Cross, the high market cross in the center of the city, was a site for official proclamations, public punishment of felons, and the like. Thus Kennedy has brought the mud of the country into the symbolic heart of the city. Compare "To the Merchants of Edinburgh" (Poem 75), lines 22–23.

213   Dunbar asserts that Kennedy has cushioned the inside of his boots with straw that sticks out through the worn spots.

219   Kennedy is mobbed by the lads of Edinburgh like an owl mobbed by crows. Compare "A Ballad of the Friar of Tungland" (Poem 54), lines 73 ff., and the note to those lines.

220   *bichis*. "Bitches" literally means "female dogs," though here it probably means "dogs" generally; it may have been chosen for the sake of the alliteration. The dogs are excited by the smell of Kennedy's deer-hide boots.

221   "Then old women cry out, 'Keep your kerchiefs in the dark'" — i.e., hide your finery, or bring in your laundry. This gibe at Kennedy as a likely thief of clothing continues in lines 223–32. One is reminded of Shakespeare's pick-purse gallows evader, Autolycus, trafficking in sheets, linens, and snapping up "unconsidered trifles" along the way (*Winter's Tale* 4.3.21–30), or Falstaff's collection of gallows-birds stealing clothing in *1 Henry IV* 4.2.42–48.

225–32   Dunbar revels in imagining the noisy uproar Kennedy's presence, with his rattling boots, creates in the midst of the city.

233–48   The verses in the final two stanzas of Dunbar's speech are filled with internal rhymes, a device popular among late medieval Scottish poets; compare Henryson's *Prayer for the Pest*, Douglas' *The Palis of Honoure* (lines 2116–42), and the final sixty-four verses of Polwart's *Flyting*. The result is that both the vocabulary and the syntax are highly inventive and unconventional. These stanzas, which reprise the main themes of Dunbar's attack, build to a grand crescendo of comic invective.

233–35   Dunbar is calling upon Kennedy to admit defeat and beg for mercy (*Cry grace*, line 235) — or else.

239   *Forflittin*. This probably means "defeated in flyting," and *barkit hyd* probably refers disparagingly to Kennedy's weathered skin.

240   *Clym ledder, fyle tedder*. The images here depict a condemned man climbing the ladder to the gallows who defiles (vomits on?) the noose around his neck.

241   *air to Hilhous*. It is not clear what is meant by being "heir to Hill House" or why it is an insult. Bawcutt suggests that it may have something to do with being a glutton

(Bw 2.445). Kennedy also refers to Hill House in line 515. Perhaps the hill house is the sheepfold or an outhouse. Whatever the sense, it is demeaning.

241–43   Several of the abusive phrases in these verses are obscure, and their precise meanings can only be guessed at — e.g., *byt buttoun*, *air to Hilhous* (line 241), and *Chittirlilling* (line 243). *DOST butto(u)n* n. cites Hume *Epistle* 145: "My breast was brusd . . . My buttons brist," where buttons might imply "nipples"; hence my gloss "nipple-biter" for *byt buttoun*.

245   *rak sauch*. "Stretched" (or "racked") sack, meaning a "gallows bird"; Bawcutt explains the phrase as "one who stretches a withy, when hanged from it on a gallows" (Bw 2.438). It is also possible that Dunbar is intimating that Kennedy stuffs his trousers with fake marks of manhood made of tallow and rocks. The phrases *cry crauch* and "cry cok" in line 248 refer to cries of submission as a defeated party admits his defeat.

247   *carlingis pet*. The phrase may simply mean "old woman's lap pet"; in this list of insults, however, that would seem surprisingly tame, and Bawcutt's suggestion of "fart" (Bw 2.438) may be closer to the mark. Compare the French word *pet* ("fart") and the expression, "hoist by his own petard."

249–50   In Numbers 16, Dathan and Abiron are important members of a group that rebel against Moses and Aaron. Their punishment involves being swallowed alive in the earth and taken to Hell. In the latter Middle Ages they were viewed as types of the seditious clergyman and were sometimes linked with the Lollards, as here. *Beliall* (line 250) was the name of a devil famed for his ability to corrupt through persuasive speech. The name originates in the phrase *filii Belial* ("sons of Belial") in Judges 19:22 and 1 Kings (1 Samuel) 2:12. See Bw 2.438.

249–552   Kennedy's main speech, which occupies the remainder of the poem, is longer than Dunbar's and more discursive; whereas Dunbar's attack on Kennedy is largely personal, Kennedy's attack on Dunbar encompasses a broader range of Scottish history and the larger history of the Dunbar family.

254   "Have I not silenced you, knave of a shepherd (or shepherd's knave?)?" The reference to Dunbar as a shepherd or shepherd's helper may reflect Kennedy's notion that this particular flyting should be viewed as a contest between a pair of pastoral poets.

255   *ryme and raif.* A contemptuous phrase for alliterative verse. Compare the statement of Chaucer's Parson, who claims that he cannot "rum, ram, ruf" (*CT* X[I]43).

257–64   Here Kennedy provides a sketch of the history of the Dunbar family, which may be traced to Gospatrick, earl of Northumberland, who relocated to Scotland in 1068 following the Conquest. Descended from him are the earls of Dunbar and March. Late in the thirteenth century, Patrick, eighth earl of Dunbar and first earl of March, had supported Edward I of England during the earlier stages in the War of Independence.

258   The earls of Dunbar held a castle at Cockburnspath in Berwickshire, a few miles to the southeast of the town of Dunbar.

259–60   Kennedy creates his own etymological explanation for the name Dunbar, suggesting that it reflects the union of a devil and a she-bear, hence the name *Dewlbeir* ("Devil-Bear," line 260) rather than Dunbar.

261   This verse may allude to an ancient Celtic tradition in which leaders copulated with horses, though here it is used to comment derisively on Dunbar's monstrous lineage. Kennedy links Dunbar to horses several times (earlier Dunbar had noted Kennedy's "horselessness"), and perhaps Kennedy's description of Dunbar as horse marshall in line 476 involves wordplay on the phrase *meir of Mar* in this verse.

262–64   Patrick's support of Edward I is the treachery that Kennedy is alluding to. Much of the information contained in verses 262–88 is probably drawn from Blind Hary's *Wallace*, Books 1 and 8.

265   Robert Bruce was the grandfather of Robert I. John Balliol was the nominal king of Scotland from 1292 to 1296, having been granted the title by Edward I of England. Compare "To Aberdeen" (Poem 33), lines 33–40, and the note to those verses.

267–68   According to Hary's *Wallace*, during the strife between the Scots and the English Patrick played a key role in opening Berwick to the English. The fall of Berwick occurred on 30 March 1296. See Hary's *Wallace* 1.94.

269–72   The Battle of Dunbar, which Kennedy calls Spottismuir, occurred on 27 April 1296. See Hary's *Wallace* 8.180.

270   Edward I was commonly known as "Longshanks" because he was unusually tall. Compare *The Wallace* 1.56.

277–78   In 1296 Edward "despoiled" (*spulyeit* — line 277) Scotland of its most highly revered treasures, including the Stone of Scone, the "Black Rood" of Holyrood House (which was believed to contain fragments of the True Cross), and the crown jewels. See Hary's *Wallace* 1.115–30.

281–88   In *The Wallace*, Book 8, Patrick refuses to attend the council called by Wallace and refers to him scornfully as "that king of Kyll" (8.21); subsequently Wallace exiles Patrick from Scotland.

287–91   Kennedy, perhaps echoing Isaias' prophecy of the fall of Babylon (13:19–22), predicts a dire future for the castle at Dunbar.

292–96   Kennedy now provides Dunbar with an ancestral mother who, after eating from the fateful apple of Paradise that was cast ashore from the sea, coupled with the devil and engendered Devil-bear.

295   The cockatrice, a fabulous monster described in medieval bestiaries, was a serpent hatched from a cock's egg; its glance was poisonous, and it was sometimes compared to women. Basilisks and cockatrices are similar (occasionally the terms are used interchangeably) in bestiaries, though the latter was considered mythical, the former real (see T. H. White, *Bestiary: A Book of Beasts* [New York: Putnam, 1960], p. 169n1).

299–304   Here Kennedy relates yet another historical anecdote that associates Dunbar's family with treachery and treason. See Bw 2.440.

309   *Thow wes prestyt and ordanit be Sathan.* Kennedy is casting aspersions on Dunbar's true ordination into the priesthood.

313–20   Kennedy suggests that Dunbar has failed to fulfill his responsibilities to his deceased ancestors, whose souls may find no rest because of it.

319   Trentals were sets of thirty masses that were said for the dead to help their souls to achieve respite from the pains of Purgatory. Compare *CT* III(D)1724–25.

321–22   Kennedy is alluding to the *Eclogue of Theodulus*, a popular Latin school text, which presents a debate between a shepherd and a shepherdess — Pseustis ("Liar"), who represents the falsehood of the pagans, and Alithia, who represents the truth of Christianity. For an English translation of the text, see Ronald E. Pepin, *An English Translation of the Auctores Octo: A Medieval Reader*, Mediaeval Studies 12 (Lewiston, NY: The Edwin Mellen Press, 1999), pp. 25–40.

325–28   Kennedy is suggesting that Dunbar should subject himself to a public act of penance for having slandered Kennedy. The Latin phrase *deliquisti quia* ("Because you have sinned") are the first words spoken by the priest to a penitent during confession.

331   *Stobo* refers to John Reid, a highly respected clerk in the royal secretariat and a figure whose death Dunbar laments in line 86 of "The Lament for the Makars" (Poem 14).

332   *Renounce thy rymis, bath ban and birn thy bill.* Kennedy calls for a public retraction of Dunbar's accusations against him; Bawcutt suggests *birn thy bill* refers to the "recantation required of heretics" (Bw 2.441).

336   *Arthuris Sete.* Arthur's Seat is the name of a high hill on the outskirts of Edinburgh not far from Holyrood Palace. This is one of the first recorded references to it.

337–44   Kennedy claims to have walked in the proper season upon the slopes of Mount Parnassus, a place sacred to the Nine Muses, been inspired by Mercury, the god of eloquence, and drunk from Hippocrene, the sacred fountain of poetic inspiration on Mount Helicon. But Dunbar, he says, came there in early spring and merely drank toad-spawn from a pool. This is a case of the traditional modesty topos being turned upside down.

343   *glod.* An adjective of uncertain meaning; perhaps "glued" or "gluey"? Or, on the basis of *glod*, a variant of *glade*, meaning "barren space" (see *OED*), the sense might be "empty language."

345   *elf.* Perhaps here meaning "dwarf," referring to Dunbar's small stature.

348   *Scota.* Bawcutt suggests that this is not a personification of Scotland but rather "the mythical daughter of Pharoah and wife to the Greek prince Gadelus, from whom Scots traced their origin" (Bw 2.441).

351   *rumplis*. The word may mean "fish tails," reflecting the legend that the people who struck St. Augustine of Canterbury with fish tails (see note to line 125) later gave birth to children having fish tails, a fitting punishment for the English.

355   *Quhare thou writis*. Kennedy is referring to Dunbar's claim in line 51.

356   *Densmen of Denmark ar of the kingis kyn*. James III had married Princess Margaret of Denmark in 1468, and thus James IV was the nephew of King Hans of Denmark (1481–1513).

358   A sling staff was a sling on a wooden shaft used to hurl stones; compare Barbour's *Bruce* 17.344.

361–68   Kennedy is here responding to the charges Dunbar had made in lines 145–52.

363–64   Compare Luke 16:20.

365   Dunbar's empty purse is mentioned in his petition poems, especially "To the King" (Poem 39).

367   *wedy teuch*. The phrase literally means "a tough (or strong) withy" but refers to the hangman's rope.

368   *Mount Falcoun*. Mount Falcon, or Montfaucon, was the name of the gallows hill near Paris. "It was a huge, several-storeyed structure, and sixty criminals could be hanged simultaneously" (Bw 2.441).

371   *Aire*. The principal city in Ayreshire, in south-western Scotland; compare "Master Andro Kennedy's Testament" (Poem 80), line 36, and the note to that verse.

378–80   Kennedy is apparently referring to the storm Dunbar described in lines 91–95. Carrying holy ashes on a sea voyage would ideally provide a measure of protection; Kennedy alleges that Dunbar lost them and then attempted, unsuccessfully, to rescue them.

383   Compare "A Dream" (Poem 41), line 14.

385–92   Kennedy argues that Dunbar's family is not related to the true Dunbars, the earls of Moray, a branch of the Dunbars with a long and valiant history of fighting for Scotland against the English.

394   *cor mundum*. A penitential formula originating from Psalm 50:12 in the Vulgate — "Create a clean heart in me, O God"; compare Lindsay, *Flyting*, line 20.

397   If Dunbar is the same person who received bachelor's and master's degrees from St. Andrews (in 1477 and 1479), these would be the degrees that Kennedy is referring to.

399   Medieval fools often had close-cropped hair cuts; compare "A Complaint against Mure" (Poem 60), line 19.

405   *Quhare thou puttis poysoun to me*. Kennedy is responding to Dunbar's charge in lines 77–78.

406–08   Kennedy challenges Dunbar to prove his allegations in personal combat, and he urges him not to try to get out of the fight by claiming benefit of clergy.

413–16   Kennedy describes a suitable coat of arms for Dunbar — a gallows, a noose, and a pin — and then suggests an appropriate inscription for the Dunbar coat of arms.

425–28   Kennedy here describes Dunbar as having been an itinerant preacher selling pardons, begging for his food, and then stealing under the cover of night. Kennedy's intention is to depict Dunbar as a clergyman of the lowest and most corrupt sort.

429–40   In order to escape Scottish ill will, Kennedy asserts, Dunbar traveled abroad under the pretense of being a wandering pilgrim — a "feigned palmer."

430   *a knycht of the felde*. The phrase may be an idiom meaning "a wandering vagabond" or perhaps "a pretended pilgrim."

431   Scallop shells indicated that a pilgrim had been to the shrine of St. James of Compostella in Spain. A *burdoun* was a pilgrim's staff; why it is described as *kelde* ("cold" or "cooled"?) is unclear, though the rhyme scheme requires such a word.

433–36   Kennedy suggests that Dunbar was too cowardly to risk crossing the mountain passes that would have allowed him to make a pilgrimage to Rome.

437–40   Kennedy portrays Dunbar as becoming the master hangman's apprentice, receiving half a frank for each person he hangs. He is referring back to line 368.

443   "You drank your savings" — Compare Whiting T253.

446   *Danskyn*. Danzig (modern Gdansk), the Baltic seaport with which Scotland regularly traded.

447   *De profundis*. The opening phrase of Psalm 129 in the Vulgate — "Out of the depths I have cried to thee, O Lord." Psalm 129 is considered one of the penitential psalms.

449–72   This extended scene in which Dunbar has an ignominious experience on a ship named the *Katherine* may contain a kernel of truth, though it may also be wholly fictitious. Kennedy here shows himself to be Dunbar's equal when it comes to excremental humor. For additional information, see Bw 2.443.

455–56   *The saulis had sonkyn throu the syn of thee / War not the peple maid sa grete prayere*. Perhaps there is an oblique allusion here to the story of Jonah, whose sin nearly caused the deaths of all on board the ship.

457   *the schip was saynit*. Ships were blessed before departing in order to ensure a safe voyage.

461   *the Bas*. Bass Rock is in the Firth of Forth, not far from Edinburgh. Dunbar apparently wasted little time in befouling the ship.

468   *tane the collum*. This phrase is difficult to construe, largely because of the term *collum*, which does not appear in *DOST*. Kinsley posits that the phrase means "captured the ship," a meaning that would require *collum* to be the result of minim confusion: the original word being *colvin*. It is tempting to read the line as "taken the column" (i.e., group of soldiers), but this usage for the word *column* is not attested until 1677 (*OED*). Other possibilities might be an odd spelling of *culum*, meaning "fundament," which accords well with the scatological nature of these lines but makes little sense with the verb *tane*. An unusual spelling of *culm*, meaning "bundle of thatch," is likewise fraught with difficulties (*MED*).

473–80   Kennedy commands Dunbar to go into exile in England, suggesting that he might try to pass himself off as a "horse marshall."

474   *botwand.* An obscure term, but possibly a type of whip that would identify him as a master of horses: i.e., a "butt-wand."

481   *Hye souverane lorde.* Kennedy is apparently addressing James IV, which underscores the likelihood that this is all a courtly entertainment.

484   *A rottyn crok, louse of the dok, thare doun.* Kennedy echoes the phrases Dunbar had used to describe him in line 248. The phrase *thare doun* seems to mean "send him down to England where he belongs!"

489   To be conceived or born during a total eclipse would have been a very ominous sign. Scholars have debated the possible biographical significance of this detail and the general consensus is that it has none. Compare line 14, and "Of a Black Moor" (Poem 71), line 13.

490   Although Mercury is usually portrayed as a beneficent deity and the god that inspires eloquence, he can also possess less positive attributes, as is apparently the case here.

497   *gukkis.* The likely meaning is "fool." Compare "In a Secret Place" (Poem 72), line 39.

500   *Rymis thou of me, of rethory the rose.* Compare *The Golden Targe* (Poem 65), line 253, where Chaucer is called the "rose rethoris all."

505–08 Kennedy's remark suggests that Dunbar's great desire to receive a benefice, a central concern in several of Dunbar's many petition poems, was a well-known fact. Bawcutt may be correct in suggesting that the allusion to Judas' bells refers to the ritual Silencing of the Bells during the three days prior to Easter, with the implication that Dunbar is only fit for minor clerical duties (Bw 2.444). The remark may also be meant as a slur against Dunbar's talent as a poet, as lines 507–08 surely are.

513   Cain, the slayer of his brother Abel (Genesis 4), was cursed to become a fugitive and vagabond. Tutivullus is the name of a demon who figures prominently in the *Towneley Plays* and in *Mankind*; he reveled in recording and spreading malicious gossip. In a late ME lyric (see Davies, p. 198), Tutivullus is "the devil of Hell."

514   Bawcutt suggests that "mermaid" implies effeminacy as well as monstrosity (Bw 2.444).

515–16   Kennedy's suggestion that Dunbar be baked and served to the lord of Hill House is probably another reference to his small size. There are many recorded examples of marvelous things being served within baked pies, including not only the four and twenty black birds of the nursery rhyme but even a small man.

521–44   In this extended catalogue of treacherous figures, Kennedy associates Dunbar with a whole host of traitors and enemies of the Christian faith that is drawn from Scripture, literature, history, mythology, and popular lore.

523   In Henryson's *Orpheus*, Pontius Pilate is placed in Hell, line 327.

524   The Lollards, an important reform movement within the church during Chaucer's time, were later condemned as heretics.

525   Simony was a serious crime that involved the buying or selling of benefices; given Dunbar's numerous pleas for a benefice, the charge has some pertinence.

526   Mohammad could be used as a synonym for Satan but could also refer to any devil.

528   Gog and Magog were thought to be allies of the Antichrist (Apocalypse 20:7) and persecutors of Christians. They are first mentioned in Ezechiel 38 and 39. Compare "Of James Dog" (Poem 57), line 19.

529   Nero was one of the great persecutors of Christians among the Roman emperors. *Golyas* usually refers to the Philistine giant Goliath whom David slew but also may suggest the Latin poet known as the Archpoet, the author of "The Archpoet's Confession." In the first case *Golyas* would suggest Dunbar as a freak of nature, and in the second it would suggest his irreverence and vulgarity.

530   Although Potiphar's wife is not named in Genesis, *Egiptia* (meaning "the Egyptian woman") is the name given to her in the apocryphal work *The Testament of Joseph*, one of the *Testaments of the Twelve Patriarchs*.

532   *Termygantis.* Termagant was often used as the name for one of the Saracen gods, though here it is probably used as a synonym for "demons" or "devils." Compare "The Dance of the Seven Deadly Sins" (Poem 77), line 115, and Henryson's

Annunciation, line 68. Vespasian was a Roman emperor, though not one of the ones especially noted for persecuting Christians.

534   *Cayphas*. The high priest at the trial of Jesus mentioned in Matthew 26:57 and John 11:49–53.

535   *Pluto*. I.e., Satan. Compare "The Merle and the Nightingale" (Poem 65), lines 125–26.

537   *Egeas*. Probably the Roman proconsul responsible for the martydom of St. Andrew.

538   *Marciane*. Probably the heretic Marcian of Sinope. See *The Golden Legend* 7.146.

        Maxencius. Probably the son of the Roman emperor Maximianus and a party to the martyrdom of St. Catherine of Alexandria. See *The Golden Legend* 7.16.

539   Antenor and Aeneas are Trojan princes who conspired with the Greeks to bring about the defeat of Troy, a story alluded to in Chaucer's *TC* but more fully told in Guido de Columnis' *Historia Destructionis Troiae*, books 28–30.

540   *Throp*. A woman or goddess whose identity remains uncertain (Criseyde and Atropos are among those suggested).

        Olibrius. Probably the Roman prefect who ordered the death of St. Margaret of Antioch.

541   *Puttidew*. The name often assigned to the figure known as the Wandering Jew who, because of his rudeness to Jesus on the *via dolorosa*, was condemned to wander the earth until the Last Day.

        Baal. A Phoenican god and pagan idol.

        Eyobulus. Probably Eubulus Aurelius, a priest of Baal under the emperor Elagabalus.

545–52   As Dunbar had done in his final stanzas (lines 232–48), Kennedy here revels in the use of internal rhymes.

546–52   The jingling effect of the triple rhymes and rhythms brings the flyting to its conclusion.

548   *lamp Lollardorum*. I.e., "chief of heretics."

551   *Tale tellare*. Probably carries both the meaning "teller of lies" and "teller of inferior tales," a final slur on Dunbar's artistry.

552   *Spynk*. A term used for a small bird such as a chaffinch. Kennedy is taking a parting shot at Dunbar's small size, as well as suggesting that he is merely a tiny, insignificant thing.

   Termagorum. Bw 2.446 mentions that this unclear word may be connected to *Termygantis* of line 532 and that the term in general may come from "ter" and "magus." (Thrice-magician — perhaps a kind of arch-fiend.) Compare Gower, *Confessio Amantis* 4.2408. Whatever the etymology, Kennedy's meaning is still clear: "go to Hell."

84. *The Tretis of the Tua Mariit Wemen and the Wedo*

The Tretis of the Tua Mariit Wemen and the Wedo is Dunbar's longest poem and also his most provocative, generating greatly differing responses from its readers. Perhaps reflecting the views of many readers is Spearing, who suggests that the *Tretis* is at once the poet's "most exciting and disturbing poem" (1985, p. 215). While critics have long viewed the poem as a satiric exposé of the vices and hypocrisy of women, several recent critics have observed that the *Tretis* is at least as revealing about men as it is about women.

   In its design the *Tretis* is simple enough: on Midsummer's Eve just after midnight the narrator, in search of amusement, squeezes himself into a hedge that surrounds a beautiful garden and eavesdrops on the private conversation of the three lovely ladies who are there entertaining themselves. What he hears is their bitter denunciation of the institution of marriage and their scathing comments about their husbands' sexual inadequacies. Their discussion is framed by a pair of ironic *demaundes d'amore*: the Widow initiates the discussion by asking the two younger wives if they do not agree that marriage is a blessed bond. Indeed they do not. Once the women have concluded their lengthy collocation and headed off home, the narrator poses the second *demaunde d'amore* to his audience — which of these three lovely ladies would you most desire to have for *your* wife?

   The *Tretis* draws upon several literary and cultural traditions. In genre it reflects aspects of the medieval debate poem, the flyting, the *chanson de mal mariée*, the comic poem in which drunken women revile their husbands (compare Dunbar's "The Twa Cummaris" [Poem 82]), and the mock sermon. The poem is greatly informed by an extensive tradition of medieval anti-feminist writings, including a special category of works about women that focuses on the vices attributed to widows. The *Tretis* is also the last great poem of the Middle Ages to be written in alliterative verse; although Dunbar often employs alliteration in his poems, this is the only one composed in the alliterative long line exclusively.

Many commentators have been struck by Dunbar's success in combining disparate elements into an artistic whole, in particular his union of elements drawn from dream-vision tradition, which comprise the poem's outer framework, with the obscene invective characteristic of the flyting in the women's conversation. One of Dunbar's chief devices in the *Tretis* involves the collision of opposites — the beautiful with the obscene, the natural with the stylized, the idealized with the starkly realistic. He does this in both large and small ways. Take, for example, the obvious contrast between the external beauty of the poem — the idealized setting of the dream vision and the physical perfection of the three lovely ladies — with the ugliness and vulgarity of their drunken conversation. Or take as a specific instance of this device line 96 — "Bot soft and soupill as the silk is his sary lume" — in which the First Wife applies the image of the soft and lovely texture of silk to her husband's lifeless penis, an arresting combination. The women are remarkable — both shocking and witty — in their invention of bawdy language as each attempts to outdo the other, a sort of one-upmanship (see Burness, pp. 210–11). Dunbar fuses "the language of the court and the language of the byre to suggest that there is no simple way — perhaps no real way — to convey in words the full significance of human sexual activity" (Burness, p. 218).

Chaucer's influence on the poem is extensive, and Chaucerian elements are drawn from several of the individual *Canterbury Tales*, especially from The Wife of Bath's Prologue and Tale and The Merchant's Tale, but also from The Miller's Tale and The Shipman's Tale. Some of these passages are pointed out in the notes that follow. Curiously, The Nun's Priest's Tale may also be pertinent to the discussion of Chaucer's influence on the *Tretis*, for it is the one tale of Chaucer's that reflects an overall structural design somewhat similar to Dunbar's poem. In both works the real is juxtaposed with the ideal for the purposes of satire. In Chaucer's tale the realistic world of the widow and her daughters encloses and sharply contrasts with the superficially beautiful and idealized world of Chauntecleer and Pertelot. In Dunbar's poem the idealized world of the garden and its three superficially lovely ladies contains an inner reality that is ugly, vulgar, and bestial.

One of the most fascinating elements of the poem is the narrator himself. What should readers make of him? Is he simply a neutral and unobtrusive narrator like the person who reports the debate he has overheard between the owl and the nightingale in the famous ME debate poem; or is he an obsessed voyeur, a peeping-tom perversely fascinated by the forbidden world he secretly intrudes upon? Should we assume that the narrator is actually the poet? And, if so, what does that reveal about Dunbar, a celibate clergyman, and his true feelings toward women? Is the narrator simply a convenient device, or might he represent a typical member of the court of James IV? Has he learned anything from the experience he reports, or is he more like one of the narrators of Chaucer's dream poems who comes away from his experience no wiser than he began?

The divisions in the text of 530 alliterative verses are editorial and follow those used by Kinsley. This composite text is based upon the texts in MF and RP. Mc47, K14, Bw3.

1   *the Midsummer Evin*. Midsummer's Eve, which was also St. John's Eve, occurred in the Middle Ages on the evening of June 23. Although the vigil preceding the Feast of the Nativity of John the Baptist should have been a time for serious reflection, Midsummer's Eve was commonly celebrated with dancing, bonfires, and other forms of revelry, activities often condemned by medieval preachers.

4   *hawthorne treis*. Hawthorns were often trimmed to create thick and thorny hedges. There may also be some pertinence to the fact that in fairy lore hawthorns are closely associated with magical occurrences.

5–7   This night-singing bird is probably the nightingale, a bird in medieval literature that often served to inspire romantic feelings. Given the nature of the feelings the three women will soon be expressing, there is irony in the use of this stock convention.

9   *dirkin efter mirthis*. "Rest quietly after merry-making"; apparently the narrator has been celebrating the evening also, which raises the possibility that what follows is a dream; often in dream-vision poems the narrator is lulled asleep by the fragrance of the flowers and the singing of birds.

10   *donkit*. Literally "dunked" but here meaning "moistened"; compare the ME *Parliament of the Three Ages*, line 10: "dewe appon dayses donkede full faire."

11   *ane holyn hevinlie grein hewit*. Like the hawthorn, the holly was also commonly associated with magic and fairy lore. In *SGGK* the Green Knight holds a holly sprig in one hand and an ax in the other (lines 206–09); that poem begins near the mid-winter festival, as this one does the mid-summer festival.

11–14   These successive verses all alliterate on the "h" sound, an example of what is sometimes called running alliteration.

14   The observer is also in close proximity to the hawthorn in *Wynnere and Wastoure* (line 36), Henryson's *Fables* (line 1729), and Lindsay's *Papyngo* (lines 187–89).

17   *arbeir.* Literally "arbor," but the word usually refers to a private grassy space located within a garden, often among trees. Compare the ME *Pearl*, lines 9–10: "Allas! I leste hyr in on erbere; / Thurgh gresse to grunde hit from me yot." Compare also *The Kingis Quair*, lines 211–24.

21–24   The women's tresses hang freely over their backs and shoulders but their heads are partially covered by kerchiefs. Their hair and their green apparel suggest the twenty-four dancing maidens in "To Princess Margaret" (Poem 32), lines 41–44. The color green may suggest freshness and innocence but also magic and fairy lore. Compare also *The Golden Targe* (Poem 65), lines 58–62.

27–29   Flower imagery is a highly traditional means of describing female beauty in medieval literature.

31   *annamalit.* Literally "enameled" but here meaning "brightly colored." Compare *The Golden Targe* (Poem 65), lines 13 and 250–51.

34–35   The table and the wine cups, like the fine ladies, are of great beauty and value.

36   *wlonkes.* This is a word often used in alliterative verse as an adjective meaning "lovely." It is commonly applied to women — compare *Pistel of Swete Susan*, line 26: "That wlonkest in weede." It is unusual for it to be used as a noun, as here.

37   *wantoun.* "Playful" or "jesting," but also "lascivious" or "lewd"; the ambiguity is surely intentional. Compare the use of the word in line 529.

39   *Thay wauchtit at the wicht wyne and waris out wourdis.* This line provides the first hint that these fine ladies may not be all that they seem, for the verb *wauchtit*, which means "quaffed" or "pulled at," does not strike a genteel note.

44   *leyd upone lyf.* I.e., (any) living person.

47   The "blessed bond that binds so fast" is of course marriage, which in the Middle Ages was considered permanent.

49–145   In these verses the first of the two married women presents her views of marriage and describes her personal experience of marriage.

53   "Chains are always to be avoided." This image of marriage as "chains" is fairly common; compare lines 9–16 of Chaucer's "Lenvoy de Chaucer a Bukton," and also Whiting C144. For the phrase "changes are sweet," compare the suggestion in line 20 of John Donne's "The Indifferent" that "love's sweetest part" is "variety."

56   *God, gif matrimony.* "God, if [only] marriage . . . "; or perhaps there should be no comma after *God*, the sense of the line being: "[It were] good if marriage were made to last for only a year," etc.

56–65 The First Wife's suggestion that marriage should only last a year reflects the fact that most species of birds re-mate on an annual basis. The springtime selection of those new mates is one of the central concerns in Chaucer's *PF*.

58   In ME texts the words *kynd* and *nature* are virtually synonymous and are often used interchangeably.

67   *curage.* The word has a wide range of meanings in ME texts, but in this poem it generally refers to "sexual desire" or "potency."

69   *gent, richt joyus and gent.* There is probably a scribal error in the repetition of *gent*.

70–75 The First Wife's behavior recalls the behavior of the Wife of Bath, who also delights in going "To prechyng eek, and to thise pilgrimages, / To pleyes of myracles, and to mariages" (*CT* III[D]557–58). Compare also line 474 below.

79   The First Wife refers to the traditional yoke of marriage (compare Chaucer's Merchant's Tale, *CT* IV[E]1283–85), but here she also likens the husband to a yoked animal used for plowing, a common metaphor for having sex.

80   *preveit his pitht.* "Proved or tested his sexual potency"; the Wife of Bath may also be using the word *pith* in the sense of "sexual vigor" in *CT* III(D)475.

81   *kirk . . . markat.* I.e., in every public place.

85–88 Note the running alliteration in these verses.

85   *forky fure.* The phrase is obscure, but the line seems to refer to a draft animal, and therefor *fure* may mean "furrow" or perhaps "furrower." The *OED* takes *forky* to be a variant of *forcy*, meaning "powerful, strong."

87   *fresche of his forme as flouris in May.* For this common simile compare the famous
      line in the description of Chaucer's Squire: "He was as fressh as is the month of
      May" (*CT* I[A]92); compare also Whiting F306.

89–145 Here the First Wife presents a portrait of her old, jealous, worthless husband — a
      literary type known as the *senex amans*. John the Carpenter in The Miller's Tale
      reflects this stock character, but the fullest literary example is January in The
      Merchant's Tale. Compare also Lydgate's *Temple of Glas*, lines 179–95.

90   *wolroun.* The term is clearly abusive, though the precise sense is uncertain.

91   Phlegm was one of the four bodily humors or fluids, and it was thought to be the
      dominant humor during old age. Compare line 272.

92   *scabbit.* Literally "having scabs" but figuratively meaning "worthless"; the word
      scutarde is obscure but may derive from the verb *scout*, "shoot, spurt," and thus may
      mean "one who pours out," i.e., "defecates"; compare the use of "schute" in line
      451 of the *Flyting* (Poem 83).

94–95 Compare January's love-making in The Merchant's Tale (*CT* IV[E]1823–27).

94   Compare the *Flyting* (Poem 83), line 184.

97   *to the syn assent.* As Bawcutt observes, this is a "sarcastic use of theological
      terminology" (Bw 2.288). Compare *The Pistel of Swete Susan.*

101–17 In these verses the First Wife portrays her husband as being a devil or an incubus
      demon.

101   *Mahowne.* Literally Muhammad, who was commonly viewed by medieval
      Christians as a pagan god, though many writers used his name as a synonym for the
      Devil. Compare the *Flyting* (Poem 83), line 233; "The Dance of the Seven Deadly
      Sins" (Poem 77), lines 6, 27, 109; and "The Antichrist" (Poem 51), line 32.

105–08 Again compare the description of January's love-making in *CT* IV(E)1823–27.

107   A heckle was an implement used to comb out flax during an early stage in the
      process of making linen. See Henryson's *Fables*, lines 1825–29.

112   *Belzebub.* I.e., Beelzebub, the "Lord of the Flies," a Syrian deity (4 Kings [2 Kings] 1:2); he was often viewed as being the devil's chief deputy, if not the devil himself. Compare also Matthew 12:24.

113   *smake smolet.* A phrase of uncertain meaning, but the context suggests something like "ugly mug" or "wicked smile."

114   "He pushes out his lower lip like a sick old horse leering at a filly." *Farcy* refers to an equine ailment involving, among other things, nasal discharge.

120   *gib.* "Cat"; in later Scots usage the term denotes a castrated tomcat.

127   *Venus werkis.* "Venus' works," i.e., "sexual acts." Compare *CT* IV[E]1971, and *Destruction of Troy*, lines 753–54.

128   May similarly "preyseth nat [January's] pleyyng worth a bene" in The Merchant's Tale (*CT* IV[E]1854).

131–41   The First Wife's refusal to grant her husband any sexual favors until she has received payment in the form of rich gifts is a tactic also employed by the Wife of Bath (*CT* III[D]407–16). Compare: *RR* 13663–14546 on the old Duenna's advice toward securing gifts.

135–36   Wordplays involving *pen* and *purse* — for penis and scrotum — are common. Compare *CT* III(D)44a–44b, and IV(E)1736–37.

141   *rousty raid.* "An armed incursion" but also "an incompetent mounting"; compare the similar suggestion of impotence implied by the Reeve's "rusty blade" in his portrait in the General Prologue (*CT* I[A]620).

142   *Johne Blunt.* Scottish slang for a simpleton ("blunt" means "dull" or "slow-witted"), but there is surely sexual double entendre here as well.

145   *syre.* It is possible to read a pun on the term *sire* as meaning not just "man," "husband," or "lord," but also "sire" in the sense of a "male parent of a quadruped," though the earliest attribution given by the *OED* for this meaning is 1523. This alternative reading is certainly fitting as the First Wife has already described her husband in bestial terms (see, for example, lines 131 and 137) and is currently describing how he "mounts" her. It hardly needs pointing out that associating him

with a stallion is here an insult to his humanity, not a compliment to his sexuality. The Widow likewise disparagingly refers to having sex with one of her deceased husbands as being "loppin with sic a lob avoir" ("mounted by such a clumsy horse" — line 387).

147   *leuch apon loft*. A common alliterative phrase; compare *Rauf Coilyear*, line 739, and Holland's *Howlat*, line 828.

161–238   The Second Wife's marital confession, which requires seventy-seven verses, is longer and more elaborate and more scurrilous than that of the First Wife; the Widow's confession, which comes last, far surpasses them both in every respect.

161   Her assertion that "there is no spy near" is of course incorrect, and serves to remind us of the narrator, securely hidden in the hedge, whose mental recorder is functioning very well.

162–67   *I sall a ragment reveil . . . that suellit wes gret*. The Second Wife employs the imagery of pregnancy, but she is only pregnant with resentment, not child. The dichotomy underscores her husband's general lack of virility.

164–67   Her sentiments here are strikingly similar to those expressed by Dunbar in his petition poem "Against the Solicitors at Court" (Poem 45), lines 85–88. Compare also the sentiments of King Midas' wife in The Wife of Bath's Tale: "Hir thoughte it swal so soore aboute hir herte / That nedely som word hire moste asterte" (*CT* III[D]967–68).

168   *hur maister*. Not a "whoremaster" in the usual sense, but rather a frequenter of whores. The Second Wife's husband is a worn-out lecher who bears some resemblance to the Wife of Bath's fourth husband, a "revelour" who had a mistress (*CT* III[D]453).

183   *Venus chalmer*. "Venus' chamber," a common sexual euphemism; compare the Wife of Bath's statement: "I koude noght withdrawe / My chambre of Venus from a good felawe" (*CT* III[D]617–18). A lady's chamber was a small private room connected to her bower (i.e., bedroom). Compare also lines 430–31.

185   I.e., "He looks like a man who would make a fine lover, though he is of little worth."

186   *dotit dog*. This is apparently a traditional figure for describing lecherous old would-be lovers. Chaucer uses it also in The Parson's Tale when he says the hound, "whan he comth by the roser . . . though he may nat pisse, yet wole he heve up his leg" (*CT* X[I]858), referring to "olde dotardes holours" (*CT* X[I]857).

195   *God wait quhat I think quhen he so thra spekis*. Compare The Merchant's Tale: "But God woot what that May thoughte in hir herte" (*CT* IV[E]1851).

197–98   The sense of these verses is difficult, and the repetition of *bot* may indicate textual corruption. Perhaps the meaning is something like: "Unless he himself one evening might make some (sexual) attempt on one of them; but he is not such a person, not one who possesses their natural powers (i.e., virility)."

201   *geit*. "Jet"; jet is a hard, dense form of coal; in Dunbar's time it was often polished into black beads used in inexpensive jewelry.

202   *He had the glemyng of gold and wes bot glase fundin*. Proverbial; compare Whiting G282.

203   *ferse*. "Fierce"; i.e., "eager with desire."

206   The earliest recorded references to St. Valentine as the patron saint of lovers and mating birds occurs in such fourteenth-century poems as Chaucer's *PF* and *The Complaint of Mars*, and Oton de Granson's *Le Songe Saint Valentin*. There is nothing in the legend of the early Christian martyr to explain why he became associated with amorous feelings, aside from the fact that his feast day occurs in the early spring on 14 February, about the time that birds would actually be selecting their new mates.

232   *geir*. For the use of this term in a sexual sense, compare "These Fair Ladies That Repair to Court" (Poem 73), line 32.

234   *straik*. "Strike" or "stroke," here clearly used as a sexual metaphor, though normally a term more appropriate for military usage.

236   *werkit*. "Worked," but here used in the sense of "ached."

238   *bird.* A common term in romance poetry for an attractive young woman. Compare Chaucer's *Romaunt*, line 1014, *Sir Degrevaunt*, line 701, or *Erle of Tolous*, line 844.

         bourd. "A jest"; the Second Wife's point is that the love-making would be so good that there would be nothing to make jokes about.

245–504   These verses contain the Widow's monologue, which has its closest counterpart, not in the confessions of the first two wives, but in the self-exposé of Chaucer's Wife of Bath.

247–50   This is the Widow's invocation, which draws upon the stock phrases of medieval preachers; indeed, what she presents to the other two wives amounts to a kind of mock-sermon, as well as a parody of a saint's life. See A. A. MacDonald, "Alliterative Poetry," p. 269

250   *And mak yow mekar to men in maneris and conditiounis.* This verse is of course ironic, for her intent is not at all to make the women she is "preaching" to be meeker in their behavior and attitudes toward men.

257   *Unto my lesson ye lyth and leir at me wit.* Here, too, the Widow presents herself as a preacher who is instructing her less experienced audience.

260–69   These verses recall the ironic advice to women contained in the *envoi* to The Clerk's Tale, *CT* IV(E)1183–1206.

262   *turtoris.* The turtle dove, one of the few species of birds that mates for life, was a symbol of marital fidelity and of constancy in love. See *PF* lines 582–83 "'Nay, God forbede a lovere shulde chaunge!' / The turtle seyde, and wex for shame al red."

         talis. For "tails" as the female sex organs, compare *CT* III(D)467 and *CT* VII(B²) 416 and 434, and *Piers Plowman* B.3.131. Kinsley cites as a further example "cocke Lorelles Bote" (ca. 1515), line 14: "Many whyte nonnes with whyte vayles / That was full wanton of theyr tayles," noting the bilingual pun on tail, from OE *tægl*, for posterior extremity of an animal, and OF *taille*, for a cut or division (p. 269).

263–64   The Widow here echoes Christ's words to the Apostles: "Be ye therefore wise as serpents and simple as doves" (Matthew 10:16–17). Like the Wife of Bath, the

Widow employs Scripture for her own purposes. The dove — possibly distinct from the "turtle" — was a symbol of meekness. Compare "To a Lady" (Poem 63), lines 36–37.

269   *nought worth a hen.* A common expression for something of little value; compare the Wife of Bath's "nat worth an hen," *CT* III(D)1112, and Whiting H347. See also the Monk's scornful "He yaf nat of that text a pulled hen" *CT* I(A)177.

270–409 In this section of her speech the Widow presents her marital autobiography; like the Wife of Bath, she successively characterizes each of her marriages — in her case two rather than five. Her first husband was senile and impotent and resembles the Wife of Bath's first three husbands (*CT* III[D]272–95).

273   *I hatit him like a hund thought I it hid prevé.* Compare Whiting H585.

274   *kissing . . . clapping.* "Kissing and clipping (embracing)" a common collocation in medieval works, especially in romances: see, e.g., The Merchant's Tale, *CT* IV(E)2413; *Emaré*, lines 212, 1020; *Floris and Blancheflour*, line 503; and Malory (*Works*, p. 168).

275   *claw his cruke bak.* "Scratch his crooked back"; i.e., to "cause him pleasure," or to "flatter him." Compare the Cook's response to the Reeve in the *Canterbury Tales*: "For joye him thoughte he clawed him on the bak" (I[A]4326).

277   *bler his . . . e.* A common expression meaning "to cheat or trick"; compare the Miller's remark in The Reeve's Tale: "They wene that no man may hem bigyle, / But by my thrift, yet shal I blere hir ye" (*CT* I[A]4048–49); and compare Henryson's *Fables*, line 2041, and Whiting E217.

283–87 The Widow boasts openly of having a youthful lover, something the Wife of Bath only hints at. The Widow's greater candor may reflect the fact that she is speaking privately to a select audience of kindred spirits, whereas the Wife of Bath is speaking publicly to a much broader audience.

284   *couth be secrete and sure and ay saif my honour.* The Widow's concern for her reputation had practical implications, but it also mirrors the discretion required of courtly lovers engaging in an affair.

289   *Bot leit the sueit ay the sour to gud sesone bring.* Compare *King Hart*, lines 657–58.

291–93   The Widow's husband, out of devotion to her, leaves his finest manor house to their child, even though he is not (unbeknownst to him) the one who had fathered the child.

296–410   The Widow now discusses her second marriage, to a wealthy middle-aged merchant whom she considered her social inferior.

298–302   Here the Widow lists the several ways in which she believed herself to be her husband's superior; and she says she made sure that he never forgot it.

305   I.e., "I appeared to be very vivacious by the time I had reached the age of maturity." The phrase *perfit eild* refers to the age at which a person is considered legally competent; for a girl this was usually twelve, for a boy fourteen.

307–08   She suggests that this clergyman has gone on to achieve considerable prominence in the church, a subtle piece of anti-clerical satire on Dunbar's part.

309   *I gert the buthman obey.* This verse, as well as many others, reflects her condescending attitude toward her lowly "shopkeeper" of a husband.

316   *never bot in a gentill hert is generit ony ruth.* This verse echoes the famous line used several times in *The Canterbury Tales* that "pitee renneth soone in gentil herte" (I[A]1761). The Widow's mercy, however, is motivated by something other than her innate nobility. Compare "To a Lady" (Poem 63), lines 41–42.

319   "He dared not disregard my summons." The Widow's statement, couched in legal terminology, demonstrates her practical wisdom in dealing with the exigencies of experience.

321–28   The Widow's comments on her "womanly nature" are similar to sentiments expressed by the Wife of Bath — that those things that are easily attained are soon despised, while things difficult to attain are greatly desired; compare the Wife of Bath in *CT* III(D)517–24.

323   *or I him faith gaif.* I.e., "before I was betrothed to him."

331   *I wald haif riddin him to Rome with raip in his heid.* The Widow's domination of her husband, reflected in the image of her riding him like a bridled horse, reverses the usual relationship between the sexes during the Middle Ages. It certainly calls

433

to mind the popular imagery of the ridden man (for example, Aristotle and Phyllis) as a misogynist visualization of women's wiles; for more on the trope, see Natalie Zemon Davis, "Women on Top," in *Society and Culture in Early Modern France* (Stanford: Stanford University Press, 1975), pp. 124–51. The phrase *to Rome* implies a very great distance (compare Whiting R182); Rome was also an important pilgrimage site for medieval Christians, one of several visited by the Wife of Bath.

332   *Wer not ruffill of my renoune and rumour of pepill.* The Widow's hostility toward her husband, she says, was only held in check by her fear of public opinion.

338   *hie burrow landis.* "Tall burgh buildings"; probably tenements within the city. The Widow's husband obviously had extensively property holdings.

344–48 The Widow has concealed her true attitude toward her husband until the legal documents conferring his property on her child were signed, sealed, and delivered. Then she permits her pent-up anger to erupt.

347   *bauchles.* The word's meaning is debated, but it seems to be a legal term pertaining to the transfer of property or money.

351–52 The reversal of their sex-roles has now been completed.

355–57 The Widow's husband has become a thoroughly subdued, properly behaving packhorse; he is no longer one that casts the baskets slung across his back into the midden (line 355), or that is skittish or nervous or skips to the side (line 357).

362   *lumbart.* "Banker" or "financier"; the term derives from Lombardy, an important center of banking during the later Middle Ages. Compare *Piers Plowman* C.4.194.

379   *pako.* The peacock was a traditional symbol of vanity; compare Whiting P280, and *CT* I(A)3926, describing Symkyn in The Reeve's Tale.

382   *papingay.* The popinjay or parrot, like the peacock, was deemed vain and proud of its colorful plumage, as well as being a bird given to the pursuit of sensuous pleasures. In contrast, the husband is called a *plukit herle* ("plucked heron"), a bird that has been stripped bare. Herons were often hunted in falconry.

384   *maid a stalwart staff to strik himselfe doune.* Compare the proverbial saying, "to make a rod with which to beat yourself"; Whiting S652.

389   *thing*. A euphemism for her sex organs. The Wife of Bath uses similar euphemisms: e.g., "oure bothe thynges smale / Were eek to knowe a femele from a male" (*CT* III[D]121–22); and "For if I wolde selle my *bele chose*, / I koude walke as fressh as is a rose" (*CT* III[D]447–48).

403   *his first wif*. Her husband, we here learn, was himself a widower when the Widow married him; this fact lends greater poignancy to her efforts to gain for her own children all of his money and property, while depriving the children of his first marriage of their inheritance.

405   *heid at feid*. Literally "had at feud" but probably meaning "held in contempt." Compare Holland's *Howlat*, line 61.

408–09   "And yet these wise men, they know that all evil wives are given to such behavior and recognized for behaving in such a fashion" — i.e., their cruel treatment of their stepchildren.

410–14   Compare the sentiments of Sprowtok in Henryson's fable of the "Cock and the Fox," *Fables*, lines 509–22.

412   Ironically, the verse carries religious overtones; compare "Be myrthfull now at all your mycht, / For passit is your dully nycht" in "On the Nativity of Christ" (Poem 1), lines 36–37.

415–21   The Widow's false mourning has many literary counterparts, but compare especially the Wife of Bath, *CT* III(D)587–92.

423   *As foxe in a lambis fleise*. A proverbial expression that originates in Matthew 7:15; compare Whiting W474. Compare also "Tidings from the Session" (Poem 74), line 37, and "A Wooing in Dunfermline" (Poem 69), line 59.

424–25   The Widow's book is probably an illuminated book of hours; she carries it more as a symbol of her noble status — i.e., for show — rather than for devotional purposes.

429   *best brand*. I.e., "the most brawny" or "the best muscled"; brawn originally referred to the chest muscles of a boar, but the word came to mean "brawny" in general.

430–31   "Or [who] has been made most powerfully to furnish a banquet / in Venus' chamber" — colorful sexual metaphors. Compare "To the Queen" (Poem 70), line 7.

433–34   Compare the description of Chaucer's Criseyde in *TC* 1.174–75.

437–39   Women were often thought to have the ability to shed tears whenever necessary —
the Wife of Bath even calls weeping one of God's three gifts to women (*CT*
III[D]401) — but the Widow's tears seems to need a bit of extra help — what A. A.
MacDonald wittily calls "do-it-yourself lachrymosity" (1994, p. 268).

443   *perle of plesance.* Compare the opening verse of the ME *Pearl*: "Perle, plesaunte
to prynces paye."

444   Compare "Women are in church saints, abroad angels, at home devils" (Tilley
W702).

452   *bejaip.* "Fool" or "deceive," often implying "to cuckold" or deceive sexually;
compare *CT* IX(H)144–45.

460   *Faith has a fair name bot falsheid faris beittir.* This verse sounds very much like a
proverbial expression.

464   *happy.* I.e., "good-fortuned" or "lucky" or "well-off."

465   The Widow heaps scorn upon the woman who has reached the age of a hundred but
continues to be a foolish girl in regard to the strategies of love and sex, especially
the importance of keeping it secret. Bawcutt notes that "this perverts a much-
glossed scriptural text (Isaiah 65:20)" (Bw 2.294).

471   *solace under serk.* "Joy beneath my gown" — i.e., good sex; there is clever word-
play on her "cair under cloke" (line 470) during the day and her "joy under gown"
during the night.

476–502   In her grand finale, the Widow touts her ability to satisfy a *thik thrang* ("thick
throng" — line 488) of would-be wooers simultaneously. Like the Wife of Bath,
who "ne loved nevere by no discrecioun, / But evere folwede myn appetit, / Al were
he short, or long, or blak, or whit" (*CT* III[D]622–24), the Widow is also happy to
bestow her favors upon virtually all comers, regardless of their social rank (lines
497–98).

479   *And fyllis me wyne wantonly with weilfair and joy.* Perhaps pertinent here is the
       Wife of Bath's observation that "In wommen vinolent is no defence," for "A
       likerous mouth moste han a likerous tayl" (*CT* III[D]467, 466).

484   Serving and carving at table were important social skills, and these duties were often
       performed by youthful squires such as Chaucer's Squire (*CT* I[A]99–100).

485–86 This vulgar behavior stands in stark contrast to the genteel behavior in the preceding
       verse.

489   *fair calling.* "Warm welcome"; compare the figure of Bialacoil in *RR*, and *The
       Golden Targe* (Poem 65), line 188.

497–502 Kinsley argues that in these verses the Widow's salon "is exposed as a brothel" (K,
       p. 273); more likely, though, the Widow is having a good time parading before her
       friends as a woman with voracious appetites and a sexual ego to match.

498   *luf unluffit.* I.e., "love without being loved in returned"; this is a common phrase to
       describe unrequited love.

500   *That he be lost or with me lak, his lif sall not danger.* One of the standard clichés
       of courtly love poetry was that the wooer would die if his ardor was not satisfied.
       Chaucer also parodies this sentiment with "hende" Nicholas' remark to Alisoun,
       "Ywis, but if ich have my wille, / For deerne love of thee, lemman, I spille" (*CT*
       I[A]3277–78).

501–02 The Widow, wittingly or unwittingly, is parodying the Beatitude from the Sermon
       on the Mount, "Blessed are the merciful, for they shall obtain mercy" (Matthew
       5:7).

502   *Sabot.* The best explanation is that this means "God" and is derived from the
       biblical phrase *Dominus Sabaoth* ("Lord God of Hosts") in Isaias 1:9, Romans 9:29,
       etc. Also, Bawcutt notes that in "Bartholomaeus Anglicus, I. 19, on the names of
       God: 'the thridde name is Sabaoth'" (Bw 2.295).

504   *legeand.* "Story," but also carrying the ironic meaning of "saint's life." Compare the
       comment of the merchant's wife to the monk in Chaucer's Shipman's Tale: "Thanne
       wolde I telle a legende of my lyf / What I have suffred sith I was a wyf" (*CT*
       VII[B^2]145–46).

507–08   The practice of women being instructed by the secret teachings of other women and then following their advice is also reflected in The Wife of Bath's Prologue: "I folwed ay my dames loore, / As wel of this as of othere thynges moore" (*CT* III[D]583–84).

512–22   The narrator returns to the opening description of nature in all of its beauty and perfection, completing the framework which surrounds the women's conversation.

515   *Silver schouris*. These are drops of dew. Compare *The Golden Targe* (Poem 65), line 14.

516–18   The birds rejoice at the coming of the dawn. Compare *The Golden Targe* (Poem 65), lines 20–21.

522   *kindill agane his curage thoght it wer cald sloknyt*. In light of all that the narrator has just overheard, his *curage* — his sexual vitality — might well have "slackened cold" and require some "rekindling."

523   *rais thir ryall rosis in ther riche wedis*. The irony in this line, too, is inescapable.

525   *I all prevély past to a plesand arber*. Could he now be occupying the very place in which the women were recently disporting themselves — a kind of amusing effort at appropriation of their private domain?

526   *with my pen did report*. I.e., "recorded in writing"; Dunbar also uses the phrase in line 69 of "A Wooing in Dunfermline" (Poem 69). (There may be some irony in the fact that earlier in the poem the word "pen" — line 135 — had been used to refer to the penis.)

527–30   Here the narrator, or perhaps Dunbar, presents his audience with the traditional *demaunde d'amore* — "which of these three lively ladies would *you* wish to marry?" The answer, of course, is not hard to come by. The ironic use of this device may have a parallel in the Franklin's question at the conclusion to his tale: "Lordynges, this question, thanne, wol I aske now, / Which was the mooste fre, as thynketh yow?" (*CT* V[F]1621–22).

Textual Notes

Abbreviations: See Explanatory Notes.

Poem 1	Base Text: Bannatyne MS, fols. 27r–27v.
8	*puer*. MS: *power*. I follow the Vulgate spelling, as do Mc, K, Bw.
24	Refrain abbreviated. So also with lines 32 and 40.
33	*fowlis*. MS: *flour* canceled; *fowlis* written after.
45–46	These verses are written in the margin.
51	*fische*. So Bw. MS: *fiche*, corrected to *fische*. Mc, K read *fishe*.
Colophon	*Finis. Quod Dumbar.*

Poem 2	Base Text: Maitland Folio, pp. 203–07; with emendations from Asloan MS, fols. 290v–292r and Arundel MS, fols. 168r–170r.
3	*And knelit*. So As, followed by Mc, K, Bw. MS: *And kneling*.
19	*ruge*. So As and Ar, followed by Mc, K, Bw. MS: *rage*.
42	*syne*. So Mc. MS: *syn*, followed by K, Bw.
51	*to*. So As, followed by Mc, K, Bw. MS: *he*.
57	*bak*. MS: *bayth* canceled before.
59	*hyd*. So As, followed by K, Bw. MS: *syd*, followed by Mc.
70	*Him all nakit*. So As and Ar, followed by Mc, K, Bw. MS: *at him all nathing*.
77	*and$_2$*. Canceled in MS, but I follow As in retaining it.
94	*As martir*. So As, followed by Mc, K. MS: *Ane martirdome*, followed by Bw.
96	As ends here with *Explicit Dunbar*.
103	*bludy*. So Ar. MS: *ane wound*, followed by Mc, K. Bw substitutes *bludy* for *ane*.
117	*The Lord*. So Ar, followed by Bw. MS: *That schort*, followed by Mc, K.
129	*Grace*. So Ar, followed by Mc, K, Bw. MS: *Grudge*.
139	*that steid*. MS: *part thair* canceled before.
Colophon	*Finis quod Dunbar.*

Poem 3	Base Text: Bannatyne MS, fol. 35r.
2	*confountit*. MS: *coun* canceled before.
11	*his*. MS: *þe* canceled before.
13	*clowis*. So K, Bw. MS: *clows*, followed by Mc.

16	Refrain is abbreviated. So also with lines 24 and 32.
20	*as a gyane.* So K, Bw. MS: *as gyane,* followed by Mc.
Colophon	*Finis quod Dunbar.*

Poem 4	Base Text: Asloan MS, fols. 303r–304v.
11	*matern.* The last three letters are barely legible in the MS, but all modern editors (Mc, K, Bw) read *matern.*
36	*irke.* MS: *il* canceled before.
63	*vyce.* So Mc, K. MS: *wyce,* followed by Bw, who glosses "wise".
Colophon	*Quod Dunbar.*

Poem 5	Base Text: Bannatyne MS, fol. 278v.
Colophon	*Quod Dumbar.*

Poem 6	Base Text: Arundel MS, fols. 161r–162v.
8	*thee.* Supplied, following Mc. K, Bw supply *the.*
11	*that.* Supplied, following Mc, K. Bw follows MS.
14	*confessour.* So K, Bw. MS: *confessioun,* followed by Mc.
19	*schrift.* So Mc, K, Bw. MS: *schift.*
48	*hert.* Supplied, following Mc, K, Bw.
Colophon	*Quod Dumbar.*

Poem 7	Base Text: Arundel MS, fols. 1r–4v; emendations from Bannatyne MS, fols. 17v–19v & Maitland Folio, pp. 199–203.
4	*schryve.* K reads *schrife.* MS: *schir.*
7	*Thy.* MS: *my* canceled before.
10	*Thy.* Supplied from B, BD, MF, following Mc, K, Bw.
	excelling. So MF, followed by Mc, Bw. K reads *exelling.* MS: *excellent.*
18	*Synnis.* So MS, followed by K, Bw. Mc reads synnys.
	schrif. So MS, followed by K, Bw. Mc reads schirryve.
27	*nor.* So B, BD, MF, followed by Mc, K, Bw. MS: *þe.*
30	*the deid.* So B, BD, MF, followed by Mc, K, Bw. MS: *I did.*
33	*Marcy.* So MF, followed by Mc, K, Bw. MS: *Mary.*
	Spirituall. MS: *and* canceled before.
34	*teching.* MS: *consall* canceled before.
35	*nor.* MS: *r* added above the line.
37	*saulis.* MS: *we* canceled before.

37	*preching.* So K. MS: *peching.* Bw follows B, BD, MF: *Nor vnto saulis support of my praying.* Mc reads (without explanation): *Nor to my rychtbowris support of my praying.*
43	*Eucarist.* So K, Bw. MS: *vnacrist.* Mc reads *Holy Supper* from B, BD.
	exellence. So K, Bw. MS: *exelling.* Emendation based on rhyme; the line is not in MF.
44	*Pennence.* So K, Bw. MS: *pennce.*
45	*Matremony.* So K, Bw. MS: *Matromony.*
63	*pointis.* So K, Bw. Mc reads *poynttis.* MS: *pontis.*
70	*quhair.* So Mc, K, Bw. MS: *quair.*
71	*befoir.* So Mc, Bw. MS: *befor*, followed by K.
85–86	These verses are transposed in MS. See Mc, Bw. The lines are not in MF, B, BD.
99	*remembring.* So Mc, K, Bw. MS: *remembing.*
100	*Hevinnis.* So K. MS five minims rather than six. Mc reads *hevenis*; Bw reads *hevinns.*
	hiddous feid. So B, MF, followed by Mc, K, Bw. BD: *hidduous sede.* MS: *having confide.*
111	*on Rude.* Supplied from B, BD, MF, followed by Mc, K, Bw.
	redeming. So B, BD, MF, followed by Mc, K, Bw. MS: *redempcioun.*
122–23	These verses are transposed in MS.
123	*gud.* So B, followed by Mc. MS: *my*, followed by K, Bw.
125	Miswritten line is canceled and then written correctly.
	invencionis bredyng. So B, BD, MF, followed by Mc, Bw. MS: *invenconis ledyng* (after canceled line), followed by K.
129	*Of.* So B, BD, MF, followed by Mc, K, Bw. MS: *O.*
141–42	These verses are transposed in MS. So K. Bw orders the lines 139, 141, 140, 142; Mc uses this same order but follows B line 140 (*In hurt or slawchter, gif I be*) as line 141.
147	*as scho.* So B, BD, MF, followed by Mc, K, Bw. MS: *eschew.*
	weipe. So K. Mc reads *weip.* MS: *veipe*, followed by Bw.
155	*unmannyit.* So Bw. MS: *vnmannrit.* Mc follows B, BD: *unmenƺeit*, glossing "unmanned." K reads *unmenƺit.*
156	*Bot felling.* So Bw. K reads *Bot feiling.* Mc follows B, BD: *Bot fall in.*
157	*hart a.* So B, BD, followed by Mc, Bw. MS: *hertis*, followed by K.
166	*sailis.* So Mc. MS: *saillis*, followed by K, Bw.
168	*I cry.* So K. MS: *I crcy.* B, BD, MF: *That cryis*, followed by Mc, Bw.
	laser. So K, Bw. Mc reads *lasar.* MS: *I laser.*
Colophon	*Heir endis the tabill of confessioun compilit be Mr William Dunbar.*

Poem 8   Base Text: Bannatyne MS, fol. 48v.
8   Refrain abbreviated. So also with lines 20, 28, 32, 36.
34   Written to the right of line 33 in MS.
Colophon *Quod Dumbar.*

Poem 9   Base Test: Bannatyne MS, fols. 47r–47v; emendations from Maitland Folio, pp. 193–94.
28   *that all devouris.* Added in a later hand in MS.
44   *dryve.* Supplied from MF, following Mc, K, Bw.
Colophon *Finis quod Dumbar.*

Poem 10 Base Text: Maitland Folio, p. 326.
Colophon *Quod Dumbar.*

Poem 11 Base Text: Maitland Folio, pp. 195–96.
22   *dissolvit.* MS: *no* canceled before.
Colophon *Finis quod Dunbar.*

Poem 12 Base Text: Maitland Folio, p. 310.
Colophon *Quod Dumbar.*

Poem 13 Base Text: Maitland Folio, pp. 5–6; emendations from Maitland Folio b, p. 315.
1   *warld.* MS: *l* inserted above the line.
7   *seasoun.* MS: written in the margin to correct *sessione.*
16   Verse supplied from MFb, following Mc, K, Bw; it has been cut away in MS.
17   *cairis.* MS: *ch* canceled before.
Colophon *Quod Dumbar.*

Poem 14 Base Text: The Rouen Print, b3r–b4v; emendations from Bannatyne MS, fols. 109r–110r and Maitland Folio, pp. 189–92.
8   Refrain abbreviated here and in most subsequent stanzas.
9   *and.* In several instances MF reads *et* for *and.* See also lines 17, 18, 22, 38, 42, 51, 54 (twice), 58, 59, and 69.
15   *vanité.* So Mc, K, Bw. Print: *vainte.*
17   *Onto.* So Mc, Bw. K: *One to.* Print: *On*, with a macron over the *n.*
21   *knychtis.* So B, MF, followed by Mc, K, Bw. Print: *knythis.*
26   *Takis.* So B, MF, followed by Mc, K, Bw. Print: *Tak.*
          on. So Mc, Bw. K: *one.* Print: *on*, with a macron over the *n.*
34   *clerk.* So Mc, K, Bw. Print: *clcerk.*

46   *pageant*. So Print, followed by Mc, K. Bw follows B, MF: *padʒanis*.

49   *hes*. So Mc. Print: *has*, followed by K, Bw.

62   *that*. So Mc, K, Bw. Print: *taht*.

70   *Slaine*. So Mc, Bw. K: *Slane*. Print: *Slame*.

71   *fle*. So B, MF, followed by Mc, K, Bw. Print: *only*.

Colophon   *Quod Dunbar quhen he wes sek.*

Poem 15   Base Text: Maitland Folio, pp. 318–19.

5   *sangis*. So Mc, K. MS: *sangs*, followed by Bw.

6   *lenthin*. Bw reads *lenth in*.

43   *blys*. So Mc, K, Bw. MS: *blyiz*.

Colophon   *Quod Dumbar.*

Poem 16   Base Text: Bannatyne MS, fols. 84r–85r; emendations from Maitland Folio, pp. 331–33.

10   *may*. So MF, followed by Mc, Bw. MS: *ma*, followed by K.

15   Refrain abbreviated here and in all subsequent stanzas.

26   *nobilité*. So MF, followed by Mc, Bw. MS: *nobiltie*. K reads *nobilitie*.

37   *lordis*. So MF, followed by Mc, K, Bw. MS: *lord*.

38   *Trewthe*. So MF, followed by Mc, Bw. MS: *trewth*, followed by K.

39   *Honour*. Supplied from MF, followed by K. Mc, Bw reject MS line entirely and follow MF: *Exylit is honour of the toun*, thereby avoiding the Latinate *exul* of MS.

43   *lukis*. So MF, followed by Mc, K, Bw. MS: *luke*.

47   *hairtis*. So MS, followed by K. MF: *hartis*, followed by Mc, Bw.

48   *ar maid of blew*. So MF, followed by Mc, K, Bw. MS: *of amiable blyth*.

72   *sunt*. Supplied from MF, following Mc, K, Bw.

84   *Tu regni da imperium*. So MS, followed by K. MF: *Bot me ressaue in regnum tuum*, followed by Mc, Bw.

Colophon   *Finis quod Dumbar.*

Poem 17   Base Text: Bannatyne MS, fol. 98v; emendations from Maitland Folio, p. 337.

8   *it*. Supplied from MF, following Mc, K, Bw.

11   *man*. So MF, followed by Mc, K, Bw. MS: *men*.

15   Refrain abbreviated here and in subsequent stanzas.

16   *Quha*. Corrected from *Quhen* in MS.

39   *frawdfull*. MS: *d* inserted above the line.

Colophon   *Quod Dunbar.*

Poem 18 Base Text: Maitland Folio, p. 307; emendations from Reidpeth.

18   *maist sall.* So R, followed by Mc, K, Bw. MS: *sall sonast it.*

28   *us imprent.* So MS, followed by Mc, K. R: *ws be lent,* followed by Bw.

Colophon   *Quod Dumbar.*

Poem 19 Base Text: Aberdeen Minute Book, III, pp. 321–22; emendations from Bannatyne MS, fols. 98r–98v.

5   *nycht.* Supplied from B, following Mc, K, Bw.

23   *michtely.* So B, MF, followed by Mc, K, Bw. MS: *michely.*

28   *thar.* Supplied from B, following Mc, K, Bw.

29   *uthiris cum.* So B, followed by Mc, K, Bw. MS: *tothir.*

31   Verse supplied from B, following Mc, Bw. K follows MF with *Thairfoir be glaid, and spend with mirrie face.*

37   *ragment.* So B, followed by Mc, K. Bw reads *regimen.* MS: *regiment.*

39   *as ony.* So B, followed by Mc, K, Bw. MS: *has.*

Poem 20 Base Text: Bannatyne MS, fols. 115v–116r.

15   Refrain is abbreviated here and in line 20.

Colophon   *Quod Dumbar.*

Poem 21 Base Text: Bannatyne MS, fols. 136r–136v. Bw uses MF as base text.

7   *it.* MS: *h* canceled before.

8   *quhill.* So Mc, K, Bw. MS: altered to *quhen.*

12   Refrain is abbreviated here and in lines 16, 20, 24, 28, and 36.

Colophon   *Quod Dumbar.*

Poem 22 Base Text: Bannatyne MS, fols. 64v–65r.

12   Refrain abbreviated here and in lines 16, 28, 32, 36, and 40.

20   Bw follows MF for this line: *Is now bot cair and covetyce.*

29   *heill.* So MF, followed by Mc, K, Bw. MS: *eill.*

30   *sald.* MS: *suld* canceled before.

Colophon   *Finis.*

Poem 23 Base Text: Bannatyne MS, fols. 63v–64r.

8   *thai.* So MF, followed by Mc, K, Bw. MS: *I.*

18   *he.* So MFb, followed by K. MS: *hie,* followed by Mc, Bw as a regular spelling for "he," though not an eye-rhyme.

21   *I.* Supplied from MF, following Mc, K, Bw.

32   *streiche.* So MF, followed by Mc, K, Bw. MS: *screiche.*

40	*tyme.* Supplied from MF, following Mc, K, Bw.
Colophon	*Finis quod Dumbar.*

Poem 24 Base Text: Maitland Folio, pp. 323–24, but with the sequence of stanzas following the arrangement in the Bannatyne MS (fols. 65v–66v). In Maitland the sequence is 1–25, 36–40, 26–30, 31–35, 41–50. The fourth stanza in Maitland is here deleted, also in accordance with Bannatyne.

3   Bw follows B: *I can not leif in no degre.*

6   *and.* So B, followed by Mc, K, Bw. MS: *ane.* Bw follows B for the entire line: *Gif I be galland, lusty, and blyth.*

14   *lad.* So Mc, K, Bw. MS: *laid.*

16   A stanza in MF is here deleted; as K observes, this stanza is not integral and disturbs the rhetorical pattern of the poem; this stanza, which is here printed (punctuation added), is not found in B:

> Be I liberall, gentill, and kynd,
> Thocht I it tak of nobill strynd,
> ȝit will thai say, baythe he and he,
> ȝon man is lyke out of his mynd:
> Lord god, how sall I gowerne me?

19   This line supplied from B, following Mc, K, Bw.

31   *gif.* So K, Bw. B: *than,* followed by Mc.

31–35   This stanza appears as stanza number six in MF, with a different first line: *And gif sum tyme rewarde gif I.*

Colophon   *finis quod Dumbar.*

Poem 25 Base Text: Bannatyne MS, fols. 68r–69r.

4   *speiche.* So Mc, K, Bw. MS: *speice.*

10   *trewth₂.* MS: *f* canceled before.

14   *vyle.* So Mc, Bw. MS: *vyld* is corrected to *vyle,* though K reads *vyld.*

40   *can.* So Mc, K, Bw. MS: *gan.*

46   *do.* So K, Bw. MS: *to,* followed by Mc.

Colophon   *Finis quod Dumbar.*

Poem 26 Base Text: Bannatyne MS, fols. 61r–61v, with emendations from Maitland Folio, pp. 259–60.

7   *Gif me.* So Mc, K. MF: *Gif me, gif me,* followed by Bw.

         rane. So MF, followed by Mc, Bw. MS: *drene,* followed by K.

15   Refrain is abbreviated here and in lines 30 and 35.

16–20   This stanza is omitted in MF.

24	*serve.* So Mc, K. MF: *suffise,* followed by Bw.
33	*or.* So Mc, K. MF, BD: *but,* followed by Bw.
36	*Ye.* Separated within the line by virgules.
38	*tyme.* MS: *tha* canceled before.
43	*Gife.* So Mc, K. Bw reads *Gif.*
44	*fecht.* So Mc, K. MF: *flytt,* followed by Bw.
Colophon	*Finis of asking. Followis discrecioun of geving.*

Poem 27	Base Text: Bannatyne MS, fols. 61v–62v, with emendations from Maitland Folio, pp. 260–61.
11	*and sum for threit.* So MF, followed by K, Bw. Mc omits *and.* MS: *sum chereit,* with *chereit* corrected from *chereitie.*
15	Refrain abbreviated here and in lines 20, 30, 35, 45, 50, and 55.
23	*And for a.* So Mc, K. BD: *And for sic,* followed by Bw.
	he. So MF, followed by Mc, K. MS: *hie,* followed by Bw.
31–35	This stanza is lacking in MF.
34	*His.* So Mc, K, Bw. MS: *Is.*
36	*faces.* So MF, followed by K, Bw. MS: *face,* followed by Mc.
38	*servandis.* So Mc, K, Bw. MS: *serwandis.*
48	*he.* So Mc, K. MS: *hie,* followed by Bw. The whole line in MF reads *he ken weill the contrarie.*
51	*thewis.* So MF, followed by Mc, Bw. K reads *kewis.* MS: *gud kewis.*
53	*knaiffis.* So MF, followed by Mc, K. Bw reads *knavis.* MS: *knaw his.*
59	*hes na wit thamselffe.* So MF, followed by Mc, K. Bw emends to *thame na wit hes thame.* MS: *he na wit hes thame.*
Colophon	*Finis of discretioun of geving. Followis discretioun in taking.*

Poem 28	Base Text: Bannatyne MS, fols. 62v–63r.
16	*mens.* So Bw. Mc, K follow MF: *menis.*
19	*Quhill.* So MF, followed by Mc, K, Bw. MS: *Quhilk.*
20	Refrain abbreviated here and in lines 25 and 30.
21	*sum.* Supplied, following K.
32	Bw follows MF: *And not ȝit can be satisfied.*
37	*Ar.* So MF, followed by Mc, K, Bw. MS: *At.*
38	*And peur.* So Mc, K. MF: *Quhair small,* followed by Bw.
Colophon	*Finis quod Dumbar.*

Poem 29	Base Text: Maitland Folio, pp. 9–10.
8	*Ane.* So K. The parchment is blemished. Mc and Bw read *A.*

8   *prosperité.* MS: *sp* canceled before.

10–11   Full line cancellation of *The theologgis sermon,* due to eyeskip.

11   *filosophicall.* MS: *off* canceled before.

12   *astronomy.* K reads *astronamy.* Mc, Bw read *astronomie.*

13   *fablis.* So Mc, K, Bw. MS: *fable.*

14   *selfe.* So Mc, Bw. MS: *salff.* K reads *selff.*

15   *flouris.* So Mc, K, Bw. MS: *floris.*

20   *owr.* So Mc, K, Bw. MS: *ʒour.*

21   *frustar is yowr.* So Mc, K, Bw. MS: corrected to *vain is all your,* but the original reading is preferable.

Colophon   *Quod Dumbar.*

Poem 30   Base Text: Bannatyne MS, fols. 342v–345r.

45–46   B repeats the phrase *full hestely* (*full hestely besene* / . . . *full haistely I went*). Most editors treat the repetition as eyeskip error and alter one line or the other. Bw emends line 45 to *full fresche and weill besene;* Mc emends line 46 to *eftir hir I went,* followed by K.

67   *scharp.* Not in MS. Schipper's emendation, followed by K, to repair the meter.

81   *seche.* So MS, followed by Bw. Mc, K emend to *feche,* an attractive alternative.

92   *full.* MS: corrected from *wes; wes* added after *terrible.*

104   *chief.* So K. MS: *cheif,* followed by Mc, Bw.

        the woddis. MS omits *the,* followed by Mc, K, Bw.

111   *for.* MS: *fow* canceled before.

115   *le.* So Mc, K, Bw. MS: *la.*

119   *parcere.* So Mc, K, Bw. MS: *proceir.*

124   *wycht.* So Mc, K, Bw. MS: *wychtcht.*

135   *hald.* So Bw. MS: *thow hald,* followed by Mc, K.

143   *thyne.* So Mc, K. Bw reads *thy.*

155   *clarefeid.* MS: *clarf* canceled before.

182   *Chryst.* So Mc, K, Bw. MS: *Crhyst.*

184   *awoilk.* MS: *wen* canceled before.

Colophon   *Explicit quod Dumbar.*

Poem 31   Base Text: British Library Royal MS 58, fols. 17v–18r.

15   *spreit.* So K. MS: *seqete.* Mc reads *secrete.*

Poem 32   Base Text: Aberdeen Minute Book, II, p. 460.

Colophon   *quod Dunbar.*

Poem 33 Base Text: Reidpeth MS, fols. 7r–7v.

3 *upheyt.* Supplied, following Bw. Mc, K add *ascendit.*

26 *with.* MS: *with* is written twice.

33 *stour.* So Mc, K. MS *stor,* followed by Bw.

35 *large.* MS: *full* canceled before.

37 *royall Stewartis.* Supplied, following K. Laing conjectured *nobill Stewartis,* followed by Mc. Bw emends to *stok ryell.*

43 *gold.* So Mc, K, Bw. MS: *cold.*

44 *all browderit.* So R, followed by Mc, Bw. K emends to *browderit all.*

   bravelie. So Mc, K, Bw. MS: *brav,* with a prior cancelation. Emendation based on rhyme.

47 *halsand.* MS: *husband.* I follow Bw's emendation; Mc and K emend to *saluand.*

51 *playit.* So Mc, K, Bw. MS: *plyayit.*

54 *schene.* Supplied, following Mc, K, Bw.

63 *Coverit.* MS is corrected from *Cunyeitt.*

Colophon *Quod Dumbar.*

Poem 34 Base Text: Bannatyne MS, fol. 238v.

10 *day the.* MS is defective; I follow K's (and Laing's) emendation. Mc omits.

21 *persoun.* MS: *renoun* canceled before.

24 Refrain is abbreviated.

37 *wyse and trew.* MS: *fair of hew* canceled before.

38 *out all.* Written twice in MS.

Colophon *Finis.*

Poem 35 Base Text: Chepman & Myllar Print, pp. 171–74.

56 *glorie.* So Mc, K. Print: *gloire,* followed by Bw.

63 *fortunate.* Print: *fortunable,* followed by Mc, K, Bw.

69 *knyghtheid.* So Mc, K, Bw. Print: *knyghteid.*

Poem 36 Base Text: Reidpeth MS, fols. 6v–7r.

3 *Stewart.* So Mc, K, Bw. MS: *stewar.*

7 *him.* Inserted above the line in MS.

13 *Turkas.* So K. MS: *turk,* followed by Mc, Bw.

21 *stour.* So Mc, K. MS: *stoir,* followed by Bw.

23 *chois.* So Mc, K. MS: *schois,* followed by Bw.

32 *chavelrie.* So Bw. Mc, K: *chevelrie.* MS: *chabelrie.*

Colophon *Quod Dumbar.*

Poem 37   Base Text: Reidpeth MS, fols. 2v–3r.

11   *Evir*. MS: *and* canceled before.

16   *New*. Supplied, following Mc, K, Bw.

Colophon   *Quod Dumbar.*

Poem 38   Base Text: Maitland Folio, pp. 194–95.

7   *hard*. So Mc, K, Bw. MS: *hart*.

Colophon   *Finis quod Dunbar.*

Poem 39   Base Text: Bannatyne MS, fols. 113v–114r.

15   Refrain abbreviated here and in line 25.

Colophon   *Quod Dumbar to the king.*

Poem 40   Base Text: Maitland Folio, p. 316 (MFb); emendations from Maitland Folio a, p. 7.

1   *of*. Supplied from MFa, following Mc, K, Bw.

8   *birst*. So MS, followed by K. Mc, Bw follow MFa: *brist*.

Colophon   *Quod Dumbar quhone mony Benefices vakit.*

Poem 41   Base Text: Maitland Folio, pp. 321–22 (MFb); emendations from Maitland Folio a, pp. 8–9.

8   *thame*. So Mc, K, Bw. MS: *thane*. So, too, lines 10, 13, 15, 18, and 20.

17   *spraidis . . . nett*. So MFa, followed by Mc, K, Bw. MS: *spendis . . . mett*.

26   *warryit*. So MFa, followed by Mc, K, Bw. MS: *variant*.

27   Bw follows MFa and R: *That men off it are neuer content.*

Colophon   *Quod Dumbar.*

Poem 42   Base Text: Reidpeth MS, fols. 3v–5r.

13   *This*. So Mc, K, Bw. MS: *Thus*.

14   *fiendlie*. So K, Bw. MS: *freindlie*, followed by Mc.

19   *eik*. So Mc, K, Bw. MS: *iek*.

     Hivines. So Mc, K, Bw. MS: *Hiwenis*.

23   *so*. MS: *full* corrected to *so*.

25   *leid*. Bw emends to *weid*, which makes good sense in terms of the withering metaphor and the pattern of alliteration.

28   *Saying*. So Mc, K, Bw. MS: *Seing*.

29   *se*. So Mc, K, Bw. MS: *sa*.

36   *glader wox*. So Mc, K. MS: *glaider wax*. Bw reads *glader vox*, the sense being "became more glad."

38   *lady*. So Mc, K, Bw. MS: *lay*.

39	*fiellis*. MS: corrected from *fellis*.
	wecht. So Mc, K, Bw. MS: *wicht*.
48	*malady*. So Mc, K. MS: *melody*, followed by Bw.
50	*his*. Supplied, following Mc, K, Bw.
56	*said*. MS: corrected from &.
65	*Thy*. MS: corrected from *The*.
	evir. MS: corrected from *neuir*.
72	*first*. MS: corrected from *be*.
73	*quoth*. So Mc, K. Bw emends to *quod*. MS: *with*.
74	*dies*. MS: corrected from *dres*.
76	*Inoportunite*. So Mc, K, Bw. MS: *Inoportunititie*.
95	*sum*. Written above the line in MS.
106	*me*. MS: *said* canceled after.
107	*humelie*. So Mc, K, Bw. MS: altered to *heuinelie*.
108	*full*. MS: *knaw* canceled, *full* written above.
109	*He*. So Mc, K, Bw. MS: *ʒe*.
112	*rak*. MS: altered to *crak* or *trak*.
115	*anon*. MS: corrected from *amen*.
Colophon	*Quod Dumbar*.

Poem 43	Base Text: Reidpeth MS, fol. 6r.
5	*scant*. Interlined.
11	*oft*. So Mc, K, Bw. MS: *off*.
Colophon	*Quod Dumbar*.

Poem 44	Base Text: Maitland Folio, pp. 178–81.
13	An extra *liell* deleted before *labour*.
17	*all*. MS: *ane* canceled before.
38	*the father*. So Mc, K, Bw. MS: *his father*.
67	*all the*. MS: repeated and then canceled.
76	Refrain abbreviated here and in lines 80 and 84.
81	*it*. Supplied, following Mc, K, Bw.
Colophon	*Finis quod Dumbar*.

Poem 45	Base Text: Maitland Folio, p. 8 (MFa).
6	*Quhill*. So MFb, followed by Mc, K, Bw. MS: *Quhilk*.
7	*singis*. MS: *d* canceled after.
Colophon	*Quod Dumbar*.

Poem 46   Base Text: Maitland Folio, pp. 196–98.
10   *flingaris*. Preceded by a blank space in MS.
11   *carvouris*. MS: *carpentaris* canceled before.
36   *eik*. Corrected from *reik* in MS.
65   *nyce*. MS: *y* canceled before.
79   *mind*. So Mc, K, Bw. MS: *mynd*.
85   *Or*. So Mc, K, Bw. MS: *And*.
Colophon   *Quod Dunbar*.

Poem 47   Base Text: Maitland Folio, pp. 16–18.
4   *All*. Corrected from *And* in MS.
16   *Cowkin*. Corrected from *Couth quhennis* in MS.
       culroun. So R, followed by Mc, K, Bw. MS: *cukoun*.
19   *dyvowris*. So Mc, K. MS: *dyowris*, followed by Bw.
21   *mastis*. Corrected from *kynd* in MS.
43   *ald*. So R, followed by Bw. MS: *all*, followed by Mc, K.
53   *clais*. MS: *plasse* canceled before.
56   *beir*. So Mc, K. R: *bere*, followed by Bw. MS: *be*.
64   *Nobles*. So Mc, K, Bw. MS: *And nobles*.
70   *That lang*. So Mc, K, Bw. MS: words are faded.
71   *I be*. So Mc, K, Bw. MS: words are faded.
Colophon   *Quod Dumbar &c.*

Poem 48   Base Text: Maitland Folio, pp. 295–96; emendations from Bannatyne MS, fols.
       94v–95v.
1   *yit*. So B, followed by Mc, K, Bw. MS: *ʒe*.
23   *at cheif*. So B, followed by Mc, K. MS: *but greif*, followed by Bw.
33   *Kyne of Rauf Colyard*. So B, followed by Mc, K. MS: *Raf Coilyearis kynd*,
       followed by Bw.
41   *suld*. so Mc, Bw. MS: *sould*, followed by K.
76–85   Recorded on p. 309 in MF; leaf misplaced.
Colophon   *Quod Dumbar*.

Poem 49   Base Text: Maitland Folio, p. 18 (for lines 1–32); Reidpeth MS, fols. 1r–1v (for
       lines 33–76).
1   *toune*. So R, followed by K, Bw. MS: *toume*.
3   *jaid aver*. MS: *ʒald auir* canceled and rewritten as *ʒaid aver*. Bw reads *ʒald aver*.
5   *Strenever*. So K, Bw. MS: *Streneverne*.
7–8   The burden, repeated at the end of each stanza, is abbreviated in both MSS.

30	Verse is faded in MS.
32	MF ends here (subsequent quire is lacking).
33–76	Verses supplied from R.
39	*curage.* Written above canceled *pleȝe* in MS.
52	*cast.* Inserted above the line in MS.
63	*clappit.* MS: altered from *chappid.*
Colophon	*Quod Dumbar.*

Poem 50	Base Text: Reidpeth, fols. 3r–3v; emendations from Bannatyne MS, fol. 66v.
4	*And.* MS: *ȝett* deleted after.
7	*he.* Supplied from B, following K, Bw. Mc omits.
10	*lusty.* So B, BD, followed by K, Bw. MS: *nobill*, followed by Mc.
15	*wame.* So B, followed by Mc, K, Bw. MS: *vane.*
23	*Quha.* So B, BD, followed by Mc, K, Bw. MS: *Quhar.*
25–30	These lines are not in B or BD. Mc ignores the refrain and ends at line 28. K, following B, ends at line 24. Bw follows MS, as do I.
Colophon	*Quod Dumbar.*

Poem 51	Base Text: Maitland Folio, pp. 334–35; emendations from Bannatyne MS, fols. 133r–134r.
2	*sterris.* B: *sternis*, followed by Mc, K, Bw.
16	*the.* So B, followed by Mc, K, Bw on metrical grounds. Omitted in MS.
31	*Saturnus.* So B, followed by Mc, K, Bw. MS: *Saturnis.*
35	*wondrus.* So MS. B reads *windir*, followed by Mc, K, Bw on grounds that *wondrus* is a modernization. But the *OED* cites an example of *wondrus* in 1509. B's *windir* means "strange, marvellous," and could well be the more likely reading. See Poem 52, line 13.
Colophon	*Quod Dumbar.*

Poem 52	Base Text: Reidpeth MS, fols. 5v–6r.
5	*rink.* MS: altered to *rank.* Mc reads *raik.*
7	*thocht.* Inserted above a deletion in MS.
16	*awin.* Inserted above the line in MS.
26	*lyflett.* In MS, a later insertion filling in a blank.
Colophon	*Quod Dumbar.*

Poem 53	Base Text: Reidpeth MS, fols. 6r–6v.
8	*clink.* Emendation for rhyme, following Mc, K, Bw. MS: *clank.*
Colophon	*Quod Dumbar.*

Poem 54   Base Text: Bannatyne MS, fols. 117r–118v; emendations from Asloan MS, fols. 211v–212v (lines 1–69 only).

Title   B: *Ane ballat of the fenʒeit freir of Tungland: how he fell in the myre fleand to Turkiland.*

30   *mony in.* MS: corrected from *in to*, followed by Mc, K. Bw adheres to the original MS reading.

56   *smowking.* MS: *k* is inserted above the line.

67   *Martis.* MS: *the* canceled before.

    blak. Supplied from As, followed by Mc, K, Bw.

104   *with.* MS: *quhi* canceled before.

111   *owtsprang.* So Bw. MS: *owsprang*, followed by Mc, K.

Colophon   *Finis quod Dumbar.*

Poem 55   Base Text: Maitland Folio, pp. 3–5; emendations from Reidpeth MS, fols. 8r–8v.

4   *giand.* So R. MS: *grand* (?).

6   Verse supplied from R, following Mc, K, Bw. MS is defective.

8   *On.* So R, followed by Mc, K, Bw. MS: *or*.

10   *comin in.* So Bw. MS, R: *com in*, followed by Mc. K emends to *com in to*, which satisfies the meter, as does *comin in*.

37–40   Verses supplied from R, following Mc, K, Bw. MS is defective.

Colophon   *Quod Dumbar.*

Poem 56   Base Text: Maitland Folio, pp. 340–41.

4   *The.* MS: corrected from *His*.

9   *culd.* MS: *man* canceled before.

23   *thair.* Interlined in MS.

36   *Dounteboir.* MS: *u* inserted above the line.

37   *louket.* MS: *u* inserted above the line.

42   *mirrear.* So Mc, K, Bw. MS: *mirrar*.

Colophon   *Quod Dunbar of a dance in the quen[is] chalmer.*

Poem 57   Base Text: Maitland Folio, p. 339.

1   *boure.* MS: *u* inserted above the line.

2   *doublett.* MS: *u* inserted above the line.

Colophon   *Quod Dunbar of James Dog Kepair of the Quenis wardrep.*

Poem 58   Base Text: Maitland Folio, pp. 339–40.

7   *all.* Inserted above the line in MS.

14   *taingis*. MS: *tang* canceled before.
Colophon   *Quod Dunbar of the said James quhen he had plesett him.*

Poem 59 Base Text: Bannatyne Draft MS, pp. 53–54; emendations from Maitland Folio,
            pp. 11–12.
20   *hes*. So MF, followed by Bw. MS: *had*, followed by Mc, K.
21   *Round ylis*. So MF, followed by Mc, K, Bw. MS: *rowme Iylis*.
24   *Now he dois*. So MF, followed by Bw. MS: *ȝitt dois he*, followed by Mc, K.
27   *licht*. MS: *slicht* written first, then canceled.
31   *fals*. So MF, followed by Mc, Bw. MS: *falis*, followed by K.
32   *all reffar*. So MF, followed by Bw. MS: *every*, followed by Mc, K.
48   *Quhill*. MS: *quyll* written first, then canceled.
Colophon   *Finis quod Dumbar for Donald Ovre Epetaphe.*

Poem 60 Base Text: Maitland Folio, pp. 10–11.
8   *dismemberit*. So R, followed by Mc, K, Bw. MS: *dismeberit*.
16   *awin*. MS: added in margin.
18   *seasoun*. MS: *ressoun* corrected in margin to *seasoun*.
Colophon   *Quod Dumbar.*

Poem 61 Base Text: Maitland Folio, p. 320.
Colophon   *Quod Dumbar.*

Poem 62 Base Text: Bannatyne MS, fols. 214r–215r; emendations from Reidpeth MS, fol.
            8r (lines 1–16 only).
11   *thame*. So R, followed by Bw. MS: *hir*, followed by Mc, K.
15   *Fresche*. Supplied from R, following Mc, K, Bw.
            said. So R, followed by Bw. MS: *sayis*, followed by Mc, K.
18   *Strangenes*. Corrected in MS from *strangens*.
30   *a feir*. So Mc, K, Bw. MS: *affeir*.
87   *Gud*. MS: *hi* canceled after.
90   *His*. MS: *h* canceled after.
            he. Supplied, following K, Bw. Mc omits.
94   *Bot*. MS: *ye* deleted after.
104   *Betuix*. MS: *the* deleted after.
Colophon   *Finis &c.*

Poem 63	Base Text: Maitland Folio, pp. 322–23.
16	*goist.* MS: *fl* canceled after.
Colophon	*Quod Dumbar quhone he list to feyne.*

Poem 64	Base Text: Bannatyne MS, fol. 212v.
22	*nor.* MS: *or to* canceled before.
Colophon	*Finis &c. Dumbar.*

Poem 65	Base Text: Chepman and Myllar Print, pp. 91–99.
Title	*Here begynnys ane litil tretie intitulit the goldyn targe compilit be Maister Wilyam Dunbar.*
14	*schuke.* So B, MF, followed by Bw. Print: *schake,* followed by Mc, K.
16	*To part.* So Mc, K. B, MF: *Depart,* followed by Bw.
19	*hoppis.* So B, MF, followed by Bw, Mc. Print: *happis,* followed by K.
31	*wyth.* So Mc, K, Bw. Print: *wyht.*
32	*The.* So B, MF, followed by Bw. Print: *That,* followed by Mc, K.
39	*emerant.* So Mc, K, Bw. Print: *emeraut.*
47	*soun.* Mc reads *sone.* K reads *soune.*
54	*falcoun.* Mc, K read *falcoune.*
64	*Discrive.* So Mc, K, Bw. Print: *Distrine.*
90	*proporcioun.* So Print, Mc, K. Bw: *proporcion.*
103	*ballettis.* So Mc, K, Bw. Print: *ballectis.*
112	*the.* So Mc, K, Bw. Print: *te.*
139	*grene.* So Mc, K. Print: *gren,* followed by Bw.
140	*bowis.* So B, MF, followed by Mc, K, Bw. Print: *lowis.*
151	*Resoun.* So Print, followed by Mc, K. Bw: *Reson.*
153	*that.* So B, MF, followed by Mc, K, Bw. Print: *thas.*
165	*Discrecioun.* So Print, followed by Mc, K. Bw: *Discrecion.*
187	*anker.* So B, MF. Print: *ankers,* followed by Mc, K. Bw emends to *ankeris.*
201	*assayit.* So B, MF, followed by Mc, K, Bw. Print: *assayes.*
203	*Quhill.* So B, MF, followed by Mc, K, Bw. Print: *Quhilk.*
228	*tuke.* So B, MF, followed by Mc, K, Bw. Print: *take.*
231	*toschuke.* So B, MF, followed by Mc, K, Bw. Print: *toschake.*
235	*schip.* So B, MF, followed by Mc, K, Bw. Print: *scip.*
254	*ane.* So B, MF, followed by Mc, K, Bw. Print: *and.*
259	*noucht.* So Mc, K, Bw. Print: *noucth.*
268	*write.* So K, Bw. Mc: *wryte.* Print: *wirte.*
274	*hes spent.* So B, followed by Mc, K, Bw. MF: *may spend.* Print: *may spent.*

Poem 66	Base Text: Bannatyne MS, fols. 283r–284v; emendations from Maitland Folio, pp. 165–68.
6	*lawry*. MS: corrected from *lawrir*.
23	*new*. MS: *noble* canceled before.
35	*faill*. So MF, followed by Mc, K, Bw. MS: *fable*.
52	*luve*. MS: *eik* canceled before.
72	*lufes*. So MF, followed by Mc, K, Bw. MS: *lufe*.
74	*Ane man may in his lady tak*. So MF, followed by Bw. MS: *Man may tak in his lady*, followed by Mc, K.
75	*bewtie*. So MF, followed by Bw. MS: *vertew*, followed by Mc, K.
90	*Sic*. So MF, followed by Mc, K, Bw. MS: *Sir*.
92	*thai*. Inserted above the line in MS.
99	*sic*. MS: *thame* canceled before.
	hardines. MS: *ignorance* canceled before.
108	*hes*. Supplied from MF, following Bw.
115	*into*. So MF, followed by Bw. MS: *ʒit*, with *maid* added above line.
116	*in rest and*. So Mc, K, Bw. MS: *in restand*, with *in* canceled.
Colophon	*Finis quod Dumbar.*

Poem 67	Base Text: Bannatyne MS, fol. 281r.
11	*the schort*. MS: corrected from *with lang*.
Colophon	*Finis quod Dumbar.*

Poem 68	Base Text: Banntyne MS, fols. 284v–285v.
4	*ay*. Interlined in MS.
19–20	The burden is abbreviated here and in subsequent stanzas.
58	*me*. Repeated in MS, then canceled.
75–76	Verses are transposed in MS; in the margin are numbers correcting their order.
84	*That*. MS: *So* canceled before.
	our. MS: *my* canceled, *our* interlined to replace it.
Colophon	*Finis quod Dumbar.*

Poem 69	Base Text: Bannatyne MS, fols. 116r–116v; emendations from Maitland Folio, pp. 335–37.
Rubric	*Follows the wowing of the king / quhen he wes in Dumfermeling.*
28	*that*. So MF, followed by Bw. MS: *this*, followed by Mc, K.
35	Refrain abbreviated here and in subsequent stanzas.
36	*hir . . . him*. So MF, followed by Mc, K, Bw. MS: *him . . . hir*, where the sense seems to be "pressed himself against her" rather than "drew her to him."

66	*bell*. So MF, followed by Mc, K. MS: *tod*, followed by Bw.
Colophon	*Quod Dumbar*.

Poem 70	Base Text: Maitland Folio, p. 342.
1	*said*. So R, followed by Mc, K, Bw. MS: *sad*.
4	*soin*. So K. Mc, Bw read *som*. R: *son*.
28	*Had*. Corrected from a cancellation in MS.
Colophon	*Quod Dunbar*.

Poem 71	Base Text: Maitland Folio, pp. 341–42; emendations from Reidpeth MS, fols. 45v–46r.
9	*schou*. Supplied from R, following Mc, K, Bw, though Mc reads *scho*.
Colophon	*Quod Dunbar of an blak moir*.

Poem 72	Base Text: Maitland Folio, p. 308 (for lines 1–28); p. 311 (for lines 29–63), following Bawcutt.
16	*I*. Inserted above the line in MS.
Colophon	*Quod Dumbar*.

Poem 73	Base Text: Maitland Folio, pp. 324–25; emendations from Bannatyne MS, fols. 261r–261v.
7	*So*. So B, followed by Mc, K, Bw. MS: *For*.
44	*evidens*. So B, followed by Mc, K, Bw. MS: *evudens*.
Colophon	*Quod Dumbar*.

Poem 74	Base Text: Maitland Folio, pp. 314–15.
Colophon	*Quod Dumbar*.

Poem 75	Base Text: Reidpeth MS, fols. 1v–2v.
7	*hurt*. So Mc, K, Bw. MS: *quyt* canceled.
11	*flyttinis*. MS: *flyttingis*, followed by Mc, K, Bw.
15	*Stull*. MS: altered to *scull*.
17	*foirstairis*. So Mc, Bw. MS: *foirstair*, followed by K.
20	*polesie*. So Mc, K, Bw. MS: *polaesie*.
25	*Jame*. So Mc, K, Bw. MS: *Iames*.
27	*ilk*. So Mc, K, Bw. MS: *ill*.
31	*serve*. MS: *schow* canceled.
33	Line 34 is mistakenly written at the end of this line, then repeated below.
37	*streitis*. So Mc, Bw. K emends to *streittis*. MS: *streit*.

38	*merchantis*. MS: *merchandis*, followed by Mc, K, Bw.
46	*rame*. MS: *lament* canceled before.
61	Continues on same line as 60.
67	*proclame*. So Mc, K, Bw. MS: *proclameid*.
73	*fynd*. MS: corrected from *send*.
77	*restor to*. Conjectural emendation to fill blank space. Mc, Bw leave the space blank. K suggests *[win bak to]*.
Colophon	*Quod Dumbar.*

Poem 76   Base Text: Bannatyne MS, fols. 115r–115v; emendations from Maitland Folio, pp. 333–34.

Title	MS: *Followis how Dumbar wes Desyrd to be ane Freir.*
29	*forder*. So MF, followed by Bw. MS: *ony*. Mc, K follow the MS, but place the whole stanza (lines 26–30) after line 15 (i.e., as the fourth stanza). It appears as the fifth stanza in MF.
30	*put*. MS: *b* canceled before.
49	*hous end*. So MF, followed by Mc, K, Bw. MS: *houshend*.
Colophon	*Quod Dumbar.*

Poem 77   Base Text: Bannatyne MS, fols. 110r–112v; emendations from Maitland Folio, pp. 12–16, and Asloan MS, fols. 210r–211v.

17	*hair*. So Mc, K. MS: *bair*, followed by Bw.
35	*into*. MS: *all* canceled before; *to* written above line.
50	*in secreit places*. So MF, followed by Mc, Bw. MS: *of sindry racis*, followed by K.
80	*Come*. Supplied from MF, following Mc, Bw. K omits.
81	*Lythenes*. So MF, followed by K, Bw. MS: *ydilnes*, followed by Mc.
99	*creissche*. MS: *creis* canceled before.
112	*Be he the*. So Mc, K, Bw. MS: *Be he þe the.*
131	*clayth*. MS: *beis* canceled before.
137	*fillis*. So MF, followed by Bw. MS: *flowis*, followed by Mc, K.
142	*come furth*. So MS, followed by Mc, K. As: *comfort*, followed by Bw.
145	*The tailyeour hecht*. So Mc, K. As: *He hecht*, followed by Bw.
149	*curage*. So As, MF, followed by K. MS: *hairt*, followed by Mc, Bw.
151	Entire verse supplied from MF, following Bw. MS: *And quhen to þe sowtar he did cum*, followed by Mc, K.
154	Entire verse supplied from As, following Bw. MS: *In harte he tuke ȝit sic ane scunner*, followed by Mc, K.

169   *talyeour*. So As, MF, followed by Bw. MS: *telȝour*, followed by Mc, K. Bw follows As, MF for the whole line: *Apon the talȝeour quhen he did luke*.

171   *Uneis he mycht*. So As, followed by Bw. MS: *He mycht nocht rycht*, followed by Mc, K.

173   *quhilk cost him*. So MF. Bw: *that cost him*. MS: *quhilk he cost*, followed by Mc, K.

174   *never*. So MF, followed by Bw. MS: *deill*, followed by Mc, K.

177   *stynk than*. So As, followed by Bw. MS: *sair syne*, followed by Mc, K.

187–88 As, MF: *Thai spurrit apon athir syde, / The horw attour the grene did glyd*, followed by Bw.

189   *Than tham*. So Mc, K. MF: *And tham*, followed by Bw.

190   *The tailyeour was*. So MF, followed by Bw. MS: *The tailȝeour þat wes*, followed by Mc, K.

193   *birnes*. So MF, followed by Bw. MS: *harnas*, followed by Mc, K.

200   *wend*. Mc, K read *went*. As: *Trowit*, followed by Bw.

       bene. MS: *ha* canceled before.

201   *stern*. So Mc, K. As: *strenyt*, followed by Bw.

204   *Quyte our from*. So As, followed by Bw. MF: *Quyte our frome*. MS: *Evin quyte frome*, followed by Mc, K.

206   *he straik till*. So Mc, K. As: *flewe to the*, followed by Bw.

207   *fartit*. So Mc, K. As, MF: *fart*, followed by Bw.

209   *The new maid knycht lay into swoun*. So As, followed by Bw. MS: *Thir new maid knychtis lay bayth in swoun*, followed by Mc, K.

210   *forswer*. So As, followed by Bw. MS: *mensweir*, followed by Mc, K.

214   *bayth*. So MS, followed by Mc, K. As: *agane*, followed by Bw. MF: *ay*.

217   *of*. MS: *writtin* canceled before.

224   *To*. MS: *And* corrected to *To*.

226   *To dyte how all this thing*. So As, followed by Bw. MS: *For this said iusting it*, followed by Mc, K.

228   *Schirris*. So As, MF, followed by Bw. MS: *Now*, followed by Mc, K.

       it. So As, MF, followed by Bw. MS: *this*, followed by Mc, K.

Colophon *Heir endis the sowtar amd tailyouris war maid be the nobill poyet maister William Dumbar.*

Poem 78 Base Text: Bannatyne MS, fols. 112v–113r; emendations from Maitland Folio, pp. 319–20.

Title   MS: *Followis the amendis maid be him to the telyouris and sowtaris for the turnament maid on thame.*

12   Refrain abbreviated here and in subsequent stanzas.

20	*Bot.* MS: *Tely* canceled before.
	tham. MS: *thame*, followed by Mc, K, Bw.
25	*swayne.* So MF, followed by Bw. MS: *man*, followed by Mc, K.
30	*gud.* So MF, followed by Mc, K, Bw. MS: *gude crafty.*
Colophon	*Quod Dumbar.*

Poem 79	Base Text: Bannatyne MS, fols. 132v–133r.
20	Refrain abbreviated here and in subsequent stanzas.
39	*cowth.* So Bw. Mc, K read *cowld.* MS: *qwith.*
Colophon	*Quod Dumbar.*

Poem 80	Base Text: Rouen Print, pp. 193–96.
1	*maister.* So Mc, K, Bw. Print: *maist.*
47	*hecht.* So Mc, K, Bw. Print: *hetht.*
71	*gif.* So Mc, K, Bw. Print: *hif.*
74	*Lego.* So Mc, K, Bw. Print: *Llego.*
104	*miscebam.* So Mc, K, Bw. Print: *missebam.*
Colophon	*Explicit.*

Poem 81	Base Text: Maitland Folio, pp. 290–92; emendations from Bannatyne MS, fols. 102r–103v.
Title	*Dumbaris Dirige to the King.*
14	*into.* So B, followed by Mc, K, Bw. MS: *in.*
34	*manis.* So Mc, K. Bw reads *mans.*
46a	*Lectio secunda.* Supplied from B, following Mc, K, Bw.
49	*saitt.* So B, followed by Mc, K, Bw. MS: *hewinlie court.*
87	*sould ye.* So B, followed by Mc, K, Bw. MS: *ye sould.*
103	*ne.* Supplied from B, following Mc, K, Bw.
Colophon	*Dumbaris dirige to the king / Bydand ouir lang in Stirling.*

Poem 82	Base Text: Aberdeen Minute Book, II, p. 460.
19	*husband.* So B, MF, followed by Mc, K, Bw. MS: *susband.*
21	*scho.* So B, MF, followed by Mc, K, Bw. MS: *sche.*
22	*is.* So B, MF, followed by Mc, K, Bw. MS: *ale.*
23	*nocht.* So B, MF, followed by Mc, K, Bw. MS: *norcht.*
24	*glas.* MS: *cop* canceled before.
	me to. So B, MF, followed by Mc, K, Bw. MS: *to me.*
Colophon	*Quod Dumbar.*

Poem 83	Base Text: Bannatyne MS, fols. 147r–154r (lines 1–315); Chepman and Myllar, pp. 137–44 (lines 316–552); emendations from Maitland Folio, pp. 53–54, 59–63, 69–72, 77–80.
18	*richt*. So MF, followed by Mc, Bw. MS: *for*, followed by K.
28	*laureat*. MS: *lane* canceled before.
48	This line is added in the left margin in MS.
51	*Denseman*. MF: *Densmen*, followed by Bw.
54	*royis*. MS: *reis* canceled before.
58	*Skitterand scorpion, scauld*. So MF, followed by Bw. MS: *Scarth fra scorpione scaldit*, followed by Mc, K.
68	*To*. So Mc, K, Bw. MS: *Tho*.
76	*cowart*. MS: added in the left margin.
83	*glengoir loun*. MF: *ganʒelon*, followed by Bw.
88	*recry it*. So MF, followed by Bw. MS: *recryat*, followed by Mc, K.
92	*us*. So MF, followed by K, Bw. MS: *wes*, followed by Mc.
	wind and. So MF, followed by Mc, K, Bw. MS: *woundis*.
95	*sey*. Supplied from MF, following K, Bw. Mc omits.
97	*rethore*. So MF, followed by Bw. MS: *rethory*, followed by Mc, K.
102	*lauchtane*. So MF, followed by Bw. MS: *lachand*, followed by Mc, K (reading *lathand*).
106	*rejoys*. MS: *reris* canceled before.
114	*pingill*. MS: *de* canceled before.
119	*gyngill*. MS: *In* canceled before.
120	*bratt*. So R, followed by Bw. MS: *club*, followed by Mc, K.
121	*loungeour, lowsy*. So MF, followed by Bw. MS: *loungeour baith lowsy*, followed by Mc, K.
123	*Lawrance*. So Mc, K, Bw. MS: *Lawarance*.
129	*Cummerwarld*. So R, followed by Bw. MS: *Commirwald*, followed by Mc, K.
133	*mair*. Corrected from *thair* in MS.
135	*for wage*. So MF, followed by Bw. MS: *ar at*, followed by Mc, K.
139	*my*. So Bw. MS: *thy*, followed by Mc, K.
152	*lymmair*. So MF, followed by Bw. MS: *lymmerfull*, followed by Mc, K.
160	*sacryne*. So MF, followed by Bw. K emends to *sacrand*. MS: *secirind*, which Mc reads as *seccrind*.
169	*linkis*. So MF, followed by Bw. MS: *lukis*, followed by Mc, K.
	lenye. So MF, followed by Bw. MS: *lene*, followed by Mc, K.
175	Entire verse supplied from MF, following Mc, K, Bw.
185	*pynhippit*. So MF, followed by K, Bw. Mc reads *purehippit*. MS: *hippit*.
197	*me*. So MF, followed by K, Bw. MS: *my*, followed by Mc.

201	*burch.* So Mc, K, Bw. MS: *burcht.*
217	*Edinburch.* So Mc, K, Bw. MS: *Edinburcht.*
218	*Hay.* So MF, followed by Bw. MS: *ay*, followed by Mc, K.
231	*skeilis.* MS: *skiilis* canceled before.
237	*fed.* Added above the line in MS.
241	*byt.* So MF, followed by Mc, K, Bw. MS: *byle.*
242	*flay.* So MF, followed by Bw. MS: *foule*, followed by Mc, K.
251	*werwoif.* MS: *werf* canceled before.
257	*forbear is.* So Bw. MS: *forbearis*, followed by Mc, K.
261	*on.* So MF, followed by Bw. MS: *of*, followed by Mc, K.
281	*Pert.* So Bw. MS: *Perth*, followed by Mc, K.
283	*disert.* So Bw. MS: *diserth*, followed by Mc, K.
289	*binkis.* MS: *abydis* canceled after.
290	*abydis.* MS: *amang* canceled after.
299	*Archebauld.* So MF, followed by Bw. Mc, K read *Archbald.* MS: *Archbard.*
316 ff.	From this point on, Chepman & Myllar Print is used.
325	*kneis.* So B, MF, followed by Mc, K, Bw. Print: *keneis.*
329	*commissare.* So Mc, K, Bw. Print: *comnissare.*
332	*bill.* So B, followed by Mc, K, Bw. Print: *bull.*
335	*and.* So B, MF, followed by Bw. Print: *or*, followed by Mc, K.
367	*For.* Supplied from B, following Bw.
386	*erlis.* So Bw. Print: *erl*, followed by Mc, K.
388	*that.* So B, MF, followed by Mc, K, Bw. Print: *tha.*
389	*wicht.* So B, MF, followed by Mc, K, Bw. Print: *wyth.*
392	*dicht.* So Mc, K, Bw. Print: *ditht.*
395	*Duerch.* So Mc, K, Bw. Print: *Duerth.*
398	*thy scule.* So Bw. Print: *the scule*, followed by Mc, K.
399	*thy hede.* So B, MF, followed by Bw. Print: *the hede*, followed by Mc, K.
400	*for.* So MF, followed by Bw. Print: *wyth*, followed by Mc, K.
408	*duerche.* So Mc, K, Bw. Print: *doerthe.*
443	*thrift.* So B, MF, followed by Mc, K, Bw. Print: *trift.*
472	*muk.* So B, MF, followed by Mc, K, Bw. Print: *mak.*
483	*Lat.* So B, MF, followed by Bw. Print: *That*, followed by Mc, K.
509	*skryp.* So Mc, K, Bw. Print: *skyrp.*
	clamschellis. So Mc, K, Bw. Print: *clanischellis.*
511	*mischance.* So Mc, K, Bw. Print: *mischanche.*
520	*tume.* So B, followed by Mc, K, Bw. Print: *tune.*
526	*manesuorne.* So Mc, K, Bw. Print: *manesuorme.*
530	*Egiptia.* So MF, followed by Bw. Print: *Egipya*, followed by Mc, K.

548	*Prikkit.* So MF, followed by Bw. Mc reads *Pickit.* K reads *Prickit.* Print: *Pirckit.*
Colophon	MF: *Quod Kennedy to Dumbar.* No colophon in CM.

Poem 84   Base Text: Maitland Folio, pp. 81–84, for lines 1–103; Rouen Print, pp. 177–89, which lacks the initial two pages, for lines 104–530, with emendations from Maitland Folio, pp. 84–96. Paragraph divisions in the text are editorially supplied, following Kinsley.

Title	MF: *Heir beginis the Tretis of the Tua Mariit Wemen and the Wedo.*
1–103	Supplied from MF, as RP is missing the initial pages.
2	*in.* Supplied, following Bw.
18	*garlandis.* MS: *gor* canceled before.
29	*Now.* So K, Bw. MS: *New,* followed by Mc.
30–38	Verses are faded and difficult to read.
36	*tua.* So Mc, K, Bw. MS: *wyth tua.*
40a	Followed in MS by *Aude viduam iam cum interrogatione sua* [Now hear the widow with her question].
48	Followed in MS by *Responsio prime vxoris ad viduam* [The reply of the first wife to the widow].
62–65	Verses are faded and final words in each are uncertain.
66	*feiris.* So Mc, K, Bw. MS: *freiris.*
89a	Followed in MS by *Aude vt dicet de viro suo* [Hear how she talks about her husband].
98	*gor.* So K, Bw. Mc emends to *goreis.* MS: *gor is.*
104	From this point on, the text is that of RP. The compositor of RP often places a *t* where a *c* would normally be required: thus printing *leuth* for *leuch* (line 147) or *rautht* for *raucht* (line 148). The compositor also has difficulty with *th* and *ght* endings, often spelling both as *tgh* (e.g., *ritgh* for *right* [line 139], *witgh* for *with* [line 152]) or simply as *gt* (e.g., *knygtis* for *knyghtis* [line 216]). Misprinting *n* for *u* or *u* for *n* is also common (e.g., *derue* for *derne* [line 192]). Such errors have been silently emended.
106	*schendis.* K, Mc follow MF, which reads *scheddis,* the sense being that the husband "parts" her lips.
116	*Than.* So Mc, K, Bw. Print: *Tan.*
124	*How.* So Mc, K, Bw. Print: *Ho.*
127	*waistit.* So Mc, K, Bw. Print: *wistit.*
141	*wod.* So MF, followed by Mc, K, Bw. Print: *wmyod.*
149	Followed in MF by *Hic bibent et inde vidua interrogat alteram mulierem et ille respondet vt sequitur* [Here they drink and then the widow questions the second wife, and she responds as follows].

150   *to.* Supplied from MF, followed by Mc, K, Bw.

        thir. So MF, followed by Bw. Print: *ther*, followed by Mc, K.

152   *man.* So Print, followed by Mc, K, Bw. MF: men.

        menskit. So Mc, K, Bw. Print: *menkit.*

156   *samyn.* So Mc, K, Bw. Print: *samy.*

157   *And.* So Mc, Bw. Print: *An*, followed by K.

        suth. So MF, followed by Bw. Print: *south*, followed by Mc, K.

172   *flurising.* So Mc, K, Bw. Print: *flurisnig.*

175   *into swoune.* So Bw. Print: *in tho swonne.* Mc, K: *in to swonne.*

182   *haris.* So Bw. Print: *hair*, followed by Mc, K.

184   *semis.* So MF, followed by Mc, K, Bw. Print: *sunys.*

186   *damys.* So Mc, K, Bw. Print: *danys.*

187   *And.* So Mc, Bw. Print: *An*, followed by K.

190   *effect.* So Mc, K, Bw. Print: *effecc.*

192   *sal be.* So Mc, K, Bw. Print: *salle.*

199   *is.* So Mc, K, Bw. Print: *iȝ.*

204   *and.* So MF, followed by Bw. Mc, K emend to *or*. Print: *ot.*

209   *haif.* Print: *I* canceled after.

        fang in myn. So Mc, Bw. Print: *faug i mynn.* K; *fang in mynn.*

212   *murnys.* So Mc, K, Bw. Print: *mrnuys.*

221   *quhy.* So Mc, K, Bw. Print: *quly.*

233   *my gud man.* So MF, followed by Mc, K, Bw. Print: *man gud my.*

236   *to that.* So Mc, K, Bw. Print: *to to that.*

240   *Loud lauchand.* So MF, followed by Bw. Mc reads *Loudly lauchand.* K reads
        Ludly lauchand. Print: *Luly rauthand.*

244   Followed in MF by *Nunc bibent et inde prime due interrogant viduam et de sua
        responsione et quomodo erat* [Now they drink and then the first two question
        the widow, and concerning her reply and how it was].

249   *your.* So Mc, K, Bw. Print: *aour.*

252   *innocent.* So MF, followed by Mc, K, Bw. Print: *i nicrit.*

259   *counterfeit.* So Mc, K, Bw. Print: *conutfeit.*

269   *hen.* So Mc, K, Bw. Print: *heun.*

275   *claw.* So MF, followed by Bw. Print: *keyth*, followed by Mc. K reads *krych.*

292   *he.* Supplied from MF, following Mc, K, Bw.

296   *merchand.* So K, Bw. Mc reads *marchand.* Print: *nichand.*

303   *tuichandly.* So Mc, K, Bw. Print: *tinchandly.*

315   *mercy.* So Mc, K, Bw. Print: *nicy.*

318   *that.* So MF, followed by Bw. Print: *for*, followed by Mc, K.

325   *ourcummyn.* So Mc, K, Bw. Print: *ourcummy.*

327	*sett*. So Mc, K, Bw. Print: *soit*.
338	*biggingis*. So Mc, K, Bw. Print: *biggnigis*.
344	*evidentis*. So Mc, K, Bw. Print: *emdentis*.
	thai. So Mc, K, Bw. Print: *ai*.
345	*that*. So Mc, K, Bw. Print: *at*.
346	*neir*. So Mc, K, Bw. Print: *meir*.
347	*bauchles*. So Mc, Bw. K reads *bauchlis*. Print: *bauthles*.
362	*misteris*. So Mc, K, Bw. Print: *nustis*.
364	*throw*. So Mc, K, Bw. Print: *thro*, with a macron over the *o*.
368	*renoune*. So Mc, K, Bw. Print: *renovue*, with a macron over the *e*.
369	*craftely*. So Mc, K, Bw. Print: *crftaely*.
371	*Thought*. So Mc, K, Bw. Print: *Tought*.
374	*precius*. So Mc, K, Bw. Print: *precnis*.
377	*dink*. So Mc, K, Bw. Print: *duik*.
396	*And*. So Mc, K, Bw. Print: *An*.
408	*thir*. So Mc, K, Bw. Print: *ther*.
409	*knawin*. So Mc, K, Bw. Print: *knawi*.
410	*dyvour*. So Mc, K, Bw. Print: *dyour*.
417	*makis*. So Mc, K, Bw. Print: *makris*.
421	*I*. Supplied from MF, following Mc, K, Bw.
431	*chalmer*. So Mc, K, Bw. Print: *chaliu*, with a macron over the *u*.
433	*throw*. So Mc, K, Bw. Print: *tro*, with a macron over the *o*.
434	*throw*. So Mc, K, Bw. Print: *thro*, with a macron over the *o*.
435	*cortly*. So Mc, K, Bw. MS: *corly*.
451	*wemen*. So MF, followed by Mc, K, Bw. Print: *men*.
453	*convoyis*. So Mc, K, Bw. Print: *gvoyis*.
456	*to*. So Mc, K, Bw. Print: *te*.
458	*thaim*. So Mc, K, Bw. Print: *þai*.
464	*woman*. So Mc, K, Bw. Print: *waman*.
466	*sobir*. So Mc, K, Bw. Print: *sovir*.
469	*service*. So Mc, K, Bw. Print: *sermce*.
480	*rownis*. So MF, followed by Mc, K, Bw. Print: *rowis*.
490	*nixt*. So Mc, K, Bw. Print: *mxt*.
491	*samin*. So Mc, K, Bw. Print: *sanu*, with a macron over the *u*.
492	*sittis*. Supplied from MF, following Mc, K, Bw.
495	*speciall*. So Mc, K, Bw. MS: *speiall*.
507	*said thai suld*. So Mc, K, Bw. Print: *suid thai sald*.
510	*going*. So Mc, K, Bw. Print: *gonig*.
516	*schill*. So MF, followed by Mc, K, Bw. Print: *still*.

518	*glorius*. So Mc, K, Bw. Print: *glornis*.
520	*and*. Supplied from MF, following Mc, Bw. K omits.
	singing. So Mc, K, Bw. Print: *singnig*.
523	*thir*. So MF, followed by Mc, K, Bw. Print: *ryer*.
524	*throw*. So Mc, K, Bw. Print: *thro*, with a macron over the *o*.
529	*thir*. So MF, followed by Mc, K, Bw. Print: *yer*.
Colophon	Print: *Quod Dunbar*; MF: *Quod Maister Williame Dunbar*.

Index of First Lines

Glossary

A Basic Note on Vocabulary

Dunbar's poetry is written in the dialect known today as Middle Scots. As such, the reader of Chaucerian Middle English will have relatively little trouble reading Scots, provided that some basic dialectal differences are borne in mind.

Vowels: (1) long vowels are often marked by combination of the vowel and a subsequent *i* in Middle Scots ("speir" for *spear* — Poem 1, line 12; "glaid" for *glad* — Poem 1, line 17; "meik" for *meek* — Poem 1, line 15); (2) Middle Scots sometimes uses an *a* where we anticipate an *o* ("lang" for *long* — Poem 2, line 49; "behald" for *behold* — Poem 2, line 102); (3) the letters *i* and *y* are interchangeable in Middle Scots ("inclyne" for *incline* — Poem 1, line 25); final -*e* is generally silent (except where accented in the text), but sometimes does act as a sign denoting a preceding long vowel ("rute" for *root* — Poem 1, line 41).

Consonants: (1) where we might expect a *gh* in Middle English, Middle Scots often substitutes a *ch* ("brycht" for *bright* — Poem 1, line 3); (2) where we might expect a *mb* we often find *mm* or simply *m* ("lymmis" for *limbs* — Poem 2, line 66); *th* is replaced by *dd* or *d* quite frequently ("fedder" for *feather* — Poem 13, line 8); Middle English *wh* is most often represented by *quh* ("quhome" for *whom* — Poem 1, line 5); final *d* is replaced by *t* ("passit" for *passed* — Poem 1, line 37); *sh* is often represented by *sch*, as is initial *s* ("schouris" for *showers* — Poem 1, line 2; "schir" for *sir* — Poem 14, line 63); initial *h* is occasionally silent and/or dropped ("armony" for *harmony* — Poem 1, line 50); vocalization of /l/ after back vowels is inconsistent ("aw" for *all* — Poem 14, line 85; but see line 51, "all"); also, metathesis is characteristic of Middle Scots ("brist" for *burst* — Poem 2, line 74).

For a brief overview of the grammar of the dialect, see C. I. MacAfee, "A Short Grammar of Older Scots," *Scottish Language* 11/12 (1992–93), 10–36. For help on the pronunciation of Scots, see Adam J. Aitken, "How to Pronounce Older Scots," in *Bards and Makars*, ed. Adam J. Aitken, et al. (Glasgow: University of Glasgow, 1977), pp. 1–21.

agane *again*
aganis *against*
ald *old*
alkin *every kind of*
allane *alone*
als *also; as*
amang *among*

and *and; if*
an(e) *a(n); one*
aneuther *another*
anis *once*
apon(e) *upon*
ar *are*
askis *asks*

Glossary

at(t)our *over, above*
Aurora *the Dawn*
avalis *avails, helps*
awin *own*
ay *always, ever*

ba(i)th *both*
be *by; when*
befoir *before*
begowthe *began*
bene *be; is; are; been*
bot; but *but; only; without*

cleir, clere *clear; bright*
come *came*
couth; culd *could*
cum *come*

dar *dare*
de *die*
deid *dead; death; deed*
deir *dear*
deit *died*
dois *does*
doun *down*
durst *dared*

e *eye, eyes*
efter *after*
eik *also*
eir *ear*
eke *also*
ellis *else*
ene *eyes*
erd *earth*

fals *false*
fane *glad; gladly*
fang *take*

feir *fear*
fer *far*
fle *fly*
flour, flouris *flower, flowers*
foryet *forget*
fra, fro *from*
fule *fool*
furth *forth*

ga *go*
gaddir *gather*
gaif *gave*
gang *go; walk*
gart *caused*
gif(f) *if; give*
gr(e)it *great*
gud(e) *good*

haif *have; keep*
haill *healthy; whole*
hale *hail*
ha(u)ld *hold*
hame *home*
hard *heard*
hart(e) *heart*
heff *have*
he(ich) *high; loud*
heir *here; hear; listen*
hes *has*
hew *hue, color*
hir *her*

ilk *each; same*
into *in; into*
invy *envy*

keip *keep*
ken *know; teach*
kest *cast*

472

kirk(e) *church*
knaw *know*

laithly *loathly, disgusting*
lang *long*
lat(t) *let; allow; prevent*
law *low*
leif *leave; live*
lik, lyk *like*
luf(f) *love*
luk(e) *look*
lusty *joyful; pleasant*

ma *more*
mair *more*
maist *most*
mak *make*
man *must; man*
mekill *much; large*
moist *most*
mon(e) *must*
mony *many*
mot *must; may*

na *no; nor; than*
nan(e) *none; not one*
nixt *next*
nocht, nought *not; nothing*
nor *nor; than*
nowder *neither*

o(u)ght *anything*
on(e) *on; in*
ony *any*
or *or; before, ere*
orient *eastern*
our *over; our*

pennis *feathers*

prys *great wealth*
pur(e) *poor*

quha *who*
quhair *where*
quhais *whose*
quham(e) *whom*
quhar(e) *where*
quhat *what*
quhen *when*
quhilk *which; who*
quhill *while; until; which*
quhit(e) *white*
quho *who*
quhois *whose*
quhom(e) *whom*
quhone *when*
quhow *how*
quhy *why*
quhyte *white*
quyk *living*
quod *said*

riale, riall *royal*
richt *very*
rin *run*

sa *so*
sal(l) *shall*
Salvatour *Savior*
sam *same*
sang *song*
sary *sorry*
schaw *show*
schene *bright; beautiful*
schir *sir*
scho(u) *she*
se *see*
seik *seek*

sen *since; then*

sic *such*

sone *son; sun; soon*

sould *should*

stan(e) *stone*

sua *so; thus*

suld *should*

sum *some*

suppois *although*

swa *so; thus*

syne *since; then; therefore; sin*

ta *the one*

ta(i)k *take*

tane *taken*

thai, thay *they; those*

thaim *them*

thair *their; there*

than *then*

thar *their*

that *who; that*

think *seem*

thir *these; them*

thocht *thought; although*

thow *thou (you)*

throw *through*

thruch *through*

til(l) *until; to; for*

togidder *together*

tother *the other*

trew *true*

trow *believe*

tua *two*

tuik *took*

twa *two*

udir, uther *other*

waild *would*

wait(t) *know(s)*

wald *would; wished*

walk *wake*

war *were*

warld *world*

weill, wele *weal; prosperity; well*

weir *war; doubt; wear*

wene *think; suppose*

wes *was*

wicht *person*

wirk *work; make*

wo *woe, misery*

wode *mad*

wrocht *made*

ye *you*

yeid *went*

yeir *year*

yit *yet; still*

yon(e) *that*

yow *you*

Volumes in the Middle English Texts Series

The Floure and the Leafe, *The Assembly of Ladies*, and *The Isle of Ladies*, ed. Derek Pearsall (1990)

Three Middle English Charlemagne Romances, ed. Alan Lupack (1990)

Six Ecclesiastical Satires, ed. James M. Dean (1991)

Heroic Women from the Old Testament in Middle English Verse, ed. Russell A. Peck (1991)

The Canterbury Tales: Fifteenth-Century Continuations and Additions, ed. John M. Bowers (1992)

Gavin Douglas, *The Palis of Honoure*, ed. David Parkinson (1992)

Wynnere and Wastoure and The Parlement of the Thre Ages, ed. Warren Ginsberg (1992)

The Shewings of Julian of Norwich, ed. Georgia Ronan Crampton (1993)

King Arthur's Death: The Middle English Stanzaic Morte Arthur and Alliterative Morte Arthure, ed. Larry D. Benson and Edward E. Foster (1994)

Lancelot of the Laik and Sir Tristrem, ed. Alan Lupack (1994)

Sir Gawain: Eleven Romances and Tales, ed. Thomas Hahn (1995)

The Middle English Breton Lays, ed. Anne Laskaya and Eve Salisbury (1995)

Sir Perceval of Galles and Ywain and Gawain, ed. Mary Flowers Braswell (1995)

Four Middle English Romances: Sir Isumbras, Octavian, Sir Eglamour of Artois, Sir Tryamour, ed. Harriet Hudson (1996)

The Poems of Laurence Minot (1333–1352), ed. Richard H. Osberg (1996)

Medieval English Political Writings, ed. James M. Dean (1996)

The Book of Margery Kempe, ed. Lynn Staley (1996)

Amis and Amiloun, Robert of Cisyle, and Sir Amadace, ed. Edward E. Foster (1997)

The Cloud of Unknowing, ed. Patrick J. Gallacher (1997)

Robin Hood and Other Outlaw Tales, ed. Stephen Knight and Thomas Ohlgren (1997)

The Poems of Robert Henryson, ed. Robert L. Kindrick (1997)

Moral Love Songs and Laments, ed. Susanna Greer Fein (1998)

John Lydgate, *Troy Book: Selections*, ed. Robert R. Edwards (1998)

Thomas Usk, *The Testament of Love*, ed. R. Allen Shoaf (1998)

Prose Merlin, ed. John Conlee (1998)

Middle English Marian Lyrics, ed. Karen Saupe (1998)

John Metham, *Amoryus and Cleopes*, ed. Stephen F. Page (1999)

Four Romances of England: King Horn, Havelok the Dane, Bevis of Hampton, Athelston, ed. Ronald B. Herzman, Graham Drake, and Eve Salisbury (1999)

The Assembly of Gods: Le Assemble de Dyeus, or Banquet of Gods and Goddesses, with the Discourse of Reason and Sensuality, ed. Jane Chance (1999)

Thomas Hoccleve, *The Regiment of Princes*, ed. Charles R. Blyth (1999)

John Capgrave, *The Life of St. Katherine*, ed. Karen Winstead (1999)

John Gower, *Confessio Amantis*, Vol. 1, ed. Russell A. Peck (2000); Vol. 2 (2003)

Richard the Redeless and *Mum and the Sothsegger*, ed. James Dean (2000)

Ancrene Wisse, ed. Robert Hasenfratz (2000)

Walter Hilton, *The Scale of Perfection*, ed. Thomas Bestul (2000)

John Lydgate, *The Siege of Thebes*, ed. Robert Edwards (2001)

Pearl, ed. Sarah Stanbury (2001)

The Trials and Joys of Marriage, ed. Eve Salisbury (2002)

Middle English Legends of Women Saints, ed. Sherry L. Reames (2003)

The Wallace: Selections, ed. Anne McKim (2003)

Three Purgatory Poems (The Gast of Gy, Sir Owain, The Vision of Tundale), ed. Edward E. Foster (2004)

William Dunbar, *The Complete Works*, ed. John Conlee (2004)

Chaucerian Dream Visions and Complaints, ed. Dana M. Symons (2004)

Other TEAMS Publications

Documents of Practice Series:

Love and Marriage in Late Medieval London, selected, translated, and introduced by Shannon McSheffrey (1995)

Sources for the History of Medicine in Late Medieval England, selected, introduced, and translated by Carole Rawcliffe (1995)

A Slice of Life: Selected Documents of Medieval English Peasant Experience, edited, translated, and with an introduction by Edwin Brezette DeWindt (1996)

Regular Life: Monastic, Canonical, and Mendicant Rules, selected with an introduction by Douglas J. McMillan and Kathryn Smith Fladenmuller (1997); second edition, selected and introduced by Daniel Marcel La Corte and Douglas J. McMillan (2004)

Women and Monasticism in Medieval Europe: Sisters and Patrons of the Cistercian Reform, selected, translated, and with an introduction by Constance H. Berman (2002)

Medieval Notaries and Their Acts: The 1327–1328 Register of Jean Holanie, introduced, edited, and translated by Kathryn L. Reyerson and Debra A. Salata (2004)

Commentary Series:

Commentary on the Book of Jonah, Haimo of Auxerre, translated with an introduction by Deborah Everhart (1993)

Medieval Exegesis in Translation: Commentaries on the Book of Ruth, translated with an introduction by Lesley Smith (1996)

Nicholas of Lyra's Apocalypse Commentary, translated with an introduction and notes by Philip D. W. Krey (1997)

Rabbi Ezra Ben Solomon of Gerona: Commentary on the Song of Songs and Other Kabbalistic Commentaries, selected, translated, and annotated by Seth Brody (1999)

John Wyclif: On the Truth of Holy Scripture, translated with an introduction and notes by Ian Christopher Levy (2001)

Second Thessalonians: Two Early Medieval Apocalyptic Commentaries, translated with an introduction by Steven R. Cartwright and Kevin L. Hughes (2001)

The Glossa Ordinaria *on the Song of Songs*, translated with an introduction and notes by Mary Dove (2004)

Medieval German Texts in Bilingual Editions Series:

Sovereignty and Salvation in the Vernacular, 1050–1150, introduction, translation, and notes by James A. Schultz (2000)

Ava's New Testament Narratives: "When the Old Law Passed Away," introduction, translations, and notes by James A. Rushing, Jr. (2003)

History as Literature: German World Chronicles of the Thirteenth Century in Verse, introduction, translations, and notes by R. Graeme Dunphy (2003)

To order please contact: MEDIEVAL INSTITUTE PUBLICATIONS
Western Michigan University
Kalamazoo, MI 49008–5432
Phone (269) 387–8755
FAX (269) 387–8750

http://www.wmich.edu/medieval/mip/index.html

Medieval Institute Publications is a program
of The Medieval Institute, College of Arts
and Sciences, Western Michigan University

Typeset in 10.5 pt. Times New Roman
with Times New Roman display
Manufactured by Cushing-Malloy, Inc.—Ann Arbor, Michigan

Medieval Institute Publications
College of Arts and Sciences
Western Michigan University
1903 W. Michigan Avenue
Kalamazoo, Michigan 49008-5432
www.wmich.edu/medieval/mip/

 WESTERN MICHIGAN UNIVERSITY